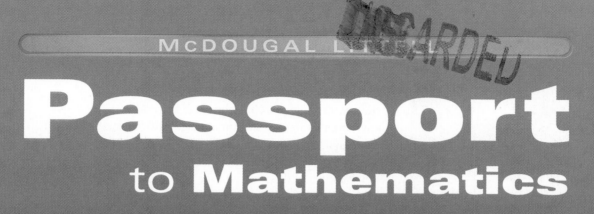

MCDOUGAL LITTELL

Passport
to **Mathematics**
BOOK 1

RON LARSON

LAURIE BOSWELL

TIMOTHY D. KANOLD

LEE STIFF

McDougal Littell
A HOUGHTON MIFFLIN COMPANY
Evanston, Illinois • Boston • Dallas

About the Cover

The Passport series brings mathematics to life with many real-life applications. The cover shows a use of mathematics in exploration and scientific research. Other examples of mathematics in exploration and scientific research are shown on pages 63, 141, 195, 202, 215, 305, 373, 379, 441, 535, and 587. The mathematical statements and diagrams on the cover show some of the material covered in this book—problem solving with fractions and decimals. Look for exciting applications of these and other topics as you study mathematics this year!

ISBN: 0-395-87982-5   456789—VJM—03 02 01 00 99

Internet Web Site: http://www.mlmath.com

Ron Larson is a professor of mathematics at the Behrend College of Pennsylvania State University at Erie. He is the author of many well-known high school and college mathematics textbooks, including *Heath: Algebra 1*, *Geometry*, *Algebra 2*, *Precalculus*, *Precalculus with Limits*, and *Calculus*. He is a pioneer in the development of interactive textbooks, and his calculus textbook is published on CD-ROM. Dr. Larson is a member of NCTM and frequently speaks at NCTM and other professional conferences.

Laurie Boswell is a mathematics teacher at Profile Junior-Senior High School in Bethlehem, New Hampshire. She is active in NCTM and local mathematics organizations. A recipient of the 1986 Presidential Award for Excellence in Mathematics Teaching, she is also the 1992 Tandy Technology Scholar and the 1991 recipient of the Richard Balomenos Mathematics Education Service Award presented by the New Hampshire Association of Teachers of Mathematics. She is an author of *Heath Geometry* and Houghton Mifflin *Math Central*.

Timothy D. Kanold is Director of Mathematics and Science and a teacher at Adlai Stevenson High School in Lincolnshire, Illinois. A 1986 recipient of the Presidential Award for Excellence in Mathematics Teaching, he is also the 1993 recipient of the Illinois Council of Teacher of Mathematics Outstanding Leadership Award. A member of NCTM, he served on NCTM's Professional Standards for Teaching Mathematics Commission. He is an author of *Heath: Algebra 1* and *Algebra 2*.

Lee Stiff is an associate professor of mathematics education in the College of Education and Psychology of North Carolina State University at Raleigh and has taught mathematics at the high school and middle school levels. A member of NCTM, he served on the Board of Directors. He is also the 1992 recipient of the W.W. Rankin Award for Excellence in Mathematics Education presented by the North Carolina Council of Teachers of Mathematics. He is an author of *Heath: Algebra 1*, *Geometry*, *Algebra 2*, and Houghton Mifflin *Math Central*.

Reviewers and Contributors

Renee Arrington
Mathematics Specialist
Alief Middle School
Houston, TX

Lyn Baier
Mathematics Teacher
Hopkins West Junior High School
Hopkins, MN

Deborah J. Barrett
Assistant Superintendent/Curriculum/
    Assessment/Technology
Wapato School District
Wapato, WA

Jeff Beatty
Mathematics Teacher
Thomas Harrison Middle School
Harrisonburg, VA

Nancy Belsky
Mathematics Teacher
Westmoreland School
Westmoreland, NH

Marianne Cavanaugh
Head Mathematics Teacher
Gideon Welles Middle School
Glastonbury, CT

Linda Cooke
Mathematics Teacher
Lincoln Middle School
Pullman, WA

Charleen M. DeRidder
Supervisor of Mathematics, K–12
Knox County School District
Knoxville, TN

Betty Erickson
Mathematics Coordinator and Teacher
Kearsarge Regional School District
Bradford, NH

Madelaine Gallin
Mathematics Teacher
Community School District #5
Manhattan, NY

Linda Gojak
Mathematics Teacher/Department Chairperson
Hawken School
Lyndhurst, OH

Margarita Gutiérrez
Curriculum Specialist
Urban Systemic Initiative
El Paso, TX

Thomas Keating
Mathematics Teacher
Chase Middle School
Spokane, WA

Betty Koleilat
Assistant Principal of Curriculum
Drew Academy
Houston, TX

Nancy W. Lewis
Mathematics Teacher
Thurmont Middle School
Thurmont, MD

Richard D. Lodholz
Mathematics Coordinator
Parkway School District
St. Louis, MO

Donna J. Long
Title I/Mathematics Coordinator
M.S.D. of Wayne Township
Indianapolis, IN

Carol Mellett
Mathematics Teacher
Lincoln School
Brookline, MA

Dee Ann Meziere
Mathematics Teacher
Putnam City Central Middle School
Oklahoma City, OK

Janice Mosley
Mathematics Teacher
Bellevue Middle School
Nashville, TN

Donna M. Ogle
Professor of Reading and Language
National-Louis University
Evanston, IL

John Peter Penick
District Mathematics Coordinator
Marcus Whitman Junior High School
Port Orchard, WA

Susan Powell
Mathematics Teacher
Burghard Elementary School
Macon, Georgia

Rochelle President-Brown
Mathematics Teacher
Burnside Scholastic Academy
Chicago, IL

Eduardo Reyna
Mathematics Teacher/Department Chairperson
Brown Middle School
McAllen, TX

Krista Rogers
Mathematics Teacher
Hutchinson Junior High School
Lubbock, TX

Marsha Rosenwasser
Mathematics Teacher/Department Head
J. Q. Adams Middle School
Metairie, LA

Frank C. Santoro
Mathematics Teacher
Lincoln School
Brookline, MA

Donna Schneller
Mathematics Teacher
Lake Riviera Middle School
Brick, NJ

Cindy H. Sellars
Mathematics Chairperson
Peet Junior High School
Conroe, TX

Cynthia G. Siebert
Mathematics Teacher
Ballenger Creek Middle School
Frederick, MD

Robyn Silbey
Mathematics Specialist
Montgomery County Public Schools
Rockville, MD

Diana G. Sullivan
Mathematics Teacher
Murray Avenue School
Huntingdon Valley, PA

William F. Tate
Associate Professor of
    Mathematics Education
University of Wisconsin
Madison, WI

Vicki Vaughan
Mathematics Teacher
Putnam City Central Middle School
Oklahoma City, OK

Beverly Weldon
Senior Mathematics Consultant
Region 10 Educational
    Service Center
Richardson, TX

Brenda Wright
Mathematics Specialist
Dozier Middle School
Newport News, VA

Student Review Panel

Laina Carlos
Greeneville Middle School
Greeneville, TN

Amelia Groeschel
Peet Junior High School
Conroe, TX

Kendra Hudgins
Brewer Middle School
Fort Worth, TX

Jennifer Karr
West Middle School
Holland, MI

Megan Keller
Marinette Middle School
Marinette, WI

Danny Kelly
Norton Middle School
Norton, OH

Frank Kincel, Jr.
West Scranton Intermediate School
Scranton, PA

Jessica Kull
Haven Middle School
Evanston, IL

Jonathan Larason
Woodbury School
Salem, NH

Rebecca Marriott
Southeastern Randolph
    Middle School
Asheboro, NC

Megan McDiffett
Wendler Middle School
Anchorage, AK

Meredith McKenna
Plymouth Community
    Intermediate School
Plymouth, MA

Gaston Prevette
Smithfield Middle School
Smithfield, NC

Gabrielle Ramos
Frederick H. Tuttle Middle School
South Burlington, VT

Reathie Rogers
Durham Magnet School
Durham, NC

Eric Roskens
Thayer Jay Hill Middle School
Naperville, IL

Arlie Sommer
Middleton Middle School
Middleton, ID

Kelly Swift
Anderson High School
Cincinnati, OH

Kelli VanDeusen
Irons Junior High School
Lubbock, TX

Sarah Zanoff
Forestwood Middle School
Lewisville, TX

Problem Solving Together

Applications
Sports 8
Computers 11
Cars 16
Business 18
Movies 19
Food 21
Woodworking 23
Quilt Patterns 24
Recycling 30
Art 31
Miniature Golf 37
Games 40
Hiking 52

Assessment
Ongoing Assessment *5, 9, 13, 17, 23, 29, 35, 39, 45*
Standardized Test Practice *7, 11, 15, 20, 25, 31, 37, 41, 47*
Spiral Review *20, 32, 42*
Mid-Chapter Assessment *21* **Chapter Assessment** *52*
Problem Solving Strategies
Applying Strategies *4, 5, 6, 12, 16, 21, 23, 27, 31, 35, 36, 38, 40, 45, 46, 47, 51, 52*
Interdisciplinary Features
Career Interview: Exhibit Designer *42*
Communicating About Mathematics: Museums *43*

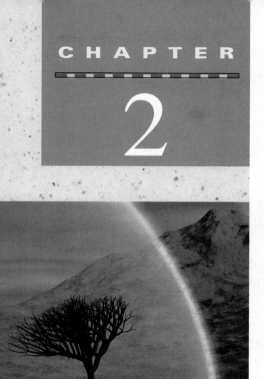

CHAPTER 2

Place-Value Systems and Operations

Applications

Assessment

CHAPTER 3

Decimals and Percent

Applications

Money 113
Dinosaurs 119
Health 120
Drafting 121
Pets 125
Travel 127
Language Skills 130
Technology 133
Olympics 135
Library Science 137
Baseball 139
Coins 141
Science 146
Music 149

Assessment

Ongoing Assessment *113, 117, 125, 129, 135, 139, 145, 149*
Standardized Test Practice *115, 119, 127, 131, 137, 142, 147, 151*
Spiral Review *120, 132, 142*
Mid-Chapter Assessment *133*   **Chapter Assessment** *156*

Problem Solving Strategies

Applying Strategies *111, 121, 125, 130, 135, 136, 142, 143, 151, 158*

Interdisciplinary Features

Career Interview: Consultant *120*
Communicating About Mathematics: Crash Course *143*

CHAPTER

4

Applications

Applications of Decimals and **Percents**

Statistics and Graphs

Applications

Assessment

CHAPTER 6

Fractions, Ratios, and Proportions

Applications

Car Safety   271
Architecture   279
Typing   281
Gasoline Mileage   285
Tiling   286
Tree House   287
Shopping   291
Bicycles   293
Swimming   295
Baking   297
Music   299
Science   305

CHAPTER 7

Adding and Subtracting Fractions

Applications

Assessment

CHAPTER 8

Multiplying and Dividing Fractions

Applications

Assessment

Problem Solving Strategies

Interdisciplinary Features

CHAPTER 9

Geometry and Patterns

Applications

Assessment

CHAPTER

10

Applications

Letter Puzzle 479
Tennis 479
Washington, DC 483
Walking 484
Cooking 494
Geography 495
Greenhouse 495
Optical Illusion 497
Soap Box Derby 503
Photography 509
Energy Sources 514
Ice Skating 515
Pets 519

Geometry and Measurement

Assessment
Ongoing Assessment *477, 481, 487, 493, 501, 507, 513, 517*
Standardized Test Practice *479, 483, 489, 495, 503, 509, 515, 519*
Spiral Review *484, 496, 510*
Mid-Chapter Assessment *497* **Chapter Assessment** *524*

Problem Solving Strategies
Applying Strategies *481, 485, 488, 491, 496, 499, 501, 507, 510, 517, 518*

Interdisciplinary Features
History Connection: Almanacs *484*
Communicating About Mathematics: Bicycles Built for View *511*

Integers and the Coordinate Plane

Applications

Assessment

CHAPTER
12

Algebra: Equations and Probability

Applications

Student Resources

You can use the reference tools in the Student Resources to help you find answers to your math questions.

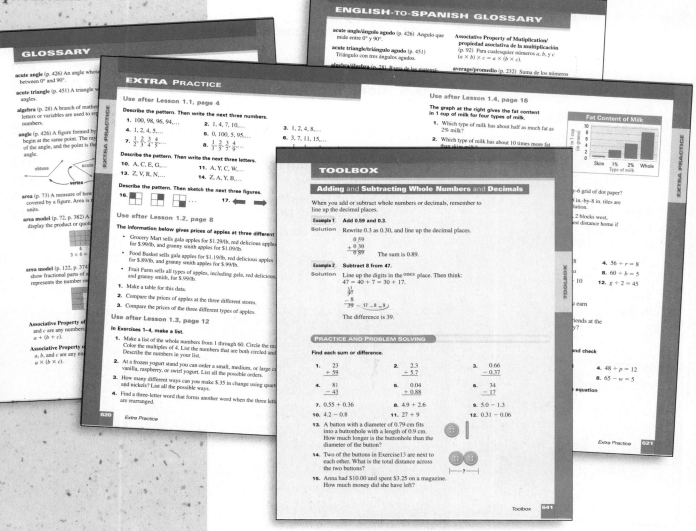

Real-Life Applications

Look through this list for things that interest you. Then find out how they are linked to mathematics.

Animals/Pets 125, 179, 206, 271, 313, 351, 357, 380, 403, 430, 519, 615, 618

Architecture 243, 279, 308, 453, 460, 470, 519

Art/Design 31, 148, 174, 179, 222, 417, 435, 509, 519, 587

Automobiles 16, 249, 271, 285, 287, 352, 398

Books/Literature 70, 191, 325, 515

Business 18, 19, 31, 71, 237, 343, 599

Calendars/Time 51, 87, 98, 239

Collections/Hobbies 1, 29, 81, 205, 244, 260, 362, 399, 615

Community Service 315, 321, 326, 333, 340, 351, 409

Computers 11, 55, 69, 104, 248, 555

Cooking 79, 297, 309, 340, 402, 404, 605

Economics 10, 42, 75, 115, 173, 175, 183, 187, 212, 244, 246, 247, 255, 356, 595

Education/School 39, 130, 137, 151, 236, 281, 285, 443, 560, 604

Engineering/Drafting 121, 433, 452, 567

Food 10, 21, 161, 167, 189, 299, 310, 378, 395, 618

Fundraising 15, 87, 91, 325, 593, 595, 604

Games 40, 51, 156, 255, 326, 575

Geography/Maps 25, 63, 74, 92, 260, 327, 350, 413, 483, 489, 495, 496, 509, 510, 527, 593, 605

Health/Nutrition 46, 120, 173, 212, 241, 377, 403, 414

Hiking 52, 345, 461

History 62, 119, 225, 341, 604

Home Improvement 73, 74, 75, 263, 349

Money 21, 107, 113, 141, 171, 179, 541

Movies 19, 52, 340, 550

Music/Radio 83, 149, 238, 254, 299, 333, 345, 393, 414, 508

Puzzles 25, 46, 137, 169, 239, 324, 339, 345, 351, 393, 479, 549

Recycling/Environment 14, 30, 150, 326, 514

Savings 21, 179, 541

Science 61, 63, 141, 146, 195, 202, 207, 222, 227, 255, 260, 305, 327, 373, 379, 429, 440, 441, 535, 548, 549, 561, 572, 587

Sewing 24, 321, 344

Shopping 10, 82, 291, 305

Sports and Athletics 8, 18, 40, 71, 135, 139, 151, 159, 169, 220, 226, 235, 239, 240, 241, 295, 339, 344, 356, 387, 479, 539, 595, 610

Surveys 186, 240, 281, 313, 394, 395

Temperature 249, 547, 551, 581

Travel/Vacation 14, 91, 127, 250, 254, 393, 515

Woodworking 23, 191, 337, 391, 441

World Cultures 127, 223, 293, 356, 494

Real Life... Real Math

You may be surprised at all the ways mathematics is connected to daily life and careers.

Real Life... Real People

Real Life... Real Facts

Welcome to the Passport series

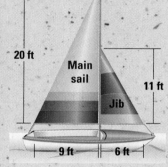

Preparing you for success in mathematics in the middle grades and beyond.

As you progress through this course you will see that:

Mathematics makes connections

In this course you will study important middle grade mathematics concepts and see how they are related. You will also find a gradual approach to understanding the underlying principles of algebra and geometry.

Mathematics is accessible

Each lesson in the *Passport* series will help you learn more about math. The interesting activities and the useful pictures, charts, graphs, and models will make it easier for you to learn.

20 ft

Main sail

11 ft

Jib

9 ft

6 ft

Mathematics is meaningful

Throughout each book in the series, you will explore and discover the importance of mathematics in daily life. In fact, you will find that many of the things you do, see, and hear are linked to mathematics.

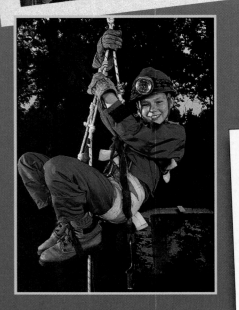

Making mathematics relevant.

The Passport series emphasizes real data and real-life applications. The series also shows how to use modeling to understand concepts and solve problems.

The value of math is highlighted through the **LESSON OBJECTIVES** which will explain what you will learn, and why it is important.

4.1 Adding Decimals

What you should learn:

Goal 1 How to add decimals

Goal 2 How to use decimal addition to solve real-life problems

Why you should learn it:

Decimal addition can be used to help you find the cost of things. An [...] the total [...]

Goal 1 ADDING DECIMALS

Example 1 Adding Decimals with Base-Ten Pieces

Use base-ten pieces to show, or *model*, 1.2 + 0.87.

Solution

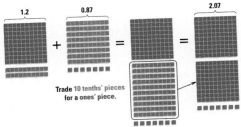

1.2 + 0.87 = = 2.07

Trade **10 tenths' pieces** for a ones' piece.

So, 1.2 + 0.87 = 2.07.

Another way to add decimals is to use vertical form. When you do this, remember to line up the decimal places. The steps are similar to those used for adding whole numbers.

Example 2 Using Vertical Form to Add

Use vertical form to add the decimals.

a. 4.72 + 2.5   **b.** 5.32 + 7   **c.** 0.247 + 1.9

Solution

a.
$$\begin{array}{r} 4.72 \\ +2.5 \\ \hline 7.22 \end{array}$$

b.
$$\begin{array}{r} 5.32 \\ +7 \\ \hline 12.32 \end{array}$$

c.
$$\begin{array}{r} 0.247 \\ +1.9 \\ \hline 2.147 \end{array}$$

NEED TO KNOW

Remember that whole numbers have an "unwritten" decimal point. For example, 5 and 5.0 are the same.

Use of **COMPUTERS** and **CALCULATORS** is often demonstrated by showing you how these everyday tools are used to solve problems.

Interesting and informative **TABLES**, **CHARTS**, and **GRAPHS** not only show the real-life value of math, but also develop your critical thinking skills.

REAL LIFE, REAL FACTS shows the everyday value and importance of mathematics.

Mathematical **MODELING** shows you math at work in real-life situations and demonstrates the problem-solving power of mathematics.

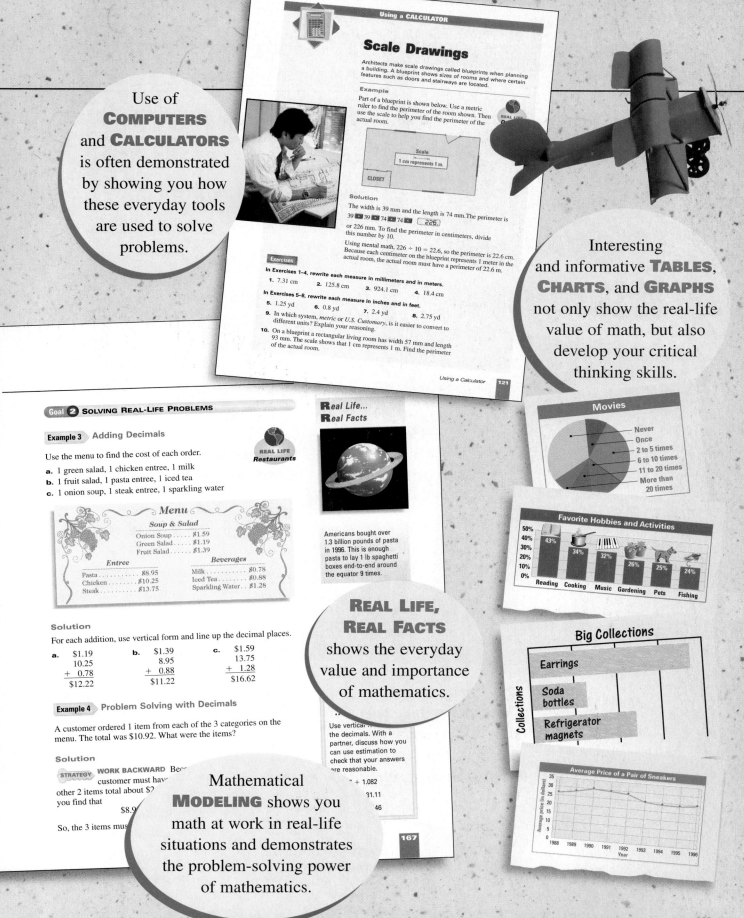

Using a Calculator **121**

Using a CALCULATOR

Scale Drawings

Architects make scale drawings called blueprints when planning a building. A blueprint shows sizes of rooms and where certain features such as doors and stairways are located.

Example

Part of a blueprint is shown below. Use a metric ruler to find the perimeter of the room shown. Then use the scale to help you find the perimeter of the actual room.

Scale
1 cm represents 1 m.

CLOSET

Solution

The width is 39 mm and the length is 74 mm. The perimeter is
39 ⊞ 39 ⊞ 74 ⊞ 74 ⊞ [226]
or 226 mm. To find the perimeter in centimeters, divide this number by 10.

Using mental math, 226 ÷ 10 = 22.6, so the perimeter is 22.6 cm. Because each centimeter on the blueprint represents 1 meter in the actual room, the actual room must have a perimeter of 22.6 m.

Exercises

In Exercises 1–4, rewrite each measure in millimeters and in meters.
1. 7.31 cm   2. 125.8 cm   3. 924.1 cm   4. 18.4 cm

In Exercises 5–8, rewrite each measure in inches and in feet.
5. 1.25 yd   6. 0.8 yd   7. 2.4 yd   8. 2.75 yd
9. In which system, *metric* or *U.S. Customary*, is it easier to convert to different units? Explain your reasoning.
10. On a blueprint a rectangular living room has width 57 mm and length 93 mm. The scale shows that 1 cm represents 1 m. Find the perimeter of the actual room.

Goal 2 SOLVING REAL-LIFE PROBLEMS

Example 3 Adding Decimals

Use the menu to find the cost of each order.
a. 1 green salad, 1 chicken entree, 1 milk
b. 1 fruit salad, 1 pasta entree, 1 iced tea
c. 1 onion soup, 1 steak entree, 1 sparkling water

REAL LIFE
Restaurants

Menu
Soup & Salad
Onion Soup $1.59
Green Salad $1.19
Fruit Salad $1.39

Entree	Beverages
Pasta $8.95	Milk $0.78
Chicken $10.25	Iced Tea $0.88
Steak $13.75	Sparkling Water . . $1.28

Solution
For each addition, use vertical form and line up the decimal places.

a. $1.19
    10.25
   + 0.78
   $12.22

b. $1.39
    8.95
   + 0.88
   $11.22

c. $1.59
    13.75
   + 1.28
   $16.62

Example 4 Problem Solving with Decimals

A customer ordered 1 item from each of the 3 categories on the menu. The total was $10.92. What were the items?

Solution

STRATEGY **WORK BACKWARD** Bec
customer must hav
other 2 items total about $2
you find that
$8.9

So, the 3 items mus

Real Life...
Real Facts

Americans bought over 1.3 billion pounds of pasta in 1996. This is enough pasta to lay 1 lb spaghetti boxes end-to-end around the equator 9 times.

Use vertical
the decimals. With a partner, discuss how you can use estimation to check that your answers
are reasonable.

? + 1.082

31.11

46

167

Movies
- Never
- Once
- 2 to 5 times
- 6 to 10 times
- 11 to 20 times
- More than 20 times

Favorite Hobbies and Activities
Reading 43%
Cooking 34%
Music 32%
Gardening 26%
Pets 25%
Fishing 24%

Big Collections
Collections
Earrings
Soda bottles
Refrigerator magnets

Average Price of a Pair of Sneakers
Average price (in dollars)
35, 30, 25, 20, 15, 10, 5, 0
1988 1989 1990 1991 1992 1993 1994 1995 1996
Year

Making mathematics easy to learn.

Throughout the Passport series, lessons and labs make even the most difficult concepts easier to understand.

Each **LESSON** has two goals: the first goal helps you to understand the math skill, the second goal shows you how the skill is applied to daily life.

Important **TERMS** are highlighted and shown in examples, making it easy to understand key math vocabulary.

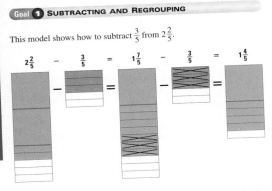

7.5 Subtracting and Regrouping: Common Denominators

What you should learn:

Goal 1 How to subtract with regrouping

Goal 2 How to use subtracting and regrouping to solve real-life problems

Why you should learn it:

Knowing how to regroup when subtracting can help you when comparing the amounts of two checks.

Goal 1 SUBTRACTING AND REGROUPING

This model shows how to subtract $\frac{3}{5}$ from $2\frac{2}{5}$.

$$2\frac{2}{5} - \frac{3}{5} = 1\frac{7}{5} - \frac{3}{5} = 1\frac{4}{5}$$

Rewriting $2\frac{2}{5}$ as $1\frac{7}{5}$ is called **regrouping**. Notice how regrouping is used in the examples below.

Example 1 Subtracting and Regrouping

Simplify the following expressions.

a. $3 - 1\frac{3}{4}$ **b.** $2\frac{1}{3} - \frac{2}{3}$ **c.** $8\frac{1}{5} - 5\frac{2}{5}$

Solution

a. $3 - 1\frac{3}{4} = 2\frac{4}{4} - 1\frac{3}{4}$ Regroup 3 as $2\frac{4}{4}$.

$\qquad\qquad = 1\frac{1}{4}$ Subtract mixed numbers.

b. $2\frac{1}{3} - \frac{2}{3} = 1\frac{4}{3} - \frac{2}{3}$ Regroup $2\frac{1}{3}$ as $1\frac{4}{3}$.

$\qquad\qquad = 1\frac{2}{3}$ Subtract.

c. $8\frac{1}{5} - 5\frac{2}{5} = 7\frac{6}{5} - 5\frac{2}{5}$ Regroup $8\frac{1}{5}$ as $7\frac{6}{5}$.

$\qquad\qquad = 2\frac{4}{5}$ Subtract mixed numbers.

STUDY TIP

In the subtraction problem

$$4 - 2\frac{5}{8}$$

4 should be regrouped as $3\frac{8}{8}$ so the fractions have a common denominator.

Chapter 7 Adding and Subtracting Fractions

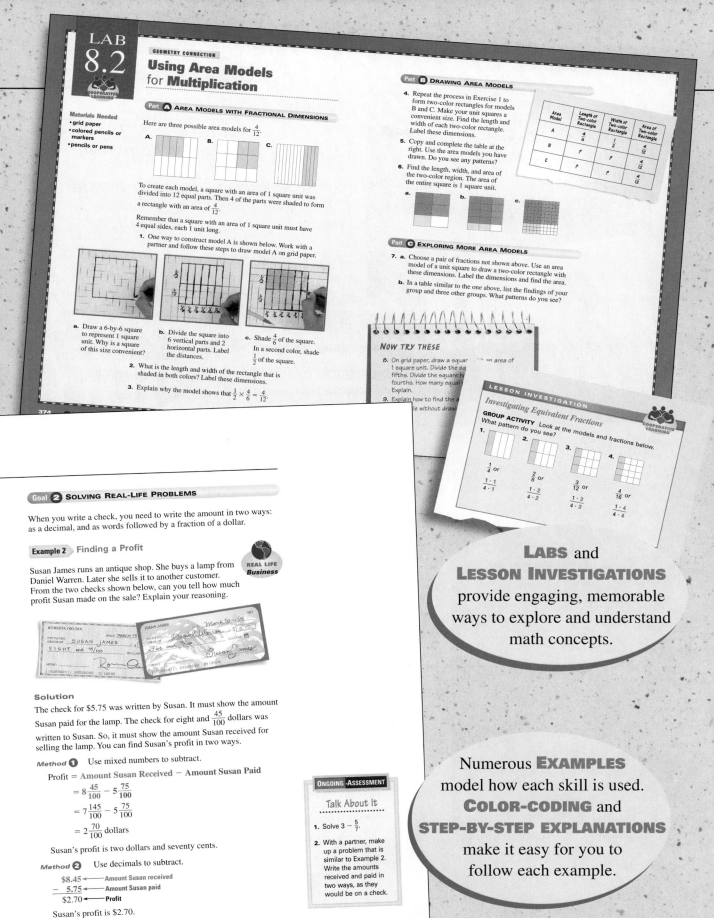

LAB 8.2
COOPERATIVE LEARNING

GEOMETRY CONNECTION

Using Area Models for Multiplication

Materials Needed
- grid paper
- colored pencils or markers
- pencils or pens

Part A AREA MODELS WITH FRACTIONAL DIMENSIONS

Here are three possible area models for $\frac{4}{12}$.

A.   B.   C.

To create each model, a square with an area of 1 square unit was divided into 12 equal parts. Then 4 of the parts were shaded to form a rectangle with an area of $\frac{4}{12}$.

Remember that a square with an area of 1 square unit must have 4 equal sides, each 1 unit long.

1. One way to construct model A is shown below. Work with a partner and follow these steps to draw model A on grid paper.

a. Draw a 6-by-6 square to represent 1 square unit. Why is a square of this size convenient?

b. Divide the square into 6 vertical parts and 2 horizontal parts. Label the distances.

c. Shade $\frac{4}{6}$ of the square. In a second color, shade $\frac{1}{2}$ of the square.

2. What is the length and width of the rectangle that is shaded in both colors? Label these dimensions.

3. Explain why the model shows that $\frac{1}{2} \times \frac{4}{6} = \frac{4}{12}$.

Part B DRAWING AREA MODELS

4. Repeat the process in Exercise 1 to form two-color rectangles for models B and C. Make your unit squares a convenient size. Find the length and width of each two-color rectangle. Label these dimensions.

5. Copy and complete the table at the right. Use the area models you have drawn. Do you see any patterns?

6. Find the length, width, and area of the two-color region. The area of the entire square is 1 square unit.

a.   **b.**   **c.**

Area Model	Length of Two-color Rectangle	Width of Two-color Rectangle	Area of Two-color Rectangle
A	$\frac{4}{6}$	$\frac{1}{2}$	$\frac{4}{12}$
B	?	?	$\frac{4}{12}$
C	?	?	$\frac{4}{12}$

Part C EXPLORING MORE AREA MODELS

7. a. Choose a pair of fractions not shown above. Use an area model of a unit square to draw a two-color rectangle with these dimensions. Label the dimensions and find the area.

b. In a table similar to the one above, list the findings of your group and three other groups. What patterns do you see?

NOW TRY THESE

8. On grid paper, draw a squar... on area of 1 square unit. Divide the eq... fifths. Divide the square h... fourths. How many equal ... Explain.

9. Explain how to find the a... ...le without draw...

374

LESSON INVESTIGATION

Investigating Equivalent Fractions

GROUP ACTIVITY Look at the models and fractions below. What pattern do you see?

1. $\frac{1}{4}$ or $\frac{1 \cdot 1}{4 \cdot 1}$

2. $\frac{2}{8}$ or $\frac{1 \cdot 2}{4 \cdot 2}$

3. $\frac{3}{12}$ or $\frac{1 \cdot 3}{4 \cdot 3}$

4. $\frac{4}{16}$ or $\frac{1 \cdot 4}{4 \cdot 4}$

COOPERATIVE LEARNING

LABS and LESSON INVESTIGATIONS provide engaging, memorable ways to explore and understand math concepts.

Goal 2 SOLVING REAL-LIFE PROBLEMS

When you write a check, you need to write the amount in two ways: as a decimal, and as words followed by a fraction of a dollar.

Example 2 Finding a Profit

REAL LIFE
Business

Susan James runs an antique shop. She buys a lamp from Daniel Warren. Later she sells it to another customer. From the two checks shown below, can you tell how much profit Susan made on the sale? Explain your reasoning.

Solution

The check for $5.75 was written by Susan. It must show the amount Susan paid for the lamp. The check for eight and $\frac{45}{100}$ dollars was written to Susan. So, it must show the amount Susan received for selling the lamp. You can find Susan's profit in two ways.

Method 1 Use mixed numbers to subtract.

$$\text{Profit} = \text{Amount Susan Received} - \text{Amount Susan Paid}$$

$$= 8\frac{45}{100} - 5\frac{75}{100}$$

$$= 7\frac{145}{100} - 5\frac{75}{100}$$

$$= 2\frac{70}{100} \text{ dollars}$$

Susan's profit is two dollars and seventy cents.

Method 2 Use decimals to subtract.

$$\begin{array}{r} \$8.45 \leftarrow \text{Amount Susan received} \\ - \ \ 5.75 \leftarrow \text{Amount Susan paid} \\ \hline \$2.70 \leftarrow \text{Profit} \end{array}$$

Susan's profit is $2.70.

ONGOING ASSESSMENT

Talk About It

1. Solve $3 - \frac{5}{7}$.

2. With a partner, make up a problem that is similar to Example 2. Write the amounts received and paid in two ways, as they would be on a check.

Numerous **EXAMPLES** model how each skill is used. **COLOR-CODING** and **STEP-BY-STEP EXPLANATIONS** make it easy for you to follow each example.

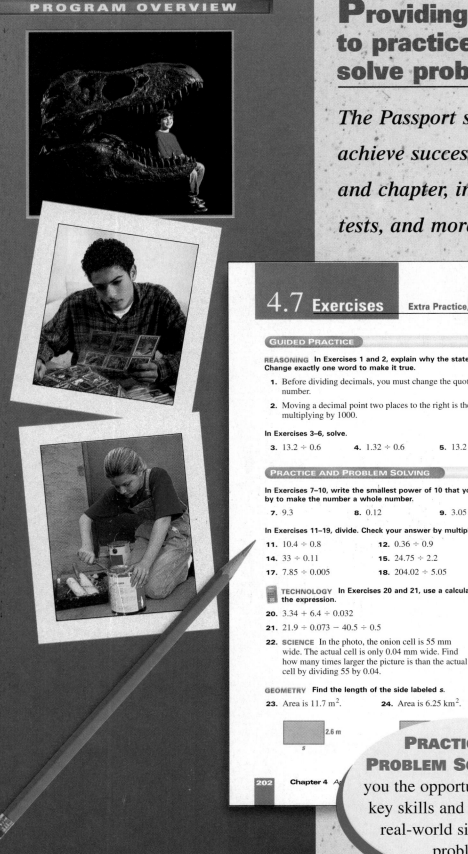

Providing opportunities to practice skills and to solve problems.

The Passport series helps you achieve success in each lesson and chapter, in standardized tests, and more.

GUIDED PRACTICE aids you and your teacher in assessing your understanding of each skill.

4.7 Exercises Extra Practice,

GUIDED PRACTICE

REASONING In Exercises 1 and 2, explain why the statement is
Change exactly one word to make it true.

1. Before dividing decimals, you must change the quotient to a whole number.

2. Moving a decimal point two places to the right is the same as multiplying by 1000.

In Exercises 3–6, solve.

3. $13.2 \div 0.6$ 4. $1.32 \div 0.6$ 5. $13.2 \div 0.06$ 6. $1.32 \div 6$

PRACTICE AND PROBLEM SOLVING

In Exercises 7–10, write the smallest power of 10 that you would multiply by to make the number a whole number.

7. 9.3 8. 0.12 9. 3.05 10. 12.001

In Exercises 11–19, divide. Check your answer by multiplying.

11. $10.4 \div 0.8$ 12. $0.36 \div 0.9$ 13. $3.14 \div 0.2$
14. $33 \div 0.11$ 15. $24.75 \div 2.2$ 16. $0.816 \div 0.68$
17. $7.85 \div 0.005$ 18. $204.02 \div 5.05$ 19. $500 \div 0.25$

TECHNOLOGY In Exercises 20 and 21, use a calculator to evaluate the expression.

20. $3.34 + 6.4 \div 0.032$

21. $21.9 \div 0.073 - 40.5 \div 0.5$

22. **SCIENCE** In the photo, the onion cell is 55 mm wide. The actual cell is only 0.04 mm wide. Find how many times larger the picture is than the actual cell by dividing 55 by 0.04.

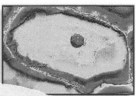

GEOMETRY Find the length of the side labeled s.

23. Area is 11.7 m^2.   24. Area is 6.25 km^2.

2.6 m

s

PRACTICE AND PROBLEM SOLVING gives you the opportunity to master key skills and apply them to real-world situations and problems.

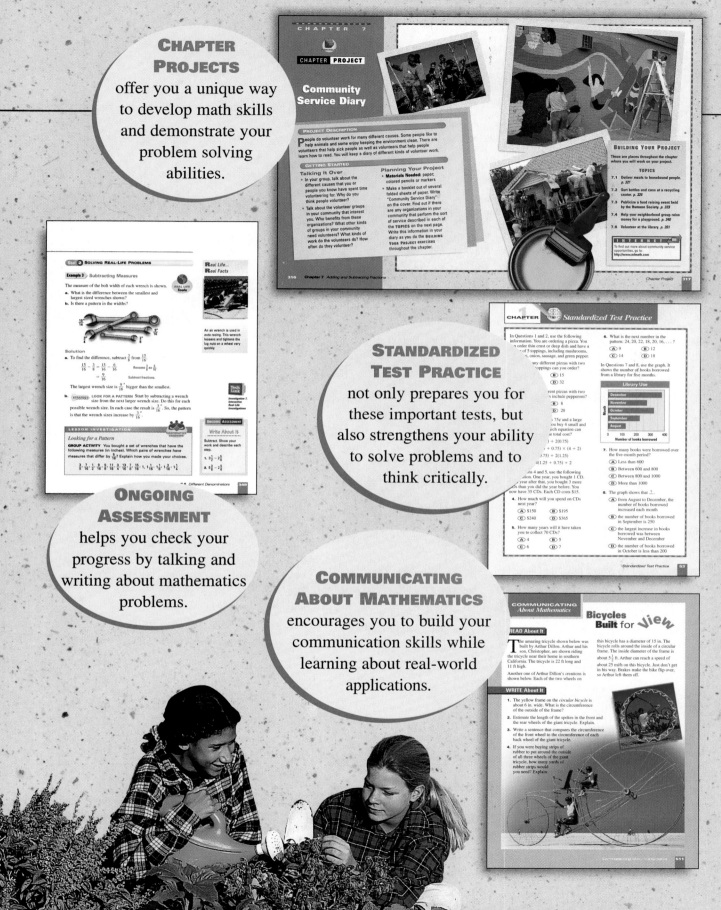

CHAPTER PROJECTS

offer you a unique way to develop math skills and demonstrate your problem solving abilities.

STANDARDIZED TEST PRACTICE

not only prepares you for these important tests, but also strengthens your ability to solve problems and to think critically.

ONGOING ASSESSMENT

helps you check your progress by talking and writing about mathematics problems.

COMMUNICATING ABOUT MATHEMATICS

encourages you to build your communication skills while learning about real-world applications.

Problem Solving Together

SCIENCE MUSEUMS contain exhibits about how things work. The collections often include things that visitors can try for themselves.

TECHNOLOGY

Technology resources accompanying this chapter:

- Interactive Real-Life Investigations
- Middle School Tutorial Software

CHAPTER THEME
Collections and Hobbies

TRANSPORTATION MUSEUMS are a kind of history museum that focuses on how we move. For example, the Motorsports Museum focuses on the history of racing cars.

HISTORY MUSEUMS often contain examples of objects from many different time periods.

REAL LIFE
Collections

Museum Exhibits

Some museums are large and display many types of collections. Other museums are smaller, and have more specialized collections. The table shows the number of items in the collections of some museums.

Museum	Type of Collection	Number of Items
Motorsports Museum	Race vehicles	100
New York Hall of Science	Science exhibits	150
U.S. Air Force Museum	Antique planes	200
Museum of Surgical Science	Surgery related objects	7000

Think and Discuss

1. How might you count a collection that contains thousands of objects?

2. Do you think the numbers in the table are exact?

3. Which of the four museums do you think occupies the most space? Why?

PORTFOLIO

CHAPTER PROJECT

Exhibiting a Class Collection

Students experiment with tops at the Children's Museum in Boston, MA.

PROJECT DESCRIPTION

Museums display collections of objects. Many museums also have educational exhibits and hands-on activities. Plan a class museum. Your museum will display collections brought in by members of your class. It will also have a booth with puzzles and activities. To organize your plans, you will use the list of **TOPICS** on the next page.

Tech Link

Investigation 1, Interactive Real-Life Investigations

GETTING STARTED

Talking It Over

- What museums have you visited? What collections and exhibits did you see? Were there activities for you to do?

- In the museums that you have visited, how were the collections displayed? Were they organized by subject? If they were, what were some of the categories? Why do you think the museum was organized in that way?

Planning Your Project

- **Materials Needed:** notebook or journal; colored pencils or markers; posterboard

- Think about where you will have your class museum. How long will it last? Who will you invite to come and see your exhibits? As you plan your museum, you will keep track of your plans in your journal. Add your answers to the **BUILDING YOUR PROJECT** questions to your journal.

STELLINGMOLEN

4+4 ct

NEDERLAND

INTERNET

To find out more about collections and museums, go to: **http://www.mlmath.com**

1.1 Looking for a Pattern

What you should learn:

Goal 1 How to use a problem solving plan

Goal 2 How to look for a pattern in data

Why you should learn it:

Finding a pattern in a set of numbers can help you organize data. For example, this strategy can help you find how many metal digits you need to buy in order to number houses.

Goal 1 A PROBLEM SOLVING PLAN

You use problem solving strategies every day. One that you use in mathematics is *looking for a pattern*. For example, you may look for patterns in *data*. A collection of numerical facts is called **data** .

Example 1 Number Patterns

Describe the pattern. Then write the next three numbers.

3, 12, 48, 192, ? , ? , ? , . . .

Solution

STRATEGY LOOK FOR A PATTERN Following the problem solving plan below can help you find the pattern.

Understand the Problem You need to find the pattern, describe it, and use it to find the next three numbers.

Make a Plan For the first few numbers, each one is four times larger than the previous one. Check to see if this is the pattern for the numbers.

Solve the Problem Each number is four times larger than the previous one. To find the next three numbers, continue multiplying by 4.

$$4 \times 3 = 12 \qquad 4 \times 192 = 768$$
$$4 \times 12 = 48 \qquad 4 \times 768 = 3072$$
$$4 \times 48 = 192 \qquad 4 \times 3072 = 12{,}288$$

Look Back Check your answer by dividing each number by the preceding number. The result is always 4.

Example 2 Geometric Patterns

Describe the pattern. Then sketch the next three figures.

Solution

To form the second triangle, turn the first triangle a one-third turn counterclockwise. Continue turning the triangle a one-third turn counterclockwise to get the other triangles in the pattern.

You can use the four steps in Example 1 to help you solve the problem in the Lesson Investigation. When you work in a group on Lesson Investigations, you should work together on each step.

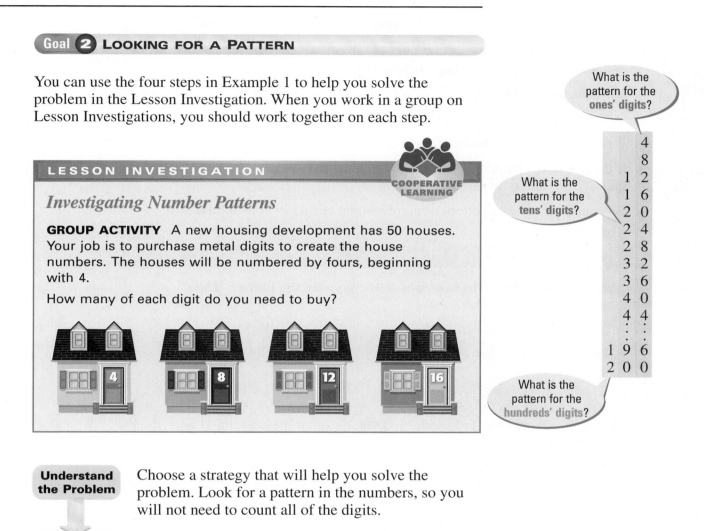

LESSON INVESTIGATION

Investigating Number Patterns

GROUP ACTIVITY A new housing development has 50 houses. Your job is to purchase metal digits to create the house numbers. The houses will be numbered by fours, beginning with 4.

How many of each digit do you need to buy?

What is the pattern for the **ones' digits?**

What is the pattern for the **tens' digits?**

What is the pattern for the **hundreds' digits?**

		4
		8
	1	2
	1	6
	2	0
	2	4
	2	8
	3	2
	3	6
	4	0
	4	4
⋮	⋮	⋮
1	9	6
2	0	0

Understand the Problem

Choose a strategy that will help you solve the problem. Look for a pattern in the numbers, so you will not need to count all of the digits.

Make a Plan

Organize the information you will use to solve the problem. Make a vertical list of the house numbers. What patterns can you find in the digits? For example, the pattern for the **ones' digits** is 4, 8, 2, 6, 0. How many times does the pattern repeat?

Solve the Problem

Use the patterns you found to decide how many of each digit you need. For example, in the **ones' digits**, each of the digits 0, 2, 4, 6, and 8 is used 10 times.

Look Back

Does your solution answer the question? Is it reasonable? How can you check your solution? For example, you can check that the total number of digits you plan to buy is the same as the total number of digits you need for all the house numbers.

ONGOING ASSESSMENT

Write About It

....

Describe the pattern. How did you find it? Use the pattern to find the next three letters.

1. B, E, H, K, . . .

2. A, B, D, G, . . .

1.1 Exercises

Extra Practice, page 620

GUIDED PRACTICE

In Exercises 1–3, use the following pattern of numbers.

8, 16, 24, 32, 40, 48, . . .

1. Describe any patterns that you see.

2. Write the next three numbers in the list.

3. If the list were continued, would 108 be in the list? Would 104 be in the list? Explain your reasoning.

4. Give an example of a pattern of numbers that occurs in your school.

PRACTICE AND PROBLEM SOLVING

LOOKING FOR A PATTERN **In Exercises 5–10, describe the pattern. Then write the next three numbers.**

5. 1, 3, 5, 7, ? , ? , ? , . . .

6. 50, 45, 40, 35, ? , ? , ? , . . .

7. 5, 15, 45, 135, ? , ? , ? , . . .

8. 3, 6, 9, 12, ? , ? , ? , . . .

9. $\frac{1}{2}, \frac{1}{4}, \frac{1}{8}, \frac{1}{16}$, ? , ? , ? , . . .

10. $1, \frac{1}{2}, \frac{1}{3}, \frac{1}{4}$, ? , ? , ? , . . .

LOOKING FOR A PATTERN **In Exercises 11–14, describe the pattern. Then write the next three letters.**

11. A, D, G, J, ? , ? , ? , . . .

12. A, Z, B, Y, ? , ? , ? , . . .

13. Z, X, V, T, ? , ? , ? , . . .

14. A, N, B, O, ? , ? , ? , . . .

GEOMETRY **In Exercises 15 and 16, sketch the next three figures.**

15.  . . .

16. 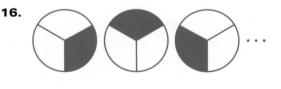 . . .

17. NUMBER THEORY The pattern of numbers at the right is called Pascal's Triangle, named after the French mathematician Blaise Pascal. Find the sum of the numbers in each row of the triangle. Complete the table. Describe the pattern for the sums.

Row	1	2	3	4	5	6	7
Sum	2	4	?	?	?	?	?

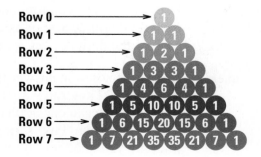

Row 0
Row 1
Row 2
Row 3
Row 4
Row 5
Row 6
Row 7

18. You begin a weight-training program. The first week you lift 12 lb. The following three weeks you lift 13, 14.5, and 16.5 lb. If the pattern continues, during which week will you first lift over 50 lb?

19. Find a pattern for multiplying each of the following numbers by itself. 1; 11; 111; 1111; 11,111; 111,111

20. **CIRCLE DESIGNS** The first four numbers that have 3 as a factor are 3, 6, 9, and 12. The ones' digits of these numbers are connected in the circle at the right.

    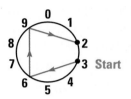

    a. Find the next seven numbers that have 3 as a factor. Copy and complete the design. What happens if you use more numbers?

    b. Create circle designs for numbers that have 4 as a factor, numbers that have 5 as a factor, and so on up to numbers that have 8 as a factor. Which circle designs are the same?

    c. What do you think the circle designs for numbers that have 43 as a factor and numbers that have 65 as a factor look like? Explain.

STANDARDIZED TEST PRACTICE

21. What number should come next in the pattern? 0, 6, 12, 18, . . .

    (A) 20   (B) 22   (C) 24   (D) 26

22. What number should come next in the pattern? 15, 13.5, 12, 10.5, . . .

    (A) 7.5   (B) 8   (C) 8.5   (D) 9

EXPLORATION AND EXTENSION

23. a. **GROUP ACTIVITY** Write three numbers that follow a pattern you have made up. (For example, if your pattern is "all numbers that have 3 as a factor," then you write down 3, 6, 9.)

    b. Have the members of your group guess the next three numbers that they think follow the pattern. Answer *yes* or *no* to each guess. The group continues to guess until one person describes the pattern.

    c. Repeat parts (a) and (b) until each person in your group has made up a pattern.

1.2 Reading and Making a Table

What you should learn:

Goal 1 How to solve problems by reading a table

Goal 2 How to solve problems by making a table

Why you should learn it:

Making a table is a strategy for organizing data for a problem. You can use a table to compare the popularity of sports by age groups.

Soccer is the most popular field sport in Europe and South America. It is becoming more popular in the United States.

Goal 1 READING A TABLE

Often data is given to you in a table. To answer questions about the data, you need to be able to read the table.

Example 1 Reading a Table

REAL LIFE
Sports

The table below shows the numbers of people (in thousands) in the United States who participate in basketball, football, soccer, softball, and swimming at least once a year. (Source: National Sporting Goods Association)

a. How many people who are 18 to 24 years old play softball?

b. In each age group, which sport is most popular?

c. Which sports are played by more people who are 12 to 17 years old than people who are 7 to 11 years old?

Sport	Age Group					
	7–11	12–17	18–24	25–34	35–44	45–54
Basketball	5,554	7,951	5,165	4,768	3,462	797
Football	3,021	4,958	3,255	2,484	1,105	271
Soccer	5,494	3,536	1,394	1,023	778	157
Softball	3,292	3,567	3,070	4,340	2,667	893
Swimming	10,669	9,335	6,565	10,645	10,470	5,261

Solution

a. Find the *column* for the 18–24 age group. Look down the column until you find the softball *row*. The number in the table shows how many thousand 18–24 year-olds play softball. So 3,070,000 people who are 18 to 24 years old play softball.

b. To find the sport that is most popular among people who are 7 to 11 years old, look at the column for the 7–11 age group. The largest number is in the swimming row.

Look at each of the other columns. In every column, the number in the swimming row is largest, so in each age group swimming is the most popular sport.

c. More people who are 12 to 17 years old play basketball, football, and softball than people who are 7 to 11 years old.

Example 2 > Making a Table

A newspaper article compared the wages in three towns.

- The average hourly wage for baby-sitting is $5.00 in Parker, $6.50 in Whittier, and $4.75 in Madison.

- The average hourly wage for mowing lawns is $5.50 in Parker, $6.00 in Whittier, and $5.00 in Madison.

- The average hourly wage for house cleaning is $7.00 in Parker, $8.25 in Whittier, and $6.75 in Madison.

- The average hourly wage for restaurant work is $6.00 in Parker, $7.25 in Whittier, and $5.50 in Madison.

Make a table for this data. Use the table to compare the wages in the three towns.

Solution

There are three towns and four different jobs. Suppose you choose to use the towns as column heads and the jobs as row heads. Then your table would look like this.

	Parker	Whittier	Madison
Baby-sitting			
Lawn Mowing			
House Cleaning			
Restaurant Work			

Row

Column

Now, use the given data to complete the table.

	Parker	Whittier	Madison
Baby-sitting	$5.00	$6.50	$4.75
Lawn Mowing	$5.50	$6.00	$5.00
House Cleaning	$7.00	$8.25	$6.75
Restaurant Work	$6.00	$7.25	$5.50

The average wages in Whittier are the greatest and the average wages in Madison are the least.

ONGOING ASSESSMENT

Talk About It
....

1. In Example 1, which sport is least popular in most age groups? Why do you think it is least popular?

2. Discuss some other conclusions you can make about the data in the Examples.

1.2 Exercises

Extra Practice, page 620

GUIDED PRACTICE

ECONOMICS In Exercises 1–3, use the information in the newspaper article at the right. The article is comparing the costs of buying various items in three towns.

1. Make a table for the data.

2. Use the table to compare the costs of the items in the three towns.

3. WRITING Use the table from Exercise 1 and the table from Example 2 on page 9 to compare the wages and the costs of items in the three towns.

- The average cost of a bicycle is $89.00 in Parker, $99.00 in Whittier, and $84.00 in Madison.

- The average cost of a movie ticket is $5.50 in Parker, $7.00 in Whittier, and $4.75 in Madison.

- The average cost of a pair of rollerblades is $48.50 in Parker, $54.00 in Whittier, and $47.25 in Madison.

PRACTICE AND PROBLEM SOLVING

4. SHOES The table at the right shows the numbers of 3 types of shoes sold in 1995 for different age groups. (Source: National Sporting Goods Association)

  a. What is the most popular shoe for people who are 17 and younger? for people who are 35 and older?

  b. Which age group buys the most running shoes?

1995 Athletic Shoe Purchases (in thousands)

	Aerobic Shoes	Sneakers	Running Shoes
Under 14	714	31,111	2988
14–17	386	9754	2728
18–24	763	4729	1992
25–34	2684	7759	4174
35–44	2674	8794	5621
45–64	2095	8942	5171

5. FOOD The table below shows the amounts of fruits (in thousands of tons) produced in 1994, 1995, and 1996. (Source: U.S. Dept. of Agriculture)

Fruit Production in the United States

	Apples	Limes	Oranges	Peaches	Pears
1994	5750	9	10,329	1257	1046
1995	5293	10	11,432	1151	948
1996	5217	14	11,723	1035	779

  a. Which fruits increased in production from 1994 to 1996?

  b. In what year was the production of oranges about 10 times the production of peaches?

COMPUTERS **In Exercises 6–9, use the following information.**
(Source: U.S. Bureau of the Census)

> • In 1993, the number of elementary schools that owned a CD-ROM computer was 4457, the number of middle schools was 2326, and the number of high schools was 4168.
>
> • In 1994, the number of elementary schools that owned a CD-ROM computer was 11,794, the number of middle schools was 4874, and the number of high schools was 7724.
>
> • In 1995, the number of elementary schools that owned a CD-ROM computer was 16,816, the number of middle schools was 6170, and the number of high schools was 9063.

6. Make a table of the data.

7. Which type of school owned the most CD-ROM computers?

8. In what year was the total number of schools that owned a CD-ROM computer more than double the previous year?

9. **WRITING** Write a short paragraph discussing other conclusions you can make from the data in the table from Exercise 6.

STANDARDIZED TEST PRACTICE

10. Juan is training for a 10K race. The table shows the number of kilometers Juan ran in the last 6 weeks. Estimate how many kilometers he ran in Week 4.

(**A**) 10   (**B**) 20

(**C**) 25   (**D**) 35

Week	1	2	3	4	5	6
Kilometers	15	21	29	?	42	50

EXPLORATION AND EXTENSION

PORTFOLIO

11. **BUILDING YOUR PROJECT** Survey your class to find out what collections each person has. Organize your data in a table. Classify the collections into categories such as toys and games, things from nature, and stamps and coins. Explain which categories you chose and why.

1.3

What you should learn:

Goal 1 How to solve problems by making a list

Goal 2 How to use lists to help you solve problems

Why you should learn it:

Making a list is another strategy for organizing data. You can use a list to help count the number of options.

Making a List

Goal 1 MAKING A LIST

Many people use lists to keep track of things that they need to remember to do. In mathematics, *making a list* is a very useful problem solving strategy.

Example 1 Making a List

You own a snack shop. You have a special for a one-pound mix of 3 different snacks for $4.95. The snacks for the special are dried fruits and nuts.

How many mixtures of three can you make? If you add walnuts (W) to the choices, how many mixtures of three can you make?

Solution

One way to solve the problem is to make a list.

First, list all the mixtures of three snacks that include raisins.

RCB	RCP	RCA
RAP	RBP	RAB

raisins, cashews, and apricots

Then list all the mixtures that include cashews but not raisins.

CAB   CAP   CPB

Then list all the mixtures that do not include cashews or raisins.

ABP

There are 10 different mixtures of three snacks.

If you add walnuts, you can make ten more mixtures.

WCB	WCP	WCR	WCA
WBP	WBR	WBA	
WPR	WPA		
WRA			

There are 10 different mixtures that include walnuts and 10 that do not. So, with walnuts, there are 20 different mixtures of three snacks.

Goal 2 USING A LIST

STUDY TIP

The pattern shown by a list can depend on how the list is written. In Example 2, the pattern would not be as clear if you used 10 columns instead of 12.

A **multiple** of a number is the product of the number and any whole number greater than zero. For example, 15 is a multiple of 5 because $5 \times 3 = 15$. Some other multiples of 5 are 5, 10, 20, and 25.

Example 2 Using a List

The list shows the whole numbers from 1 through 72.

1	2	3	4	5	6	7	8	9	10	11	12
13	14	15	16	17	18	19	20	21	22	23	24
25	26	27	28	29	30	31	32	33	34	35	36
37	38	39	40	41	42	43	44	45	46	47	48
49	50	51	52	53	54	55	56	57	58	59	60
61	62	63	64	65	66	67	68	69	70	71	72

a. Copy the list and circle all the multiples of 4.

b. Color all the multiples of 6 blue.

c. Describe the numbers that are circled and blue.

Solution

a. The multiples of 4 consist of the 4th, 8th, and 12th columns.

b. The multiples of 6 consist of the 6th and 12th columns.

1	2	3	④	5	6	7	⑧	9	10	11	⑫
13	14	15	⑯	17	18	19	⑳	21	22	23	㉔
25	26	27	㉘	29	30	31	㉜	33	34	35	㊱
37	38	39	㊵	41	42	43	㊹	45	46	47	㊽
49	50	51	㊼	53	54	55	㊻	57	58	59	㉠
61	62	63	㉔	65	66	67	㉨	69	70	71	㉒

c. The numbers that are circled and blue are the numbers in the 12th column. They are all multiples of 12. So, in general you can say that if a number is both a multiple of 4 and a multiple of 6, then it is a multiple of 12.

ONGOING ASSESSMENT

Write About It

List the whole numbers from 1 through 36.

1. Circle the multiples of 2.

2. Color the multiples of 3.

3. Describe the numbers that are circled and colored.

GUIDED PRACTICE

1. Make a list of the whole numbers from 1 through 50. Circle the multiples of 5. Color the multiples of 2. Describe the numbers that are circled and colored.

2. List all of the different ways that you can rearrange the letters in the word *STAR*. How many ways did you find?

VACATION You are packing clothes for a weekend vacation trip. You pack a pair of shorts, a pair of jeans, a pair of sweatpants, a blue T-shirt, a white T-shirt, and a knit shirt in your suitcase.

3. Make a list of the different outfits you could wear during your trip.

4. You also pack sandals, sneakers, and casual shoes for your trip. How many different outfits, including footwear, could you wear during your trip? Use a list to help find the solution.

PRACTICE AND PROBLEM SOLVING

NUMBER THEORY In Exercises 5–7, make a list with several examples of the indicated types of numbers. Is the sum *even* or *odd*?

5. even + even = _?_   6. odd + odd = _?_   7. even + odd = _?_

NUMBER THEORY In Exercises 8–10, copy the list of whole numbers 1 to 72 on page 13.

8. Find all the numbers that are divisible by 12 and whose digits add up to 6.

9. Find all the numbers that are multiples of 2, 3, and 5. Are these numbers all multiples of 6? of 9? of 30?

10. Are all of the multiples of 6 also multiples of 2? Use a list of numbers to explain your answer.

11. **PROBABILITY** A bag contains five marbles numbered 1 to 5. You choose three marbles and determine the sum of the numbers on the marbles. List the possible sums.

12. **SHELLS** You are giving your friend part of your shell collection. You have 3 scallop shells, 2 olive shells, and 3 conch shells. If you choose one of each type, how many different combinations of shells could you give your friend?

REASONING In Exercises 13 and 14, name the number in the list below that is described by the clues.

6248	7232	8426	374	6482	6314
2648	338	1661	4640	8642	518
5135	6062	684	4514	1822	1580

13. No two digits are alike. None of the digits are odd. The number is a multiple of 6.

14. The sum of the digits is 14. The number is divisible by 2. The number has more than three digits. The number is less than 5000. The number is a multiple of 8.

15. REASONING You have forgotten your friend's phone number. You do remember that the first three digits are 621 and the last four digits contain the numbers 1, 3, 5, and 9. List the possible phone numbers. How many did you find?

16. FUND RAISING You are selling items at a snack sale. A customer buys a bag of popcorn for $.35 and gives you $1.00.

    a. List the different ways that you can give the customer change if you have quarters, dimes, and nickels.

    b. Which way uses the fewest coins? Which uses the most?

STANDARDIZED TEST PRACTICE

17. Theresa has a three-digit access code for her computer and has forgotten the code. If she knows that the first digit is a 2, how many numbers must she enter before she is sure to enter the correct code?

    (A) 20   **(B)** 80   **(C)** 100   **(D)** 200

EXPLORATION AND EXTENSION

PORTFOLIO

18. BUILDING YOUR PROJECT Use your results from the Building Your Project in Lesson 1.2 on page 11. Suppose that you can fit three collections on each table and two collections on each desk. What is the minimum number of tables and desks that you will need to display all the collections? Is it possible to fill each of the tables and desks that you use? Explain.

Tech Link

Investigation 1 Interactive Real-Life Investigations

1.4

Using a Graph

What you should learn:

Goal 1 How to solve problems using a graph

Goal 2 How to color code a map

Why you should learn it:

Using a graph is a strategy for comparing data. It can be used, for example, to compare the average gasoline expenses in different parts of the country.

In 1993, retail gasoline sales in the United States were more than $130,000 million.

TOOLBOX

Reading a Bar Graph, page 659

Goal 1 USING A GRAPH

Graphs, pictures, and diagrams help you interpret data. For example, the **bar graph** below shows the average amount per person per year spent on gasoline in different regions in the United States.

Example 1 Using a Graph

Use the graph to estimate the average gasoline expense in each region. Order the averages from least to greatest.

REAL LIFE
Cars

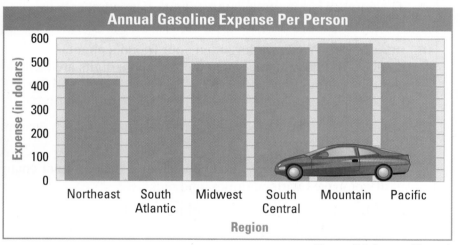

(Source: U.S. Bureau of Census)

Solution

The shortest bar has the lowest expense, and the tallest bar has the greatest expense. You can use this to help put your estimates in order. The bar for the Northeast states is the shortest. It reaches halfway between the horizontal bars for $400 and $450. Continue to compare the heights of the bars to complete the list.

Northeast	About $425
Midwest	Just under $500
Pacific	About $500
South Atlantic	About $525
South Central	Just over $550
Mountain	About $575

Example 2 Color Coding a Map

You can also use a color-coded map to show the data in the list in Example 1. Begin by choosing different spending ranges. Because the averages vary from $425 to $575, you could choose to have the spending ranges begin at $400 and increase by $50 to $599.

Range	Color	Regions
$400–449	(Color 1)	Northeast
$450–499	(Color 2)	Midwest
$500–549	(Color 3)	Pacific, South Atlantic
$550–599	(Color 4)	South Central, Mountain

Using this information, you can color the map as shown below.

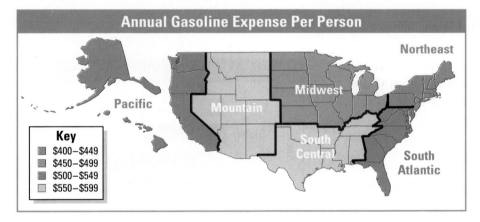

Annual Gasoline Expense Per Person

Key
- $400–$449
- $450–$499
- $500–$549
- $550–$599

Example 3 Reading a Circle Graph

In a **circle graph**, the area of the section of the circle represents a part of the whole. The graph at the right shows the types of fuel used by cars and trucks in the United States in 1996.

The section for gasoline is about four times as large as the section for diesel, so vehicles in the United States used about four times as much gasoline as diesel fuel.

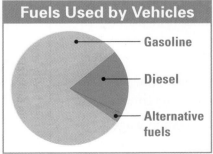

Fuels Used by Vehicles
- Gasoline
- Diesel
- Alternative fuels

TOOLBOX
Reading a Circle Graph, page 660

ONGOING ASSESSMENT

Talk About It

1. Discuss the advantages and disadvantages of the presentations in Examples 1 and 2.

2. Why do you think the average spending in the Northeast is lower than in the Mountain states?

GUIDED PRACTICE

1. Give an example of data that you could represent using a bar graph.

2. Give an example of data that you could represent by color coding a map of your state.

DATA ANALYSIS In Exercises 3 and 4, use the graph at the right. It shows the results of a survey that asked 100 people about how often they misplace the remote control for their television each week.

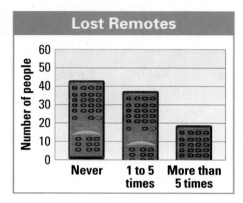

3. From the graph, estimate the number of people out of 100 surveyed who say they never misplace the remote.

4. What number of people out of 100 surveyed say that they misplace the remote at least once a week?

PRACTICE AND PROBLEM SOLVING

5. **SPORTS** The bar graph at the right shows the number of vacationers out of 100 surveyed who participated in four outdoor sports. (Source: U.S.A. Today)

   a. What sport was about 3 times more popular than sailing?

   b. List the sports from most popular to least popular.

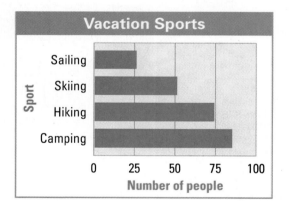

6. **BUSINESS** The bar graph at the right shows the average wages of production workers in manufacturing industries in three states for 1980 and 1995. (Source: U.S. Bureau of Labor Statistics)

   a. In which state did the average wage increase the most during this time?

   b. In which state did the average wage increase the least?

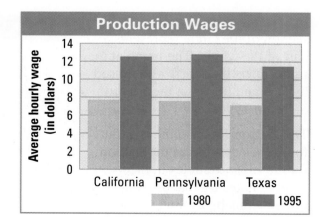

7. **MOVIES** In a survey, 1255 Americans were asked how often they went to the movies in the last year. The circle graph shows the results of the survey. (Source: Survey Research Consultants International)

   a. What was the most common response? How do you know?

   b. Is it reasonable to say that the number of people who said "once" was about the same as the number of people who said "11 to 20 times"? Explain why or why not.

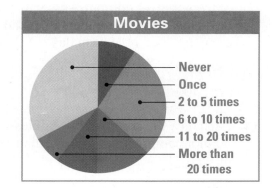

Movies

- Never
- Once
- 2 to 5 times
- 6 to 10 times
- 11 to 20 times
- More than 20 times

8. **BUSINESS** Use the list of the number of shopping centers in the United States to color code a map. Use the ranges 0–2499, 2500–4999, 5000–7499, and 7500–9999. (Source: U.S. Bureau of the Census)

Region	Shopping Centers
Northeast	6517
Midwest	8308
South Atlantic	9027
South Central	7144
Mountain	2681
Pacific	6691

9. **WRITING** The bar graph below shows some data. Estimate the height of each bar. Then make up a story about what the numbers might mean.

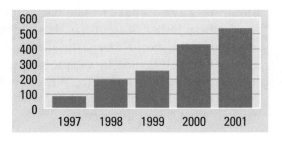

NATIONAL DEFENSE The table and the bar graph show the number of people serving in four branches of the U.S. military for 1990 and 1996.

	1990	1996
U.S. Army	746,220	493,330
U.S. Navy	604,562	436,608
U.S. Marine Corps	196,652	172,287
U.S. Air Force	535,233	389,400

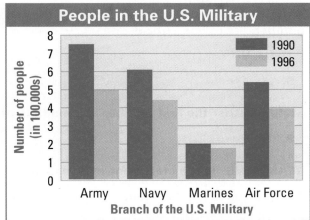

10. How many more people served in the U.S. Army in 1990 than in 1996? Is it easier to find this information in the table or from the graph?

11. Did the number of people serving in the U.S. Marine Corps decline more or less than the number of people serving in the U.S. Navy? Is it easier to find this information in the table or from the graph?

12. A company assembles six types of computers. The graph shows the number of each type of computer assembled each day. How many computers does the company assemble each day?

    (A) 200   **(B)** 300

    (C) 400   **(D)** 500

13. Each day, the company assembles 30 more computers of type 2 than of type **?** .

    (A) 1   **(B)** 3

    (C) 5   **(D)** 6

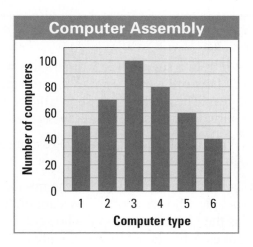

EXPLORATION AND EXTENSION

PORTFOLIO

14. BUILDING YOUR PROJECT The bar graph shows the number of items (in thousands) in some of the world's largest collections as of 1996. You decide to use the graph in a display in your museum. Write a few sentences to go with the graph that explain what the graph means.

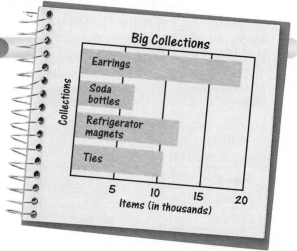

SPIRAL REVIEW

Write the first number as a product of the second number and another number. (Toolbox, page 642)

  1. 63, 9   **2.** 16, 2   **3.** 36, 4   **4.** 51, 3

  5. 56, 8   **6.** 81, 27   **7.** 75, 5   **8.** 63, 21

State whether the first number is a multiple of the second. (1.3)

  9. 18, 3   **10.** 28, 3   **11.** 54, 6   **12.** 40, 6

REASONING Is the statement reasonable? (Toolbox, page 655)

13. A book is 5 meters long.   **14.** A nickel weighs 5 grams.

15. The race is 5 kilometers long.   **16.** A can holds 5 milliliters.

17. You have a job mowing lawns. You earn $12 per lawn. If you mow 3 lawns each day, how much money will you earn in 3 days? **(1.3)**

Take this test as you would take a test in class. The answers to the exercises are given in the back of the book.

LOOKING FOR A PATTERN In Exercises 1–3, match the description with the pattern. (1.1)

1. 3, 8, 13, 18, . . .

A. Each number is 5 times the number before it.

2. 3, 15, 75, 375, . . .

B. Each number is 5 more than the number before it.

3. 3, 8, 11, 19, . . .

C. Each number is the sum of the two numbers before it.

4. SAVINGS You deposit money into your bank account each week to save for a computer game. The computer game costs $65. You deposit $2 the first week, $4 the second week, and $8 the third week. For how many weeks do you need to save to buy the computer game? (1.1)

FOOD In Exercises 5 and 6, use the table at the right. It lists the prices of 4 foods from 1992 to 1995. (bread: 1 pound; eggs: 1 dozen; chicken: 1 pound; oranges: 1 pound) (1.2)
(Source: U.S. Bureau of Labor Statistics)

	1992	1993	1994	1995
Bread	$0.74	$0.76	$0.75	$0.84
Eggs	$0.93	$0.87	$0.87	$1.16
Chicken	$2.08	$2.17	$1.91	$1.95
Oranges	$0.52	$0.56	$0.55	$0.64

5. Which foods cost more in 1995 than in 1992?

6. In which years did each of these four foods cost the most?

7. MAKING A LIST You are taking a true-false quiz with five questions. How many different ways can you answer all the questions on the quiz? (1.3)

FRIENDSHIP In a survey, 100 people told what is important to a friendship. The bar graph at the right shows the results. (1.4)
(Source: MCI Communications)

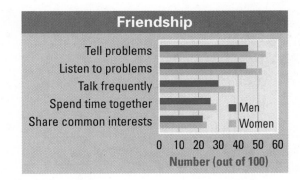

8. What part of friendship is considered most important by both men and women?

9. Do men and women have the same views about friendship? Explain.

10. MAKING A LIST As a fund raiser, your class is selling sandwiches. A sandwich can be made with white or wheat bread. It can be a ham, turkey, vegetarian, or combo. It can have Swiss, American, provolone, or mozzarella cheese. How many different kinds of sandwiches can your class sell? (1.3)

1.5

What you should learn:

Goal 1 How to solve problems by drawing a diagram

Goal 2 How to use a diagram to help you solve real-life problems

Why you should learn it:

Drawing a diagram is a strategy for collecting data for a problem. You can use it, for example, to find how much wood you need to build a storage box for CDs.

Drawing a Diagram

Goal 1 DRAWING A DIAGRAM

In Lesson 1.4, you used graphs to help you solve problems. Now you will use diagrams or pictures to help you solve problems.

A **quadrilateral** is a figure with four sides.

Quadrilateral

A **parallelogram** is a quadrilateral that has two pairs of parallel sides.

Parallelogram

Example 1 Drawing a Diagram

How many different shapes of quadrilaterals can be drawn in a 3-by-3 grid of dot paper? How many are parallelograms?

Solution

On a sheet of dot paper, draw a box around several 3-by-3 grids. Then draw as many different shapes of quadrilaterals as you can.

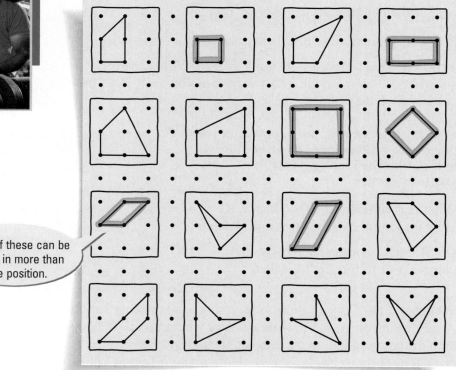

Many of these can be drawn in more than one position.

Of the 16 quadrilaterals, the 6 green ones are parallelograms.

Example 2 Drawing a Diagram

You are planning to build a storage box for your CD collection, as shown at the right. You plan to cut the pieces from a board that is 12 in. wide. How long should the board be?

REAL LIFE
Woodworking

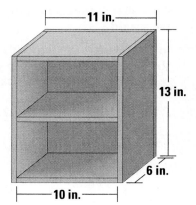

Solution

STRATEGY **DRAW A DIAGRAM**
The storage box has 6 pieces. One way to arrange the pieces on a board that is 12 in. wide is shown at the right. To find how long the board should be, find the sum of the lengths.

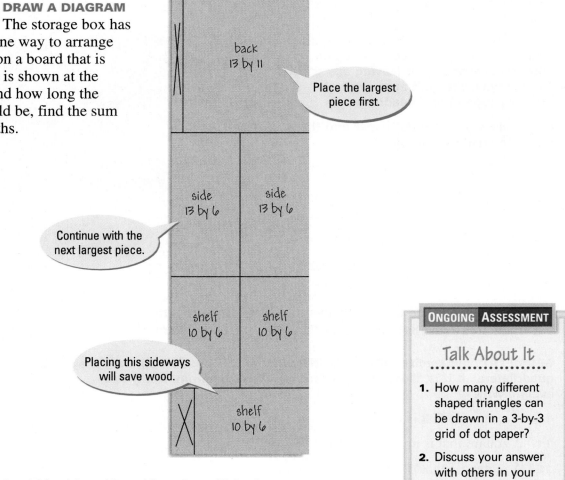

back
13 by 11

Place the largest piece first.

side
13 by 6

side
13 by 6

Continue with the next largest piece.

shelf
10 by 6

shelf
10 by 6

Placing this sideways will save wood.

shelf
10 by 6

The board should be 13 + 13 + 10 + 6, or 42 in. long.

ONGOING ASSESSMENT

Talk About It

1. How many different shaped triangles can be drawn in a 3-by-3 grid of dot paper?

2. Discuss your answer with others in your class.

GUIDED PRACTICE

GEOMETRY The large trapezoid at the right is drawn using 4 smaller trapezoids that are the same shape as the large trapezoid.

In Exercises 1–4, use dot paper. Use four quadrilaterals that are the size and shape of the given one to draw a larger quadrilateral that is the same shape.

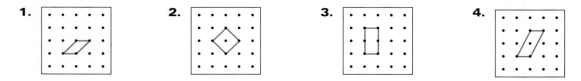

1.   2.   3.   4.

PRACTICE AND PROBLEM SOLVING

QUILT PATTERNS The pieces of a quilt pattern fit together to cover a region without overlapping or leaving any gaps. For example, the quilt at the right is made by repeating a quadrilateral.

In Exercises 5–8, use dot paper and the figure to create a quilt pattern.

5.   6.   7.   8.

9. Draw a quadrilateral on dot paper that is different from the ones in Exercises 7 and 8. Use your quadrilateral to create a pattern.

GEOMETRY In Exercises 10–13, decide whether it is possible to draw the quadrilateral. If it is, illustrate your answer with a diagram. If it is not, explain why.

10. A rectangle that is not a square

11. A square that is not a rectangle

12. A rectangle that is not a parallelogram

13. A quadrilateral that is not a square, a rectangle, or a parallelogram

MAPS You and six friends live in the same city within several blocks of one another. The table shows the number of blocks to your friends' homes from your home. (You live on the corner of a block.)

Friend	Distance (in blocks)
Luis	2 West, 3 North
Carmen	4 East, 3 North
Yoko	3 North
Steve	2 West, 5 South
Sue Ellen	2 East, 3 South
Jesse	6 East, 1 South

14. Use grid paper to draw a diagram that shows the locations of all the homes.

15. Which friend lives closest to you? How many blocks away does he or she live?

16. Which two friends live closest to each other? How many blocks apart do they live?

17. Describe the path from Carmen's home to Yoko's home.

18. How many blocks do Luis and Steve live from one another?

19. Which statement is *not* true?

(A) All rectangles are parallelograms.

(B) All rectangles are quadrilaterals.

(C) All parallelograms are quadrilaterals.

(D) All parallelograms are rectangles.

EXPLORATION AND EXTENSION

PORTFOLIO

WORD PUZZLE In Exercises 20–22, copy the grid of letters at the right. Use the clues to discover each word.

A	B	C	D	E
F	G	H	I	J
K	L	M	N	O
P	Q	R	S	T
U	V	W	X	Z

20. Start at M.
Left 2, up 2.
Right 4, down 3.
Left 2, up 2.

21. Start at I.
Down 2.

22. Start at F.
Down 3.
Right 3, up 2.

23. **BUILDING YOUR PROJECT** Design a poster to advertise your class museum. What size paper will you put it on? How high will the headlines be? Will you include a picture, and if so, how large will it be? What other information will you need to put on the advertisement? Sketch the layout of the ad to use as a model. Then make your poster.

LAB
1.6

COOPERATIVE
LEARNING

Classifying and Grouping

Materials Needed
• paper
• pencils

1. In your group, solve each problem on a separate sheet of paper. Then sort the problems into two piles that you have labeled *Addition Problems* and *Subtraction Problems*. Be prepared to explain how your group decided to classify each problem.

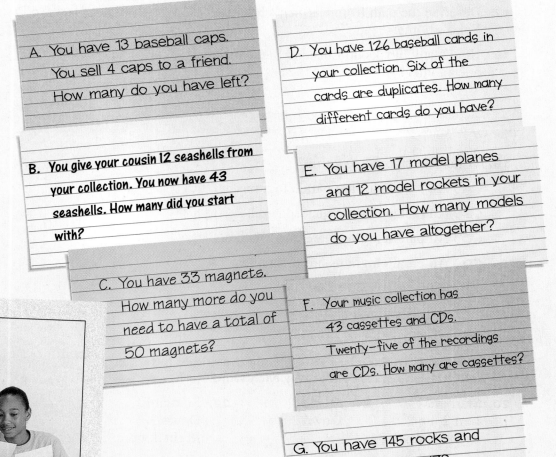

A. You have 13 baseball caps. You sell 4 caps to a friend. How many do you have left?

D. You have 126 baseball cards in your collection. Six of the cards are duplicates. How many different cards do you have?

B. You give your cousin 12 seashells from your collection. You now have 43 seashells. How many did you start with?

E. You have 17 model planes and 12 model rockets in your collection. How many models do you have altogether?

C. You have 33 magnets. How many more do you need to have a total of 50 magnets?

F. Your music collection has 43 cassettes and CDs. Twenty-five of the recordings are CDs. How many are cassettes?

G. You have 145 rocks and your friend has 178. How many more does your friend have than you?

Compare the way your group classified the seven problems with the ways other groups classified them.

2. Are there some problems that your group classified as addition but other groups classified as subtraction? Discuss your reasoning.

Here are two number sentences that you could have used to solve Problem A.

Addition Number Sentence

$$4 + \boxed{?} = 13$$

Subtraction Number Sentence

$$13 - 4 = \boxed{?}$$

In each number sentence, $\boxed{?}$ represents the number of caps you have left.

3. Make a table that shows how each of the other six problems can be represented as an addition number sentence *and* a subtraction number sentence.

	Addition Sentence	Subtraction Sentence
Problem A	4 + ? = 13	13 - 4 = ?
Problem B		
Problem C		
Problem D		
Problem E		
Problem F		
Problem G		

NOW TRY THESE

4. ALGEBRA Solve each problem. After you solve the problem, decide whether you would classify it as a multiplication problem or a division problem. Explain your reasoning.

   a. You have 4 boxes of football cards. Each box has 85 cards. How many cards do you have?

   b. Your collection of 39 model cars is displayed on 3 shelves. Each shelf has the same number of cars. How many are on each shelf?

5. WRITING NUMBER SENTENCES Write each of the problems in Exercise 4 as a multiplication number sentence and as a division number sentence.

1.6

What you should learn:

Goal 1 How to use mental math to solve addition and subtraction equations

Goal 2 How to use mental math to solve multiplication and division equations

Why you should learn it:

In algebra you will use symbols to solve problems. Learning to write equations for real-life problems can help you solve them.

Algebra and Equations

Goal 1 ADDITION AND SUBTRACTION EQUATIONS

In this lesson, you will learn how to use *algebra* to solve a problem. Here is an example.

> You have **13** baseball caps. You sell **4** caps to a friend. How many caps do you have left?

This problem can be solved using a sentence called a **verbal model** that can be rewritten as an **equation**. An equation is a mathematical sentence with an equal sign "=" in it.

| **Verbal Model** | Number of caps left | = | Number of caps you started with | − | Number of caps sold |

Equation   ? $= 13 - 4$

In this equation, ? stands for the number of caps left. In algebra, this number is represented by a letter, such as c.

Algebraic Equation $c = 13 - 4$

The value of c that makes the equation true is the **solution** of the equation. The solution of this equation is **9**. You can check this by replacing c by **9** in the original equation.

$c = 13 - 4$	Original equation
$9 \overset{?}{=} 13 - 4$	Replace c by 9.
$9 = 9$ ✔	Solution is correct.

Example 1 Solving Equations with Mental Math

Solve the equation.

a. $n + 4 = 19$ **b.** $20 - y = 12$

c. $x - 4 = 14$ **d.** $7 + p = 23$

Solution

a. The solution is $n = 15$, because $15 + 4 = 19$.

b. The solution is $y = 8$, because $20 - 8 = 12$.

c. The solution is $x = 18$, because $18 - 4 = 14$.

d. The solution is $p = 16$, because $7 + 16 = 23$.

STUDY TIP

Any letter can be used in an equation. To help remember what the letter represents, you can use letters such as c for cards, t for time, and p for price.

Goal 2 MULTIPLICATION AND DIVISION EQUATIONS

You can also use mental math to solve multiplication and division equations. Multiplication can be written with the symbol " · " or "×". Some calculators use the symbol " ∗ " for multiplication.

Example 2 Solving Equations with Mental Math

Solve the equation.

a. $8 \cdot p = 56$ **b.** $m \div 5 = 10$ **c.** $72 \div x = 8$

Solution

a. The solution is $p = 7$, because $8 \cdot 7 = 56$.
b. The solution is $m = 50$, because $50 \div 5 = 10$.
c. The solution is $x = 9$, because $72 \div 9 = 8$.

Example 3 Writing an Equation

REAL LIFE
Collecting

You are shopping for rocks for your collection. You find some that cost $1.65 each and decide to buy five of them.

a. Write an equation that can be used to find the total cost for five of the rocks.

b. You pay for your rocks with a ten dollar bill. Write an equation for the amount of change you will receive.

Solution

a. You can use a verbal model to write the equation.

> **Verbal Model**   **Total cost = Number of rocks × Price per rock**
>
> **Equation** $T = 5 \times 1.65$

Because 5×1.65 is 8.25, the total cost is $8.25.

b. Use a verbal model to write the equation.

> **Verbal Model**   **Change = Payment − Cost**
>
> **Equation** $C = 10 - 8.25$

Because $10 - 8.25 = 1.75$, you will receive $1.75 in change.

Real Life...
Real Facts

Fluorite crystals are often in the shape of a cube or octahedron. These crystals can be found in many parts of the United States.

ONGOING ASSESSMENT

Write About It

1. Which equation is easier to read?

$12 \cdot x = 60$

$12 \times x = 60$

Explain your reasoning.

2. Write a real-life problem that could be represented by the equation above.

GUIDED PRACTICE

In Exercises 1 and 2, use the problem below. Complete the statement with the word *equation* or *solution*.

> You are bowling and knock down 8 of the 10 pins. To get a *spare*, you must knock down the remaining pins. How many more pins must you knock down?

1. The __?__ that shows this problem is $p = 10 - 8$.

2. The __?__ is $p = 2$.

3. Your cat eats 2 cans of cat food every day. What letter would you use to stand for the number of cans of cat food you must buy every week? Why did you select that letter?

RECYCLING One recycled aluminum can saves enough energy to keep a 100-watt light bulb burning for $3\frac{1}{2}$ hours. You recycle 336 aluminum cans. The amount of energy saved is enough to keep a 100-watt light bulb burning for how many hours?

4. Complete the verbal model for the problem.

   Total hours $= $ __?__ $\times$ __?__

5. Write an equation that can be used to find the total number of hours the bulb will burn. Solve it.

6. **MENTAL MATH** Solve the equation $140 \div m = 14$ using mental math.

PRACTICE AND PROBLEM SOLVING

ALGEBRA AND MENTAL MATH   Use mental math to solve.

7. $18 + m = 25$ 8. $x + 36 = 42$ 9. $18 - s = 11$

10. $122 + 33 = t$ 11. $p - 11 = 12$ 12. $50 - 15 = d$

13. $9 \cdot y = 54$ 14. $40 \div b = 10$ 15. $n \times 15 = 45$

16. $x \div 5 = 7$ 17. $r \div 4 = 8$ 18. $m \cdot m = 16$

EQUATIONS   Write an equation for the problem. Then solve.

19. What number can you subtract from 17 to get 5?

20. What number can you multiply by 5 to get 40?

21. What number can you divide by 2 to get 18?

LOOKING FOR A PATTERN In Exercises 22–25, solve the equation. Then describe the pattern for *d*.

22. $2 + d = 10$
$4 + d = 10$
$6 + d = 10$
$8 + d = 10$

23. $d - 5 = 10$
$d - 5 = 15$
$d - 5 = 20$
$d - 5 = 25$

24. $d \cdot 5 = 25$
$d \cdot 5 = 30$
$d \cdot 5 = 35$
$d \cdot 5 = 40$

25. $d \div 2 = 7$
$d \div 2 = 8$
$d \div 2 = 9$
$d \div 2 = 10$

26. **ART** You sign up for a pottery class that costs $7 for each lesson. How many lessons can you take if you have $84? Use the following verbal sentence to write an equation for the problem. Then solve the equation.

Money you have ÷ Number of lessons = Cost per lesson

27. **BUSINESS** You ordered 350 T-shirts to sell at your store. You counted that you have 134 of them left. Write an equation that you can use to find out how many of the T-shirts you have sold. Then solve the equation.

In Exercises 28–31, write an equation for the problem. Then solve.

28. At the end of fifth grade, you were 59 in. tall. At the beginning of sixth grade, you were 61 in. tall. How many inches did you grow?

29. **TABLE TENNIS** In table tennis, the first player to get 21 points wins the game. Your score is 14. How many more points do you need to win?

30. **SWIMMING** Each day at swim team practice you must swim one mile. If one-half mile is 36 lengths of the pool, how many lengths must you swim each day at practice?

31. You are taking a standardized test. The test is in 6 equal parts, and the total time for the test is 180 minutes. How long is each part of the test?

Real Life...
Real Facts

Table Tennis

Players from more than 100 countries belong to the International Table Tennis Federation.

STANDARDIZED TEST PRACTICE

32. Which is the solution of $64 \div t = 4$?

   A $t = 12$ **B** $t = 14$ **C** $t = 16$ **D** $t = 18$

33. Which is the solution of $n \cdot 8 = 56$?

   A $n = 6$ **B** $n = 7$ **C** $n = 8$ **D** $n = 9$

34. **BUILDING YOUR PROJECT** To cover the costs of
your museum, you charge 10¢ admission.

a. At the beginning of the first day, you have
$1.00 in the cash box so you can make
change. At the end of the day, you have $3.30
in the cash box. Use the verbal model below
to write an equation that can be used to find
how much money you collected that day.
Use mental math to solve the equation.

$$\begin{matrix} \text{Cash at} \\ \text{beginning} \end{matrix} + \begin{matrix} \text{Money} \\ \text{collected} \end{matrix} = \begin{matrix} \text{Cash at end} \\ \text{of day} \end{matrix}$$

b. Use the verbal model below to write an equation that can
be used to find how many people came to the museum that day.
Use mental math to solve the equation.

Admission per person × Number of people = Money collected

c. Discuss in your group whether you should charge admission to
your museum. What did the group decide? Why?

35. **COMMUNICATING ABOUT MATHEMATICS** (page 43) The
Pennsylvania College of Podiatric Medicine's Shoe Museum has
about 800 pairs of shoes. About 250 pairs are on display. Write an
equation that you could use to estimate the number of pairs of shoes
that are not on display. Then solve your equation.

SPIRAL REVIEW

Add, subtract, multiply or divide. (Toolbox, page 641)

1. $40.1 + 13.7$
2. $12.22 - 10.01$
3. $1.8 + 12$
4. $4.5 + 9$
5. $33.18 + 21.55$
6. $120.21 - 50.34$
7. $1.67 + 15$
8. $78.15 - 15$

MEASUREMENT **Measure the length of each item to the nearest inch.**
(Toolbox, page 654)

9. Math book
10. Quarter
11. Unsharpened pencil

Use the number line below to find the distance between the points.
(Toolbox, page 641)

```
              A            B         C         D
  ←────┼──┼──┼──┼──┼──┼──┼──┼──┼──┼──┼──→
    15.75  16  16.25  16.5  16.75  17  17.25  17.5  17.75  18  18.25
```

12. A and B
13. B and C
14. B and D
15. A and D

16. You want to ride a rollercoaster at an amusement park. The ride
is 3 min long. If you wait in line 15 min each time you ride the
rollercoaster, how many times can you ride it in one hour? (1.6)

Multiplying Decimals

Many real-life problems contain decimal numbers. One way to solve such problems is to use a calculator.

Example

You buy 12 gallons of gasoline that cost $1.249 per gallon. You have $16. Is that enough to pay for the gasoline?

Solution

When you use a calculator, you should first think about what a reasonable answer would be. For this problem, you can use mental math to estimate the total cost of the 12 gallons of gasoline. Because $1.249 is about $1.25, you can estimate the total cost as follows.

Multiply 12 times $1 and 12 times $.25 separately.

$$12 \times 1.00 = 12 \qquad\qquad 12 \times 0.25 = 3$$

Then add the products.

$$12 + 3 = 15$$

So 12 gallons should cost about $15. To find the product with a calculator, enter the following keystrokes.

12 ✕ 1 . 249 = ⬛ 14.988

The calculator should display 14.988, which is less than $16. So, you do have enough to pay for the gasoline.

STUDY TIP

You will study how to add, subtract, multiply, and divide decimal numbers by hand in Chapter 4. Here is an example of how to multiply decimal numbers.

$$
\begin{array}{r}
1.249 \\
\times\ \ \ \ 12 \\
\hline
2\,498 \\
12\,49 \\
\hline
14.988 \\
\end{array}
$$

Exercises

In Exercises 1–8, first use mental math to estimate the answer. Then, use a calculator to add, subtract, multiply, or divide.

1. $1.248 + 1.456$
2. $4.509 + 6.826$
3. $8.408 - 6.507$
4. $7.532 - 5.002$
5. 1.23×3.2
6. 4.25×8.12
7. $5.36 - 1.2$
8. $6.58 \div 2.3$

9. You buy 15 gallons of gasoline that cost $1.199 per gallon. You have $18. Is that enough to pay for the gasoline? Answer the question first by estimating, and then use a calculator.

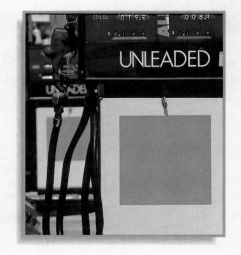

1.7 Working Backward

What you should learn:

Goal 1 How to work backward to solve an equation

Goal 2 How to work backward to solve real-life problems

Why you should learn it:

You can work backward when you want to know the original amount of something. An example is finding the amount of money you started with at a water park.

In 1997, there were more than 900 water parks in the United States.

Goal 1 WORKING BACKWARD

What reasoning can you use to solve this equation?

$n \div 2 = 7$ **Original equation**

One way is to think of the equation as a question.

What **number** can you **divide** by 2 to get 7?

To find the answer, you can *work backward*. To undo the division in the question, you can multiply, as follows.

*Start with 7 and **multiply** by 2 to get 14.*

The solution is $n = 14$.

You can use the same strategy to solve other types of equations. For example, use subtraction to undo addition.

Example 1 › Solving Equations

Write each equation as a question. Then solve the equation by working backward.

a. $x + 83 = 94$ **b.** $m - 5 = 21$ **c.** $11 \cdot p = 99$

Solution

a. Equation $x + 83 = 94$

Question What **number** can you **add** to 83 to get 94?

Work Backward Start with 94 and **subtract** 83 to get **11**.

The solution is $x = 11$.

b. Equation $m - 5 = 21$

Question What **number** can you **subtract** 5 from to get 21?

Work Backward Start with 21 and **add** 5 to get **26**.

The solution is $m = 26$.

c. Equation $11 \cdot p = 99$

Question What **number** can you **multiply** by 11 to get 99?

Work Backward Start with 99 and **divide** by 11 to get **9**.

The solution is $p = 9$.

Example 2 Combining Strategies

REAL LIFE
Recreation

You went to a water park with a friend. You spent half of your money on admission to the park. You forgot to bring a towel, so you spent half the money that was left on a new one. Then you had $4 left, which you spent on lunch. How much money did you take to the water park?

Solution

STRATEGY **DRAW A DIAGRAM** To begin, draw a diagram that represents the problem.

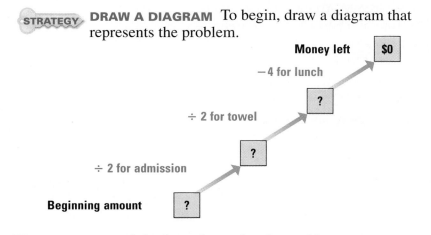

Now, you can work backward to solve the problem.

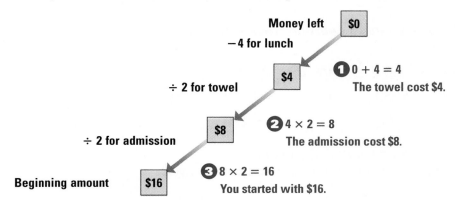

✓**Check:** You can check this as follows.

$16 \div 2 = 8$ You paid $8 for admission and still have $8.

$8 \div 2 = 4$ You paid $4 for a towel and still have $4.

$4 - 4 = 0$ You paid $4 for lunch and have no more money.

ONGOING ASSESSMENT

Write About It
·····················

Write each equation as a question. Then solve the equation by working backward.

1. $9 + y = 14$

2. $m \cdot 4 = 36$

3. $17 - x = 8$

4. $n \div 6 = 48$

GUIDED PRACTICE

1. Copy and complete the diagram below. Work backward to solve. Explain your steps.

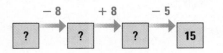

In Exercises 2–5, rewrite the equation as a question. Then solve the equation and check your answer.

2. $78 + n = 93$ **3.** $54 - p = 48$ **4.** $3 \cdot y = 39$ **5.** $42 \div b = 6$

6. You have a gymnastics class at 10:30 A.M. You want to get there 15 minutes early. Your bus ride from home to class is 25 minutes. What time should you leave home?

PRACTICE AND PROBLEM SOLVING

WORKING BACKWARD   In Exercises 7–10, copy and complete the diagram.

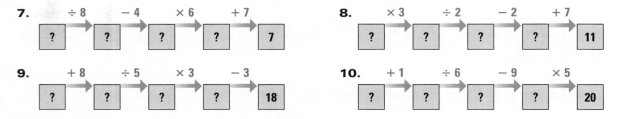

In Exercises 11–22, rewrite the equation as a question. Then solve the equation and check your answer.

11. $x + 5 = 24$ **12.** $18 - y = 6$ **13.** $a - 32 = 51$ **14.** $6 + n = 45$

15. $t + 55 = 66$ **16.** $68 - d = 52$ **17.** $8 \cdot b = 48$ **18.** $p \div 7 = 10$

19. $c \div 8 = 14$ **20.** $m \times 4 = 112$ **21.** $63 \cdot x = 189$ **22.** $156 \div y = 12$

WRITING EQUATIONS   In Exercises 23–27, write an equation that represents the question. Then solve the equation and check your answer.

23. What number can be added to 18 to get 27?

24. What number can be subtracted from 95 to get 23?

25. What number can be multiplied by 7 to get 105?

26. What number can be divided by 4 to get 17?

27. What number can be multiplied by 12 to get 60?

GEOMETRY In Exercises 28 and 29, find the measure labeled *x*.

28. Length: 48 m

21 m

x

29. Length: 125 m

83 m

x

30. MINIATURE GOLF You play in a nine hole miniature golf tournament. Your scores for the last seven holes are shown below. You forgot your scores for the first two holes. You do remember that the score of the first hole was one stroke less than the score for the second hole. Your total score is 22. What were the scores for the first and second holes?

Hole	1	2	3	4	5	6	7	8	9
Score	?	?	2	3	4	2	3	1	2

STANDARDIZED TEST PRACTICE

31. Solve $n - 5 = 14$.

  A 9   **B** 12   **C** 19   **D** 21

32. Solve $p \div 3 = 42$.

  A 14   **B** 39   **C** 45   **D** 126

EXPLORATION AND EXTENSION

PORTFOLIO

33. BUILDING YOUR PROJECT You include the puzzle at the right about collections in the puzzles and activities booth of your museum.

Work backward to find the answer to the puzzle so that you can have it available at the museum. Write a similar puzzle based on your classmates' collections. Exchange puzzles with another member of your class and solve each other's puzzle. Explain to the other members of your group how you created your puzzle.

> There are half as many dolls as there are basketball cards. There are 8 more action figures than there are dolls. There are 6 times as many postage stamps as action figures, and there are 10 times as many postage stamps as there are glass statues. There are 15 glass statues. How many items are in each of the collections?

1.8 Solving a Simpler Problem

What you should learn:

 Goal 1 How to solve a simpler problem

Goal 2 How to solve real-life problems by solving a simpler problem

Why you should learn it:

You can often solve a simpler problem when a real-life problem is complex and confusing.

In a round-robin tournament each team plays each of the other teams. How many games will there be in a round-robin tournament with eight teams?

Goal 1 SOLVING A SIMPLER PROBLEM

You can solve some problems by first *solving a simpler problem.* You may find a pattern that will help solve the original problem.

LESSON INVESTIGATION

Counting Routes to School

GROUP ACTIVITY The grid shows a 2-by-4 block region. Your home and school are shown. How many blocks do you have to walk to get to school? How many different ways can you walk this number of blocks?

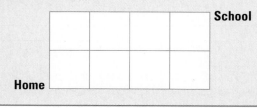

You can begin by solving the following simpler problem.

Count the number of ways to walk to the corners near your home.

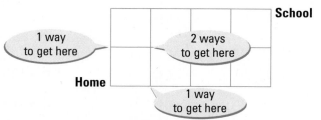

Count the number of ways to walk to nearby corners. The number of ways to walk to a corner is the sum of the number of ways to get to the corner one block to the left and the corner one block down. Why?

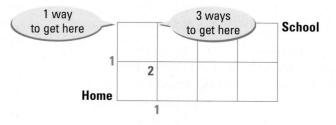

Continue finding the number of ways to walk to each corner until you get to school.

Goal 2 SOLVING REAL-LIFE PROBLEMS

Example 1 Counting Combinations

REAL LIFE
School

Each day, your teacher asks two students to write solutions to homework problems on the board. There are 20 students in your class. How many different pairs of students are there? There are 150 days in the year when homework is assigned. Can a different pair of students write solutions each day?

Solution

One way to solve this problem is to *solve a simpler problem*. You can draw diagrams to count the number of pairs with smaller numbers of students.

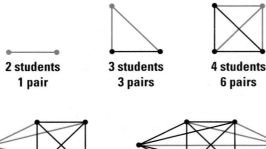

2 students
1 pair

3 students
3 pairs

4 students
6 pairs

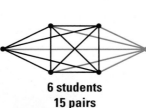

5 students
10 pairs

6 students
15 pairs

It appears that the pattern is as follows.

2 students	1 pair
3 students	$1 + 2 = 3$ pairs
4 students	$1 + 2 + 3 = 6$ pairs
5 students	$1 + 2 + 3 + 4 = 10$ pairs
6 students	$1 + 2 + 3 + 4 + 5 = 15$ pairs

Use this pattern to predict the number of pairs with 20 students.

20 students $1 + 2 + 3 + 4 + 5 + \ldots + 19 = 190$ pairs

There are more pairs of students than days when homework is assigned, so a different pair of students can be assigned to write solutions on the board each day.

ONGOING ASSESSMENT

Talk About It
. . . .

1. If you doubled the number of students in your class, would the number of different pairs double? Explain your reasoning.

2. Give an example of a real-life situation where solving a simpler problem can help you solve a more complicated one.

GUIDED PRACTICE

CHOOSING A STRATEGY In Exercises 1–3, which strategy is the best to use to solve the problem? Choose from: *make a list, solve a simpler problem,* and *draw a diagram*.

1. A stack of quarters is worth $1000. How high is the stack?

2. How many squares can be drawn on a 3-by-3 grid of dot paper?

3. In how many different orders can five people stand in a line?

In Exercises 4 and 5, describe a simpler problem that you could solve.

4. **SPORTS** An exercise program requires you to do one sit-up the first day and double the number you do each day for seven days. How many sit-ups will you do on the sixth day?

5. **FRIENDSHIP CLUB** You form a club with six people. Each member is to exchange a friendship ring with each other member. How many rings will be exchanged?

PRACTICE AND PROBLEM SOLVING

6. Triangular numbers can be represented by dots arranged in a triangle, as shown at the right. Predict the number of dots in the eighth triangular number.

7. **GAMES** Look at the 5-by-5 checkerboard at the right. To find the total number of squares of different sizes on the board, begin by solving simpler problems.

    a. How many 1-by-1 squares are there?

    b. How many 2-by-2 squares are there?

    c. What other size squares do you need to count? How many of each size can you find?

    d. How many squares did you find in all?

8. **GEOMETRY** The first four figures of a pattern are shown below. Describe the pattern for the lengths. Predict the length of the 15th figure.

$n = 4$ $n = 8$ $n = 12$ $n = 16$

Figure 1   **Figure 2**   **Figure 3**   **Figure 4**

9. Copy the diagram at the right. Then put the numbers 1 through 19 in the circles so that each row of 3 numbers has the same sum. (One number is already used.)

10. **TOURNAMENTS** You are scheduling the chess club tournament. There are seven members and they play each other once. How many games must you schedule?

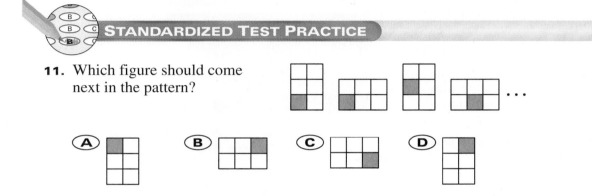

11. Which figure should come next in the pattern?

...

(A) (B) (C) (D)

EXPLORATION AND EXTENSION

12. **TECHNOLOGY** To solve the *Calculator Crossword,* do the calculation and then turn the calculator upside down to find the word.

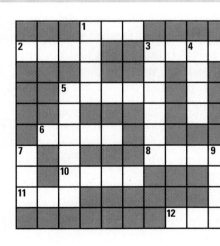

0-O	5-S
1-I	6-g
2-Z	7-L
3-E	8-B
4-h	9-G

ACROSS

1. $1000 - 396$ A farm animal
2. $2161 + 1412$ Do it or **?** !
3. $4910 - 1205$ Bottom of a shoe
5. $25,487 + 12,589$ Model of the world
6. $30,800 \div 10$ Musical instrument
8. $384.5 \cdot 12$ Opposite of low
10. $8305.5 \div 1.5$ More or **?**
11. $83.8 + 251.2$ Homonym of sea
12. $1110 - 377$ Can be electric

DOWN

1. $25,669 \div 3.5$ Part of a foot
3. $3691 \cdot 125$ Has jingle bells
4. $7 \cdot 501$ Misplace
5. $227,509 + 151,297$ A barnyard noise
7. $2020 \div 4$ A distress signal
9. $2624 + 5090$ Opposite of valley

In Exercises 1–6, add or subtract. (Toolbox, page 641)

1. $1329 + 3255$
2. $645 - 436$
3. $895 + 327$
4. $8740 - 235$
5. $985 + 12{,}499$
6. $43{,}866 - 32{,}114$

RECREATION One hundred students who are 7 to 12 years old were asked about their favorite things to do. The results are shown in the graph. (1.4)

7. What activity was chosen more often than any other?

8. About how many said *playing outside*?

9. **ECONOMICS** You go to the video arcade and spend $5 to buy tokens that cost 25¢ each to play the games. When it is time to go home, you still have 6 tokens left. How many tokens have you used at the arcade? (1.6)

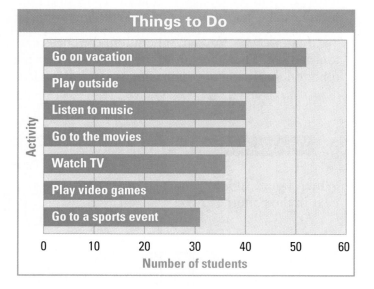

CAREER Interview

EXHIBIT DESIGNER

Richard Sheffield has been an exhibit designer at the Museum of Science, Boston for more than 40 years. Working with other people and computers, he designs exhibits for the museum.

Q. What led you to this career?
I decided I wanted to work in a museum when I was 11. I joined the staff at the Museum of Science after finishing college and have been here ever since.

Q. How does math help you with your job?
You have to think in three dimensions to use the space in a museum to best advantage. I do a lot of area and volume calculations. There is no way in the world you could do my job without using math.

Q. What can you tell students about the importance of studying math?
Every professional job I know of involves some kind of calculations. Math doesn't have to be your favorite thing, but you need to be able to use it readily or it will hold you up. Although I wasn't a great math student in high school, I have become better through on-the-job training.

NOT YOUR EVERYdAY
MUSEUM

READ About It

Usually when people think about museums, they think of art museums or natural history museums, but there are many other kinds.

For example, the Hall of Flame celebrates the history of fire fighting equipment. This museum contains 130 vehicles used for fighting fires as well as 12,000 smaller items. Some of the vehicles are horse drawn or hand drawn. Only 45 of them are motorized.

The Carole and Barry Kaye Museum of Miniatures contains the largest collection of miniatures in the world. The Museum opened with about 100 exhibits, and today it has 400 items. About 350 miniatures are on display at any one time.

Other unusual museums in the United States include the American Sanitary Plumbing Museum, the Museum of Ancient Brick, the Museum of Bad Art, the Mustard Museum, and the Barbed Wire Hall of Fame!

WRITE About It

1. How many of the vehicles at the Hall of Flame are either hand drawn or horse drawn?

2. The table below contains information about the pumping capabilities of several of the pumpers at the Hall of Flame. Which one can pump the most gallons of water per minute?

Fire Engine Model	Year	Pumping rate (in gal/min)
Howe/Ford Model T	1918	350
Mack Model 1	1951	550
Rumsey "Village Fire Engine"	1865	30
Seagrave Standard	1927	750

3. The table lists the pumpers in alphabetical order. Rewrite the table with the pumpers in order by the year they were built.

4. About how many miniatures have been added to the collection of the Miniature Museum since it opened? How many pieces are *not* on display at any one time?

1.9

What you should learn:

Goal 1 How to decide which problem solving strategies to use

Goal 2 How to use problem solving strategies to solve puzzles

Why you should learn it:

Problem solving is important in all parts of life. Learning to solve problems in mathematics can help you solve many problems in everyday living.

A Summary of Problem Solving Strategies

Goal 1 PROBLEM SOLVING STRATEGIES

In this chapter, you studied many problem solving strategies.

STRATEGIES FOR SOLVING PROBLEMS	
Looking for a Pattern	**Lesson 1.1**
Reading and Making a Table	**Lesson 1.2**
Making a List	**Lesson 1.3**
Using a Graph	**Lesson 1.4**
Drawing a Diagram	**Lesson 1.5**
Classifying and Grouping Data	**Lab 1.6**
Working Backward	**Lesson 1.7**
Solving a Simpler Problem	**Lesson 1.8**

Example 1 shows another useful strategy: *Guess, Check, and Revise.*

Example 1 Using Guess, Check, and Revise

Two whole numbers are *consecutive* if their difference is 1. For example, 1 and 2 are consecutive and 5 and 6 are consecutive. What two consecutive numbers have a product of 342?

TOOLBOX
Multiplying Whole Numbers, page 642

Solution

One way to solve this problem is to guess the numbers, check to see if their product is 342, and revise your guess, if necessary.

Choose 23 and 24. — First guess.
$23 \times 24 = 552$ — Check. Product is too large.

Choose 16 and 17. — Revise guess.
$16 \times 17 = 272$ — Check. Product is too small.

Choose 17 and 18. — Revise guess.
$17 \times 18 = 306$ — Check. Product is too small.

Choose 18 and 19. — Revise guess.
$18 \times 19 = 342$ — Check. Guess is correct.

So, the two numbers are 18 and 19.

Example 2 Choosing a Strategy

One by one, 4 students walk by a bowl of apples.

- Mary takes $\frac{1}{4}$ of the apples.

- Carlos takes $\frac{1}{3}$ of what Mary left.

- Elsa takes half of what Carlos left.

- James takes the remaining 2 apples.

How many apples were originally in the bowl?

Solution

STRATEGY **DRAW A DIAGRAM** One way to solve this problem is to draw a diagram and work backward.

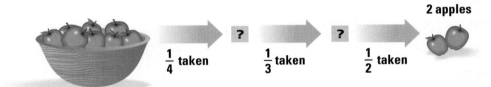

Now, you can work backward as follows.

- James took 2 apples, so start with 2 apples.

- Elsa took half of the apples, so half remain. 2 is half of 4. There were 4 apples in the bowl before Elsa took 2 apples.

- Carlos took $\frac{1}{3}$ of the apples, so $\frac{2}{3}$ remain. 4 is $\frac{2}{3}$ of what number? Use *Guess, Check, and Revise.* There were 6 apples before Carlos took 2.

- Mary took $\frac{1}{4}$ of the apples, so $\frac{3}{4}$ remain. 6 is $\frac{3}{4}$ of what number? Use *Guess, Check, and Revise.* There were 8 apples before Mary took 2.

There were 8 apples in the bowl originally.

ONGOING ASSESSMENT

Write About It

. . . .

1. Write a puzzle like the one in Example 2.

2. Trade puzzles with another student in your class. Solve the puzzle you received.

3. Discuss with your class the strategies that you used.

Extra Practice, page 622

GUIDED PRACTICE

CHOOSING A STRATEGY   **In Exercises 1 and 2, name two strategies that you could use to solve the problem. Tell why you chose them.**

1. In Minnesota, to get from Meadowlands to Zim, you must go through either Tiovola or Kelsey. A road connects Tiovola and Kelsey. Describe the routes you could take.

2. At an Italian restaurant, you have a choice of lasagna, ravioli, or spaghetti for a main course and a choice of cannoli or spumoni for dessert. How many different meals can you have?

3. Give an example of a problem that you could solve using the strategy of *Guess, Check, and Revise.*

4. Which problem solving strategy do you like best? Why?

PRACTICE AND PROBLEM SOLVING

GUESS, CHECK, AND REVISE   **In Exercises 5 and 6, solve the problem using the strategy of *Guess, Check, and Revise.***

5. Find numbers that satisfy the statement.

   a. The sum of two consecutive numbers is 293.

   b. The product of two consecutive numbers is 702.

   c. The product of three consecutive numbers is 2184.

6. **NUMBER PUZZLE**   The sum of two numbers is 50. The product of the two numbers is 481. What are the numbers?

   $$a + b = 50$$
   $$a \times b = 481$$

In Exercises 7 and 8, solve the problem using any strategy. State the strategy or strategies you used and why.

7. **FITNESS**   You are helping the coach tape lines on the gym floor to divide the length of the gym into 8 lanes of the same size. If it takes one minute to tape a line, how long will it take to do the job?

8. **REASONING**   You are playing the card game Crazy Eights. During the game, you pick up twice as many cards as you lay down, and you lay down 7 cards. If you now have 15 cards in your hand, how many cards did you start with?

In Exercises 9 and 10, use the graph at the right about 5–17 year-old students. It shows the average number of days of school missed per student for five years. (Source: U.S. Center for Health Statistics)

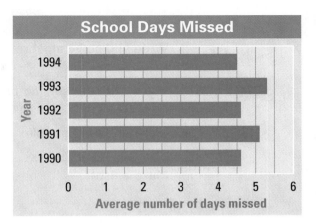

School Days Missed

9. Estimate the number of days missed in each year, to the nearest half day.

10. In 1990, about 46,000,000 students in the United States were 5 to 17 years old. Use this number to estimate the *total* number of days missed by students in 1990. Explain.

11. With 1 straight cut, you can cut a circle into two pieces. The figures at the right show the results of using 2 and 3 straight cuts. What is the largest number of pieces you can make using 5 straight cuts? Draw a diagram to show your solution.

STANDARDIZED TEST PRACTICE

12. If $x - 8 = 17$, then $x = $? .

 (A) 9 (B) 11 (C) 21 (D) 25

EXPLORATION AND EXTENSION

PORTFOLIO

13. Copy the table at the right. Use the clues below to determine who collects what. Mark an X in the table when it cannot be true and an O in the table when it can.

 a. Most of Manuel's collection came on soda bottles.

 b. Larry could not use his collection to eat soup.

 c. Yuki uses her collection to display photos she took herself.

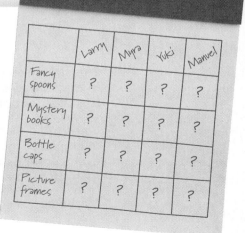

14. **BUILDING YOUR PROJECT** Make a logic puzzle like the one in Exercise 13 about the collections in your class's museum.

WHAT *did you learn?*   **WHY** *did you learn it?*

		WHAT	**WHY**

Skills

1.6	Write and solve algebra equations.	Solve real-life problems, such as finding total cost.

Strategies

1.1	Use a problem solving plan and look for a pattern.	Solve real-life problems such as making purchases.
1.2	Make and read a table.	Analyze data, such as the popularity of sports.
1.3	Make a list.	Organize data for solving problems.
1.4	Use a bar graph, a circle graph, and a colored map.	Analyze data, such as gasoline expenses.
1.5	Draw a diagram.	Find the amount of wood to purchase for a project.
1.6	Use mental math to solve equations.	Solve real-life problems such as finding the cost of a purchase.
1.7	Work backward to solve problems.	Solve problems where you need to find the amount you started with.
1.8	Solve a simpler problem.	Solve complex problems by finding a pattern.
1.9	Choose an appropriate strategy. Use Guess, Check, and Revise.	Solve mathematical and real-life problems.

Using Data

1.1–1.9	Use tables, lists, and graphs.	Organize data and solve problems.

HOW *does it fit in the bigger picture of mathematics?*

The strategies you have learned in this chapter will help you solve problems in mathematics and in real life. You may need to use more than one strategy to solve a problem.

You should always be willing to try a new approach to a problem if your first attempt doesn't work. Some problems in mathematics have taken years or even centuries to solve. These problems required the people working on them to try many different approaches and strategies for solving them.

Mathematics is still developing. Some problems are still unsolved.

VOCABULARY

- data (p. 4)
- multiple (p. 13)
- bar graph (p. 16)

- circle graph (p. 17)
- quadrilateral (p. 22)
- parallelogram (p. 22)

- verbal model (p. 28)
- equation (p. 28)
- solution (p. 28)

1.1 LOOKING FOR A PATTERN

Example In the pattern 3, 6, 12, 24, [?], [?], [?], . . . each number is two times the number before it. The next three numbers in this pattern are 48, 96, and 192.

1. Describe the pattern in the numbers below. Write the next three numbers in the pattern.

   35, 40, 46, 53, [?], [?], [?], . . .

1.2 USING A TABLE

Example From the table, you can see that people spent more time watching broadcast television than cable television in all three years. The time spent watching cable television increased over these years. (Source: Veronis, Suhler & Associates)

Time Spent Watching Television (hours per person)

	Broadcast Television	Cable Television
1993	1082	453
1994	1091	469
1995	1019	556

2. In each year in the table, about how much more time did people spend watching broadcast television than they spent watching cable television?

3. The source of the data shown in the table predicts that in the year 2000, people will watch 999 hours of broadcast television and 651 hours of cable television. Copy the table and add this information.

1.3 MAKING A LIST

Example Use a list to find the number of different kinds of sandwiches you can make using ham or turkey, and cheese or no cheese.

    ham, no cheese   ham, cheese

    turkey, no cheese   turkey, cheese

You can make four different kinds of sandwiches.

4. In the example, if you had rolls and bread to use for the sandwiches, how many different kinds of sandwiches could you make?

1.4 USING A GRAPH

Example The bar graph shows the consumption (in gallons) of bottled water and fruit juice in the United States. It shows that consumption of bottled water increased during each two-year period from 1988 to 1994. (Source: U.S. Bureau of the Census)

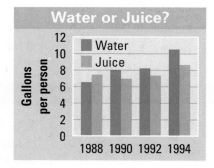

5. What was the first year that more bottled water was consumed than fruit juice?

6. Estimate how much bottled water a person drank in 1993.

1.5 DRAWING A DIAGRAM

Example You can draw a diagram to show that not all quadrilaterals are parallelograms.

This quadrilateral is a parallelogram.

This quadrilateral is not a parallelogram.

7. You have a piece of poster paper 12 in. by 18 in. You want to cut out flash cards that are 3 in. by 4 in. How many flash cards can you make? Draw a diagram to help you plan your solution.

1.6 ALGEBRA AND EQUATIONS

Example Together, you and a friend caught 26 fish. You caught 15. How many did your friend catch?

Total Fish = Fish your friend caught + Fish you caught

$$26 = \boxed{?} + 15$$

$$26 = n + 15$$

The solution is $n = 11$ because $26 = 11 + 15$.

In Exercises 8–10, use mental math to solve. Check your solution.

8. $x + 5 = 13$ **9.** $m \div 6 = 9$ **10.** $p - 4 = 49$

11. Write an equation you can use to solve the problem. Then solve it. You take $25 to a hockey game. You leave the game with $9. How much have you spent?

1.7 WORKING BACKWARD

Example **Equation** $x \div 4 = 12$

Question What **number** can you **divide** by 4 to get 12?

Work Backward Start with 12 and **multiply** by 4 to get **48**.

In Exercises 12–14, rewrite each equation as a question. Solve the equation. Check your answer.

12. $8 \cdot x = 128$ **13.** $y \div 3 = 21$ **14.** $m - 16 = 52$

1.8 SOLVING A SIMPLER PROBLEM

Example To find the number of hours you spend each year traveling to school, you can start by solving a simpler problem. Find the number of hours you spend traveling to school each week. Then you can multiply this number by the number of weeks of school to find the total.

15. TIME Describe a simpler problem you could solve to help you find the number of seconds in a year.

16. GAMES You are planning a backgammon tournament for five people. If each person plays one game against each of the other people, how many games must you schedule?

1.9 A SUMMARY OF STRATEGIES

You may want to review the list of Problem Solving Strategies on page 44. Another strategy you can use is *Guess, Check, and Revise.*

Example Find two consecutive numbers whose product is 462.

Choose 20 and 21.   First guess.

$20 \times 21 = 420$ Check. Product is too small.

Choose 21 and 22.   Revise guess.

$21 \times 22 = 462$ Check. Guess is correct.

The two numbers are 21 and 22.

17. A dime is about 18 mm wide. How long is a row of dimes worth $12?

18. The sum of two numbers is 15. The product of the two numbers is 36. Use *Guess, Check, and Revise* to find the numbers.

LOOKING FOR A PATTERN Describe the pattern. Then write the next 3 numbers or letters.

1. 60, 59, 56, 51, ? , ? , ? , . . .

2. 1, 2, 4, 7, ? , ? , ? , . . .

3. $\frac{1}{10}, \frac{2}{10}, \frac{4}{10}, \frac{8}{10}$, ? , ? , ? , . . .

4. A, D, G, J, ? , ? , ? , . . .

ALGEBRA AND MENTAL MATH Use mental math to solve.

5. $4 + b = 22$

6. $x - 15 = 34$

7. $78 \div y = 13$

8. $14 \cdot n = 70$

ALGEBRA In Exercises 9 and 10, write the equation as a question. Solve the equation by answering the question. Check your result.

9. $p - 45 = 110$

10. $a \div 3 = 14$

11. REASONING At a restaurant, you have a choice of 6 cheeseburger toppings. The toppings are lettuce (L), tomato (T), ketchup (K), mustard (M), pickle (P), and mayonnaise (Y). Make a list to find the number of combinations of two different toppings you can have on your cheeseburger.

12. Draw five triangles with different measurements on a 3-by-3 grid of dot paper.

13. JEWELRY Tina is arranging beads on a necklace. She first uses 1 yellow bead, then 2 green beads, then 3 red beads, and finally 2 blue beads. If she continues this pattern of beads on the necklace, what is the color of the 18th bead?

14. HIKING At 7:45 A.M., you begin a 12 mile hike. At 8:20 A.M., you have walked one mile. If you hike at the same speed the entire day, how many more hours will it take you to finish your hike?

MOVIES In Exercises 15–17, use the bar graph. It shows the average number of hours per year that people watch movies at home on videos and in theaters.
(Source: Veronis, Suhler, and Associates)

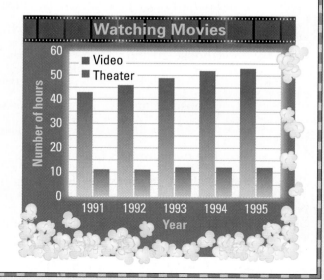

15. Estimate the average number of hours people watched movies in the theater and at home on videos in 1991.

16. Estimate the average number of hours people watched movies in the theater and at home on videos in 1995.

17. Did people spend more time watching movies in 1991 or 1995? Explain.

In Questions 1 and 2, use the following information. You are ordering a pizza. You can order thin crust or deep dish and have a choice of 5 toppings, including mushrooms, pepperoni, onion, sausage, and green pepper.

1. How many different pizzas with two different toppings can you order?

   (A) 10   **(B)** 15

   (C) 20   **(D)** 32

2. How many different pizzas with two different toppings include pepperoni?

   (A) 4   **(B)** 8

   (C) 10   **(D)** 20

3. A small juice costs 75¢ and a large one costs $1.25. You buy 4 small and 2 large juices. Which equation can you use to find the total cost?

   (A) $c = 4(1.25) + 2(0.75)$

   (B) $c = (1.25 + 0.75) \times (4 + 2)$

   (C) $c = 4(0.75) + 2(1.25)$

   (D) $c = 4(1.25 + 0.75) + 2$

In Questions 4 and 5, use the following information. One year, you bought 1 CD. Each year after that, you bought 3 more CDs than you did the year before. You now have 35 CDs. Each CD costs $15.

4. How much will you spend on CDs next year?

   (A) $150   **(B)** $195

   (C) $240   **(D)** $365

5. How many years will it have taken you to collect 70 CDs?

   (A) 4   **(B)** 5

   (C) 6   **(D)** 7

6. What is the next number in the pattern: 24, 20, 22, 18, 20, 16, . . . ?

   (A) 9   **(B)** 12

   (C) 14   **(D)** 18

In Questions 7 and 8, use the graph. It shows the number of books borrowed from a library for five months.

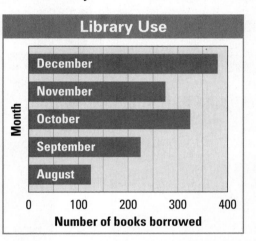

Library Use — Month / Number of books borrowed

7. How many books were borrowed over the five-month period?

   (A) Less than 600

   (B) Between 600 and 800

   (C) Between 800 and 1000

   (D) More than 1000

8. The graph shows that _?_.

   (A) from August to December, the number of books borrowed increased each month

   (B) the number of books borrowed in September is 225

   (C) the largest increase in books borrowed was between November and December

   (D) the number of books borrowed in October is less than 200

CHAPTER

2

TECHNOLOGY

Technology resources accompanying this chapter:

- Interactive Real-Life Investigations
- Middle School Tutorial Software

Place-Value Systems and Operations

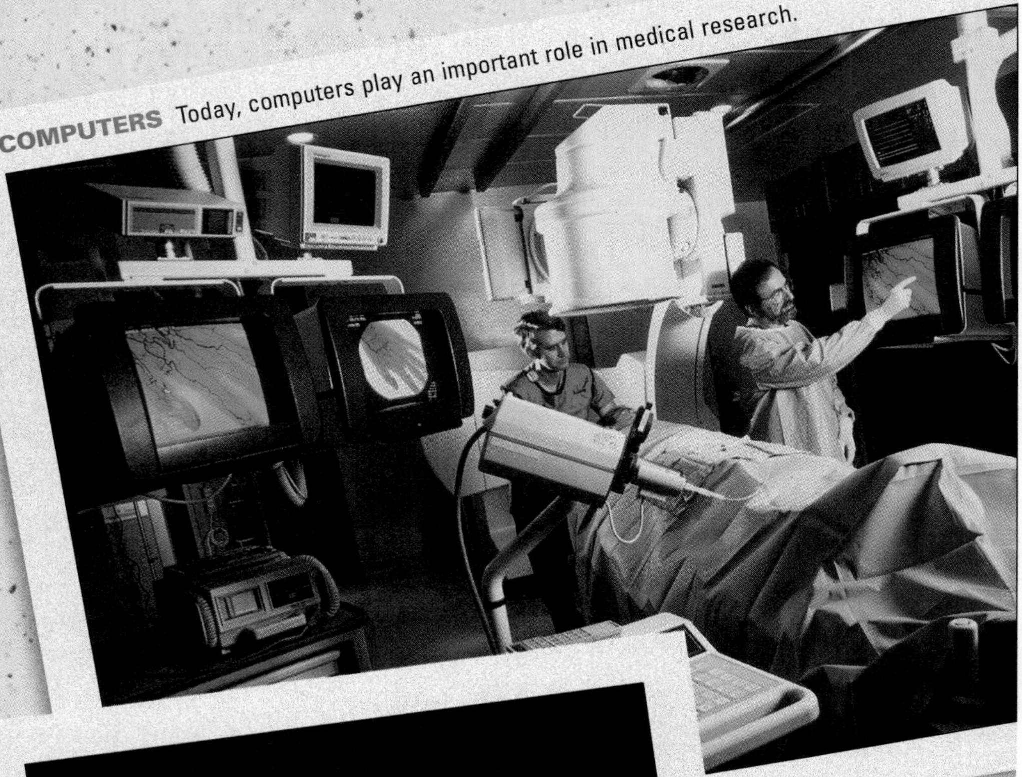

COMPUTERS Today, computers play an important role in medical research.

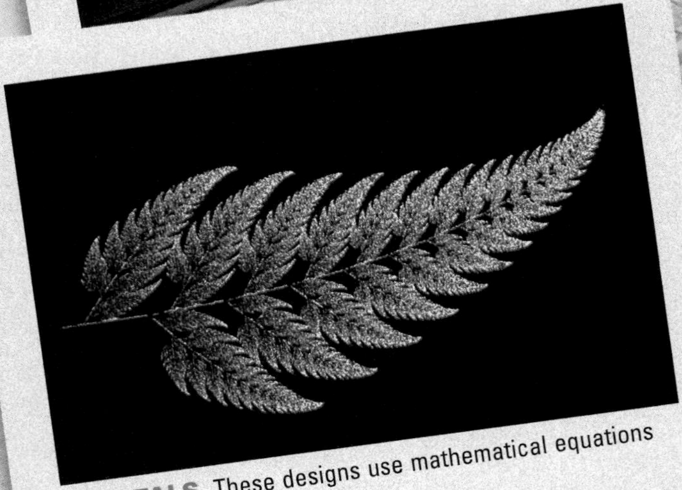

FRACTALS These designs use mathematical equations to create pieces of art.

CHAPTER THEME

Computers

FRACTAL LANDSCAPE This landscape is made up of complex, self-repeating, computer-generated patterns.

Fractals

REAL LIFE
Computers

An **algorithm** is a description of a process that is done exactly the same way each time it is repeated. For example, there is an algorithm for addition or multiplication of whole numbers. Computers have made it possible to apply algorithms to any kind of repeating process like fractals. A Polish mathematician named Waclaw Sierpinski (1882–1969) gave the world one of the first fractals.

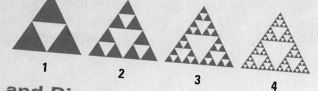

1   2   3   4

Think and Discuss

1. Look at the series of figures. Describe an algorithm for creating the Sierpinski gasket shown above.

2. What number patterns do you notice in the series of figures?

PORTFOLIO

CHAPTER PROJECT

Managing a Software Company

PROJECT DESCRIPTION

Imagine starting a company that makes computer games. Once you have some good computer games, you have to tell people about them. You will make a publicity booklet that shows some of your products. It will also contain a sample bill and some information about computers. To organize your booklet, you will use the **TOPICS** on the next page.

GETTING STARTED

Talking It Over

- In your group, discuss the tasks that computers help people with every day. How were these tasks done before there were any computers?

- What do you use a computer for? What are the features of a good computer program? If you could write any kind of computer program you wanted to, what would it be like?

Planning Your Project

- **Materials Needed:** paper, pens, colored pencils or markers

- Make a booklet using several sheets of paper. Think of a name for your company and design a logo. Put this information on the cover of the booklet. Add more information to your booklet as you do the **BUILDING YOUR PROJECT** exercises in this chapter.

BUILDING YOUR PROJECT

These are places throughout the chapter where you will work on your project.

TOPICS

2.2 Design a game that uses addition and subtraction. *p. 69*

2.3 Make a form for a bill and fill it out. *p. 75*

2.4 Prepare diskettes to be shipped. *p. 82*

2.6 Calculate the sum of several orders for your products. *p. 92*

2.7 Crack a code used in a computer game. *p. 99*

INTERNET

To find out about managing a software company, go to: **http://www.mlmath.com**

LAB 2.1

COOPERATIVE LEARNING

Materials Needed
- paper
- colored pencils

Representing Numbers

The first way that people wrote numbers is with tally marks. For example, the cave drawing at the right probably meant that 7 deer had been killed in a hunt.

Writing larger numbers such as 34 with tally marks is difficult. So people began to group tally marks. The groups usually had 5 or 10 tally marks.

34 marks	Grouped by 5's	Grouped by 10's

The ancient Egyptian number system grouped by 10's. The system included symbols for 1, 10, 100, 1000, and so on.

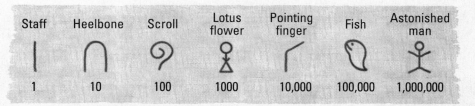

Staff	Heelbone	Scroll	Lotus flower	Pointing finger	Fish	Astonished man
1	10	100	1000	10,000	100,000	1,000,000

Here are two examples of numbers that are written with the ancient Egyptian number system.

354   1,312,240

Part A THE TALLY SYSTEM

1. In your group, show the number 28 in three different tally systems. Which system do you think is best? Explain.

2. Suppose you found some ancient writing that uses two number systems. You believe that both numbers are the same. Describe the second system, shown at the right below.

3. The numbers below are written using the ancient Egyptian number system. Write the numbers using our number system.

a.

b. ꧋

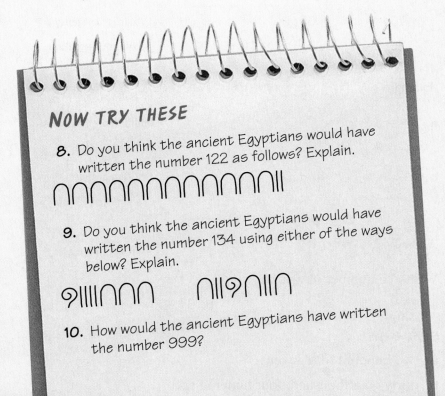

4. Write the numbers 304 and 2,210,008 in the Egyptian number system.

5. How do you think the Egyptians might have written the following sum?

$$453 + 734 = 1187$$

6. Discuss some problems of the ancient Egyptian system.

Part **C** CREATING A NUMBER SYSTEM

7. With your partner or group, design a number system that does not have the problems of the tally system or the ancient Egyptian number system.

NOW TRY THESE

8. Do you think the ancient Egyptians would have written the number 122 as follows? Explain.

∩∩∩∩∩∩∩∩∩∩∩∩II

9. Do you think the ancient Egyptians would have written the number 134 using either of the ways below? Explain.

ꟿIIII∩∩∩   ∩IIꟿ∩II∩

10. How would the ancient Egyptians have written the number 999?

2.1 The Base-Ten Place-Value System

What you should learn:

Goal 1 How to write base-ten place-value numbers in expanded notation

Goal 2 How to use base-ten place-value numbers to solve real-life problems

Why you should learn it:

An understanding of base-ten place-value systems will help you understand the operations that are used in our number system.

TOOLBOX

Multiplying and Dividing Whole Numbers, page 642

STUDY TIP

Because the ancient Egyptian number system was not a place-value system, it did not need a symbol for zero. In a place-value system, a symbol for zero is a placeholder that allows you to tell the difference between numbers such as 38, 380, and 308.

Goal 1 PLACE-VALUE SYSTEMS

Our number system is a **place-value system**. This means that the value of a digit is determined by its place in a number. For example, the 7 in 174 shows 7 tens, or seventy. But the 7 in 147 shows 7 ones, or simply seven.

Our number system is also a **base-ten system**. This means that as you move to the left, each place gets 10 times larger.

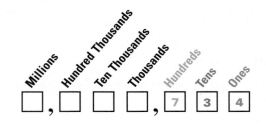

The place-value position of 7 tells you it is 7 hundreds, or seven hundred.

Our number system has an addition property, which allows numbers to be written in **expanded notation**.

$$734 = 700 + 30 + 4 \qquad \text{Addition property}$$
$$= 7 \times 100 + 3 \times 10 + 4 \times 1 \qquad \text{Expanded notation}$$

Example 1 Writing Expanded Notation

a. $83 = 80 + 3$ Addition property
$$= 8 \times 10 + 3 \times 1 \qquad \text{Expanded notation}$$

b. $542 = 500 + 40 + 2$ Addition property
$$= 5 \times 100 + 4 \times 10 + 2 \times 1 \qquad \text{Expanded notation}$$

Example 2 Writing Numbers

Write the number in words.

a. 257   **b.** 34,406

Solution

a. two hundred fifty-seven

b. thirty-four thousand, four hundred six

Example 3 Using Estimation to Order Distances

Match the real-life description with its distance.

CONNECTION
Science

Real-Life Description	Distance (mi)
Diameter (width) of Earth	93,000,000
Distance from Earth to Sun	865,000
Distance from Earth to Moon	8,000
Diameter (width) of Sun	239,000

Real Life...
Real Facts

Planets
Mars is the fourth planet from the sun. It has two small moons named Phobos and Deimos.

Solution

Understand the Problem	The first table gives descriptions of distances and diameters involving Earth, the sun, and the moon.
Make a Plan	**DRAW A DIAGRAM** Use a diagram to help order the descriptions, then order the numbers.

Solve the Problem

Distance from Earth to Moon
Diameter of Earth
Distance from Earth to Sun Diameter of Sun

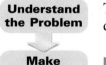

Not drawn to scale

Real-Life Description	Distance (mi)
Diameter (width) of Earth	8,000
Distance from Earth to Moon	239,000
Diameter (width) of Sun	865,000
Distance from Earth to Sun	93,000,000

Look Back The table shows both lists from least to greatest.

In Example 3, the diameter of the sun can be written as eight hundred sixty-five thousand miles. The distance from Earth to the sun can be written as ninety-three million miles.

ONGOING ASSESSMENT

Write About It

Write each number in words.

1. 8,000
2. 293,000
3. 10,904
4. 1,240,052

2.1 Exercises

Extra Practice, page 622

GUIDED PRACTICE

HISTORY In Exercises 1–3, use the Roman numeral system shown at the right.

1. Is the Roman system a base-ten system? Explain.

2. Is the Roman system a place-value system? Explain.

3. Write the number 362 in Roman numerals.

4. Write the number 102,681 in words.

1000 500 100 50 10 5 1

COMMUNICATING In Exercises 5 and 6, is the statement *true* or *false*? Explain.

5. In a base-ten system, each place in a number gets 10 times larger as you move to the right.

6. There are 10 hundreds in 1000.

PRACTICE AND PROBLEM SOLVING

In Exercises 7–10, write the number given by the expanded notation.

7. $6 \times 100 + 4 \times 10$

8. $5 \times 10,000 + 3 \times 100 + 7 \times 1$

9. $4 \times 10,000 + 4 \times 1000 + 4 \times 10$

10. $2 \times 1,000,000 + 3 \times 10,000 + 1 \times 100$

In Exercises 11–14, fill in the blanks with words.

11. $5200 = \underline{?}$ thousand $\underline{?}$ hundred

12. $1020 = \underline{?}$ thousand $\underline{?}$

13. $325,000 = \underline{?}$ hundred $\underline{?}$-$\underline{?}$ thousand

14. $2,030,000 = \underline{?}$ million, $\underline{?}$ thousand

In Exercises 15–18, match the number with its description.

A. Two million, sixteen thousand, five hundred

B. Two hundred ten thousand, six hundred fifty

C. Twenty thousand, one hundred sixty

D. Two hundred one thousand, six hundred fifty

15. 201,650

16. 2,016,500

17. 20,160

18. 210,650

REASONING In Exercises 19–22, use the digits 3, 5, 6, and 8 no more than once, to form the 3-digit numbers described.

19. The largest

20. The smallest

21. The closest to 400

22. The numbers between 400 and 700

23. CANADA The areas (in square miles) of some provinces in Canada are listed below. Write the provinces in order from smallest to largest area. For each province's area, write the place-value position for the digit 5.

Province	Area (mi^2)
British Columbia	366,158
Manitoba	251,000
New Brunswick	28,354
Nova Scotia	21,425
Quebec	594,860
Saskatchewan	251,700

SCIENCE In Exercises 24–26, write the number.

24. Neptune has a diameter of thirty thousand, eight hundred miles.

25. Saturn's year has ten thousand, seven hundred fifty-nine days.

26. The distance from Venus to the sun is sixty-seven million, two hundred thirty thousand miles.

STANDARDIZED TEST PRACTICE

27. Which is the best estimate for 557 + 893?

A 1400 **B** 1450 **C** 1500 **D** 2000

28. Estimate the distance from A to B.

A 5 millimeters

B 5 centimeters

C 5 decimeters

D 5 meters

A• B•

EXPLORATION AND EXTENSION

COMMUNICATING ABOUT MATHEMATICS In Exercises 29–31, write the Arabic numerals in Modern Arabic. Then write the numbers in words. Use the information in *Communicating About Mathematics* on page 93.

29. 50 **30.** 358 **31.** 5922

LAB 2.2

COOPERATIVE LEARNING

Materials Needed
- base-ten pieces
- graph paper

Using Base-Ten Pieces

Part A BASE-TEN PIECES

You can use base-ten pieces to show addition and subtraction of whole numbers. Base-ten pieces come in three sizes, as follows.

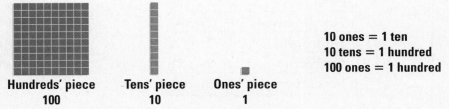

Hundreds' piece
100

Tens' piece
10

Ones' piece
1

10 ones = 1 ten
10 tens = 1 hundred
100 ones = 1 hundred

You can use base-ten pieces to show the sum 27 + 14. To begin, arrange models for 27 and 14, as shown below. To add the numbers, combine the pieces.

Trade these for one tens' piece.

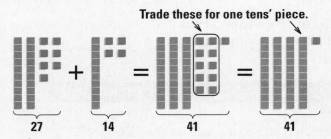

27   14   41   41

In Exercises 1 and 2, write the addition problem that is shown by the base-ten pieces. Use base-ten pieces to solve the problem.

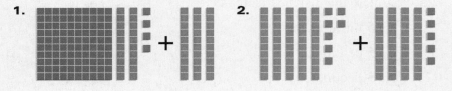

1.

2.

Part B ADDING WITH BASE-TEN PIECES

In Exercises 3–6, use base-ten pieces to find the sum. Describe any pieces that you traded.

3. 152 + 43   **4.** 141 + 236

5. 255 + 138   **6.** 135 + 267

You can use base-ten pieces to show the difference
53 − 28. To begin, arrange models for 53 and 28, as
shown below. To subtract the numbers, remove as many
pieces from the first group as are in the second group.
Notice that in the first group, you must trade 1 of the
tens' pieces for 10 ones' pieces.

Trade one tens'   Remove these pieces
piece for these.   from the first group.

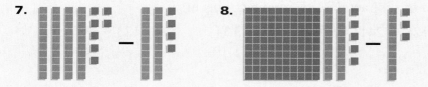

53   28   25

**In Exercises 7 and 8, write the subtraction problem that is shown by
the base-ten pieces. Use base-ten pieces to solve the problem.**

7.

8.

**In Exercises 9 and 10, use base-ten pieces to find the difference.
Describe any pieces that you traded.**

9. 124 − 18   **10.** 236 − 187

NOW TRY THESE

In Exercises 11–18, use base-ten pieces to find the
sum or difference. Record the steps on graph
paper. Did you need to trade any pieces? If you did,
describe the pieces that you traded.

11. 145 + 154   **12.** 23 + 56

13. 213 + 175   **14.** 122 + 173

15. 97 − 65   **16.** 33 − 11

17. 103 − 85   **18.** 129 − 41

2.2

What you should learn:

Goal 1 How to add and subtract whole numbers by regrouping.

Goal 2 How to find the perimeter of a geometric figure.

Why you should learn it:

You can use addition and subtraction to compare the perimeters of real-life objects, such as regions that need fencing.

Addition and Subtraction

Goal 1 OPERATIONS WITH REGROUPING

When adding or subtracting whole numbers, you may need to use a method called **regrouping**. For example, to subtract 18 from 37, you need to regroup, or rewrite, the 37 as 20 + 17. The steps for completing this problem are shown below.

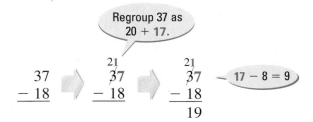

Regroup 37 as 20 + 17.

$$\begin{array}{r} 37 \\ -18 \end{array} \Rightarrow \begin{array}{r} \overset{2}{\cancel{3}}\overset{1}{7} \\ -18 \end{array} \Rightarrow \begin{array}{r} \overset{2}{\cancel{3}}\overset{1}{7} \\ -18 \\ \hline 19 \end{array}$$ 17 − 8 = 9

Example 1 Regrouping

Add or subtract. Use regrouping, if necessary.

a. 128 + 241   **b.** 458 + 154   **c.** 123 − 36

Solution

a. For this problem, regrouping is not necessary.

$$\begin{array}{r} 128 \\ + 241 \\ \hline 369 \end{array}$$

b. For this problem, regrouping is necessary.

$$\begin{array}{r} \overset{1}{} \overset{1}{} \\ 458 \\ + 154 \\ \hline 612 \end{array}$$

1 + 5 + 5 = 11 — 6**12** — 8 + 4 = 12

c. For this problem, regrouping is necessary.

11 − 3 = 8 — $\begin{array}{r} \overset{0}{\cancel{1}}\overset{1}{1}1 \\ \cancel{1}23 \\ - 36 \\ \hline 87 \end{array}$ — 13 − 6 = 7

✔**Check:** MAKE AN ESTIMATE
Because 120 − 35 = 85, you know that 87 is a reasonable answer.

Goal 2 FINDING THE PERIMETER OF A FIGURE

TOOLBOX

Perimeter, page 652

The distance around a figure is called the **perimeter**. To find the perimeter of a figure, find the sum of the lengths of all of its sides.

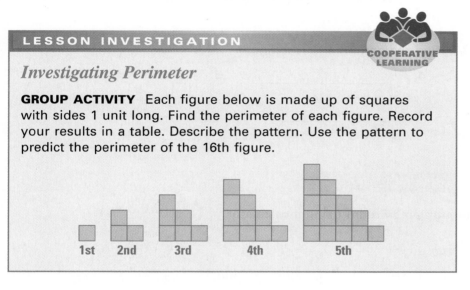

LESSON INVESTIGATION

COOPERATIVE LEARNING

Investigating Perimeter

GROUP ACTIVITY Each figure below is made up of squares with sides 1 unit long. Find the perimeter of each figure. Record your results in a table. Describe the pattern. Use the pattern to predict the perimeter of the 16th figure.

1st   2nd   3rd   4th   5th

Example 2 ▷ Finding Perimeters

CONNECTION
Geometry

You are buying fencing materials for each region. How much fencing do you need for each? Which region uses the most fencing? (The side lengths are in feet.)

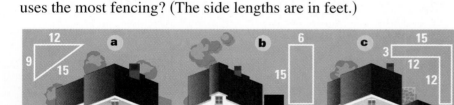

Solution

a. Perimeter = 15 + 12 + 9 = 36 ft

b. Perimeter = 15 + 6 + 15 + 6 = 42 ft

c. Perimeter = 15 + 12 + 3 + 15 + 12 + 3 = 60 ft

The region in part (c) has the greatest perimeter. So, it uses the most fencing.

ONGOING ASSESSMENT

Talk About It

Use mental math to find each sum or difference. Record your answers. Then, talk with others in your group about how you got your answers.

1. 432 − 203

2. 125 + 376

3. 524 − 99

GUIDED PRACTICE

1. Give examples of two addition problems: one that uses regrouping and one that does not.

2. Give examples of two subtraction problems: one that uses regrouping and one that does not.

GEOMETRY In Exercises 3–5, find the perimeter of the figure.

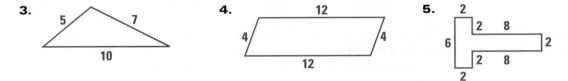

3. 5 7 10

4. 12 4 4 12

5. 2 2 8 6 2 2 8 2

PRACTICE AND PROBLEM SOLVING

In Exercises 6–13, solve the problem without using a calculator.
Show your work.

6. $135 + 62$ 7. $387 - 123$ 8. $243 + 68$ 9. $125 - 87$

10. $980 - 198$ 11. $764 + 397$ 12. $4324 + 2999$ 13. $8001 - 5667$

NUMBER SENSE In Exercises 14–17, find the missing digits.

14.
$$
\begin{array}{r}
?\,?4 \\
+\ 33\,? \\
\hline
533
\end{array}
$$

15.
$$
\begin{array}{r}
5\,?\,? \\
-\ 246 \\
\hline
?24
\end{array}
$$

16.
$$
\begin{array}{r}
5\,?5\,? \\
+\ ?7\,?2 \\
\hline
7016
\end{array}
$$

17.
$$
\begin{array}{r}
?2\,?8 \\
-\ \ ?8\,? \\
\hline
4587
\end{array}
$$

ALGEBRA In Exercises 18–23, use mental math to solve.

18. $m + 25 = 65$ 19. $80 - s = 29$ 20. $c + 146 = 245$

21. $325 + p = 500$ 22. $1000 - b = 202$ 23. $w - 998 = 4002$

In Exercises 24–26, find the length of the side labeled *x*.

24. Perimeter = 24 ft

x 6 ft 8 ft

25. Perimeter = 4.8 m

2 m *x* *x* 2 m

26. Perimeter = 153 cm

24 cm 24 cm *x* 61 cm

REASONING In Exercises 27–29, choose two numbers from 16, 25, 35, 38, 43, and 49 to make the statement true.

27. $? + ? = 84$ 28. $? - ? > 30$ 29. $? - ? = 9$

COMPUTERS In Exercises 30–32, use the bar graph at the right. It shows the sales of software (in millions of dollars) for 1995. Decide whether the statement is *true* or *false*. (Source: U.S. Bureau of the Census)

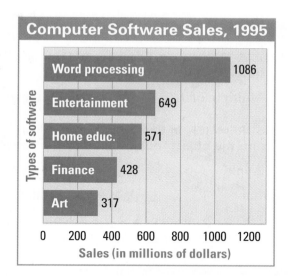

Computer Software Sales, 1995

Types of software	Sales (in millions of dollars)
Word processing	1086
Entertainment	649
Home educ.	571
Finance	428
Art	317

30. More money is spent on finance and word processing software than on entertainment, home education, and art software.

31. The difference between the amount spent on finance software and on home education software is 144 million dollars.

32. More than 3000 million dollars was spent on computer software in 1995.

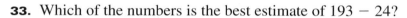

STANDARDIZED TEST PRACTICE

33. Which of the numbers is the best estimate of $193 - 24$?

   A 175   **B** 170   **C** 165   **D** 160

34. Use mental math to solve the equation $32 - x = 20$.

   A 52   **B** 22   **C** 12   **D** 8

35. The sides of a triangular region measure 13 ft, 12 ft, and 5 ft. What is the perimeter of this region?

   A 20 ft   **B** 30 ft   **C** 31 ft   **D** 33 ft

EXPLORATION AND EXTENSION

PORTFOLIO

36. BUILDING YOUR PROJECT Your computer company designs and sells educational computer games.

a. Design a game that uses addition and subtraction. Your game should have different levels of difficulty.

b. Draw a computer screen of what your game will look like, and write a description of how it works. Think of a name for your game.

In Exercises 1–8, use mental math to solve. (Toolbox, page 642)

1. 42×100　　2. 500×10　　3. 5×100　　4. 25×1000

5. $660 \div 10$　　6. $7200 \div 100$　　7. $800 \div 100$　　8. $7500 \div 10$

NUMBER THEORY In Exercises 9–11, find all the numbers from 1 to 50 that have the given property (Toolbox, page 642)

9. Multiple of 4　　10. Factor of 7　　11. Multiple of both 2 and 5

MEASUREMENT In Exercises 12–17, which unit would you use to measure the object: *ounces*, *pounds*, or *tons*? (Toolbox, page 654)

12. Apple　　13. Person　　14. Sheet of paper

15. Car　　16. Feather　　17. Pencil

18. **BOOKS** You spent $14 at a discount book store. Each of the books that you bought cost $2. How many books did you buy? (1.6)

HISTORY Connection

COMPUTERS

Ada Lovelace predicted computer music a whole century before it was actually produced.

Ada Byron Lovelace, the daughter of the famous British poet, Lord Byron, is credited with being the first computer programmer. She was one of the few people that helped and understood the English mathematician, Charles Babbage.

In 1822, Babbage recognized that many mathematical computations were algorithmic, or repetitious. So, he proposed to invent a machine that would perform repeating tasks. Lovelace wrote about Babbage's Analytical Engine and provided programs it could use. She also predicted the uses and limitations of computers. The programming language ADA is named after her.

1. You are writing a program that instructs a computer to subtract any three-digit number from 1000. Write out steps that you could use to tell the computer to do so that it can solve this problem.

2. Create three problems that can be solved by this program. Solve them using the steps.

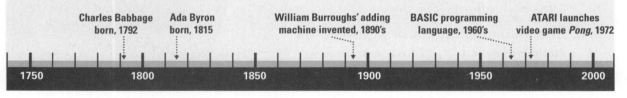

Charles Babbage born, 1792　　Ada Byron born, 1815　　William Burroughs' adding machine invented, 1890's　　BASIC programming language, 1960's　　ATARI launches video game *Pong*, 1972

1750　　1800　　1850　　1900　　1950　　2000

Adding It Up

When you add long lists of numbers, it is easy to make a mistake. Most people who add long lists of numbers in their job use a calculator.

REAL LIFE
Accounting

CALCULATOR TIP

Many calculators have a clear key labeled **C** or **CE**. If you press this key once, it will clear the number on the screen. If you press this key twice, it will clear all the previously entered numbers. Try one of these keys on your calculator.

Example

You do the accounting for a small business that has 14 employees. The following list shows the number of hours that the employees worked during the week. Find the total number of hours.

40, 32, 40, 44, 42, 24, 20,
48, 40, 32, 44, 42, 36, 40

Solution

One way to find the total is to use a calculator.

40 **+** 32 **+** 40 **+** 44 **+** 42 **+** 24 **+** 20 **+**

48 **+** 40 **+** 32 **+** 44 **+** 42 **+** 36 **+** 40 **=**

After entering these keystrokes, your calculator should display 524. The total number of hours worked by the 14 employees is 524.

Exercises

In Exercises 1–6, use a calculator to find the sum.

1. $32 + 56 + 48 + 78 + 26 + 68$

2. $124 + 145 + 150 + 136 + 243 + 208$

3. $37 + 35 + 69 + 89 + 14 + 72$

4. $346 + 298 + 435 + 789 + 356 + 456$

5. $256 + 146 + 128 + 340 + 204 + 206$

6. $1567 + 1341 + 2078 + 1450 + 1254$

7. NUMBER SENSE Without adding the numbers, how do you know that each total in Exercises 1–6 must be an even number?

8. ESTIMATION Without adding the numbers, explain why the totals in Exercises 1 and 3 are less than 600.

9. BASKETBALL In one season you play 18 basketball games. The points you scored each game are shown below. How many points did you score over the entire season?

12, 18, 14, 18, 12, 15, 16, 21, 15,
14, 18, 15, 16, 16, 17, 10, 15, 20

2.3

What you should learn:

Goal 1 How to use area models to show whole-number multiplication

Goal 2 How to find the area of a rectangle

Why you should learn it:

Multiplication can help you find the amount of materials you need for a project. An example is finding the number of tiles needed to cover a given area.

Multiplication and Area

Goal 1 USING AREA MODELS

You can use an area model to show the **product** of two whole numbers. For example, the product $5 \times 3 = 15$ is shown at the right, since there are 15 square units in the area model.

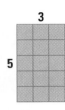

Example 1 Drawing an Area Model

Use an area model to find the product of 8×12.

Solution

Draw a rectangle that is 12 units long and 8 units wide.

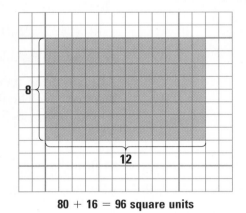

$80 + 16 = 96$ square units

To find the area, think of the rectangle as having two parts. One part is 10 by 8 and has an area of 80 square units. The other is 8 by 2 and has an area of 16 square units. The total area of the two parts is 96 square units, or 96 units^2.

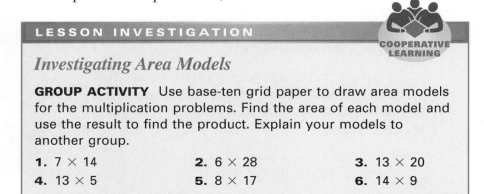

LESSON INVESTIGATION

COOPERATIVE LEARNING

Investigating Area Models

GROUP ACTIVITY Use base-ten grid paper to draw area models for the multiplication problems. Find the area of each model and use the result to find the product. Explain your models to another group.

1. 7×14 **2.** 6×28 **3.** 13×20
4. 13×5 **5.** 8×17 **6.** 14×9

The **area** of a rectangle is given by the product of the length and width of the rectangle.

Example 2 Finding Areas

You work in a store that sells floor tiles. You are asked to find the number of 1 ft-by-1 ft tiles that are needed to cover the rooms shown below. In the diagram, each square is 1 ft by 1 ft.

REAL LIFE
Tiling

a. Explain how you would solve this problem.

b. Suppose you decide to use 6 in.-by-6 in. tiles. Will it take twice as many tiles?

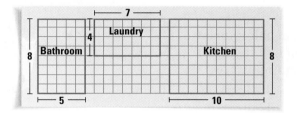

Solution

a. You can find the area of each room by multiplying the room's length by its width.

$$8 \times 5 = 40 \text{ ft}^2 \qquad \text{Area of bathroom}$$

$$7 \times 4 = 28 \text{ ft}^2 \qquad \text{Area of laundry room}$$

$$10 \times 8 = 80 \text{ ft}^2 \qquad \text{Area of kitchen}$$

The total area of the three rooms is

$$40 + 28 + 80 = 148 \text{ ft}^2.$$

Because each tile has an area of 1 ft², 148 tiles are needed.

b. Each 1 ft-by-1 ft tile covers the same area as four 6 in.-by-6 in. tiles. So, you need four times as many tiles, or

$$4 \times 148 = 592 \text{ tiles.}$$

Notice that using tiles whose sides are half as long does not double the number of tiles.

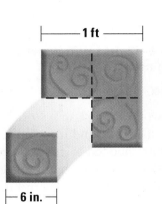

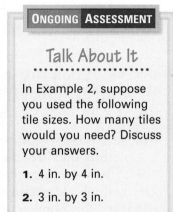

├── 1 ft ──┤

├ 6 in. ┤

ONGOING ASSESSMENT

Talk About It
• • • • • • • • • • • • • • •

In Example 2, suppose you used the following tile sizes. How many tiles would you need? Discuss your answers.

1. 4 in. by 4 in.

2. 3 in. by 3 in.

GUIDED PRACTICE

In Exercises 1 and 2, write the multiplication problem that is shown by the area model.

1. Area is 63 square units.

2. Area is 44 square units.

3. GEOGRAPHY Use the scale drawing at the right to estimate the area of Wyoming. Each square is 25 mi by 25 mi.

4. Use base-ten grid paper to draw a model for 7×11. Find the area.

5. Cut a square piece of paper. Fold it in half to make a rectangle. Then fold the rectangle in half to make a square. Unfold the paper. Write a multiplication problem that can be modeled by the paper.

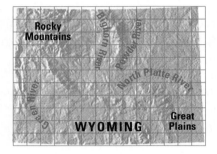

PRACTICE AND PROBLEM SOLVING

In Exercises 6–8, write the multiplication problem that is shown by the area model.

6. Area is 50 square units.

7. Area is 48 square units.

8. Area is 21 square units.

GEOMETRY In Exercises 9–12, use grid paper to sketch an area model for the problem. What is the area?

9. 4×12 **10.** 11×11 **11.** 4×13 **12.** 15×3

13. HOME IMPROVEMENT You work in a store that sells ceiling tiles. You are asked to find the number of 2 ft-by-1 ft tiles that are needed to cover three ceilings. The dimensions are shown at the right. Find this number and explain how you did it.

Room	Dimension (ft)
Bathroom	6×9
Laundry	4×7
Hallway	4×9

ALGEBRA In Exercises 14–16, use mental math to solve.

14. $3 \cdot s = 33$ **15.** $5 \cdot d = 25$ **16.** $4 \cdot n = 16$

NUMBER SENSE In Exercises 17–19, is the product *even* or *odd*? Give examples to support your answer.

17. even × even   **18.** even × odd   **19.** odd × odd

In Exercises 20 and 21, solve the equations. Describe a pattern for *n*.

20. $2 \times 22 = n, 4 \times 22 = n, 8 \times 22 = n$

21. $n \times 6 = 12, n \times 6 = 24, n \times 6 = 48$

22. YARDWORK You are raking leaves that cover a rectangular part of your yard that is 8 ft by 9 ft. Can you complete the job in an hour if it takes you 10 minutes to rake an area that is 12 ft^2? Draw a diagram of the problem.

23. CONSUMER ECONOMICS Video game system A costs $200, and each game costs $50. System B costs $150 with each game costing $60. Which system with three games costs less?

Real Life... Real Facts

Virtual Reality
Special equipment is needed to play a virtual reality video game. The head-mounted display lets the player see objects as they would appear in the physical world.

STANDARDIZED TEST PRACTICE

24. What is the area of the figure?

  A 3 cm^2 **B** 7 cm   **C** 10 cm^2 **D** 15 cm^2

2 cm
5 cm

25. Choose the symbol that makes the following a true statement: $23 - 14 \; ? \; 12 + 9$.

  A >   **B** <   **C** =   **D** None of the above

EXPLORATION AND EXTENSION

PORTFOLIO

26. BUILDING YOUR PROJECT A computer store wants to buy the following software from your company.

  6 games at $55 each   12 games at $45 each
  8 games at $50 each   10 games at $60 each

Design a company bill that you can use to charge the store. Your bill should include the amount the store is spending on each type of game. Total the bill after all of the information is in place.

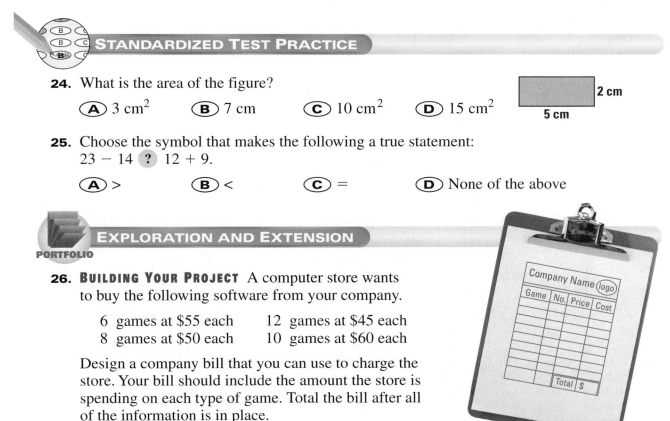

Company Name (logo)

Game	No.	Price	Cost
		Total	$

LAB 2.4

COOPERATIVE LEARNING

Materials Needed
- **counters**
- **paper**
- **pencils**

Using Division Models

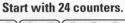

Part A MODELS FOR DIVISION

SET MODEL Consider the following question.

A class of 24 students is divided into groups of 4 to work on a project. Each group needs a computer. How many computers does the class need?

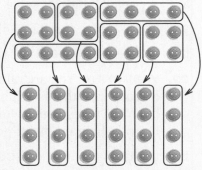

Start with 24 counters.

Start with 24 counters. Take out sets of 4 counters until all 24 counters have been used. You get 6 sets of 4 counters, so there are 6 groups. Therefore, the class needs 6 computers.

The question can also be answered with division.

$$24 \div 4 = 6$$

Put the counters into groups of 4.

SHARING MODEL Consider the following question.

A class of 30 students is divided into 6 teams. Each team has the same number of students. How many students are on each team?

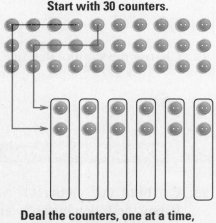

Start with 30 counters.

Start with 30 counters. Then deal the counters, one at a time, into 6 groups. There will be 5 counters in each of the 6 groups, so there are 5 students on each team.

The question can also be answered with division.

$$30 \div 6 = 5$$

Deal the counters, one at a time, into 6 groups.

1. Explain the differences between using a set model and a sharing model.

Part B DRAWING MODELS

In Exercises 2–4, use counters to make a model that shows the question. Did you use a set model or a sharing model? Explain your choice. Write the question as a division problem.

2. You are given 28 floppy disks and are asked to put 4 disks with each computer in your classroom. How many computers are in your classroom?

3. Your class receives several boxes that contain a total of 42 computer programs. Each box contains 6 programs. How many boxes are there?

4. Your class receives a shipment of 36 calculators that are packed in 9 boxes. How many calculators are in each box?

Part C MODELS IN REAL LIFE

5. Write a real-life problem that can be shown using a set model for division. Then write another problem that can be shown using a sharing model for division.

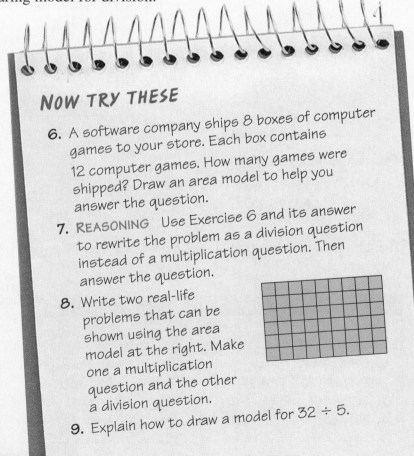

NOW TRY THESE

6. A software company ships 8 boxes of computer games to your store. Each box contains 12 computer games. How many games were shipped? Draw an area model to help you answer the question.

7. REASONING Use Exercise 6 and its answer to rewrite the problem as a division question instead of a multiplication question. Then answer the question.

8. Write two real-life problems that can be shown using the area model at the right. Make one a multiplication question and the other a division question.

9. Explain how to draw a model for $32 \div 5$.

2.4 Exploring Whole-Number Division

What you should learn:

Goal 1 How to write answers to division problems that have remainders

Goal 2 How to use division to solve real-life problems

Why you should learn it:

Division can help you when cooking. An example is finding one fourth of a recipe ingredient.

Goal 1 QUOTIENTS WITH REMAINDERS

Each number in a division problem has a name.

$$\underset{\text{Divisor}}{\overset{\text{Dividend}}{24 \div 3}} = \underset{\text{Quotient}}{8}$$

Here, 3 *divides evenly* into 24 because the quotient is a whole number. Quotients that are not whole numbers can be written with a remainder or with a fraction.

Example 1 ▸ Dividing Whole Numbers

Solve $80 \div 7$ and write the quotient in two ways. Draw an area model to show the division.

Solution

Divide 7 into 80.

$$\begin{array}{r} 11 \\ 7\overline{)80} \\ \underline{7} \\ 10 \\ \underline{7} \\ 3 \end{array} \longleftarrow \textbf{Remainder}$$

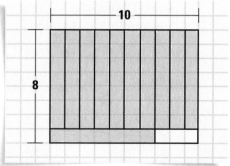

This can be written in two ways.

$80 \div 7 = 11 \text{ R}3$ with a remainder

$80 \div 7 = 11\frac{3}{7}$ with a fraction

The area model shows that 80 can be divided into 11 groups of 7 with 3 squares left over.

LESSON INVESTIGATION

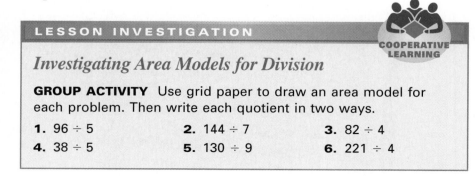

Investigating Area Models for Division

GROUP ACTIVITY Use grid paper to draw an area model for each problem. Then write each quotient in two ways.

1. $96 \div 5$ **2.** $144 \div 7$ **3.** $82 \div 4$

4. $38 \div 5$ **5.** $130 \div 9$ **6.** $221 \div 4$

Goal 2 SOLVING REAL-LIFE PROBLEMS

Example 2 Writing Quotients with Fractions

REAL LIFE
Cooking

You are cooking a stir-fry dinner for your family of four. The recipe card is shown below.

a. How many teaspoons of oil are in one serving?

b. For a meal to be considered low in sodium it must have less than 140 mg of sodium per serving. Is this a low-sodium meal?

Gingered Chicken with Mushrooms

Ingredients	Serves 4
• 5 t. oil	• 4 oz chicken broth
• 12 oz chicken	• 2 t. cornstarch
• 8 oz mushrooms	• 3 cloves of garlic
• 4 oz snowpeas	• 2 in. piece of ginger

Recipe contains 976 calories, 58 g fat, 32 g carbohydrates, and 237 mg sodium.

Solution

a. To find the amount of oil in one serving, divide the oil in the recipe by 4. Use mental math.

$$5 \div 4 = 1\frac{1}{4}$$

Each serving contains $1\frac{1}{4}$ t. of oil.

✔**Check:** DRAW A DIAGRAM

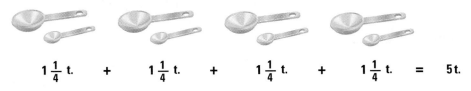

$1\frac{1}{4}$ t. + $1\frac{1}{4}$ t. + $1\frac{1}{4}$ t. + $1\frac{1}{4}$ t. = 5 t.

b. To find the amount of sodium in one serving, divide 237 by 4.

$$237 \div 4 = 59\frac{1}{4}$$

One serving contains $59\frac{1}{4}$ mg of sodium. It is a low-sodium meal, since $59\frac{1}{4}$ mg is less than 140 mg.

TOOLBOX

Dividing Whole Numbers, page 642

ONGOING ASSESSMENT

Write About It

Solve each division problem. Write each answer in two ways.

1. $7 \div 3$

2. $22 \div 8$

3. $83 \div 5$

4. $39 \div 12$

2.4 Exercises

GUIDED PRACTICE

In Exercises 1–3, use the division problem 27 ÷ 4.

1. Name the dividend and the divisor in the problem.

2. Sketch an area model to show the problem.

3. Find the quotient. Write your answer in two ways.

In Exercises 4–6, match the division problem with its area model. Then write the quotient in two ways.

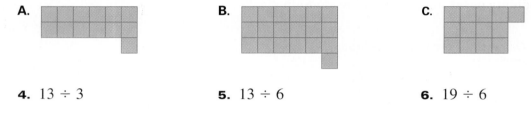

A.   **B.**   **C.**

4. $13 \div 3$ **5.** $13 \div 6$ **6.** $19 \div 6$

PRACTICE AND PROBLEM SOLVING

WRITING EXPRESSIONS **In Exercises 7 and 8, write a division problem shown by the statement. Then divide to solve the problem.**

7. You have 52 basketball cards. You separate them into 4 piles. Each pile has the same number of cards. How many cards are in each pile?

8. You and some friends have a box of 60 stickers. After all the stickers are divided equally, each person in the group has 15 stickers. How many people are in the group?

In Exercises 9–16, divide. Then write the quotient in two ways.

9. $39 \div 4$ **10.** $77 \div 9$ **11.** $43 \div 3$ **12.** $76 \div 6$

13. $119 \div 5$ **14.** $128 \div 3$ **15.** $245 \div 4$ **16.** $385 \div 14$

In Exercises 17 and 18, write the division problem shown.

17.   **18.**

In Exercises 19–21, sketch an area model. Then find the quotient.

19. $14 \div 5$ **20.** $21 \div 4$ **21.** $30 \div 8$

In Exercises 22 and 23, find the length of the side labeled x.

22. Area = 45 cm^2

23. Area = 29 ft^2

8 cm

4 ft

x

x

24. **NUMBER SENSE** Solve $140 \div 10$. Then solve $280 \div 10$. What happens to the quotient if you double the dividend? Explain.

25. **ERROR ANALYSIS** Your friend is using a calculator to solve $720 \div 45$. The result on the display is 0.0625. What did your friend do wrong? What should the display be?

26. **TECHNOLOGY** Find the quotients and describe any patterns that you see. Write the next two problems that follow the pattern.

$$9 \div 9 = \boxed{?}, \qquad 108 \div 9 = \boxed{?},$$
$$1107 \div 9 = \boxed{?}, \qquad 11{,}106 \div 9 = \boxed{?}, \ldots$$

27. **IN-LINE SKATING** You are skating on a path. In two hours, you travel a total distance of five miles. Find your average speed by solving the following division problem. Should you write the quotient with a *remainder* or with a *fraction*? Explain.

(5 miles) $\div$ (2 hours) $= \boxed{?}$ miles per hour

28. **BABY-SITTING** You baby-sit for 4 hours and earn \$11. Find the amount you earned per hour by solving the following problem. Should you write the quotient with a *remainder* or with a *fraction*? Explain.

(11 dollars) $\div$ (4 hours) $= \boxed{?}$ dollars per hour

STANDARDIZED TEST PRACTICE

29. Which of the following is *not* correct?

(A) 1 pound = 16 ounces

(B) 36 inches = 3 feet

(C) 5 years = 50 months

(D) 2 hours = 120 minutes

30. Use mental math to solve $n + 6 = 20$.

(A) $n = 26$ **(B)** $n = 16$ **(C)** $n = 14$ **(D)** $n = 4$

EXPLORATION AND EXTENSION

PORTFOLIO

31. BUILDING YOUR PROJECT Your computer company has taken some orders that need to be filled. You have to ship the diskettes to a packaging company before the diskettes go to your customers. Each diskette is 90 mm by 93 mm and 3 mm thick. Each shipping box is 90 mm by 93 mm and 60 mm thick.

a. Write a division problem to see how many diskettes can be put into each shipping box.

b. You have a total of 150 diskettes to ship. If each shipping box must be full, will you be able to ship all the diskettes? If not, how many will you have left over? Explain.

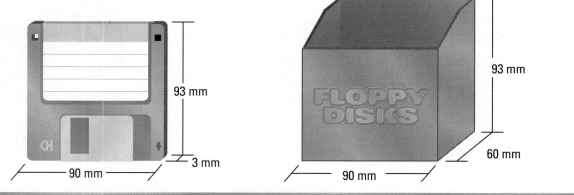

SPIRAL REVIEW

In Exercises 1–4, you are given the dimensions of a rectangle. Find its perimeter and area. (2.2, 2.3)

1. 6 in. by 11 in.　　**2.** 11 cm by 4 cm　　**3.** 7 ft by 7 ft　　**4.** 4 m by 10 m

ALGEBRA AND MENTAL MATH Solve the equation. **(1.6, 2.2, 2.3, 2.4)**

5. $s + 119 = 229$　　**6.** $m + 189 = 500$　　**7.** $110 - d = 40$　　**8.** $t - 71 = 69$

9. $5 \cdot s = 125$　　**10.** $116 \times p = 232$　　**11.** $500 \div k = 10$　　**12.** $121 \div a = 11$

In Exercises 13–18, round the number to the given place value.
(Toolbox, page 648)

13. 74 (tens)　　**14.** 129 (hundreds)　　**15.** 1107 (tens)

16. 1877 (hundreds)　　**17.** 2499 (thousands)　　**18.** 2990 (thousands)

In Exercises 19 and 20, describe the pattern. Then write the next three numbers in the pattern. (1.1)

19. 3, 11, 19, ?, ?, ?, . . .　　　　**20.** 1, 4, 9, 16, ?, ?, ?, . . .

21. **SHOPPING** You go to the school store with 80¢ to buy pencils. Each pencil costs 15¢. Write an equation that can be used to find how many pencils you can buy. Solve the equation. Should you write the quotient with a *remainder* or with a *fraction*? Explain. **(1.6, 2.4)**

Take this test as you would take a test in class. The answers to the exercises are given in the back of the book.

In Exercises 1–3, write the number given by the expanded notation. (2.1)

1. $4 \times 10,000 + 1 \times 1000 + 3 \times 10 + 5 \times 1$

2. $6 \times 1000 + 2 \times 100 + 9 \times 1$

3. $5 \times 100 + 9 \times 10 + 0 \times 1$

In Exercises 4–6, write the number in words. (2.1)

4. 4054   **5.** 30,870   **6.** 652,001

In Exercises 7 and 8, find the perimeter of the given figures. (2.2)

7.

8.

In Exercises 9–12, make a sketch of the problem. (2.3, 2.4)

9. A 9×7 area model.

10. A $40 \div 5$ set model.

11. A 6×13 area model.

12. A $65 \div 7$ set model.

ALGEBRA   **In Exercises 13–18, use mental math to solve. (2.2, 2.3, 2.4)**

13. $x + 42 = 62$ **14.** $50 - y = 14$ **15.** $p - 47 = 38$

16. $5 \cdot a = 35$ **17.** $b \cdot 25 = 100$ **18.** $q \div 5 = 10$

ESTIMATION The bar graph at the right compares the numbers of different types of radio stations in the United States in 1990 and 1995. **(2.2)**

19. About how many more country stations were there in 1995 than there were in 1990?

20. Which type of station had fewer stations in 1995 than in 1990? About how many fewer?

21. Were there more rock or contemporary stations in 1995? About how many more?

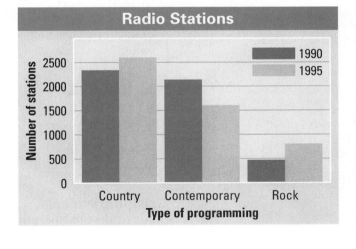

2.5

What you should learn:

Goal 1 How to evaluate an expression

Goal 2 How to use order of operations

Why you should learn it:

When more than one operation is used in an expression, it is important to know the order in which the operations must be performed.

The final appearance of an actor depends on the order in which the make-up artist completes each task.

Order of Operations

Goal 1 EVALUATING AN EXPRESSION

A **numerical expression** is a collection of numbers that can be linked by addition, subtraction, multiplication, and division. Finding the value of the expression is **evaluating** the expression.

Example 1 Evaluating Expressions

Evaluate the expression.

a. $13 - 8$ **b.** 4×12 **c.** $8 \div 2$ **d.** $6 + 7$

Solution

a. The value of $13 - 8$ is 5.   **b.** The value of 4×12 is 48.

c. The value of $8 \div 2$ is 4.   **d.** The value of $6 + 7$ is 13.

Each expression in Example 1 has only one *operation,* such as addition or multiplication. When an expression has two or more operations, its value can depend on the order in which you do the operations.

LESSON INVESTIGATION

Investigating Order of Operations

GROUP ACTIVITY Evaluate each expression. Does the value of the expression depend on the order in which you do the operations? Discuss which order you think gives the correct value.

1. $2 \times 4 + 5$ **2.** $3 + 4 \times 6$

3. $16 \div 4 \times 2$ **4.** $4 \times 12 \div 3$

5. $12 + 8 - 5$ **6.** $23 - 5 + 8$

7. $2 \times 6 - 2 \times 2$ **8.** $20 - 4 \times 3 + 2$

9. $20 \div 5 \times 4$ **10.** $13 + 7 \times 2$

Grouping symbols, such as parentheses, help you decide in which order to do the operations. Here are some examples.

$$3 \times (2 + 4) = 3 \times 6 = 18$$
$$(12 - 4) \div 2 = 8 \div 2 = 4$$
$$2 \times (5 \times 3) = 2 \times 15 = 30$$

Goal **2** USING ORDER OF OPERATIONS

To make sure everyone gets the same number when an expression is evaluated, mathematicians have established the following **order of operations** .

> ### ORDER OF OPERATIONS
>
> **1.** Evaluate expressions within grouping symbols.
> **2.** Multiply and divide from left to right.
> **3.** Add and subtract from left to right.

Example 2 **Using Order of Operations**

a. $20 - 4 \times 3 = 20 - 12$ **Multiply 4 by 3.**
$ = 8$ **Subtract 12 from 20.**

b. $48 \div (6 \div 2) = 48 \div 3$ **Divide 6 by 2.**
$ = 16$ **Divide 48 by 3.**

c. $48 \div 6 \div 2 = 8 \div 2$ **Divide 48 by 6.**
$ = 4$ **Divide 8 by 2.**

Example 3 **Using a Calculator**

Use a calculator to evaluate $6 + 24 \div 3$.

Solution

Without using a calculator, the value of this expression is $6 + 8$, or 14. Entering the keystrokes from left to right on a calculator may or may not give the correct value.

If the calculator follows the order of operations, then you will get the following.

If the calculator does not follow the order of operations, then you need to change the order you use to enter the keystrokes. Enter the division first. Then add.

What happens if you don't change the order of the keystrokes?

Extra Practice, page 623

GUIDED PRACTICE

In Exercises 1–4, match the expression with its value.

A. 53   **B.** 23   **C.** 16   **D.** 25

1. $6 \times 3 + 10 - 5$ **2.** $6 \div 3 \times 10 + 5$ **3.** $6 - 3 + 10 \times 5$ **4.** $6 \times 3 - 10 \div 5$

5. Add parentheses to the statement to make it true.

$$5 \times 9 - 3 + 12 \div 6 = 32$$

PRACTICE AND PROBLEM SOLVING

In Exercises 6–14, evaluate the expression.

6. $11 + 5 \times 2$ **7.** $26 - 8 \times 3$ **8.** $20 - (4 + 8)$

9. $4 \times 7 \times 2$ **10.** $32 \div (4 \times 2)$ **11.** $54 \div 9 \div 2$

12. $8 + 5 \times (4 \div 2)$ **13.** $12 \times 3 - 6 \times 3$ **14.** $72 \div 9 + 56 \div 7$

TECHNOLOGY In Exercises 15–20, use a calculator to evaluate the expression. Does your calculator use order of operations? Explain.

15. $44 + 66 \div 11$ **16.** $12 \times 13 - 12$ **17.** $75 \div 5 \div 5$

18. $128 \div 8 \times 5 + 20$ **19.** $23 \times 5 - 20 \times 5$ **20.** $144 \div 16 - 54 \div 6$

WRITING EXPRESSIONS In Exercises 21–23, write the expression that is described. Use parentheses if necessary. Then evaluate.

21. Subtract 8 from 17, then multiply the difference by 5.

22. Add 4 to the product of 8 and 4.

23. Subtract the product of 4 and 5 from 25.

In Exercises 24–27, use the numbers 2, 4, 5, 7, and 9 to make the statement true.

24. $\boxed{?} \times \boxed{?} - \boxed{?} = 26$ **25.** $\boxed{?} + \boxed{?} \times \boxed{?} = 25$

26. $\boxed{?} \times \boxed{?} \div \boxed{?} = 18$ **27.** $\boxed{?} + \boxed{?} \div \boxed{?} = 11$

28. **TECHNOLOGY** You evaluate the expression $2 + 12 \div 2 \times 3$ using your calculator and get a display of 21. Did your calculator use order of operations? Explain.

In Exercises 29–32, complete the statement. Use $+$, $-$, $\times$, or $\div$.

29. $9 \; ? \; 7 \; ? \; 2 \; ? \; 6 = 17$ **30.** $6 \; ? \; 2 \; ? \; 6 \; ? \; 4 = 14$

31. $5 \; ? \; 3 \; ? \; 8 \; ? \; 2 = 19$ **32.** $3 \; ? \; 3 \; ? \; 3 \; ? \; 3 = 9$

THEME PARKS At Busch Gardens in Williamsburg, Virginia, a 3-day pass costs $43. The hotel costs $30 per person per night. A family of 4 is going to Busch Gardens for 3 days and 2 nights.

33. Write an expression that shows how much the family will pay for 3-day passes and the hotel.

34. The family plans to spend $700 on the trip. Write an expression that shows the amount the family has left after paying for the 3-day passes and the hotel.

35. **CALENDARS** The Maya Indians in Mexico used a calendar that had 18 months, each month having 20 days. Five extra days were added at the end of the year. Write and evaluate an expression that calculates the number of days in a Maya year. Compare your answer with the length of our year.

Tech Link

Investigation 2, Interactive Real-Life Investigations

STANDARDIZED TEST PRACTICE

36. A cable TV company charges $24 for basic service and $7 for each pay station. You decide to get 3 pay stations along with your basic service. Which expression shows how much you will pay?

(A) 3×7 **(B)** $24 + 3 \times 7$

(C) $(24 + 3) \times 7$ **(D)** $7 + 24 \times 3$

EXPLORATION AND EXTENSION

37. **CAR WASH** The following algorithm, or process, is written out of order. It describes the process of a car wash. Use the phrasing of the steps and key words to help you put the algorithm back in order. Think of another example of a real-life algorithm and write out the steps it takes.

Water is sprayed on the dirty car.

Soap is rinsed off the car.

The wet car is dried off with towels.

The dirty car drives up.

The clean car drives away.

The car is washed with soapy water.

What you should learn:

Goal 1 How to use the distributive property

Goal 2 How to evaluate variable expressions

Why you should learn it:

The distributive property can help you use mental math to evaluate expressions, such as finding the cost of a field trip.

The Distributive Property

Goal 1 THE DISTRIBUTIVE PROPERTY

You already know two symbols for multiplication, "·" and "×." Multiplication can also be symbolized by parentheses. An example is $3(4) = 12$.

> **THE DISTRIBUTIVE PROPERTY**
>
> Let a, b, and c be numbers.
> $$a(b + c) = a \times b + a \times c$$
> For example: $5(11 + 2) = 5 \times 11 + 5 \times 2$

In English, to *distribute* means to give something to everyone in a group. In mathematics, the meaning of *distribute* is similar.

Example 1 Finding the Area of a Room

A hallway is 8 ft wide and 27 ft long. Explain how to use mental math to find the area of the hallway.

Solution

STRATEGY **DRAW A DIAGRAM** One way is to think of the length as 20 + 7, as the diagram below shows. Then instead of multiplying 8 by 27, you can multiply 8 by 20 and 8 by 7 and add the results.

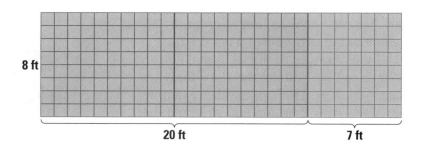

8 ft

20 ft   7 ft

$$8 \times 27 = 8(20 + 7)$$ **Rewrite 27 as 20 + 7.**

$$= 8 \times 20 + 8 \times 7$$ **Use the distributive property.**

$$= 160 + 56$$ **Use mental math.**

$$= 216$$ **Use mental math.**

The total area of the hallway is 216 ft^2.

> **TOOLBOX**
> Area, page 653

In algebra, a letter that can be replaced by any number is a **variable**. A **variable expression** is an expression that has one or more variables. Substituting numbers for the variables is evaluating the expression.

Example 2 Evaluating Expressions

Find the value of the expression when $n = 3$.

a. $7 \times n$ **b.** $7(n + 2)$

Solution

a. $7 \times n = 7(3)$ Substitute 3 for *n*.

         $= 21$ Multiply 7 and 3.

b. $7(n + 2) = 7(3 + 2)$ Substitute 3 for *n*.

           $= 7(5)$ Add 3 and 2.

           $= 35$ Multiply 7 and 5.

Example 3 Using the Distributive Property

Your class of 30 students is taking a field trip to a science museum. Admission per student is $5 for the museum and $2 for the laser show. How much money will the class spend for the field trip if everyone goes to the museum and the laser show?

Solution

Method **1** Total cost = **Number of students × Cost per student**

                    $= 30(5 + 2)$ The cost per student is $5 + $2.

                    $= 30(7)$ Simplify within the grouping symbols.

                    $= \$210$ Multiply.

Your class will spend $210 for the field trip.

Method **2** Total cost = **Cost for museum + Cost for laser show**

                    $= 30 \times 5 + 30 \times 2$

                    $= 150 + 60$ Use mental math.

                    $= \$210$ Add.

Your class will spend $210 for the field trip.

Real Life... Real Facts

Museum Exhibit
The wave shown in the exhibit was made from a machine. Waves in the ocean are a result of Earth's gravitational pull.

ONGOING ASSESSMENT

Talk About It

In Exercises 1 and 2, evaluate the expression when $m = 2$.

1. $4(m + 5)$

2. $18 + 6m$

3. In Example 3, which method uses the distributive property? Which method would you rather use in the example?

GUIDED PRACTICE

1. **COMMUNICATING** Why is the order of operations important when using the distributive property? Give examples.

2. **ERROR ANALYSIS** Find and correct the error on the piece of paper at right.

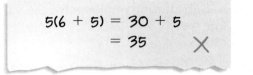

$$5(6 + 5) = 30 + 5$$
$$= 35 \quad \times$$

3. Evaluate $7(10 + 8)$ in two ways. Which way do you prefer?

4. **AREA MODEL** The purple model shows the product $4(4 + 2)$. What product is shown by the green model? What product is shown by the orange model? Write an equation for the area models. Then evaluate the numerical expression on each side of the equation.

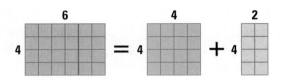

PRACTICE AND PROBLEM SOLVING

In Exercises 5–12, evaluate the expression in two ways.

5. $3(4 + 7)$ 6. $2(5 + 9)$ 7. $6(8 + 1)$ 8. $9(6 + 3)$

9. $4(25 + 5)$ 10. $7(10 + 11)$ 11. $2(15 + 50)$ 12. $8(40 + 1)$

In Exercises 13–16, match the expression with an equivalent expression. Then evaluate both expressions when $n = 4$. What can you conclude?

A. $6 \times 5 + 6 \times n$ **B.** $5 \times n + 5 \times 6$ **C.** $3 \times 8 + 3 \times n$ **D.** $8 \times n + 8 \times 3$

13. $3(8 + n)$ 14. $5(n + 6)$ 15. $8(n + 3)$ 16. $6(5 + n)$

In Exercises 17 and 18, write an equation for the area models.

17.   18.

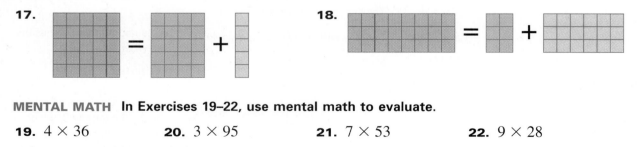

MENTAL MATH In Exercises 19–22, use mental math to evaluate.

19. 4×36 20. 3×95 21. 7×53 22. 9×28

ALGEBRA AND MENTAL MATH In Exercises 23–26, solve. Explain the strategy you used.

23. $3(n + 6) = 30$ 24. $7(5 + x) = 63$ 25. $8(7 + y) = 88$ 26. $4(a + 4) = 28$

27. MENTAL MATH For your computer company, you rent an office that is 60 ft by 72 ft. Explain how you can use mental math with the distributive property to find the area of the office.

28. FUNDRAISING Your class is selling cards and posters to raise $600 for a class picnic. It costs $115 for materials. Your class sells 112 posters and 220 cards, each for $2. How much money was raised? Did your class raise the $600?

29. FIELD TRIP Your class of 75 students and 5 teachers takes a field trip to the aquarium.

  a. The admission costs are $7 for adults and $5 for students. How much does it cost for everyone to be admitted?

  b. For lunch, each person gets a sandwich for $2 and a juice for $1. How much does it cost for the entire group to eat lunch?

Dolphins
The dolphin shown here is a bottle-nosed dolphin. This kind of dolphin lives in all oceans and reaches a length of 15 ft.

STANDARDIZED TEST PRACTICE

30. You decide to divide 38 marbles evenly between 3 of your friends and keep those that are left over for yourself. How many will you keep?

 (A) 13 **(B)** 12 **(C)** 3 **(D)** 2

31. Evaluate $5(10 + 2)$.

 (A) 20 **(B)** 50 **(C)** 52 **(D)** 60

32. Ted is determining traffic flow on Main Street. He determines that the average number of cars that travel on the street each hour is 145. The average number of trucks per hour is 55. On average, how many vehicles travel on Main Street in a three-hour period?

 (A) 145 **(B)** 200 **(C)** 600 **(D)** 900

33. What is the value of $2 + y \div 5$, when $y = 10$?

 (A) 10 **(B)** 9 **(C)** 4 **(D)** 1

PROPERTIES OF ALGEBRA In Exercises 34–37, describe the property in your own words.

34. $1 + 2 = 2 + 1$ **Commutative Property of Addition**

35. $1 \cdot 2 = 2 \cdot 1$ **Commutative Property of Multiplication**

36. $(1 + 2) + 3 = 1 + (2 + 3)$ **Associative Property of Addition**

37. $(1 \cdot 2) \cdot 3 = 1 \cdot (2 \cdot 3)$ **Associative Property of Multiplication**

38. BUILDING YOUR PROJECT Your company has developed two new computer games. One is a math game that costs \$32. The other is a spelling game that costs \$38. The table at the right shows how many of each game Stores A, B, and C want to buy.

	A	B	C
Math	22	28	19
Spelling	22	20	22

a. Show how the distributive property can be used to find the total amount you will receive from the three stores for the math game.

b. Use the company bill you designed in the *Building Your Project* on page 75 to write bills to the three stores. The bills should include the amount spent on each type of game.

SPIRAL REVIEW

1. TREASURE MAP Using the treasure map at the right, find out if the following steps will lead you to the treasure. Write out another set of directions with at least 5 steps that will lead you to the treasure. Each square is 1 ft by 1 ft. **(1.5)**

> 5 ft east, 2 ft north, 2 ft west, 7 ft south, 4 ft west, 1 ft south, 10 ft east

2. Evaluate the expression $5 + 3 \times 4 + 2$. **(2.5)**

ALGEBRA In Exercises 3–5, rewrite the equation as a question. Then solve the equation and check your answer. **(1.7)**

3. $4 \times t = 60$ **4.** $114 - m = 84$ **5.** $g - 32 = 8$

6. Today you went to the mall where you spent half your money on a tape. Then you spent \$1 on a drink and \$2 on a soft pretzel. When you got home, you had \$4 left in your pocket. How much money did you start with? How much did the tape cost? **(1.7)**

In Exercises 7–9, write the number in words. **(2.1)**

7. 327   **8.** 600,000   **9.** 56,400

A Family of Numbers

READ About It

The base-ten number system that we use today was first used by people who lived in India more than 2000 years ago. Later, people in Arabia began using the system and it came to be known as the Arabic number system. This system is an example of a place-value system.

The Arabic number system is currently used in many parts of the world. People in Egypt, Turkey, Iran, and other countries in the Middle East use a system of numerals called East Arabic or Modern Arabic. Like the system with which you are familiar, the Modern Arabic system is a place-value system that uses ten as its base.

COL DU TICHKA
ALT. 2260

Arabic Numerals	0	1	2	3	4	5	6	7	8	9
Modern Arabic Numerals	٠	١	٢	٣	٤	٥	٦	٧	٨	٩

WRITE About It

1. Which numbers use symbols that are almost the same in both systems? Explain.

2. Write the following numbers using Modern Arabic numerals.

   a. 49 **b.** 3732 **c.** 4420

3. Write the following Modern Arabic numbers using Arabic numerals.

   a. ٦٠ **b.** ٨٥٩ **c.** ٤٢٠١

4. Explain why having a symbol for zero is an advantage in a number system.

5. Solve in Arabic numerals. Notice that the operation sign is on the right.

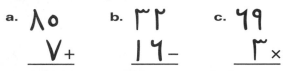

   a. ٨٥
       ٧+

   b. ٣٢
       ١٦−

   c. ٦٩
       ٣×

LAB 2.7

COOPERATIVE LEARNING

Materials Needed
• paper
• pencils
• base-five pieces

Investigating Different Bases

Part A DESCRIBING BASE-FIVE PIECES

Look at the 3 pieces shown below. With others in your group, answer the questions.

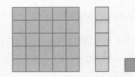

1. Describe the shape of each piece.

2. How many small squares are in each piece?

3. What would be good names for these pieces? Why?

Part B USING BASE-FIVE PIECES

Form a collection of base-five pieces like that shown below. This collection has a total number of 12 pieces.

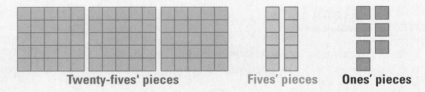

Twenty-fives' pieces   Fives' pieces   Ones' pieces

The total number of ones' pieces, or small squares, is

$$(3 \times 25) + (2 \times 5) + (7 \times 1) = 75 + 10 + 7$$
$$= 92.$$

4. Find other collections of base-five pieces that have a total of 92 ones' pieces. Use at least one large square. Record your results in a table.

5. How many different collections can you find that have a total of 73 ones' pieces? Record your results in a new table.

6. Look back at your two tables. In each table, circle the collection that contains the fewest pieces. Describe the method you used to find the smallest collections.

Part C WRITING NUMBERS IN BASE FIVE

Base-five notation shows the smallest collection of base-five pieces for a given number. Here are two examples.

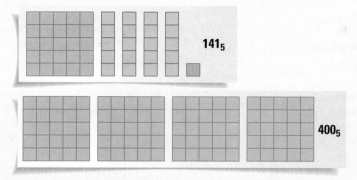

141_5

400_5

7. In base-five notation, does the number 274_5 make sense? Explain.

8. Write the base-five notation for 121 ones' pieces, 89 ones' pieces, and 42 ones' pieces.

9. What digits are used in base-five notation?

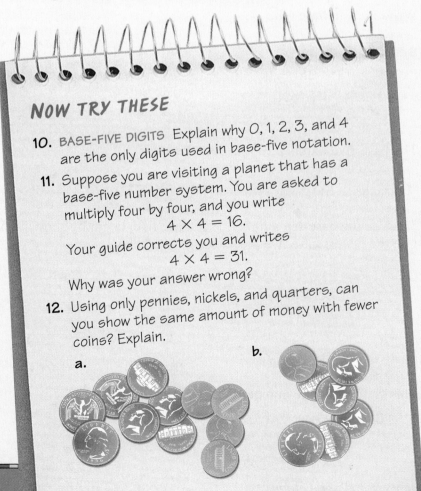

NOW TRY THESE

10. BASE-FIVE DIGITS Explain why 0, 1, 2, 3, and 4 are the only digits used in base-five notation.

11. Suppose you are visiting a planet that has a base-five number system. You are asked to multiply four by four, and you write
$$4 \times 4 = 16.$$
Your guide corrects you and writes
$$4 \times 4 = 31.$$
Why was your answer wrong?

12. Using only pennies, nickels, and quarters, can you show the same amount of money with fewer coins? Explain.

a.

b.

2.7

What you should learn:

Goal 1 How to read and write numbers in base five

Goal 2 How to read and write numbers in other bases

Why you should learn it:

Understanding the way numbers are written in different bases helps you get a better understanding of the base-ten system.

The objects that archeologists recover help us understand what number systems past cultures used.

Goal 1 READING AND WRITING IN BASE FIVE

In the base-ten place-value system, each place value is 10 times larger than the place value to its right. In the base-five place-value system, each place value is five times larger, as shown below.

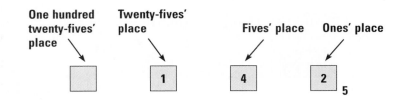

Notice that base-five numbers, such as 142_5, are written with a 5 at the lower right.

Example 1 Reading Numbers in Base Five

Write 203_5 in base ten.

Solution

$$203_5 = (2 \times 25) + (0 \times 5) + (3 \times 1)$$
$$= 50 + 0 + 3$$
$$= 53$$

The base-five number 203_5 is 53 in base ten.

Example 2 Writing Numbers in Base Five

To write the base-ten number 58 in base five, begin by showing 58. Use the fewest base five pieces, as shown below.

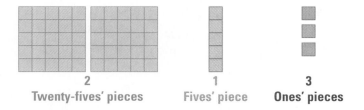

2	1	3
Twenty-fives' pieces	Fives' piece	Ones' pieces

This shows that the number is 213_5, in base five.

✔**Check:** WORK BACKWARD

$$(2 \times 25) + (1 \times 5) + (3 \times 1) = 58 ✔$$

Today, the base-two system is the most commonly used base other than base ten. In base two, each place value is two times larger.

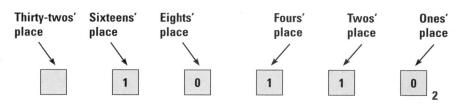

| Thirty-twos' place | Sixteens' place | Eights' place | | Fours' place | Twos' place | | Ones' place |

To show numbers in base two, you can also use base-two pieces.

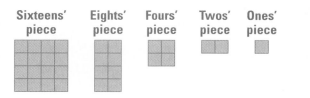

Sixteens' piece   Eights' piece   Fours' piece   Twos' piece   Ones' piece

Base two is used by computers to store numbers. Computer memories have thousands of tiny switches that can be *on* (1) or *off* (0). Each base-two number lets the computer know which switches need to be on or off.

Example 3 Reading Numbers in Base Two

In computer memory, what number does the following show?

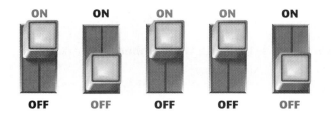

ON   ON   ON   ON   ON

OFF   OFF   OFF   OFF   OFF

Solution

The figure shows the base-two number 10110_2.

$$10110_2 = (1 \times 16) + (1 \times 4) + (1 \times 2)$$
$$= 16 + 4 + 2$$
$$= 22$$

In base ten, the number is 22.

Real Life...
Real Facts

Babylonians
A Babylonian clay tablet is shown above. The ancient Babylonian number system had base 60.

ONGOING ASSESSMENT

Write About It
· · · · · · · · · · · · · · · · ·
Write each number in base two. Write a sentence describing how to tell whether a base-two number is even or odd.

1. 7   **2.** 31   **3.** 12

2.7 Exercises

GUIDED PRACTICE

1. Which of the models better shows 67 in base five?

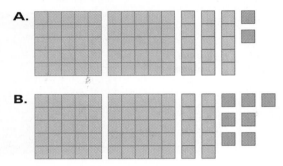

A.

B.

2. Write the base-five number that has 77 ones' pieces.

3. Write the number 38 in base five.

4. What base-ten number is shown by 10011_2?

5. In the base-six system, what digits can you use?

6. Sketch a picture of what you think base-four pieces look like.

7. **ERROR ANALYSIS** Explain why 16123_5 is not a base-five number.

PRACTICE AND PROBLEM SOLVING

READING BASE-FIVE NUMBERS In Exercises 8–13, write the number in base ten. (*Hint:* How many ones' pieces would the number be?)

8. 122_5

9. 303_5

10. 444_5

11. 1412_5

12. 2003_5

13. 4444_5

WRITING BASE-FIVE NUMBERS In Exercises 14–19, write the number in base five.

14. 27

15. 75

16. 89

17. 144

18. 525

19. 310

20. **TIME** You have two movies that you want to watch. The first has a running time of 133 min 38 s and the second has a running time of 147 min 41 s.

   a. If you watch the movies back to back, starting at exactly 5:00 P.M., at what time will the second movie end?

   b. Explain how an understanding of different bases helps you solve the problem.

READING BASE-TWO NUMBERS In Exercises 21–26, write the number in base ten.

21. 1001_2 **22.** 1010_2 **23.** 1111_2

24. 11010_2 **25.** 10001_2 **26.** 11111_2

WRITING BASE-TWO NUMBERS In Exercises 27–30, write the number in base two.

27. 11 **28.** 23 **29.** 31 **30.** 59

In Exercises 31–33, use the base-eight number system described below. Write the number in base ten.

Sixty-fours' place   Eights' place   Ones' place

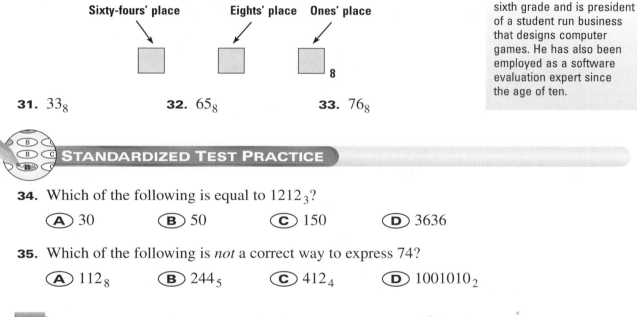

31. 33_8 **32.** 65_8 **33.** 76_8

STANDARDIZED TEST PRACTICE

34. Which of the following is equal to 1212_3?

Ⓐ 30   Ⓑ 50   Ⓒ 150   Ⓓ 3636

35. Which of the following is *not* a correct way to express 74?

Ⓐ 112_8 Ⓑ 244_5 Ⓒ 412_4 Ⓓ 1001010_2

EXPLORATION AND EXTENSION

PORTFOLIO

36. BUILDING YOUR PROJECT Your company writes an adventure game featuring teenage sleuths Matt and Mara. They write messages to each other using a secret code.

In the code, each letter is assigned a number. The letter A is 65, B is 66, and so forth. A space is 32. The numbers are then put into base two. The message at the right is sent by Mara and Matt to the player at the end of the game. Can you crack the code? The first letter is done for you.

```
0 1 0 1 1 0 0 1 ←Y
0 1 0 0 1 1 1 1
0 1 0 1 0 1 0 1
0 0 1 0 0 0 0 0
0 1 0 0 0 0 0 1
0 1 0 1 0 0 1 0
0 1 0 0 0 1 0 1
0 0 1 0 0 0 0 0
0 1 0 1 0 0 1 1
0 1 0 0 1 1 0 1
0 1 0 0 0 0 0 1
0 1 0 1 0 0 1 0
0 1 0 1 0 1 0 0
```

WHAT *did you learn?*

WHY *did you learn it?*

Skills

2.1	Write base-ten place-value numbers in expanded notation.	Order distances by comparing place values.
2.2	Add and subtract whole numbers, using regrouping.	Find the perimeter of a geometric shape.
2.3	Multiply whole numbers.	Find the area of a rectangle, such as a floor.
2.4	Write answers to division problems that have remainders.	Find a fraction of a whole.
2.5	Evaluate a variable expression using order of operations.	Simplify expressions by doing operations in a given order.
2.6	Evaluate a variable expression using the distributive property.	Simplify expressions using mental math.
2.7	Read and write numbers in different bases.	Read and write base-two computer codes.

Strategies 2.1–2.7 Use problem solving strategies.   Solve a wide variety of real-life problems.

Using Data 2.1–2.7 Use tables and graphs.   Organize data and solve problems.

HOW *does it fit in the bigger picture of mathematics?*

In mathematics, knowing *how* to do something is only half the story. It is also important to know *why* the procedure works.

Example   Shown below is *how* and *why* $5 \times 14 = 70$

How

$$\begin{array}{r} 2 \\ 14 \\ \times\ 5 \\ \hline 70 \end{array}$$

Why

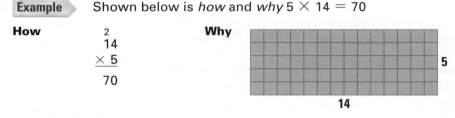

In order to apply multiplication to real-life problems, such as finding area, you have to know why it works. This is shown by the use of the area model above. This is also true for addition, subtraction, and division.

Number operations can be shown using diagrams that help you understand the operations.

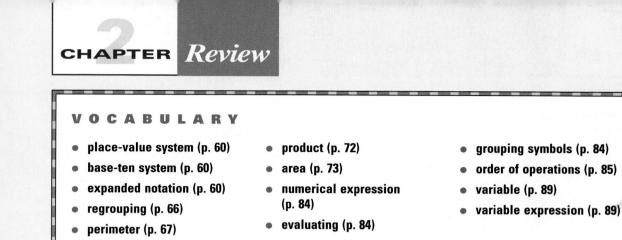

VOCABULARY

- place-value system (p. 60)
- base-ten system (p. 60)
- expanded notation (p. 60)
- regrouping (p. 66)
- perimeter (p. 67)

- product (p. 72)
- area (p. 73)
- numerical expression (p. 84)
- evaluating (p. 84)

- grouping symbols (p. 84)
- order of operations (p. 85)
- variable (p. 89)
- variable expression (p. 89)

2.1 THE BASE-TEN PLACE-VALUE SYSTEM

Write a number in expanded notation as the sum of each digit multiplied by the power of ten for its place value.

Example

$$367 = 300 + 60 + 7$$
$$= 3 \times 100 + 6 \times 10 + 7 \times 1$$

1. Write 680,201 in words.

2. Write 35,790 in expanded notation.

In Exercises 3 and 4, write the number given by the expanded notation.

3. $5 \times 1000 + 3 \times 1$

4. $6 \times 100 + 7 \times 10 + 2 \times 1$

2.2 ADDITION AND SUBTRACTION

Find the perimeter of a figure by adding the lengths of the sides.

Find the sum or difference of whole numbers by regrouping 1 ten as 10 ones, and 1 hundred as 10 tens.

Examples

$$\begin{array}{r} \overset{1\;1}{} \\ 127 \\ + 396 \\ \hline 523 \end{array}$$

$1 + 2 + 9 = 12$ $7 + 6 = 13$

$15 - 8 = 7$

$$\begin{array}{r} \overset{6\,1\,5\,1}{764} \\ - 89 \\ \hline 675 \end{array}$$

$14 - 9 = 5$

5. Find the sum of 159 and 87.

6. Find the difference of 306 and 28.

In Exercises 7 and 8, find the perimeter of the figure.

7.

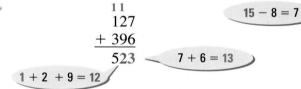

2 ft   2 ft   4 ft
3 ft   3 ft
7 ft

8.

5 in.
2 in.
5 in.
4 in.
2 in.

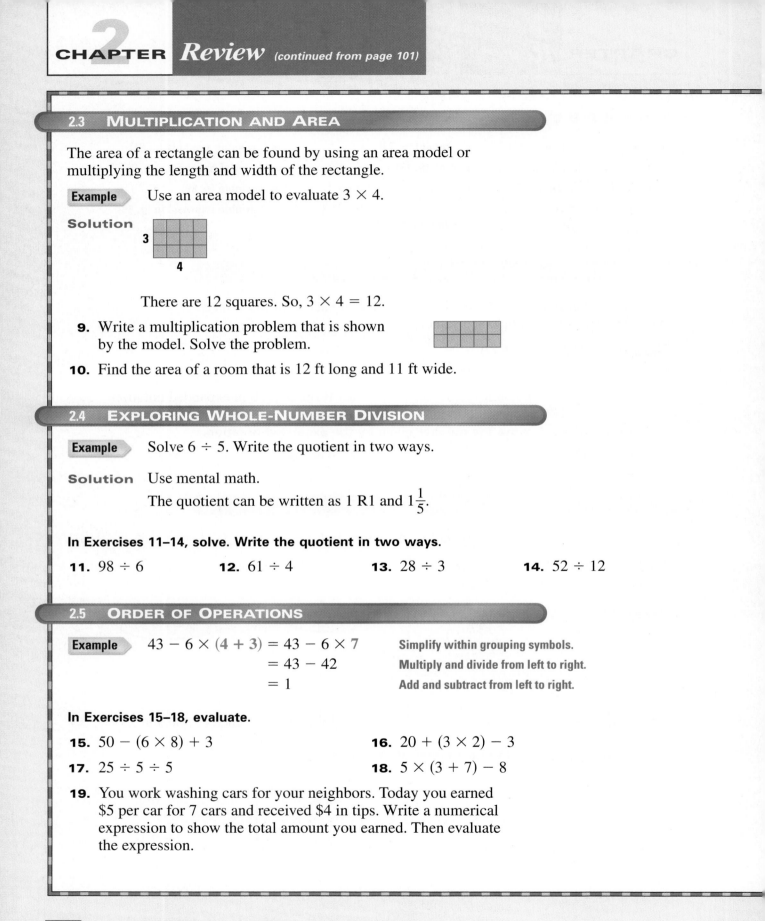

2.3 MULTIPLICATION AND AREA

The area of a rectangle can be found by using an area model or multiplying the length and width of the rectangle.

Example Use an area model to evaluate 3×4.

Solution

3

4

There are 12 squares. So, $3 \times 4 = 12$.

9. Write a multiplication problem that is shown by the model. Solve the problem.

10. Find the area of a room that is 12 ft long and 11 ft wide.

2.4 EXPLORING WHOLE-NUMBER DIVISION

Example Solve $6 \div 5$. Write the quotient in two ways.

Solution Use mental math.

The quotient can be written as 1 R1 and $1\frac{1}{5}$.

In Exercises 11–14, solve. Write the quotient in two ways.

11. $98 \div 6$ **12.** $61 \div 4$ **13.** $28 \div 3$ **14.** $52 \div 12$

2.5 ORDER OF OPERATIONS

Example

$$43 - 6 \times (4 + 3) = 43 - 6 \times 7$$ Simplify within grouping symbols.

$$= 43 - 42$$ Multiply and divide from left to right.

$$= 1$$ Add and subtract from left to right.

In Exercises 15–18, evaluate.

15. $50 - (6 \times 8) + 3$ **16.** $20 + (3 \times 2) - 3$

17. $25 \div 5 \div 5$ **18.** $5 \times (3 + 7) - 8$

19. You work washing cars for your neighbors. Today you earned $5 per car for 7 cars and received $4 in tips. Write a numerical expression to show the total amount you earned. Then evaluate the expression.

2.6 THE DISTRIBUTIVE PROPERTY

To use mental math to evaluate an expression, use the distributive property.

Example Use mental math to evaluate 6×57.

Solution

$6 \times 57 = 6(50 + 7)$	Rewrite 57 as 50 + 7.
$= 6 \times 50 + 6 \times 7$	Use the distributive property.
$= 300 + 42$	Use mental math.
$= 342$	Use mental math.

20. Evaluate $6(11 + 5)$ in two ways.

21. Evaluate $8(n + 2)$ when $n = 5$.

22. Use mental math to evaluate 3×32.

23. Use mental math to solve $6(5 + x) = 54$.

2.7 EXPLORING DIFFERENT BASES

Examples

a.

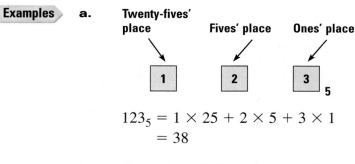

$$123_5 = 1 \times 25 + 2 \times 5 + 3 \times 1$$
$$= 38$$

b.

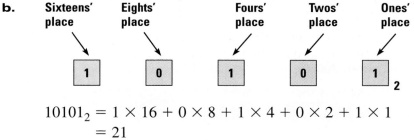

$$10101_2 = 1 \times 16 + 0 \times 8 + 1 \times 4 + 0 \times 2 + 1 \times 1$$
$$= 21$$

24. Write the number 423_5 in base ten.

25. Write the number 11110_2 in base ten.

In Exercises 26–29, write the base-ten number in base two and base five.

26. 15   **27.** 60   **28.** 38   **29.** 11

In Exercises 1–4, write the number in words and in expanded notation.

1. 5110   **2.** 19,003   **3.** 3472   **4.** 29,308

In Exercises 5–8, add or subtract. State whether you used regrouping.

5. $124 + 711$ **6.** $1310 - 219$ **7.** $556 + 968$ **8.** $3124 + 1901$

In Exercises 9 and 10, write the multiplication problem shown.

9. Area is 60 square units.

10. Area is 60 square units.

In Exercises 11–14, divide. Write the quotient in two ways.

11. $37 \div 5$ **12.** $88 \div 3$ **13.** $255 \div 4$ **14.** $27 \div 2$

In Exercises 15–18, simplify the expression.

15. $(10 + 5) \times 4$ **16.** $57 - 45 \div 3$ **17.** $(27 - 3) \div 8$ **18.** $2 \times 10 + 3$

In Exercises 19–22, rewrite the number in base ten.

19. 4431_5 **20.** 10011_2 **21.** 221_5 **22.** 1111_2

23. Find the area and the perimeter of the rectangle.

3 yd

7 yd

In Exercises 24 and 25, use the table below. It shows the number of people employed in computer-related jobs in 1994 and the number expected to be employed in 2005. (Source: U.S. Bureau of Labor Statistics)

	Computer Engineer	Computer Operator	Systems Analyst	Computer Programmer
1994	195,000	259,000	483,000	537,000
2005	372,000	162,000	928,000	601,000

24. How many fewer computer operators are expected in 2005 than in 1994?

25. How many more computer programmers are expected in 2005 than in 1994?

1. The following is expanded notation for what number?

   $$3 \times 10,000 + 2 \times 100 + 4 \times 1$$

   (A) 32,004   (B) 30,204

   (C) 3204   (D) 324

2. The number 3,300,000 is 33 _?_.

   (A) millions

   (B) hundred thousands

   (C) ten thousands

   (D) thousands

3. The following is an example of _?_.

   $$3 \times 32 = 3 \times (30 + 2)$$
   $$= 90 + 6$$
   $$= 96$$

   (A) modeling multiplication

   (B) the distributive property

   (C) regrouping

   (D) base-three numbers

4. Use mental math to solve $21 - n = 7$.

   (A) $n = 28$ (B) $n = 14$

   (C) $n = 4$ (D) $n = 3$

5. You have 101101_2 marbles. Jack has 140_5 marbles. Jill has 45 marbles. Who has the most marbles?

   (A) You   (B) Jack

   (C) Jill   (D) You have the same.

6. $7 \times 3 + 4 - 2 \times 5 =$ ❓

   (A) 135   (B) 115

   (C) 39   (D) 15

7. Name the dividend and divisor in the problem $40 \div 10 = 4$.

   (A) dividend 10, divisor 4

   (B) dividend 4, divisor 40

   (C) dividend 10, divisor 40

   (D) dividend 40, divisor 10

8. $14 - 3 \times 2 + 8 \div 2 =$ ❓

   (A) 15 R1   (B) 15

   (C) 12   (D) 8

9. In the number 154,873, what place value does the 5 have?

   (A) millions

   (B) hundred thousands

   (C) ten thousands

   (D) thousands

10. In base two, the number 28 is written as ❓ .

    (A) 14_2 (B) 11212_2

    (C) 11100_2 (D) 110_2

11. One hundred fifty thousand, five hundred is the same as what number?

    (A) 155,000   (B) 150,500

    (C) 105,500   (D) 100,550

12. You have 36 trading cards and want to divide them among yourself and 3 friends. If you divide them evenly, how many cards will each of your friends receive?

    (A) 33   (B) 32

    (C) 12   (D) 9

Decimals
and Percent

FLAGS of every member nation fly in front of the United Nations buildings in New York City.

DOLLAR SIGN The widely accepted explanation for the origin of the "$" is that it came from the Mexican or Spanish "P's" for *pesos*. The "s" gradually was written over the "P."

CHAPTER THEME
Money of the World

TECHNOLOGY

Technology resources accompanying this chapter:

- Interactive Real-Life Investigations
- Middle School Tutorial Software

MONEY EXCHANGE Many banks and travel agencies display up-to-the-minute rates of currency exchange, for the convenience of their customers.

CURRENCY EXCHANGE RATES

		WE BUY AT	WE SELL AT
≡ USA	USD		
AUSTRALIA	A$		
AUSTRIA	AS		
BELGIUM	BFR		
CANADA	CAD		
DENMARK	KNR		
UNITED KINGDOM	GBP		
FRANCE	FRF		
GERMANY	DEM		
THE NETHERLANDS	NLG		
HONG KONG	HKD		

Units of Money

REAL LIFE
Foreign Money

When visiting a foreign country, you need to have foreign money. The table below shows about how much one unit of foreign currency is worth in United States dollars and how much one United States dollar is worth in each country. (Source: *Wall Street Journal*, 1997)

	In United States $	Currency per United States $
yen (Japan)	0.008	124.25
pound (U.K.)	1.631	0.613
mark (Germany)	0.596	1.679
rand (South Africa)	0.226	4.424
drachma (Greece)	0.004	265.80

Think and Discuss

1. Which is worth more: a mark or a rand? Explain your reasoning.
2. How many pounds do you get for 100 United States dollars? Explain.

E PORTFOLIO

CHAPTER PROJECT

Making a Travel Handbook

PROJECT DESCRIPTION

When people plan a trip to another country, they should learn as much about that country as they can before they leave home. You will make a handbook of travel tips for people who are planning an international trip. To organize your handbook, you will use the list of **TOPICS** on the next page.

GETTING STARTED

Talking It Over

- In your group, talk about which countries you would like to visit. What sights would you like to see while you are there? Think of any kinds of food that come from that country.

- Talk about planning a vacation to the country you would like to visit. How would you get there? How would you know what kind of clothes to pack? Where will you stay while you are there? How will you know how much money you will need?

Planning Your Project

- **Materials:** paper, pencils or pens, colored pencils or markers

- Make a booklet out of folded pieces of paper. Research the flags of each country mentioned in the **TOPICS** list. Design a cover for your handbook using some or all of the flags. Be sure to include your name and the title of the handbook on the cover. As you answer the **BUILDING YOUR PROJECT** questions, add your results to your handbook. Add pictures that represent countries you write about.

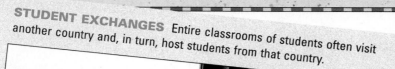

STUDENT EXCHANGES Entire classrooms of students often visit another country and, in turn, host students from that country.

EXCHANGE MACHINES This student is using a machine that will automatically exchange currency of one country for currency of another country.

BUILDING YOUR PROJECT

These are places throughout the chapter where you will work on your project.

TOPICS

I N T E R N E T

To find out more about travel, go to:
http://www.mlmath.com

Investigating Decimals and Base-Ten Pieces

Materials Needed
- base-ten pieces
- paper
- pencils

In Chapter 2, you learned how to use base-ten pieces to represent whole numbers. For example, the number 328 can be modeled with 3 large squares, 2 strips, and 8 small squares.

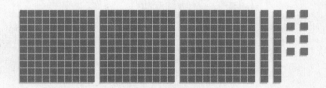

In this Lab, you will learn how to use base-ten pieces to model decimals.

Part A MODELING DECIMALS

1. Let a large square represent the number 1. Suppose that the square is divided into 10 equal strips. What number (or fraction of the square) does each strip represent? Say the number in words. Then discuss how to write the number as a decimal.

The large square represents one.

2. Now, suppose one of the strips is divided into 10 small squares. What number does each small square represent? Say the number *in words*. Then discuss how to write the number as a decimal.

3. How many small squares does it take to make one large square?

4. If a small square is divided into 10 small strips, what number would each small strip represent?

5. Use base-ten pieces to model these numbers: 3.2, 3.02, and 0.32. Draw a sketch of each model.

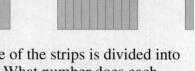

6. The base-ten pieces below represent 7 tenths and 13 hundredths. Find other ways that you can use base-ten pieces to represent the same number. Organize your results in a table like that shown below.

7 tenths　　　　**13 hundredths**

Tenths	Hundredths	Total Number of Pieces
7	13	20
8	3	?
?	?	?
?	?	?
?	?	?

7. What patterns do you see in the table?

8. Which collection has the fewest pieces? How is this collection related to the decimal form of the number?

Part **C** REGROUPING

Form each collection of base-ten pieces. Then trade pieces to form a collection with the fewest pieces. Write the decimal number shown by your collection with the fewest pieces.

9. 1 ones, 12 tenths, 16 hundredths

10. 15 tenths

11. 347 hundredths

12. 2 ones, 48 hundredths

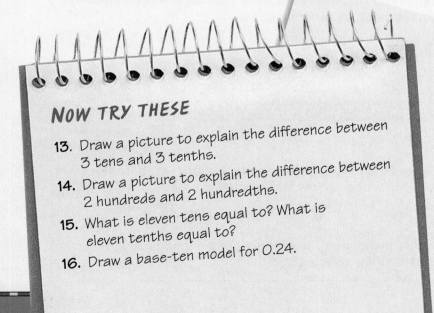

NOW TRY THESE

13. Draw a picture to explain the difference between 3 tens and 3 tenths.

14. Draw a picture to explain the difference between 2 hundreds and 2 hundredths.

15. What is eleven tens equal to? What is eleven tenths equal to?

16. Draw a base-ten model for 0.24.

=0.15

3.1 Exploring Decimal Representation

What you should learn:

Goal 1 How to write decimals in expanded notation

Goal 2 How the choice of a unit changes the decimal representation of a number

Why you should learn it:

An understanding of the base-ten place-value system will help you understand the decimal form of numbers. For example, $.75 and 75¢ represent the same amount of money.

Goal 1 EXPANDED NOTATION OF DECIMALS

In Chapter 2, you wrote whole numbers in the base-ten place-value system. In this chapter, you will study decimal numbers such as the one shown below. It is read as "two and fifty-eight hundredths." You will learn to represent decimals using base-ten pieces and expanded notation.

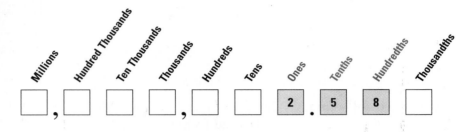

Example 1 Using Base-Ten Pieces

Use base-ten pieces to write 2.58 in expanded notation.

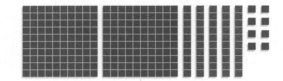

Solution

To write a number in expanded notation, each digit is multiplied by a number representing its place value.

$$2.58 = 2 + 0.5 + 0.08$$
$$= (2 \times 1) + (5 \times 0.1) + (8 \times 0.01)$$

STUDY TIP

The way you write a number depends on the units that you select. The number in Example 1 can be written in the following ways.

258 small squares or 258 hundredths

25.8 strips or 25.8 tenths

2.58 large squares or 2.58 ones

LESSON INVESTIGATION

COOPERATIVE LEARNING

Investigating Representations of Decimals

Draw each base-ten model using the fewest pieces. Write three names for the number that is represented.

1. 134 small squares

2. 1.02 large squares

3. 23.1 strips

How does the position of the decimal point change depending on the units that are selected?

Prices can be written in two ways: dollars and cents. It is helpful to be able to use both units.

Example 2 Naming Amounts of Money

REAL LIFE
Money

Suppose you sell fruits and vegetables. You mark your prices different ways, depending on the size of the sign. Write each lettered price in dollars and in cents.

Solution

a. The dollar price can be written as $1.99 or 199¢.

b. The dollar price can be written as $1.00 or 100¢.

c. The cents price can be written as $.79 or 79¢.

d. The cents price can be written as $.69 or 69¢.

You can state the results of Example 2 as follows.

1. *Dollars to cents:* Move the decimal point two places to the right.

2. *Cents to dollars:* Move the decimal point two places to the left.

GUIDED PRACTICE

In Exercises 1–3, use the values for base-ten pieces shown at the right to match the name with the model.

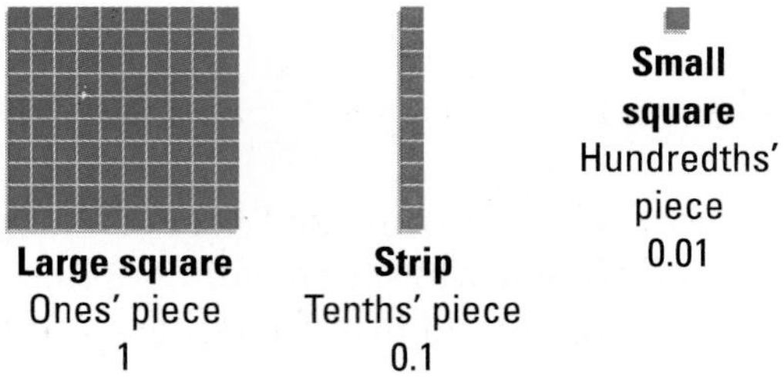

1. Ones   **A.** Strips

2. Hundredths   **B.** Small squares

3. Tenths   **C.** Large squares

4. Write a number that has a 7 in the thousands' place *and* a 7 in the thousandths' place.

5. Write 6.78 dollars in cent units.

6. Write 25 cents using both ¢ and $.

Large square Ones' piece 1   **Strip** Tenths' piece 0.1   **Small square** Hundredths' piece 0.01

In Exercises 7–9, sketch the base-ten model using the fewest pieces. Then write three names for the number that is represented.

7. 1.12 large squares   8. 15.6 strips   9. 121 small squares

PRACTICE AND PROBLEM SOLVING

In Exercises 10–12, write two names for the number represented by the base-ten pieces. Use the values for base-ten pieces shown above.

10.   11.    12.

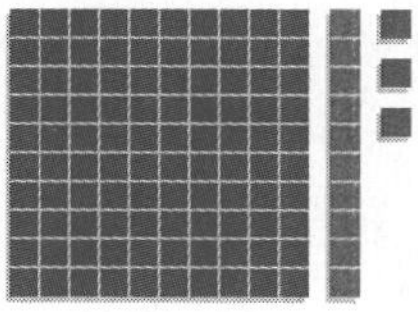

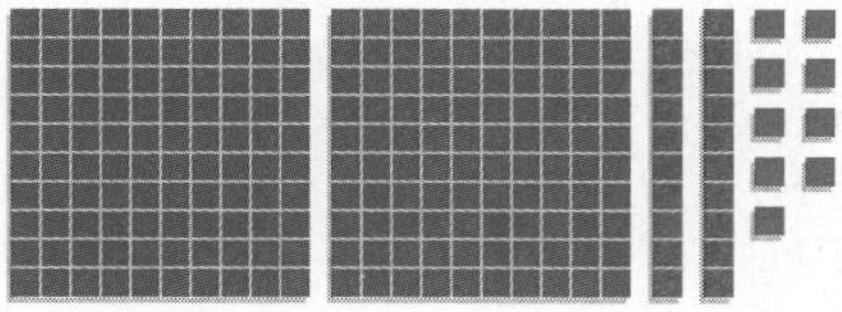

In Exercises 13–15, use the model at the right. Complete the statement with the words *ones*, *tenths*, or *hundredths*. Use the values for base-ten pieces shown above.

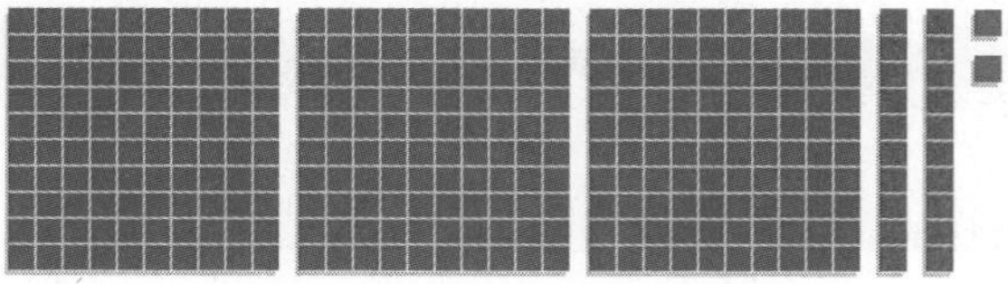

13. 3.22 ?   14. 322 ?   15. 32.2 ?

COMMUNICATING In Exercises 16–21, write the number using numerals.

16. Three and four tenths

17. Twelve and fifty-two hundredths

18. Two hundred twenty thousandths

19. Five hundred and three hundredths

20. Four and seventeen hundredths

21. Five thousandths

In Exercises 22–24, write the number in expanded notation.

22. 5.48   23. 23.936   24. 101.021

In Exercises 25–28, decide whether the statement is *true* or *false*.

25. 100 tenths = 10 ones

26. 10 hundredths = 100 tenths

27. 10 hundredths = 1 tenth

28. 1000 thousandths = 1 one

GASOLINE PRICES In Exercises 29–32, use the graph at the right. It shows average prices of gasoline. Write the amounts in dollars and in cents. (Source: Energy Information Administration)

29. The cost of 1 gallon of gas in 1975

30. The cost of 10 gallons of gas in 1983

31. The cost of 100 gallons of gas in 1995

32. The cost of 1000 gallons of gas in 1991

33. **REASONING** Which would you rather have: $5 or 5000¢? Explain.

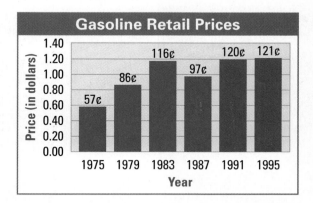

Gasoline Retail Prices

34. Which number could the base-ten pieces *not* represent?

   (A) 202 hundredths   **(B)** 20.2 tenths

   (C) 2.02 ones   **(D)** 2.2 ones

35. Which number is equal to 3.22 tenths?

   (A) 32.2 hundredths   **(B)** 3220 thousandths

   (C) 0.322 hundredths   **(D)** 32.2 ones

EXPLORATION AND EXTENSION

PORTFOLIO

36. **BUILDING YOUR PROJECT** Which price might you expect to pay for a pencil in Norway?

   A. 4.6 krone   **B.** 46 øre

   C. 460 øre   **D.** 460 krone

Answer this question, and write it as a tip for your travel handbook. Use the information to write another tip for travelers to Norway in your travel handbook.

Tech Link

Investigation 3, Interactive Real-Life Investigations

1 krone = $.13
100 øre = 1 krone

3.2

Measuring Length: the Metric System

What you should learn:

Goal 1 How to measure length in the metric system

Goal 2 How to change units of length in the metric system

Why you should learn it:

The metric system is used in most countries of the world. It is also used in the United States—especially in science.

To comfortably use the metric system, it helps to relate the lengths to real-life objects. For example, the thickness of a dime is about one millimeter.

Goal 1 USING THE METRIC SYSTEM

The metric system is about 200 years old. Before that, many measuring systems were used in the world. In the United States, *two* measuring systems are used—the metric system and the U.S. Customary system (inches, feet, miles).

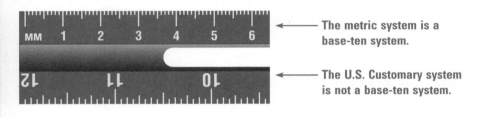

The metric system is a base-ten system.

The U.S. Customary system is not a base-ten system.

THE METRIC SYSTEM OF LENGTH			
Unit	Symbol	Prefix Meaning	Notation
Millimeter	mm	Thousandth	0.001 m
Centimeter	cm	Hundredth	0.01 m
Decimeter	dm	Tenth	0.1 m
Meter	m	—	1.0 m
Decameter	dam	Ten	10.0 m
Hectometer	hm	Hundred	100.0 m
Kilometer	km	Thousand	1000.0 m

Example 1 Estimating Lengths

Unit	Real-Life Object
a. Millimeter	About the thickness of a dime
b. Centimeter	About the width of a fingernail
c. Decimeter	About the width of a hand
d. Meter	About the height of a kitchen counter
e. Decameter	About the width of a classroom
f. Hectometer	About the width of two football fields
g. Kilometer	About the length of five city blocks

Goal 2 CHANGING METRIC UNITS

To change units in the metric system, it is helpful to remember that it is a base-ten system.

CHANGING METRIC UNITS
10 millimeters = 1 centimeter
10 centimeters = 1 decimeter
10 decimeters = 1 meter
100 centimeters = 1 meter
1000 millimeters = 1 meter
1000 meters = 1 kilometer

Example 2 **Changing Metric Units**

Rewrite the measures in the given metric unit.

a. Elaine is 150 cm tall. (meters)

b. A pencil is 0.006 m wide. (millimeters)

c. You went on a 3000 m subway ride. (kilometers)

Solution

a. To convert from centimeters to meters, divide by **100**.

$$150 \text{ centimeters} = (150 \div 100) \text{ meters}$$
$$= 1.5 \text{ meters}$$

So, Elaine is 1.5 m tall.

b. To convert from meters to millimeters, multiply by **1000**.

$$0.006 \text{ meter} = (0.006 \times 1000) \text{ millimeters}$$
$$= 6 \text{ millimeters}$$

So, the pencil is 6 mm wide.

c. To convert from meters to kilometers, divide by **1000**.

$$3000 \text{ meters} = (3000 \div 1000) \text{ kilometers}$$
$$= 3 \text{ kilometers}$$

So, you went on a 3 km subway ride.

ONGOING ASSESSMENT

Write About It

Rewrite each measure in the given metric unit. Then write a sentence that uses the measure.

1. 250 cm (meters)

2. 250 mm (meters)

3. 4000 m (kilometers)

4. 0.02 m (millimeters)

GUIDED PRACTICE

1. Is the U.S. Customary system of length (inches, feet, yards, miles) a base-ten system? Explain.

Fill in the missing metric unit for the length of the actual object.

2. 13.2 ?   **3.** 50 ?   **4.** 25 ?   **5.** 15 ?

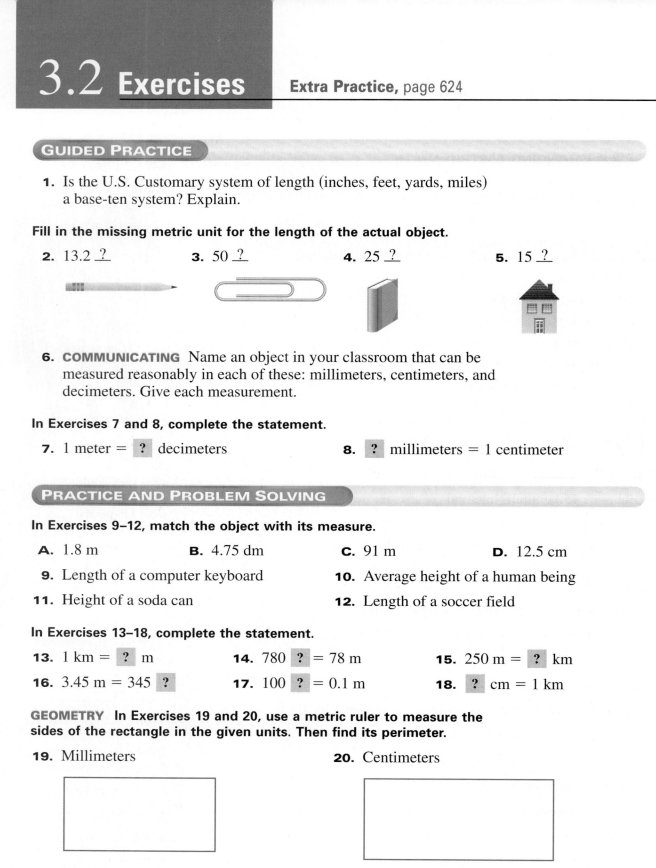

6. COMMUNICATING Name an object in your classroom that can be measured reasonably in each of these: millimeters, centimeters, and decimeters. Give each measurement.

In Exercises 7 and 8, complete the statement.

7. 1 meter = ? decimeters

8. ? millimeters = 1 centimeter

PRACTICE AND PROBLEM SOLVING

In Exercises 9–12, match the object with its measure.

A. 1.8 m   **B.** 4.75 dm   **C.** 91 m   **D.** 12.5 cm

9. Length of a computer keyboard   **10.** Average height of a human being

11. Height of a soda can   **12.** Length of a soccer field

In Exercises 13–18, complete the statement.

13. 1 km = ? m   **14.** 780 ? = 78 m   **15.** 250 m = ? km

16. 3.45 m = 345 ?   **17.** 100 ? = 0.1 m   **18.** ? cm = 1 km

GEOMETRY In Exercises 19 and 20, use a metric ruler to measure the sides of the rectangle in the given units. Then find its perimeter.

19. Millimeters   **20.** Centimeters

21. Measure the four sides of your mathematics book's cover. Use a reasonable metric unit. Then find the perimeter of the cover.

WRITING In Exercises 22–27, rewrite the length in the given metric unit. Then write a sentence that uses the rewritten measure and describes a real-life object.

22. 57 cm (meters)
23. 6500 mm (meters)
24. 0.28 km (meters)
25. 3600 m (kilometers)
26. 0.004 m (millimeters)
27. 1000 cm (meters)

NUMBER SENSE In Exercises 28–33, complete the statement using >, <, or =.

28. 1 mm ? 1000 m
29. 0.1 km ? 10,000 cm
30. 35 cm ? 3.5 mm
31. 0.68 km ? 68 cm
32. 4 m ? 40 cm
33. 2 km ? 2000 mm

DINOSAURS In Exercises 34 and 35, use the following dinosaur lengths.

Dinosaur	Length
Apatosaurus	2100 cm
Ornitholestes	1.8 m
Stegosaurus	0.0076 km
Allosaurus	9000 mm
Tyrannosaurus rex	0.012 km

34. Rewrite each length in meters. List the dinosaurs from shortest to longest.

35. Which dinosaur is five times as long as another?

Tyrannosaurus rex skull

STANDARDIZED TEST PRACTICE

36. Your friend tells you that he and his family traveled 40 km yesterday. Which is the most reasonable assumption?

    (A) They drove across town.   **(B)** They drove for most of the day.

    (C) They walked around a block.   **(D)** They rode bicycles for three hours.

EXPLORATION AND EXTENSION

37. **HISTORY OF A METER** A meter was first defined to be $\frac{1}{10,000,000}$ of the distance between the equator and the North Pole. What is the distance between the equator and the North Pole in kilometers?

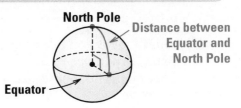

North Pole

Distance between Equator and North Pole

Equator

In Exercises 1–4, write the number in words. (2.1, 3.1)

1. 1432   **2.** 18,067   **3.** 9.55   **4.** 16.043

In Exercises 5–10, write the number in expanded notation. (2.1)

5. 2167   **6.** 8098   **7.** 20,450

8. 97,902   **9.** 306,520   **10.** 1,001,010

**ALGEBRA   In Exercises 11–16, use mental math to solve the equation.
(1.6, 1.7)**

11. $x + 13 = 27$ **12.** $36 - y = 25$ **13.** $16 \cdot p = 48$

14. $q \div 10 = 12$ **15.** $950 \div n = 95$ **16.** $2.2 \cdot m = 220$

**GEOMETRY   In Exercises 17–20, sketch an area model for the problem.
(2.3, 2.4)**

17. 4×6 **18.** 9×8 **19.** $40 \div 3$ **20.** $9 \div 3$

21. **HEALTH** You decide to join a health club. The initiation fee is $25 and membership is $45 a month. Write an expression that represents how much you will pay for a one-year membership. Simplify the expression. **(2.5)**

CAREER Interview

CONSULTANT

Stephanie Fan works for PEACH Corporation in Boston, Massachusetts. She is hired by organizations to help them for a short time when they have a problem.

Q What types of things are you hired to do?
I might do accounting work, hire new employees, or give workshops about the diversity in the community.

Q What math skills do you use in your job?
I use all the basic math skills and estimation, especially when I work with an organization's finances.

Q Do you use mathematical reasoning?
My job is problem solving. Organizations hire me when they have a problem. I go in, study it, and help find a solution. The problems are always different.

Q What would you like to tell kids about math?
There is so much to learn. Schooling doesn't end at twelfth grade. It is a lifelong experience. Learning keeps you energized and young forever.

Scale Drawings

Architects make scale drawings called blueprints when planning a building. A blueprint shows sizes of rooms and where certain features such as doors and stairways are located.

Example

Part of a blueprint is shown below. Use a metric ruler to find the perimeter of the room shown. Then use the scale to help you find the perimeter of the actual room.

REAL LIFE
Drafting

Scale

1 cm represents 1 m.

CLOSET

Solution

The width is 39 mm and the length is 74 mm. The perimeter is

39 ➕ 39 ➕ 74 ➕ 74 ➖ (226.)

or 226 mm. To find the perimeter in centimeters, divide this number by 10.

Using mental math, $226 \div 10 = 22.6$, so the perimeter is 22.6 cm. Because each centimeter on the blueprint represents 1 meter in the actual room, the actual room must have a perimeter of 22.6 m.

Exercises

In Exercises 1–4, rewrite each measure in millimeters and in meters.

1. 7.31 cm   **2.** 125.8 cm   **3.** 924.1 cm   **4.** 18.4 cm

In Exercises 5–8, rewrite each measure in inches and in feet.

5. 1.25 yd   **6.** 0.8 yd   **7.** 2.4 yd   **8.** 2.75 yd

9. In which system, *metric* or *U.S. Customary*, is it easier to convert to different units? Explain your reasoning.

10. On a blueprint a rectangular living room has width 57 mm and length 93 mm. The scale shows that 1 cm represents 1 m. Find the perimeter of the actual room.

LAB 3.3

COOPERATIVE LEARNING

Materials Needed
- base-ten grid paper
- plain paper
- pencils

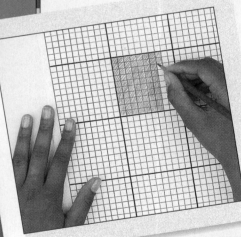

Investigating Area Models

In this chapter, you have seen that numbers can have different names. For example, you can read 2500 as "2.5 thousand" or "25 hundred."

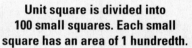

Part A DECIMALS LESS THAN 1

The shaded regions are the same size, so $0.3 = 0.30$.

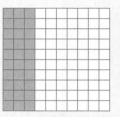

Unit square is divided into 10 strips. Each strip has an area of 1 tenth.

Unit square is divided into 100 small squares. Each small square has an area of 1 hundredth.

1. How many tenths are shown by the shaded region? How many hundredths? Redraw the model on base-ten grid paper. Sketch the number as hundredths.

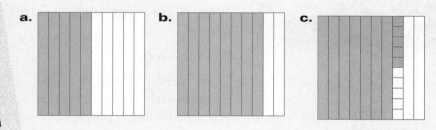

a.   b.   c.

2. How many hundredths are shown by the shaded region? How many tenths? Redraw the model on base-ten grid paper. Sketch the number as tenths.

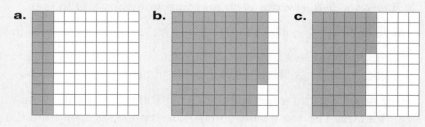

a.   b.   c.

3. The area model represents 3.14 ones. Name the number as tenths and as hundredths.

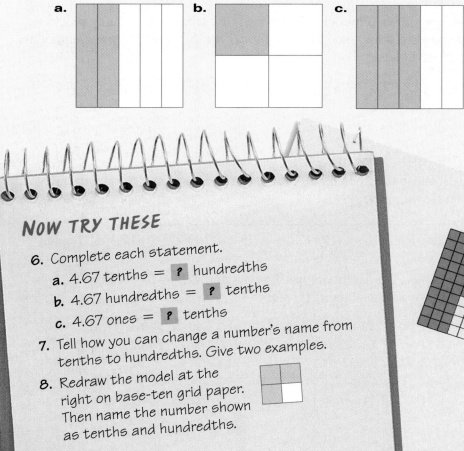

4. Draw a model for 2.32 ones. Name the number as tenths and as hundredths.

Part **C** AREA MODELS

In each model below, a unit square has been divided into smaller regions that each have the same area.

5. Redraw the model on base-ten grid paper. All sides should be 10 units long. Then name the number shown by the shaded region as tenths and hundredths.

a.

b.

c.

NOW TRY THESE

6. Complete each statement.
   a. 4.67 tenths = **?** hundredths
   b. 4.67 hundredths = **?** tenths
   c. 4.67 ones = **?** tenths

7. Tell how you can change a number's name from tenths to hundredths. Give two examples.

8. Redraw the model at the right on base-ten grid paper. Then name the number shown as tenths and hundredths.

3.3

Modeling Decimals

What you should learn:

Goal 1 How to represent decimals with number-line models and set models

Goal 2 How to use decimals to solve real-life problems

Why you should learn it:

Decimals can be used to represent data from a survey. An example is the portion of households who own a dog.

In the United States, 36.5 million households own dogs and 30.9 million households own cats. Many of these own two or more pets.

Goal 1 MODELING DECIMALS

In this chapter, you have shown decimals with base-ten pieces and area models. You can also show decimals with number-line models and set models.

The following models each have 3 of the 10 parts colored, so they are models for 0.3, or 3 tenths. In the models, you can think of 0.3 as a portion of the whole (which is 1).

Number-Line Model

Set Model

3 tenths

Example 1 ▷ Drawing Models

You are shown a model for a portion of a whole. How many pieces do you need to draw to complete a model for the whole? Draw the model for the whole.

a.
```
|---+---+---+---|
0               0.4
```

b.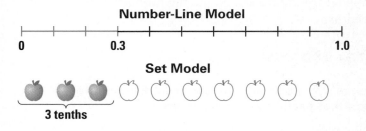
0.13

Solution

a. Because the line shows 4 tenths and has 4 parts, the whole must have 10 parts.

b. Because the set model has 13 stars and shows 13 hundredths, the whole must have 100 stars.

☆☆☆☆☆☆☆☆☆☆☆☆☆☆☆☆☆☆☆☆
☆☆☆☆☆☆☆☆☆☆☆☆☆☆☆☆☆☆☆☆
☆☆☆☆☆☆☆☆☆☆☆☆☆☆☆☆☆☆☆☆
☆☆☆☆☆☆☆☆☆☆☆☆☆☆☆☆☆☆☆☆
☆☆☆☆☆☆☆☆☆☆☆☆☆☆☆☆☆☆☆☆

Goal 2 SOLVING REAL-LIFE PROBLEMS

Example 2 Interpreting a Survey

One hundred people were asked which types of pets they have. The results are shown in the graph. Estimate the portion that have a dog. Give your answer as a decimal. How many people said they had a dog as a pet?

REAL LIFE
Pets

Portion of People Who Own Pets									
Each symbol is 0.1 of the people surveyed.									

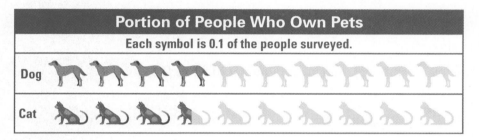

Solution

Understand the Problem

To find the number of people surveyed who have a dog, first use the graph to estimate the portion.

Make a Plan

🔑 STRATEGY **DRAW A DIAGRAM** From the graph, about $\frac{4}{10}$, or 0.4, of the 100 people have a dog. To find the number of people, draw a diagram to show 100 people and circle $\frac{4}{10}$ of them.

Solve the Problem

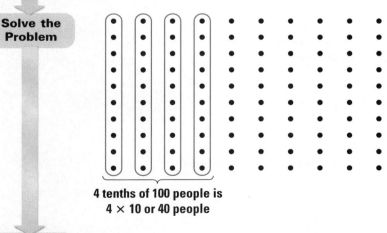

4 tenths of 100 people is
4 × 10 or 40 people

Look Back

40 people are circled, so 40 people have a dog.

Four tenths, or 0.4, of 100 is 40.

ONGOING ASSESSMENT

Talk About It
· · · · · · · · · · · · · · · · · · · ·

Use the information in Example 2 to answer the question. Discuss the solution.

1. In Example 2, how many people own a cat?

2. If the survey involved 200 people, how many people do you think would have replied *dog*?

GUIDED PRACTICE

In Exercises 1–3, the entire drawing represents 1. What portion does the red part represent?

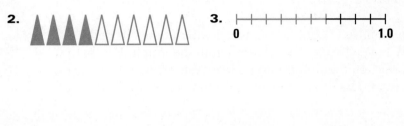

1.

2.

3.

4. Draw an area model to show 0.8.

5. Draw a number-line model, a set model, and an area model to show 0.6.

PRACTICE AND PROBLEM SOLVING

6. NUMBER SENSE Draw a number-line model to show 0.2.

7. NUMBER SENSE Draw a set model to show 0.9.

8. GEOMETRY Draw an area model to show 0.45.

In Exercises 9–11, you are shown a model for a portion of a whole. Describe a model of the whole.

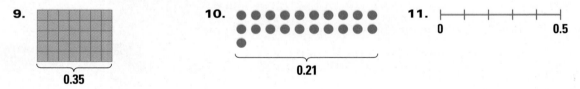

9.

0.35

10.

0.21

11.

0   0.5

GEOMETRY In Exercises 12–14, the model shows a portion of a whole. Draw two rectangles that could represent the whole.

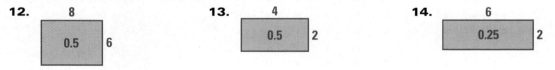

12.

8

0.5   6

13.

4

0.5   2

14.

6

0.25   2

ALGEBRA In Exercises 15 and 16, write an equation represented by the models.

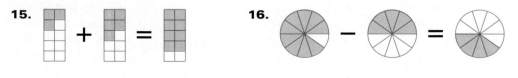

15.

16.

TRAVEL A survey of 100 students was taken. They were asked whether they were interested in traveling to various foreign countries.

Students Who Travel

Each symbol is 0.1 of the students surveyed.

Country	Portion of students
Great Britain	
Italy	
Japan	
Australia	

Portion of students

17. Estimate the portion who said they had an interest in traveling to each country. List your answers as decimals.

18. How many students surveyed were interested in traveling to Japan?

STANDARDIZED TEST PRACTICE

19. In a model, 8 shaded squares represent 0.16. The entire model represents 1. How many squares are in the model?

(A) 16   **(B)** 42   **(C)** 50   **(D)** 92

20. What decimal number is represented by the model?

(A) 0.005   **(B)** 0.05   **(C)** 0.5   **(D)** 5

EXPLORATION AND EXTENSION

PORTFOLIO

21. BUILDING YOUR PROJECT You find that an average hotel room in Japan costs about 20,000 yen a night. How many dollars can a traveler expect to pay for a hotel? Answer this question, then write it as a tip for your travel handbook. Use the graph to write another tip for travelers to Japan.

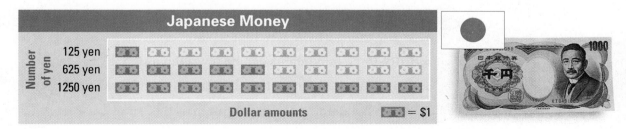

Japanese Money

Number of yen	Dollar amounts
125 yen	
625 yen	
1250 yen	

Dollar amounts   = $1

Decimals, Fractions, and Percents

Many students volunteer their time, helping in community projects.

Goal 1 REWRITING DECIMALS AS FRACTIONS

In this lesson, you will learn how to rewrite decimals: (1) as fractions and (2) as percents. Here are examples of decimals that are rewritten as fractions. In the first example, the decimal 0.7 and the fraction $\frac{7}{10}$ are both read as "seven tenths."

0.7, or $\frac{7}{10}$, of the marbles are red.

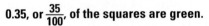

0.35, or $\frac{35}{100}$, of the squares are green.

Example 1 Rewriting Decimals as Fractions

Rewrite each decimal in words and as a fraction.

a. 0.7 **b.** 0.31 **c.** 0.027

Solution

a. 0.7 can be rewritten as seven tenths, or $\frac{7}{10}$.

b. 0.31 can be rewritten as thirty-one hundredths, or $\frac{31}{100}$.

c. 0.027 can be rewritten as twenty-seven thousandths, or $\frac{27}{1000}$.

Example 2 Rewriting Fractions as Decimals

Rewrite each fraction in words and as a decimal.

a. $\frac{8}{10}$ **b.** $\frac{53}{100}$ **c.** $\frac{739}{1000}$ **d.** $\frac{7}{100}$

Solution

a. Eight tenths can be rewritten as 0.8.

b. Fifty-three hundredths can be rewritten as 0.53.

c. Seven hundred thirty-nine thousandths can be rewritten as 0.739.

d. Seven hundredths can be rewritten as 0.07.

Goal 2 REWRITING DECIMALS AS PERCENTS

TOOLBOX
Percent, page 657

In real-life problems, decimals are often rewritten as **percents**. Here are three examples.

$$0.62 = 62\% \qquad 0.4 = 0.40 = 40\% \qquad 0.03 = 3\%$$

The *cent* in percent means hundred. So, you can think of *percent* as "per hundred."

Example 3 · Writing Decimals as Percents

Write each decimal as a percent.

a. 0.33

b. 0.5

Solution

a. In words, 0.33 is 33 hundredths. So, $0.33 = 33\%$.

b. To write 0.5 as a percent, begin by rewriting 0.5 as hundredths.

$$0.5 = 0.50 \qquad \text{Rewrite 5 tenths as 50 hundredths.}$$
$$ = 50\% \qquad \text{50 hundredths means 50 per hundred.}$$

Example 4 · Writing Percents

In a survey, 50 girls and 50 boys were asked to name their favorite rainbow color (purple, blue, green, yellow, orange, or red). The results are shown in the diagram below.

a. What percent named red?

b. What percent are boys who named red?

c. What percent are girls who named yellow?

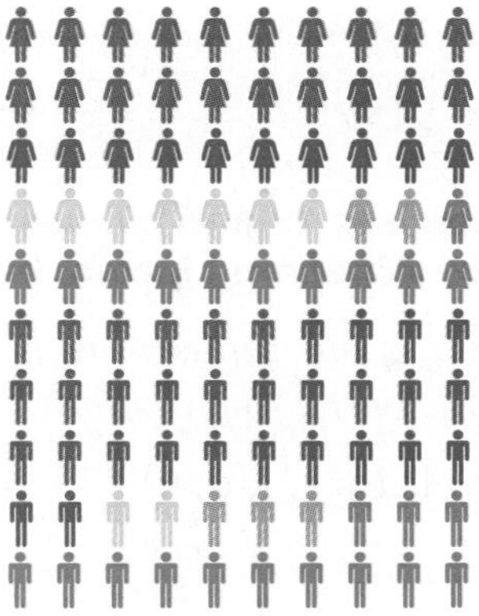

Solution

a. Because 24 of the 100 figures are red, 0.24, or 24% named red.

b. Because 13 of the 100 figures are red and boys, 0.13, or 13% are boys who named red.

c. Because 7 of the 100 figures are yellow and girls, 0.07, or 7% are girls who named yellow.

ONGOING ASSESSMENT

Write About It

Use the diagram in Example 4 to answer the questions.

1. What percent named orange?

2. What percent did not name blue?

3. Write another question that can be answered by the diagram.

3.4 Exercises

Extra Practice, page 625

GUIDED PRACTICE

In Exercises 1–3, write the number of blue dots in the model at the right in each of the following forms.

1. A decimal portion of the total

2. A fractional portion of the total

3. A percent of the total

In Exercises 4–6, write each number in words.

4. 67%   5. $\frac{15}{100}$ 6. 0.45

READING A GRAPH In Exercises 7 and 8, use the following information. The graph shows the monthly recording times for people who own video cameras. (Source: *USA Today*)

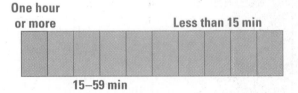

7. What portion records less than 15 min per month? Write this result as a decimal, a percent, and a fraction.

8. What portion records 1 hour or more per month? Write this result as a decimal, a percent, and a fraction.

PRACTICE AND PROBLEM SOLVING

In Exercises 9 and 10, write the decimal, fraction, and percent shown by the blue portion of the model.

9. 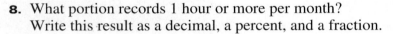   10.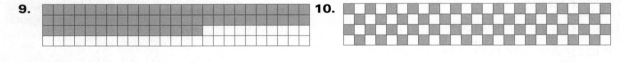

In Exercises 11–18, rewrite the number as a fraction.

11. 0.55   12. 18%   13. 43%   14. 0.129

15. 0.401   16. 91%   17. 0.49%   18. 87%

LANGUAGE SKILLS In Exercises 19 and 20, use the first 100 letters of *The Gettysburg Address*, by Abraham Lincoln, below.

Fourscore and seven years ago our fathers brought forth on this continent, a new nation, conceived in Liberty, and dedicat. . .

19. What fraction are vowels (a, e, i, o, u)?

20. What percent are *t*'s?

In Exercises 21–28, is the statement *true* or *false*? If false, correct it.

21. $\dfrac{53}{100} = 53\%$ **22.** $\dfrac{2}{100} = 20\%$ **23.** $9\% = \dfrac{9}{100}$ **24.** $42\% = \dfrac{402}{1000}$

25. $0.01 = 10\%$ **26.** $0.25 = 25\%$ **27.** $80\% = 0.8$ **28.** $99\% = \dfrac{999}{1000}$

In Exercises 29–36, rewrite the number as a percent.

29. 0.24 **30.** $\dfrac{33}{100}$ **31.** $\dfrac{85}{100}$ **32.** 0.12

33. $\dfrac{7}{100}$ **34.** 0.09 **35.** 0.6 **36.** $\dfrac{1}{10}$

In Exercises 37–40, use the model. Write the green portion of the rectangle as a fraction and as a percent.

37.   **38.**   **39.**   **40.**

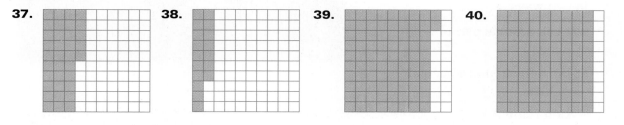

In Exercises 41–44, use the diagram at the right.

41. What percent are yellow?

42. What percent are green or red?

43. What percent are not blue?

44. What percent are not orange or green?

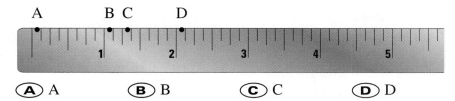

STANDARDIZED TEST PRACTICE

45. Which point on the ruler best represents 2.1 in.?

    (A) A   **(B)** B   **(C)** C   **(D)** D

46. You buy a pair of shoes on sale and pay only 80% of the original price. What fraction of the original price did you pay?

    (A) $\dfrac{8}{1000}$ **(B)** $\dfrac{8}{100}$ **(C)** $\dfrac{8}{10}$ **(D)** $\dfrac{2}{5}$

47. BUILDING YOUR PROJECT At a shop in Mexico City, piñatas cost 75 pesos. In your travel handbook, advise a traveler how much one of these piñatas would cost in United States dollars. Then write another travel tip about the Mexican peso in your handbook.

8 pesos = $1

48. COMMUNICATING ABOUT MATHEMATICS Use the information on page 143, about car crashes that manufacturers create on purpose. The planned car crashes, such as the one shown at the right, are witnessed by a camera that photographs each crash. How often does each camera take a picture? Explain your answer. Write your answer in two ways:

a. As a decimal part of a second

b. As a fraction of a second

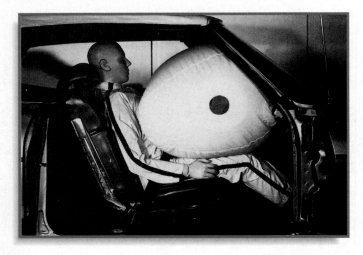

SPIRAL REVIEW

1. You have a coupon to buy a sandwich at a local restaurant. You have a choice of white or wheat bread, and five different fillings: ham salad, egg salad, tuna salad, chicken salad, and corned beef. How many different sandwiches could you order? **(1.3)**

2. Use four copies of the figure at the right to create a larger figure having the same shape. **(1.5)**

NUMBER SENSE In Exercises 3 and 4, find the missing digits. **(2.2)**

3.
$$\begin{array}{r} 2\;?\;8 \\ -\;?\,0\,? \\ \hline 1\,6\,1 \end{array}$$

4.
$$\begin{array}{r} 6\,4\,7 \\ -\;4\;?\;? \\ \hline ?\,0\,8 \end{array}$$

In Exercises 5–10, evaluate the expression in two ways. **(2.6)**

5. $4(5 + 2)$

6. $3(6 + 7)$

7. $8(9 + 11)$

8. $5(4 + 3)$

9. $7(9 + 2)$

10. $9(18 + 8)$

In Exercises 11–14, complete the statement. **(3.2)**

11. $12.5 \text{ mm} = 1.25$ **?**

12. **?** $\text{m} = 0.03 \text{ km}$

13. $50 \text{ cm} =$ **?** m

14. $2000 \text{ mm} =$ **?** m

Take this test as you would take a test in class. The answers to the exercises are given in the back of the book.

In Exercises 1–3, sketch a model of the number using the fewest base-ten pieces. (3.1)

1. 1.43   **2.** 1.89   **3.** 2.65

In Exercises 4–9, complete the statement. (3.1, 3.2)

4. $2.05 = \boxed{?}$ cents   **5.** 30¢ = $ $\boxed{?}$ **6.** 515¢ = $ $\boxed{?}$

7. 56 cm = $\boxed{?}$ mm   **8.** 1.78 $\boxed{?}$ = 1780 mm   **9.** $\boxed{?}$ km = 12.3 m

In Exercises 10–12, you are shown a model for a portion of a whole. Draw a model of the whole. (3.3)

10.
```
|-+-+-+-+-+-+-+-|
0               0.7
```

11.
```
● ● ● ● ● ● ● ● ● ●
 ● ● ● ● ● ● ● ● ●
   ⎵_____⎵
      0.18
```

12.
```
        9
 ┌──────────┐
 │   0.5    │ 5
 └──────────┘
```

In Exercises 13–15, write the portion that is green as a decimal, a fraction, and a percent of the whole. (3.4)

13. **14.** **15.**

WORLD RECORDS The table shows three of the men's and women's international track-and-field records.
(Source: *The Universal Almanac 1997*) (3.4)

Event	Men's	Women's
High jump	245 cm	2090 mm
Long jump	8950 mm	752 cm
Discus	0.0741 km	7680 cm

16. Rewrite the table using meters.

17. In which event does a woman have a better world record than a man?

18. **TECHNOLOGY** In a survey people were asked to name a recent type of technology that has made life easier. The results are shown in the graph at the right. Estimate the percent of the people who named each type of technology.

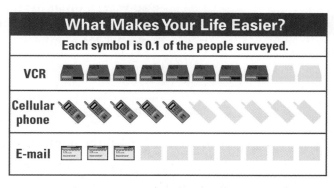

What Makes Your Life Easier?

Each symbol is 0.1 of the people surveyed.

VCR

Cellular phone

E-mail

3.5

Comparing and Ordering Decimals

What you should learn:

Goal 1 How to order decimals

Goal 2 How to use ordering of decimals to solve real-life problems

Why you should learn it:

Decimals can be used to compare quantities, such as the winning times in an Olympic race.

United States women's Olympic swim team, 1996

Goal 1 ORDERING DECIMALS

You already know how to locate whole numbers on a number line. For example, the number line below shows the locations of 2, 7, and 9. To order the numbers from least to greatest, read them from left to right. Notice that the numbers get larger as you move from left to right.

Number Line

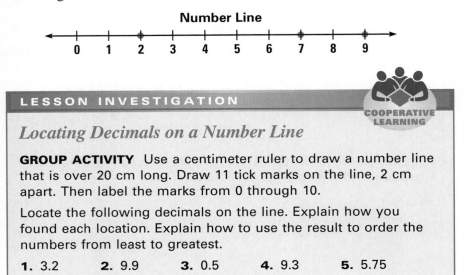

LESSON INVESTIGATION

COOPERATIVE LEARNING

Locating Decimals on a Number Line

GROUP ACTIVITY Use a centimeter ruler to draw a number line that is over 20 cm long. Draw 11 tick marks on the line, 2 cm apart. Then label the marks from 0 through 10.

Locate the following decimals on the line. Explain how you found each location. Explain how to use the result to order the numbers from least to greatest.

1. 3.2   **2.** 9.9   **3.** 0.5   **4.** 9.3   **5.** 5.75

Example 1 Ordering Decimals

Order the numbers from least to greatest.

2.3,   2.09,   2.32,   2.27,   2.37

Solution

One way to order the numbers is to locate them on a number line. You order decimals on a number line the same way you order whole numbers.

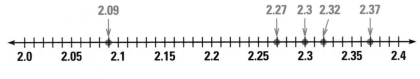

In order, the numbers are

2.09,   2.27,   2.3,   2.32,   and   2.37.

Example 2 Comparing Times

The winning times for the women's 100 meter freestyle swimming race in the Olympics from 1976 to 1996 are given in the bar graph. Order the times from least to greatest.

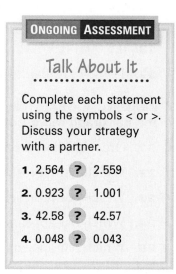

REAL LIFE
Olympics

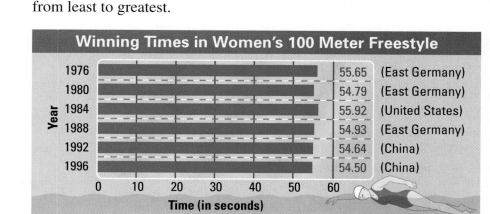

Winning Times in Women's 100 Meter Freestyle

Year	Time (in seconds)	Country
1976	55.65	(East Germany)
1980	54.79	(East Germany)
1984	55.92	(United States)
1988	54.93	(East Germany)
1992	54.64	(China)
1996	54.50	(China)

Solution

From the graph, you can see that the times are

  55.65, 54.79, 55.92, 54.93, 54.64, 54.50.

You can compare two decimals by comparing their place values from left to right. For example, you can compare 54.79 and 54.64 as follows.

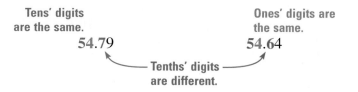

Tens' digits are the same.   Ones' digits are the same.

  54.79   54.64

  Tenths' digits are different.

From left to right, the first digits that are different are in the tenths' place. Because 7 is greater than 6, it follows that 54.79 is greater than 54.64. This can be written as   54.79 > 54.64   or   54.64 < 54.79.

Written from least to greatest, the winning times are

  54.50, 54.64, 54.79, 54.93, 55.65, 55.92

In the bar graph, notice that the shortest time has the shortest bar and the longest time has the longest bar.

STUDY TIP

On a number line, the number to the right of another number is greater. For example, 6.7 is greater than 6.4, which can be written as

6.7 > 6.4
or
6.4 < 6.7.

6.4 6.5 6.6 6.7

ONGOING ASSESSMENT

Talk About It

Complete each statement using the symbols < or >. Discuss your strategy with a partner.

1. 2.564 **?** 2.559

2. 0.923 **?** 1.001

3. 42.58 **?** 42.57

4. 0.048 **?** 0.043

3.5 Exercises

Extra Practice, page 625

GUIDED PRACTICE

1. Name the numbers represented by the letters on the number line.

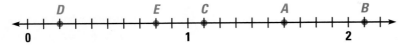

2. Draw a number line from 0.6 to 0.7. Add 9 tick marks to divide the line into 10 equal parts. Label each tick mark. Name three numbers on the line that are greater than 0.67.

3. Write three numbers that are greater than 6.5 and less than 6.6.

4. Order the following decimals from least to greatest.

   0.5,   0.4,   0.04,   0.54,   0.45

PRACTICE AND PROBLEM SOLVING

NUMBER SENSE In Exercises 5–8, order the numbers from least to greatest.

5. 0.25,   0.5,   2.5,   0.2,   0.02

6. 0.10,   0.07,   0.17,   1.7,   0.7

7. 6.82,   6.08,   6.8,   6.18,   6.12

8. 4.1,   4.39,   4.03,   4.4,   4.13

REASONING Write the numbers in order.

9. 0.026,   0.26,   0.126,   0.06,   0.2

10. 5.143,   5.14,   5.13,   5.104,   5.1

11. 1.69,   1.107,   1.9,   1.709,   1.76

12. 4.281,   4.18,   4.118,   4.218,   4.081

NUMBER SENSE In Exercises 13–20, complete each statement using >, <, or =.

13. 0.5 ? 0.3

14. 0.18 ? 0.2

15. 6.7 ? 6.72

16. 3.109 ? 3.011

17. 1.5 ? 1.50

18. 0.06 ? 0.6

19. 0.40 ? 0.4

20. 2.35 ? 2.305

READING A GRAPH In Exercises 21–25, each bar of the bar graph represents a decimal between 0 and 1.

21. Order the bars from shortest to longest.

22. Which bar represents 0.7?

23. Which bar represents 0.15?

24. Which bar appears about twice as long as another?

25. Which bar appears about four times as long as another?

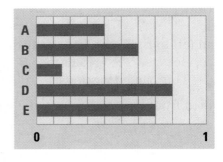

In Exercises 26–28, write the decimal shown by the model.

26.

27.

28.

29. Order the decimals found in Exercises 26–28 from least to greatest.

30. Draw a number line from 3.2 to 3.3. Divide the line into 10 equal parts and label each tick mark. In what place value is each tick mark?

31. **LIBRARY SCIENCE** Many libraries use the Dewey decimal call number classification to classify books. The system gives a decimal to a book according to the subject of the book. Put the books in order by ordering their call numbers from least to greatest.

32. A surveyor determines the size, in acres, of four different properties. Which size property is the largest?

Property A: 5.555 acres   Property B: 5.500 acres

Property C: 5.550 acres   Property D: 5.505 acres

(A) 5.555   (B) 5.500   (C) 5.550   (D) 5.505

EXPLORATION AND EXTENSION

33. **DECIMAL TIC-TAC-TOE** The tic-tac-toe game at the right can be won only if the three numbers in a row, column, or diagonal are in order. They can be in order from least to greatest or from greatest to least. Copy the game and draw lines through the possible ways to win.

0.9	0.71	0.6
0.04	0.5	0.65
0.05	0.34	0.45

3.6

Rounding Decimals

What you should learn:

Goal 1 How to round decimals

Goal 2 How to use rounding of decimals to solve real-life problems

Why you should learn it:

Many times in real life, you need to round decimals. Examples include buying gasoline or finding baseball averages.

Goal 1 ROUNDING DECIMALS

In many real-life situations, decimals may have more digits than are appropriate. For example, if you buy 6 gallons of gasoline at $1.339 per gallon, then the exact total would be 6 × 1.339 or $8.034. You can't really pay this amount, so you round to the nearest cent.

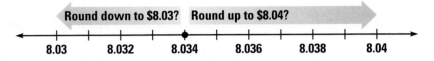

Because $8.034 is closer to $8.03 than to $8.04, you should *round down* to $8.03.

ROUNDING NUMBERS

To round to a given place, look at the digit to its right.

1. If the digit is 4 or less, round down.

2. If the digit is 5 or more, round up.

Example 1 Rounding Numbers

	Round to Nearest	Original Number	Round Up or Down?	Rounded Number
a.	Ten	983	Round down.	980
b.	Ten	3146	Round up.	3150
c.	Hundred	6058	Round up.	6100
d.	Thousand	71,479	Round down.	71,000

Example 2 Rounding Decimals

	Round to Nearest	Original Number	Round Up or Down?	Rounded Number
a.	Thousandth	1.2852	Round down.	1.285
b.	Hundredth	3.157	Round up.	3.16
c.	Tenth	12.449	Round down.	12.4
d.	One	1359.5	Round up.	1360

Example 3 Making a Decision

Ted Williams was a famous baseball player who played for the Boston Red Sox for 19 seasons between 1939 and 1960. Here is a story that involves Ted Williams and rounding numbers.

REAL LIFE
Baseball

> *It was the night before the last game of the season in 1941. Ted Williams had a batting average of 0.39955. (Up to this point in the season, he had 179 hits out of 448 times at bat.) If he decided not to play the game, his batting average would round up to 0.400. If he decided to play the game, his average could drop below 0.400.*
>
> *No major league player had finished a season with a batting average of 0.400 or more in more than a decade.*

a. Explain how Williams might have lowered his batting average by playing the game.

b. Williams decided to play and had six hits out of eight times at bat. What was his final batting average?

Solution

a. Williams might have lowered his batting average if he came to bat four times and got only one hit.

$$\text{Batting average} = \frac{\text{Number of hits}}{\text{Times at bat}}$$

$$= \frac{(179 + 1)}{(448 + 4)} \qquad \text{1 more hit and 4 more times at bat}$$

$$= \frac{180}{452} \qquad \text{Add.}$$

$$\approx 0.39823 \qquad \text{Rounds to 0.398}$$

b. $\text{Batting average} = \dfrac{(179 + 6)}{(448 + 8)} \qquad$ **6 more hits and 8 more times at bat**

$$= \frac{185}{456} \qquad \text{Add.}$$

$$\approx 0.40570 \qquad \text{Rounds to 0.406}$$

By taking a chance and playing for his team, Ted Williams ended the season with a batting average over 0.400.

Ted Williams won six American League batting titles and led the league in home runs four times. He was an outfielder with the Boston Red Sox.

ONGOING ASSESSMENT

Talk About It
....

1. Suppose that Ted Williams came up to bat four times on the last day. What are the possible batting averages he could end up with? Use a calculator to find the averages and round to three decimal places.

GUIDED PRACTICE

1. **COMMUNICATING** Give two examples of real-life situations in which you would round a decimal.

2. Draw a model that helps show how to round 0.24 to the nearest tenth.

In Exercises 3–6, round 4.5239 to the given place value.

3. Thousandths   4. Hundredths   5. Tenths   6. Ones

7. **ERROR ANALYSIS** A friend of yours is asked to round 6.3487 to the nearest tenth. Your friend first rounded to the nearest hundredth to get 6.35, and then rounded to the nearest tenth to get 6.4. Was your friend correct? Explain your reasoning.

PRACTICE AND PROBLEM SOLVING

In Exercises 8–10, draw a number line. Show how to round 6.263 to the given place value.

8. Hundredths   9. Tenths   10. Ones

NUMBER SENSE Round each whole number to the given place value.

11. 269 (tens)   12. 34,575 (thousands)   13. 411,990 (hundreds)

NUMBER SENSE Round each decimal to the given place value.

14. 5.41 (tenths)   15. 20.7 (ones)   16. 8.5165 (thousandths)

Decide whether the statement is *true* or *false*. If false, correct the red number.

17. 2.15 rounded to the nearest one is 2.

18. 13,099 rounded to the nearest thousand is 13,000.

19. 5.445 rounded to the nearest tenth is 5.5.

20. 4.999 rounded to the nearest hundredth is 5.00.

Round the instrument reading to the given place value.

21. Odometer (hundreds)   22. Thermometer (ones)   23. Digital scale (tens)

In Exercises 24–32, round to the nearest dollar.

24. $32.25   **25.** $25.49   **26.** $611.50

27. $1.79   **28.** $89.19   **29.** $95.11

30. $8.83   **31.** $66.60   **32.** $21.49

33. COINS The bar graph at the right shows the cost of making different coins. Round the number shown by each bar to the nearest tenth. (Source: United States Mint)

Costs of Making Coins

SCIENCE To identify a solution as an acid or a base, scientists use a number from 0 to 14 called pH. A pH below 7 means that the solution is an acid. A pH above 7 means that the solution is a base. Round the pH number to the nearest one. Is the substance an acid or a base?

34. Apples 3.1   **35.** Sea water 8.5   **36.** Eggs 7.8

37. Lemons 2.3   **38.** Tomatoes 4.2   **39.** Milk 6.5

In Exercises 40–48, use a calculator to evaluate the expression. Round the result to the nearest whole number.

40. 2.3×7 **41.** 12×1.2 **42.** 0.7×125

43. 0.02×2065 **44.** $\dfrac{456}{11}$ **45.** $\dfrac{45.6}{7}$

46. $\dfrac{979}{44}$ **47.** $\dfrac{55}{8}$ **48.** 1.6×1.6

GEOMETRY In Exercises 49–52, use the figure below to find the indicated measure. Round each answer to the nearest tenth.

49. Length AB

50. Length BC

51. Measure of angle A

52. Measure of angle C

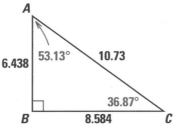

53. What is 8.049 rounded to the nearest tenth?

    A 8.05   **B** 8.0   **C** 8.1   **D** 10.0

54. Evan weighs mail packages and records their weights to the nearest pound. He weighs a package and determines that it weighs 2.5 lb. What weight should he record?

    A 2 lb   **B** 2.5 lb   **C** 3 lb   **D** 10 lb

EXPLORATION AND EXTENSION

PORTFOLIO

55. BUILDING YOUR PROJECT A friend has told you of a restaurant in Bombay, India, that offers a curry dish for 105 rupees. In what years would the restaurant have accepted $3 for the dish? Do you think that $3 will be enough to pay for the dish in the future, if the price in rupees stays the same? Explain why or why not. Write about the restaurant as a tip in your travel handbook. Then write another travel tip about Indian money in your handbook.

Year	Number Rupees = $1
1991	22.712
1992	28.158
1993	31.291
1994	31.370
1995	32.418
1996	35.510
1997	35.895

SPIRAL REVIEW

1. Lee, Chris, and Pat are going to the movies. Make a list of all of the different orders in which they can purchase their tickets. (1.3)

Divide. (2.4)

  2. $45 \div 6$ **3.** $33 \div 4$ **4.** $121 \div 5$ **5.** $220 \div 9$

Evaluate the expression. (2.5)

  6. $10 + 16 \div 8$ **7.** $24 - 8 \times 2$ **8.** $(14 + 13) \div 9$ **9.** $54 \div 9 \times 2$

Write the number in base ten. (2.7)

10. 13_5 **11.** 414_5 **12.** 1101_2 **13.** 11011_2

Write the number in numerals. (3.1)

14. One and five tenths   **15.** Four and fifty-seven hundredths

16. One hundred and one hundredth   **17.** Ten and fifty thousandths

18. WORKING BACKWARD Lupe buys a bag of apples and gives $\frac{2}{3}$ of the apples to Dale. Dale gives $\frac{1}{4}$ of the apples he received to Sue. Sue receives two apples. How many apples were in the bag? (1.9)

CRASH Course

READ About It

Not all car wrecks are accidents. Car manufacturers crash about 500 cars every year, and they do it on purpose.

The cars contain dummies that send data to a computer. This data helps the manufacturer make cars that are safe. Some dummies are the size of a child and others are as large as a 170-pound adult. The dummies cost about $100,000 each.

The cars are pulled by a cable straight into a concrete wall. The wall is anchored 15 ft underground and weighs over a million pounds. It only takes 10 seconds for the car to travel 520 ft to the wall.

In the last two fifths of a second, each dummy sends about 4000 pieces of information to the computer. During this time, high-speed cameras each take photographs at a rate of about 1000 pictures per second.

WRITE About It

1. For what percent of a second do the dummies send information to the computer? Explain your reasoning.

2. How many pictures does each high-speed camera take during the last two fifths of a second before the crash? Explain your reasoning.

3. Why do you think each dummy costs so much? What type of data do you think the dummy sends to the computer?

4. The concrete wall stands 5 ft high above the ground. Draw a diagram of the wall. What percent of the wall is anchored underground? Explain your answer.

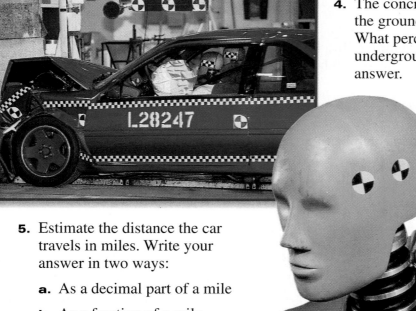

L.28247

5. Estimate the distance the car travels in miles. Write your answer in two ways:

   a. As a decimal part of a mile

   b. As a fraction of a mile

3.7

What you should learn:

Goal 1 How to use exponents to write powers

Goal 2 How to evaluate expressions that have exponents

Why you should learn it:

Exponents allow you to write mathematical expressions in simpler ways. For example, $10 \times 10 \times 10$ can be written as 10^3.

Using telescopes, astronomers proved that Earth rotates around the sun at an average distance of 1.488×10^9 km.

Powers and Exponents

Goal 1 USING EXPONENTS TO WRITE POWERS

You can write the product $10 \times 10 \times 10$ as a **power**, with a **base** of 10 and an **exponent** of 3.

$$\underbrace{10 \times 10 \times 10}_{\text{Factors}} = 10^{\overset{\text{Exponent}}{\downarrow}3} \Big\} \text{ Power}$$
$$\text{Base}$$

Example 1 Writing Powers

	Number	Product	Power
a.	16	4×4	4^2

The power is read as "4 to the 2nd power" or "4 squared."

b.	125	$5 \times 5 \times 5$	5^3

The power is read as "5 to the 3rd power" or "5 cubed."

c.	10,000	$10 \times 10 \times 10 \times 10$	10^4

The power is read as "10 to the 4th power."

The numbers 10^2, 10^3, 10^4, and so on are called **powers of 10**. Powers of 10 can be used to write numbers in expanded notation.

Example 2 Numbers in Expanded Notation

Write the number in expanded notation using powers of 10.

a. 1453   **b.** 36,728   **c.** 11,016

Solution

a. $1453 = (1 \times 1000) + (4 \times 100) + (5 \times 10) + (3 \times 1)$
$= \left(1 \times 10^3\right) + \left(4 \times 10^2\right) + (5 \times 10) + (3 \times 1)$

b. $36{,}728 = (3 \times 10{,}000) + (6 \times 1000) + (7 \times 100) + (2 \times 10) + (8 \times 1)$
$= \left(3 \times 10^4\right) + \left(6 \times 10^3\right) + \left(7 \times 10^2\right) + (2 \times 10) + (8 \times 1)$

c. $11{,}016 = (1 \times 10{,}000) + (1 \times 1000) + (1 \times 10) + (6 \times 1)$
$= \left(1 \times 10^4\right) + \left(1 \times 10^3\right) + (1 \times 10) + (6 \times 1)$

Goal 2 **EVALUATING EXPRESSIONS**

Example 3 **Evaluating an Expression**

If the length of the side of a square is x cm, then the area of the square is x^2 cm^2. Evaluate the expression x^2 when x is equal to 1, 2, and 3. Show your results with a diagram.

CONNECTION
Geometry

Solution

Value of x	Expression	Substitute	Area
$x = 1$	x^2	1^2	1 cm^2
$x = 2$	x^2	2^2	4 cm^2
$x = 3$	x^2	3^2	9 cm^2

A diagram of the three squares is shown below.

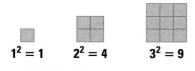

$1^2 = 1$ $2^2 = 4$ $3^2 = 9$

Powers need to be added to the list of order of operations.

ORDER OF OPERATIONS

1. First do operations within grouping symbols.
2. Then evaluate powers.
3. Then multiply and divide from left to right.
4. Finally add and subtract from left to right.

Example 4 **Using Order of Operations**

a. $(3 + 2)^2 \times 2 = 5^2 \times 2$ Add inside parentheses.

$\qquad\qquad\quad = 25 \times 2$ Evaluate power.

$\qquad\qquad\quad = 50$ Multiply.

b. $3 + 2^2 \times 2 = 3 + 4 \times 2$ Evaluate power.

$\qquad\qquad\quad = 3 + 8$ Multiply.

$\qquad\qquad\quad = 11$ Add.

Real Life...
Real People

Darryl Stanford is the chairman of the astronomy department at the City College of San Francisco. He first began using a telescope when he was eight years old in East Harlem, New York.

TOOLBOX

Area, page 653

ONGOING ASSESSMENT

Write About It

Evaluate each expression using the solutions in Example 4 as a model. Label each step with a written statement.

1. $(5 - 1)^3 \div 8$

2. $3 \times 2^4 \div 6$

3. $(10 \div 2)^2 \div 5$

GUIDED PRACTICE

In Exercises 1–3, name each of the following in the expression 22^6.

1. Base   2. Exponent   3. Power

4. Write the values of 10^2, 10^3, 10^4, 10^5, and 10^6.

5. Write the number 2993 in expanded notation using powers of ten.

6. Is it true to say that the value of the expression $4^3 - 6 \times 10 + 5$ is 585? If not, what is the value?

PRACTICE AND PROBLEM SOLVING

In Exercises 7–10, find the value of the exponent.

7. $36 = 6^{?}$ 8. $16 = 2^{?}$ 9. $27 = 3^{?}$ 10. $\dfrac{1}{1000} = \dfrac{1}{10^{?}}$

In Exercises 11–14, find the value of the base.

11. $81 = \boxed{?}^{\,2}$ 12. $64 = \boxed{?}^{\,3}$ 13. $32 = \boxed{?}^{\,5}$ 14. $\dfrac{1}{10,000} = \dfrac{1}{\boxed{?}^{\,4}}$

In Exercises 15–20, evaluate the power.

15. 5^4 16. 3^6 17. 9^3 18. $\dfrac{1}{10^4}$ 19. $\dfrac{1}{100^3}$ 20. 7^3

In Exercises 21–28, use a calculator to evaluate the power. The Sample shows two methods you can use.

Sample: $8^3 = 8 \;\boxed{\times}\; 8 \;\boxed{\times}\; 8 \;\boxed{=}\;$ or $8^3 = 8 \;\boxed{y^x}\; 3 \;\boxed{=}\;$

21. 23^3 22. 125^2 23. 11^4 24. 50^3

25. 9^8 26. 16^5 27. 44^4 28. 6^8

SCIENCE In Exercises 29–32, use the table below. Write the number in expanded notation using powers of ten.

Animal	Speed (cm/s)
Goldfish	75
Penguin	380
Dolphin	1030
Yellowfin tuna	2080

29. Goldfish   30. Penguin

31. Dolphin   32. Yellowfin tuna

In Exercises 33–36, evaluate the power. Then round the number to the nearest ten.

33. 7^2
34. 5^3
35. 13^3
36. 24^2

GEOMETRY **In Exercises 37–40, you are given the area of a square. Find the lengths of the sides.**

37. 64 cm^2
38. 49 in.^2
39. 100 mm^2
40. 121 ft^2

In Exercises 41 and 42, complete the statement.

41. $10^4 = \boxed{?} \times 10^2$
42. $10^5 = \boxed{?} \times 10^2$

In Exercises 43–46, evaluate the expression.

43. $(4 - 2)^5 - 5$
44. $8 + 2 \times 9^2$
45. $6 + 2^3 \div 8$
46. $30 + (11 - 1)^2$

47. **REASONING** The ski club sets up a telephone tree. The first person in the tree calls 4 people. The 4 people each call 4 other people. They each call 4 other people. How many people have been called?

48. You are working in a warehouse. You can stack boxes in a room so that they are 12 high, 12 wide, and 12 long. How many boxes can you fit in the room? Write your answer as a power.

STANDARDIZED TEST PRACTICE

49. Which expression is equal to 25?

(A) $(4 + 3)^2$
(B) $\left(4^2 + 3^2\right)^2$
(C) $4^2 + 3^2$
(D) $2(4 + 3)$

50. Evaluate $(6 + 1)^2 - 6$.

(A) 1
(B) 30
(C) 43
(D) 55

EXPLORATION AND EXTENSION

PORTFOLIO

51. **BUILDING YOUR PROJECT** Your friend is helping you write your travel handbook. Your friend suggests that 10×10^2 centavos is equal to two cents. You say that it is about 10,000 centavos. Who is correct? Why?

100 centavos = 1 peso
10 pesos = $.02

Explain the value of Chilean money in your travel handbook. Then write another travel tip about Chilean money in your handbook.

3.8

Using Decimals, Fractions, and Percents

What you should learn:

Goal 1 How to use fractions to solve real-life problems

Goal 2 How to use percents to solve real-life problems

Why you should learn it:

Decimals can be written as fractions or percents. You need to use all three forms to be an effective problem solver.

The average person in the United States consumes about 13 pounds of oranges per year.

Goal 1 USING FRACTIONS IN REAL LIFE

Remember that decimals can be written as fractions or as percents. Here is an example.

Decimal Form	Fraction Form	Percent Form
0.3	$\frac{3}{10}$	30%

Many real-life problems have questions of the form, "What is $\frac{3}{10}$ of 20 cars?" or "What is 30% of 20 cars?" One way to answer this question is to use a set model, like that shown below. In the model, each group represents one tenth. So three tenths contains six cars.

$\frac{3}{10}$

Example 1 Using Fractions in Real Life

An advertisement states that $\frac{7}{10}$ of all middle school students drink orange juice at least once a week. There are 30 students in your class. According to the ad, how many drink orange juice at least once a week?

REAL LIFE
Advertising

Solution

One way to solve this problem is to use a set model and divide the 30 students into 10 groups. Each group represents one tenth of the class.

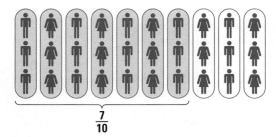

$\frac{7}{10}$

Because seven tenths contains 21 students, 21 students drink orange juice at least once a week.

Goal 2 USING PERCENTS IN REAL LIFE

Example 2 Using Percents in Real Life

In a survey, 200 people were asked if they played a musical instrument. Thirty-five percent said they did. How many people said they played a musical instrument?

REAL LIFE
Music

Solution

Remember that 35% can be written as $\frac{35}{100}$. To find 35% of 200, divide a collection of 200 objects into 100 groups. Count the number of objects in 35 of the groups. You can see that 35% of 200 is 70. Thus, 70 people said they played a musical instrument.

Real Life...
Real Facts

The balalaika is a Russian stringed instrument that became popular in the early 1700's. It comes in six sizes, and the largest must rest on the floor when played.

Example 3 Decimals, Fractions, and Percents

The set model below shows a group of guitars, trumpets, and drums. What portion of the instruments are trumpets? Write your answer as a decimal, a fraction, and a percent.

Solution

Of the 20 instruments, 10 are trumpets. So, half of the instruments are trumpets. Here are three ways to write this.

As a decimal, 0.5 of the instruments are trumpets.

Rewrite 0.5 as a fraction. $\frac{5}{10}$ of the instruments are trumpets.

Rewrite 0.5 as a percent. 50% of the instruments are trumpets.

ONGOING ASSESSMENT

Write About It

Use the set model in Example 3. Write each answer as a decimal, a fraction, and a percent.

1. What portion of the instruments are guitars?

2. What portion of the instruments are drums?

GUIDED PRACTICE

1. The area model at the right shows 39% of 1000 students who do an after-school activity. How many students does this represent?

2. Use a set model to find 60% of 40 strawberries.

STATISTICS A survey was taken of 20 students who were asked to name their favorite juice flavor: apple, orange, or grape. The results are shown in the figure at the right. Write each answer as a decimal, a fraction, and a percent.

3. What portion of the students like apple juice best?

4. What portion of the students like orange juice best?

5. What portion of the students like grape juice best?

apple orange grape

PRACTICE AND PROBLEM SOLVING

In Exercises 6 and 7, write the decimal, the fraction, and the percent that the green portion of the figure represents.

6.

7.

In Exercises 8 and 9, use a set model to help you answer the question.

8. What is 70% of 20 baseballs?

9. What is 30% of $30?

Use the area model to help you find the number.

10. 15% of 300

11. 40% of 500

12. **RECYCLING** On an average day, $\frac{24}{100}$ of all glass waste is recycled. If 200 tons of glass waste is generated in one day, how much is recycled? (Source: Franklin Associates, Ltd.)

13. EDUCATION A class of 50 students took a test. The portions of students who received each letter grade are shown in the table. Use a set model to find the number of students that received each grade.

A	$\frac{4}{10}$
B	30%
C	0.20
D	10%

14. READING A GRAPH On each work day, about 35 million United States coins are minted. The portions of these that are pennies, nickels, dimes, and quarters are shown in the graph below. Write each portion as a decimal, as a fraction, and as a percent.

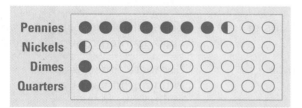

(Source: United States Mint)

15. WATCHING FOOTBALL A survey asked 200 people if they prefer watching a football game at home or at a stadium. Fifty-five percent said they prefer watching football at home. Was this more than 100 people? Explain.

STANDARDIZED TEST PRACTICE

16. In a reading contest, Ray read eight books. This represented 20% of the class total. What fraction of the class total did Ray read?

   A $\frac{1}{2}$ **B** $\frac{1}{4}$ **C** $\frac{1}{5}$ **D** $\frac{1}{20}$

17. Which number is not equal to the others?

   A $\frac{25}{10}$ **B** 25%   **C** $\frac{1}{4}$ **D** 0.25

EXPLORATION AND EXTENSION

PORTFOLIO

18. BUILDING YOUR PROJECT You have a friend who took 6650 drachmas to buy souvenirs in Greece. Your friend tells you that each souvenir costs about 20% of the 6650 drachmas. Use this to write a statement in your travel handbook about how much a tourist in Greece might pay for a souvenir. Then write another tip about Greek money in your handbook.

6650 drachmas = $25

WHAT *did you learn?*

WHY *did you learn it?*

Skills

3.1	Write decimals in expanded notation.	Use decimals to represent amounts of money.
3.2	Measure lengths in the metric system. Change units of length in the metric system.	Use the metric system in science.
3.3	Show decimals with number-line models and set models.	Interpret graphs about real-life situations.
3.4	Rewrite decimals as fractions or percents.	Solve problems using percents, such as interpreting diagrams.
3.5	Compare and order decimals.	Compare times, such as winning times for a swimming race.
3.6	Round decimals.	Make a decision about a real-life situation.
3.7	Use exponents to write powers. Evaluate expressions that have exponents.	Write expressions in simpler ways.
3.8	Use fractions and percents to solve real-life problems.	Use fractions, percents, and decimals in decision-making.

Strategies 3.1–3.8 Use problem solving strategies. Solve a wide variety of real-life problems.

Using Data 3.1–3.8 Use tables and graphs. Organize data and solve problems.

HOW *does it fit in the bigger picture of mathematics?*

In this chapter you learned how to write some numbers as decimals, fractions, and percents and to use models to represent each of them.

$$0.30 = \frac{30}{100} = 30\%$$

Area Model

Number-Line Model

0   1

Understanding the different ways to write numbers will make you a better problem solver, because it gives you more choices.

VOCABULARY

- millimeter (p. 116)
- centimeter (p. 116)
- meter (p. 116)
- kilometer (p. 116)
- percents (p. 129)
- power (p. 144)
- base (p. 144)
- exponent (p. 144)
- powers of 10 (p. 144)

3.1 WRITING DECIMALS

Use base-ten pieces to help write a decimal in expanded notation. In expanded notation, the number is the sum of each digit multiplied by the power of ten for its place value.

Example
$$2.35 = 2 + 0.3 + 0.05$$
$$= (2 \times 1) + (3 \times 0.1)$$
$$+ (5 \times 0.01)$$

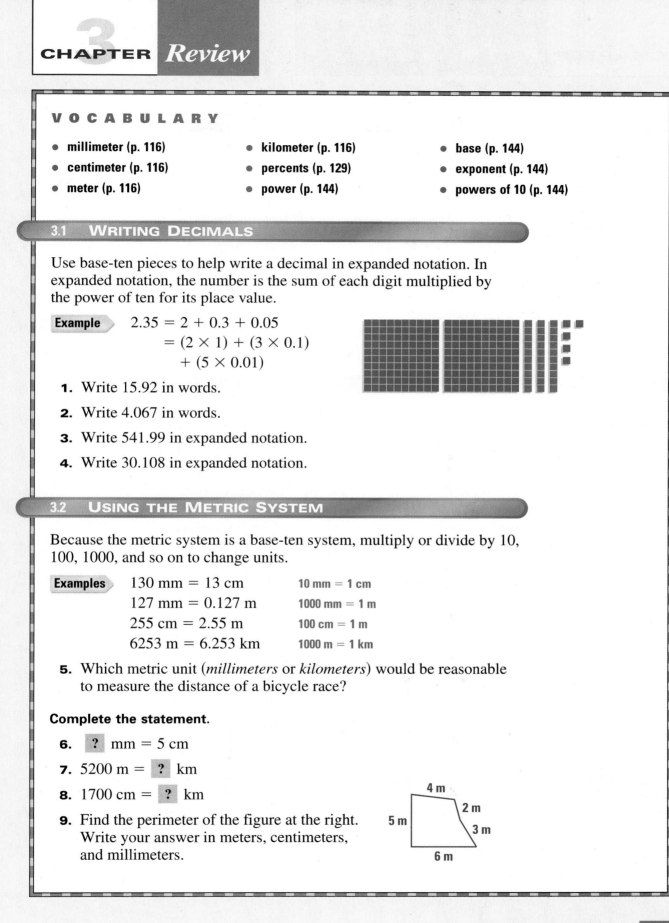

1. Write 15.92 in words.

2. Write 4.067 in words.

3. Write 541.99 in expanded notation.

4. Write 30.108 in expanded notation.

3.2 USING THE METRIC SYSTEM

Because the metric system is a base-ten system, multiply or divide by 10, 100, 1000, and so on to change units.

Examples
130 mm = 13 cm	10 mm = 1 cm
127 mm = 0.127 m	1000 mm = 1 m
255 cm = 2.55 m	100 cm = 1 m
6253 m = 6.253 km	1000 m = 1 km

5. Which metric unit (*millimeters* or *kilometers*) would be reasonable to measure the distance of a bicycle race?

Complete the statement.

6. ? mm = 5 cm

7. 5200 m = ? km

8. 1700 cm = ? km

9. Find the perimeter of the figure at the right. Write your answer in meters, centimeters, and millimeters.

4 m
2 m
5 m
3 m
6 m

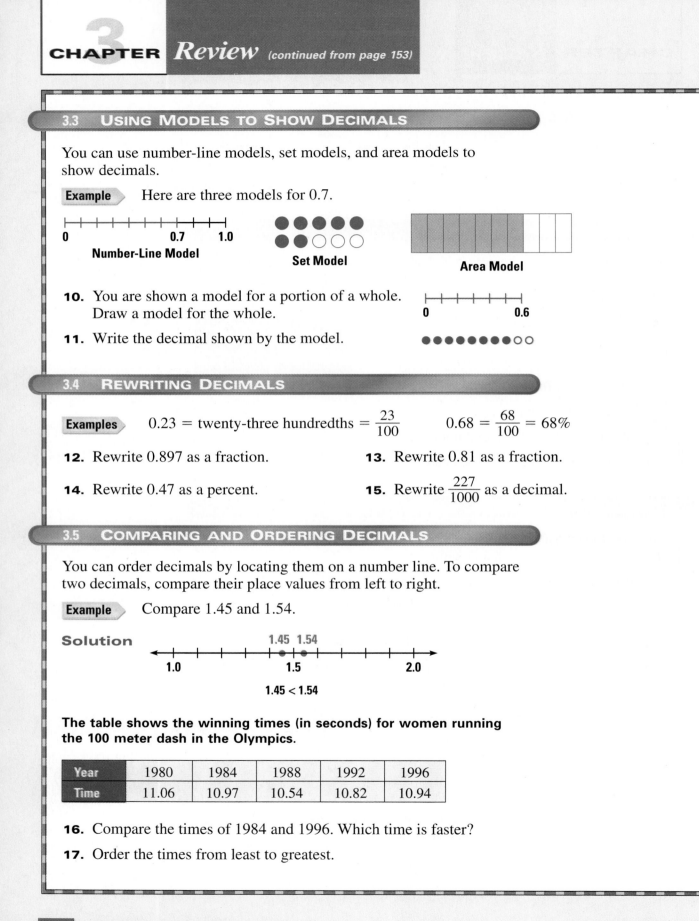

3.3 USING MODELS TO SHOW DECIMALS

You can use number-line models, set models, and area models to show decimals.

Example   Here are three models for 0.7.

0   0.7   1.0
Number-Line Model

Set Model

Area Model

10. You are shown a model for a portion of a whole. Draw a model for the whole.

0   0.6

11. Write the decimal shown by the model.

3.4 REWRITING DECIMALS

Examples $0.23 =$ twenty-three hundredths $= \dfrac{23}{100}$ $0.68 = \dfrac{68}{100} = 68\%$

12. Rewrite 0.897 as a fraction.   **13.** Rewrite 0.81 as a fraction.

14. Rewrite 0.47 as a percent.   **15.** Rewrite $\dfrac{227}{1000}$ as a decimal.

3.5 COMPARING AND ORDERING DECIMALS

You can order decimals by locating them on a number line. To compare two decimals, compare their place values from left to right.

Example   Compare 1.45 and 1.54.

Solution

1.45 1.54

1.0   1.5   2.0

$1.45 < 1.54$

The table shows the winning times (in seconds) for women running the 100 meter dash in the Olympics.

Year	1980	1984	1988	1992	1996
Time	11.06	10.97	10.54	10.82	10.94

16. Compare the times of 1984 and 1996. Which time is faster?

17. Order the times from least to greatest.

3.6 ROUNDING DECIMALS

To round a number to a given place value, look at the digit to its right. Round down if the digit is 4 or less. Round up if the digit is 5 or more.

Examples 2.1**7**7 rounds up to 2.18. 11.**4**4 rounds down to 11.4.

18. The prices of toothpaste in different cities of the world are shown in the table. Round each price to the nearest dollar.

City	Paris	Tokyo	London	Sydney	Mexico City
Price of Toothpaste	$3.63	$4.12	$3.62	$2.42	$1.33

3.7 USING EXPONENTS

Exponent

Example $8 \times 8 \times 8 \times 8 = 8^4 \big\}$ **Power**

Factors Base

When evaluating expressions with powers, use the order of operations.

Example
$$(6 + 7) - 3 \times 2^2 = 13 - 3 \times 2^2$$ **First do operations within grouping symbols.**
$$= 13 - 3 \times 4$$ **Then evaluate powers.**
$$= 13 - 12$$ **Then multiply and divide from left to right.**
$$= 1$$ **Finally add and subtract from left to right.**

19. Evaluate 6^3.   **20.** Evaluate 3^6.   **21.** Evaluate $25 + 3^3 \times 2$.

22. You invite 3 friends to join a club. Each friend invites 3 people, and each of these people invites 3 other people. Not counting yourself, how many people are in the club?

3.8 SOLVING REAL-LIFE PROBLEMS

Example You can use a set model to help describe real-life situations.

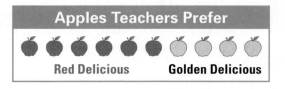

Apples Teachers Prefer

Red Delicious   Golden Delicious

$\frac{6}{10}$ prefer Red Delicious.   40% prefer Golden Delicious.

23. What is 30% of 60 books?   **24.** What is 25% of 200 pages?

In Exercises 1–4, write the number using numerals.

1. Six and nine tenths

2. Fourteen and five hundredths

3. Six hundred twelve thousandths

4. Three hundred and three hundredths

In Exercises 5–9, complete the statement.

5. 1.45 ones = ? tenths

6. ? hundredths = 30 thousandths

7. 205 m = ? km

8. 0.71 = ? %

9. $\dfrac{?}{100} = 0.06$

In Exercises 10 and 11, you are given a model for a portion of a whole. Draw the model for the whole.

10.

```
|—+—+—+—+—+—+—|
0                    0.7
```

11.

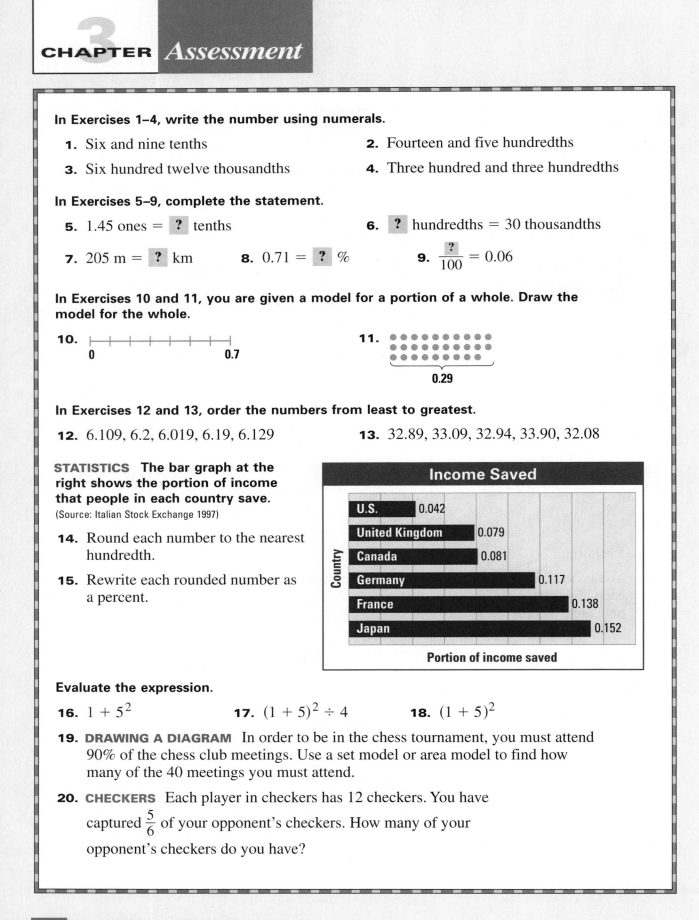

0.29

In Exercises 12 and 13, order the numbers from least to greatest.

12. 6.109, 6.2, 6.019, 6.19, 6.129

13. 32.89, 33.09, 32.94, 33.90, 32.08

STATISTICS The bar graph at the right shows the portion of income that people in each country save. (Source: Italian Stock Exchange 1997)

Income Saved

Country	Portion of income saved
U.S.	0.042
United Kingdom	0.079
Canada	0.081
Germany	0.117
France	0.138
Japan	0.152

14. Round each number to the nearest hundredth.

15. Rewrite each rounded number as a percent.

Evaluate the expression.

16. $1 + 5^2$

17. $(1 + 5)^2 \div 4$

18. $(1 + 5)^2$

19. **DRAWING A DIAGRAM** In order to be in the chess tournament, you must attend 90% of the chess club meetings. Use a set model or area model to find how many of the 40 meetings you must attend.

20. **CHECKERS** Each player in checkers has 12 checkers. You have captured $\dfrac{5}{6}$ of your opponent's checkers. How many of your opponent's checkers do you have?

1. Four tenths is the same as 400 _?_ .

   Ⓐ ones   Ⓑ hundredths
   Ⓒ thousandths Ⓓ ten thousandths

2. Two hundredths is the same as how many thousandths?

   Ⓐ 2   Ⓑ 20
   Ⓒ 200   Ⓓ 2000

3. $4 \times 1000 + 2 \times 1 + 5 \times 0.01 =$ **?**

   Ⓐ 425   Ⓑ 4002.05
   Ⓒ 4002.5   Ⓓ 4020.05

4. Which metric measurement would be the most reasonable to measure the width of your little fingernail?

   Ⓐ Millimeter Ⓑ Centimeter
   Ⓒ Meter   Ⓓ Kilometer

5. What is 20% of $50?

   Ⓐ $5   Ⓑ $10
   Ⓒ $20   Ⓓ $30

6. Write 62% as a decimal.

   Ⓐ 0.062   Ⓑ 0.602
   Ⓒ 0.62   Ⓓ 6.2

7. Write $\frac{3}{5}$ as a decimal.

   Ⓐ 0.06   Ⓑ 0.35
   Ⓒ 0.6   Ⓓ 3.5

8. $3^4 =$ **?**

   Ⓐ 12   Ⓑ 27
   Ⓒ 64   Ⓓ 81

9. Write 84.3 in expanded notation.

   Ⓐ $8 \times 1 + 4 \times 0.1 + 3 \times 0.1$
   Ⓑ $8 \times 10 + 4 \times 0.1 + 3 \times 0.1$
   Ⓒ $8 \times 10 + 4 \times 1 + 3 \times 0.1$
   Ⓓ $8 \times 10 + 4 \times 10 + 3 \times 1$

10. You have 2^6 basketball cards. Ramona has 6^2 basketball cards. Richard has 6×2 basketball cards. Who has the most cards?

    Ⓐ You   Ⓑ Ramona
    Ⓒ Richard   Ⓓ You all have the same number.

11. Your friend gives you 40% of his marble collection. If he had 60 marbles to begin with, he gave you _?_ .

    Ⓐ 12 marbles Ⓑ 20 marbles
    Ⓒ 24 marbles Ⓓ 40 marbles

12. Write 4% as a fraction.

    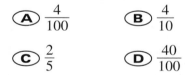

    Ⓐ $\frac{4}{100}$ Ⓑ $\frac{4}{10}$
    Ⓒ $\frac{2}{5}$ Ⓓ $\frac{40}{100}$

13. Which metric measurement would be the most reasonable to measure the height of a two-story house?

    Ⓐ Millimeter Ⓑ Centimeter
    Ⓒ Meter   Ⓓ Kilometer

14. If $5 is 10% of what you had made on your delivery route, how much money did you make?

    Ⓐ $20   Ⓑ $25
    Ⓒ $50   Ⓓ $500

LOOK FOR A PATTERN In Exercises 1 and 2, the first three figures of a pattern are shown. Make a table of their perimeters and areas. Describe the pattern. Find the perimeter and area of the next three figures. Check your answer with sketches. **(1.1, 1.2)**

1.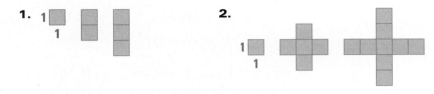

2.

QUADRILATERALS In Exercises 3 and 4, decide whether it is possible to draw the quadrilateral. If it is, illustrate your answer with a diagram. If not, explain why. **(1.5)**

3. A parallelogram that is not a quadrilateral

4. A quadrilateral that is not a parallelogram

ALGEBRA AND MENTAL MATH Use mental math to solve.
(1.6, 1.7, 2.3, 2.6)

5. $x - 14 = 12$ **6.** $b \cdot 12 = 48$ **7.** $27 \div t = 1$

8. $d \div 4 = 60$ **9.** $2(x + 1) = 14$ **10.** $5(3 + y) = 30$

WORKING BACKWARD Copy and complete the model. **(1.7)**

11.

$$\times 7 \qquad \div 5 \qquad -6 \qquad +8$$

| ? | → | ? | → | ? | → | ? | → | 16 |

12.

$$-7 \qquad \div 3 \qquad +4 \qquad \times 2$$

| ? | → | ? | → | ? | → | ? | → | 38 |

In Exercises 13–15, complete the statement. **(2.1, 3.2)**

13. $8150 = $ **?** tens   **14.** $0.392 \text{ km} = $ **?** m   **15.** **?** mm $= 5.75 \text{ cm}$

In Exercises 16 and 17, complete the statement with the words *large squares*, *strips*, or *small squares*. **(3.1)**

16. 31.5 ?   **17.** 315 ?

Evaluate the expression. (2.5, 3.7)

18. $2^3 + 3 \times 4$ **19.** $33 \div 3 + 2 \times 7$ **20.** $37 - 3^4 \div 9$

Evaluate the expression in two ways. (2.6)

21. $4(9 + 6)$ **22.** $3(12 + 10)$ **23.** $7(8 + 12)$ **24.** $3(13 + 2)$

In Exercises 25 and 26, you are shown a model for a portion of a whole. Draw a model of the whole. (3.3)

25.

0.24

26.

0.56

In Exercises 27–30, decide whether the statement is *true* or *false*. Explain your reasoning. (3.4)

27. $\dfrac{9}{10} = 90\%$ **28.** $30\% = \dfrac{3}{100}$ **29.** $\dfrac{8}{10} = 0.08$ **30.** $70\% = 0.7$

Round each number to the given place value. (3.6)

31. 6.93 (tenths)   **32.** 24.8 (ones)   **33.** 7511 (thousands)

34. PROBABILITY You flip a coin three times. List the different outcomes of heads (h) and tails (t) you could get. (1.3)

BASKETBALL The bar graphs below show the percent of games won by the top five teams in the NBA Eastern Conference Atlantic Division for the 1995–96 season. (Source: *The Universal Almanac 1997*) (1.4, 3.4–3.6)

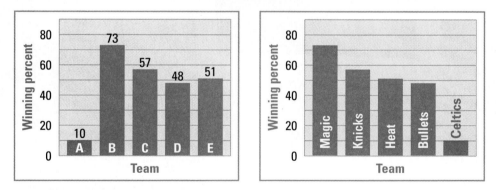

35. Match the teams with their winning percents.

36. Change each percent to a decimal.

37. Order the decimals from least to greatest.

38. Round each decimal to the nearest tenth.

39. SAVING You save to buy a radio for $50. Each week you earn $20. The first week you save 40% of your earnings. Each week you save 10% more than the week before. How many weeks will it take you to save enough money? (1.8, 1.9, 3.8)

Applications of Decimals and Percents

TECHNOLOGY

Technology resources accompanying this chapter:

• Interactive Real-Life Investigations

• Middle School Tutorial Software

FAMILY restaurants seat you at a table where a waiter or waitress takes your order, and then serves your meal.

FAST FOOD restaurants serve quick meals to people on the go.

CHAPTER THEME
Restaurants

GOURMET restaurants stress the importance of the appearance and presentation of a meal, as well as its taste.

Dining Out

REAL LIFE
Restaurants

When you increase the number of steps in making a product, you usually need to increase the cost of the product. So a meal prepared in a restaurant will usually cost more than the same food purchased fresh, prepared, and cooked at home.

Consider the cost of a cheeseburger, fries, and drink at three different restaurants.

Fast Food Hut	Dee's Diner	Waterfront Haven
$2.99	$4.50 + tip	$6.95 + tip

Think and Discuss

1. Since the preparation time is about the same, what do you think causes the different prices?

2. Besides food and equipment, what other costs do you think a restaurant has?

CHAPTER PROJECT

Making an Employee Training Manual

PROJECT DESCRIPTION

Imagine that you own a restaurant. You need to make an employee training manual to explain basic duties to new employees. To organize your manual, you will use the list of **TOPICS** on the next page.

GETTING STARTED

Talking It Over

- In your groups, talk about differences between restaurants that you have visited. If you owned a restaurant, what would you want it to be like? What kind of food would it serve? Would you have food servers or would people get their own food from a counter or buffet?

- What kind of employees would you have at your restaurant? What would the duties of each be? As the owner and manager, what would your duties be?

Planning Your Project

- **Materials Needed:** paper, pencils or pens, colored pencils or markers

- Make a booklet from several sheets of paper, and write *Employee Training Manual* on the cover. Make up a name and logo for your restaurant and add them to the cover. On the first page, make a menu for your restaurant. Include pictures if you wish. As you answer the **BUILDING YOUR PROJECT** questions, add the results to your manual.

Tech Link

Investigation 4,
Interactive
Real-Life
Investigations

BUILDING YOUR PROJECT

These are places throughout the chapter where you will work on your project.

TOPICS

4.1 Write a sample bill with its total. *p. 169*

4.2 Demonstrate how to make change for a customer. *p. 173*

4.4 Explain how to calculate a tip. *p. 186*

4.5 Find the amount of ground meat needed to make a hamburger. *p. 191*

4.7 Decide which item is the better buy. *p. 203*

4.8 Calculate an employee's wages. *p. 207*

INTERNET

To find out more about owning a restaurant, go to: **http://www.mlmath.com**

Investigating Decimal Addition and Subtraction

Materials Needed
- **base-ten pieces or grid paper**
- **paper**
- **pencils**

You can use base-ten pieces to show decimal numbers. Use a large square for a one, a strip for a tenth, and a small square for a hundredth.

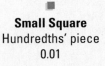

Large Square
Ones' piece
1

Strip
Tenths' piece
0.1

Small Square
Hundredths' piece
0.01

Part A MODELING ADDITION WITH BASE-TEN PIECES

Base-ten pieces can be used to show addition of decimals. The example below shows 2.4 + 1.3 = 3.7.

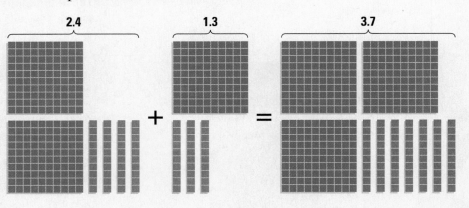

2.4   1.3   3.7

1. Use base-ten pieces to show each addition problem.

   a. 3.2 + 1.4   **b.** 0.62 + 0.37
   c. 3 + 0.33   **d.** 1.36 + 2.47

2. In part (b) above, suppose you added 1 hundredths' piece to the answer. What would you get? Explain.

3. In part (c) above, write the problem in correct vertical form.

4. How is the addition problem in part (d) above different from the other three addition problems? How did you solve it?

Base-ten pieces can also be used to show subtraction of decimals.
The example below shows $2.5 - 1.3 = 1.2$.

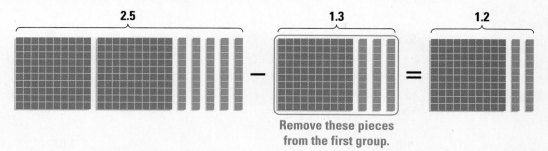

2.5   **1.3**   **1.2**

Remove these pieces
from the first group.

5. Use base-ten pieces to show each subtraction problem.

　　a. $3.4 - 1.2$　　**b.** $0.67 - 0.36$　　**c.** $3.2 - 0.2$　　**d.** $3.36 - 2.27$

6. In part (b) above, suppose you subtracted 1 hundredths' piece
from the answer. What would you get?

7. In part (c) above, write the problem in correct vertical form.

8. How is the subtraction problem in part (d) above different from
the other three subtraction problems? How did you solve it?

Part **C** MAKING CONNECTIONS

9. Use the drawing at the right. If a large
square represents one, what addition
problem is shown? If a large square
represents 1 hundred, what addition
problem is shown?

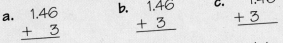

NOW TRY THESE

10. Draw a sketch of base-ten pieces to help you
add or subtract.

　　a. $2.75 + 1.34$　　**b.** $2 + 1.04$　　**c.** $4.04 - 0.4$

11. Which do you think is the best vertical form of
$1.46 + 3$? Explain your reasoning.

　　a. $\begin{array}{r} 1.46 \\ + \ \ 3 \\ \hline \end{array}$　　**b.** $\begin{array}{r} 1.46 \\ + 3 \\ \hline \end{array}$　　**c.** $\begin{array}{r} 1.46 \\ + 3 \\ \hline \end{array}$

12. Write $13.2 - 0.28$ in vertical form. Explain why
the form is correct.

4.1

Adding Decimals

What you should learn:

Goal 1 How to add decimals

Goal 2 How to use decimal addition to solve real-life problems

Why you should learn it:

Decimal addition can be used to help you find the total cost of things. An example is finding the total of a restaurant bill.

Goal 1 ADDING DECIMALS

Example 1 Adding Decimals with Base-Ten Pieces

Use base-ten pieces to show, or *model*, 1.2 + 0.87.

Solution

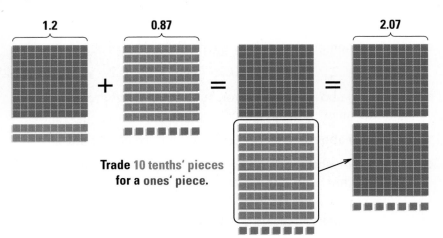

Trade **10 tenths' pieces** for a **ones' piece.**

So, 1.2 + 0.87 = 2.07.

Another way to add decimals is to use vertical form. When you do this, remember to line up the decimal places. The steps are similar to those used for adding whole numbers.

Example 2 Using Vertical Form to Add

Use vertical form to add the decimals.

a. 4.72 + 2.5   **b.** 5.32 + 7   **c.** 0.247 + 1.9

Solution

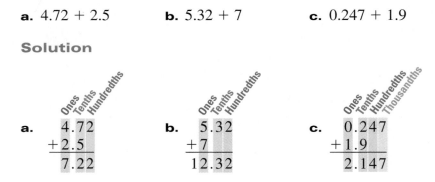

NEED TO KNOW

Remember that whole numbers have an "unwritten" decimal point. For example, 5 and 5.0 are the same.

Goal 2 SOLVING REAL-LIFE PROBLEMS

Example 3 Adding Decimals

Use the menu to find the cost of each order.

a. 1 green salad, 1 chicken entree, 1 milk
b. 1 fruit salad, 1 pasta entree, 1 iced tea
c. 1 onion soup, 1 steak entree, 1 sparkling water

REAL LIFE
Restaurants

Menu

Soup & Salad

Onion Soup $1.59
Green Salad $1.19
Fruit Salad $1.39

Entree

Pasta $8.95
Chicken $10.25
Steak $13.75

Beverages

Milk $0.78
Iced Tea $0.88
Sparkling Water . . $1.28

Pasta

Americans bought over 1.3 billion pounds of pasta in 1996. This is enough pasta to lay 1 lb spaghetti boxes end-to-end around the equator 9 times.

Solution

For each addition, use vertical form and line up the decimal places.

a.	**b.**	**c.**
$1.19	$1.39	$1.59
10.25	8.95	13.75
+ 0.78	+ 0.88	+ 1.28
$12.22	$11.22	$16.62

Example 4 Problem Solving with Decimals

A customer ordered 1 item from each of the 3 categories on the menu. The total was $10.92. What were the items?

Solution

STRATEGY **WORK BACKWARD** Because the total is $10.92, the customer must have ordered the pasta for $8.95. So the other 2 items total about $2. By trying the green salad and milk, you find that

$$\$8.95 + \$1.19 + \$0.78 = \$10.92.$$

So, the 3 items must have been pasta, green salad, and milk.

ONGOING ASSESSMENT

Talk About It

Use vertical form to add the decimals. With a partner, discuss how you can use estimation to check that your answers are reasonable.

1. 0.36 + 1.082

2. 2.508 + 31.11

3. 9.005 + 0.046

GUIDED PRACTICE

1. Copy and complete the base-ten model. Write the problem in vertical form and solve. (Large square = 1 unit)

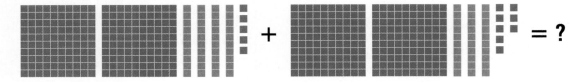

2. **ERROR ANALYSIS** Describe the error at the right. Then write a similar problem that *does* have 2 as its sum.

$$\begin{array}{r} 1\ 6 \\ +\ 0.4 \\ \hline 2.0\ \times \end{array}$$

3. Write three different addition problems whose sum is 10.45.

PRACTICE AND PROBLEM SOLVING

In Exercises 4 and 5, copy and complete the model. Write and solve in vertical form. (Large square = 1 unit)

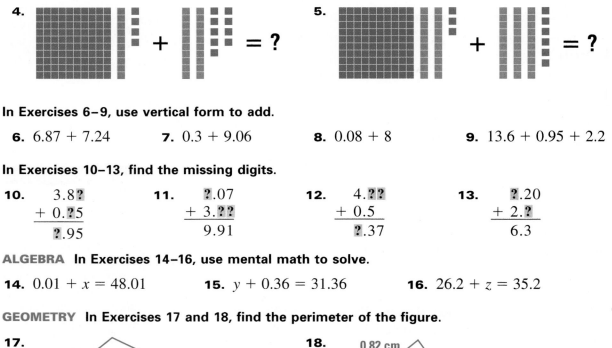

In Exercises 6–9, use vertical form to add.

6. $6.87 + 7.24$ 7. $0.3 + 9.06$ 8. $0.08 + 8$ 9. $13.6 + 0.95 + 2.2$

In Exercises 10–13, find the missing digits.

10. $\begin{array}{r} 3.8\ ? \\ +\ 0.?5 \\ \hline ?.95 \end{array}$ 11. $\begin{array}{r} ?.07 \\ +\ 3.?? \\ \hline 9.91 \end{array}$ 12. $\begin{array}{r} 4.?? \\ +\ 0.5 \\ \hline ?.37 \end{array}$ 13. $\begin{array}{r} ?.20 \\ +\ 2.? \\ \hline 6.3 \end{array}$

ALGEBRA **In Exercises 14–16, use mental math to solve.**

14. $0.01 + x = 48.01$ 15. $y + 0.36 = 31.36$ 16. $26.2 + z = 35.2$

GEOMETRY **In Exercises 17 and 18, find the perimeter of the figure.**

17. 4.19 m, 6.05 m, 8.7 m

18. 0.82 cm, 1.8 cm, 1.06 cm, 2.14 cm

TECHNOLOGY In Exercises 19 and 20, use a calculator to add. Describe any patterns that you see. Write the next 2 problems in the pattern.

19. $28.012 + 94.3 = $?

$29.123 + 94.3 = $?

$30.234 + 94.3 = $?

20. $545.45 + 565.55 = $?

$656.56 + 1565.44 = $?

$767.67 + 2565.33 = $?

21. NUMBER PUZZLE Copy and complete the pyramid. Each number is the sum of the two numbers below it.

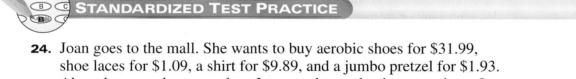

		?		
	?		?	
	?	?	?	
4.52	?	?	?	
1.02	3.5	0.9	0.04	1.6

Real Life...
Real People

Ski Jumping

Lindsay Van, 12, from Park City, Utah, won the ski jumping event for ages 15 and under at the 1996 Nordic Junior Olympics.

SKI JUMPING You are an Olympic ski-jumper. You participate in three different jumps. Your points for the three jumps are 85.39, 92.6, and 89.07. To win a medal, your total points must be at least the following: Gold—270.08, Silver—265.54, and Bronze—263.1.

22. What is your total score? What medal did you win?

23. Use mental math to find how many more points you needed to win a gold medal.

STANDARDIZED TEST PRACTICE

24. Joan goes to the mall. She wants to buy aerobic shoes for $31.99, shoe laces for $1.09, a shirt for $9.89, and a jumbo pretzel for $1.93. About how much money does Joan need to make these purchases?

(**A**) $42   (**B**) $43   (**C**) $44   (**D**) $45

EXPLORATION AND EXTENSION

PORTFOLIO

25. BUILDING YOUR PROJECT For your restaurant's *Employee Training Manual,* write a menu that shows some or all of the items you will serve. Include the price of each item.

Then write a sample bill that shows how your employees should total a bill. Include at least 3 menu items on the bill.

4.2

Subtracting Decimals

What you should learn:

Goal 1 How to subtract decimals

Goal 2 How to use decimal subtraction to solve real-life problems

Why you should learn it:

Decimal subtraction can be used to help you make change with money. An example is finding your change when you pay for a purchase.

Goal 1 SUBTRACTING DECIMALS

Example 1 Subtracting Decimals with Base-Ten Pieces

Use base-ten pieces to model $1.6 - 0.32$.

Solution

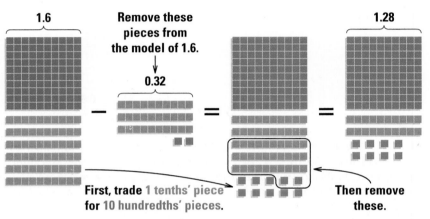

1.6 — Remove these pieces from the model of 1.6. — 0.32 — = — = — 1.28

First, trade 1 tenths' piece for 10 hundredths' pieces. — Then remove these.

Start with 1.6. Exchange 1 tenths' piece for 10 hundredths' pieces, so that you can remove 0.32 from the model. 1.28 is left.

....

You can use vertical form to subtract decimals. When doing this, remember to line up the decimal places.

Example 2 Subtracting with Vertical Form

Use vertical form to subtract the decimals.

a. $3.42 - 2.4$ **b.** $4.63 - 3$ **c.** $8 - 0.308$

Solution

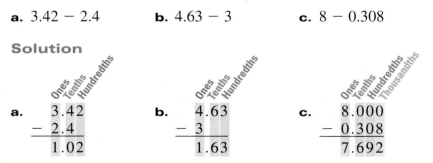

a.
$$\begin{array}{r} 3.42 \\ -\ 2.4 \\ \hline 1.02 \end{array}$$

b.
$$\begin{array}{r} 4.63 \\ -\ 3 \\ \hline 1.63 \end{array}$$

c.
$$\begin{array}{r} 8.000 \\ -\ 0.308 \\ \hline 7.692 \end{array}$$

When you subtract a decimal from a whole number, as in part (c), it helps to write a decimal point and one or more zeros with the whole number.

Example 3 Making Change

You buy a T-shirt for $12.69. You give the sales clerk $20. How much change do you get back?

REAL LIFE
Money

Solution

Method **1** Using Vertical Form

$20.00	Amount you gave clerk
− 12.69	Cost of the T-shirt
$ 7.31	Change

✔**Check:** Add to check the result of a subtraction problem.

$12.69	Cost of the T-shirt
+ 7.31	Change
$20.00	Amount you gave clerk ✔

Method **2** Counting the Change

Some sales clerks use this technique to count the amount of change they give. Here is how a sales clerk might count your change.

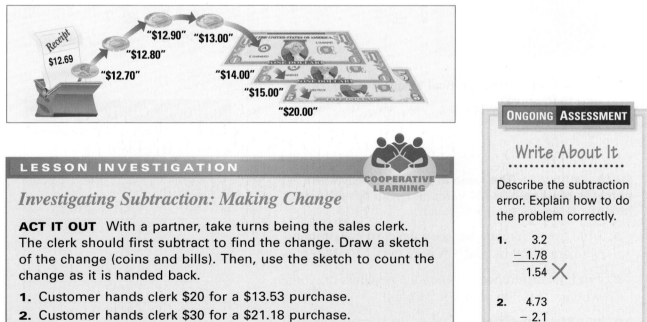

LESSON INVESTIGATION

COOPERATIVE
LEARNING

Investigating Subtraction: Making Change

ACT IT OUT With a partner, take turns being the sales clerk. The clerk should first subtract to find the change. Draw a sketch of the change (coins and bills). Then, use the sketch to count the change as it is handed back.

1. Customer hands clerk $20 for a $13.53 purchase.

2. Customer hands clerk $30 for a $21.18 purchase.

3. Customer hands clerk $20.10 for a $10.06 purchase.

ONGOING ASSESSMENT

Write About It

Describe the subtraction error. Explain how to do the problem correctly.

1.
	3.2
−	1.78
	1.54 ✗

2.
	4.73
−	2.1
	4.52 ✗

4.2 Exercises Extra Practice, page 626

GUIDED PRACTICE

1. What subtraction problem is modeled by the base-ten pieces below? Solve the problem. (Large square = 1 unit)

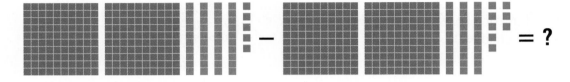

ERROR ANALYSIS In Exercises 2–4, decide whether the vertical form is correct. If not, correct the form and solve.

2.
```
  0.86
- 0.2
```

3.
```
  3.00
- 2.85
```

4.
```
  10.5
- .82
```

PRACTICE AND PROBLEM SOLVING

In Exercises 5 and 6, write the decimal problem shown by the model in vertical form and then solve. (Large square = 1 unit)

5.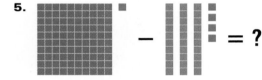

6.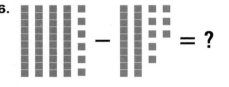

7. Choose the correct vertical form for 2 − 0.81, and then solve.

   A.
```
    2
- 0.81
```
   B.
```
  2.00
- 0.81
```

DATA ANALYSIS The table at the right shows the percents of people 18–24 years old who are different heights. (Source: U.S. Bureau of the Census)

8. Find the difference between the percents of men who are 5 ft 9 in. and 5 ft 8 in. tall.

9. Find the difference between the percents of women who are 5 ft 3 in. and 5 ft 2 in. tall.

10. **REASONING** Find the sum of the percents in each percent column. Why are the totals less than 100%?

Height	Percent of Men	Percent of Women
5' 2"	0.16	8.62
5' 3"	0.27	11.31
5' 4"	1.76	12.75
5' 5"	1.48	16.28
5' 6"	4.39	16.67
5' 7"	7.94	10.61
5' 8"	10.50	6.93
5' 9"	12.21	3.93
5' 10"	14.77	2.11
5' 11"	14.59	1.04

In Exercises 11–18, use vertical form to subtract.

11. $6.75 - 2.3$ **12.** $4.33 - 3.9$ **13.** $7.619 - 3.8$ **14.** $5.452 - 2.91$

15. $5 - 2.89$ **16.** $12 - 7.652$ **17.** $0.88 - 0.39$ **18.** $1.25 - 0.056$

TECHNOLOGY **In Exercises 19–22, use a calculator to evaluate the expression.**

19. $3.421 - 1.42 + 1.301$ **20.** $7.56 - 2.019 + 5.451$

21. $2.25 + 7.789 - 4.342$ **22.** $11.010 + 5.672 - 8.999$

NUTRITION **The map at the right shows the average number of gallons of bottled water that people drink in a year.** (Source: International Bottled Water Association)

U.S. Bottled Water Use
(gallons per person)

20.1 11.3 5.7 4.5 4.4 16.4 6.3

■ Pacific   ■ East Central
■ West   ■ Northeast
■ West Central ■ South
■ Southwest

23. Where do people drink the most bottled water? Where do they drink the least? What is the difference between the amounts used in these two regions?

24. How many more gallons of bottled water do people in the Southwest drink than people in the Northeast?

25. What might be a reason for differences in bottled water use between regions?

CONSUMER SPENDING **Was the correct change given? Explain.**

26. You give the clerk a $20 bill and receive a $10 bill and 2 dimes in change for a purchase of $10.80.

27. You use $20 to buy a concert ticket for $18.74. The clerk counts your $1.26 change as "$18.75, $19.00, $20.00."

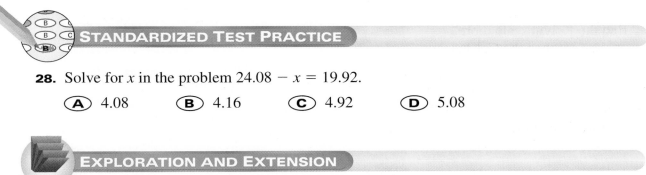

STANDARDIZED TEST PRACTICE

28. Solve for x in the problem $24.08 - x = 19.92$.

    Ⓐ 4.08   **Ⓑ** 4.16   **Ⓒ** 4.92   **Ⓓ** 5.08

EXPLORATION AND EXTENSION

PORTFOLIO

29. **BUILDING YOUR PROJECT** For your restaurant's *Employee Training Manual*, write two samples that show how to find the amount of change a customer should get. Include items from your menu.

In Exercises 1 and 2, describe the pattern. Then write the next three numbers. (1.1)

1. $\frac{1}{3}, \frac{1}{6}, \frac{1}{9}$, **?** , **?** , **?** , . . .   **2.** 9.25, 9.5, 9.75, **?** , **?** , **?** , . . .

In Exercises 3–6, find the missing digits. Use a calculator to check. (2.2–2.4)

3. **?**6**?**
 + 1**?**5
 ‾‾‾‾‾‾
  604

4.   65**?**
 − 3**?**7
 ‾‾‾‾‾
  ?78

5.   **?**9
 × **?**
 ‾‾‾‾
  ?78

6. $\dfrac{3\textbf{?}}{}$
 1**?**)456

7. GEOGRAPHY The height of Angel Falls, in Venezuela, is 3212 ft. Write this number in words. (2.1)

In Exercises 8–10, round to the given place value. (3.6)

8. 7.094 (tenths)   **9.** 169.5 (ones)   **10.** 23.1845 (hundredths)

11. ART CLASS In art class you are carving sculptures from blocks of wood. The new blocks of wood come in cartons. In each carton, the blocks are arranged 5 long, 5 wide, and 5 high. How many blocks are there in each carton? Express your answer as a power. (3.7)

Science Connection

KELVIN TEMPERATURE SCALE

The Kelvin temperature scale begins at *absolute zero*, a temperature so cold that molecules have almost no energy of motion. There are no temperature readings below zero in the Kelvin scale. For many formulas and equations, scientists find the Kelvin scale more convenient than the Celsius or Fahrenheit scales.

To convert Kelvin temperature to Celsius, subtract 273.16.

In Exercises 1–5, give the missing Celsius temperatures.

		°K	°C
1.	Aluminum melts	933.53	?
2.	Muffins bake	450.16	?
	Water boils	373.16	100
3.	Highest recorded temperature in California	329.83	?
4.	Normal human body temperature	310.16	?
5.	Butter melts	303.72	?
	Water freezes	273.16	0

"...check, please!"

Restaurant bills are often written and totaled by hand. It's a good idea to check for errors.

....

Example

You are checking the bills that were written at your restaurant during the day. Two are shown below. Are the bills correct?

REAL LIFE
Economics

Solution

The fifth item on the first bill is wrong. Using a calculator, you can find that the 2 orders of milk should cost $1.78.

Keystrokes	Display
▬.89 ➕ ▬.89 ═	1.78

Early Bird Restaurant

Number	Description	Amount
1	Grilled cheese	$ 2.19
1	Cole slaw	$1.19
1	French fries	$1.29
2	Fish & chips $4.69 each	$9.38
2	Milk $.89 each	$2.89
1	Chicken salad	$4.39
3	Green salad with French dressing $.95 each	$2.85
2	Iced tea $1.45 each	$1.45
Total		$ 25.63

Early Bird Restaurant

Number	Description	Amount
3	Cole slaw $1.19 each	$ 3.57
3	Tomato soup $1.29 each	$ 2.58
1	Mashed potatoes	$1.29
2	White rice $.89 each	$0.89
1	Pork chop dinner	$6.89
1	Mixed vegetable plate	$6.89
3	Vegetables with cheese	$4.69
	Tea $1.10 each	$3.10
Total		$ 29.90

Exercises

1. Each description on the first bill is correct. Are the amounts correct? If not, copy the bill and write the correct amounts and total.

2. Each description on the second bill is correct. Are the amounts correct? If not, copy the bill and write the correct amounts and total.

Estimating Sums and **Differences**

What you should learn:

Goal 1 How to estimate sums and differences by rounding

Goal 2 How to use front-end estimation

Why you should learn it:

You can estimate to help make decisions quickly using mental math. An example is deciding if you have enough money to pay for your groceries.

Goal 1 USING ROUNDING TO ESTIMATE

One way to estimate sums and differences is to use **rounding**.

Example 1 Buying Groceries

You take $5 to a convenience store. You need to buy bread, eggs, and milk. If you have enough money, you also want to buy a package of frozen waffles. Use the prices below to decide whether you can buy the waffles.

Loaf of bread	$1.39	**Dozen eggs**	$.89
Half gallon of milk	$1.79	**Package of waffles**	$1.65

Solution

One way to make your decision is to round each of the prices to the nearest half-dollar.

	Exact Amount	**Rounded Estimate**
Bread	$1.39	$1.50
Eggs	$0.89	1.00
Milk	$1.79	2.00
Waffles	$1.65	+ 1.50
		$6.00

Your estimate indicates that you do not have enough money to buy the waffles.

Example 2 Estimating the Difference

You buy some clothes for $23.16. You give a clerk $30 to pay for the clothes. Estimate your change.

Solution

By rounding the cost of the clothes to the nearest dollar, you can estimate your change to be

$$\$30 - \$23 = \$7.$$

Is your estimate for the change too low, or is it too high? How can you tell?

TOOLBOX

Estimating Sums, page 648

Goal 2 USING FRONT-END ESTIMATION

Front-end estimation is another useful method for estimating.

Example 3 Using Estimation in Real Life

You are driving a 12,450 lb truck with loads of 5750 lb and 3490 lb. Should you cross a bridge with a weight limit of 20,000 lb?

REAL LIFE
Weight Limits

Solution

Estimate the total weight using only the front digits of each weight.

	Exact Weight	Estimate
Truck	12,450	12,000
Load 1	5,750	5,000
Load 2	3,490	+ 3,000
		at least 20,000 lb

Your estimate indicates that you should not cross the bridge.

Example 4 Making Your Estimate Better

Now suppose your truck weighs 11,450 lb. Should you cross the bridge? Using front-end estimation leaves you unsure.

$$11,000 + 5000 + 3000 = at\ least\ 19,000\ lb$$

The total weight is *at least* 19,000 lb. This is close to the weight limit. Improve your estimate by using the **front** and **next** digits.

Add front digits.	Add next digits.	Add estimates.
11,450	11,450	
5,750	5,750	*at least* 19,000
+ 3,490	+ 3,490	*at least* + 1,500
19,000	1,500	*at least* 20,500

The improved estimate shows that the total weight must be *at least* 20,500 lb, so you should not cross the bridge. Although this method takes longer, it is more accurate.

ONGOING ASSESSMENT

Write About It

1. Write about a real-life problem that you can solve by using rounding.

2. Write about a real-life problem that you can solve by using estimation.

GUIDED PRACTICE

1. Name two strategies for estimating sums and differences. Give a real-life situation where you could use each type.

In Exercises 2–7, round to the given place value.

2. 8.547 (ones)

3. 13.015 (hundredths)

4. 19,620 (thousands)

5. 58.34 (tens)

6. 2.645 (tenths)

7. 675.082 (hundreds)

8. You and a friend go bowling. You have to be home in $2\frac{1}{2}$ h. It takes about 13 min each way to ride your bike to and from the bowling lanes. It takes about 25 min to bowl a game. About how many games can you plan to bowl?

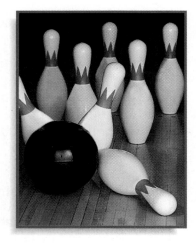

PRACTICE AND PROBLEM SOLVING

In Exercises 9–14, round the values to the nearest hundred and estimate the answer.

9. $675 - 589$

10. $422 + 451$

11. $8362 + 941$

12. $1084 - 179$

13. $3615 - 663$

14. $27 + 149$

In Exercises 15–20, round the values to the nearest dollar and estimate the answer. Then estimate again by rounding to the nearest half dollar.

15. $13.28 + $11.85

16. $14.79 - $2.65

17. $2.27 + $9.80

18. $19.94 + $3.31

19. $18.56 - $10.27

20. $258.74 - $63.29

In Exercises 21–26, estimate the answer by using front-end estimation. Then make your estimate better by using the "front" and "next" digits.

21. $287 + 165$

22. $3.84 - 1.68$

23. $172 - 112$

24. $46.18 + 34.42$

25. $4886 - 3117$

26. $4672 + 1807$

GEOMETRY In Exercises 27–29, you are given the perimeter of the figure. By rounding, estimate the length of the side labeled *x*.

27. Perimeter = 28 units

28. Perimeter = 46.5 units

29. Perimeter = 24.5 units

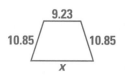

4.76

x

9.23

10.85   10.85

x

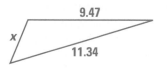

9.47

x

11.34

In Exercises 30–32, round the values to the nearest half dollar.

30. PETS You go to the pet store with $25. You decide to buy 2 fish for $3.69 each and fish food for $4.19. Rounded tanks are $11.48. Square-shaped tanks are $14.89. Estimate your total cost to find which tank you can buy. About how much money will you have left?

31. ART SUPPLIES You go to the art supply store to buy paint and brushes. You need one brush for each container of paint. Each brush is $1.27 and each container of paint is $2.85. About how many sets can you buy if you have $15?

32. SAVINGS You have a summer job mowing lawns. The amount of money you earned and spent for three weeks is shown at the right. Estimate the amount you saved each week. Then estimate your total savings.

Savings Record

STANDARDIZED TEST PRACTICE

33. A square has a perimeter of 28.6 in. The length of one side of the square is *about* __?__.

(A) 5.9 in.   **(B)** 6.3 in.   **(C)** 6.8 in.   **(D)** 7.1 in.

EXPLORATION AND EXTENSION

34. a. GROUP ACTIVITY Copy the list of 20 numbers at the right. Choose 2 of the numbers and use them to write an addition or subtraction problem. Estimate an answer and score points according to the scoring chart. (Cross off numbers after they are used).

b. Take turns repeating the procedure until all of the numbers have been used. Compare your total points with other groups.

c. What strategies might lead to high scores? Try playing again.

1.86	24.6	7.35	6.28	31.01
16.9	3.42	9.89	0.63	4.14
58.16	15.19	0.88	41.8	13.53
5.77	38.2	25.07	19.11	7.9

Estimated Range	Points
1–20	2 points
20.1–40	4 points
40.1–60	5 points
60.1–80	4 points
80.1–100	2 points

LAB
4.4

COOPERATIVE
LEARNING

Materials Needed
- **base-ten grid paper**
- **paper**
- **pencils**

Investigating Decimal Multiplication

In Chapter 2, you learned how to use base-ten grid paper to model multiplication of whole numbers. For example, the product of 6 and 7 can be modeled as shown below at the left. The same diagram can be used to model the product of 0.6 and 0.7.

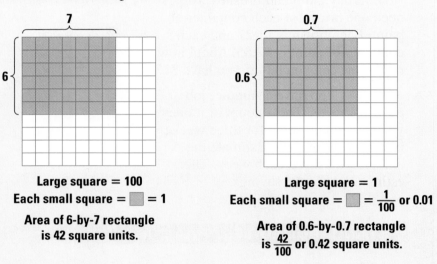

Large square = 100
Each small square = ▨ = 1

Area of 6-by-7 rectangle
is 42 square units.

Large square = 1
Each small square = □ = $\frac{1}{100}$ or 0.01

Area of 0.6-by-0.7 rectangle
is $\frac{42}{100}$ or 0.42 square units.

Part A MAKING CONNECTIONS

1. Write *two* products that could be modeled by each base-ten sketch: one with two whole numbers and one with two decimals. For each of your two products, tell what a small square represents. Then count the number of small squares and write the answer.

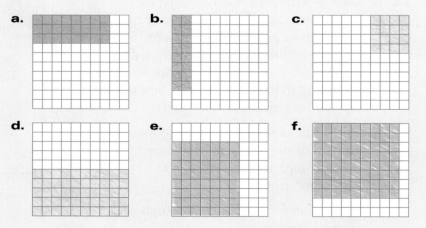

a.   b.   c.

d.   e.   f.

Part B USING AREA MODELS

The base-ten grid shows a model of the multiplication problem 1.6 × 2.7. Use the model to find the product.

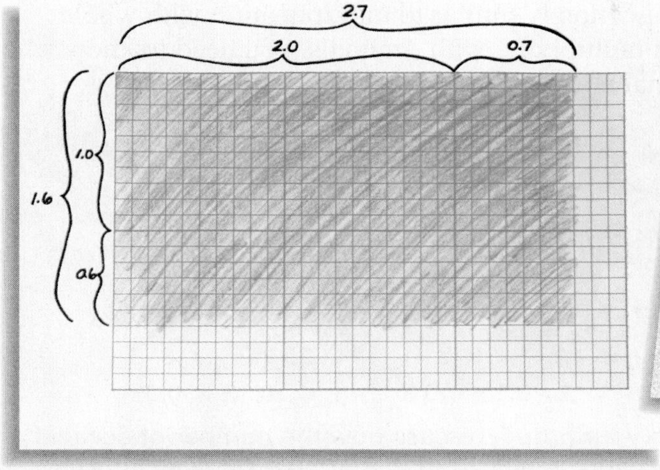

2. On base-ten grid paper, sketch a model to find the product.

a. 0.3 × 0.6 **b.** 1.4 × 3.0 **c.** 1.8 × 1.4

Part C MAKING CONNECTIONS

3. On base-ten grid paper, sketch a model to find the product. Tell what each small square represents.

a. 12 × 3

b. 1.2 × 3

c. 1.2 × 0.3

NOW TRY THESE

In Exercises 4–6, find each product.

4. a. 0.1 × 0.7 **5. a.** 0.3 × 0.8 **6. a.** 0.9 × 0.2
 b. 1.2 × 0.7 **b.** 1.3 × 0.8 **b.** 0.9 × 1.2

7. Complete the statement with *sometimes, always,* or *never.* Give two examples of each.

a. If two numbers are less than 1, their product is _?_ less than 1.

b. If one number is less than 1 and another is greater than 1, their product is _?_ less than 1.

c. If two numbers are greater than 1, their product is _?_ greater than 1.

4.4

Decimal Multiplication and Percent

What you should learn:

Goal 1 How to multiply decimals

Goal 2 How to use decimal multiplication to find a percent of a number

Why you should learn it:

Decimal multiplication can be used to help find your total cost when you buy something. An example is finding the sales tax on the items you buy.

TOOLBOX

Multiplying Decimals, page 643

Goal 1 MULTIPLYING DECIMALS

Decimal multiplication is similar to multiplication with whole numbers. When multiplying with decimals, you need to know where to put the decimal point.

LESSON INVESTIGATION

Investigating Decimal Multiplication

GROUP ACTIVITY Use a calculator to find each product.

1. 12×3 **2.** 1.2×3 **3.** 1.2×0.3
4. 0.12×3 **5.** 0.12×0.3 **6.** 0.12×0.03

With others in your group, discuss how the number of decimal places in the factors is related to the number of decimal places in the product.

Test your conclusion with the product 0.12×0.003.

As you may have discovered in the investigation, the number of decimal places in the product is equal to the sum of the number of decimal places in the factors.

Example 1 Multiplying Decimals

Find the product.

a. 3.06×1.4 **b.** 1.46×0.02

Solution

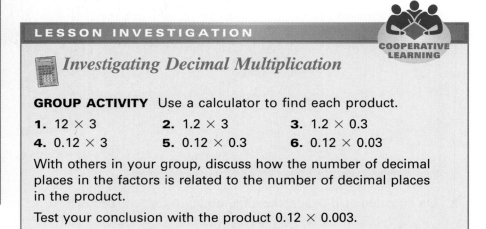

a.
$$\begin{array}{r} 3.06 \\ \times\ 1.4 \\ \hline 1224 \\ 306 \\ \hline 4.284 \end{array}$$

2 decimal places
1 decimal place

$2 + 1 = 3$, so the product has 3 decimal places.

b.
$$\begin{array}{r} 1.46 \\ \times\ 0.02 \\ \hline 0.0292 \end{array}$$

2 decimal places
2 decimal places

$2 + 2 = 4$, so the product has 4 decimal places.

Write 0 to make 4 decimal places in the product.

STUDY TIP

When you multiply decimals, use estimation to check that your answer is reasonable. In part (a) at the right, the answer seems reasonable because it is greater than 1×3, or 3, and less than 2×3, or 6.

Goal 2 MULTIPLYING TO FIND A PERCENT

To find a decimal, percent, or fractional amount *of* a number, you multiply. For example, to find 0.4 *of* 2, you multiply to get $0.4 \times 2 = 0.8$. Percents and fractions can be written as decimals.

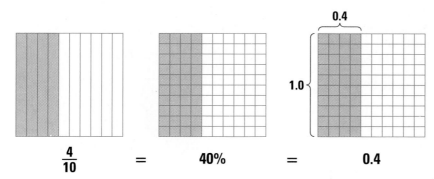

$$\frac{4}{10} \quad = \quad 40\% \quad = \quad 0.4$$

In real-life problems, you can find a percent of an amount by rewriting the percent as a decimal, and using decimal multiplication.

Example 2 Finding a Percent of a Number

REAL LIFE
Sales Tax

Most states have a sales tax, expressed as a percent. For example, if the sales tax *rate* is 6%, this means that for each dollar you pay, you must pay an extra six cents in tax.

What is the amount of tax on the following items?

a. Jeans bought for $24.95 in Colorado (3% tax rate)

b. A bicycle bought for $139.90 in Vermont (5% tax rate)

Solution

To find the amount of tax, rewrite the **tax rate** as a decimal. Multiply the **cost** of the item by the **tax rate**.

a.
$$\begin{array}{r} \$24.95 \\ \times\ 0.03 \\ \hline \$0.7485 \end{array}$$
Rewrite 3% as 0.03.

b.
$$\begin{array}{r} \$139.90 \\ \times\ 0.05 \\ \hline \$6.9950 \end{array}$$
Rewrite 5% as 0.05.

The product has 4 decimal places. Rounded to the nearest cent, the sales tax is $0.75.

The product has 4 decimal places. Rounded to the nearest cent, the sales tax is $7.00.

Real Life... Real Facts

Taxes
Taxes are used to fund government services like police and fire departments, and public schools.

TOOLBOX

Finding a Percent of a Number, page 657

ONGOING ASSESSMENT

Talk About It
....

Find the sales tax on each item.

1. 5% sales tax on a car that costs $16,540.

2. 7% sales tax on a coat that costs $56.89.

4.4 Exercises

Extra Practice, page 626

GUIDED PRACTICE

In Exercises 1–3, without multiplying, state how many decimal places are in the product.

1. 0.08×5.2

2. 12.23×4.563

3. 44.358×3.001

In Exercises 4–6, use the graph at the right. Two hundred households were asked how many phones they have. The survey results are shown as percents in the circle graph. (Source: *USA Today*)

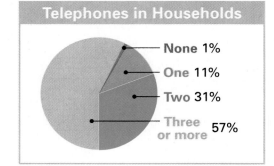

Telephones in Households
None 1%
One 11%
Two 31%
Three or more 57%

4. What number of the households surveyed have only one phone?

5. What number of the households surveyed have more than one phone?

6. What number of the households surveyed have two or more phones?

PRACTICE AND PROBLEM SOLVING

In Exercises 7–10, without multiplying, match the multiplication problem with its answer. Explain your reasoning.

A. 12.22 **B.** 1.222 **C.** 122.2 **D.** 0.1222

7. 52×2.35

8. 0.52×0.235

9. 5.2×0.235

10. 5.2×2.35

In Exercises 11–14, place the decimal point in the product.

11. $4.1 \times 2.5 \stackrel{?}{=} 1025$

12. $6.113 \times 31 \stackrel{?}{=} 189503$

13. $2.01 \times 8.01 \stackrel{?}{=} 161001$

14. $5.6 \times 2.115 \stackrel{?}{=} 118440$

15. **REASONING** Multiply 2000 by 0.2, 0.5, 0.8, 0.9, 0.95, and 0.99. What happens to the product as the second factor gets closer and closer to 1?

ALGEBRA AND MENTAL MATH In Exercises 16–18, solve.

16. $0.15 \times m = 0.45$

17. $n \times 2.01 = 6.03$

18. $2 \times 2.2 = t$

GEOMETRY In Exercises 19–21, find the area of the figure.

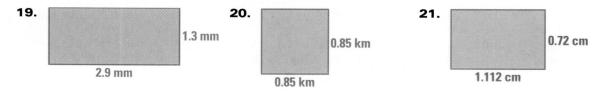

19.

1.3 mm
2.9 mm

20.

0.85 km
0.85 km

21.

0.72 cm
1.112 cm

MAKING AN ESTIMATE In Exercises 22–30, find the product. Use estimation to check that your answer is reasonable.

22. 2.25×5.61

23. 0.41×3.507

24. 5.89×1.125

25. 7.72×0.08

26. 6.643×1.495

27. 0.034×8.802

28. 0.985×2.5

29. 7.71×9.44

30. 5.1×0.02

MEASUREMENT Use a calculator to rewrite the length in centimeters. Use 1 in. = 2.54 cm. (Sample: 2 in. = 2 × 2.54 cm = 5.08 cm)

31. 4 in.

32. 6.9 in.

33. 0.4 in.

34. 0.561 in.

35. 20 in.

36. 0.1 in.

37. 1 ft

38. 2.5 ft

In Exercises 39–44, write a multiplication problem that you could use to answer the question. Then answer the question.

39. What is $\frac{3}{10}$ of 6?

40. What is 12% of 80?

41. What is 48% of 6.75?

42. What is 74% of 74?

43. What is $\frac{43}{100}$ of 9.5?

44. What is $\frac{9}{10}$ of 8.1?

CAREERS In Exercises 45 and 46, use the following information. The table at the right shows the average hourly pay for a college graduate just starting a career. (Source: Postsecondary Education Opportunity, 1995)

45. Find the weekly pay for an engineering major who works 40 hours per week.

46. Find the amount of money saved for every hour of work by a business major who saves 20% of his or her pay.

Degree	Hourly pay
Engineering	$17.09
Business	$13.68
Education	$10.91
Communications	$10.49

STANDARDIZED TEST PRACTICE

47. What percent of the diagram shown at the right is shaded?

A 2%   **B** 5%   **C** 10%   **D** 20%

48. What percent of the diagram shown at the right is *not* shaded?

A 12%   **B** 18%   **C** 80%   **D** 90%

49. Which of the four amounts is *not* equal to any of the other three?

A 25% of 80   **B** 5% of 200   **C** 40% of 50   **D** 16% of 125

50. BUILDING YOUR PROJECT For your restaurant's *Employee Training Manual,* explain how to calculate a 15% tip for a bill. Use the bill at the right as an example. What should the tip be for this bill?

Show another sample bill for which the tip is about $2. Show a third sample bill for which the tip is about $5.

51. COMMUNICATING ABOUT MATHEMATICS (page 197) Colored cotton has natural defenses against insects. Suppose growers can raise crops using only 5% of the pesticides needed for raising white cotton. If it costs $250 per acre of white cotton for pesticides, how much would you expect to spend per acre of colored cotton?

	DUSTY SOMBRERO	
2	burritos 1.50 each	3.00
1	rice 1.25	1.25
2	beans 1.30 each	2.60
2	iced tea 0.75 each	1.50
	Total: _____	

Thank You

SPIRAL REVIEW

ALGEBRA AND MENTAL MATH In Exercises 1–4, solve. (1.6)

1. $x + 15 = 33$ **2.** $54 - y = 45$ **3.** $4.5 \cdot m = 45$ **4.** $n \div 100 = 0.64$

In Exercises 5–7, insert parentheses to make the statement true. (2.5)

5. $27 - 9 - 4 + 2 = 24$ **6.** $8 + 2 \times 6 \div 4 = 15$ **7.** $12 \div 6 + 6 \times 7 = 7$

In Exercises 8 and 9, order the numbers from least to greatest. (3.5)

8. 1.13, 1.03, 1.30, 1.02   **9.** 9.45, 9.4, 9.54, 9.5

In Exercises 10–13, complete the statement. (3.7)

10. $3^4 = \boxed{?}$ **11.** $6^{\boxed{?}} = 216$ **12.** $\boxed{?}^{\,6} = 64$ **13.** $\boxed{?}^{\,3} = 125$

In Exercises 14–16, sketch a model that represents the decimal. (3.5)

14. 0.65   **15.** 0.87   **16.** 0.32

17. LUNCH SURVEY In a survey, 150 sixth-grade students were asked if they bring or buy their lunches for school. Thirty-eight percent said they bring their lunches. How many students is this? How many students buy their lunches? (3.8)

Take this test as you would take a test in class. The answers to the exercises are given in the back of the book.

In Exercises 1–6, use vertical form to add or subtract. (4.1, 4.2)

1. $3.09 + 6.14$

2. $\$7.59 - \$3.16$

3. $3.1 + 0.85$

4. $14 - 4.82$

5. $27.96 - 16.34$

6. $\$4.75 + \$19.30 + \$0.22$

In Exercises 7–9, estimate. Describe the estimation procedure you used. (4.3)

7. $\$6.43 + \$5.29$

8. $33,840 - 7800$

9. $\$9.17 + \$8.05 + \$12.36$

ALGEBRA In Exercises 10–15, use mental math or paper and pencil to solve. (4.1–4.4)

10. $4.75 + x = 8.25$

11. $5.79 - y = 1.23$

12. $m - 25.05 = 10.85$

13. $n + 0.58 = 3.64$

14. $z \times 0.1 = 0.054$

15. $2.4 \times p = 0.12$

GEOMETRY In Exercises 16–18, find the value of x. (4.1–4.4)

16. Perimeter is 27.5 units.

17. Perimeter is x units.

18. Area is x square units.

In Exercises 19–21, write a multiplication problem that you could use to answer the question. Then answer the question. (4.4)

19. What is 0.8 of 75?

20. What is $\dfrac{5}{10}$ of 37?

21. What is 35% of 46?

CONSUMER ECONOMICS In Exercises 22–24, use the menu at the right. (4.1–4.4)

22. Estimate the cost of a garden salad, a ravioli dinner, and a glass of iced tea. You have $9 to spend on your meal and don't need to leave a tip. What dessert can you order?

23. Find 4 items from the menu that total $11.18. Explain how you solved the problem.

24. You order a lasagna dinner, a Caesar salad, and a glass of soda. You give the server a tip that is 15% of your total bill. How much did you spend?

Dinners

Spaghetti.....	$4.95
Lasagna.......	$6.25
Ravioli..........	$5.45

Drinks

Milk.............	$0.68
Soda............	$1.05
Iced Tea.......	$0.79

Salads

Garden..........	$1.29
Caesar..........	$2.85

Desserts

Pie.................	$2.59
Ice Cream......	$1.18

4.5

Dividing a Decimal by a Whole Number

What you should learn:

Goal 1 How to divide a decimal by a whole number

Goal 2 How to use decimal division to solve real-life problems

Why you should learn it:

Decimal division can be used to help split the cost of something with others. An example is finding a person's share of a restaurant bill.

Goal 1 DIVIDING DECIMALS

Example 1 ▷ Modeling Decimal Division

You can use base-ten pieces to model $2.8 \div 2$.

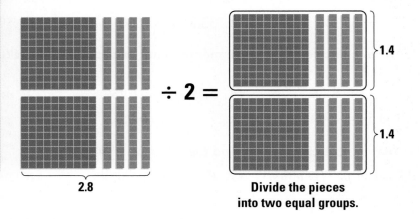

$\div 2 =$

| 2.8 | | Divide the pieces into two equal groups. |

1.4

1.4

From the model, you can see that $2.8 \div 2 = 1.4$.

Another way to divide decimals is to use long division. When you do long division with decimals, line up the decimal places in the quotient with the decimal places in the dividend.

Example 2 ▷ Using Long Division

Use long division to find $6.9 \div 3$.

Solution

$$\begin{array}{r} 2.3 \\ 3\overline{)6.9} \\ \underline{6.\!\downarrow} \\ 0.9 \\ \underline{0.9} \\ 0 \end{array}$$

Line up the decimal places.

$2 \times 3 = 6$

Bring down the 9.

$3 \times 0.3 = 0.9$

Notice that the steps for dividing decimals using long division are the same as the steps for long division with whole numbers.

STUDY TIP

When you divide with decimals, you can use estimation to check whether you have put the decimal point in the right position. In Example 2, since $6 \div 3 = 2$, you know that the answer is about 2, not 0.2 or 20.

Goal 2 SOLVING REAL-LIFE PROBLEMS

Example 3 ▷ **Dividing Decimals**

Two groups of people are in a restaurant. How much should each person pay?

REAL LIFE
Restaurants

a. 6 people are sharing a bill of $43.08.

b. 12 people are sharing a bill of $118.32.

Solution

a. To find each person's share, divide $43.08 by 6. Line up the decimal places in the quotient with the decimal places in the dividend.

$$
\begin{array}{r}
7.18 \\
6)\overline{43.08} \\
\underline{42.} \\
1.0 \\
\underline{.6} \\
.48 \\
\underline{.48} \\
0
\end{array}
$$

Line up the decimal places.

$6 \times 7 = 42$

Bring down the 0.

$6 \times 0.1 = 0.6$

Bring down the 8.

$6 \times 0.08 = 0.48$

TOOLBOX

Estimating and Division, page 651

✔**Check:** Because $42 \div 6 = 7$, you know that the answer is about 7. Your answer is reasonable. Each person's share is $7.18.

b. To find each person's share, divide $118.32 by 12. Line up the decimal places in the quotient with the decimal places in the dividend.

$$
\begin{array}{r}
9.86 \\
12)\overline{118.32} \\
\underline{108.} \\
10.3 \\
\underline{9.6} \\
.72 \\
\underline{.72} \\
0
\end{array}
$$

Line up the decimal places.

$12 \times 9 = 108$

Bring down the 3.

$12 \times 0.8 = 9.6$

Bring down the 2.

$12 \times 0.06 = 0.72$

ONGOING ASSESSMENT

Talk About It
· · · · · · · · · · · · · · · · · ·

Draw a base-ten model of a division problem that you have made up. Exchange drawings with a partner.

1. Draw the solution to the model.

2. Check your results using long division.

✔**Check:** Because $120 \div 12 = 10$, you know that the answer is about 10. Each person's share is $9.86.

GUIDED PRACTICE

1. Write the division problem shown by the base-ten pieces. (Large square = 1 unit)

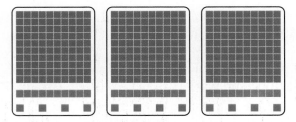

2. Draw a sketch of 4.8 ÷ 3. Then solve.

3. **WRITING** Explain how to divide a decimal by a whole number using long division.

In Exercises 4–7, estimate the answer. Then draw a sketch to find the exact answer. Write and solve using long division.

4. 10.8 ÷ 4   5. 6.5 ÷ 2   6. 9.9 ÷ 3   7. 4.6 ÷ 4

PRACTICE AND PROBLEM SOLVING

In Exercises 8 and 9, write the problem shown by the base-ten pieces. (Large square = 1 unit)

8. 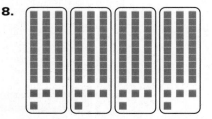   9.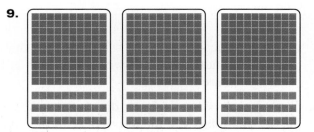

In Exercises 10–13, use long division to solve. Use estimation to evaluate the solution for reasonableness.

10. 8.25 ÷ 5   11. 17.4 ÷ 3   12. 133.6 ÷ 8   13. 100.38 ÷ 21

ALGEBRA AND MENTAL MATH In Exercises 14–16, solve.

14. $x \div 2 = 4.5$ 15. $12.6 \div y = 4.2$ 16. $n \div 4 = 2.5$

17. Consider the following division problems. What happens to the quotient when the divisor is doubled?

    48 ÷ 2, 48 ÷ 4, 48 ÷ 8, 48 ÷ 16

18. **ERROR ANALYSIS** Find and correct the error in the problem at the right. How can you tell that the answer is wrong?

$$
\begin{array}{r}
80.3 \\
7\overline{)56.21} \\
56 \\
\hline
021 \\
21 \\
\hline
0 \\
\end{array}
$$

REASONING In Exercises 19 and 20, complete the statement with *sometimes, always,* or *never.* Give an example.

19. A number less than 1 divided by a whole number is _?_ greater than 1.

20. A decimal divided by a whole number is _?_ a decimal.

READING HABITS In Exercises 21–23, use the table at the right. It shows the amount of money spent per year per person on reading material from 1993 through 1995 in the United States. (Source: Veronis, Suhler & Associates)

Year	1993	1994	1995
Newspapers	$48.25	$49.12	$48.85
Magazines	$35.27	$36.36	$36.10
Books	$75.28	$79.69	$80.62

21. Find the amount spent *per week* on books in 1993. (Use 52 weeks in a year.)

22. Find the amount spent *per month* in each category in 1995.

23. Which category increased the most from 1993 to 1994?

24. **WOODWORKING** You are building a birdhouse from a piece of wood that is 56.88 in. long and 9.48 in. wide. You divide the wood into 6 equal-sized pieces. Draw a diagram of this division. What are the dimensions of each piece?

STANDARDIZED TEST PRACTICE

25. Determine the length of the side labeled *x.*

(**A**) 1.01 cm   (**B**) 2.5 cm

(**C**) 5.5 cm   (**D**) 10.1 cm

Area = 20.2 cm² | 2 cm

x

EXPLORATION AND EXTENSION

PORTFOLIO

26. **BUILDING YOUR PROJECT** Hamburger meat loses about 20% of its weight when cooked. In your restaurant's *Employee Training Manual,* draw a diagram for your employees to explain why they need to begin with 5 oz of uncooked hamburger meat to end up with $\frac{1}{4}$ lb of cooked meat.

$\left(Hint: 16 \text{ oz} = 1 \text{ lb}; 4 \text{ oz} = \frac{1}{4} \text{ lb}\right)$

Using Powers of Ten to **Multiply** and **Divide**

Goal 1 How to multiply a decimal by a power of ten

Goal 2 How to divide a decimal by a power of ten

Why you should learn it:

Knowing how to multiply and divide by powers of ten can help you evaluate large and small numbers. An example is the power of a flash of lightning.

Goal 1 MULTIPLYING BY POWERS OF TEN

In Lesson 3.7, you studied how to use exponents to write powers of 10. Here are some examples.

$$10^2 = 100 \qquad 10^3 = 1000 \qquad 10^4 = 10{,}000$$

What happens to a number when you multiply it by a power of 10?

LESSON INVESTIGATION

Investigating Multiplication by Powers of Ten

GROUP ACTIVITY Use a calculator to solve each problem. Record each problem and answer.

1. 14×10 **2.** 14×100 **3.** 14×1000
4. 2.73×10 **5.** 2.73×100 **6.** 2.73×1000

With each of the following, try to predict the answer before using your calculator.

7. 300×1000 **8.** 20.9×100 **9.** 0.002×10

In your group, discuss how to mentally multiply a whole number or a decimal by a power of 10.

As you may have discovered, you can multiply a number by a power of 10 by moving the decimal point one place *to the right* for each zero in the power of 10.

Example 1 Multiplying by Powers of Ten

a. $2.4 \times 1000 = 2400.0$ 1000 has 3 zeros. Move decimal point 3 places to the right.

b. $3.42 \times 10 = 34.2$ 10 has 1 zero. Move decimal point 1 place to the right.

c. $0.035 \times 100 = 03.5$ 100 has 2 zeros. Move decimal point 2 places to the right.

d. $1.04 \times 10^3 = 1040.0$ 10^3, or 1000, has 3 zeros. Move decimal point 3 places to the right.

e. $57.8 \times 10^2 = 5780.0$ 10^2, or 100, has 2 zeros. Move decimal point 2 places to the right.

When you multiply by a power of 10, the decimal point moves to the right. What happens when you *divide* by a power of 10?

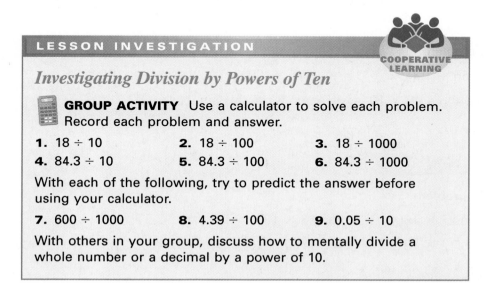

LESSON INVESTIGATION

COOPERATIVE LEARNING

Investigating Division by Powers of Ten

GROUP ACTIVITY Use a calculator to solve each problem. Record each problem and answer.

1. 18 ÷ 10   **2.** 18 ÷ 100   **3.** 18 ÷ 1000
4. 84.3 ÷ 10   **5.** 84.3 ÷ 100   **6.** 84.3 ÷ 1000

With each of the following, try to predict the answer before using your calculator.

7. 600 ÷ 1000   **8.** 4.39 ÷ 100   **9.** 0.05 ÷ 10

With others in your group, discuss how to mentally divide a whole number or a decimal by a power of 10.

As you may have discovered, you can divide a number by a power of 10 by moving the decimal point one place *to the left* for each zero in the power of 10.

Example 2 Dividing by Powers of Ten

Solve the division problem.

a. 48.3 ÷ 1000   **b.** 6.57 ÷ 10

c. 29.2 ÷ 100   **d.** $3.91 \div 10^2$

Solution

a. 48.3 ÷ 1000 = 0.0483   1000 has 3 zeros. Move decimal point 3 places to the left.

b. 6.57 ÷ 10 = 0.657   10 has 1 zero. Move decimal point 1 place to the left.

c. 29.2 ÷ 100 = 0.292   100 has 2 zeros. Move decimal point 2 places to the left.

d. $3.91 \div 10^2 = 0.0391$ 10^2, or 100, has 2 zeros. Move decimal point 2 places to the left.

ONGOING ASSESSMENT

Write About It

Use mental math to solve each equation. Discuss your answers with a partner. Then use a calculator to check your answers.

1. $3.4 \cdot n = 340$

2. $42 \cdot m = 42,000$

3. $5.6 \div x = 0.56$

4. $97.2 \div c = 0.972$

4.6 Exercises

Extra Practice, page 627

GUIDED PRACTICE

1. Explain how to multiply and divide a number by a power of 10. Give examples to support your answer.

2. Explain how to remember which way to move the decimal point when multiplying or dividing by a power of 10.

In Exercises 3–6, solve the problem.

3. 0.42×10
4. $56 \div 1000$
5. $170 \div 100$
6. 8.3×10^3

7. **SCIENCE** Humans have about 90×10^2 taste buds. Write this number in decimal form.

PRACTICE AND PROBLEM SOLVING

In Exercises 8–15, solve the problem.

8. 850×100
9. 0.23×1000
10. 63×100
11. 2.37×10
12. 0.019×100
13. 0.12×10^4
14. 1450×10^2
15. 110×10^3

In Exercises 16–23, solve the problem.

16. $320 \div 10$
17. $4 \div 1000$
18. $0.4 \div 100$
19. $799 \div 10$
20. $0.46 \div 100$
21. $462 \div 10^3$
22. $8000 \div 10^4$
23. $52 \div 10^2$

REAL-LIFE NUMBERS In Exercises 24–30, write the number in decimal form.

24. A 12 ounce jar of peanut butter is made from $5480 \div 10$ peanuts.

25. A half-hour TV cartoon is made up of 18×1000 drawings.

26. Caterpillars have more than 0.2×10^4 muscles.

27. A bee flaps its wings about $25{,}000 \div 100$ times per second.

28. By the time they are 70 years old, most people have slept 220×10^3 hours.

29. The human body has over $40{,}000 \div 1000$ miles of nerves.

30. A flash of lightning can release as much as 3.75×10^9 kilowatts of energy.

ALGEBRA AND MENTAL MATH In Exercises 31–36, use mental math to solve. Then use a calculator to check.

31. $7 \div x = 0.7$

32. $y \times 1000 = 39$

33. $z \times 100 = 51,800$

34. $0.55 \times t = 550$

35. $4600 \div m = 4.6$

36. $n \div 10,000 = 0.09876$

NUMBER SENSE In Exercises 37–42, complete the statement using >, <, or =.

37. 0.46×10 ? $46 \div 100$

38. 0.018×1000 ? $280 \div 100$

39. $25 \div 100$? $30 \div 10$

40. 0.505×1000 ? 50.5×10

41. 1.43×10^3 ? 200×10

42. 3.7×10^4 ? 3700

43. **GEOMETRY** A square mile has 640 acres. If a square mile is divided evenly among 100 people, how many acres will each person get?

44. **ASTRONOMY** The nearest star (other than the sun) is about 25 million million miles away. Write this number in decimal form. How many zeros does it have?

45. a. **BIOLOGY** There are approximately 50×10^{12} cells in the human body. Write this number in decimal form.

   b. The human body has about 100 billion nerve cells in the brain. Write this number in decimal form. What percent of the cells in the human body are nerve cells in the brain?

Real Life...
Real People

Biology
Carrie Shilyansky of San Marino, CA, won a 1997 *Westinghouse Science Talent Search* scholarship. It was awarded for her biological study of marine mollusks.

STANDARDIZED TEST PRACTICE

46. Which of the following numbers is the largest?

   A 2,000,000   **B** 2×10^5 **C** 20×10^4 **D** $200 \times 10 \times 10^2$

47. Which of the following statements is *not* true?

   A 10 kilograms = 10^4 grams   **B** 100 centimeters = 1×10^3 millimeters

   C 10^2 meters = 1 kilometer   **D** 10^2 liters = 1×10^5 milliliters

48. Dave saves 10^3 pennies each week. If he saves this amount each week for 10 years, how much money will he save?

   A $520   **B** $5200   **C** $52,000   **D** $520,000

49. WORLD POPULATIONS Write each country's population in decimal form. Then order the populations from least to greatest.

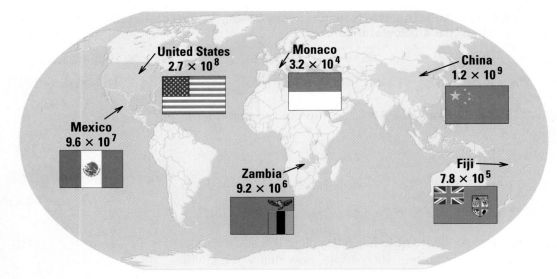

United States
2.7×10^8

Monaco
3.2×10^4

China
1.2×10^9

Mexico
9.6×10^7

Zambia
9.2×10^6

Fiji
7.8×10^5

SPIRAL REVIEW

USING A GRAPH In Exercises 1–3, use the graph at the right, that shows the number of people out of 100 who buy different writing instruments. (Source: Writing Instrument Manufacturers Association) **(1.4, 3.4)**

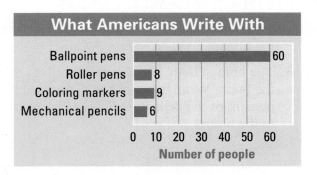

What Americans Write With

Ballpoint pens	60
Roller pens	8
Coloring markers	9
Mechanical pencils	6

0 10 20 30 40 50 60
Number of people

1. How many more people chose ballpoint pens than roller pens?

2. What fraction of the people chose coloring markers?

3. What percent of the people chose mechanical pencils?

GUESS, CHECK, AND REVISE In Exercises 4 and 5, complete the statement using +, −, ×, or ÷. **(2.5)**

4. $8 + 12$ **?** $4 - 1 = 10$ 5. $6 \times 3 + 9$ **?** $9 = 18$

NUMBER SENSE In Exercises 6–8, complete the statement using >, <, or =. **(3.5)**

6. 2.30 **?** 2.3 7. 0.16 **?** 0.61 8. 4.7 **?** 4.07

In Exercises 9–12, evaluate the power. **(3.7)**

9. 2^6 10. 3^5 11. 6^3 12. 4^4

Source of a Different Color

READ About It

The idea for Sally Fox's business started when she planted some brown cotton seeds in her backyard. When the cotton plants grew, Sally was surprised that instead of being all brown, the cotton grew in various shades of tan, brown, green, and even pink! Over the next few years, Sally cross-bred the plants to get many other colors. Now she grows about 600 acres of the colored cotton, and has recruited other growers who raise about 5000 more acres.

White cotton yields 2.5 bales per acre and colored cotton only yields 2 bales per acre. But manufacturers will pay twice as much for the colored kind. It costs $1.95 to spin a pound of colored cotton and only $1.75 to spin a pound of white cotton. But dyeing the white cotton costs $2.00 per pound, and the natural colors don't need to be dyed.

WRITE About It

1. In the United States, there are about 1.7×10^7 acres of white cotton. How many bales of white cotton are grown? Explain.

2. Use the data in Exercise 1. What fraction of the total land area used to raise cotton is used to raise colored cotton? Explain your reasoning.

3. How much more white cotton than colored cotton can be grown per acre of land? Draw a bar graph to represent your result.

4. A bale of cotton weighs 500 pounds. How much would it cost to spin and dye a bale of white cotton? Explain.

5. What percent of the colored cotton grown in this country is grown on Sally Fox's own fields? Write your answer as a sentence.

LAB 4.7

COOPERATIVE LEARNING

Investigating Decimal Division

You can use base-ten grid paper to model division problems. What the model means depends on what you let each small square represent. Here are two examples.

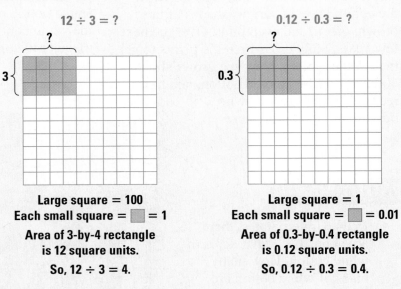

$$12 \div 3 = ?$$

3 { ?

Large square = 100
Each small square = ☐ = 1
Area of 3-by-4 rectangle
is 12 square units.
So, 12 ÷ 3 = 4.

$$0.12 \div 0.3 = ?$$

0.3 { ?

Large square = 1
Each small square = ☐ = 0.01
Area of 0.3-by-0.4 rectangle
is 0.12 square units.
So, 0.12 ÷ 0.3 = 0.4.

Materials Needed
- calculator
- base-ten grid paper
- pencils

Part A USING AREA MODELS

1. Write *two* division problems that can be modeled by each base-ten sketch: one with two whole numbers and one with two decimals. For each of your two problems, tell what a large square and a small square represent. Write the answer.

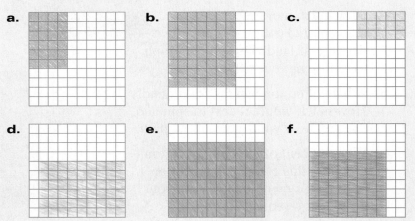

a. b. c.

d. e. f.

2. Use a calculator to divide. With others in your group, discuss any patterns that you see.

    a. $0.012 \div 0.003$ **b.** $21 \div 0.42$ **c.** $0.0472 \div 0.04$
        $1.2 \div 0.3$ $210 \div 4.2$ $0.472 \div 0.4$
        $12 \div 3$ $2100 \div 42$ $4.72 \div 4$

3. Use the patterns you saw above. Write 3 division problems that have the same answer. Which is easiest for you to solve? Why?

Part **C** MAKING CONNECTIONS

4. Solve the division problems. Use a calculator to check your answers. Explain how the two division problems are related.

    Decimal divisor   **Whole number divisor**

    a. $0.02\overline{)84.4}$ $2\overline{)8440}$

    b. $0.7\overline{)2.87}$ $7\overline{)28.7}$

5. You may have discovered that you need to rewrite a division problem that has a decimal divisor. What rules can you follow to rewrite the problem so that it has a whole number divisor?

6. Solve each division problem. First write a division problem with a whole number divisor that has the same answer.

    a. $0.03\overline{)25.8}$ **b.** $0.4\overline{)32.8}$ **c.** $1.2\overline{)1.44}$

NOW TRY THESE

In Exercises 7–12, write a division problem with a whole number divisor that has the same answer. Then solve.

7. $1.2 \div 0.6$ 8. $1.2 \div 0.06$ 9. $0.12 \div 0.6$

10. $12 \div 0.6$ 11. $120 \div 0.6$ 12. $12 \div 0.06$

13. Explain which division problem has the greatest answer without dividing.

    A. $3.2 \div 8$ B. $3.2 \div 0.8$ C. $3.2 \div 0.08$

14. Solve using mental math. Use a calculator to check your answers.

    a. $1.6 \div n = 4$ **b.** $1.6 \div n = 40$ **c.** $1.6 \div n = 400$

4.7

Dividing with **Decimals**

What you should learn:

Goal ① How to divide decimals

Goal ② How to use decimal division to solve real-life problems

Why you should learn it:

Decimal division can be used to help you compare the cost of two items that are different sizes. An example is finding the price per ounce of cans of soup.

Goal ① DIVIDING DECIMALS

To divide *by* a decimal, convert the division problem to a related one with a whole number divisor that has the same answer.

DIVIDING BY A DECIMAL

In both divisor and dividend, move the decimal point the same number of places in the same direction. To do this, multiply both by the power of ten that will make the divisor a whole number.

Example 1 Dividing Decimals

Solve each division problem.

a. $2.46 \div 0.3$ **b.** $28 \div 0.02$

Solution

a. Multiply the divisor and dividend by **10**.

$0.3 \overline{)2.46}$ — Move decimal points **1** place.

Solve the related division by a whole number.

$$\begin{array}{r} 8.2 \\ 3\overline{)24.6} \\ \underline{24}\downarrow \\ 06 \\ \underline{6} \\ 0 \end{array}$$

Because $24.6 \div 3 = 8.2$, $2.46 \div 0.3 = 8.2$.

✔**Check:** Multiply quotient and divisor.

$$\begin{array}{r} 8.2 \quad \text{Quotient} \\ \times\ 0.3 \quad \text{Divisor} \\ \hline 2.46 \quad \text{Dividend ✔} \end{array}$$

b. Multiply the divisor and dividend by **100**.

$0.02 \overline{)28.00}$ — Move decimal points **2** places.

Solve the related division by a whole number.

$$\begin{array}{r} 1400. \\ 2\overline{)2800.} \\ \underline{2}\downarrow \\ 08 \\ \underline{8} \\ 0 \end{array}$$
Fill quotient with **zeros** up to decimal point.

Because $2800 \div 2 = 1400$, $28 \div 0.02 = 1400$.

✔**Check:** Multiply quotient and divisor.

$$\begin{array}{r} 1400 \quad \text{Quotient} \\ \times\ 0.02 \quad \text{Divisor} \\ \hline 28.00 \quad \text{Dividend ✔} \end{array}$$

Example 2 Using Decimal Division

You have $12.35 to buy drinks for a picnic. Each bottle costs $0.65. How many bottles can you buy?

Solution

Divide $12.35 by $0.65.

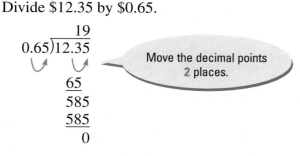

```
        19
0.65)12.35
      65
      585
      585
        0
```

Move the decimal points **2** places.

So, you can buy 19 bottles.

Example 3 Estimating with Decimal Division

A jar full of marbles weighs 2.5 kilograms (kg). The empty jar weighs 0.45 kg. About how many marbles do you think are in the jar?

Solution

Find the **weight of the marbles** by subtracting the **weight of the jar** from the **total weight**.

Weight of marbles = 2.5 kg − 0.45 kg = 2.05 kg

To estimate the number of marbles, you weigh a similar marble and find that its weight is 0.025 kg. Estimate the total number of marbles by dividing the weight of the marbles by 0.025.

```
          82
0.025)2.050
        200
         50
         50
          0
```

Add 0 to dividend and move decimal point **3** places.

So, there are about 82 marbles in the jar.

ONGOING ASSESSMENT

Write About It

Write a real-life problem that can be solved by the division problem.

1. 15.6 ÷ 0.3

2. 3.42 ÷ 0.29

Extra Practice, page 627

GUIDED PRACTICE

REASONING In Exercises 1 and 2, explain why the statement is false. Change exactly one word to make it true.

1. Before dividing decimals, you must change the quotient to a whole number.

2. Moving a decimal point two places to the right is the same as multiplying by 1000.

In Exercises 3–6, solve.

3. $13.2 \div 0.6$ 4. $1.32 \div 0.6$ 5. $13.2 \div 0.06$ 6. $1.32 \div 6$

PRACTICE AND PROBLEM SOLVING

In Exercises 7–10, write the smallest power of 10 that you would multiply by to make the number a whole number.

7. 9.3 8. 0.12 9. 3.05 10. 12.001

In Exercises 11–19, divide. Check your answer by multiplying.

11. $10.4 \div 0.8$ 12. $0.36 \div 0.9$ 13. $3.14 \div 0.2$

14. $33 \div 0.11$ 15. $24.75 \div 2.2$ 16. $0.816 \div 0.68$

17. $7.85 \div 0.005$ 18. $204.02 \div 5.05$ 19. $500 \div 0.25$

TECHNOLOGY In Exercises 20 and 21, use a calculator to evaluate the expression.

20. $3.34 + 6.4 \div 0.032$

21. $21.9 \div 0.073 - 40.5 \div 0.5$

22. **SCIENCE** In the photo, the onion cell is 55 mm wide. The actual cell is only 0.04 mm wide. Find how many times larger the picture is than the actual cell by dividing 55 by 0.04.

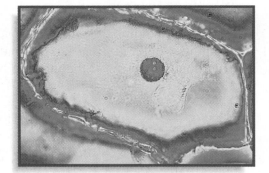

GEOMETRY Find the length of the side labeled s.

23. Area is 11.7 m^2.

24. Area is 6.25 km^2.

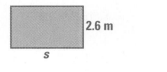
2.6 m
s

s
s

25. LARGEST VEGETABLES Six of the world records for vegetable weights are listed. Find the approximate weights in pounds by dividing by 0.45. (1 lb ≈ 0.45 kg) (Source: *Guinness Book of Records*)

Vegetable	Weight	Vegetable	Weight
Carrot	7.0 kg	Cucumber	9.1 kg
Onion	5.6 kg	Radish	17.2 kg
Pumpkin	449.0 kg	Zucchini	29.3 kg

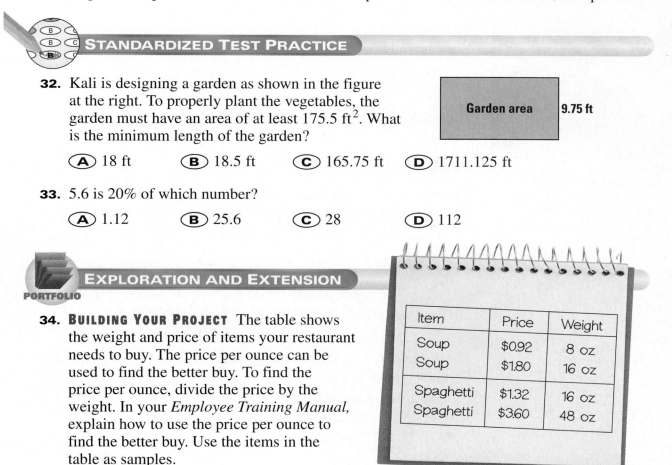

ALGEBRA AND MENTAL MATH In Exercises 26–28, use mental math to evaluate the expression when $b = 10$ and when $b = 100$.

26. $6.5 \div b$ **27.** $b \div 0.5$ **28.** $3 \times b \div 0.3$

In Exercises 29–31, find the price per meter by dividing by 0.305. (1 ft = 0.305 m)

29. Rope: $1.64 per foot   **30.** Ribbon: $0.41 per foot   **31.** Pine board: $2.46 per foot

STANDARDIZED TEST PRACTICE

32. Kali is designing a garden as shown in the figure at the right. To properly plant the vegetables, the garden must have an area of at least 175.5 ft^2. What is the minimum length of the garden?

Garden area	9.75 ft

   A 18 ft   **B** 18.5 ft   **C** 165.75 ft   **D** 1711.125 ft

33. 5.6 is 20% of which number?

   A 1.12   **B** 25.6   **C** 28   **D** 112

EXPLORATION AND EXTENSION

PORTFOLIO

34. BUILDING YOUR PROJECT The table shows the weight and price of items your restaurant needs to buy. The price per ounce can be used to find the better buy. To find the price per ounce, divide the price by the weight. In your *Employee Training Manual,* explain how to use the price per ounce to find the better buy. Use the items in the table as samples.

Item	Price	Weight
Soup	$0.92	8 oz
Soup	$1.80	16 oz
Spaghetti	$1.32	16 oz
Spaghetti	$3.60	48 oz

4.8

Problem Solving with Decimals and Percents

What you should learn:

Goal 1 How to solve real-life percent problems

Goal 2 How to solve problems with a bar graph

Why you should learn it:

Percents are used to help you analyze data. An example is reading a bar graph that shows people's favorite hobbies.

In 1994, the average American household spent $342 on their lawns and gardens. That was a 10% increase over 1993.

Goal 1 USING PERCENT IN REAL LIFE

In Lesson 4.4, you learned that you can use decimal multiplication to find a percent of a number.

Question What is 15% of 60?

Plan Rewrite 15% as 0.15. Then multiply.

Answer $0.15 \times 60 = 9$

You can solve many real-life problems by finding a percent of a number.

Example 1 ⟩ Finding Percents of Numbers

A school has 420 students. Because of the flu, 20% of the students are absent. How many are absent?

Solution

You can find how many are absent by finding 20% of 420.

$$20\% \times 420 = 0.2 \times 420 \qquad \text{Rewrite 20\% as 0.2.}$$
$$= 84 \qquad\qquad\quad \text{Multiply.}$$

There are 84 students absent from school.

Example 2 ⟩ Buying Something on Sale

The regular price of a video game is $49.80. It is on sale for 25% off the regular price. What is the discount? What is the sale price?

Solution

$$\textbf{Discount} = \textbf{Percent off} \times \textbf{Regular price}$$
$$= \mathbf{25\% \times \$49.80}$$
$$= \mathbf{0.25 \times \$49.80} \qquad \text{Rewrite 25\% as 0.25.}$$
$$= 12.45 \qquad\qquad\quad \text{Multiply.}$$

The discount is $12.45. To find the sale price, subtract the discount from the regular price.

$$
\begin{array}{ll}
\quad \$49.80 & \text{Regular price} \\
\underline{-\ 12.45} & \text{Discount} \\
\quad \$37.35 & \text{Sale price}
\end{array}
$$

The sale price is $37.35.

Goal 2 BAR GRAPHS AND PERCENTS

Example 3 Reading a Bar Graph

In a survey, 200 people were asked to name their favorite hobbies or activities. The 6 most popular are shown in the bar graph below. Find the number of people who named each hobby or activity.

REAL LIFE
Hobbies

Favorite Hobbies and Activities

	Reading	Cooking	Music	Gardening	Pets	Fishing
	43%	34%	32%	26%	25%	24%

Solution

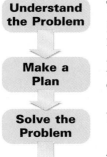

Understand the Problem

There were 200 people in the survey. Multiply the **percent** by 200 to find the **number of people who named each activity**.

Make a Plan

Multiply each **percent** by 200. Use a table to organize your results.

Solve the Problem

Use your plan.

Activity	Percent	Number Who Named Activity
Reading	43%	$0.43 \times 200 = 86$
Cooking	34%	$0.34 \times 200 = 68$
Music	32%	$0.32 \times 200 = 64$
Gardening	26%	$0.26 \times 200 = 52$
Pets	25%	$0.25 \times 200 = 50$
Fishing	24%	$0.24 \times 200 = 48$

Look Back

✔**Check:** Divide the **number of people who named each activity** by 200. This should equal the **percent given in the graph**. For example:

Reading: $86 \div 200 = 0.43 = 43\%$ ✔

ONGOING ASSESSMENT

Talk About It
. . . .
Use multiplication to answer each question. Then, discuss how you could use a model to answer the questions.

1. 25% of 60 = ?

2. 15% of 200 = ?

3. 60% of 30 = ?

GUIDED PRACTICE

In Exercises 1–3, match the shaded portion of the figure with the percent that it shows.

A. 25%   **B.** 10%   **C.** 50%

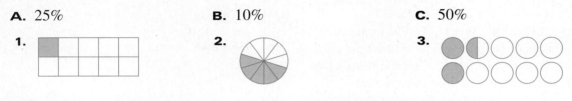

1.   **2.**   **3.**

In Exercises 4 and 5, you are given the number that is represented by the whole model. What number is shown by the shaded portion?

4. The whole is 120.   **5.** The whole is 75.

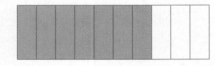

6. **PARTNER ACTIVITY** Write a problem about buying something on sale. Include the regular price and the percent discount. Exchange problems with a partner and solve.

PRACTICE AND PROBLEM SOLVING

In Exercises 7–10, find the number.

7. 30% of 80   **8.** 55% of 125   **9.** 15% of 240   **10.** 85% of 300

11. The regular price of a baseball bat is $37.50. It is on sale for 40% off the regular price. How much is the discount? What is the sale price?

12. It costs $8.00 per hour to rent skates at a park. Students get a 20% discount. How much is the discount? How much do students pay?

13. The drama club is having a dance. The admission is $4, but is increased by 25% if you don't wear a mask. How much is the increase? Without a mask, what is the admission?

14. You work at a restaurant for $5 per hour. You are given an 8% raise. What is your new hourly wage?

PETS **In Exercises 15–17, given the percent, find the number of dogs that can perform the trick. About 25,000,000 dogs in the United States can do some type of trick.** (Source: Frosty Paws)

15. Sit: 20%   **16.** Roll over: 10%   **17.** Fetch newspaper: 2%

SCIENCE The graph shows some of the factors that students in grades 3–12 say influence their interest in science. Find the number of students that listed the factor.
(Source: Purdue University National Science Outreach Survey)

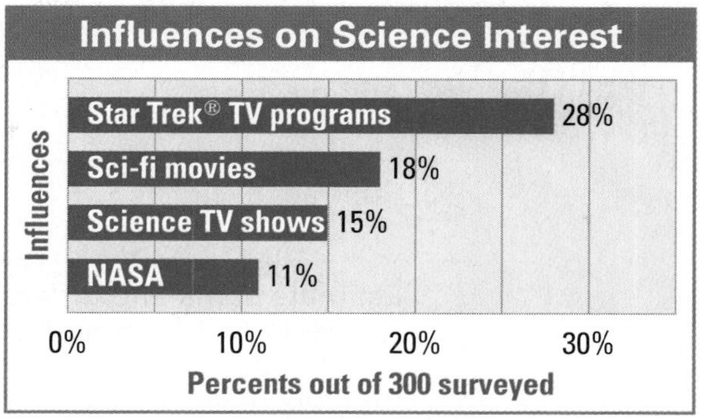

18. Star Trek® TV programs

19. Science fiction movies

20. Science TV shows

21. NASA

Influences on Science Interest

Influences	
Star Trek® TV programs	28%
Sci-fi movies	18%
Science TV shows	15%
NASA	11%

0%   10%   20%   30%
Percents out of 300 surveyed

RURAL LIVING The table below shows the percent of the population who live in rural areas for different states. You are given the population for the entire state. Find the number of people who live in rural areas.

State	Percent
Tennessee	39%
New Jersey	11%
Washington	24%
Kansas	31%

22. Tennessee 4,897,000

23. New Jersey 7,749,000

24. Washington 4,888,000

25. Kansas 2,478,000

STANDARDIZED TEST PRACTICE

26. Which of the four numbers is *not* equal to any of the other numbers?

   (A) 0.25   (B) $\frac{25}{100}$ (C) 2.5%   (D) 25%

27. Which of the four numbers is *not* equal to any of the other numbers?

   (A) 0.0089   (B) 0.089   (C) $\frac{89}{1000}$ (D) 8.9%

EXPLORATION AND EXTENSION

PORTFOLIO

28. **BUILDING YOUR PROJECT** In your *Employee Training Manual*, show how your employees can calculate their total pay. Then show them how to estimate their take-home pay by subtracting 20% from their total pay. Use the table, which shows the number of hours worked by four of your employees for one week.

Employee	Position	Hours	Hourly Wage
Sonya	Cook	32.0	$10.60
Tom	Dishwasher	38.5	$8.25
Alicia	Food Server	24.5	$5.75
Luis	Food Server	18.5	$5.75

WHAT *did you learn?*   **WHY** *did you learn it?*

		WHAT did you learn?	WHY did you learn it?
Skills	4.1	Add decimals.	Find the total of a restaurant bill.
	4.2	Subtract decimals.	Find the amount of change when making a purchase.
	4.3	Estimate sums and differences using rounding and front-end estimation.	Estimate how many items you can buy.
	4.4	Multiply decimals and find a percent of a number.	Find the sales tax for a purchase.
	4.5	Divide a decimal by a whole number.	Determine each person's share of a bill.
	4.6	Multiply and divide a decimal by a power of 10.	Find the distance from Earth to a distant star.
	4.7	Divide a number by a decimal.	Estimate the number of items, given information about one item.
	4.8	Use percents in real life.	Find the discount price of an item.
Strategies	4.1–4.8	Use problem solving strategies.	Solve a wide variety of real-life problems.
Using Data	4.1–4.8	Use tables and graphs.	Organize data and solve problems.

HOW *does it fit in the bigger picture of mathematics?*

In this chapter, you studied *operations* with decimals. In mathematics, the four basic operations are addition, subtraction, multiplication, and division.

You now know how to add, subtract, multiply, and divide whole numbers and decimals. In Chapters 7 and 8, you will learn how to add, subtract, multiply, and divide fractions. In Chapter 11, you will learn how to add and subtract integers.

As you study other chapters, remember to look for similarities in the ways different types of numbers are added, subtracted, multiplied, and divided. For example, adding $13 + 26$ is similar to adding the decimals $1.3 + 2.6$.

VOCABULARY

- rounding (p. 176)
- front-end estimation (p. 177)
- discount (p. 204)

4.1–4.2 ADDING AND SUBTRACTING DECIMALS

Example

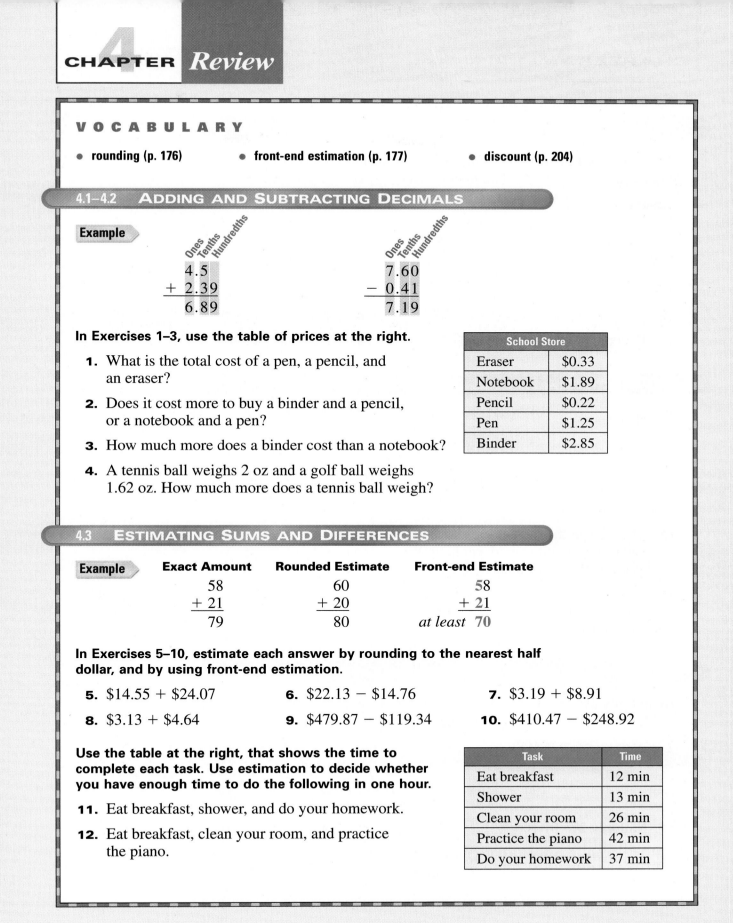

$$
\begin{array}{r}
4.5 \\
+\ 2.39 \\
\hline
6.89
\end{array}
\qquad
\begin{array}{r}
7.60 \\
-\ 0.41 \\
\hline
7.19
\end{array}
$$

Ones Tenths Hundredths

In Exercises 1–3, use the table of prices at the right.

School Store	
Eraser	$0.33
Notebook	$1.89
Pencil	$0.22
Pen	$1.25
Binder	$2.85

1. What is the total cost of a pen, a pencil, and an eraser?

2. Does it cost more to buy a binder and a pencil, or a notebook and a pen?

3. How much more does a binder cost than a notebook?

4. A tennis ball weighs 2 oz and a golf ball weighs 1.62 oz. How much more does a tennis ball weigh?

4.3 ESTIMATING SUMS AND DIFFERENCES

Example

Exact Amount	Rounded Estimate	Front-end Estimate
58	60	58
+ 21	+ 20	+ 21
79	80	*at least* 70

In Exercises 5–10, estimate each answer by rounding to the nearest half dollar, and by using front-end estimation.

5. $14.55 + $24.07

6. $22.13 − $14.76

7. $3.19 + $8.91

8. $3.13 + $4.64

9. $479.87 − $119.34

10. $410.47 − $248.92

Use the table at the right, that shows the time to complete each task. Use estimation to decide whether you have enough time to do the following in one hour.

Task	Time
Eat breakfast	12 min
Shower	13 min
Clean your room	26 min
Practice the piano	42 min
Do your homework	37 min

11. Eat breakfast, shower, and do your homework.

12. Eat breakfast, clean your room, and practice the piano.

4.4 MULTIPLYING DECIMALS AND FINDING PERCENT

When you multiply decimals, the number of decimal places in the product is equal to the total number of decimal places in the factors.

Example

$$\begin{array}{r} 0.25 \\ \times\ 1.3 \\ \hline 0.325 \end{array}$$

2 decimal places
1 decimal place
$2 + 1 = 3$, so the answer has 3 decimal places.

To find the percent of a number, write the percent as a decimal and multiply.

Example   What is 25% of 16? $0.25 \times 16 = 4$

13. Find the product of 4.52 and 12.35.

14. What is 15% of 24?

15. Find the product of 1300 and 0.06.

16. What is 40% of 80?

4.5 DIVIDING A DECIMAL BY A WHOLE NUMBER

Example

$$\begin{array}{r} 2.1 \\ 3\overline{)6.3} \\ \underline{6.} \\ 0.3 \\ \underline{.3} \\ 0 \end{array}$$

Line up the decimal places.

$3 \times 2 = 6$
Bring down the 3.
$3 \times 0.1 = 0.3$

17. The table at the right shows the flying speed of birds and insects in kilometers per hour. Write each speed as kilometers per minute.

18. The average American eats 2.8 lb of peanut butter per year. How much is this per month?
(Source: National Peanut Council, Inc.)

Animal	Speed
Pigeon	96.54
Monarch Butterfly	32.18
Honeybee	16.09

4.6 USING POWERS OF TEN TO MULTIPLY AND DIVIDE

To multiply by a power of 10, move the decimal point to the *right*. To divide by a power of 10, move the decimal point to the *left*.

Examples $35.21 \times 1000 = 35,210.0$

1000 has 3 zeros, so move the decimal point 3 places to the right.

$27.4 \div 100 = 0.274$

100 has 2 zeros, so move the decimal point 2 places to the left.

19. Multiply 275 by 100.

20. Divide 14.55 by 1000.

21. The average cost of a homemade Thanksgiving meal for 10 people is $31.66. How much is this per person? (Source: The American Farm Bureau)

4.7 DIVIDING WITH DECIMALS

Before dividing decimals, make sure that you move the decimal point the same number of places in the divisor and dividend.

Example

$$0.45\overline{)1.395}$$ gives 3.1

Multiply divisor and dividend by 100. Move the decimal points 2 places to the right.

22. The area of the rectangle is 6.25 m². Find the length of the side labeled x.

1.25 m

x

In Exercises 23–28, find the quotient.

23. $2.89 \div 0.08$

24. $8.37 \div 0.27$

25. $4.047 \div 0.095$

26. $57.3 \div 0.003$

27. $231.84 \div 12.6$

28. $42.37 \div 1.9$

4.8 PROBLEM SOLVING

To find the discount of an item on sale, write the percent marked off the regular price as a decimal. Multiply this by the regular price to get the discount. To find the sale price, subtract the discount from the regular price.

Example

Regular price: **$4.00**

Discount: **20%** of **$4.00** = **0.20 × $4.00**
                         = **$0.80**

Sale price: **$4.00 − $0.80 = $3.20**

29. A CD regularly sells for $16.50 and is marked 40% off. How much is the discount?

30. Find the sale price for a pair of sneakers that regularly sells for $54.00 and is marked 25% off.

31. Your school wants to order sets of counting cubes to use in math classes. The table shows the discount the school will receive for ordering sets of 100, 500, or 1000. What is the sale price for a set of each size?

Number in Set	100	500	1000
Regular Price	$12.50	$61.50	$125.00
Discount	8%	18%	27%

In Exercises 1–8, solve.

1. $3.45 + 7.02$ **2.** $14.75 - 4.52$ **3.** $4.55 + 5.401$ **4.** $16.001 - 4.98$

5. 3.5×6.15 **6.** $46.8 \div 8$ **7.** 2.25×4.45 **8.** $19.08 \div 2.65$

GEOMETRY **In Exercises 9–11, find the indicated measurement.**

9. Perimeter = ? **10.** Area = ? **11.** s = ?

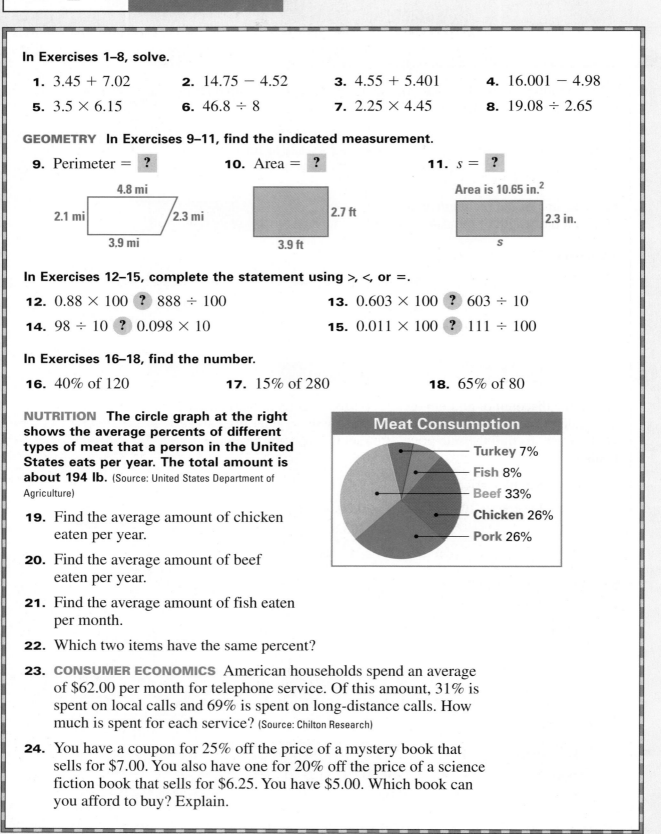

4.8 mi

2.1 mi 2.3 mi

3.9 mi

2.7 ft

3.9 ft

Area is 10.65 in.²

2.3 in.

s

In Exercises 12–15, complete the statement using >, <, or =.

12. 0.88×100 ? $888 \div 100$

13. 0.603×100 ? $603 \div 10$

14. $98 \div 10$? 0.098×10

15. 0.011×100 ? $111 \div 100$

In Exercises 16–18, find the number.

16. 40% of 120

17. 15% of 280

18. 65% of 80

NUTRITION The circle graph at the right shows the average percents of different types of meat that a person in the United States eats per year. The total amount is about 194 lb. (Source: United States Department of Agriculture)

Meat Consumption

Turkey 7%
Fish 8%
Beef 33%
Chicken 26%
Pork 26%

19. Find the average amount of chicken eaten per year.

20. Find the average amount of beef eaten per year.

21. Find the average amount of fish eaten per month.

22. Which two items have the same percent?

23. **CONSUMER ECONOMICS** American households spend an average of $62.00 per month for telephone service. Of this amount, 31% is spent on local calls and 69% is spent on long-distance calls. How much is spent for each service? (Source: Chilton Research)

24. You have a coupon for 25% off the price of a mystery book that sells for $7.00. You also have one for 20% off the price of a science fiction book that sells for $6.25. You have $5.00. Which book can you afford to buy? Explain.

1. You take $30 to the amusement park. It costs $17.49 to get into the park. At the park, you play 12 games that cost $.75 each. Which equation can be used to find C, your change at the end of the day?

   A $17.49 + 12(0.75) + C = 30$
   B $12(17.49 + 0.75) = 30 + C$
   C $17.49 + 12 + 0.75 + C = 30$
   D $17.49 + 0.75 + C = 30$

2. You bought 2 shirts that cost $14.95 each and a pair of jeans that cost $21.99. Sales tax on the items was $2.59. How much did you spend?

   A $39.53   **B** $49.38
   C $54.48   **D** $62.53

3. Tom can run a mile in 5.5 min. He runs at this pace in a 26.2 mi marathon. How long will it take Tom to run the marathon?

   A 31.7 min   **B** 143 min
   C 144.1 min   **D** 1441 min

4. Ashley walks 10 mi every week. The following data shows the number of miles she has walked so far this week. How many more miles will Ashley have to walk to complete her goal?

Sunday	1.3 mi
Monday	1.8 mi
Tuesday	2.1 mi
Wednesday	1.6 mi
Thursday	1.5 mi
Friday	1.1 mi

   A 0.6 mi   **B** 1.6 mi
   C 6.6 mi   **D** 9.4 mi

In Questions 5–7, use the following information. A music store sold 300 cassette tapes last month. Of these, 25% were country, 30% were rock, and 22% were rap.

5. These three types of music represent what percent of cassette tapes sold last month?

   A 87%   **B** 77%
   C 55%   **D** 23%

6. How many rock cassette tapes were sold last month?

   A 60   **B** 66
   C 90   **D** 100

7. How many more country cassette tapes were sold last month than rap cassette tapes?

   A 3   **B** 9
   C 12   **D** 15

8. A store is having a sale on jackets. A jacket that costs $59.95 is discounted 25%. Without tax, the cost of the jacket is *about* ? .

   A $15   **B** $35
   C $45   **D** $55

9. Kristen Brechter makes $1000 per week. The following deductions are taken out of her paycheck. What are her total weekly deductions?

Federal Income Tax	$115.29
State Income Tax	$62.72
Social Security	$41.27
Insurance	$32.88

   A $747.84   **B** $251.16
   C $252.06   **D** $252.16

Statistics
and Graphs

COLLECTING AND ANALYZING DATA about the animals and plants living in and around a stream can help you understand the ecology of the area.

TECHNOLOGY

Technology resources accompanying this chapter:

- Interactive Real-Life Investigations
- Middle School Tutorial Software

CHAPTER THEME
Data Collection

MARKET RESEARCHERS survey people about products and services that they use and what they would like to have available.

SCIENCE The study of science is based on the careful collection and analysis of data.

Right or Left?

REAL LIFE
Data Collection

Perform the following experiment. Cut a hole in a sheet of paper. Hold the paper at arm's length and look through the hole at a small object. Close only your right eye, then only your left eye. Through which eye did you see the object? This is called your *dominant* eye. Collect the results for everyone in your class.

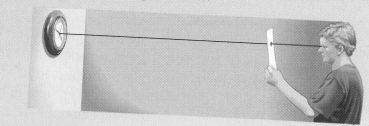

Think and Discuss

1. How many of your classmates are right-handed? left-handed?

2. How many people in your class have their left thumb on top when they fold their hands? their right? Compare these results with the dominant-eye results. Do you see any patterns?

3. How could you best display these results? Explain your reasoning.

PORTFOLIO

CHAPTER **PROJECT**

Our Class Survey

PROJECT DESCRIPTION

One way to gather information about a group of people is to conduct a survey. You will conduct a survey of your class and make a poster to display the results. You will ask the questions on the notebook on page 217. Your display will contain the data you collected in your survey. You will use the **TOPICS** on the next page to present your data.

GETTING STARTED

Talking It Over

- Have you ever been asked to answer a survey? What sorts of questions were you asked?

- Why do people conduct surveys? What kind of information would you like to know about people that you could find out by conducting a survey?

- If you surveyed the students in your class, do you think the results would be the same as if you surveyed another sixth grade class in your school? in another state? a third grade class? Why or why not?

Planning Your Project

- **Materials Needed:** poster board, paper, pens, colored pencils or markers, metric rulers

- Answer each of the questions on the notebook on page 217 on a separate sheet of paper. Divide the class into five groups. Each group should collect and tally the results of one question. Share the results with other groups. Each group should get a piece of poster board and write the title "Our Class Survey" on it. As you do the **BUILDING YOUR PROJECT** exercises throughout the chapter, you will add information to your poster.

Our Class Survey

1. How many letters are in your first name?

2. On what date of the month is your birthday?

3. On a scale of 1 to 5, with 1 being as often as possible and 5 being never, how often do you read for enjoyment?

4. What is your handspan in centimeters?

5. Choose your favorite of the subjects math, science, English, and social studies.

INTERNET

To find out about more surveys and data collection, go to: **http://www.mlmath.com**

LAB 5.1

COOPERATIVE LEARNING

Gathering and Organizing Data

Part A CONDUCTING A SURVEY

Materials Needed
- paper
- pencils

Niki read that the top five qualities that people look for in a friend are intelligence, loyalty, fun to be with, likes the person, and likes the same things. She decided to ask each of her classmates to name his or her most admired quality in a friend. Everyone gave an answer. She recorded the results on a tally sheet.

Is intelligent	IIII
Is loyal to me	HHT II
Is fun to be with	HHT I
Likes me	HHT HHT I
Likes same things	III
Is popular	II

After making the tally sheet, Niki counted the tallies and made a table.

Most Admired	Frequency
Is intelligent	4
Is loyal to me	7
Is fun to be with	6
Likes me	11
Likes same things	3
Is popular	2

1. How many students are in Niki's class?

2. What observations can you make from the frequency table?

3. Do the results in Niki's class agree with those she read? If not, why do you think they are different?

Part B ORGANIZING DATA

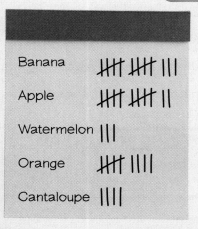

Banana	HHT HHT III
Apple	HHT HHT II
Watermelon	III
Orange	HHT IIII
Cantaloupe	IIII

David asked members of his class about their favorite fruits. Two students in the class were absent and did not answer. His tally sheet is shown at the left.

4. Use David's tally sheet to make a frequency table.

5. How many students are in David's class?

6. Which fruit is the most popular in David's class?

7. The next day, David asked the two students who missed class. The results changed the favorite fruit. Which fruit did they choose? Explain.

Loren asked his classmates about their favorite zoo animals.
The results are shown below.

Elephant	*Monkey*	*Lion*
Giraffe	*Elephant*	*Zebra*
Gorilla	*Monkey*	*Bear*
Lion	*Giraffe*	*Monkey*
Zebra	*Zebra*	*Elephant*
Monkey	*Bear*	*Monkey*
Lion	*Giraffe*	*Lion*
Zebra	*Gorilla*	*Monkey*
Elephant	*Lion*	*Lion*
Zebra	*Bear*	*Monkey*

San Diego Wild Animal Park

8. Organize the results with a tally sheet.

9. Use your tally sheet to help you make a frequency table.

10. In Loren's class, which zoo animal is most popular?

11. Suppose 200 more people are surveyed. Name three other animals you think might be selected.

NOW TRY THESE

COLLECTING DATA In Exercises 12 and 13, use the following information. The twelve most commonly used words in written English are:
the, be, of, and, to, a, in, he, have, it, for, I.

12. Choose a portion of a newspaper, magazine, or novel. The portion should have at least 300 words. Tally each time one of these twelve words is used. Make a frequency table that shows your results. Tell where you found your data.

13. Which of the twelve words occurred most often?

14. Which five letters of the alphabet do you think are the most commonly used? Describe how you could test your answer. Then test it.

Daily News

VOLUME 135, ISSUE 35

Counting Words

by John Agate

You can't just count every English word ever written to find the most commonly used words, so how do you do it? First, you make a selection of works that represent the written language. These may include a variety of newspapers, fiction, nonfiction, and government documents. You [are] to choose from a [vari]ety of sources be[caus]e the words used in [m]athematics text-book are different from the words used in a newspaper or novel. Once you have made this selection, you can have a computer make a tally of every word that appears in the text. The *Frequency Analysis of English Usage* used 500 works that included more than one million words. It determined that the most frequently used words are *the, be, of,* and *to.*

5.1

Line Plots

What you should learn:

Goal 1 How to draw a line plot

Goal 2 How to interpret a line plot

Why you should learn it:

Line plots can help you organize sports data, such as the number of games played in the World Series from 1976 through 1996.

Goal 1 DRAWING A LINE PLOT

Many real-life problems contain unorganized data or numbers. One way you can organize data is with a **line plot**.

Example 1 Drawing a Line Plot

REAL LIFE
Baseball

In the World Series, two baseball teams play from 4 to 7 games. The first team to win 4 games wins the World Series. The numbers of games played in each World Series held from 1976 to 1996 are shown below.

Year	Games	Year	Games	Year	Games	Year	Games
1976	4	1981	6	1986	7	1991	7
1977	6	1982	7	1987	7	1992	6
1978	6	1983	5	1988	5	1993	6
1979	7	1984	5	1989	4	1995	6
1980	6	1985	7	1990	4	1996	6

(Source: Major League Baseball)

Use a line plot to organize the numbers of games played.

Solution

To begin, draw a number line that includes the numbers in the data: 4, 5, 6, and 7. Below the number line, write a title that explains what is being counted.

Number of Games in the World Series (1976–1996)

Next, read through the data. As you read each number, draw an ✕ above the number.

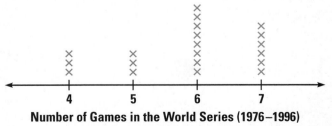

Number of Games in the World Series (1976–1996)

The most common number of games is 6. Also, the World Series is 6 or 7 games more often than it is 4 or 5 games.

Goal 2 INTERPRETING A LINE PLOT

The difference between the greatest number and the least number in a set of data is called the **range** of the data.

Example 2 Interpreting a Line Plot

You work for the Park Service. During one hour you net and weigh the sockeye salmon that climb one fish ladder and then return them to the fish ladder. What is the range of the weights?

Tech Link

Investigation 5,
Interactive
Real-Life
Investigations

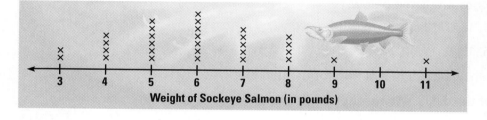

Weight of Sockeye Salmon (in pounds)

Solution

Range = Greatest weight − Smallest weight

= 11 − 3 = 8

The range is 8 pounds.

Example 3 Comparing Line Plots

Your friend collected the data below about coho salmon at another river. In general, are sockeye salmon or coho salmon heavier?

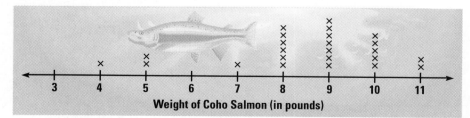

Weight of Coho Salmon (in pounds)

Solution

Most of the sockeye salmon weighed 5, 6, or 7 pounds. Most of the coho salmon weighed 8, 9, or 10 pounds. In general, the coho salmon are heavier.

Real Life...
Real Facts

Fish Ladders
A fish ladder is a series of ponds that allows a fish to climb over a dam.

TOOLBOX
Range, page 658

ONGOING ASSESSMENT

Talk About It

Use the line plots in Examples 2 and 3.

1. How many salmon did you weigh?

2. What is the range of weights of the coho salmon?

3. What else can you tell about the sockeye and coho salmon?

GUIDED PRACTICE

In Exercises 1–3, match the line plot with the description of the data.

A. Includes 10 numbers.   **B.** Has a range of 4.   **C.** Most common number is 5.

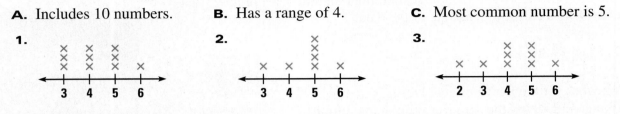

1.   **2.**   **3.**

4. WRITING Describe real-life data that you could organize using a line plot.

CARTOONS You asked the ages of 25 people who watch Saturday morning cartoons. The ages are listed below.

14, 8, 19, 12, 9, 7, 11, 16, 6, 18, 13, 12, 8,

10, 8, 18, 10, 7, 6, 15, 19, 8, 11, 12, 13

5. Make a line plot of the data. Include a title for the line plot.

6. What is the range of the data? What is the most common age?

PRACTICE AND PROBLEM SOLVING

In Exercises 7–9, make a line plot of the data. Find the most common number, the smallest and largest numbers, and the range of the data.

7. 6, 8, 5, 7, 11, 7, 10, 8, 5, 7

8. 36, 37, 36, 35, 37, 37, 36, 35, 38, 36

9. 1.4, 1.6, 1.6, 1.1, 1.6, 1.3, 1.4, 1.7, 1.6, 1.4

SCIENCE In Exercises 10 and 11, use the line plot below about meat-eating mammals. (Source: *Peterson Field Guide*)

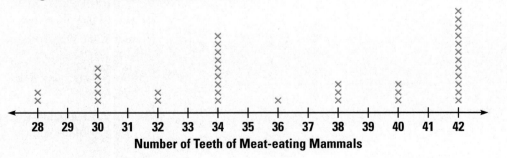

Number of Teeth of Meat-eating Mammals

10. What are the two most common numbers of teeth for meat-eating mammals?

11. Why do you think there are no odd numbers of teeth in the data?

BRAILLE In Exercises 12–14, use the table of Braille letters at the right.

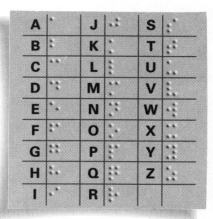

12. Create a line plot that shows the numbers of dots in each letter.

13. What are the two most common numbers of dots?

14. Write two statements that describe the data.

15. **FLAGS** Make a line plot that shows the number of colors used in each flag. What is the range of the data?

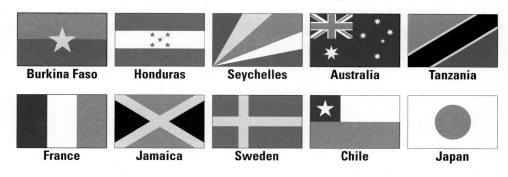

| Burkina Faso | Honduras | Seychelles | Australia | Tanzania |

| France | Jamaica | Sweden | Chile | Japan |

16. **RESEARCH** Find pictures of the flags of at least three more countries and add these data to your line plot from Exercise 15.

STANDARDIZED TEST PRACTICE

17. Use the line plot at the right to decide which of the statements is *not* true.

(A) The line plot contains 15 data values.

(B) The range of the data is 6.

(C) The most common data value is 7.

(D) Most of the data is greater than 6.

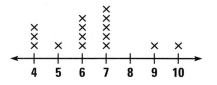

EXPLORATION AND EXTENSION

PORTFOLIO

18. **BUILDING YOUR PROJECT** The first question of your class survey was *How many letters are in your first name?* Use the results to make a line plot. What is the most common number of letters? How many letters are in the shortest name? How many letters are in the longest name?

5.2

Stem-and-Leaf Plots

What you should learn:

Goal 1 How to draw a stem-and-leaf plot

Goal 2 How to use a stem-and-leaf plot to solve real-life problems

Why you should learn it:

Stem-and-leaf plots can help you organize data, such as ordering the ages of a group of people.

Goal 1 DRAWING A STEM-AND-LEAF PLOT

Example 1 Drawing a Stem-and-Leaf Plot

Use a stem-and-leaf plot to order the following ages of family members at a reunion.

42, 12, 36, 43, 18, 21, 39, 24, 47, 55, 51, 26,

30, 45, 40, 27, 16, 28, 32, 29, 29, 22, 35, 44

Solution

First you need to create the stem of the stem-and-leaf plot. Use the tens' digits for the stem. The tens' digits are 1, 2, 3, 4, and 5. Write these digits in a column. Draw a line to the right of the digits.

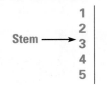

To create the leaves, you need to add the ones' digit of each age. Place the ones' digit to the right of the tens' digit for each number. For example, to plot 42, place a 2 to the right of the 4 in the stem.

```
1 | 2 8 6
2 | 1 4 6 7 8 9 9 2  ⎫
3 | 6 9 0 2 5         ⎬ Leaves
4 | 2 3 7 5 0 4       ⎭
5 | 5 1
```

To create an *ordered* stem-and-leaf plot, arrange the numbers in the leaves from least to greatest. Add a **key** that explains what the numbers in the stem and leaves represent.

```
1 | 2 6 8
2 | 1 2 4 6 7 8 9 9
3 | 0 2 5 6 9
4 | 0 2 3 4 5 7
5 | 1 5
```

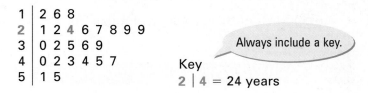

Always include a key.

Key
2 | 4 = 24 years

Use the stem-and-leaf plot to write the ages in order.

12, 16, 18, 21, 22, 24, 26, 27, 28, 29, 29, 30,

32, 35, 36, 39, 40, 42, 43, 44, 45, 47, 51, 55

Goal 2 STEM-AND-LEAF PLOTS IN REAL LIFE

Example 2 Drawing a Stem-and-Leaf Plot

REAL LIFE
History

The name of each First Lady from 1885 through 1997 and her age when she became First Lady are listed below. Make an ordered stem-and-leaf plot of the ages.

First Lady	Age	First Lady	Age
Frances Cleveland	21	Elizabeth Truman	60
Caroline Harrison	56	Mamie Eisenhower	56
Ida McKinley	49	Jacqueline Kennedy	31
Edith Roosevelt	39	Claudia Johnson	50
Helen Taft	47	Pat Nixon	56
Ellen Wilson	52	Elizabeth Ford	56
Florence Harding	60	Rosalynn Carter	49
Grace Coolidge	44	Nancy Reagan	59
Lou Hoover	54	Barbara Bush	63
Eleanor Roosevelt	48	Hillary Rodham Clinton	45

Real Life...
Real People

The youngest woman to serve as First Lady was Frances Cleveland. She married President Grover Cleveland one year after he was elected in 1884.

Solution

First, make an unordered stem-and-leaf plot of the data.

Stem   Leaves

```
2 | 1
3 | 9 1
4 | 9 7 4 8 9 5
5 | 6 2 4 6 0 6 6 9
6 | 0 0 3
```

Arrange the numbers in the leaves from least to greatest to create an ordered stem-and-leaf plot. Add a key that explains what the numbers in the stem and leaves represent.

```
2 | 1
3 | 1 9
4 | 4 5 7 8 9 9
5 | 0 2 4 6 6 6 6 9      Key
6 | 0 0 3                4 | 8 = 48 years
```

GUIDED PRACTICE

1. Describe how to make the stem and leaves of a stem-and-leaf plot.

2. Use the stem-and-leaf plot at the right. Redraw it so that it is ordered. Then write the data from least to greatest.

```
0 | 5 2 1
1 | 1 0 8 4 6
2 | 6 2 1 7 9      Key
3 | 3 9 3 5          1 | 6 = 16
```

3. The stem-and-leaf plot at the right represents *decimals*. The stem represents the ones' digits, and the leaves represent the tenths' digits. Write the numbers in increasing order.

```
7 | 1 2 7
8 | 2 5 6 8 9      Key
9 | 0 3 4 4 8        9 | 3 = 9.3
```

PRACTICE AND PROBLEM SOLVING

In Exercises 4–6, match the stem-and-leaf plot with its data.

A. 58, 61, 39, 55, 53, 32, 42, 67, 38, 43, 52, 41, 54, 42

B. 42, 55, 41, 56, 67, 52, 43, 46, 58, 42, 54, 61, 53

C. 67, 56, 43, 52, 42, 54, 42, 39, 61, 32, 55, 41, 53, 38

4.
```
3 | 2 8 9
4 | 1 2 2 3
5 | 2 3 4 5 6
6 | 1 7
        Key
        5 | 2 = 52
```

5.
```
4 | 1 2 2 3 6
5 | 2 3 4 5 6 8
6 | 1 7
        Key
        5 | 2 = 52
```

6.
```
3 | 2 8 9
4 | 1 2 2 3
5 | 2 3 4 5 8
6 | 1 7
        Key
        5 | 2 = 52
```

In Exercises 7–9, use the data below and the plot at the right.

17, 5, 2, 24, 31, 42, 30, 15, 56, 9,

31, 59, 34, 10, 16, 38, 59, 39, 23, 3

```
0 | 2 5
1 | 7
2 | 4
```

7. What numbers are missing from the stem?

8. Give a key for the stem-and-leaf plot. Is this the only key you could use?

9. Copy and complete the stem-and-leaf plot.

10. **BASKETBALL** The stem-and-leaf plot below shows unordered data of the heights (in inches) of players on a high school basketball team. Order the data in a new stem-and-leaf plot.

```
5 | 9 8
6 | 5 2 3 8 6 9 4 5 4 4 6 2 4      Key
7 | 0 2 1 0 1 1 0 0                  7 | 0 = 70 in.
```

WEATHER In Exercises 11–13, use the list below. It shows the record high temperature (°F) in December for each state that borders the Atlantic Ocean.

AL	85	FL	90	ME	69	MS	84	NY	74	SC	83
CT	74	GA	83	MD	77	NH	68	NC	81	TX	94
DE	74	LA	85	MA	73	NJ	75	RI	70	VA	80

11. Make an ordered stem-and-leaf plot of the temperatures. Remember to include a title.

12. Which state has the highest record high temperature?

13. What is the most common record high temperature?

14. **GEOMETRY** The dimensions of the rectangles that can be made on a 5-by-5 geoboard are shown below. Use a geoboard to help you find the perimeter of each rectangle. Then order the perimeters in a stem-and-leaf plot.

    1 by 1

    1 by 2   2 by 2

    1 by 3   2 by 3   3 by 3

    1 by 4   2 by 4   3 by 4   4 by 4

STANDARDIZED TEST PRACTICE

15. Round 105 to the nearest tens.

  (A) 100   **(B)** 105   **(C)** 110   **(D)** 200

16. Which of the following expressions is true?

  (A) $85 > 91$ **(B)** $0.1 < 0.01$ **(C)** $\frac{1}{10} < \frac{1}{5}$ **(D)** $54.9 > 55.1$

EXPLORATION AND EXTENSION

PORTFOLIO

17. **BUILDING YOUR PROJECT** The second question of your class survey was *On what date of the month is your birthday?* Use a stem-and-leaf plot to order the data. How many other people have a birthday on the same date of the month as yours?

Write an equation to solve the problem. Then solve. (1.6)

1. What number can you add to 5 to get 27?

2. What number can you multiply by 4 to get 48?

Write the number in expanded notation. (2.1, 3.1)

3. 3205   4. 602,920   5. 8.25   6. 12.044

MEASUREMENT Rewrite the length in meters. (3.2)

7. 440 cm   8. 0.03 km   9. 1250 mm   10. 22 mm

Rewrite the number as a fraction. (3.4)

11. 0.54   12. 0.095   13. 87%   14. 12%

15. A store is having a 25% off sale on all of its jeans. You decide to buy a pair with an original price of $34.99. How much is the discount? What is the sale price of the jeans? (4.4, 4.8)

CAREER Interview

PROFESSOR

Professor Cooper gathers data about how people perform on their jobs. In his research and teaching, he creates mathematical and statistical models to help people understand what they can do to perform better.

Q What led you to this career?
I first became interested in business when I was five years old. In eighth grade, my brother and I started our own camping equipment company. We sold certificates representing shares of stock to raise money for our business. With the money we made, we rented an airplane and flew our stockholders around New York state.

Q Why are math skills important in your work?
One reason is that to become a successful businessperson, you need to be able to predict your customers' needs. Mathematics and statistics help you do this.

Q Can the math concepts you teach be used in everyday situations?
Yes, math and statistics can help you answer questions such as: "How can I become a better athlete?" and "Will the amount of time I study affect my future career?"

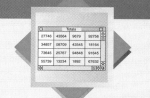

Sorting Birthdays

If you ask 15 people what date of the month they were born, almost every time, at least two of the people will tell you the same date of the month.

Example

To test the statement above, you ask 15 people what date of the month they were born. The answers are listed below.

5, 21, 7, 4, 25, 17, 14, 24, 11, 1, 19, 24, 24, 15, 30

Use a computer to write these numbers in order. How many duplicates are in the list?

Solution

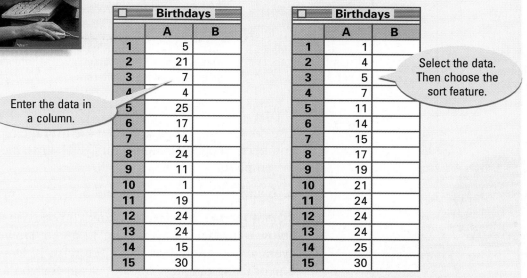

Birthdays	A	B
1	5	
2	21	
3	7	
4	4	
5	25	
6	17	
7	14	
8	24	
9	11	
10	1	
11	19	
12	24	
13	24	
14	15	
15	30	

Enter the data in a column.

Birthdays	A	B
1	1	
2	4	
3	5	
4	7	
5	11	
6	14	
7	15	
8	17	
9	19	
10	21	
11	24	
12	24	
13	24	
14	25	
15	30	

Select the data. Then choose the sort feature.

There are duplicates. Three of the people have their birthday on the 24th of the month.

Exercises

1. List the dates of the month that your classmates have birthdays. Use a spreadsheet to list the data in ascending order. Are there any duplicates in the first 15 numbers in your unsorted list?

2. Without looking, open this book 20 times. Each time record the right-hand page number and then find the sum of its digits. Enter the sums as data in a spreadsheet. Order the data. Did you get any duplicates?

LAB 5.3

COOPERATIVE LEARNING

Investigating Averages

Materials Needed
- counters or coins
- plain paper
- pencils

One way you can find the *average* of two numbers, such as 16 and 10, is to use stacks of counters. For example, you can use the steps below to find the average of 16 and 10.

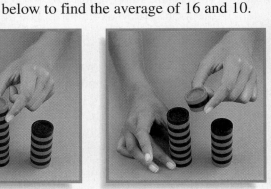

One stack has 16 counters and one stack has 10 counters.

Make the stacks the same height by moving counters.

Both stacks now have 13 counters.

The average of 16 and 10 is 13.

1. Use counters or coins to model the average of the two numbers. Sketch the steps you used. Write the average of the numbers.

   a. 6 and 10   **b.** 11 and 5   **c.** 9 and 3

2. **COMMUNICATING** Explain how you can use the number line below to model the average of 11 and 5. Do you get the same average you got in part (b) of Exercise 1? Does using a number line or using counters make it easier for you to find the average?

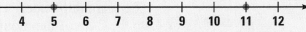

4   5   6   7   8   9   10   11   12

3. **NUMBER SENSE** Find a pair of numbers whose average is 3.5. Then find two more pairs. Explain your strategy.

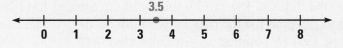

3.5

0   1   2   3   4   5   6   7   8

4. Use a number line to find the average of the numbers.

   a. 6 and 11   **b.** 7 and 8   **c.** 10 and 13

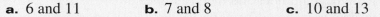

Part B FINDING THE AVERAGE OF THREE NUMBERS

You can use the steps below to find the average of 17, 13, and 12.

17 13 12 Make the stacks the same height. Each stack now has 14 counters.

The average of 17, 13, and 12 is 14.

5. Use counters or coins to find the average of the numbers.

a. 4, 8, 9 **b.** 8, 11, 14 **c.** 6, 13, 20

6. Can you find the average of 12, 13, and 18 using stacks of counters? Explain how you can or why you cannot.

NOW TRY THESE

In Exercises 7–9, draw a sketch to help you find the average of the numbers.

7. 7 and 15 **8.** 7 and 16 **9.** 8, 12, 13

10. If possible, find two numbers that fit the description.

 a. Two even numbers whose average is 10

 b. Two odd numbers whose average is 10

 c. Two numbers, one even and one odd, whose average is 10

11. Consider the three numbers, 4, ? , and 12.

 a. Find a value for ? so that the average is 9.

 b. Find a value for ? so that the average is 10.

 c. Find a value for ? so that the average is 11.

 d. What is the pattern for the numbers found in (a), (b), and (c)?

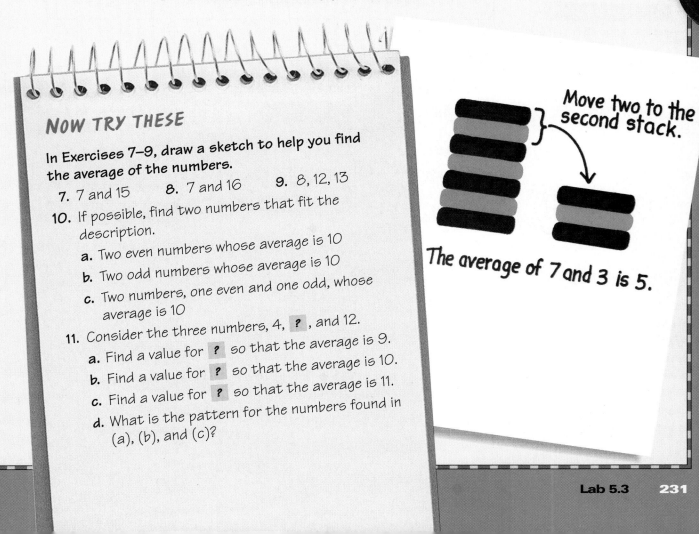

Move two to the second stack.

The average of 7 and 3 is 5.

5.3

Computing Averages

What you should learn:

Goal 1 How to find the average, or mean, of two or more numbers

Goal 2 How to use averages to solve real-life problems

Why you should learn it:

Averages can help you make decisions about scores. An example is finding the score you need on an English test.

TOOLBOX

Average, page 658

Goal 1 FINDING AN AVERAGE, OR MEAN

You can use stacks of coins to find the average of some sets of numbers. Here is one way to find the average of 8, 3, and 7.

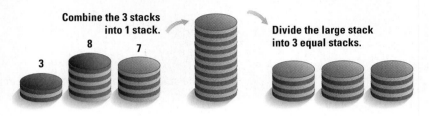

The average is 6.

FINDING AN AVERAGE, OR MEAN

To find the **average** of a set of numbers, add the numbers and divide the sum by how many numbers are in the set. The average is also called the **mean**.

Example 1 Finding Averages or Means

Find the average, or mean, of the numbers.

a. 34, 48   **b.** 97, 88, 82   **c.** 102, 145, 168, 169

Solution

a. Average $= \dfrac{34 + 48}{2}$ *Divide by the number of numbers.*

$= \dfrac{82}{2}$

$= 41$

b. Average $= \dfrac{97 + 88 + 82}{3}$

$= \dfrac{267}{3}$

$= 89$

c. Average $= \dfrac{102 + 145 + 168 + 169}{4}$

$= \dfrac{584}{4}$

$= 146$

STUDY TIP

You can check that an average is reasonable by checking that it is between the least and greatest numbers in the set. In part (b) of Example 1, the average is between 82 and 97.

Example 2 Guess, Check, and Revise

So far in English class, your test scores are 82, 75, 89, and 92. What score do you need to get on your fifth test to get a mean of 85?

Solution

Understand the Problem

You need to find a score that will make the mean of the five scores equal 85.

Make a Plan

You can use *Guess, Check and Revise* with a calculator to find the right score.

Solve the Problem

Guess that you need an 83 on the fifth test.

82 ⊞ 75 ⊞ 89 ⊞ 92 ⊞ 83 ⊟ ⌐421⌐

⌐421⌐ ⊟ 5 ⊟ ⌐84.2⌐

This is less than 85. Try a larger number, say 87.

82 ⊞ 75 ⊞ 89 ⊞ 92 ⊞ 87 ⊟ ⌐425⌐

⌐425⌐ ⊟ 5 ⊟ ⌐85⌐

You need an 87 on the fifth test.

Look Back

The mean of 82, 75, 89, and 92 is 84.5. It makes sense to need a score higher than 85 to raise the mean.

Example 3 Finding a Mean

Tim works at the driver's license bureau in a state where you must be at least 16 years old to get a driver's license. He says that yesterday 11 people got their licenses for the first time, and their average age was 22. Is this possible?

Solution

Suppose that one of the people was much older than the others. The ages could have been 16, 16, 16, 16, 17, 18, 16, 17, 18, 16, and 76.

The sum of these ages is 242. Find the mean.

$$\text{Mean} = \frac{242}{11} = 22$$

Tim's statement is possible.

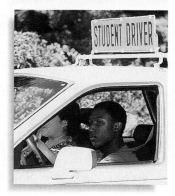

Real Life...
Real Facts

Driving
In 1997, you could get your driver's license at the age of 16 in 27 states. Thirteen states would grant a restricted license at the age of 14.

ONGOING ASSESSMENT

Talk About It
· · · · · · · · · · · · · · · · · ·
What value of *n* do you need to make the mean of *n*, 12, 28, 8, 7, and 31 equal to

1. 22?

2. 23?

3. 24?

5.3 Exercises

Extra Practice, page 628

GUIDED PRACTICE

1. Use the number line to help you find the average, or mean, of 3 and 11.

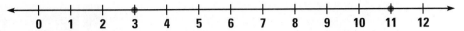

2. Use the model below to complete the statement.

The average, or mean, of **?** and **?** is **?** .

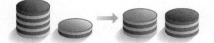

In Exercises 3–6, find the mean of the numbers.

3. 14, 26, 59

4. 35, 38, 45, 46

5. 6.8, 3.7, 8.1

6. 81, 97, 106, 125, 161

PRACTICE AND PROBLEM SOLVING

In Exercises 7–9, use the model to find the mean of the numbers.

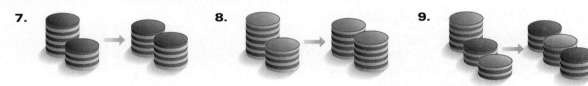

7.

8.

9.

REASONING **In Exercises 10–15, find the mean of the numbers. Then check whether your answer is reasonable.**

10. 52, 68

11. 29, 41, 38

12. 90, 105, 117

13. 63, 68, 34, 51

14. 22, 36, 143, 95

15. 79, 85, 92, 103, 106

In Exercises 16–18, use a calculator to find the mean of the numbers.

16. 11, 513

17. 90, 176, 304

18. 43, 266, 521, 910

GUESS, CHECK, AND REVISE **In Exercises 19 and 20, use *Guess, Check, and Revise* to find the value of ? .**

19. $\frac{84 + ?}{2} = 57$

20. $\frac{30 + ? + 6}{3} = 21$

21. **WRITING** Find a set of five different numbers whose mean is 10. Explain how you arrived at your list of numbers.

22. RUNNING You are practicing for a race. The bar graph shows the number of miles you ran each week for six weeks. Use the bar graph to estimate the mean number of miles you ran in a week. Then compute the mean. How close was your estimate?

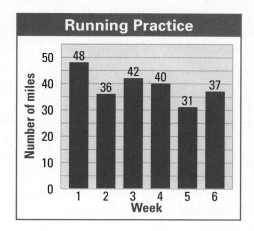

Running Practice

23. TECHNOLOGY You manage an Internet site. During the last six weeks, the site recorded 110, 134, 129, 148, 116, and 155 visitors. What is the mean number of visitors in a week? How many visitors are needed in the seventh week to achieve a mean of 135?

STANDARDIZED TEST PRACTICE

24. The distance from your home to school is 3 mi. The distance from home to school for three of your friends is 2 mi, 7 mi, and 8 mi. What is the mean distance from the school?

(A) 3 mi **(B)** 4 mi **(C)** 5 mi **(D)** 20 mi

25. The mean of 8, 15, and ? is 12.

(A) 36 **(B)** 13 **(C)** 12 **(D)** 9

EXPLORATION AND EXTENSION

PORTFOLIO

26. BUILDING YOUR PROJECT Find the mean of the responses to the third question of your class survey: *On a scale of 1 to 5, with 1 being as often as possible, how often do you read for enjoyment?* How does the class mean compare with the mean of the five numbers of the survey? What does this tell you about the results?

5.4

Exploring Median and Mode

What you should learn:

Goal 1 How to find the median of a set of numbers

Goal 2 How to find the mode of a set of numbers

Why you should learn it:

For some sets of numbers, the mean does not describe the set very well. The median or mode may describe the set better.

Goal 1 THE MEDIAN OF A SET OF NUMBERS

A mean is one way to describe a set of data. In this lesson, you will study two other ways to describe data: the *median* and the *mode*.

FINDING A MEDIAN

To find the **median** of a set of numbers, first write the numbers in order. The median is the middle number or the mean of the two middle numbers.

Example 1 Finding a Median

a. If there are an odd number of numbers in the list, the median is the middle number of the ordered list.

32, 35, 36, **37**, 41, 41, 51

The **median** is **37**.

b. If there are an even number of numbers in the list, the median is the mean of the two middle numbers.

32, 35, 36, **37**, **41**, 41, 51, 53

The median is the mean of 37 and 41.

$$\frac{37 + 41}{2} = 39$$

The **median** is **39**.

STUDY TIP

In Example 2, you could use an ordered stem-and-leaf plot to find the median. The tenth leaf is the median.

1	4	Key
2	4	2 | 4 = 24
3	3 7	
6	8	
7	2 4 5	
8	1 **2** 3 4 4 4 8	
9	1 3 8 9	

Example 2 Finding a Median

You are a teacher and give a test to your students. The scores are shown below. Find the median score.

82, 99, 33, 88, 37, 84, 68, 74, 75, 83,

24, 84, 72, 84, 14, 91, 98, 81, 93

REAL LIFE
Teaching

Solution

To find the median, write the numbers in order.

14, 24, 33, 37, 68, 72, 74, 75, 81, **82**,

83, 84, 84, 84, 88, 91, 93, 98, 99

Find the middle number.

The median is **82**.

Goal 2 THE MODE OF A SET OF NUMBERS

FINDING A MODE

To find the **mode** of a set of numbers, put the numbers in order. The mode is the number that appears most often.

Not all sets of data have a mode. For example, the set 4, 7, 9, and 11 does not have a mode because no number occurs more often than the others. A set of data can have more than one mode. For example, in the set 5, 5, 7, 7, and 9, both 5 and 7 are modes.

Example 3 Finding a Mean, Median, and Mode

REAL LIFE
Business

You started a business one year ago, and now you have 13 employees. The times (in months) that they have worked for you is shown in the line plot. Find the mean, median, and mode of the data. Which of these best describes the typical number of months of service?

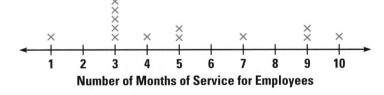

Number of Months of Service for Employees

Solution

$$\text{Mean} = \frac{1 + 3 + 3 + 3 + 3 + 3 + 4 + 5 + 5 + 7 + 9 + 9 + 10}{13}$$

$$= \frac{65}{13}$$

$$= 5$$

To find the median and mode, write the numbers in order.

  1, **3, 3, 3, 3, 3**, **4**, 5, 5, 7, 9, 9, 10

The median is **4** months.

The mode is **3** months, because 3 occurs most often.

Of these three, the mode of 3 months is probably most typical because about one third of the employees have worked that long.

Real Life...
Real People

Michelle Tees started selling plants when she was 10 years old. After two years, her greenhouse was selling over 100 kinds of plants.

ONGOING ASSESSMENT

Write About It

The hourly wages of your employees are $6, $9, $7, $7, $6, $6, $8, $6, $11, $6, $18, $8, and $6.

1. Find the range, mean, median, and mode of the data.

2. What information about the wages do you get from finding the median? the mode? Which one best describes a typical wage? Why?

5.4 *Exploring Median and Mode*   **237**

GUIDED PRACTICE

1. **SCIENCE** Use the table at the right. It shows the longest recorded life spans (in years) of several animals. Find the range, median, and mode(s) of the data. Use a calculator to find the mean of the data.

Animal	Age	Animal	Age
Tortoise	152	Lobster	50
Clam	100	Cow	40
Whale	90	Pigeon	35
Oyster	80	Cat	34
Cockatoo	70	Dog	29
Condor	70	Sheep	20
Elephant	70	Goat	18
Ostrich	62	Rabbit	18
Horse	62	Hamster	10
Chimpanzee	50		

REASONING In Exercises 2–4, decide whether the statement is *true* or *false*. If false, explain why.

2. The median and the mean of the data set 21, 27, 27, 29, 31 are both 27.

3. The mode of the data set 5, 7, 11, 18, 21 is 11.

4. The median of the data set 4, 5, 6, 7, 8, 9 is 7.

PRACTICE AND PROBLEM SOLVING

In Exercises 5–7, find the median and mode(s) of the data.

5. Numbers of students who wore red to school
   45, 36, 38, 48, 42, 45, 60, 54, 72, 45, 48, 42, 66, 54

6. Lengths of movies in minutes
   151, 175, 188, 140, 117, 155, 122, 135, 113, 122, 125, 133

7. Ages of players on a school soccer team
   11, 13, 11, 12, 12, 12, 12, 11, 13, 12, 11, 12, 10, 11, 11

In Exercises 8–10, match the description with the data set.

A. 50, 49, 49, 54, 46, 45, 57   **B.** 50, 52, 48, 47, 43, 52, 51   **C.** 50, 57, 50, 56, 46, 53, 52

8. The mode is 50.   9. The median is 50.   10. The mean is 50.

MUSIC In Exercises 11–13, use the data below. They show the lengths (in seconds) of the songs on the CD *Aladdin*. (Source: Walt Disney Music Company)

79, 85, 143, 113, 60, 146, 99, 171, 160, 163, 68,
95, 111, 175, 46, 156, 297, 111, 218, 251, 247

11. Find the range, median, and mode(s) of the song lengths.

12. What information about the song lengths do you get from finding the median? the mode?

13. Which do you think best represents the length of a song? Why?

14. BASKETBALL The data below show the number of wins of the National Basketball Association's teams for the 1995–96 season. Find the range, median, and mode(s) of the data. Use a calculator to find the mean of the data. (Source: National Basketball Association)

60, 47, 42, 39, 33, 30, 18, 72, 52, 47,
46, 46, 41, 25, 21, 59, 55, 48, 35, 26,
26, 15, 64, 53, 44, 41, 39, 36, 29

15. NUMBER RIDDLE There are 5 numbers in a set. One of the numbers is 25. The mode is 28. The median and mean are both 26. What are the numbers?

16. WRITING The ages of people in the chorus room are listed below. Find the mean, median, and mode(s) of the ages. Explain why the mean is not the best way to describe the ages.

12, 13, 12, 10, 13, 10, 12, 52, 12, 10,
12, 13, 11, 10, 10, 10, 12, 12, 11, 13

17. TIME MANAGEMENT You keep a list of the numbers of minutes you spend doing homework for 10 days. Find the mean, median, and mode(s) of the numbers. Explain why the mode is not the best way to describe the time spent.

25, 20, 29, 40, 40, 18, 21, 23, 24, 20

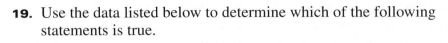

STANDARDIZED TEST PRACTICE

18. Find the mean of the data represented in the line plot at the right.

(**A**) 7   (**B**) 7.9   (**C**) 8   (**D**) 10

19. Use the data listed below to determine which of the following statements is true.

3, 3, 4, 4, 4, 5, 5, 7, 7, 8

(**A**) The mean is 4.5.   (**B**) The median is 4.5.

(**C**) The mode is 4.5.   (**D**) The range is 4.5.

20. Which of the following is the mode of the data set?

11, 22, 22, 44, 77, 11, 22, 88, 55, 77, 66

(**A**) 11   (**B**) 22   (**C**) 45   (**D**) 77

EXPLORATION AND EXTENSION

21. GROUP ACTIVITY Use a telephone book. Choose 40 last names, each from a different page. Choose the names randomly. Then count the letters in the last names. Find the median and mode of the number of letters. Which best describes the number of letters? Share your results with other groups.

22. BUILDING YOUR PROJECT The fourth question of your class survey was *What is your handspan in centimeters?* Find the range, median, and mode of the data. Which best describes the typical handspan of students in your class? Explain.

SPIRAL REVIEW

1. TILING PATTERNS Use dot paper and the figure at the right to create a tiling pattern. **(1.5)**

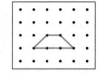

GEOMETRY In Exercises 2 and 3, the model shows a portion of a whole. Draw two rectangles that could represent the whole. **(3.3)**

2.

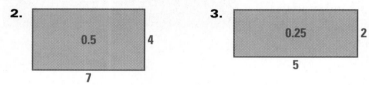

4. SURVEY A survey asked a class of 25 students if they participate in an after-school activity. Three fifths said yes. How many students participate? How many students do not participate in an after-school activity? **(3.8)**

In Exercises 5–7, divide. Check your answer by multiplying. **(4.7)**

5. $2.8 \div 1.4$ **6.** $17.94 \div 5.2$ **7.** $39 \div 0.6$

8. HOCKEY The data in the table show the number of games played in each Stanley Cup Championship for the 1980–1981 hockey season through the 1995–1996 hockey season. Use a line plot to organize the numbers of games played. Write a statement that describes the data. **(5.1)**

Season	Games	Season	Games	Season	Games	Season	Games
1980–81	5	1984–85	5	1988–89	6	1992–93	5
1981–82	4	1985–86	5	1989–90	5	1993–94	7
1982–83	4	1986–87	7	1990–91	5	1994–95	4
1983–84	5	1987–88	4	1991–92	4	1995–96	4

Take this test as you would take a test in class. The answers to the exercises are given in the back of the book.

In Exercises 1–3, match the data with the description. (5.1–5.4)

A. The data include 12 numbers.   **B.** The mode of the data is 12.

C. The mean of the numbers is 21.

1.
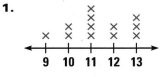

2. 31, 16, 7, 12, 37, 25, 22, 12, 39, 16, 14

3.
```
0 | 8 9
1 | 2 2 2 4
2 | 3 7 5
3 | 1 6 6        Key
4 | 5 5          1 | 4 = 14
```

FOOTBALL In Exercises 4–9, use the table below. It shows the number of Super Bowls (through 1997) won by each team and the number of points by which they beat their opponent. (5.1, 5.2, 5.4)

4. Make a line plot of the number of Super Bowls won by each team.

5. Write a description of the data in the line plot.

6. What is the mode of the number of Super Bowls won? What does this number tell you about the data?

7. Use a stem-and-leaf plot to order the number of points by which each team beat its opponent.

8. Which team beat its opponent by the most points?

9. Which team won the closest scoring game? Explain.

Team	No. of Super Bowls	Points Won by
Packers	3	25, 19, 14
Chiefs	1	16
Colts	1	3
Cowboys	5	21, 17, 35, 17, 10
Dolphins	2	7, 17
Steelers	4	10, 4, 4, 12
Raiders	3	18, 17, 29
49ers	5	5, 22, 4, 45, 23
Redskins	3	10, 32, 13
Bears	1	36
Giants	2	19, 1
Jets	1	9

GUESS, CHECK, AND REVISE In Exercises 10–12, find the unknown number. (5.3)

10. $\dfrac{54 + \boxed{?}}{2} = 49$

11. $\dfrac{\boxed{?} + 26 + 21}{3} = 25$

12. $\dfrac{40 + 53 + \boxed{?} + 41}{4} = 52$

13. NUTRITION The table at the right shows the number of calories in one serving of vegetables commonly found in salads. Find the mean, median, and mode of the data. Which best describes the data? Explain. (5.3, 5.4)

Broccoli	36	Celery	10
Carrot	23	Cucumber	8
Cauliflower	14	Lettuce	10
Onion	4	Tomato	22

5.5

Bar Graphs

What you should learn:

Goal 1 How to draw a bar graph

Goal 2 How to choose a scale for a bar graph

Why you should learn it:

A bar graph helps you quickly see information about data such as career choices.

One public service career is being a member of the police force.

Goal 1 GUIDELINES FOR DRAWING BAR GRAPHS

You already know how to *read* information from bar graphs. Here are some guidelines for *drawing* bar graphs.

GUIDELINES FOR DRAWING A BAR GRAPH

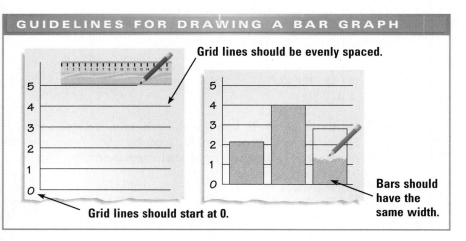

Grid lines should be evenly spaced.

Grid lines should start at 0.

Bars should have the same width.

Example 1 Drawing a Horizontal Bar Graph

Marsha asked 25 students if they want to work in public service, business, entertainment, or technology when they grow up. The responses she received were: business, 9; entertainment, 8; public service, 5; and technology, 3. Make a bar graph of her data.

Solution

One way to draw the bar graph is shown below.

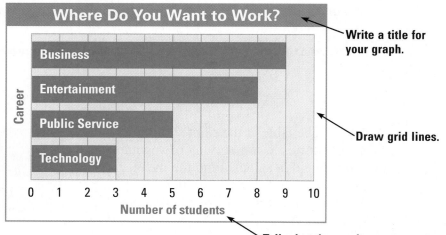

Write a title for your graph.

Draw grid lines.

Tell what the numbers mean.

Goal 2 CHOOSING A SCALE

The numbers on a bar graph are its **scale**. In Example 1, the scale increases by ones. When data contain large numbers, it may be better to choose a scale that increases by some other number. The scale should always go a little bit beyond the longest bar.

Example 2 · Choosing a Scale

a. To make a bar graph of the data below, you can choose to make the scale increase from 0 to 10 by ones.

4.1, 2.7, 6, 9.2

b. To make a bar graph of the data below, you can choose to make the scale increase from 0 to 200 by 25's.

56, 72, 45, 115, 173, 190

The bar graph in Example 1 is a **horizontal bar graph**. But you could also have used a **vertical bar graph**.

Example 3 · Drawing a Vertical Bar Graph

You can use a vertical bar graph to show the heights of the six tallest buildings in Charlotte, NC.

REAL LIFE
Architecture

Building	Height	Building	Height
NationsBank Corp. Center	871 ft	Interstate Tower	462 ft
1 First Union Center	580 ft	2 First Union Center	433 ft
NationsBank Plaza	503 ft	Wachovia Center	420 ft

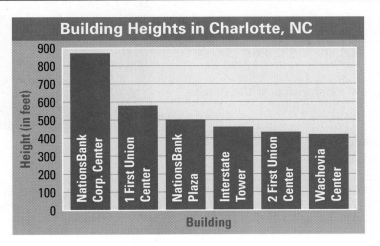

5.5 Exercises

Extra Practice, page 628

GUIDED PRACTICE

HOBBIES In Exercises 1 and 2, suppose you surveyed 328 people about their favorite winter activity. You want to show the results with a bar graph.

1. What scale should you use?

2. Draw a bar graph of the data.

3. **TRUE OR FALSE?** The scale on a bar graph should always increase by ones.

Activity	Number of People
Skiing	62
Ice Skating	89
Sledding	120
Snowmobiling	57

ERROR ANALYSIS In Exercises 4–6, what is wrong with the bar graph?

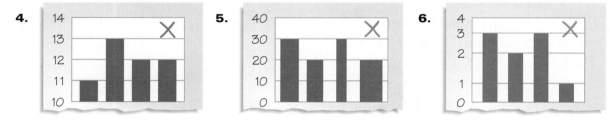

4.
5.
6.

PRACTICE AND PROBLEM SOLVING

In Exercises 7–9, match the data with the scale that fits best.

7. 550, 330, 570, 225, 100   **A.** Increase by 100's

8. 975, 2450, 825, 4100   **B.** Increase by 10's

9. 45, 62, 88, 10, 32   **C.** Increase by 1000's

CONSUMER SPENDING In Exercises 10 and 11, use the table below. It shows the mean response in a survey of how much money students spend each week.

Age	6–8	9–11	12–14	15–17
Average Weekly Spending	$3.80	$4.80	$22.00	$43.00

10. What scale would you use to draw a bar graph of the data?

11. Draw a bar graph of the data.

12. **CAVES** The table below lists some of the world's deepest caves. Draw a bar graph of the data.

Country	France	Spain	Mexico	Austria	Italy
Depth (ft)	5256	4728	4439	3999	3986

Real Life...
Real People

Leah Brown is a spelunker (cave explorer). She broke the women's world record for a 120 m climb when she was 12 years old.

13. WRITING The data below show the results of a survey of students who responded to the question *What changes would you make if you were principal for a day?* Explain why a bar graph is a better representation of these data than a line plot. Then make a bar graph of the data. (Source: *USA Today*)

Raise money for homeless	935
Have pizza party for lunch	890
Cancel classes for day	845
Get new equipment and books	725

STANDARDIZED TEST PRACTICE

14. A student used the data below to draw the bar graph at the right. Which statement about the bar graph is true?

R, R, R, G, B, B, Y, Y, Y, Y

(A) It represents the data and is drawn correctly.

(B) It does not represent the data but is drawn correctly.

(C) It represents the data but is not drawn correctly.

(D) It does not represent the data and is not drawn correctly.

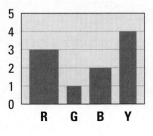

EXPLORATION AND EXTENSION

PORTFOLIO

15. BUILDING YOUR PROJECT The fifth question of your class survey was *Choose your favorite of the subjects math, science, English, and social studies.* Make a bar graph of the data. What is the most popular subject? What is the least popular subject?

16. COMMUNICATING ABOUT MATHEMATICS A double bar graph is used to compare two things by using different color bars. Look at Exercise 6 on page 18 for an example. Use the information on page 251 to make a double bar graph that compares the amount of money spent and saved by boys and girls in the 12–19 age group.

5.6

Line Graphs

What you should learn:

Goal 1 How to draw a line graph

Goal 2 How to use a line graph to recognize a trend in real-life data

Why you should learn it:

A line graph helps you analyze data over time. An example is comparing the prices of pairs of sneakers from 1988 to 1996.

TOOLBOX
Reading a Line Graph, page 660

Goal 1 DRAWING A LINE GRAPH

In this lesson, you will learn how to use a **line graph** to represent data that are changing over time.

Example 1 Drawing a Line Graph

CONNECTION
Economics

The average prices for a pair of sneakers are shown for 1988 through 1996. Draw a line graph for the data. Between which years did the price change the most? the least? (Source: National Sporting Goods Association)

Year	Price	Year	Price	Year	Price
1988	$26.46	1991	$29.21	1994	$23.78
1989	$27.88	1992	$28.39	1995	$23.56
1990	$29.92	1993	$24.62	1996	$24.41

Solution

Start by drawing a grid. Be sure the grid lines are evenly spaced. Label the axes. Then place a dot on the grid for each pair of numbers in the data set. Connect the points.

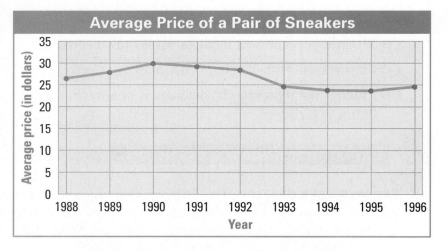

The line between two years is steepest between 1992 and 1993, so the price changed the most between 1992 and 1993. You know the price decreased because the line slants down.

The line between 1994 and 1995 is the closest to horizontal, so the price changed the least between these two years.

Goal **2** USING A LINE GRAPH

Line graphs often can be used to estimate prices or other values that will occur in the future.

Example 2 Using a Line Graph

REAL LIFE
Wages

The average hourly wages for manufacturing workers from 1988 through 1996 are shown below. Draw a line graph for the data. Use the graph to estimate the average hourly wage in 1998. (Source: Bureau of Labor Statistics)

Year	Wage	Year	Wage	Year	Wage
1988	$10.19	1991	$11.18	1994	$12.07
1989	$10.48	1992	$11.46	1995	$12.37
1990	$10.83	1993	$11.74	1996	$12.78

Solution

One way to draw the line graph is shown below.

From the graph, you can see that the hourly wage is increasing by about the same amount each year. In a typical year, the wage increased about $.30. You can use this to estimate the average hourly wage for 1998.

$$1998 \text{ hourly wage} \approx 1996 \text{ hourly wage} + \$.30 + \$.30$$
$$= 12.78 + 0.30 + 0.30$$
$$= \$13.38 \text{ per hour}$$

ONGOING ASSESSMENT

Write About It

1. Explain how to use the data in the two graphs to show that a manufacturing worker who earned the average hourly wage in 1988 had to work about 2.6 h to earn enough to buy a pair of sneakers.

2. How many hours did it take in 1995? What can you conclude?

GUIDED PRACTICE

ERROR ANALYSIS In Exercises 1 and 2, describe the error.

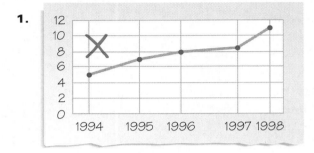

INTERNET In Exercises 3 and 4, use the line graph at the right. It shows the numbers of households that subscribed to on-line services from 1989–1995.

(Source: Veronis, Suhler, & Associates)

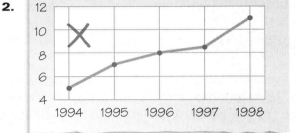

3. Did the number of subscribers increase each year? How can you tell?

4. In 1996, do you think it is more likely that there were *14 million* or *10 million* subscribers? Why?

PRACTICE AND PROBLEM SOLVING

In Exercises 5 and 6, estimate the amount for 1996.

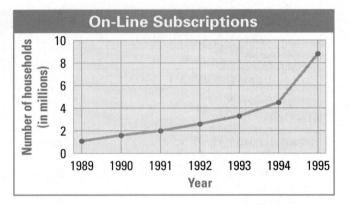

7. Make a line graph of the data in the table. It tells how many gallons of fruit juice the average person in the United States drank each year.

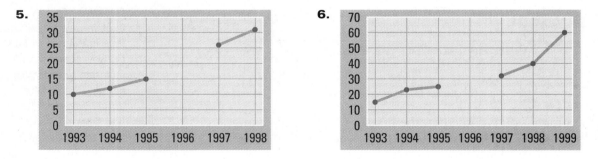

Year	1990	1991	1992	1993	1994
Juice (in gallons)	6.9	7.9	7.3	8.4	8.6

8. TEMPERATURE The table below shows the average monthly temperatures (°F) for Juneau, Alaska. Draw a line graph for the data. Use the graph to find in which month the average monthly temperature increases the most. (Source: National Oceanic and Atmospheric Administration)

Month	J	F	M	A	M	J	J	A	S	O	N	D
Temp (°F)	24	28	32	39	47	53	56	54	49	42	33	27

CARS The line graph at the right shows the amount of money spent on new and used cars from 1989–1995.
(Source: *World Almanac: 1997*)

9. Describe the trends for the amount of money spent on new and used cars.

10. Estimate the amount of money spent on used cars in 1998.

11. Do you think the amount of money spent on used cars will ever be greater than the amount of money spent on new cars? Explain.

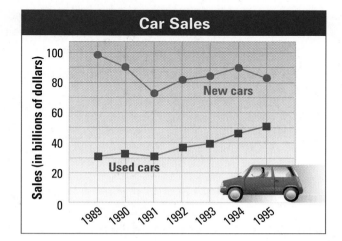

In Exercises 12 and 13, use the line graph at the right. The line graph shows the life expectancies of males and females from 1920–1990.
(Source: National Center for Health Statistics)

12. In which year was the life expectancy of a male slightly greater than 60 years?

    (A) 1930   (B) 1940

    (C) 1950   (D) 1960

13. In which of the following years was the difference in life expectancies between males and females the greatest?

    (A) 1920   (B) 1930

    (C) 1950   (D) 1970

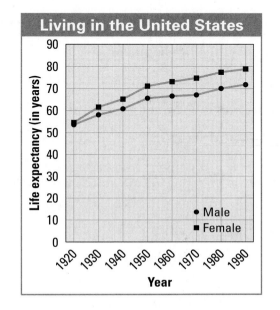

14. a. The estimated total income for people aged 12 to 19 in the United States is given in the table. Make a line graph of the data. What can you say about the amount of teen income in this time period?

b. Make an estimate of teen income in 1995. Explain how you made your estimate. How accurate do you think your estimate is?

Year	1987	1988	1989	1990	1991	1992	1993	1994
Income (in billions)	$89	$91	$94	$106	$102	$93	$88	$96

15. a. Use the data below to make a line graph of the percent of television characters who were male for the given years. On the same graph, make a line graph of the percent of television characters who were female for the same years. (Source: Broadcast Education Association)

b. Write a statement about the trends in the percents.

Year	1982	1984	1986	1988	1990	1992
Male characters	71%	51%	59%	60%	63%	58%
Female characters	29%	49%	41%	40%	37%	42%

SPIRAL REVIEW

ALGEBRA In Exercises 1–4, evaluate the expression when $t = 3$. (2.6)

1. $4 \cdot (6 - t)$ **2.** $4 \cdot t + 12$ **3.** $30 - t \cdot 4$ **4.** $45 \div 9 \cdot t$

In Exercises 5–8, round the decimal to the nearest tenth. (3.6)

5. 34.54   **6.** 1.05   **7.** 3.761   **8.** 5.549

In Exercises 9–12, find the missing number. (3.7)

9. $49 = 7^{?}$ **10.** $125 = \boxed{?}^{\,3}$ **11.** $\boxed{?} = 3^3$ **12.** $1000 = 10^{?}$

In Exercises 13–16, add or subtract. (4.1, 4.2)

13. $5.34 + 8.98$ **14.** $13.76 - 3.22$ **15.** $9 - 0.23$ **16.** $5 + 0.08$

NUMBER SENSE Is the statement *true* or *false*? If false, change the right-hand side of the equation so the statement is true. (4.6)

17. $48 \div 1000 = 48,000$ **18.** $48 \times 100 = 4800$

19. $4.8 \div 10 = 0.48$ **20.** $4.8 \times 100 = 4800$

21. TRAVEL The data show the number of states visited by 20 students. Use a stem-and-leaf plot to order the data. (5.2)

22, 38, 6, 14, 20, 8, 11, 6, 15, 2, 27, 9, 13, 40, 5, 31, 14, 3, 1, 18

TEEN
Spending

READ About It

Recently, there were about 29 million people in the United States in the 12–19 age group. As a group, these teenagers earn and spend a lot of money. Boys between the ages of 12 and 19 earn an average of $76 a week. They spend an average of $44 a week. Girls between the ages of 12 and 19 earn an average of $58 a week. They spend an average of $34 a week.

About two thirds of teens today have savings accounts. Twenty percent have checking accounts. Seventeen percent own stocks or bonds and almost one in ten has a certificate of deposit.

Besides their own money, in a year teenagers spend about $36 billion of family money. Half of the girls and one third of the boys do some of the food shopping. Teens also influence what brands other family members buy, even on major purchases such as cars.

Where Teens Get Their Cash

47%	45%	32%	26%	11%	3%
As needed from parents	Odd jobs	Allowance	Part-time job	Full-time job	Own business

Source: American Demographics

WRITE About It

1. Do some teenagers get income from more than one source? How can you tell?

2. About how many teenagers in the United States receive money from

   a. odd jobs?   **b.** part-time jobs?

3. Make a graph that compares the $99 billion of their own money that teens spend each year with the amount of family money they spend. Why did you choose this kind of graph?

4. Make a graph showing how many teenagers have savings accounts, checking accounts, stocks and bonds, and certificates of deposit. Why did you choose this kind of graph?

5.7 Choosing an Appropriate Graph

What you should learn:

Goal 1 How to draw a pictograph

Goal 2 How to choose an appropriate graph

Why you should learn it:

There are many ways to represent data with a graph. By choosing an appropriate graph, you make the data easier to understand.

In 1994, 31% of households in the United States grew some of their own vegetables.

Goal 1 DRAWING A PICTOGRAPH

A **pictograph** is similar to a bar graph except that a pictograph represents data with symbols instead of bars.

Here are some guidelines for making pictographs.

- Use symbols that are about the same size.
- If each symbol represents more than one item, include a key to show how many items it represents.

Example 1 Drawing a Pictograph

Eighty people were given a list of eight vegetables and asked to choose their least favorite. The results are shown below. Represent these results with a pictograph.

Vegetable	Number	Vegetable	Number
Mushrooms	18	Peas	8
Beets	14	Tomatoes	8
Peppers	12	Broccoli	7
Cabbage	9	Onions	4

Solution

One way to draw the pictograph is shown.

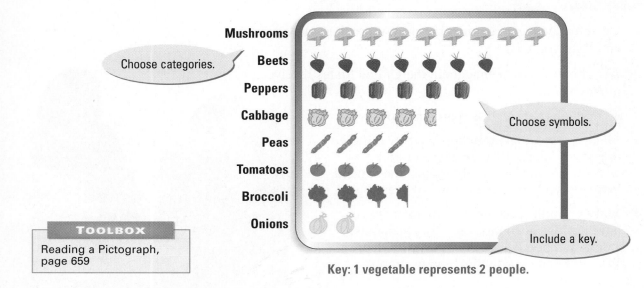

Choose categories.

Choose symbols.

Include a key.

Key: 1 vegetable represents 2 people.

TOOLBOX

Reading a Pictograph, page 659

Goal 2 CHOOSING AN APPROPRIATE GRAPH

In this chapter, you have studied five types of plots or graphs.

PLOTS AND GRAPHS

Line Plots Use to show the frequency of each number when the data have a small range. **(5.1)**

Stem-and-Leaf Plots Use to order a set of numbers. They can be used with data that have a large range. **(5.2)**

Bar Graphs Use to compare data that are in categories. Bar graphs are used in business because they are easy to read. **(5.5)**

Line Graphs Use to show how data change over time. When the line goes up, the data are increasing. **(5.6)**

Pictographs Use to compare data that are in categories. Pictographs are usually more artistic than bar graphs. **(5.7)**

Real Life...
Real Facts

Public Transportation
More than 5.5 million people in the United States use public transportation to get to work.

Example 2 Choosing an Appropriate Graph

Public transportation systems in the United States charge many different fares to adult riders. Choose a way to plot or graph the data about the number of systems that charge the most common fares.

Adult Fare	$.50	$.75	$.85	$1.00	$1.25
Number of Systems	23	55	21	91	22

Solution

One way to represent the data is with a bar graph.

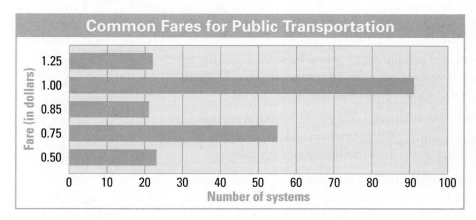

Common Fares for Public Transportation

ONGOING ASSESSMENT

Talk About It

1. Can you use another type of graph or plot to represent the data in Example 2? Explain how you could or why you cannot.

2. Give an example of data you would represent using a line graph.

GUIDED PRACTICE

In Exercises 1–3, decide whether the pictograph is misleading. If the pictograph is misleading, explain why.

1.

| Tulips | 🌷 🌷 |
| Daisies | 🌼 🌼 🌼 |

One symbol represents two flowers.

2.

| Tulips | 🌷 🌷 |
| Daisies | 🌼 🌼 🌼 |

One symbol represents two flowers.

3.

| Tulips | 🌷 🌷 |
| Daisies | 🌼 🌼 🌼 |

In Exercises 4–6, name the type of graph. Then describe a real-life situation that the graph could represent.

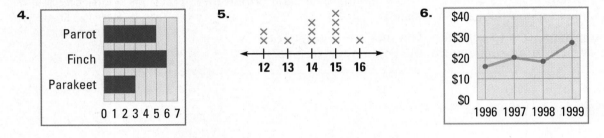

4.

Parrot, Finch, Parakeet

0 1 2 3 4 5 6 7

5.

12 13 14 15 16

6.

$40 $30 $20 $10 $0

1996 1997 1998 1999

PRACTICE AND PROBLEM SOLVING

In Exercises 7–11, match the description with the type of graph.

7. Represents data that change over time

8. Represents data with symbols

9. Uses an ✕ to represent a number

10. Used to order data

11. Can be horizontal or vertical

A. Line plot

B. Stem-and-leaf plot

C. Bar graph

D. Line graph

E. Pictograph

12. VACATIONS In a survey, 20 people were asked how they got to their summer vacations. The results were: car, 13; plane, 4; bus, 2; train, 1. Draw a pictograph of these data.

13. MUSICIANS The number (in millions) of people who play a musical instrument are: piano, 21; guitar, 14; drum, 4; flute, 3; clarinet, 2. Draw a pictograph of these data. (Source: American Music Conference)

14. In a survey, students were asked if they had attended a professional sports event. The results were: baseball, 372; basketball, 162; football, 162; hockey, 90. Draw an appropriate graph of the data.

15. GAMES The data below are the numbers of board games owned by 30 students. Organize the data using a stem-and-leaf plot or a line plot. Why did you select the graph that you did?

5, 3, 3, 5, 10, 2, 4, 3, 3, 4, 5, 4, 7, 2, 1,
3, 4, 3, 6, 3, 1, 3, 3, 4, 4, 3, 6, 8, 3, 3

16. ECONOMICS The table below shows the average amount of money a person spent on reading materials in 1990–1995. Draw two different plots or graphs of this data. Which do you think shows better how the data changed?

Year	1990	1991	1992	1993	1994	1995
Amount	$153	$163	$162	$166	$165	$162

17. SCIENCE The average daily high temperatures (in °F) each month in Baltimore, MD, are Jan., 40°; Feb., 44°; Mar., 54°; Apr., 64°; May, 74°; June, 83°; July, 87°; Aug., 85°; Sept., 79°; Oct., 67°; Nov., 56°; and Dec., 45°. Draw and compare two different plots or graphs of this data.

STANDARDIZED TEST PRACTICE

18. Which graph or plot does not represent the same data as the others?

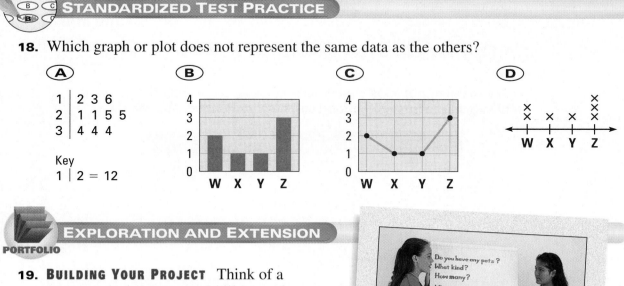

(A)

```
1 | 2 3 6
2 | 1 1 5 5
3 | 4 4 4

Key
1 | 2 = 12
```

(B)

(C)

(D)

X X X
X X X X X
W X Y Z

EXPLORATION AND EXTENSION

PORTFOLIO

19. BUILDING YOUR PROJECT Think of a survey question you would like to ask your classmates. Collect the data. Draw a graph or plot that you think would be best to display the data. Explain why you chose this kind of display.

WHAT *did you learn?* **WHY** *did you learn it?*

Skills	5.1	Use a line plot to organize data. Find the range of a set of data.	Analyze data, such as the weights of fish.
	5.2	Use a stem-and-leaf plot to organize data.	Order data, such as the ages of people in a group.
	5.3	Find the average, or mean, of a set of numbers.	Estimate averages, such as your final grade for a class.
	5.4	Find the median and mode of a set of numbers.	Analyze data, such as how long employees have worked.
	5.5	Draw a bar graph.	Compare data in categories, such as heights of buildings.
	5.6	Draw a line graph.	See how data change over time, such as prices or wages.
	5.7	Draw a pictograph.	Display data, such as the results of a survey.
Strategies	5.1–5.7	Use problem solving strategies.	Solve a wide variety of real-life problems.
Using Data	5.1–5.7	Use tables and graphs.	Organize data and solve problems.

HOW *does it fit in the bigger picture of mathematics?*

Many real-life problems contain sets of data. Organizing the data and representing them with a graph can help you understand the data.

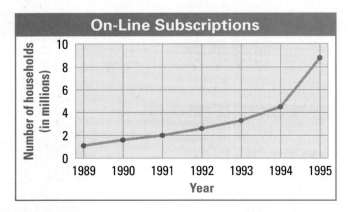

On-Line Subscriptions

Statistics is one of many areas of mathematics. Others you will study are algebra, geometry, probability, and coordinate geometry.

VOCABULARY

- line plot (p. 220)
- range (p. 221)
- key (p. 224)
- average (p. 232)

- mean (p. 232)
- median (p. 236)
- mode (p. 237)
- scale (p. 243)

- horizontal bar graph (p. 243)
- vertical bar graph (p. 243)
- line graph (p. 246)
- pictograph (p. 252)

5.1 LINE PLOTS

Example ▸ The weights in pounds of ten turkeys are 12, 10, 14, 10, 11, 12, 10, 16, 14, and 12. You can use a line plot to organize these data.

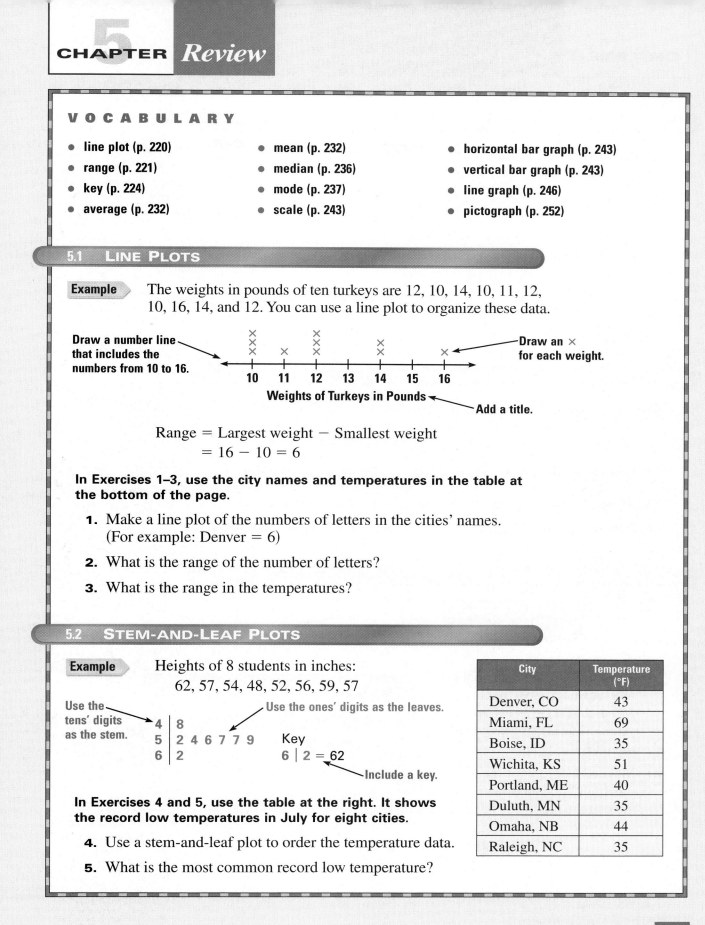

Draw a number line that includes the numbers from 10 to 16.

Draw an × for each weight.

10 11 12 13 14 15 16

Weights of Turkeys in Pounds

Add a title.

Range = Largest weight − Smallest weight
= 16 − 10 = 6

In Exercises 1–3, use the city names and temperatures in the table at the bottom of the page.

1. Make a line plot of the numbers of letters in the cities' names. (For example: Denver = 6)

2. What is the range of the number of letters?

3. What is the range in the temperatures?

5.2 STEM-AND-LEAF PLOTS

Example ▸ Heights of 8 students in inches:
62, 57, 54, 48, 52, 56, 59, 57

Use the tens' digits as the stem.

Use the ones' digits as the leaves.

```
4 | 8
5 | 2 4 6 7 7 9     Key
6 | 2               6 | 2 = 62
```

Include a key.

In Exercises 4 and 5, use the table at the right. It shows the record low temperatures in July for eight cities.

4. Use a stem-and-leaf plot to order the temperature data.

5. What is the most common record low temperature?

City	Temperature (°F)
Denver, CO	43
Miami, FL	69
Boise, ID	35
Wichita, KS	51
Portland, ME	40
Duluth, MN	35
Omaha, NB	44
Raleigh, NC	35

5.3 COMPUTING AVERAGES

Example Number of minutes you read per day:

15, 10, 20, 19, 15, 32, 15, 20, 25

$$\text{Mean} = \frac{\text{Sum of the numbers}}{\text{Number of numbers}}$$

$$= \frac{15 + 10 + 20 + 19 + 15 + 32 + 15 + 20 + 25}{9}$$

$$= \frac{171}{9} = 19$$

The mean number of minutes you read per day is 19.

Normal Precipitation in El Paso, TX

Month	Precipitation (in.)
Jun	0.69
Jul	1.29
Aug	1.19
Sep	1.14
Oct	0.85
Nov	0.33

6. Find the mean of the precipitation data in the table at the right.

5.4 EXPLORING MEDIAN AND MODE

Example To find the median and mode of the reading data shown above, write the numbers in order.

10, **15**, **15**, **15**, **19**, 20, 20, 25, 32

The mode is the most common number, or 15.   The median is the middle number, or 19.

In Exercises 7 and 8, use the precipitation data shown above.

7. Find the median.   **8.** Find the mode.

5.5 BAR GRAPHS

Example

Denomination (in dollars)	1	5	10	20
Lifespan (in years)	1.5	2	3	4

9. The source of the data about U.S. currency says that both $50 and $100 bills last nine years. Make a bar graph that includes these data.

10. Make a bar graph of the precipitation data in the table at the top of the page.

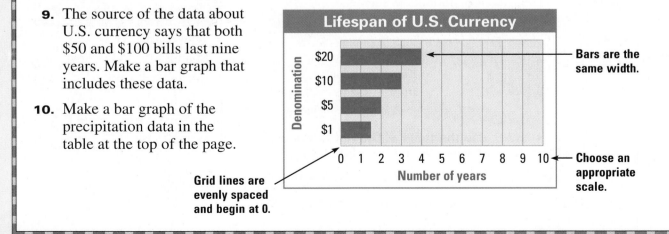

Example Make a line graph of the data below about the average farm size in the United States. (Source: *The World Almanac: 1996*)

Year	1940	1950	1960	1970	1980	1990
Number of acres	174	215	302	390	445	461

Solution

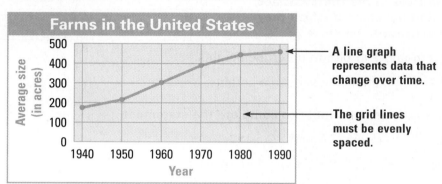

A line graph represents data that change over time.

The grid lines must be evenly spaced.

11. Make a graph of the data in the table. Which year had the greatest increase? (Source: U.S. Bureau of the Census)

Average Price per Pound for Lemons (dollars)

Year	1990	1991	1992	1993	1994	1995
Price	$.97	$1.21	$.90	$1.05	$1.04	$1.12

5.7 CHOOSING AN APPROPRIATE GRAPH

In a pictograph, the symbols that represent the data should be about the same size. Include a key that tells what each symbol represents.

Example

Food	Protein (grams)
Hamburger	24
Hot dog	12
Tuna fish sandwich	15
Grilled cheese	20

Protein in Foods

One symbol represents 4 grams of protein.

Hamburger	🍔🍔🍔🍔🍔🍔
Hot dog	🌭🌭🌭
Tuna fish sandwich	🥪🥪🥪🥪
Grilled cheese	🥪🥪🥪🥪🥪

12. Americans buy about 5000 hockey sticks, 3000 pairs of bowling shoes, 4000 soccer balls, 500 skateboards, and 6000 basketballs on an average day. Draw a pictograph of the data. (Source: National Sporting Goods Assoc.)

In Exercises 1 and 2, use the number of days in each month of the year.

1. Make a line plot of the data.

2. List two features of the data.

Pine	Height (yd)	State
Digger	54	CA
Eastern White	67	MI
Jeffrey	66	CA
Ponderosa	74	CA
Sugar	77	CA
Washoe	54	CA

SCIENCE The table at the right shows six of the tallest pine trees in the United States, their heights, and the state in which they grow. (Source: American Forestry Association)

3. Make a stem-and-leaf plot to order the heights.

4. Draw a bar graph that shows the tree heights.

In Exercises 5 and 6, use a number to complete the statement.

5. The mean of 85, 45, 66, 21, and [?] is 52.

6. The mode of 44, 54, 75, 89, 75, 44, and [?] is 75.

7. The numbers of glasses of milk that 25 students drank last week are shown below. Find the range, mean, median, and mode(s) of the data.

10, 14, 25, 16, 15, 16, 22, 18, 11, 5, 14, 16, 17, 21, 10, 14, 12, 11, 12, 15, 22, 20, 16, 18, 20

8. GEOGRAPHY The table below shows the lengths of some of the world's rivers. Make a bar graph of the data. (Source: U.S. Department of Commerce)

The Nile River, Egypt

River	Nile	Amazon	Mississippi	Rio Grande
Length (in miles)	4145	4000	2348	1885

9. MAIL The average number of pieces of mail received by each person is listed in the table for every 5 years from 1970 to 1995. Make a line graph of the data. What five-year period had the greatest increase? (Source: U.S. Postal Service)

Year	1970	1975	1980	1985	1990	1995
Mail	411	411	463	585	662	683

10. GARDENING These data give the numbers out of 100 surveyed who grew each type of flower in their gardens: marigolds, 60; roses, 60; geraniums, 58; impatiens, 56; and tulips, 52. Draw a pictograph of the data.

1. In the last 5 basketball games, the team scored 83 points, 64 points, 75 points, 89 points, and 82 points. Find the mean score for the last 5 games.

    (A) 76.3 points   (B) 76.8 points

    (C) 78.3 points   (D) 78.6 points

2. Ms. Johnson made a tally sheet of each student's grade on the social studies quiz. One student did not take the quiz. Which of the following statements is true?

Score	Tally
5	II
4	++++ I
3	++++ II
2	III
1	II

    (A) The mode of the scores was 4.

    (B) There are 20 students in the class.

    (C) The average quiz score was 3.

    (D) If Jill's score was 4, she did better than over one half of the class.

3. Your class held a car wash. The number of cars washed each day were 20, 8, 9, 4, 7, 10, and 12. You charged $2 per car. What was the mean amount of money raised in one day?

    (A) $28   (B) $17

    (C) $20   (D) $18

In Questions 4 and 5, use the following information. Your boss gave each employee a raise. The amounts are $.50, $.50, $.75, $.25, $.25, $.50, $.75, $1.00, $.50, $.25.

4. What was the mode of the raises?

    (A) $.25   (B) $1.00

    (C) $.50   (D) $5.25

5. What was the mean raise given?

    (A) $.75   (B) $.53

    (C) $.63   (D) $.50

6. Sandy asked her classmates to name their favorite kind of movie. The results are shown below. Which of the following statements is *false*?

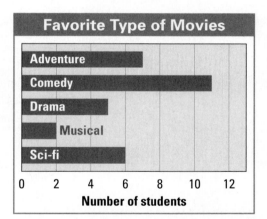

Favorite Type of Movies

    (A) Half as many students prefer science fiction movies to comedies.

    (B) In Sandy's class, adventure movies are less popular than comedies.

    (C) More than 15% of Sandy's class prefer dramas.

    (D) Less than 10% of Sandy's class prefer musicals.

Fractions, Ratios, and Proportions

TECHNOLOGY

Technology resources accompanying this chapter:
• Interactive Real-Life Investigations
• Middle School Tutorial Software

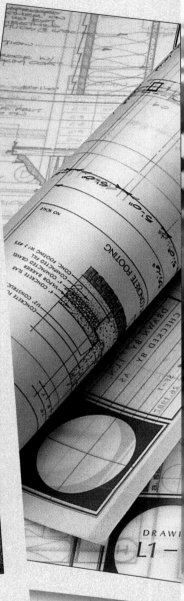

OWNING A HOME For a typical home-owning family, the home accounts for more than half of the family's total wealth.

CHAPTER THEME
Architecture

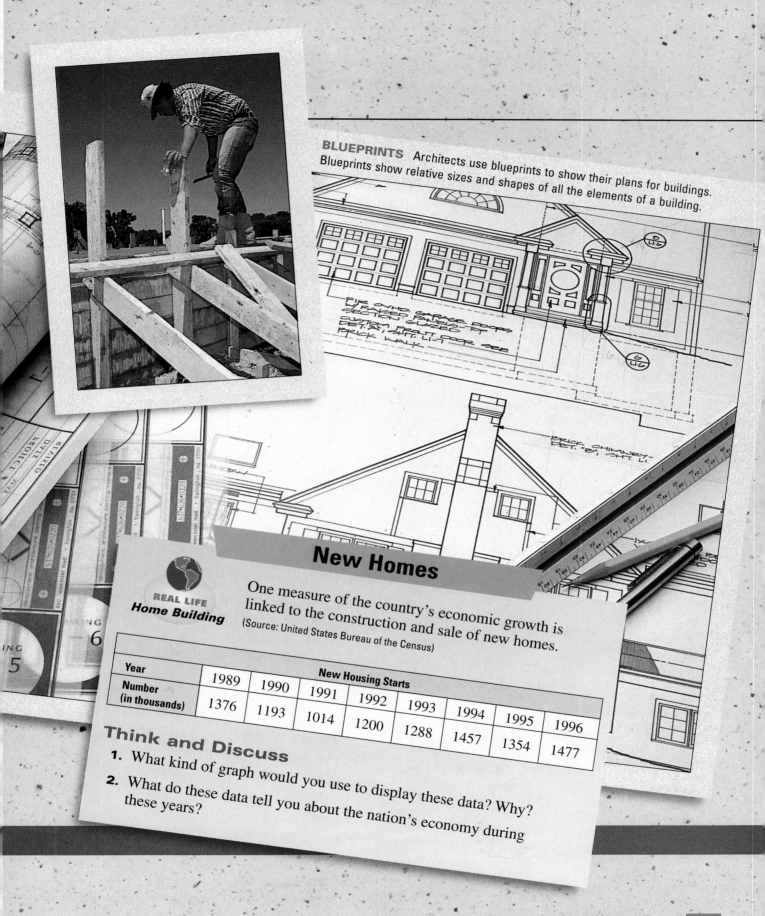

BLUEPRINTS Architects use blueprints to show their plans for buildings. Blueprints show relative sizes and shapes of all the elements of a building.

New Homes

REAL LIFE
Home Building

One measure of the country's economic growth is linked to the construction and sale of new homes. (Source: United States Bureau of the Census)

Year	New Housing Starts							
	1989	1990	1991	1992	1993	1994	1995	1996
Number (in thousands)	1376	1193	1014	1200	1288	1457	1354	1477

Think and Discuss

1. What kind of graph would you use to display these data? Why?

2. What do these data tell you about the nation's economy during these years?

PORTFOLIO

CHAPTER PROJECT

Planning an Apartment

PROJECT DESCRIPTION

Architects are people who design buildings. They draw blueprints that show what the building would look like if you sliced off the ceiling and looked at the arrangement of rooms from above. You will design and draw a blueprint of an apartment that has five rooms.

GETTING STARTED

Talking It Over

- In your groups, talk about what purpose a blueprint might serve. What building problems could it prevent? What would be some of the information you would expect to find on a blueprint? Who, besides the architect, might use the blueprint?

- Discuss what sorts of things you would want to think about before starting your apartment design. How would each factor affect your design?

Planning Your Project

- **Materials Needed:** one-inch grid paper, ruler, colored pencils

- Place a sheet of grid paper and four sheets of plain paper in your portfolio. You will use these papers and the **TOPICS** list on the next page to design your apartment and solve the related problems. Your project should include answers to the **BUILDING YOUR PROJECT** questions that appear throughout the chapter.

BUILDING YOUR PROJECT

These are places throughout the chapter where you will work on your project.

TOPICS

6.1 Make a scale drawing of the design. *p. 271*

6.2 Compare the width-to-length ratios in the blueprint of the rooms. *p. 277*

6.3 Compare the blueprint to the actual apartment. *p. 281*

6.4 Find the number of rolls of wallpaper you need. *p. 285*

6.5 Compare the sizes of the five rooms in the apartment. *p. 294*

6.6 Find the number of boxes of tiles needed to cover the floors. *p. 300*

INTERNET

To find out more about architecture, go to: **http://www.mlmath.com**

LAB 6.1

COOPERATIVE LEARNING

Materials Needed
• grid paper
• centimeter ruler
• colored pencils, pens, or markers

Investigating Part-to-Whole Models

Part **A** FOLDING PAPER IN HALVES

Fold a sheet of paper in half. Then fold it in half a second and a third time. Finally, unfold the paper. Two ways to do this are shown below.

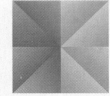

1. How many small regions are on your sheet? Are all the regions the same size?
2. What fraction of the whole does each small region represent?
3. Shade three of the regions. What fraction of the whole do the shaded regions represent?

Part **B** COMPARING FRACTIONS

There are many ways to draw a part-to-whole model for $\frac{3}{4}$ on grid paper. You can use a 1-by-4 rectangle, a 1-by-8 rectangle, or a 1-by-12 rectangle. In each case, divide the rectangle into four equal parts and shade three parts. The shaded part represents $\frac{3}{4}$ of the rectangle.

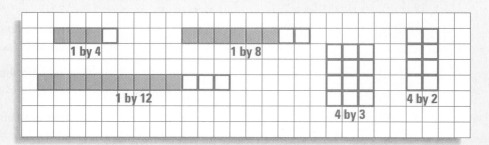

1 by 4　　1 by 8

1 by 12　　4 by 3　　4 by 2

4. Use a 2-by-4 rectangle to draw a part-to-whole model for $\frac{3}{4}$.
5. Use a 3-by-4 rectangle to draw a part-to-whole model for $\frac{3}{4}$.
6. Write a sentence that describes what all of these models for $\frac{3}{4}$ have in common.

7. Decide whether the figure is a correct part-to-whole model of the fraction $\frac{1}{3}$. Explain your reasoning.

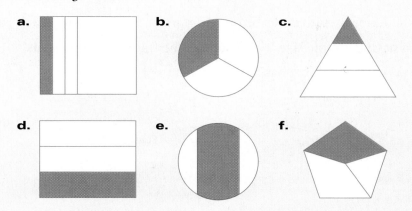

a. **b.** **c.**

d. **e.** **f.**

8. Look at the models above. What must be true of a part-to-whole model of the fraction $\frac{1}{3}$?

NOW TRY THESE

In Exercises 9–14, write the fraction that is shown by the part-to-whole model.

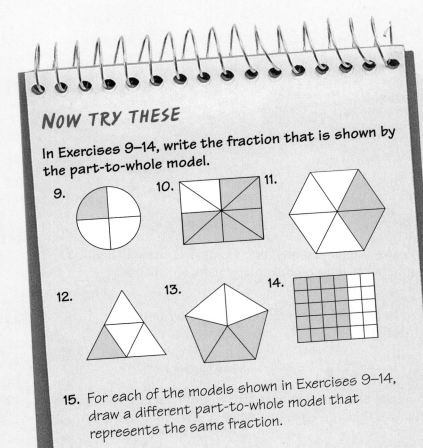

9. **10.** **11.**

12. **13.** **14.**

15. For each of the models shown in Exercises 9–14, draw a different part-to-whole model that represents the same fraction.

6.1

Fundamental Fraction Concepts

What you should learn:

Goal 1 How to write fractions

Goal 2 How to use fractions to solve real-life problems

Why you should learn it:

Fractions can help you compare sets. An example is comparing groups of students.

NEED TO KNOW

Any number that can be written as a fraction is a "rational number." The number 3 is a rational number because it can be written as the fraction $\frac{3}{1}$.

Goal 1 WRITING FRACTIONS

A fraction is used to describe one or more parts of a whole. Each part must have the same size. For example, the fraction $\frac{2}{5}$ represents 2 parts of a whole that has 5 equal parts.

Numerator ⟶ $\frac{2}{5}$
Denominator ⟶

Fraction Model

Example 1 Looking for a Pattern

The shaded parts of each circle represent a fraction of the circle. Name each fraction using fourths. What do the denominators and numerators represent?

a. b. c.

d. e.

Solution

The fractions are

a. $\frac{1}{4}$ **b.** $\frac{2}{4}$ **c.** $\frac{3}{4}$ **d.** $\frac{4}{4}$ **e.** $\frac{5}{4}$.

The denominator 4 tells you how many parts the circle is divided into. The numerators tell you how many parts are shaded.

In part (e) of Example 1, the fraction $\frac{5}{4}$ can be written as a **mixed number**.

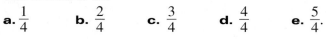

Fraction ⟶ $\frac{5}{4} = 1\frac{1}{4}$ ⟵ Mixed number

The fraction tells you that you have five fourths circles. The mixed number tells you that you have one whole circle, plus one fourth of another circle. So, $\frac{5}{4} = 1 + \frac{1}{4} = 1\frac{1}{4}$.

Example 2 ▷ **Representing Portions with Fractions**

You are helping to teach two first-grade classes to spell. Each class has 24 students.

a. In the first class, you divide the students into 6 equal groups. Five groups spell all the words correctly.

b. In the second class, you divide the students into 8 equal groups. Five groups spell all the words correctly.

c. Did one class do better than the other? Explain.

Solution

STRATEGY **DRAW A DIAGRAM** A diagram can help you answer the question.

a.

5 out of 6 groups

b.

5 out of 8 groups

c. So, $\frac{5}{6}$ of the first class, or 20 students, spelled all the words correctly, and $\frac{5}{8}$ of the second class, or 15 students, spelled all the words correctly. The first class did better.

Example 3 ▷ **Using Fractions in Real Life**

A digital clock uses one unit of electricity to light the entire block of squares at the right. The fractions below show how much electricity is used to light each digit from 0 to 4.

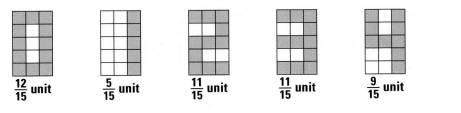

$\frac{12}{15}$ unit $\frac{5}{15}$ unit $\frac{11}{15}$ unit $\frac{11}{15}$ unit $\frac{9}{15}$ unit

---

ONGOING ASSESSMENT

Write About It
. . . .

1. A class of 15 students is divided into 5 equal groups, and 3 groups go to the science lab. What fraction goes to science lab?

2. Another class of 15 students is divided into 3 equal groups, and 2 groups go to the science lab. Which class has more students in the science lab?

GUIDED PRACTICE

1. Does the diagram at the right represent the fraction $\frac{4}{6}$? Explain your reasoning.

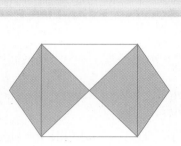

In Exercises 2–4, complete the statement.

2. In the fraction $\frac{6}{7}$, 6 is the ? and 7 is the ? .

3. The number $2\frac{2}{3}$ is a ? .

4. The denominator of the fraction $\frac{5}{12}$ is ? .

GEOMETRY   In Exercises 5–7, match the fraction with its model.

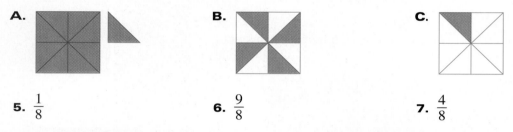

A.   **B.**   **C.**

5. $\frac{1}{8}$ 6. $\frac{9}{8}$ 7. $\frac{4}{8}$

8. **COMMUNICATING** Describe three situations in real life in which you would use a mixed number.

PRACTICE AND PROBLEM SOLVING

In Exercises 9–14, is the diagram a good model to use for a fraction? If it is, what fraction of the model is shaded? If it isn't, explain why.

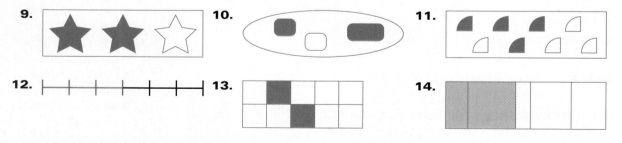

9.   10.   11.

12.   13.   14.

15. **MEASUREMENT** Draw a line that is 12 cm long. On the line, mark each centimeter. Then shade the part of the line that represents the fraction $\frac{7}{12}$.

16. **a.** Draw a model for $\frac{5}{6}$.   **b.** Draw a model for $\frac{7}{6}$.

17. CAR SAFETY In 1987, the fraction of cars and vans with driver's side air bags was $\frac{1}{20}$. In 1994, the fraction was $\frac{9}{10}$. Draw a model to represent each fraction. (Source: Insurance Institute for Highway Safety)

GUINEA PIGS A guinea pig had two litters. In the first, 2 of 3 babies were brown. In the second, 3 of 4 babies were brown.

18. For each litter, write the fraction that was brown.

19. In which litter was the fraction of brown baby guinea pigs larger? Use the diagram to help you decide.

20. Write three fractions that are close to 0 and three fractions that are close to 1.

21. Draw 20 circles. Group them by 4's. Color three of the groups blue. Draw another 20 circles and group them by 5's. Color three of the groups blue. On which group of 20 did you color more circles?

22. Use Exercise 21 to explain which fraction is larger, $\frac{3}{4}$ or $\frac{3}{5}$.

STANDARDIZED TEST PRACTICE

23. One inch is what fraction of a yard?

  A $\frac{1}{3}$ **B** $\frac{1}{12}$ **C** $\frac{1}{24}$ **D** $\frac{1}{36}$

24. Twenty seconds is what fraction of a minute?

  A $\frac{2}{3}$ **B** $\frac{20}{30}$ **C** $\frac{20}{60}$ **D** $\frac{3}{20}$

EXPLORATION AND EXTENSION

PORTFOLIO

25. BUILDING YOUR PROJECT Draw a model of an apartment on a 5 in.-by-5 in. grid of 25 squares. The sizes of the rooms are: kitchen (2-by-2), bathroom (1-by-2), living room (3-by-3), bedroom A (2-by-3), and bedroom B (2-by-2). The living room should connect to each of the other rooms. For each room, write the fraction that its area is of the apartment's area.

Investigating Set Models

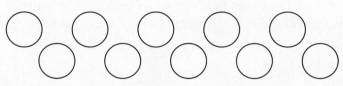

Part A DRAWING SET MODELS

Materials Needed
- plain paper
- colored pencils
  or markers

1. Copy the circles on a sheet of paper. Color $\frac{7}{10}$ of the circles green. Color the rest brown. What fraction of the circles are brown?

2. Copy the triangles on a sheet of paper. Color $\frac{1}{4}$ of the triangles red. Color the rest blue. What fraction of the triangles are blue?

3. Draw 15 squares of the same size.

  a. Is it possible to color $\frac{1}{3}$ of the squares yellow? Explain.

  b. Is it possible to color $\frac{1}{4}$ of the squares blue? Explain.

  c. Is it possible to color $\frac{1}{5}$ of the squares green? Explain.

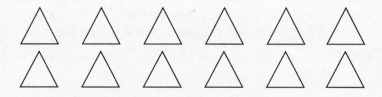

Part B PROBLEM SOLVING

4. Draw a set model to help you solve each problem.

  a. You have 12 model airplanes. One fourth of them have engines. How many have engines?

  b. You have $18. You spend four ninths of it for a T-shirt. How much did you spend?

  c. You have 8 pairs of jeans. One fourth are dark blue. How many *are not* dark blue?

5. You are asked to take one and one half dozen oranges to a school picnic. Explain how the set model shown below can help you find how many oranges you need to take.

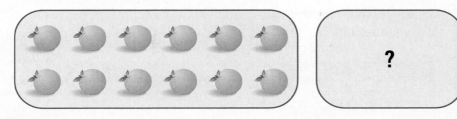

6. You have 16 baseball caps. Your friend has $\frac{5}{4}$ as many. Use a set model to find how many caps your friend has.

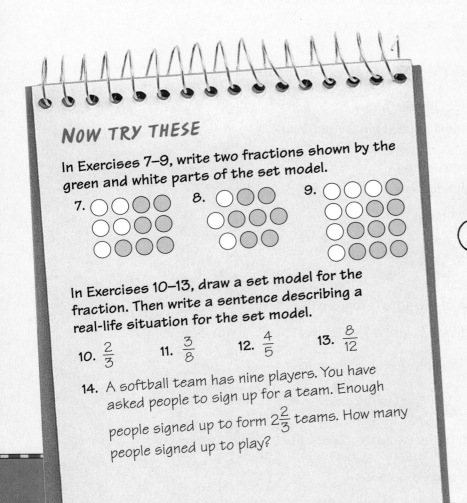

NOW TRY THESE

In Exercises 7–9, write two fractions shown by the green and white parts of the set model.

7.

8.

9.

In Exercises 10–13, draw a set model for the fraction. Then write a sentence describing a real-life situation for the set model.

10. $\frac{2}{3}$ 11. $\frac{3}{8}$ 12. $\frac{4}{5}$ 13. $\frac{8}{12}$

14. A softball team has nine players. You have asked people to sign up for a team. Enough people signed up to form $2\frac{2}{3}$ teams. How many people signed up to play?

$\frac{1}{8}$, $\frac{7}{8}$

6.2

Exploring Division and Ratios

What you should learn:

Goal 1 How fractions are related to division

Goal 2 How to write ratios

Why you should learn it:

Fractions can help you divide things evenly. An example is finding how 5 people can equally share 3 pizzas.

Goal 1 FRACTIONS AND DIVISION

In this lesson, you will learn another way to represent the result of a division problem.

LESSON INVESTIGATION

Investigating Division

GROUP ACTIVITY You are having a sleepover with 4 friends. For supper, you make 3 pizzas. Draw a diagram to show how you could cut the pizzas so that each person would get the same amount.

What portion of a whole pizza would each person get?

There are several ways you might have solved the pizza problem above. One way is to use *division*. Because 3 pizzas are shared among 5 people, you could divide 3 by 5 and conclude that each person would get $\frac{3}{5}$ of a pizza.

Example 1 Solving Division Problems

a. Divide 3 hours into 4 equal parts.

b. Divide 5 apples into 2 equal parts.

Solution

a. To divide 3 hours into 4 equal parts, divide 3 by 4.

$$(3 \text{ hours}) \div 4 = \frac{3}{4} \text{ hour}$$

Each of the 4 parts represents $\frac{3}{4}$ hour.

b. To divide 5 apples into 2 equal parts, divide 5 by 2.

$$(5 \text{ apples}) \div 2 = \frac{5}{2} \text{ apples}$$

Each of the two parts represents $\frac{5}{2}$, or $2\frac{1}{2}$, apples.

NEED TO KNOW

In earlier chapters you studied three ways to write the result of a division problem.

$5 \div 2 = 2 \text{ R}1$ With a Remainder

$5 \div 2 = 2\frac{1}{2}$ Mixed Number

$5 \div 2 = 2.5$ Decimal

Example 1 shows a fourth way to write a division problem: as a fraction.

$5 \div 2 = \frac{5}{2}$ Fraction

Goal 2 WRITING A RATIO

Writing a *ratio* can be a useful way to compare quantities. Ratios are often used in advertising. For example, a company may claim that "4 out of 5 doctors" recommend their product.

WRITING A RATIO

A **ratio** is a comparison of two numbers by division. The two numbers must have the same unit of measure.

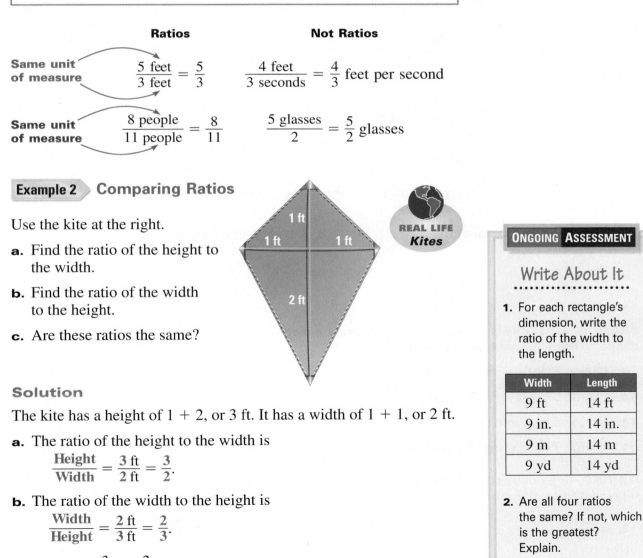

Ratios

Same unit of measure $\dfrac{5 \text{ feet}}{3 \text{ feet}} = \dfrac{5}{3}$

Same unit of measure $\dfrac{8 \text{ people}}{11 \text{ people}} = \dfrac{8}{11}$

Not Ratios

$\dfrac{4 \text{ feet}}{3 \text{ seconds}} = \dfrac{4}{3}$ feet per second

$\dfrac{5 \text{ glasses}}{2} = \dfrac{5}{2}$ glasses

Example 2 **Comparing Ratios**

Use the kite at the right.

a. Find the ratio of the height to the width.

b. Find the ratio of the width to the height.

c. Are these ratios the same?

REAL LIFE
Kites

1 ft

1 ft   1 ft

2 ft

Solution

The kite has a height of $1 + 2$, or 3 ft. It has a width of $1 + 1$, or 2 ft.

a. The ratio of the height to the width is
$$\frac{\text{Height}}{\text{Width}} = \frac{3 \text{ ft}}{2 \text{ ft}} = \frac{3}{2}.$$

b. The ratio of the width to the height is
$$\frac{\text{Width}}{\text{Height}} = \frac{2 \text{ ft}}{3 \text{ ft}} = \frac{2}{3}.$$

c. The ratios $\dfrac{3}{2}$ and $\dfrac{2}{3}$ are not the same.

ONGOING ASSESSMENT

Write About It

1. For each rectangle's dimension, write the ratio of the width to the length.

Width	Length
9 ft	14 ft
9 in.	14 in.
9 m	14 m
9 yd	14 yd

2. Are all four ratios the same? If not, which is the greatest? Explain.

GUIDED PRACTICE

1. Suppose there are 4 large sandwiches to be divided equally among 5 people. How could the sandwiches be divided equally? What fraction of a sandwich does each person get?

2. The model at the right shows how to divide 3 into 2 equal parts. What fraction of the model is each part?

3. Use a diagram to divide 7 apples equally among 4 people. What fraction of an apple does each person get?

4. Explain how to write a ratio. Give an example.

PRACTICE AND PROBLEM SOLVING

In Exercises 5 and 6, use a diagram to answer the question.

5. You have 32 one-dollar coins. One fourth are Susan B. Anthony coins. How many are another type of one-dollar coin?

6. You are flying on a 500 mi trip. You have flown two fifths of the distance. How far have you flown?

VISUAL THINKING   **In Exercises 7 and 8, use the model to divide. Write your answer as a fraction.**

7. Divide 3 into 5 equal parts.

8. Divide 5 into 3 equal parts.

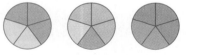

DRAWING A DIAGRAM   **In Exercises 9–12, draw a diagram to help you divide. Write your answer as a fraction.**

9. Divide 2 dollars into 4 equal parts.

10. Divide 5 pizzas into 7 equal parts.

11. Divide 8 pies into 6 equal parts.

12. Divide 7 boards into 6 equal parts.

WRITING   **In Exercises 13–15, describe a real-life situation that can be represented by the ratio.**

13. $\dfrac{16 \text{ miles}}{45 \text{ miles}}$

14. $\dfrac{7 \text{ books}}{9 \text{ books}}$

15. $\dfrac{8 \text{ meters}}{15 \text{ meters}}$

GEOMETRY In Exercises 16 and 17, write the ratio of the width to the length of the rectangle.

16.
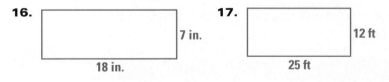
7 in.
18 in.

17.
12 ft
25 ft

MARBLES In Exercises 18–20, use the set model below that shows a collection of colored marbles.

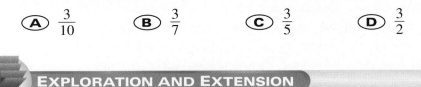

18. What is the ratio of purple marbles to total marbles?

19. What is the ratio of red marbles to yellow marbles?

20. What is the ratio of blue marbles to red marbles?

21. Measure the width and length of the photo above to the nearest millimeter. Write the ratio of the width to the length.

STANDARDIZED TEST PRACTICE

22. The athletes in a race run 3 mi, swim 2 mi, and cycle 5 mi. What is the ratio of the distance run to the total length of the race?

(A) $\frac{3}{10}$ (B) $\frac{3}{7}$ (C) $\frac{3}{5}$ (D) $\frac{3}{2}$

EXPLORATION AND EXTENSION

PORTFOLIO

23. BUILDING YOUR PROJECT For each room in your apartment, write the ratio of the length of the short side to the length of the long side. What can you say about the ratios of the rooms that are square?

24. COMMUNICATING ABOUT MATHEMATICS (page 301) Four sculptures of large badminton shuttlecocks by Claes Oldenburg are displayed in Kansas City, MO. The height of each sculpture is 18 ft. A smaller model of the sculpture is 27 in. high. What is the ratio of the height of the sculpture to the height of the model?

6.3

Equivalent Fractions and **Ratios**

What you should learn:

Goal 1 How to decide if two fractions are equivalent

Goal 2 How to decide whether two ratios are equivalent

Why you should learn it:

Fractions can be written in different forms. To be a problem solver, you need to be able to recognize equivalent forms.

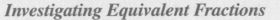

Goal 1 EQUIVALENT FRACTIONS

In this lesson, you will see that fractions can be written in various forms.

LESSON INVESTIGATION

Investigating Equivalent Fractions

GROUP ACTIVITY Look at the models and fractions below. What pattern do you see?

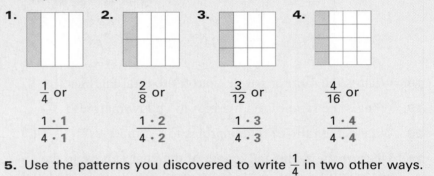

1. $\frac{1}{4}$ or $\frac{1 \cdot 1}{4 \cdot 1}$ 2. $\frac{2}{8}$ or $\frac{1 \cdot 2}{4 \cdot 2}$ 3. $\frac{3}{12}$ or $\frac{1 \cdot 3}{4 \cdot 3}$ 4. $\frac{4}{16}$ or $\frac{1 \cdot 4}{4 \cdot 4}$

5. Use the patterns you discovered to write $\frac{1}{4}$ in two other ways.

In the investigation, you may have discovered that all the models have the same ratio of shaded parts to total parts. The fractions shown by the models are *equivalent fractions*.

TOOLBOX

Equivalent Fractions, page 644

EQUIVALENT FRACTIONS

Multiplying the numerator and the denominator of a fraction by the *same* nonzero number produces an **equivalent fraction**.

STUDY TIP

To find an equivalent fraction, multiply the numerator and denominator by the same nonzero number.

$$\frac{2}{3} = \frac{2 \cdot 4}{3 \cdot 4} = \frac{8}{12}$$

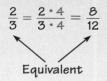

Equivalent

Example 1 Equivalent Fractions

Show that $\frac{2}{3}$ and $\frac{8}{12}$ are equivalent fractions.

Solution

$$\frac{2}{3} = \frac{2 \cdot 4}{3 \cdot 4} = \frac{8}{12}$$ Multiply numerator and denominator by 4.

The fractions $\frac{2}{3}$ and $\frac{8}{12}$ are equivalent.

Ratios are equivalent if they are equivalent as fractions. For example, the following ratios are equivalent.

$$\frac{3 \text{ in.}}{6 \text{ in.}} = \frac{3}{6} = \frac{1}{2}$$

$$\frac{4 \text{ ft}}{8 \text{ ft}} = \frac{4}{8} = \frac{1}{2}$$

A **rate** is a fraction in which the numerator and denominator have different units of measure. Here are some examples of rates:

$$\frac{45 \text{ mi}}{\text{hour}} \qquad \frac{\$36}{3 \text{ hours}}$$

Example 2 > **Writing Equivalent Ratios**

REAL LIFE
Architecture

Find the dimensions of the scale drawing of the kitchen. Compare the width-to-length ratios of the *scale drawing* and of the *actual kitchen*. What can you conclude?

9 ft

Kitchen

Living Room

12 ft

15 ft   12 ft

Solution

In the scale drawing, the kitchen is 3 cm by 5 cm.

$$\frac{\text{Width}}{\text{Length}} = \frac{3 \text{ cm}}{5 \text{ cm}} = \frac{3}{5} \qquad \textbf{Scale drawing}$$

The actual kitchen is 9 ft by 15 ft.

$$\frac{\text{Width}}{\text{Length}} = \frac{9 \text{ ft}}{15 \text{ ft}} = \frac{9}{15} \qquad \textbf{Actual kitchen}$$

The two ratios are equivalent because $\frac{3}{5} = \frac{3 \cdot 3}{5 \cdot 3} = \frac{9}{15}$.

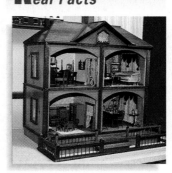

Real Life...
Real Facts

Dollhouses became popular in the 17th and 18th centuries in Europe. Dollhouses are still popular collectibles among today's children and adults.

TOOLBOX

Ratio, page 656

ONGOING ASSESSMENT

Write About It
....

1. In Example 2, find the width-to-length ratios of the scale drawing of the living room and the actual living room.

2. Compare the ratios. What can you conclude?

GUIDED PRACTICE

1. Write two equivalent fractions represented by the diagram at the right.

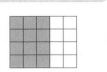

2. Draw a diagram that shows why the fractions $\frac{4}{5}$ and $\frac{8}{10}$ are equivalent.

3. Draw a diagram that shows why the fractions $\frac{3}{4}$ and $\frac{9}{12}$ are equivalent.

4. **GEOMETRY** Use a centimeter ruler to measure the width and length of the rectangles below. For each rectangle, find the ratio of the width to the length. Are the ratios equivalent?

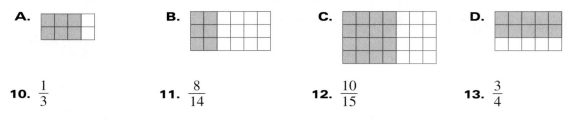

REASONING In Exercises 5–8, decide whether the fractions are equivalent. Explain why or why not.

5. $\frac{1}{6}, \frac{2}{12}$ 6. $\frac{1}{2}, \frac{4}{6}$ 7. $\frac{5}{8}, \frac{15}{24}$ 8. $\frac{2}{5}, \frac{4}{9}$

9. Find and correct the error: $\frac{2}{3} = \frac{2}{3} \cdot \frac{2}{3} = \frac{4}{9}$.

PRACTICE AND PROBLEM SOLVING

In Exercises 10–13, match the fraction with its diagram. Write an equivalent fraction that is represented by the diagram.

A.   B.   C.   D.

10. $\frac{1}{3}$ 11. $\frac{8}{14}$ 12. $\frac{10}{15}$ 13. $\frac{3}{4}$

GUESS, CHECK, AND REVISE In Exercises 14–17, find the missing number.

14. $\frac{2}{5} = \frac{?}{25}$ 15. $\frac{3}{18} = \frac{?}{6}$ 16. $\frac{8}{36} = \frac{2}{?}$ 17. $\frac{4}{7} = \frac{24}{?}$

Write three equivalent fractions. Tell why they are equivalent.

18. $\frac{7}{8}$ 19. $\frac{4}{11}$ 20. $\frac{15}{18}$ 21. $\frac{4}{36}$

In Exercises 22–24, is the statement *true* or *false*? If it is false, change the red number to make the statement true.

22. $\dfrac{2 \text{ m}}{3 \text{ m}} = \dfrac{8 \text{ km}}{18 \text{ km}}$ **23.** $\dfrac{200 \text{ mi}}{4 \text{ h}} = \dfrac{100 \text{ mi}}{2 \text{ h}}$ **24.** $\dfrac{9 \text{ ft}}{12 \text{ ft}} = \dfrac{18 \text{ ft}}{24 \text{ ft}}$

SCHOOL SURVEY A survey asked 24 students to name their favorite subject. One fourth chose science, one third chose English, and one sixth chose computer science. The rest chose math.

25. Use a set model to determine the number of students who chose each subject as their favorite.

26. Write the fraction of students who chose math.

27. How many students chose computer science?

28. **WALKING** Suzy walked 6 mi in 2 h. Ricardo walked 12 mi in 3 h. Did they walk at the same rate? Explain.

29. **TYPING** Mark types 6 pages in 36 min. Melissa types 5 pages in 30 min. Do they type at the same rate? Explain.

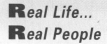

STANDARDIZED TEST PRACTICE

30. Which ratio is equivalent to $\dfrac{24}{36}$?

   (A) $\dfrac{2}{3}$ **(B)** $\dfrac{4}{9}$ **(C)** $\dfrac{3}{18}$ **(D)** $\dfrac{3}{24}$

31. In your coin collection, you have 9 buffalo nickels and 30 Lincoln pennies. What is the ratio of buffalo nickels to Lincoln pennies?

   (A) $\dfrac{9}{15}$ **(B)** $\dfrac{3}{9}$ **(C)** $\dfrac{3}{10}$ **(D)** $\dfrac{1}{13}$

EXPLORATION AND EXTENSION

PORTFOLIO

32. **BUILDING YOUR PROJECT** In the scale drawing of your apartment, let each segment represent 6 ft. Label each room with its actual length and width. (This means that the actual apartment is 30 ft by 30 ft.) Copy and complete the table below. What can you conclude?

Room	Kitchen	Living Room	Bathroom	Bedroom A	Bedroom B
Model Width-to-Length Ratio	?	?	?	?	?
Actual Width-to-Length Ratio	?	?	?	?	?

6.4

Exploring Proportions

What you should learn:

Goal 1 How to simplify a fraction

Goal 2 How to solve a proportion

Why you should learn it:

Proportions can be used to find the rate at which you work. An example is finding how many words per minute you can type.

To qualify for jobs in the federal government, you need to type at least 40 words per minute.

TOOLBOX

Equivalent Fractions, page 644

Goal 1 SIMPLIFYING FRACTIONS

How many fractions are equivalent to $\frac{4}{10}$? The answer is that there are more than you can count! Here are a few.

$$\frac{2}{5}, \frac{4}{10}, \frac{6}{15}, \frac{8}{20}, \frac{10}{25}, \frac{12}{30}, \frac{14}{35}, \cdots$$ **Equivalent fractions**

These models show that $\frac{4}{10} = \frac{2}{5}$.

Four tenths of the marbles are red.

Two fifths of the marbles are red.

The fraction in **simplest form** is $\frac{2}{5}$ because its numerator and denominator have no common factor other than one. To **simplify a fraction** means to rewrite it in its simplest form.

Example 1 **Simplifying Fractions**

Simplify the fraction.

a. $\frac{4}{8}$　　　　**b.** $\frac{14}{6}$　　　　**c.** $\frac{10}{5}$

Solution

To simplify a fraction, divide its numerator and denominator by a common factor.

a. $\frac{4}{8} = \frac{4 \div 4}{8 \div 4}$　　　Factor numerator and denominator.

$= \frac{1}{2}$　　　Simplify the fraction.

b. $\frac{14}{6} = \frac{14 \div 2}{6 \div 2}$　　　Factor numerator and denominator.

$= \frac{7}{3}$　　　Simplify the fraction.

c. $\frac{10}{5} = \frac{10 \div 5}{5 \div 5}$　　　Use 5 as the common factor.

$= \frac{2}{1}$　　　Simplify the fraction.

$= 2$　　　Write as a whole number.

A **proportion** is an equation stating that two ratios are equivalent. If there is a variable, you **solve a proportion** by finding the value of the variable.

Example 2 ▷ Solving a Proportion

To solve the proportion $\frac{2}{3} = \frac{x}{9}$, you need to find a value of x so that $\frac{x}{9}$ is equivalent to $\frac{2}{3}$.

Method **1**   Use mental math to write an equivalent fraction.

$$\frac{2}{3} = \frac{2 \cdot 3}{3 \cdot 3} = \frac{6}{9}$$ **Multiply numerator and denominator by 3.**

So, $x = 6$.

Method **2**   Use a fraction model. There are 6 shaded parts in the new model, so $x = 6$.

Model for $\frac{2}{3}$ Model divided into 9 parts

Example 3 ▷ Using a Proportion

You worked 2 hours and earned $28. Janet did the same work for 3 hours and earned $42. Did you get paid at the same rate?

Solution

Understand the Problem   You got paid at the same rate if the following proportion is true:

$$\frac{\text{Your hours}}{\text{Your pay}} = \frac{\text{Janet's hours}}{\text{Janet's pay}}$$

Make a Plan   Check whether the proportion is true.

Solve the Problem

$$\frac{2}{28} \stackrel{?}{=} \frac{3}{42}$$

$$\frac{2 \div 2}{28 \div 2} \stackrel{?}{=} \frac{3 \div 3}{42 \div 3}$$

$$\frac{1}{14} = \frac{1}{14} \checkmark$$

Look Back   You did get paid at the same rate.

Talk About It
....

In Exercises 1 and 2, use the methods in Example 2 to solve the proportion.

1. $\frac{m}{16} = \frac{3}{4}$

2. $\frac{9}{12} = \frac{n}{4}$

3. Which method do you prefer? Why?

GUIDED PRACTICE

NUMBER SENSE In Exercises 1–4, match the fraction with its model.

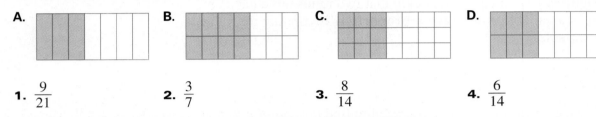

A.   **B.**   **C.**   **D.**

1. $\dfrac{9}{21}$ **2.** $\dfrac{3}{7}$ **3.** $\dfrac{8}{14}$ **4.** $\dfrac{6}{14}$

5. In Exercises 1–4, which three fractions are equivalent? Of these, which is in simplest form?

6. Write the fraction that is represented by the model at the right. Then simplify the fraction.

7. Solve the proportion $\dfrac{4}{5} = \dfrac{n}{15}$ by drawing a diagram.

8. **GROUP ACTIVITY** On a sheet of paper, write a proportion that has one variable. Exchange papers with your partner. Solve the proportion that your partner wrote. Explain your reasoning. Then check each other's work.

PRACTICE AND PROBLEM SOLVING

In Exercises 9–11, write the fraction that is represented by the model. Then simplify if possible.

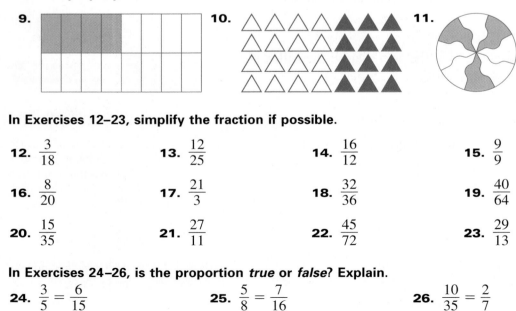

9.   **10.**   **11.**

In Exercises 12–23, simplify the fraction if possible.

12. $\dfrac{3}{18}$ **13.** $\dfrac{12}{25}$ **14.** $\dfrac{16}{12}$ **15.** $\dfrac{9}{9}$

16. $\dfrac{8}{20}$ **17.** $\dfrac{21}{3}$ **18.** $\dfrac{32}{36}$ **19.** $\dfrac{40}{64}$

20. $\dfrac{15}{35}$ **21.** $\dfrac{27}{11}$ **22.** $\dfrac{45}{72}$ **23.** $\dfrac{29}{13}$

In Exercises 24–26, is the proportion *true* or *false*? Explain.

24. $\dfrac{3}{5} = \dfrac{6}{15}$ **25.** $\dfrac{5}{8} = \dfrac{7}{16}$ **26.** $\dfrac{10}{35} = \dfrac{2}{7}$

In Exercises 27–32, solve the proportion.

27. $\dfrac{3}{10} = \dfrac{9}{m}$

28. $\dfrac{16}{28} = \dfrac{4}{n}$

29. $\dfrac{a}{40} = \dfrac{1}{5}$

30. $\dfrac{6}{x} = \dfrac{30}{55}$

31. $\dfrac{2}{9} = \dfrac{y}{54}$

32. $\dfrac{d}{72} = \dfrac{7}{8}$

GEOMETRY In Exercises 33 and 34, the figures are similar. Write a proportion that you can use to find the missing length. Then solve the proportion.

33.

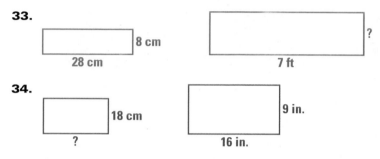

34.

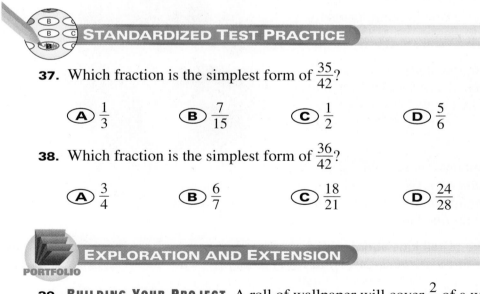

35. GASOLINE MILEAGE Jon drove 100 mi and used 5 gal of gasoline. Maura drove 150 mi and used 8 gal of gasoline. Did they use gasoline at the same rate? Explain.

36. TYPING After taking a class in typing, you find that you can type 155 words in 5 minutes. How many words per minute can you type?

STANDARDIZED TEST PRACTICE

37. Which fraction is the simplest form of $\dfrac{35}{42}$?

A $\dfrac{1}{3}$ **B** $\dfrac{7}{15}$ **C** $\dfrac{1}{2}$ **D** $\dfrac{5}{6}$

38. Which fraction is the simplest form of $\dfrac{36}{42}$?

A $\dfrac{3}{4}$ **B** $\dfrac{6}{7}$ **C** $\dfrac{18}{21}$ **D** $\dfrac{24}{28}$

EXPLORATION AND EXTENSION

PORTFOLIO

39. BUILDING YOUR PROJECT A roll of wallpaper will cover $\dfrac{2}{3}$ of a wall.

How many rolls cover four walls? Use a diagram to help answer the question. Ignore any doors or windows in the walls.

GEOMETRY **In Exercises 1 and 2, draw the figure on a 6-by-6 grid of dot paper. (1.5)**

1. A square with an area of 25 square units

2. Two rectangles, each with a perimeter of 14 units

3. **TILING** Your family is buying tiles for the kitchen floor. The kitchen measures 8 ft-by-10 ft. How many 2 ft-by-2 ft tiles does your family need to buy? **(2.3)**

4. What is 80% of 16? **(4.4)**

5. What is 0.3 of 4.5? **(4.4)**

VISUAL THINKING **Write the fraction of the diagram that is shaded. (6.1)**

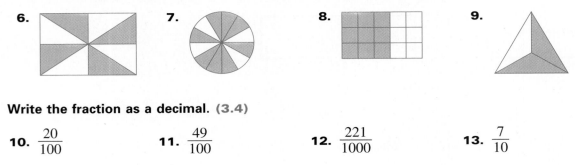

6.

7.

8.

9.

Write the fraction as a decimal. (3.4)

10. $\dfrac{20}{100}$

11. $\dfrac{49}{100}$

12. $\dfrac{221}{1000}$

13. $\dfrac{7}{10}$

CAREER Interview

CITY PLANNER

Maria Resendiz puts her degree in architecture to work as a city planner. Resendiz's responsibilities include reviewing permit requests for new construction and designing building plans for local community businesses.

Q What math skills do you apply in your work?
Ratios, division, area, and perimeter, to name a few. For example, I calculate the square footage of land lots and then figure out how they can be divided into smaller lots.

Q Do you use mathematical reasoning?
Yes, I recently had to predict the shadow of a planned office tower using a sun dial and a math formula. I had to decide if the shadow would affect the homes and buildings around it.

Q What would you like to tell kids about math?
During my first few years of college, we did a lot of math problems. I couldn't understand why. Then in my last semester, I took a class on architectural technology and I finally saw how everything applied to building. All the time I spent learning math was worth it.

Take this test as you would take a test in class. The answers to the exercises are given in the back of the book.

In Exercises 1–4, write the fraction of the figure that is shaded. Then match the fraction with its description (6.1)

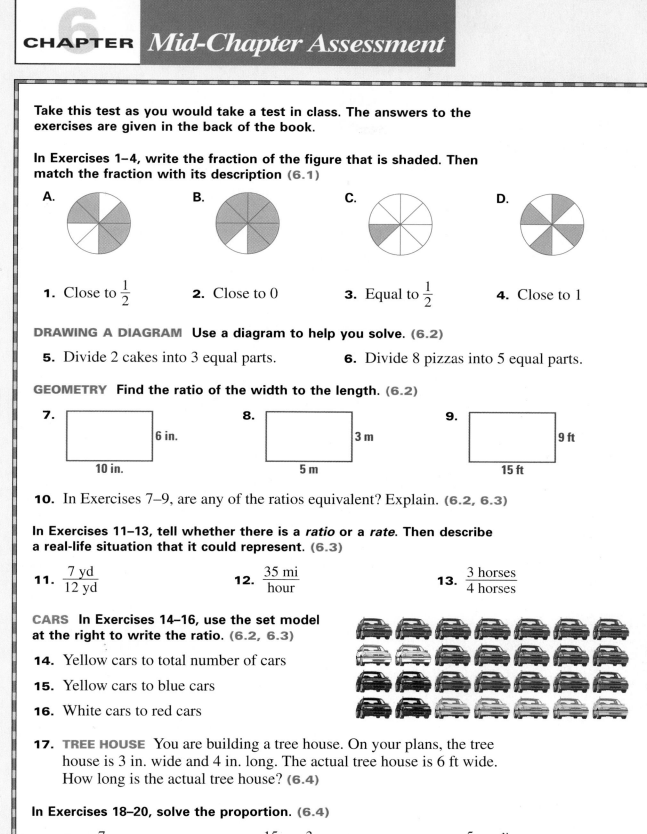

A.

B.

C.

D.

1. Close to $\frac{1}{2}$

2. Close to 0

3. Equal to $\frac{1}{2}$

4. Close to 1

DRAWING A DIAGRAM Use a diagram to help you solve. (6.2)

5. Divide 2 cakes into 3 equal parts.

6. Divide 8 pizzas into 5 equal parts.

GEOMETRY Find the ratio of the width to the length. (6.2)

7. 6 in. 10 in.

8. 3 m 5 m

9. 9 ft 15 ft

10. In Exercises 7–9, are any of the ratios equivalent? Explain. (6.2, 6.3)

In Exercises 11–13, tell whether there is a *ratio* or a *rate*. Then describe a real-life situation that it could represent. (6.3)

11. $\frac{7 \text{ yd}}{12 \text{ yd}}$

12. $\frac{35 \text{ mi}}{\text{hour}}$

13. $\frac{3 \text{ horses}}{4 \text{ horses}}$

CARS In Exercises 14–16, use the set model at the right to write the ratio. (6.2, 6.3)

14. Yellow cars to total number of cars

15. Yellow cars to blue cars

16. White cars to red cars

17. **TREE HOUSE** You are building a tree house. On your plans, the tree house is 3 in. wide and 4 in. long. The actual tree house is 6 ft wide. How long is the actual tree house? (6.4)

In Exercises 18–20, solve the proportion. (6.4)

18. $\frac{x}{4} = \frac{7}{28}$

19. $\frac{15}{n} = \frac{3}{10}$

20. $\frac{5}{8} = \frac{y}{72}$

LAB 6.5

COOPERATIVE LEARNING

Investigating Comparisons of Fractions

Materials Needed
- plain paper
- pencils
- ruler
- calculator

1. Which is greater: $\frac{1}{3}$ or $\frac{2}{5}$? One way you can decide is to use rectangular fraction models. The denominators are 3 and 5, so draw two 3-by-5 models. The grids must divide each model into 15 rectangles of the same size.

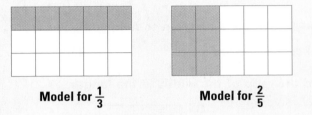

Model for $\frac{1}{3}$ Model for $\frac{2}{5}$

Explain how to decide which fraction is greater.

Part **B** MAKING CONNECTIONS

2. Copy the two fraction models below. Write the fraction for each model. Look at the denominators. Add lines to each model so that both models have the same number of regions. Then compare the two fractions. Which is greater?

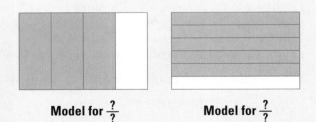

Model for $\frac{?}{?}$ Model for $\frac{?}{?}$

Draw a rectangular model for each fraction. Then use the models to decide which fraction is greater.

3. Which is greater: $\frac{3}{4}$ or $\frac{4}{5}$? Use rectangular models that have 4 units on one side and 5 units on the other side.

4. Which is greater: $\frac{3}{8}$ or $\frac{2}{5}$? Use rectangular models that have 8 units on one side and 5 units on the other side.

5. Another way to compare fractions is to rewrite them as decimals. To see which decimal is greater, plot them on a number line. (*Hint:* You can use a calculator to rewrite $\frac{5}{8}$ as 0.625.) Which is greater: $\frac{6}{10}$ or $\frac{5}{8}$?

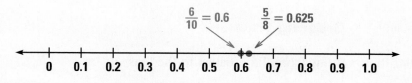

$$\frac{6}{10} = 0.6 \qquad \frac{5}{8} = 0.625$$

6. Copy the following number line. Using mental math or a calculator, rewrite the fractions $\frac{3}{10}, \frac{3}{8}, \frac{2}{5}, \frac{1}{2}$, and $\frac{7}{16}$ as decimals. Plot and label the decimals on the number line. Decide which fraction is greater.

a. $\frac{3}{10}, \frac{3}{8}$ b. $\frac{2}{5}, \frac{7}{16}$ c. $\frac{3}{8}, \frac{1}{2}$ d. $\frac{1}{2}, \frac{7}{16}$

NOW TRY THESE

In Exercises 7 and 8, draw a model for each fraction. Then use the result to decide which fraction is greater.

7. $\frac{3}{7}, \frac{1}{2}$ 8. $\frac{3}{5}, \frac{5}{8}$

Use a calculator to rewrite the fractions as decimals. Then use a number line to decide which fraction is greater.

9. $\frac{7}{10}, \frac{5}{8}$ 10. $\frac{7}{10}, \frac{4}{5}$

11. $\frac{3}{4}, \frac{4}{5}$ 12. $\frac{13}{16}, \frac{3}{4}$

6.5 Comparing and Ordering Fractions

What you should learn:

Goal 1 How to compare and order fractions

Goal 2 How to compare fractions to solve real-life problems

Why you should learn it:

Comparing fractions can help you be a smart consumer. An example is comparing the prices of two remote control cars that are on sale.

Goal 1 COMPARING AND ORDERING FRACTIONS

When you decide that one fraction is greater or lesser than another, you are **comparing fractions**.

Example 1 Ordering Fractions

Order the fractions from the greatest to the least.

a. $\frac{2}{5}$ and $\frac{3}{5}$

b. $\frac{2}{5}$, $\frac{2}{3}$, and $\frac{2}{4}$

Solution

a. For fractions with the same **denominator**, the fraction with the greater **numerator** is greater.

$$\frac{2}{5}, \frac{3}{5} \longrightarrow \frac{3}{5} > \frac{2}{5}$$

Because $\frac{3}{5} > \frac{2}{5}$, the order is $\frac{3}{5}, \frac{2}{5}$.

b. For fractions with the same **numerator**, the fraction with the lesser **denominator** is greater.

$$\frac{2}{5}, \frac{2}{3}, \frac{2}{4} \longrightarrow \frac{2}{3} > \frac{2}{4} > \frac{2}{5}$$

Because $\frac{2}{3} > \frac{2}{4} > \frac{2}{5}$, the order is $\frac{2}{3}, \frac{2}{4}, \frac{2}{5}$.

Example 2 Comparing Fractions

Compare the fractions $\frac{3}{4}$ and $\frac{2}{3}$.

Solution

List the equivalent fractions and find two with the same denominator.

Original Fraction	Equivalent Fractions
$\frac{3}{4}$	$\frac{3}{4} = \frac{6}{8} = \frac{9}{12} = \frac{12}{16}$
$\frac{2}{3}$	$\frac{2}{3} = \frac{4}{6} = \frac{6}{9} = \frac{8}{12}$

Using the fractions $\frac{9}{12}$ and $\frac{8}{12}$, it follows that $\frac{3}{4} > \frac{2}{3}$.

STUDY TIP

Another way to compare the fractions you see in Example 2 is to use fraction models.

$\frac{3}{4} = \frac{9}{12}$ $\frac{2}{3} = \frac{8}{12}$

So $\frac{3}{4} > \frac{2}{3}$.

Example 3 Comparing Fractions

You want to buy a remote control car. Which is the better buy?

Remote Controls are used not only with model racecars but also with model airplanes, automatic garage doors, televisions, and theme park attractions.

Real Life...
Real Facts

Solution

Method ❶ *Compare fractions.*

$\frac{1}{3} > \frac{1}{4}$, so Bob's Car Land is the better buy.

Method ❷ *Use set models.* At Bob's Car Land, the sale price is $16. At Mary's Toy Land, the sale price is $18. So, Bob's Car Land is the better buy.

Bob's Car Land   **Mary's Toy Land**

$16 $18

Example 4 Ordering Fractions

Use a ruler to order the fractions $\frac{3}{8}$, $\frac{1}{2}$, $\frac{1}{4}$, and $\frac{3}{4}$.

Solution

$\frac{1}{4}$ $\frac{3}{8}$ $\frac{1}{2}$ $\frac{3}{4}$

The order is $\frac{1}{4}, \frac{3}{8}, \frac{1}{2}, \frac{3}{4}$.

ONGOING ASSESSMENT

Talk About It
· · · · · · · · · · · · · · · ·
Draw a number line with 13 tick marks. Label the tick marks as 0, $\frac{1}{12}$, $\frac{2}{12}$, $\frac{3}{12}$, and so on, up to $\frac{12}{12}$, or 1. Use the number line to order the fractions from least to greatest.

1. $\frac{1}{3}, \frac{5}{6}, \frac{3}{4}$

2. $\frac{2}{3}, \frac{1}{2}, \frac{7}{12}$

GUIDED PRACTICE

1. **COMMUNICATING** Describe three ways to compare and order fractions. Which way do you prefer? Explain.

2. Name the fractions that are shown by the models. Which fraction is greater?

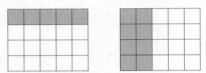

3. **DRAWING A DIAGRAM** Draw a diagram to explain why $\frac{1}{5}$ is greater than $\frac{1}{6}$. What does this tell you about $\frac{4}{5}$ and $\frac{5}{6}$? Explain.

REASONING In Exercises 4–6, compare each fraction to $\frac{1}{2}$. Then use the result to decide which fraction is greater.

4. $\frac{4}{9}, \frac{5}{9}$

5. $\frac{1}{3}, \frac{3}{4}$

6. $\frac{2}{3}, \frac{3}{7}$

PRACTICE AND PROBLEM SOLVING

GEOMETRY In Exercises 7 and 8, name the fractions that are shown by the models. Which fraction is greater?

7.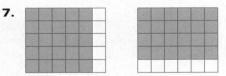

8.

NUMBER SENSE In Exercises 9–12, compare each fraction to $\frac{1}{2}$. Then use the result to decide which fraction is greater.

9. $\frac{2}{4}, \frac{3}{4}$

10. $\frac{3}{5}, \frac{3}{6}$

11. $\frac{4}{6}, \frac{3}{8}$

12. $\frac{5}{9}, \frac{6}{13}$

In Exercises 13–15, copy the number line. Locate and label the four fractions on the line. Then order the fractions from least to greatest.

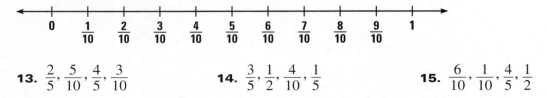

13. $\frac{2}{5}, \frac{5}{10}, \frac{4}{5}, \frac{3}{10}$

14. $\frac{3}{5}, \frac{1}{2}, \frac{4}{10}, \frac{1}{5}$

15. $\frac{6}{10}, \frac{1}{10}, \frac{4}{5}, \frac{1}{2}$

In Exercises 16–19, complete the statement using > or <.

16. $\frac{2}{6}$ **?** $\frac{3}{4}$ **17.** $\frac{5}{6}$ **?** $\frac{2}{3}$ **18.** $\frac{3}{8}$ **?** $\frac{1}{2}$ **19.** $\frac{5}{9}$ **?** $\frac{3}{6}$

NUMBER SENSE **In Exercises 20–23, find a fraction that makes the statement true.**

20. **?** $< \frac{1}{2}$ **21.** **?** $> \frac{8}{10}$ **22.** $\frac{5}{7} <$ **?**   **23.** $\frac{6}{11} >$ **?**

24. **SPANISH** Randy finished $\frac{3}{4}$ of an 80-question Spanish test. Gina finished $\frac{4}{5}$ of the same test. Who finished more of the test? Explain.

NUMBER SENSE **In Exercises 25–27, find a fraction that is greater than the first fraction and less than the second fraction.**

25. $\frac{1}{6}, \frac{3}{6}$ **26.** $\frac{3}{8}, \frac{5}{8}$ **27.** $\frac{3}{10}, \frac{1}{2}$

28. Of the fractions $\frac{7}{8}, \frac{7}{9}, \frac{7}{10}, \frac{7}{11}$, which is closest to 1? Explain.

29. Of the fractions $\frac{1}{4}, \frac{1}{5}, \frac{1}{6}$, and $\frac{1}{7}$, which is closest to 0? Explain.

VISUAL THINKING **In Exercises 30–32, write the fraction that is shown by the model.**

30.   **31.**   **32.**

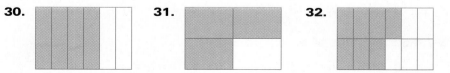

33. Order the three fractions in Exercises 30–32 from least to greatest.

34. **BICYCLES** On a bicycle, the ratio of teeth on the pedal gear to teeth on the axle gear is called the *gear ratio*. The smaller the ratio, the easier it is to turn the pedal. Find the gear ratio of the gears. Which set makes it easier to turn the pedal?

    a. 52 teeth on pedal gear, 28 teeth on axle gear

    b. 52 teeth on pedal gear, 24 teeth on axle gear

35. **GEOMETRY** The width of a rectangle is 2 in. The length is 4 in. Is the length-to-width ratio greater than or less than $\frac{5}{12}$?

Investigation 6,
Interactive
Real-Life
Investigations

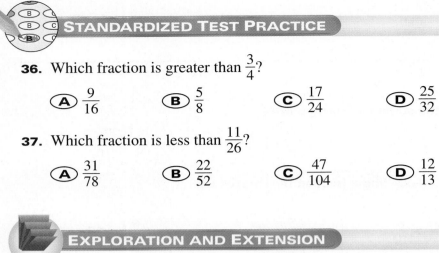
36. Which fraction is greater than $\frac{3}{4}$?

(A) $\frac{9}{16}$ **(B)** $\frac{5}{8}$ **(C)** $\frac{17}{24}$ **(D)** $\frac{25}{32}$

37. Which fraction is less than $\frac{11}{26}$?

(A) $\frac{31}{78}$ **(B)** $\frac{22}{52}$ **(C)** $\frac{47}{104}$ **(D)** $\frac{12}{13}$

PORTFOLIO

EXPLORATION AND EXTENSION

38. **BUILDING YOUR PROJECT** Refer to your answer from Building Your Project in Lesson 6.1 on page 271 to determine the fraction of the total apartment's area for each room. Use the fractions to order the rooms from smallest to largest. Explain why some rooms are larger than others.

SPIRAL REVIEW

1. **DINNER** You are choosing a meal at an Italian restaurant. You have a choice of spaghetti, rigatoni, ziti, cavatelli, ravioli, or manicotti topped with meat sauce or marinara sauce. You can choose a tossed salad or an antipasto salad. How many different meals, including salad, can you choose? **(1.3)**

MENTAL MATH Solve. (2.6)

2. $2(x + 6) = 18$ **3.** $8(5 + y) = 48$ **4.** $4(n + 9) = 64$

GEOMETRY In Exercises 5–7, find the value of *x*. (3.7, 4.1–4.4)

5. Area = x **6.** Perimeter = 30.24   **7.** Area = x

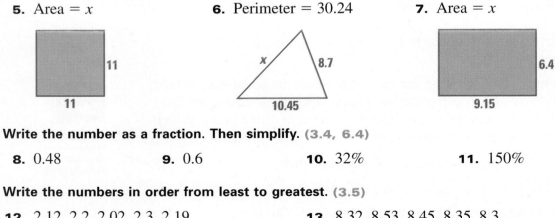

Write the number as a fraction. Then simplify. (3.4, 6.4)

8. 0.48   **9.** 0.6   **10.** 32%   **11.** 150%

Write the numbers in order from least to greatest. (3.5)

12. 2.12, 2.2, 2.02, 2.3, 2.19   **13.** 8.32, 8.53, 8.45, 8.35, 8.3

14. 0.19, 0.09, 0.6, 0.05, 0.009   **15.** 2.15, 2.105, 2.05, 2.015, 2.01

Ordering Fractions

One way to compare fractions is to rewrite them as decimals. After you do this, you need to look at the place value of the digits. Compare the digits from left to right until the digits are different.

CALCULATOR TIP

It is helpful to know some decimal equivalents of fractions, so you can order numbers more quickly.

$$\frac{1}{5} = 0.2$$

$$\frac{1}{4} = 0.25$$

$$\frac{1}{2} = 0.5$$

$$\frac{3}{4} = 0.75$$

Example

Use a calculator to help you decide which fraction is greater: $\frac{1}{3}$ or $\frac{3}{8}$.

Solution

Fraction	Key Strokes	Display
$\frac{1}{3}$	1 ÷ 3 =	0.333333
$\frac{3}{8}$	3 ÷ 8 =	0.375

To decide which is greater, compare the digits from left to right. From the hundredths place, you can tell that $\frac{3}{8}$ is greater than $\frac{1}{3}$.

Exercises

In Exercises 1–8, use a calculator to decide which fraction is greater. Which decimal place did you use to decide?

1. $\frac{8}{11}, \frac{13}{18}$ **2.** $\frac{5}{16}, \frac{6}{19}$ **3.** $\frac{3}{22}, \frac{2}{15}$ **4.** $\frac{5}{12}, \frac{7}{17}$

5. $\frac{4}{7}, \frac{11}{19}$ **6.** $\frac{10}{7}, \frac{13}{9}$ **7.** $\frac{8}{21}, \frac{9}{23}$ **8.** $\frac{1}{12}, \frac{2}{23}$

In Exercises 9–12, use a calculator to help you decide whether the fractions are equivalent. Explain your reasoning.

9. $\frac{7}{9}, \frac{14}{18}$ **10.** $\frac{9}{17}, \frac{10}{19}$ **11.** $\frac{6}{7}, \frac{18}{21}$ **12.** $\frac{12}{22}, \frac{5}{9}$

13. SWIMMING You and a friend each give a survey about swimming. You survey 37 people and find 16 swim at least six times a year. Your friend surveys 31 people and finds 17 swim at least six times a year. Which survey has a larger fraction of people who swim at least six times a year? Explain.

6.6

Modeling Fractions Greater Than One

What you should learn:

Goal 1 How to rewrite improper fractions and mixed numbers

Goal 2 How to use fractions greater than one to solve real-life problems

Why you should learn it:

Fractions that are greater than one often occur in cooking. An example is in recipes for baking bread.

Goal 1 FRACTIONS AND MIXED NUMBERS

A fraction that is greater than or equal to 1 is called an **improper fraction** . Here are some examples.

$$\frac{9}{4}, \frac{11}{10}, \frac{3}{2}, \frac{6}{6}$$ Improper fraction: Numerator is greater than or equal to denominator.

$$\frac{3}{4}, \frac{7}{10}, \frac{1}{2}, \frac{5}{6}$$ Proper fraction: Numerator is less than denominator.

LESSON INVESTIGATION

COOPERATIVE LEARNING

Investigating Mixed Numbers

GROUP ACTIVITY Copy the model for the mixed number $2\frac{1}{4}$. Add lines so that each whole is divided into four equal parts. Then rewrite $2\frac{1}{4}$ as an improper fraction.

Draw a model for each mixed number. Then rewrite each mixed number as an improper fraction.

1. $1\frac{1}{2}$ **2.** $1\frac{2}{3}$ **3.** $2\frac{1}{5}$ **4.** $3\frac{1}{4}$

Example 1 Rewriting Improper Fractions

Show how you can use a fraction model to rewrite the improper fraction $\frac{8}{3}$ as a mixed number.

Solution

Start by drawing rectangles to represent wholes. The denominator shows that you want to model thirds, so divide each whole into 3 parts. The numerator shows that you want to represent 8 of the thirds. So shade 8 parts.

The model represents $2\frac{2}{3}$, so $\frac{8}{3} = 2\frac{2}{3}$.

Example 2 Rewriting a Mixed Number

The recipe below makes two loaves of Boston brown bread. You have fourth-cup, third-cup, and half-cup measures, but you can't find the one-cup measure. How many third-cup measures of raisins do you need?

REAL LIFE
Baking

Boston Brown Bread	
$2\frac{1}{2}$ c. whole wheat flour	2 t. baking soda
$1\frac{1}{4}$ c. rye flour	2 c. buttermilk
1 c. corn meal	$\frac{3}{4}$ c. molasses
$2\frac{1}{2}$ t. baking powder	$1\frac{2}{3}$ c. raisins
$1\frac{1}{4}$ t. salt	

Solution

You need to find how many third-cup measures equal $1\frac{2}{3}$ cups. Fill the third-cup measure three times, to equal 1 cup.

Fill it two more times for $\frac{2}{3}$ cup.

So you need five third-cup measures, or $\frac{5}{3}$ cups, to equal $1\frac{2}{3}$ cups.

ONGOING ASSESSMENT

Write About It

Use only a fourth-cup measure and a half-cup measure. Explain how you could measure the following ingredients used in the Boston brown bread recipe.

1. Whole wheat flour

2. Rye flour

3. Molasses

GUIDED PRACTICE

1. How is an improper fraction different from a proper fraction?

WRITING EXPRESSIONS **In Exercises 2 and 3, use the diagram below.**

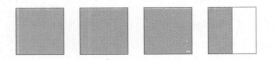

2. Write the mixed number represented by the model. Explain how each part of the mixed number relates to the model.

3. Write the improper fraction represented by the model.

4. Draw a model to represent $2\frac{1}{4}$. Then use the model to rewrite $2\frac{1}{4}$ as an improper fraction. Explain your steps.

5. Rewrite $\frac{17}{3}$ as a mixed number.

6. Rewrite $4\frac{3}{4}$ as an improper fraction.

PRACTICE AND PROBLEM SOLVING

REASONING **In Exercises 7–9, complete the statement using *sometimes, always,* or *never*.**

7. A mixed number is __?__ greater than 1.

8. A proper fraction is __?__ greater than 1.

9. An improper fraction is __?__ a whole number.

WRITING EXPRESSIONS **In Exercises 10 and 11, write the mixed number and the improper fraction represented by the model.**

10.    **11.**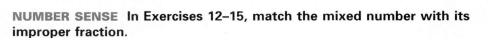

NUMBER SENSE **In Exercises 12–15, match the mixed number with its improper fraction.**

A. $\frac{14}{4}$ **B.** $\frac{11}{4}$ **C.** $\frac{25}{4}$ **D.** $\frac{7}{4}$

12. $2\frac{3}{4}$ **13.** $1\frac{3}{4}$ **14.** $3\frac{1}{2}$ **15.** $6\frac{1}{4}$

In Exercises 16–23, draw a model to represent the improper fraction. Then rewrite the fraction as a mixed number.

16. $\dfrac{7}{5}$ **17.** $\dfrac{14}{9}$ **18.** $\dfrac{23}{7}$ **19.** $\dfrac{7}{2}$

20. $\dfrac{16}{3}$ **21.** $\dfrac{11}{8}$ **22.** $\dfrac{15}{4}$ **23.** $\dfrac{29}{6}$

In Exercises 24–31, draw a model to represent the mixed number. Then rewrite the mixed number as an improper fraction.

24. $2\dfrac{1}{2}$ **25.** $1\dfrac{3}{4}$ **26.** $2\dfrac{3}{5}$ **27.** $3\dfrac{2}{3}$

28. $1\dfrac{4}{7}$ **29.** $2\dfrac{1}{6}$ **30.** $3\dfrac{1}{4}$ **31.** $3\dfrac{5}{6}$

32. FOOTBAG You practiced with your footbag half an hour every day for nine days. Write an improper fraction that shows the total number of hours you practiced. Rewrite the improper fraction as a mixed number. Which number best represents the answer? Explain.

33. MUSIC You practice for your piano recital for $\dfrac{2}{3}$ of an hour each day. Draw a model to find how many hours you practice in five days. Would you write your answer as an improper fraction or as a mixed number? Explain.

34. RESTAURANTS You work in a restaurant that serves quiche. The standard serving size is $\dfrac{1}{6}$ of a quiche. When you start your shift, you see that there are $2\dfrac{5}{6}$ quiches in the refrigerator. How many servings is this? Explain how writing $2\dfrac{5}{6}$ as an improper fraction can help answer the question.

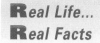

Footbag
Champions in the game of footbag have been known to practice five hours a day to become expert footbag players.

STANDARDIZED TEST PRACTICE

35. Jerome can read one chapter of a book in $\dfrac{1}{3}$ of an hour. How many hours will it take to read 13 chapters?

Ⓐ $1\dfrac{1}{3}$ Ⓑ $4\dfrac{1}{3}$ Ⓒ $13\dfrac{1}{3}$ Ⓓ $14\dfrac{1}{3}$

36. Which fraction is equivalent to $3\dfrac{3}{8}$?

Ⓐ $\dfrac{6}{8}$ Ⓑ $\dfrac{9}{8}$ Ⓒ $\dfrac{27}{8}$ Ⓓ $\dfrac{33}{8}$

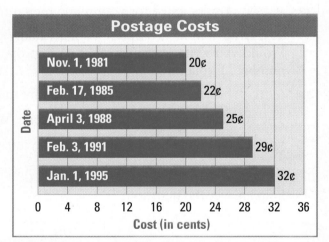

37. BUILDING YOUR PROJECT In your apartment, it takes $2\frac{1}{2}$ boxes of tile to cover the bathroom floor. How many boxes of tile would it take to cover the floor of each of the other four rooms? Explain your reasoning.

SPIRAL REVIEW

1. WORKING BACKWARD You are going to the aquarium. You realize that you don't have any money, so you stop at a bank. You spend $9.00 on admission into the aquarium. You spend two thirds of the money you have left for a souvenir. You then spend half of the money you have left on lunch. This leaves you with $3.50. How much money did you get at the bank? **(1.7)**

GEOMETRY In Exercises 2 and 3, find the value of x. (4.7)

2. Area $= 13.05$ mm^2

3. Area $= 1.96$ in.^{2}

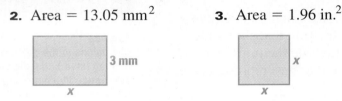

In Exercises 4 and 5, use the bar graph at the right. It shows the cost (in cents) of a stamp for a letter for each date the cost increased from November 1, 1981, to January 1, 1995. (Source: U.S Postal Service) **(5.5)**

4. On which date did the cost of a stamp increase the most from the previous cost?

5. How much more did a stamp cost on January 1, 1995, than on April 3, 1988?

6. The table below shows the number of hours spent per person watching videos for 1990 through 1996.

(Source: Veronis, Suhler & Associates Inc.) **(5.6)**

Year	1990	1991	1992	1993	1994	1995	1996
Hours	42	43	46	49	52	53	54

a. Make a line graph of the data.

b. Write a statement that describes the data.

READ About It

The remarkable piece of sculpture shown here were done by Claes Oldenburg. Born in Sweden in 1929, he and his family came to live in the United States when he was seven. Oldenburg's interest in art started with painting and progressed to sculpture. Many of his sculptures resemble everyday objects such as sinks, hamburgers, and ice cream bars. Traveling by airplane often and looking down at Earth led him to think about representing objects on a larger-than-life scale.

Shuttlecocks, 1994; aluminum and fiberglass-reinforced plastic painted with polyurethane enamel. Four shuttlecocks, each 17 ft $10\frac{3}{4}$ in. $\times$ 15 ft $\frac{3}{4}$ in. crown diameter and 4 ft nose diameter.

WRITE About It

Shuttlecock–Fabrication Model, 1994; aluminum, cardboard, felt, resin, and urethane enamel; $27 \times 24\frac{1}{2}$ in. diameter. Aluminum base: $\frac{1}{2} \times 18 \times 18$ in.

1. The sculpture of a badminton shuttle is about 18 ft tall. An actual shuttle is only about 3 in. tall. What is the ratio of the sculpture to the actual shuttle?

2. Before making the actual sculpture, Oldenburg made a model of it. In the model, the diameter of the shuttle is 2 ft wide. The diameter of the actual sculpture is 16 ft. What is the ratio of the model's diameter to the actual diameter?

3. Claes Oldenburg made a sculpture of a clothespin that is about 54 ft tall. A real clothespin is only about 3 in. tall. Write a ratio that describes the relation between the height of a real clothespin and the height of the sculpture.

Introduction to Probability

What you should learn:

Goal 1 How to use ratios to find probabilities

Goal 2 How to interpret probabilities

Why you should learn it:

Probability can be used to predict outcomes. An example is predicting on which color a spinner will land.

Goal 1 USING RATIOS TO FIND PROBABILITIES

In this lesson, you will see how ratios can be used to express probabilities. You will also use ratios and decimals to help you interpret probabilities.

LESSON INVESTIGATION

Investigating Experimental Probability

GROUP ACTIVITY Make a cardboard spinner as shown at the right. Spin the paper clip 20 times and record your results. Add your results to those of four other groups. Your totals should add up to 100. Copy and complete the table. On which color is the paper clip most likely to land? least likely to land? Explain.

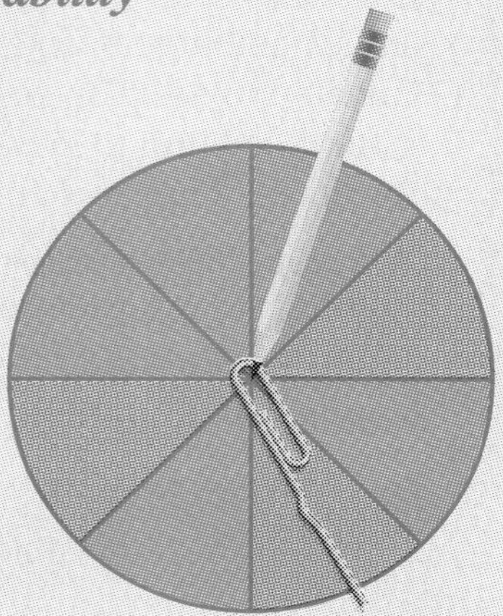

	Red	Blue
Number of spins on color	?	?
Ratio	$\frac{?}{100}$	$\frac{?}{100}$

Each ratio you found above is an **experimental probability**. The **theoretical probability** of an event tells you how likely it is that the event will happen.

Example 1 Finding Probabilities

Find the probability that the spinner above will land on the color.

a. Red **b.** Blue

Solution

In each case, the theoretical probability is a ratio.

a. Probability of **red** $= \dfrac{\text{Number of red regions}}{\text{Total number of regions}} = \dfrac{5}{8}$

b. Probability of **blue** $= \dfrac{\text{Number of blue regions}}{\text{Total number of regions}} = \dfrac{3}{8}$

STUDY TIP

You need to be careful to notice which probability you are using, experimental or theoretical. Experimental probability is found as the result of doing an experiment.

INTERPRETING PROBABILITIES

The probability that *any* event occurs is a number from 0 to 1. The closer the probability is to 0, the less likely the event is to occur. The closer the probability is to 1, the more likely the event is to occur.

Cannot occur   **Equally likely to occur or not occur**   Must occur

0   Not likely to occur   0.5 or $\frac{1}{2}$ Likely to occur   1

STUDY TIP

A "simple event" is an event whose outcome does not affect other events.

Example 2   Interpreting Probabilities

A small button is tossed onto regions like those shown below. If the button lands on a line, the toss is not counted. Find the probability that the button will land on a blue region. Interpret the results.

a. **b.**

Solution

a. Probability of **blue** $= \dfrac{\text{Number of blue regions}}{\text{Total number of regions}} = \dfrac{1}{12}$

Because the theoretical probability is close to 0, it is not very likely that the button will land on a blue region.

b. Probability of **blue** $= \dfrac{\text{Number of blue regions}}{\text{Total number of regions}} = \dfrac{6}{12} = \dfrac{1}{2}$

Because the theoretical probability is one half, it is equally likely that the button will land on a blue region or on another color.

In part (a) of Example 2, the probability that a button will *not* land on blue is the **complement** of the probability that it will land on blue. The sum of the probabilities is 1.

Probability of blue + Probability of *not* blue = 1, so

Probability of *not* blue $= 1 -$ Probability of blue

$$= 1 - \frac{1}{12} = \frac{11}{12}$$

Because the probability of *not* blue is close to 1, it is likely that the button will not land on blue.

ONGOING ASSESSMENT

Write About It

In Example 2, find the probability that the button will land on a red region when it is tossed onto the following. Show your work.

1. Region in part (a)

2. Region in part (b)

GUIDED PRACTICE

In Exercises 1–5, refer to the spinner at the right. Find the probability that the arrow will land on the number described.

1. A number divisible by 3

2. A number less than 4

3. An odd number

4. An even number

5. Is your answer to Exercise 4 the complement of your answer to Exercise 3? Explain.

In Exercises 6–8, match the probability with its description.

6. 0.02

A. Very likely to occur

7. 0.5

B. Not likely to occur

8. 0.97

C. Equally likely to occur or not

9. GROUP ACTIVITY Toss a paper cup in the air. Did the cup land on its side, upside down, or upright? Repeat the experiment 20 times. Record your results. Use your results to estimate the probabilities of each of the possible outcomes. Compare your results with other groups' results.

10. Tape a penny to the inside bottom of the cup in Exercise 9. Then repeat the experiment. How do your results change?

PRACTICE AND PROBLEM SOLVING

MARBLES **In Exercises 11–14, suppose you have a bag that contains the marbles shown. Without looking, you draw one marble from the bag. What is the probability that the marble is blue?**

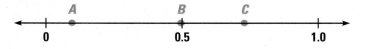

11. **12.** **13.** **14.**

Match the event with the letter of its probability.

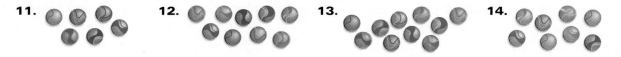

15. You correctly guess the answer to a true-false question.

16. A student you pick from your class is left-handed.

17. A phone number ends in the digit 1, 2, 3, 4, 5, 6, or 7.

18. SHOPPING Use the graph at the right. What is the probability that a person has the following favorite day to shop?

   a. Saturday   **b.** Tuesday

In Exercises 19 and 20, make a circular spinner. Divide the spinner into four equal regions. Color one of the regions green and three yellow.

19. Find the probability that the spinner will land on green. Write the probability as a fraction and a decimal.

20. Spin the spinner 40 times and record your results. Find the experimental probability of landing on green.

SCIENCE **The color of a snapdragon depends on the genes of its** *parent* **flowers. The diagram at the right shows possible colors when both parents are pink, with one red (R) and one white (W) gene. Find the probability.**

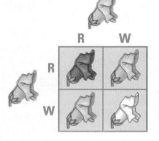

21. The flower color is pink.   **22.** The flower color is not white.

STANDARDIZED TEST PRACTICE

23. There are 6 pink roses and 10 white roses in a bouquet. If you choose a rose at random, what is the probability that you will pick a white one?

  A $\frac{3}{8}$ **B** $\frac{3}{5}$ **C** $\frac{5}{8}$ **D** $\frac{5}{3}$

24. At an intersection, you can go straight, turn right, or turn left. Two ways will take you where you want to go. If you don't know the way, what is the probability that you will choose the correct way?

  A $66\frac{2}{3}\%$ **B** 50%   **C** $33\frac{1}{3}\%$ **D** 25%

EXPLORATION AND EXTENSION

MAKING PREDICTIONS **You can use theoretical probability and ratios to make predictions.**

25. The probability of drawing a green marble from a bag is $\frac{1}{3}$. If you chose a marble 30 times, how many times would you expect it to be green?

26. The probability of drawing a red marble from a bag is 0.4. If you chose a marble 50 times, how many times would you expect it to be red?

WHAT *did you learn?*

WHY *did you learn it?*

Skills

6.1	Identify the numerator and denominator of a fraction.	Compare results, such as grades in two classes.
6.2	Rewrite a fraction as a division problem. Use a ratio to compare two values.	Find ways to share things equally.
6.3	Decide whether two fractions or ratios are equivalent.	Compare ratios, such as dimensions of a room.
6.4	Simplify a fraction. Solve a proportion.	Find a rate at which you work.
6.5	Compare and order two or more fractions.	Make decisions about purchases.
6.6	Rewrite mixed numbers and improper fractions.	Rewrite measures, such as those in a recipe.
6.7	Find experimental and theoretical probabilities.	Make predictions about outcomes.

Strategies 6.1–6.7 Use problem solving strategies. | Solve a wide variety of real-life problems.

Using Data 6.1–6.7 Use tables and graphs. | Organize data and solve problems.

HOW *does it fit in the bigger picture of mathematics?*

In this chapter, fractions were modeled and used to write ratios and proportions.

$$\frac{5}{6} \qquad = \qquad \frac{10}{12}$$

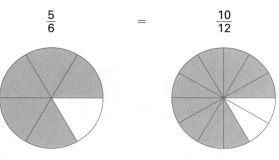

In Chapters 7 and 8, you will see how models can help you understand operations, such as addition and multiplication.

VOCABULARY

- mixed number (p. 268)
- ratio (p. 275)
- equivalent fraction (p. 278)
- rate (p. 279)
- simplest form (p. 282)

- simplify a fraction (p. 282)
- proportion (p. 283)
- solve a proportion (p. 283)
- compare fractions (p. 290)
- improper fraction (p. 296)

- experimental probability (p. 302)
- theoretical probability (p. 302)
- complement (p. 303)

6.1 FUNDAMENTAL FRACTION CONCEPTS

Example

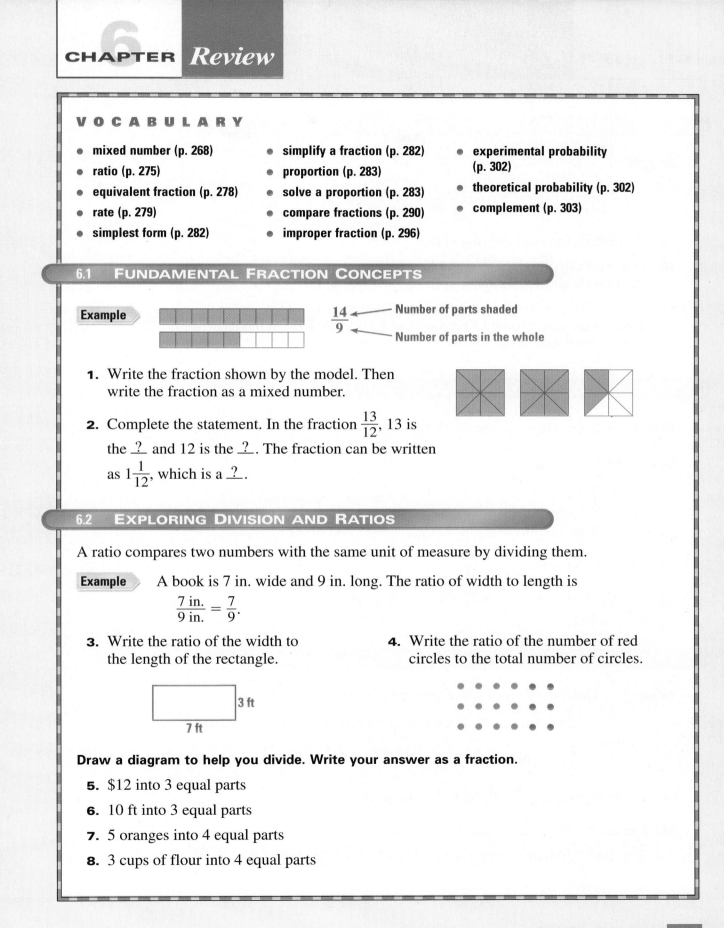

$\dfrac{14}{9}$ ← Number of parts shaded ← Number of parts in the whole

1. Write the fraction shown by the model. Then write the fraction as a mixed number.

2. Complete the statement. In the fraction $\dfrac{13}{12}$, 13 is the ? and 12 is the ?. The fraction can be written as $1\dfrac{1}{12}$, which is a ?.

6.2 EXPLORING DIVISION AND RATIOS

A ratio compares two numbers with the same unit of measure by dividing them.

Example   A book is 7 in. wide and 9 in. long. The ratio of width to length is
$$\frac{7 \text{ in.}}{9 \text{ in.}} = \frac{7}{9}.$$

3. Write the ratio of the width to the length of the rectangle.

3 ft
7 ft

4. Write the ratio of the number of red circles to the total number of circles.

Draw a diagram to help you divide. Write your answer as a fraction.

5. $12 into 3 equal parts

6. 10 ft into 3 equal parts

7. 5 oranges into 4 equal parts

8. 3 cups of flour into 4 equal parts

6.3 EQUIVALENT FRACTIONS AND RATIOS

Example
$$\frac{5}{6} = \frac{5 \cdot 3}{6 \cdot 3} = \frac{15}{18}$$

The fractions $\frac{5}{6}$ and $\frac{15}{18}$ are equivalent.

9. Write three fractions equivalent to $\frac{6}{7}$.

10. Find the ratio of the width to the length of a videotape that is 28 cm wide and 48 cm long.

11. **ARCHITECTURE** You are building a model of your school's gymnasium. The gym is 120 ft long and 40 ft wide. In your model, the length of the gym is 1 ft. How wide should your model be?

6.4 EXPLORING PROPORTIONS

Example Solve the proportion $\frac{7}{8} = \frac{x}{40}$.

Solution

$$\frac{7}{8} = \frac{7 \cdot 5}{8 \cdot 5} = \frac{35}{40}$$ **Multiply the numerator and denominator by 5**

The solution is 35.

12. Solve the proportion $\frac{4}{n} = \frac{16}{28}$.

13. You buy two pencils for $.12. Use a proportion to find the cost of six pencils.

6.5 COMPARING AND ORDERING FRACTIONS

Example Order the fractions from greater to lesser.

$\frac{7}{12}, \frac{5}{12}$ **The denominators are the same, so compare the numerators.**

$7 > 5$, so the order is $\frac{7}{12}, \frac{5}{12}$.

14. Of the fractions $\frac{3}{4}, \frac{7}{8}, \frac{15}{16}$, and $\frac{31}{32}$, which is closest to 1?

15. Use the number line to order the fractions $\frac{2}{3}, \frac{5}{6}$, and $\frac{1}{2}$ from least to greatest.

Example The model shows that the improper fraction $\frac{5}{4}$ equals the mixed number $1\frac{1}{4}$.

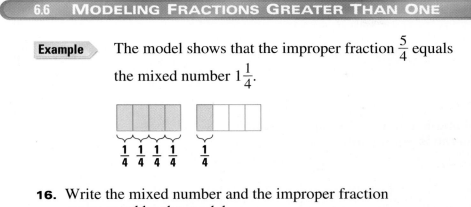

$$\frac{1}{4} \quad \frac{1}{4} \quad \frac{1}{4} \quad \frac{1}{4} \qquad \frac{1}{4}$$

16. Write the mixed number and the improper fraction represented by the model.

17. Draw a model to represent $1\frac{5}{6}$. Then rewrite the mixed number as an improper fraction.

18. **BAKING** A recipe calls for $1\frac{3}{4}$ cups of flour. Write $1\frac{3}{4}$ as an improper fraction. If you used only a quarter-cup measuring cup, how many times would you have to fill it to measure the flour?

The probability of an event is a ratio of the number of favorable outcomes to the number of possible outcomes. Probabilities are between 0 and 1.

Example

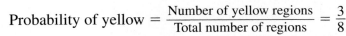

Probability of yellow $= \dfrac{\text{Number of yellow regions}}{\text{Total number of regions}} = \dfrac{3}{8}$

19. You throw a dart at the board at the right. What is the probability of landing on an orange square?

Complete each statement with 0, $\frac{1}{2}$, or 1.

20. If an event is impossible, its probability is ？ .

21. A probability can be no greater than ？ .

22. When flipping a coin, the probability of heads is ？ .

In Exercises 1–3, write three equivalent fractions represented by the red portion of the figure.

1.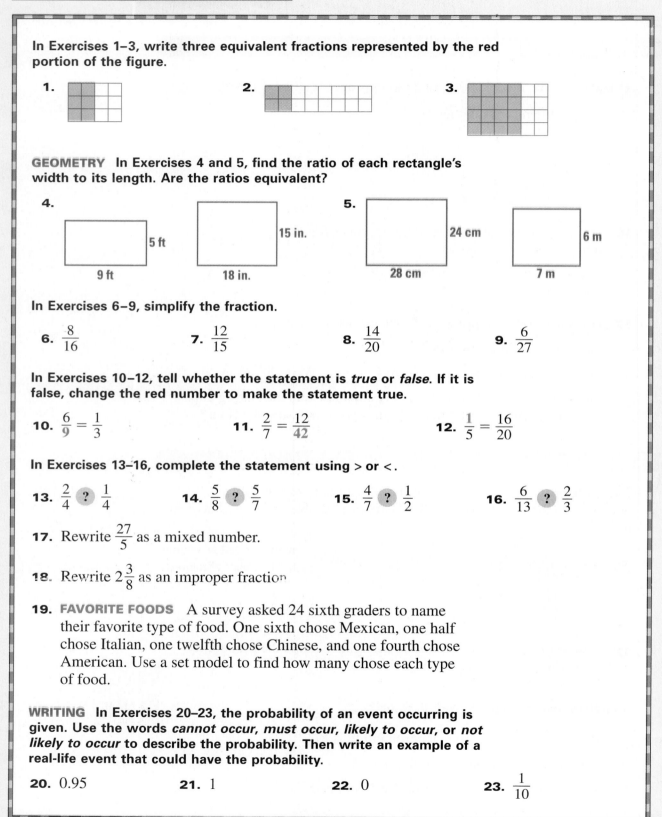

2.

3.

GEOMETRY In Exercises 4 and 5, find the ratio of each rectangle's width to its length. Are the ratios equivalent?

4.
5 ft
9 ft

15 in.
18 in.

5.
24 cm
28 cm

6 m
7 m

In Exercises 6–9, simplify the fraction.

6. $\dfrac{8}{16}$　　　7. $\dfrac{12}{15}$　　　8. $\dfrac{14}{20}$　　　9. $\dfrac{6}{27}$

In Exercises 10–12, tell whether the statement is *true* or *false*. If it is false, change the red number to make the statement true.

10. $\dfrac{6}{9} = \dfrac{1}{3}$　　　11. $\dfrac{2}{7} = \dfrac{12}{42}$　　　12. $\dfrac{1}{5} = \dfrac{16}{20}$

In Exercises 13–16, complete the statement using > or < .

13. $\dfrac{2}{4}$? $\dfrac{1}{4}$　　　14. $\dfrac{5}{8}$? $\dfrac{5}{7}$　　　15. $\dfrac{4}{7}$? $\dfrac{1}{2}$　　　16. $\dfrac{6}{13}$? $\dfrac{2}{3}$

17. Rewrite $\dfrac{27}{5}$ as a mixed number.

18. Rewrite $2\dfrac{3}{8}$ as an improper fraction.

19. **FAVORITE FOODS** A survey asked 24 sixth graders to name their favorite type of food. One sixth chose Mexican, one half chose Italian, one twelfth chose Chinese, and one fourth chose American. Use a set model to find how many chose each type of food.

WRITING In Exercises 20–23, the probability of an event occurring is given. Use the words *cannot occur, must occur, likely to occur,* or *not likely to occur* to describe the probability. Then write an example of a real-life event that could have the probability.

20. 0.95　　　21. 1　　　22. 0　　　23. $\dfrac{1}{10}$

1. Your English teacher gives a test with three equal parts. If you have 50 min, how long should you spend on each part?

   A 10 min   **B** 15 min

   C $16\frac{2}{3}$ min   **D** $18\frac{1}{3}$ min

2. Louie earned $8 for mowing three lawns. At the same rate, how much will he earn if he mows 12 lawns?

   A $12   **B** $32

   C $36   **D** $48

3. A box is 24 in. long. Its depth is 16 in., and its width is 18 in. What is the ratio of the length to the width of the box?

   A $\frac{2}{3}$ **B** $\frac{3}{4}$

   C $\frac{4}{3}$ **D** $\frac{3}{2}$

4. You earn $60 and deposit $20 into your savings account. If you earn $33, which proportion can be used to find x, the amount you would deposit?

   A $\frac{20}{60} = \frac{x}{33}$ **B** $\frac{20}{60} = \frac{33}{x}$

   C $\frac{60}{33} = \frac{x}{20}$ **D** $\frac{60}{x} = \frac{33}{20}$

5. You have read $\frac{3}{4}$ of a mystery, $\frac{3}{5}$ of a biography, and $\frac{2}{3}$ of a science fiction book. Which fractions show the order of the books from least to greatest?

   A $\frac{2}{3}, \frac{3}{4}, \frac{3}{5}$ **B** $\frac{2}{3}, \frac{3}{5}, \frac{3}{4}$

   C $\frac{3}{4}, \frac{2}{3}, \frac{3}{5}$ **D** $\frac{3}{5}, \frac{2}{3}, \frac{3}{4}$

6. Which percent is equal to $\frac{3}{5}$?

   A 5%   **B** 30%

   C 60%   **D** 80%

7. A shuffled deck of playing cards has 52 cards, with four aces. What are the chances of drawing an ace?

   A $\frac{1}{52}$ **B** $\frac{1}{13}$

   C $\frac{1}{4}$ **D** $\frac{4}{13}$

8. You have 30 socks in a drawer and randomly pick two socks. You have 18 white socks, 6 blue, and 6 brown. What is the probability of picking a white sock on your first pick?

   A $\frac{1}{30}$ **B** $\frac{1}{18}$

   C $\frac{2}{5}$ **D** $\frac{3}{5}$

9. You need 12 oz of chocolate chips to make cookies. If you double the recipe, how many pounds of chocolate chips do you need? (16 oz = 1 lb)

   A $\frac{3}{4}$ lb   **B** $1\frac{1}{3}$ lb

   C $1\frac{1}{2}$ lb   **D** 2 lb

10. One shirt costs $25 and is not on sale. A second shirt costs $39 but is on sale for $\frac{1}{3}$ off. What is the difference between shirt prices?

    A $1   **B** $6

    C $13   **D** $14

ALGEBRA AND MENTAL MATH In Exercises 1–6, solve.
(1.6, 2.2–2.4, 4.6)

1. $x + 6 = 18$

2. $20 - y = 9$

3. $12 \cdot n = 60$

4. $m \div 5 = 7$

5. $4(a + 5) = 32$

6. $0.45 \cdot b = 45$

In Exercises 7–12, evaluate the expression. (2.1, 2.5, 2.7, 3.7)

7. $(2 \times 3^2) \div 6$

8. $4 + 24 \div 2 - 8$

9. $5 \times 10 - 2^5 - 2$

10. $9 \times 1000 + 5 \times 10$

11. 11011_2

12. 143_5

In Exercises 13–15, write the decimal or fraction shown by the model.
(3.1, 3.3, 6.1)

13.

large square = 1 unit

14.

$$\begin{array}{c} \vdash\!\!\!+\!\!\!+\!\!\!+\!\!\!+\!\!\!+\!\!\!+\!\!\!+\!\!\!+\!\!\!+\!\!\!+\!\!\!\dashv \\ 0 \qquad\qquad\qquad\qquad 1 \end{array}$$

15.

In Exercises 16–21, complete the statement. (3.2, 3.4, 6.2–6.4, 6.6)

16. ? m = 2.8 km

17. $\dfrac{7}{10} = ? \%$

18. ? % = 0.92

19. $\dfrac{7}{8} = \dfrac{42}{?}$

20. $\dfrac{2 \text{ pears}}{5 \text{ pears}} = \dfrac{6 \text{ apples}}{? \text{ apples}}$

21. $\dfrac{?}{5} = 2\dfrac{4}{5}$

In Exercises 22–25, order the numbers from least to greatest. (3.5, 6.5)

22. 3.12, 3.2, 3.02, 3.22, 3.19

23. 0.02, 0.11, 0.011, 0.01, 0.1

24. $\dfrac{3}{8}, \dfrac{3}{5}, \dfrac{3}{4}, \dfrac{4}{8}$

25. $\dfrac{4}{7}, \dfrac{4}{5}, \dfrac{1}{2}, \dfrac{2}{3}$

In Exercises 26–31, round each number to the given place value. (3.6)

26. 947 (tens)

27. 1620 (hundreds)

28. 83,510 (thousands)

29. 14.8 (ones)

30. 0.53 (tenths)

31. 7.846 (hundredths)

GEOMETRY In Exercises 32–34, find the value of *x*. (4.1, 4.2, 4.4, 4.5, 4.7)

32. Perimeter = 20.42

33. Area = 45.9

34. Area = *x*

STATISTICS Find the range, the median, and the mode of the data. Use a calculator to find the mean. **(5.3, 5.4)**

35. 15, 12, 12, 16, 14, 15, 14, 11, 17, 14

36. 43, 39, 37, 41, 41, 39, 39, 42, 39

37. **WRITING** Name three ways of organizing or graphing data. Write a sentence about each and the type of data that each would best display. **(1.2, 1.3, 5.1, 5.2, 5.5–5.7)**

38. You have 32 markers. Three fourths are worn out. How many of your markers are worn out? **(6.1)**

SPORTING DOGS The list below shows the average maximum weights (in pounds) of breeds of sporting dogs. (Source: *World Book Encyclopedia*) **(5.2)**

45, 40, 80, 85, 28, 80, 34, 70, 55, 50, 75, 70,
65, 75, 80, 70, 65, 75, 75, 45, 50, 80, 40, 60

39. Organize the data in a stem-and-leaf plot.

40. What are the most common maximum weights of sporting dogs?

41. What is the lightest maximum weight of sporting dogs?

MOVIE SURVEY The table at the right shows the results of a survey that asked 100 people to name their favorite type of movie. **(1.2, 1.4, 3.4, 5.5, 6.3)**

42. Represent the data with a bar graph.

43. What percent of the people surveyed chose *Action*?

44. What type of movie was chosen by one fourth of the people?

Movie type	Number
Comedy	32
Action	27
Drama	25
Western	16

CELLULAR PHONES In Exercises 45 and 46, use the list at the right that shows the number of cellular telephone systems from 1988 through 1995.
(Source: U.S. Bureau of the Census, 1996) **(5.7)**

45. Choose an appropriate graph to display the data. Explain why you chose that type of graph.

46. Which year had the largest increase in the number of cellular telephone systems?

47. **TELEPHONE CALLS** You received 18 phone calls on Saturday and Sunday. One third were on Sunday. How many were on Saturday? **(6.4)**

Year	Number of systems
1988	517
1989	584
1990	751
1991	1252
1992	1506
1993	1529
1994	1581
1995	1627

Adding and Subtracting Fractions

TECHNOLOGY

Technology resources accompanying this chapter:

- Interactive Real-Life Investigations
- Middle School Tutorial Software

EDUCATION AND YOUTH DEVELOPMENT Some volunteer organizations concentrate on helping young people. The YMCA and YWCA are examples of such organizations.

HEALTH AND HUMAN SERVICES Local organizations help service the needs of the people of a community. For example, some groups deliver meals to homebound people.

CHAPTER THEME
Community Service

POLITICAL OR RELIGIOUS This wall was painted by the artist
Wyland. He paints these murals all over the world, without asking to be paid.
His walls show the importance and beauty of the creatures of the ocean.

Community Service

REAL LIFE
Volunteering

Volunteers are people who help others for no pay.
People volunteer for many different types of activities.
Almost one half of all adults in the United States do
some form of volunteer work. The table below shows the fraction of
the United States population that volunteers for certain kinds of
organizations.

Organization	Fraction
Education and youth development	$\frac{40}{100}$
Health and human services	$\frac{20}{100}$
Political or religious organizations	$\frac{28}{100}$

Think and Discuss

1. Compare the three fractions shown in the table.

2. Reduce each of the fractions to its simplest form. Does this make it
easier to compare the fractions? Explain.

PORTFOLIO

CHAPTER PROJECT

Community Service Diary

PROJECT DESCRIPTION

People do volunteer work for many different causes. Some people like to help animals and some enjoy keeping the environment clean. There are volunteers that help sick people as well as volunteers that help people learn how to read. You will keep a diary of different kinds of volunteer work.

GETTING STARTED

Talking It Over

- In your group, talk about the different causes that you or people you know have spent time volunteering for. Why do you think people volunteer?

- Talk about the volunteer groups in your community that interest you. Who benefits from these organizations? What other kinds of groups in your community need volunteers? What kinds of work do the volunteers do? How often do they volunteer?

Planning Your Project

- **Materials Needed:** paper; colored pencils or markers

- Make a booklet out of several folded sheets of paper. Write "Community Service Diary" on the cover. Find out if there are any organizations in your community that perform the sort of service described in each of the **TOPICS** on the next page. Write this information in your diary as you do the **BUILDING YOUR PROJECT** exercises throughout the chapter.

BUILDING YOUR PROJECT

These are places throughout the chapter where you will work on your project.

TOPICS

7.1 Deliver meals to homebound people. *p. 321*

7.2 Sort bottles and cans at a recycling center. *p. 326*

7.3 Publicize a fund raising event held by the Humane Society. *p. 333*

7.4 Help your neighborhood group raise money for a playground. *p. 340*

7.6 Volunteer at the library. *p. 351*

I N T E R N E T

To find out more about community service opportunities, go to:
http://www.mlmath.com

7.1

Measuring Length in the U.S. Customary System

What you should learn:

Goal 1 How to measure lengths with U.S. Customary units

Goal 2 How to rewrite measurements of length

Why you should learn it:

Knowing how to use the U.S. Customary system can help you when measuring. An example is measuring a piece of fabric.

Goal 1 MEASURING LENGTHS

In Lesson 6.6, you saw that rewriting fractions can help you when you are cooking. It can also be helpful when you are measuring lengths.

Example 1 Rewriting Fractions

a. $\dfrac{13}{3} = 13 \div 3 = 4\dfrac{1}{3}$

b. $\dfrac{22}{8} = 22 \div 8 = 2\dfrac{6}{8} = 2\dfrac{3}{4}$

Example 2 Measuring Lengths

Write the length of each rectangle as a mixed number.

CONNECTION
Geometry

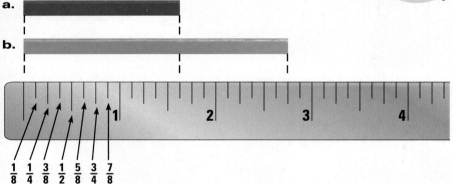

Solution

a. This rectangle is $1\dfrac{5}{8}$ in., or $\dfrac{13}{8}$ in. long.

b. This rectangle is $2\dfrac{3}{4}$ in., or $\dfrac{11}{4}$ in. long.

LESSON INVESTIGATION

COOPERATIVE LEARNING

Investigating Fractional Measures of Length

GROUP ACTIVITY Use a ruler to draw line segments that have the following lengths.

1. $\dfrac{7}{8}$ in. **2.** $1\dfrac{1}{2}$ in. **3.** $3\dfrac{3}{8}$ in. **4.** $2\dfrac{1}{4}$ in.

Choose two of the measurements given above. Explain how you can use a ruler to find the sum of these lengths.

Goal 2 REWRITING MEASURES OF LENGTH

In the metric system, units of measure increase by multiples of 10. For example, a centimeter is 10 times as long as a millimeter. This is not true in the U.S. Customary system.

> **TOOLBOX**
> Equivalent Measures, page 654

THE U.S. CUSTOMARY SYSTEM	
12 inches (in.) = 1 foot (ft)	36 inches = 1 yard
3 feet = 1 yard (yd)	5280 feet = 1 mile (mi)

The symbol ′ means feet and the symbol ″ means inches. So, 5′2″ is read as "five feet, two inches."

Example 3 Measuring a Person's Height

The heights of three people are shown below. Write each measurement in the given units.

a. $5'4\frac{1}{2}''$, inches

b. 4 ft 11 in., inches

c. 63″, feet and inches

Solution

You can change feet to inches by multiplying the number of feet by 12, because there are 12 inches in a foot.

a. $5'4\frac{1}{2}'' = (5 \cdot 12)'' + 4\frac{1}{2}'' = 60'' + 4\frac{1}{2}'' = 64\frac{1}{2}''$

b. 4 ft 11 in. = (4 · 12) in. + 11 in. = **48** in. + 11 in. = 59 in.

c. You can change inches to feet and inches by finding the largest multiple of 12 that is less than the measurement in inches. Then regroup, using the multiple of 12. List the multiples of 12, as follows.

Multiples of 12: 12, 24, 36, 48, 60, 72, . . .

Regroup 63 as 60 + 3, since 60 is the largest multiple of 12 that is less than 63.

$63'' = 60'' + 3'' = (5 \cdot 12)'' + 3'' = 5' + 3'' = 5'3''$

> **ONGOING ASSESSMENT**
>
> **Write About It**
>
> **1.** Write the measurement in the given units.
>
> **a.** 5′11″, inches
>
> **b.** 6′, inches
>
> **c.** 74″, feet and inches
>
> **2.** Which of the measurements given above is the largest?

GUIDED PRACTICE

In Exercises 1 and 2, write the length of the paperclip to the nearest $\frac{1}{8}$ in.

1.

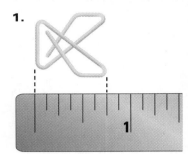

2.

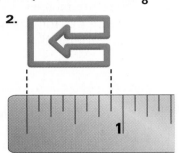

3. Write each of the following as eighths. What is the pattern?

$$\frac{1}{8}, \ \frac{1}{4}, \ \frac{3}{8}, \ \frac{1}{2}, \ \frac{5}{8}, \ \frac{3}{4}, \ \frac{7}{8}, \ 1$$

4. GEOMETRY Use a ruler to measure the dimensions of this textbook to the nearest $\frac{1}{8}$ in. Find the perimeter.

In Exercises 5 and 6, complete the statement.

5. 24 in. = <u>?</u> ft

6. $2\frac{1}{2}$ ft = <u>?</u> in.

PRACTICE AND PROBLEM SOLVING

MEASUREMENT In Exercises 7–11, write the fraction as a mixed number. Then match the fraction with its location on the ruler.

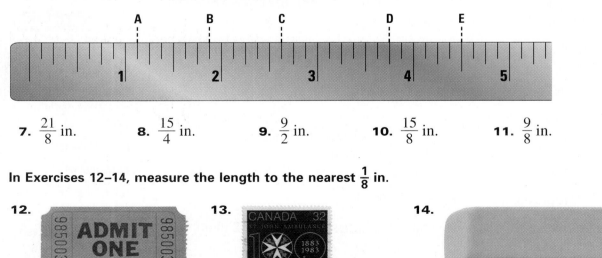

7. $\frac{21}{8}$ in.

8. $\frac{15}{4}$ in.

9. $\frac{9}{2}$ in.

10. $\frac{15}{8}$ in.

11. $\frac{9}{8}$ in.

In Exercises 12–14, measure the length to the nearest $\frac{1}{8}$ in.

12.

13.

14.

REASONING In Exercises 15–18, name a real-life object that could have the given length.

15. 65 in. **16.** 100 yd **17.** 2 ft **18.** 50 ft

In Exercises 19–22, write the height in feet and inches.

19. 75″ **20.** 71 in. **21.** $53\frac{1}{2}''$ **22.** $67\frac{3}{4}''$

In Exercises 23–28, complete the statement.

23. 1 yd = ? ft

24. 60 in. = ? ft

25. ? in. = 5 yd

26. ? yd = 27 ft

27. $\frac{1}{2}$ yd = ? in.

28. ? in. = $\frac{1}{4}$ ft

In Exercises 29–31, find the perimeter of the figure.

29. $5\frac{3}{4}$ yd $5\frac{3}{4}$ yd

30. $1\frac{7}{8}$ ft $4\frac{3}{8}$ ft

31. $2\frac{1}{4}$ in. $1\frac{5}{8}$ in. $3\frac{4}{8}$ in.

32. **SEWING** For a sewing project you need a piece of material that is 114 in. long and 30 in. wide. Write the dimensions in yards.

STANDARDIZED TEST PRACTICE

33. Which of the following is equal to 8 in.?

A $\frac{3}{4}$ ft **B** $\frac{1}{3}$ yd **C** $\frac{1}{9}$ yd **D** $\frac{2}{3}$ ft

EXPLORATION AND EXTENSION

PORTFOLIO

34. **BUILDING YOUR PROJECT** You have volunteered to deliver meals to homebound people. You will ride your bicycle from the kitchen to each of the homes on your route, and then back to the kitchen.

a. Use a ruler to measure the distances on the map.

b. If 1 inch is equal to 1 mile, estimate the distance that you will ride your bicycle. Write this information in your diary.

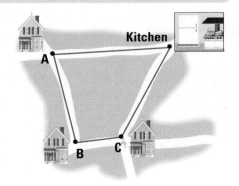

Least Common Denominators

What you should learn:

Goal 1 How to find common denominators of two fractions

Goal 2 How to find the least common denominator of two fractions

Why you should learn it:

Knowing how to find common denominators helps you compare and order fractions.

Goal 1 **FINDING COMMON DENOMINATORS**

Fractions with the same denominator have a **common denominator**. For example, $\frac{3}{6}$ and $\frac{2}{6}$ have a common denominator of 6.

LESSON INVESTIGATION

Investigating Equivalent Fractions

GROUP ACTIVITY The models show fractions equivalent to $\frac{1}{4}$. Write the fractions. Describe any patterns.

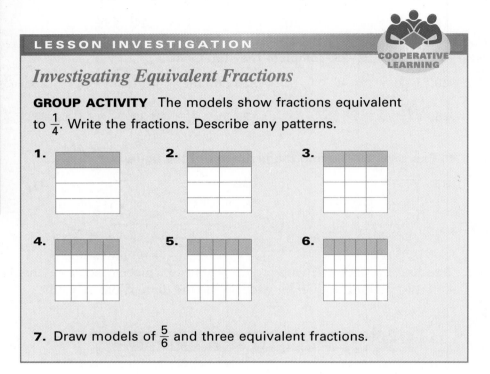

7. Draw models of $\frac{5}{6}$ and three equivalent fractions.

Example 1 **Finding a Common Denominator**

Rewrite the fractions with a common denominator of 36.

a. $\frac{1}{4}$, $\frac{5}{6}$ **b.** $\frac{1}{9}$, $\frac{5}{12}$

Solution

a. $\frac{1}{4} = \frac{1 \cdot 9}{4 \cdot 9} = \frac{9}{36}$ Multiply by $\frac{9}{9}$.

$\frac{5}{6} = \frac{5 \cdot 6}{6 \cdot 6} = \frac{30}{36}$ Multiply by $\frac{6}{6}$.

b. $\frac{1}{9} = \frac{1 \cdot 4}{9 \cdot 4} = \frac{4}{36}$ Multiply by $\frac{4}{4}$.

$\frac{5}{12} = \frac{5 \cdot 3}{12 \cdot 3} = \frac{15}{36}$ Multiply by $\frac{3}{3}$.

STUDY TIP

You can form equivalent fractions by multiplying the numerator and denominator of a fraction by the same number. For example, the fractions $\frac{2}{3}$ and $\frac{4}{6}$ are equivalent because

$$\frac{2}{3} = \frac{2 \cdot 2}{3 \cdot 2} = \frac{4}{6}.$$

In Example 1, notice that the common denominator of 36 is a multiple of the original denominators of 4 and 6. This is also true of the denominators 9 and 12.

> **LEAST COMMON DENOMINATOR**
>
> The **least common multiple** of two numbers is the smallest multiple that they have in common.
>
> The **least common denominator** of two fractions is the least common multiple of their denominators.

Example 2 Finding a Least Common Denominator

Find the least common denominator of the fractions. Then rewrite the fractions with the least common denominator.

a. $\dfrac{3}{5}, \dfrac{1}{2}$ **b.** $\dfrac{5}{8}, \dfrac{1}{6}$

Solution

a. Begin by finding the least common multiple of 2 and 5.

Multiples of 2: 2, 4, 6, 8, **10**, 12, 14, 16, 18, 20, . . .
Multiples of 5: 5, **10**, 15, 20, 25, . . .

The least common multiple of 2 and 5 is **10**, because it is the smallest multiple that appears in both lists.

Now, rewrite each fraction with a denominator of **10**.

$$\frac{3}{5} = \frac{3 \cdot 2}{5 \cdot 2} = \frac{6}{10} \qquad \text{Multiply by } \tfrac{2}{2}.$$

$$\frac{1}{2} = \frac{1 \cdot 5}{2 \cdot 5} = \frac{5}{10} \qquad \text{Multiply by } \tfrac{5}{5}.$$

b. The least common multiple of 6 and 8 is **24**. Rewrite each fraction with a denominator of **24**.

$$\frac{5}{8} = \frac{5 \cdot 3}{8 \cdot 3} = \frac{15}{24} \qquad \text{Multiply by } \tfrac{3}{3}.$$

$$\frac{1}{6} = \frac{1 \cdot 4}{6 \cdot 4} = \frac{4}{24} \qquad \text{Multiply by } \tfrac{4}{4}.$$

> **ONGOING ASSESSMENT**
>
> **Talk About It**
>
> **1.** Rewrite $\dfrac{3}{8}, \dfrac{5}{6}$, and $\dfrac{7}{12}$ with a least common denominator. Discuss your steps with a partner.
>
> **2.** How will the least common denominator help you order the fractions $\dfrac{3}{8}, \dfrac{5}{6}$, and $\dfrac{7}{12}$?

GUIDED PRACTICE

1. Which model shows a fraction *not* equivalent to $\frac{1}{3}$? Explain.

A.   **B.**   **C.**   **D.**

In Exercises 2–5, tell whether the statement is *true* or *false*. Explain.

2. Two common multiples of 3 and 5 are 30 and 45.

3. The least common multiple of 3 and 5 is 30.

4. The least common denominator of $\frac{2}{3}$ and $\frac{2}{5}$ is 15.

5. The least common multiple of any 2 numbers is their product.

6. **REASONING** Which is larger, $\frac{3}{10}$ or $\frac{2}{5}$? How did you decide?

PRACTICE AND PROBLEM SOLVING

In Exercises 7–10, list the first ten multiples of each number. Then find the least common multiple of the two numbers.

7. 5, 8   **8.** 10, 4   **9.** 5, 6   **10.** 12, 10

In Exercises 11–14, draw models of two fractions that are equivalent to the given fraction.

11. $\frac{1}{6}$ **12.** $\frac{3}{8}$ **13.** $\frac{4}{5}$ **14.** $\frac{5}{12}$

In Exercises 15–18, find the least common denominator. Then rewrite the fractions with the least common denominator.

15. $\frac{1}{3}, \frac{11}{12}$ **16.** $\frac{2}{3}, \frac{7}{8}$ **17.** $\frac{1}{6}, \frac{7}{10}$ **18.** $\frac{3}{15}, \frac{1}{2}$

19. **SECRET MESSAGE** Order the fractions from least to greatest. Then copy the diagram and write the ordered letters in the boxes. What is the message? (*Hint:* Rewrite the fractions with a common denominator.)

$\frac{1}{6}$ – E, $\frac{5}{12}$ – L, $\frac{11}{12}$ – E, $\frac{5}{6}$ – O, $\frac{3}{8}$ – L, $\frac{7}{8}$ – N, $\frac{2}{3}$ – D, $\frac{1}{12}$ – W

| ? | ? | ? | ? | | ? | ? | ? | ? |

20. WALKING You walked $\frac{5}{8}$ mi in $\frac{3}{5}$ h. Your friend walked $\frac{7}{12}$ mi in $\frac{2}{3}$ h. Who walked farther? a longer time? faster? Explain your reasoning.

21. PROBABILITY Make a circular spinner that has 10 equal pie-cut regions. Write the following fractions in the regions.

$$\frac{1}{2}, \ \frac{1}{3}, \ \frac{1}{4}, \ \frac{2}{4}, \ \frac{2}{6}, \ \frac{2}{8}, \ \frac{3}{9}, \ \frac{3}{12}, \ \frac{4}{12}, \ \frac{6}{12}$$

What is the probability that the spinner will land on a fraction equivalent to $\frac{1}{3}$? $\frac{1}{4}$? $\frac{1}{2}$?

POETRY In Exercises 22 and 23, count the number of three-letter words in the poem, not including the title. Then write the fraction of words that have three letters.

Walking

People help raise money for charities by walking. A walk for the March of Dimes is shown above.

22.
The Purple Cow

I never saw a Purple Cow;
   I never Hope to See One;
But I can Tell you Anyhow,
   I'd rather See than Be One.

Gelett Burgess

23.
Amidst the grassland
Sings a skylark
Free and disengaged from all things.

Matsuo Basho

24. In which poem is the fraction of three-letter words larger?

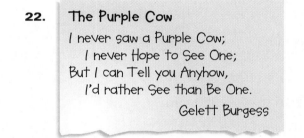

STANDARDIZED TEST PRACTICE

25. Which of the following is *not* equivalent to the fraction $\frac{5}{6}$?

A $\frac{40}{48}$ **B** $\frac{25}{36}$ **C** $\frac{25}{30}$ **D** $\frac{30}{36}$

26. On a class trip to the zoo, you see 58 different kinds of animals. Later, you learn that the zoo has 126 different kinds of animals altogether. Which of the following statements is true?

A You saw less than half of the animals.

B You saw more than half of the animals.

C You saw exactly half of the animals.

D You need more information to determine the answer.

27. BUILDING YOUR PROJECT The local recycling center estimates that $\frac{1}{2}$ of the bottles and cans it takes in are aluminum cans, $\frac{1}{3}$ are plastic bottles, and $\frac{1}{6}$ are glass bottles.

On a day when you are at the center, they receive 85 aluminum cans, 25 plastic bottles, and 12 glass bottles. Do these numbers agree with the estimates given above? Explain. Add your answer to your diary.

SPIRAL REVIEW

1. GAMES You and your friend go to a game room. Air hockey costs $.75 per game, each video game costs $.50 per game, and skeeball costs $.25 per game. Together, you play a total of 3 games of air hockey, 4 games of skeeball, and 2 video games. **(2.5, 4.4)**

a. Write an expression that shows the amount that you and your friend spent at the game room.

b. How much money did you and your friend spend?

In Exercises 2–5, complete the statement using >, <, or =. (3.2)

2. 0.75 km ? 75 m

3. 1.25 m ? 1250 mm

4. 0.23 cm ? 2.3 mm

5. 0.2 mm ? 2.0 cm

In Exercises 6–9, use vertical form to add or subtract. (4.1, 4.2)

6. $4.5 + 3.35$ **7.** $16 - 3.54$ **8.** $12.92 + 3.56$ **9.** $10.66 - 8.98$

TECHNOLOGY In Exercises 10–13, use mental math to solve. Then use a calculator to check your answers. (4.6)

10. $m \times 0.03 = 3$ **11.** $50 \div t = 0.05$ **12.** $n \div 100 = 0.32$ **13.** $0.4 \times b = 4000$

14. Make a line plot of the data below. Find the mode and range. Make up a story about what the data could be. **(5.1, 5.4)**

22, 25, 18, 17, 16, 17, 23, 18, 17, 18, 20, 17

In Exercises 15–16, use a diagram to answer the question. (6.2)

15. You have 16 pens. One fourth are blue and the rest are black. How many black pens do you have?

16. You are painting a wall that is 10 yd^2 in area. You have painted one fifth of the wall. How many square yards are left to paint?

Units in the U.S. Customary System

In Lesson 7.1, you learned about measurements of length in the U.S. Customary System. There are also units for area, capacity, and weight that you use every day. A table of these measures can be found on page 661.

A table of these measures can be found on page 661.

STUDY TIP

Remember that the word *of* often means to multiply. An example is shown below.

$$0.2 \text{ of } 12 = 0.2 \times 12$$
$$= 2.4$$

Example

You are using a recipe that calls for $\frac{3}{4}$ of a cup of milk. You only have a cup that measures fluid ounces (fl oz). How do you know how much milk to use?

Solution

You need to convert $\frac{3}{4}$ of a cup to fluid ounces. First, convert $\frac{3}{4}$ to a decimal. Then multiply.

$\frac{3}{4}$ of a cup $= 0.75$ of a cup	Rewrite $\frac{3}{4}$.
$= 0.75 \times (1 \text{ c})$	Multiply.
$= 0.75 \times (8 \text{ fl oz})$	Rewrite 1 c.
$= 6 \text{ fl oz}$	Use a calculator.

Exercises

In Exercises 1–3, match the real-life description with its appropriate measure.

1. ton   **A.** an area of land

2. gallon   **B.** the weight of a truck

3. acre   **C.** the amount of water in a fish tank

In Exercises 4–9, use a calculator to help you complete the statement.

4. $1 \text{ qt} = \boxed{?} \text{ c}$ **5.** $1\frac{3}{4} \text{ gal} = \boxed{?} \text{ qt}$ **6.** $62 \text{ lb} = \boxed{?} \text{ oz}$

7. $2\frac{1}{2} \text{ c} = \boxed{?} \text{ fl oz}$ **8.** $\frac{1}{4} \text{ lb} = \boxed{?} \text{ oz}$ **9.** $1\frac{1}{2} \text{ gal} = \boxed{?} \text{ qt}$

10. **GEOGRAPHY** Colorado has an area of 66,618,240 acres and New Mexico has an area of 121,593 mi^2. Which state is larger?

11. **SPACE SHUTTLE** To help the space shuttle *Atlantis* launch, it needs two rocket boosters and an external fuel tank. Each rocket booster weighs 650 tons and the external fuel tank weighs 827.8 tons. If *Atlantis* weighs 171,205 lb, then how much will the entire shuttle system weigh before a launch?

LAB 7.3

COOPERATIVE LEARNING

Materials Needed
• paper
• colored pencils
• markers or pens
• fraction strips

Investigating Operations with Fractions

Part A ADDING FRACTIONS

Write the addition problem that the model shows.

1.

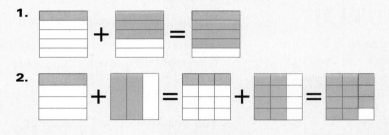

2.

In Exercises 3–8, draw a model of the problem and find the sum.

3. $\dfrac{1}{3} + \dfrac{2}{3}$ **4.** $\dfrac{1}{6} + \dfrac{4}{6}$ **5.** $\dfrac{2}{4} + \dfrac{1}{4}$

6. $\dfrac{1}{3} + \dfrac{2}{4}$ **7.** $\dfrac{3}{5} + \dfrac{1}{3}$ **8.** $\dfrac{1}{2} + \dfrac{2}{3}$

9. Use the results from above, explain how to add two fractions that have different denominators.

Part B SUBTRACTING FRACTIONS

Write the subtraction problem that the model shows.

10.

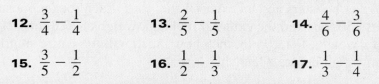

11.

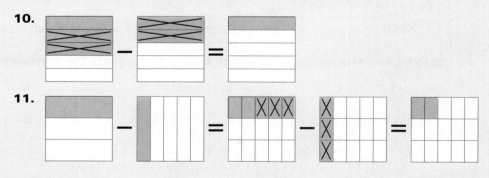

In Exercises 12–17, draw a model of the problem and find the difference.

12. $\dfrac{3}{4} - \dfrac{1}{4}$ **13.** $\dfrac{2}{5} - \dfrac{1}{5}$ **14.** $\dfrac{4}{6} - \dfrac{3}{6}$

15. $\dfrac{3}{5} - \dfrac{1}{2}$ **16.** $\dfrac{1}{2} - \dfrac{1}{3}$ **17.** $\dfrac{1}{3} - \dfrac{1}{4}$

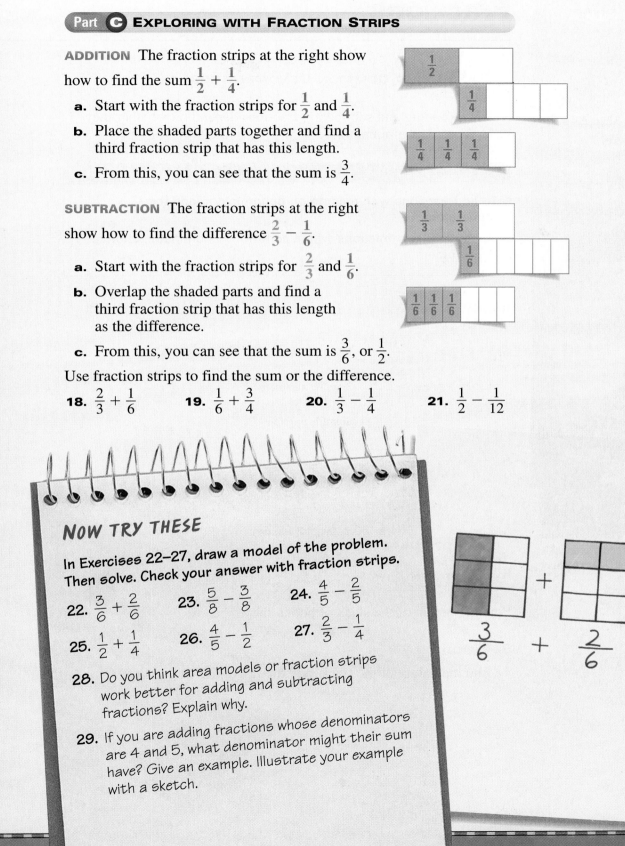

Part C EXPLORING WITH FRACTION STRIPS

ADDITION The fraction strips at the right show how to find the sum $\frac{1}{2} + \frac{1}{4}$.

a. Start with the fraction strips for $\frac{1}{2}$ and $\frac{1}{4}$.

b. Place the shaded parts together and find a third fraction strip that has this length.

c. From this, you can see that the sum is $\frac{3}{4}$.

SUBTRACTION The fraction strips at the right show how to find the difference $\frac{2}{3} - \frac{1}{6}$.

a. Start with the fraction strips for $\frac{2}{3}$ and $\frac{1}{6}$.

b. Overlap the shaded parts and find a third fraction strip that has this length as the difference.

c. From this, you can see that the sum is $\frac{3}{6}$, or $\frac{1}{2}$.

Use fraction strips to find the sum or the difference.

18. $\frac{2}{3} + \frac{1}{6}$ **19.** $\frac{1}{6} + \frac{3}{4}$ **20.** $\frac{1}{3} - \frac{1}{4}$ **21.** $\frac{1}{2} - \frac{1}{12}$

NOW TRY THESE

In Exercises 22–27, draw a model of the problem. Then solve. Check your answer with fraction strips.

22. $\frac{3}{6} + \frac{2}{6}$ **23.** $\frac{5}{8} - \frac{3}{8}$ **24.** $\frac{4}{5} - \frac{2}{5}$

25. $\frac{1}{2} + \frac{1}{4}$ **26.** $\frac{4}{5} - \frac{1}{2}$ **27.** $\frac{2}{3} - \frac{1}{4}$

28. Do you think area models or fraction strips work better for adding and subtracting fractions? Explain why.

29. If you are adding fractions whose denominators are 4 and 5, what denominator might their sum have? Give an example. Illustrate your example with a sketch.

$$\frac{3}{6} + \frac{2}{6} =$$

7.3 Adding and Subtracting Fractions

What you should learn:

Goal 1 How to add and subtract fractions with a common denominator

Goal 2 How to add and subtract fractions with different denominators

Why you should learn it:

Fractions may need to be added or subtracted when working with measurements.

Knowing how to add fractions can help you when learning how to read music.

Goal 1 USING COMMON DENOMINATORS

Rules for adding and subtracting fractions depend on whether they have the same denominators.

FRACTIONS WITH A COMMON DENOMINATOR

To **add** fractions with a common denominator, add their numerators.

To **subtract** two fractions with a common denominator, subtract their numerators.

Example 1 Adding and Subtracting Fractions

a. $\dfrac{1}{8} + \dfrac{3}{8} = \dfrac{1+3}{8}$ Add numerators.

$= \dfrac{4}{8}$ Simplify numerator.

$= \dfrac{1}{2}$ Simplify fraction.

b. $\dfrac{7}{10} - \dfrac{3}{10} = \dfrac{7-3}{10}$ Subtract numerators.

$= \dfrac{4}{10}$ Simplify numerator.

$= \dfrac{2}{5}$ Simplify fraction.

Example 2 Adding Fractions

Find the height of the stack of books shown below.

REAL LIFE
Measurement

Solution

To find the height of the stack, add the fractions.

$$\frac{3}{8} + \frac{7}{8} = \frac{3+7}{8}$$

$$= \frac{10}{8}$$

$$= \frac{5}{4}$$

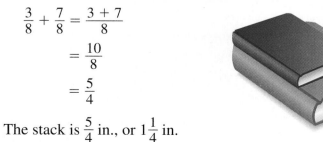

$\frac{3}{8}$ in.

$\frac{7}{8}$ in.

The stack is $\dfrac{5}{4}$ in., or $1\dfrac{1}{4}$ in.

Adding and subtracting fractions with different denominators uses a problem-solving strategy called solving a simpler problem.

FRACTIONS WITH DIFFERENT DENOMINATORS

To **add** or **subtract** fractions with different denominators, follow these steps:

1. Rewrite the fractions using a common denominator.

2. Add or subtract the numerators.

Example 3 Adding and Subtracting Fractions

a. $\dfrac{1}{4} + \dfrac{2}{5} = \dfrac{1 \cdot 5}{4 \cdot 5} + \dfrac{2 \cdot 4}{5 \cdot 4}$ **A common denominator is 20.**

$= \dfrac{5}{20} + \dfrac{8}{20}$ **Simplify.**

$= \dfrac{5 + 8}{20}$ **Add numerators.**

$= \dfrac{13}{20}$ **Simplify numerator.**

b. $\dfrac{3}{4} - \dfrac{1}{6} = \dfrac{3 \cdot 3}{4 \cdot 3} - \dfrac{1 \cdot 2}{6 \cdot 2}$ **A common denominator is 12.**

$= \dfrac{9}{12} - \dfrac{2}{12}$ **Simplify.**

$= \dfrac{9 - 2}{12}$ **Subtract numerators.**

$= \dfrac{7}{12}$ **Simplify numerator.**

c. Find the sum of one fourth, three eighths, and seven eighths.

$\dfrac{1}{4} + \dfrac{3}{8} + \dfrac{7}{8} = \dfrac{1 \cdot 2}{4 \cdot 2} + \dfrac{3 \cdot 1}{8 \cdot 1} + \dfrac{7 \cdot 1}{8 \cdot 1}$ **A common denominator is 8.**

$= \dfrac{2}{8} + \dfrac{3}{8} + \dfrac{7}{8}$ **Simplify.**

$= \dfrac{2 + 3 + 7}{8}$ **Add numerators.**

$= \dfrac{12}{8}$ **Simplify numerator.**

$= \dfrac{3}{2}$ **Simplify fraction.**

ONGOING ASSESSMENT

Talk About It

Add or subtract. Compare your answers with a partner. Discuss any differences.

1. $\dfrac{4}{5} + \dfrac{2}{3}$

2. $\dfrac{7}{8} - \dfrac{1}{2}$

3. $\dfrac{1}{3} + \dfrac{1}{2} + \dfrac{1}{6}$

GUIDED PRACTICE

LOGICAL REASONING In Exercises 1–3, complete the statement with *sometimes, always,* or *never.* Give examples to support your answer.

1. The difference of two fractions that are each less than 1 is ___?___ less than 1.

2. The sum of three fractions that are each less than 1 is ___?___ greater than 1.

3. The least common denominator of two fractions is ___?___ the product of the two denominators.

4. WRITING Explain how to add or subtract two fractions with a common denominator *and* with different denominators. Give examples to support your explanations.

5. ERROR ANALYSIS Describe and correct the error.

a.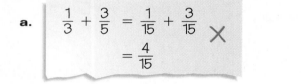

b.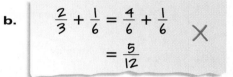

PRACTICE AND PROBLEM SOLVING

In Exercises 6 and 7, copy and complete the model. Then check your answer by using another method.

6. 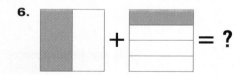   **7.**

In Exercises 8–13, add or subtract. Then write your answer in words.

8. $\dfrac{3}{6} + \dfrac{5}{6}$ **9.** $\dfrac{2}{4} - \dfrac{2}{5}$ **10.** $\dfrac{6}{9} - \dfrac{1}{6}$

11. $\dfrac{1}{2} + \dfrac{4}{5} + \dfrac{3}{10}$ **12.** $\dfrac{1}{7} + \dfrac{3}{7} + \dfrac{1}{14}$ **13.** $\dfrac{5}{7} - \dfrac{1}{3}$

ALGEBRA AND MENTAL MATH In Exercises 14–19, complete the statement. (There may be more than one correct answer.)

14. $\boxed{?} + \dfrac{3}{7} = 1$ **15.** $\dfrac{8}{10} - \boxed{?} = \dfrac{1}{2}$ **16.** $\boxed{?} - \boxed{?} = \dfrac{2}{3}$

17. $\boxed{?} + \boxed{?} = \dfrac{1}{4}$ **18.** $\boxed{?} - \dfrac{1}{4} = \dfrac{1}{8}$ **19.** $\dfrac{1}{3} + \boxed{?} = \dfrac{1}{2}$

GEOMETRY In Exercises 20–22, find the value of *x*.

20. Perimeter = *x*

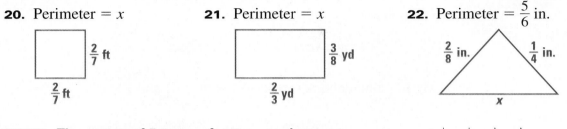

$\frac{2}{7}$ ft

$\frac{2}{7}$ ft

21. Perimeter = *x*

$\frac{3}{8}$ yd

$\frac{2}{3}$ yd

22. Perimeter = $\frac{5}{6}$ in.

$\frac{2}{8}$ in. $\frac{1}{4}$ in.

x

MUSIC The names of 5 types of notes are shown at the right. In Exercises 23–25, find the sum of the notes. In $\frac{4}{4}$ time it should equal 1. Does it?

Whole $\frac{1}{2}$ $\frac{1}{4}$ $\frac{1}{8}$ $\frac{1}{16}$

23.

24.

25.

26. Which of the following does *not* have a sum of 1?

A $\frac{5}{6} + \frac{1}{9} + \frac{1}{18}$ **B** $\frac{1}{2} + \frac{1}{3} + \frac{1}{6}$ **C** $\frac{1}{4} + \frac{1}{8} + \frac{1}{16}$ **D** $\frac{4}{16} + \frac{3}{4}$

EXPLORATION AND EXTENSION

PORTFOLIO

27. BUILDING YOUR PROJECT The local Humane Society is sponsoring a vaccination clinic for dogs. They are sending out invitations to publicize the clinic. You and another volunteer stuff the invitations into the envelopes. You stuff $\frac{2}{5}$ of the envelopes. Your partner stuffs $\frac{1}{3}$ of the envelopes.

a. Who stuffed a greater fraction of the envelopes? How much greater?

b. If there are 600 invitations being mailed, how many envelopes are left to be stuffed? Add this information to your booklet.

LAB 7.4

COOPERATIVE LEARNING

Materials Needed
- paper
- colored pencils
- markers or pens

Investigating Mixed Numbers

Part A COMMON DENOMINATORS

Here is a model that shows how to add $1\frac{1}{4}$ and $1\frac{2}{4}$.

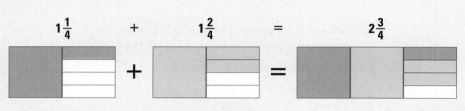

$$1\frac{1}{4} \quad + \quad 1\frac{2}{4} \quad = \quad 2\frac{3}{4}$$

1. Draw a model for the problem. Then find the sum or difference.

   a. $1\frac{1}{5} + 1\frac{3}{5}$ **b.** $1\frac{3}{6} + 1\frac{2}{6}$ **c.** $2\frac{5}{6} - 1\frac{3}{6}$

2. Use the results of Exercise 1 to explain how to add or subtract two mixed numbers that have the same denominator.

Part B DIFFERENT DENOMINATORS

Here is a model that shows how to add $1\frac{1}{4}$ and $1\frac{2}{3}$.

$$1\frac{1}{4} \quad + \quad 1\frac{2}{3} \quad = \quad 1\frac{3}{12} \quad + \quad 1\frac{8}{12} \quad = \quad 2\frac{11}{12}$$

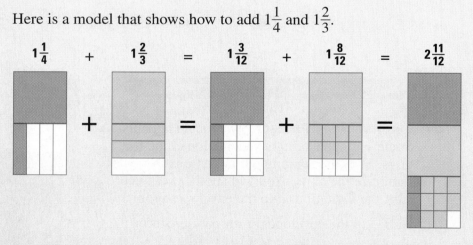

3. Draw a model for the problem. Then find the sum or difference.

   a. $1\frac{1}{3} + 1\frac{1}{2}$ **b.** $1\frac{1}{4} + 1\frac{2}{5}$ **c.** $2\frac{5}{6} - 1\frac{1}{2}$

4. Use the results of Exercise 3 to explain how to add or subtract two mixed numbers that have different denominators.

5. Write the mixed-number addition problem shown by the model.

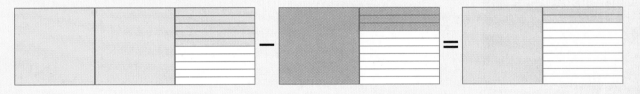

6. Write the decimal addition problem shown by the model above.

7. Write each decimal problem as a mixed-number problem. Solve each version. Compare your answers.

    a. $3.2 + 1.4$ **b.** $1.25 + 1.6$ **c.** $4.7 + 2.5$

8. Write the mixed-number subtraction problem shown by the model.

9. Write the decimal subtraction problem shown by the model above.

NOW TRY THESE

In Exercises 10–13, draw a sketch of the problem. Then solve.

10. $1\frac{3}{6} + 1\frac{2}{6}$

11. $2\frac{3}{5} - 1\frac{3}{5}$

12. $1\frac{1}{2} + 1\frac{1}{4}$

13. $2\frac{4}{5} - 1\frac{1}{2}$

In Exercises 14–17, estimate the answer.

14. $8\frac{2}{3} + 4\frac{1}{6}$

15. $5\frac{4}{5} + 3\frac{1}{4}$

16. $7\frac{2}{3} - 4\frac{1}{4}$

17. $2\frac{7}{8} - 1\frac{5}{6}$

18. REASONING Solve the problem $2.8 - 1.4$ using vertical form. How does "lining up the decimal points" relate to the problem $2\frac{8}{10} - 1\frac{4}{10}$?

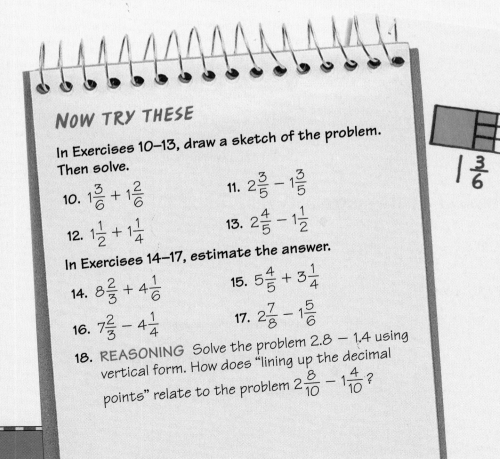

$1\frac{3}{6} + 1\frac{2}{6} =$

7.4 Adding and Subtracting Mixed Numbers

What you should learn:

Goal 1 How to add mixed numbers

Goal 2 How to subtract mixed numbers

Why you should learn it:

Addition and subtraction of mixed numbers is often used in woodworking. An example is finding dimensions to complete a project.

Goal 1 ADDING MIXED NUMBERS

Adding mixed numbers with common denominators is similar to adding fractions with common denominators.

ADDING MIXED NUMBERS

To **add** mixed numbers, do the following:

1. Add the fractions.
2. Add the whole numbers.
3. Simplify if necessary.

Example 1 Common Denominators

Add $3\frac{5}{8} + 4\frac{6}{8}$.

Solution

$$3\frac{5}{8} + 4\frac{6}{8} = 7\frac{11}{8}$$ Add the fractions. Then add the whole numbers.

$$= 7 + \frac{8}{8} + \frac{3}{8}$$ Regroup $\frac{11}{8}$ as $\frac{8}{8} + \frac{3}{8}$.

$$= 7 + 1 + \frac{3}{8}$$ Rewrite $\frac{8}{8}$ as 1.

$$= 8 + \frac{3}{8}$$ Add $7 + 1$ to get 8.

$$= 8\frac{3}{8}$$ Rewrite as mixed number.

Example 2 Different Denominators

Add $8\frac{1}{3} + 4\frac{1}{6}$.

Solution

$$8\frac{1}{3} + 4\frac{1}{6} = 8\frac{2}{6} + 4\frac{1}{6}$$ Rewrite with common denominator.

$$= 12\frac{3}{6}$$ Add the fractions. Then add the whole numbers.

$$= 12\frac{1}{2}$$ Simplify.

Goal 2 SUBTRACTING MIXED NUMBERS

SUBTRACTING MIXED NUMBERS

To **subtract** two mixed numbers, do the following:

1. Subtract the second fraction from the first.
2. Subtract the second whole number from the first.
3. Simplify if necessary.

Example 3 **Common Denominators**

$$5\frac{7}{9} - 3\frac{4}{9} = 2\frac{3}{9}$$ Subtract the fractions. Then subtract the whole numbers.

$$= 2\frac{1}{3}$$ Simplify.

Example 4 **Subtracting Mixed Numbers**

You are designing a wooden box with an inlaid design. Find the height of the flowered part of the lid.

REAL LIFE
Woodworking

$1\frac{3}{8}$ in.

$1\frac{3}{4}$ in.

$4\frac{1}{2}$ in.

Solution

To begin, add the heights of the top and bottom parts.

$$1\frac{3}{8} + 1\frac{3}{4} = 1\frac{3}{8} + 1\frac{6}{8} = 2\frac{9}{8} = 2 + \frac{8}{8} + \frac{1}{8} = 3\frac{1}{8}$$

Now, subtract this sum from the total height.

$$4\frac{1}{2} - 3\frac{1}{8} = 4\frac{4}{8} - 3\frac{1}{8} = 1\frac{3}{8}$$

The height of the flowered part is $1\frac{3}{8}$ in.

**Real Life...
Real Facts**

Wood Design

An inlaid wood design is made by setting a decorative design into the surface of the wood.

ONGOING ASSESSMENT

Write About It

Add or subtract. Show your work and describe each step.

1. $3\frac{3}{4} + 2\frac{3}{4}$

2. $6\frac{5}{6} - 4\frac{1}{2}$

1. **MEASUREMENT** Draw and measure line segments with lengths of $5\frac{5}{8}$ in. and $3\frac{1}{4}$ in. Use a ruler to find the sum and difference of the two. Explain your methods.

In Exercises 2 and 3, describe each step of the solution.

2. $2\frac{5}{7} + 6\frac{4}{7} = 8\frac{9}{7}$

$$= 8 + \frac{7}{7} + \frac{2}{7}$$

$$= 9\frac{2}{7}$$

3. $4\frac{5}{6} - 2\frac{1}{3} = 4\frac{5}{6} - 2\frac{2}{6}$

$$= 2\frac{3}{6}$$

$$= 2\frac{1}{2}$$

ESTIMATION In Exercises 4–7, match the sum or difference with the numbers that can be used to make an estimate.

A. $9 - 1$ **B.** $4 + 2$ **C.** $7 + 1$ **D.** $5\frac{1}{2} - \frac{1}{2}$

4. $3\frac{9}{10} + 2\frac{1}{8}$ 5. $6\frac{5}{6} + \frac{7}{8}$ 6. $5\frac{4}{9} - \frac{4}{7}$ 7. $9\frac{1}{6} - \frac{7}{8}$

In Exercises 8–11, write the problem shown by the phrase. Then solve the problem.

8. The sum of two and three fifths and five and one fourth

9. The difference of six and eight ninths and two and four ninths

10. The difference of seven and three sixths and four and one sixth

11. The sum of three and six eighths and one and one half

In Exercises 12–19, add or subtract.

12. $7\frac{3}{5} + 5\frac{1}{5}$ 13. $6\frac{5}{8} - 3\frac{1}{8}$ 14. $8\frac{2}{3} - 1\frac{2}{9}$ 15. $2\frac{7}{10} + 8\frac{1}{2}$

16. $3\frac{2}{3} + 4\frac{3}{4}$ 17. $6\frac{2}{5} - 2\frac{1}{3}$ 18. $9\frac{3}{6} - 4\frac{1}{4}$ 19. $6\frac{5}{8} + 3\frac{1}{6}$

20. **REASONING** During a bike ride, you drank $1\frac{2}{3}$ bottles of spring water. Your friend drank $1\frac{7}{10}$ of the same size bottles. Who drank more water? how much more?

ALGEBRA AND MENTAL MATH In Exercises 21–26, solve.

21. $7\frac{6}{7} - x = 1\frac{6}{7}$

22. $y + 1\frac{1}{3} = 10\frac{2}{3}$

23. $m + 2\frac{1}{8} = 3\frac{3}{8}$

24. $4\frac{3}{4} - n = 4\frac{1}{2}$

25. $3\frac{4}{5} + a = 4$

26. $4\frac{1}{2} - b = 2$

FINDING A PATTERN In Exercises 27–29, solve each problem. Then describe any patterns that you see.

27. $6\frac{7}{8} - 5\frac{1}{8} = n$

$6\frac{7}{8} - 5\frac{1}{4} = n$

$6\frac{7}{8} - 5\frac{3}{8} = n$

28. $9\frac{5}{6} - 1\frac{1}{6} = d$

$9\frac{5}{6} - 1\frac{1}{3} = d$

$9\frac{5}{6} - 1\frac{1}{2} = d$

29. $12 - 3\frac{4}{5} = t$

$12 - 3\frac{3}{5} = t$

$12 - 3\frac{2}{5} = t$

NUMBER RIDDLES In Exercises 30 and 31, solve the riddle.

30. I am a number between 4 and 5. When added to myself, I equal a whole number. What number am I?

31. The sum of two mixed numbers is $5\frac{4}{5}$. The difference of the numbers is $1\frac{2}{5}$. Both numbers have a denominator of 5. Find the numbers.

32. **GYMNASTICS** The diagram below shows a set of uneven parallel bars, used in gymnastics. What is the height from the floor to the lower bar?

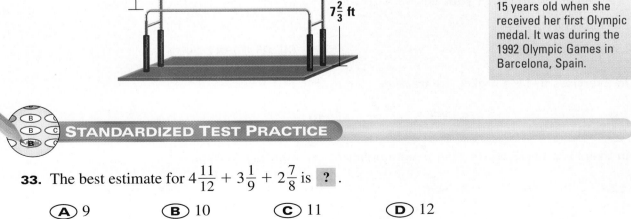

$3\frac{1}{3}$ ft

$7\frac{2}{3}$ ft

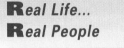

Dominique Dawes was 15 years old when she received her first Olympic medal. It was during the 1992 Olympic Games in Barcelona, Spain.

STANDARDIZED TEST PRACTICE

33. The best estimate for $4\frac{11}{12} + 3\frac{1}{9} + 2\frac{7}{8}$ is [?] .

(A) 9   (B) 10   (C) 11   (D) 12

34. BUILDING YOUR PROJECT Your neighborhood group is holding a bake sale to raise money for a new playground. You are baking three kinds of muffins to help out. Using the list of common ingredients shown below, find out how much of the following you will need to bake all three kinds of muffins.

a. flour (in cups)   **b.** sugar (in cups)

c. oil (in cups)   **d.** baking powder (in teaspoons)

Common Ingredients	Bran	Apple	Blueberry
Flour	$1\frac{3}{4}$ c.	$2\frac{1}{2}$ c.	$1\frac{1}{2}$ c.
Sugar	$\frac{1}{4}$ c.	$1\frac{1}{4}$ c.	$\frac{1}{2}$ c.
Baking powder	$2\frac{1}{2}$ t.	—	2 t.
Oil	$\frac{1}{3}$ c.	$\frac{1}{2}$ c.	$\frac{1}{4}$ c.

SPIRAL REVIEW

1. MOVIES A group of 4 friends goes to the movie theater. In how many ways can the friends sit in a row of 5 seats? **(1.8)**

In Exercises 2 and 3, you are shown a model for a portion of a whole. Describe a model for the whole. **(3.3)**

2.  = 0.6

3. ▲▲▲▲▲▲▲▲▲
▲▲▲▲▲▲▲▲▲ = 0.16

STATISTICS In Exercises 4–7, find the mean of the numbers. Use a calculator to check your answers. **(5.3)**

4. 56, 89, 23   **5.** 111, 123, 90, 93, 113

6. 192, 533, 250   **7.** 89, 95, 77, 87, 82

In Exercises 8–11, simplify the fraction. **(6.4)**

8. $\frac{6}{54}$ **9.** $\frac{15}{30}$ **10.** $\frac{35}{7}$ **11.** $\frac{12}{60}$

In Exercises 12–15, write the mixed number as an improper fraction. **(6.6)**

12. $2\frac{4}{5}$ **13.** $4\frac{1}{9}$ **14.** $3\frac{11}{12}$ **15.** $6\frac{7}{10}$

Take this test as you would take a test in class. The answers to the exercises are given in the back of the book.

In Exercises 1 and 2, measure the length of the object to the nearest $\frac{1}{8}$ in. Write the length as a mixed number and as an improper fraction. **(7.1)**

1.

2.

3. HISTORY The tallest president was Abraham Lincoln. His height was 6 ft 4 in. Write Lincoln's height in inches. **(7.1)**

In Exercises 4–7, decide whether the fractions are equivalent. **(7.2)**

4. $\frac{9}{36}, \frac{1}{3}$ **5.** $\frac{10}{16}, \frac{15}{24}$ **6.** $\frac{15}{25}, \frac{8}{10}$ **7.** $\frac{18}{27}, \frac{6}{9}$

In Exercises 8–13, match the pair of fractions with its description. **(7.2, 7.3, 7.4)**

A. Difference is four sevenths. **B.** Both can be simplified. **C.** They are equivalent.

D. Both are mixed numbers. **E.** Sum is 2. **F.** Sum is 1.

8. $\frac{7}{9}, 1\frac{2}{9}$ **9.** $\frac{3}{8}, \frac{9}{24}$ **10.** $1\frac{2}{3}, 2\frac{1}{8}$

11. $\frac{5}{7}, \frac{1}{7}$ **12.** $\frac{1}{4}, \frac{6}{8}$ **13.** $\frac{4}{12}, \frac{6}{12}$

In Exercises 14–22, add or subtract. **(7.3, 7.4)**

14. $\frac{7}{12} + \frac{5}{12}$ **15.** $\frac{11}{15} - \frac{7}{15}$ **16.** $\frac{1}{2} - \frac{1}{9}$

17. $\frac{1}{6} + \frac{3}{4}$ **18.** $\frac{1}{2} + \frac{1}{3} + \frac{1}{6}$ **19.** $\frac{1}{12} + \frac{1}{6} + \frac{1}{8}$

20. $3\frac{1}{8} + 2\frac{7}{8}$ **21.** $4\frac{1}{3} + 3\frac{1}{6}$ **22.** $5\frac{7}{10} - 1\frac{1}{10}$

23. REASONING When your cousin was six years old, she lost one fifth of her baby teeth. When she was seven years old, she lost one fourth of her baby teeth. During the two years, did she lose more or less than half her baby teeth? Explain your reasoning. **(7.3)**

7.5

Subtracting and Regrouping: Common Denominators

What you should learn:

Goal 1 How to subtract with regrouping

Goal 2 How to use subtracting and regrouping to solve real-life problems

Why you should learn it:

Knowing how to regroup when subtracting can help you when comparing the amounts of two checks.

Goal 1 SUBTRACTING AND REGROUPING

This model shows how to subtract $\frac{3}{5}$ from $2\frac{2}{5}$.

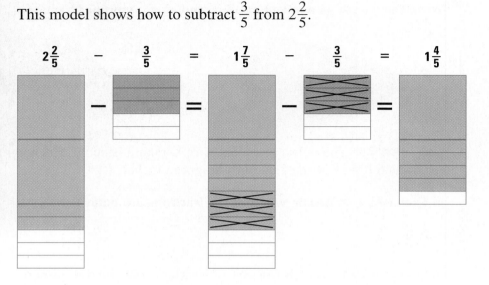

$$2\frac{2}{5} \quad - \quad \frac{3}{5} \quad = \quad 1\frac{7}{5} \quad - \quad \frac{3}{5} \quad = \quad 1\frac{4}{5}$$

Rewriting $2\frac{2}{5}$ as $1\frac{7}{5}$ is called **regrouping**. Notice how regrouping is used in the examples below.

Example 1 Subtracting and Regrouping

Simplify the following expressions.

a. $3 - 1\frac{3}{4}$ **b.** $2\frac{1}{3} - \frac{2}{3}$ **c.** $8\frac{1}{5} - 5\frac{2}{5}$

Solution

a. $3 - 1\frac{3}{4} = 2\frac{4}{4} - 1\frac{3}{4}$ Regroup 3 as $2\frac{4}{4}$.

$\qquad\qquad = 1\frac{1}{4}$ Subtract mixed numbers.

b. $2\frac{1}{3} - \frac{2}{3} = 1\frac{4}{3} - \frac{2}{3}$ Regroup $2\frac{1}{3}$ as $1\frac{4}{3}$.

$\qquad\qquad = 1\frac{2}{3}$ Subtract.

c. $8\frac{1}{5} - 5\frac{2}{5} = 7\frac{6}{5} - 5\frac{2}{5}$ Regroup $8\frac{1}{5}$ as $7\frac{6}{5}$.

$\qquad\qquad = 2\frac{4}{5}$ Subtract mixed numbers.

STUDY TIP

In the subtraction problem

$$4 - 2\frac{5}{8}$$

4 should be regrouped as $3\frac{8}{8}$ so the fractions have a common denominator.

Goal 2 SOLVING REAL-LIFE PROBLEMS

When you write a check, you need to write the amount in two ways: as a decimal, and as words followed by a fraction of a dollar.

Example 2 Finding a Profit

REAL LIFE *Business*

Susan James runs an antique shop. She buys a lamp from Daniel Warren. Later she sells it to another customer. From the two checks shown below, can you tell how much profit Susan made on the sale? Explain your reasoning.

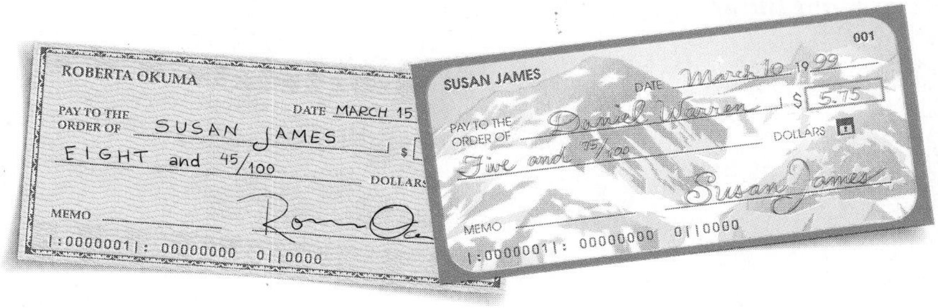

Solution

The check for \$5.75 was written by Susan. It must show the amount Susan paid for the lamp. The check for eight and $\frac{45}{100}$ dollars was written to Susan. So, it must show the amount Susan received for selling the lamp. You can find Susan's profit in two ways.

Method 1 Use mixed numbers to subtract.

Profit = **Amount Susan Received** − **Amount Susan Paid**

$$= 8\frac{45}{100} - 5\frac{75}{100}$$

$$= 7\frac{145}{100} - 5\frac{75}{100}$$

$$= 2\frac{70}{100} \text{ dollars}$$

Susan's profit is two dollars and seventy cents.

Method 2 Use decimals to subtract.

\$8.45 ←	**Amount Susan received**
− 5.75 ←	**Amount Susan paid**
\$2.70 ←	**Profit**

Susan's profit is \$2.70.

ONGOING ASSESSMENT

Talk About It

1. Solve $3 - \frac{5}{7}$.
2. With a partner, make up a problem that is similar to Example 2. Write the amounts received and paid in two ways, as they would be on a check.

GUIDED PRACTICE

In Exercises 1–3, match the subtraction problem with the best way to regroup the whole number.

A. $2\frac{3}{3}$

B. $2\frac{8}{8}$

C. $2\frac{12}{12}$

1. $3 - 1\frac{5}{8}$

2. $3 - \frac{11}{12}$

3. $3 - \frac{2}{3}$

4. Subtract $1.35 from $5.00 using decimals and then using fractions. Which method do you like better? Why?

SEWING In Exercises 5 and 6, each quilt has an area of $4\frac{1}{8}$ yd^2 of fabric. How many square yards of fabric are *not* blue?

5.

6.

$1\frac{3}{8}$ yd^2 are blue.

$2\frac{5}{8}$ yd^2 are blue.

PRACTICE AND PROBLEM SOLVING

ALGEBRA In Exercises 7–10, use regrouping to solve.

7. $3 = 2\frac{a}{8}$

8. $4\frac{1}{6} = 3\frac{x}{6}$

9. $6\frac{1}{4} = 5\frac{t}{4}$

10. $2\frac{3}{5} = 1\frac{m}{5}$

In Exercises 11–14, complete the statement using <, >, or =.

11. $4\frac{3}{4}$? $3\frac{7}{4}$

12. $5\frac{1}{6}$? $4\frac{6}{6}$

13. $3\frac{4}{8}$? $3\frac{12}{8}$

14. $6\frac{3}{5}$? $5\frac{8}{5}$

15. SPORTS Use the diagram below to find the difference between the length and the width of a basketball court.

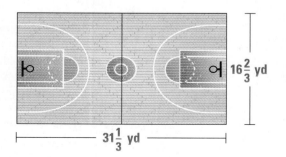

$16\frac{2}{3}$ yd

$31\frac{1}{3}$ yd

Real Life... **R**eal Facts

Basketball was invented in 1891 and was originally played with a soccer ball.

In Exercises 16–23, subtract. Then simplify, if possible.

16. $3 - 1\frac{1}{8}$ **17.** $4 - 1\frac{7}{12}$ **18.** $3\frac{1}{4} - \frac{3}{4}$ **19.** $2\frac{2}{5} - \frac{3}{5}$

20. $1\frac{5}{8} - \frac{7}{8}$ **21.** $7\frac{4}{9} - 5\frac{5}{9}$ **22.** $6\frac{1}{6} - 3\frac{5}{6}$ **23.** $9\frac{3}{10} - 6\frac{7}{10}$

MUSIC Your music teacher asked four music students to keep track of the number of hours they practiced during the week. Find the difference between the practice times for the students.

24. Thelma and Leroy

25. Thelma and Caitlin

26. Arnold and Leroy

27. The student who practiced the most and the student who practiced the least.

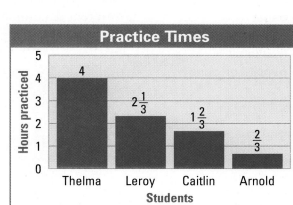

28. **HIKING** You are hiking on a 6 mi trail that is marked every $\frac{1}{10}$ mi. The marker you have just passed says $3\frac{7}{10}$ mi. How many miles can you hike until you reach the end of the trail? Solve the problem using both fractions and decimals.

STANDARDIZED TEST PRACTICE

29. Generally, a lane at a bowling alley is 26 yd long and $1\frac{1}{6}$ yd wide. How much longer is the lane than it is wide?

(A) $24\frac{5}{6}$ yd **(B)** $25\frac{5}{6}$ yd **(C)** $26\frac{5}{6}$ yd **(D)** $27\frac{1}{6}$ yd

EXPLORATION AND EXTENSION

FRACTION WORDS In Exercises 30–33, make a new word using fractional parts of words. For example, the first $\frac{2}{5}$ of *green* plus the last $\frac{3}{4}$ of *neat* makes the word *great*.

30. first $\frac{3}{6}$ of *muscle*, last $\frac{2}{5}$ of *tonic*

31. first $\frac{2}{5}$ of *money*, last $\frac{3}{5}$ of *amuse*

32. first $\frac{1}{5}$ of *baker*, last $\frac{3}{4}$ of *clue*

33. Make a "fraction word" of your own.

LAB 7.6

COOPERATIVE LEARNING

Investigating Regrouping: Different Denominators

Part A USING MODELS TO SUBTRACT

Materials Needed
• paper
• colored pencils
• markers
• pencils or pens

Here is a model that shows how to subtract mixed numbers that have different denominators.

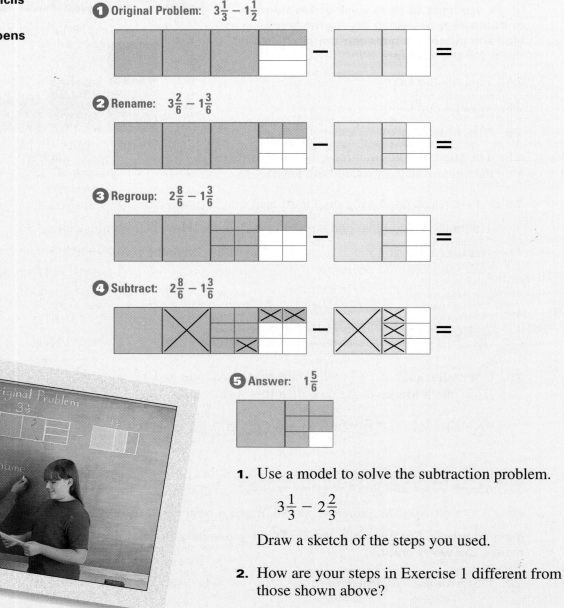

❶ Original Problem: $3\frac{1}{3} - 1\frac{1}{2}$

❷ Rename: $3\frac{2}{6} - 1\frac{3}{6}$

❸ Regroup: $2\frac{8}{6} - 1\frac{3}{6}$

❹ Subtract: $2\frac{8}{6} - 1\frac{3}{6}$

❺ Answer: $1\frac{5}{6}$

1. Use a model to solve the subtraction problem.

$$3\frac{1}{3} - 2\frac{2}{3}$$

Draw a sketch of the steps you used.

2. How are your steps in Exercise 1 different from those shown above?

3. Write a summary of steps for the subtraction problem that is shown below. Explain each step.

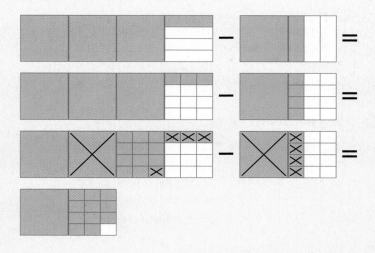

4. Use a model to help you solve each subtraction problem. Write a summary of steps.

    a. $3\frac{1}{4} - 2\frac{2}{3}$ **b.** $2\frac{2}{5} - 1\frac{3}{4}$ **c.** $4\frac{1}{3} - 3\frac{3}{4}$ **d.** $6\frac{1}{6} - 4\frac{1}{4}$

5. With others in your group, discuss how to tell that a subtraction problem needs renaming, regrouping, or both.

NOW TRY THESE

Match the problem with the phrase that describes it. Then use a model to help you solve the problem.

  A. Needs renaming but not regrouping.
  B. Needs regrouping but not renaming.
  C. Needs renaming and regrouping.
  D. Does not need renaming or regrouping.

6. $3\frac{2}{3} - \frac{1}{3}$ **7.** $3\frac{3}{4} - 2\frac{2}{3}$

8. $3\frac{2}{3} - 2\frac{3}{4}$ **9.** $3\frac{1}{3} - 2\frac{2}{3}$

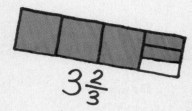

$3\frac{2}{3}$

7.6

Subtracting and Regrouping: Different Denominators

What you should learn:

Goal 1 How to regroup to subtract

Goal 2 How to use subtraction and regrouping to solve real-life problems

Why you should learn it:

Subtraction and regrouping can help you compare measurements. An example is comparing wrench measures.

Goal 1 SUBTRACTING AND REGROUPING

Subtracting mixed numbers with different denominators is similar to subtracting mixed numbers with common denominators.

Example 1 Subtracting Two Ways

Method **1** Use horizontal form.

$$4\frac{1}{2} - 2\frac{5}{8} = 4\frac{4}{8} - 2\frac{5}{8}$$ Rename $\frac{1}{2}$ as $\frac{4}{8}$.

$$= 3\frac{12}{8} - 2\frac{5}{8}$$ Regroup $4\frac{4}{8}$ as $3\frac{12}{8}$.

$$= 1\frac{7}{8}$$ Subtract mixed numbers.

Method **2** Use vertical form.

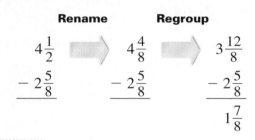

Rename   **Regroup**

$$4\frac{1}{2} \qquad 4\frac{4}{8} \qquad 3\frac{12}{8}$$
$$-2\frac{5}{8} \qquad -2\frac{5}{8} \qquad -2\frac{5}{8}$$
$$\qquad\qquad\qquad\qquad\qquad 1\frac{7}{8}$$

In Example 1, notice how to tell that you need to rename *and* regroup.

1. You need to rename because the denominators are different.

2. You need to regroup because $\frac{4}{8}$ is less than $\frac{5}{8}$.

Example 2 Subtracting, Renaming, Regrouping

Solve $10\frac{1}{6} - 8\frac{1}{4}$.

Solution

$$10\frac{1}{6} - 8\frac{1}{4} = 10\frac{2}{12} - 8\frac{3}{12}$$ Rename $\frac{1}{6}$ as $\frac{2}{12}$ and $\frac{1}{4}$ as $\frac{3}{12}$.

$$= 9\frac{14}{12} - 8\frac{3}{12}$$ Regroup $10\frac{2}{12}$ as $9\frac{14}{12}$.

$$= 1\frac{11}{12}$$ Subtract mixed numbers.

STUDY TIP

In vertical form, the whole numbers "line up" and the fractions "line up."

$$3\frac{4}{5}$$
$$-2\frac{3}{5}$$
$$\overline{\quad 1\frac{1}{5}}$$

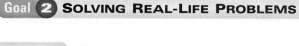

Example 3 > Subtracting Measures

The measure of the bolt width of each wrench is shown.

a. What is the difference between the smallest and largest sized wrenches shown?

b. Is there a pattern in the widths?

REAL LIFE Tools

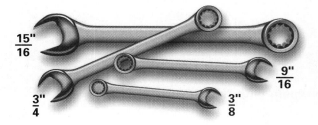

$\frac{15"}{16}$

$\frac{9"}{16}$

$\frac{3"}{4}$

$3\frac{"}{8}$

Solution

a. To find the difference, subtract $\frac{3}{8}$ from $\frac{15}{16}$.

$$\frac{15}{16} - \frac{3}{8} = \frac{15}{16} - \frac{6}{16} \qquad \text{Rename } \frac{3}{8} \text{ as } \frac{6}{16}.$$

$$= \frac{9}{16} \qquad \text{Subtract fractions.}$$

The largest wrench size is $\frac{9}{16}''$ bigger than the smallest.

b. STRATEGY **LOOK FOR A PATTERN** Start by subtracting a wrench size from the next larger wrench size. Do this for each possible wrench size. In each case the result is $\frac{3}{16}''$. So, the pattern is that the wrench sizes increase by $\frac{3}{16}''$.

LESSON INVESTIGATION

COOPERATIVE LEARNING

Looking for a Pattern

GROUP ACTIVITY You bought a set of wrenches that have the following measures (in inches). Which pairs of wrenches have measures that differ by $\frac{5}{16}$? Explain how you made your choices.

$$\frac{3}{8}, \frac{7}{16}, \frac{1}{2}, \frac{9}{16}, \frac{5}{8}, \frac{11}{16}, \frac{3}{4}, \frac{13}{16}, \frac{7}{8}, \frac{15}{16}, 1, 1\frac{1}{16}, 1\frac{1}{8}, 1\frac{3}{16}, 1\frac{1}{4}$$

Real Life...
Real Facts

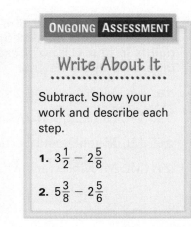

Wrenches

An air wrench is used in auto racing. This wrench loosens and tightens the lug nuts on a wheel very quickly.

Tech Link

Investigation 7, Interactive Real-Life Investigations

ONGOING ASSESSMENT

Write About It
....

Subtract. Show your work and describe each step.

1. $3\frac{1}{2} - 2\frac{5}{8}$

2. $5\frac{3}{8} - 2\frac{5}{6}$

GUIDED PRACTICE

In Exercises 1–3, decide whether you need to *rename* or *regroup*. Explain your reasoning. Then solve.

1. $2\frac{2}{3} - \frac{1}{4}$ **2.** $1\frac{1}{8} - \frac{5}{8}$ **3.** $3\frac{7}{12} - 2\frac{1}{3}$

4. REASONING Give an example of a subtraction problem in which you need to regroup but not rename.

5. The steps below are those used to solve $5\frac{2}{3} - 3\frac{4}{5}$. Put the steps in the correct order.

   A. $1\frac{13}{15}$ **B.** $5\frac{10}{15} - 3\frac{12}{15}$ **C.** $4\frac{25}{15} - 3\frac{12}{15}$ **D.** $5\frac{2}{3} - 3\frac{4}{5}$

PRACTICE AND PROBLEM SOLVING

REASONING In Exercises 6–9, match the problem with the phrase that describes it.

   A. Needs renaming only

   B. Needs regrouping only

   C. Does not need renaming or regrouping

   D. Needs both renaming and regrouping

6. $1\frac{5}{16} - 3\frac{7}{8}$ **7.** $4\frac{5}{16} - 3\frac{3}{16}$ **8.** $4\frac{5}{16} - 3\frac{7}{16}$ **9.** $4\frac{5}{16} - 3\frac{1}{8}$

In Exercises 10–17, subtract. Then simplify, if possible.

10. $7\frac{2}{5} - 3\frac{7}{8}$ **11.** $3\frac{3}{8} - \frac{7}{12}$ **12.** $4\frac{3}{10} - 2\frac{4}{5}$ **13.** $5\frac{5}{12} - 2\frac{7}{8}$

14. $2\frac{1}{9} - 1\frac{2}{3}$ **15.** $12\frac{4}{15} - \frac{4}{5}$ **16.** $15\frac{1}{16} - 12\frac{3}{4}$ **17.** $14\frac{4}{9} - 9\frac{11}{18}$

GEOGRAPHY The bar graph at the right shows the approximate heights (in miles) of the highest points in four states. In Exercises 18–21, find the difference in the heights.

18. Mt. McKinley and Spruce Knob

19. Mt. Hood and Mt. Mitchell

20. Mt. Mitchell and Spruce Knob

21. Mt. McKinley and Mt. Hood

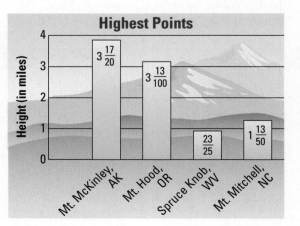

Highest Points

BIRDS The table at the right shows the lengths of four birds. In Exercises 22 and 23, find the difference in lengths of the given birds.

(Source: Peterson Field Guide)

22. Saw-whet owl and ruby-throated hummingbird

23. Snow bunting and magnolia warbler

Snow Bunting	Ruby-throated Hummingbird	Magnolia Warbler	Saw-whet Owl
$7\frac{1}{4}$ in.	$3\frac{3}{4}$ in.	$4\frac{3}{4}$ in.	$8\frac{1}{2}$ in.

24. **FRACTION PUZZLE** Copy and cut out the squares. Fit the pieces together so the fractions on the touching sides are equivalent. Name the shape the pieces form.

1 $\frac{2}{4}$ $\frac{1}{7}$	$\frac{4}{12}$ $\frac{2}{10}$	2 $\frac{3}{2}$ $\frac{1}{8}$	3 $\frac{3}{7}$	$\frac{1}{4}$	$\frac{2}{3}$ $\frac{10}{16}$	$\frac{6}{16}$ $\frac{2}{6}$	5	$\frac{6}{8}$ $\frac{12}{24}$	$\frac{10}{12}$ $2\frac{6}{6}$	$1\frac{1}{2}$ $\frac{1}{5}$ $\frac{6}{14}$ $4\frac{3}{3}$
$\frac{2}{12}$ $\frac{3}{5}$	$\frac{8}{10}$ $\frac{5}{3}$ $\frac{6}{3}$	$3\frac{3}{3}$ $\frac{2}{16}$ $\frac{2}{14}$ $\frac{3}{4}$	$\frac{5}{8}$ $1\frac{1}{2}$ $\frac{1}{3}$	$\frac{4}{6}$ $1\frac{2}{3}$ $\frac{17}{9}$	$\frac{2}{8}$ $\frac{4}{5}$ $\frac{5}{6}$	$1\frac{8}{9}$ $\frac{1}{2}$	$\frac{1}{6}$ $\frac{1}{3}$ $\frac{6}{10}$ $\frac{3}{8}$			

STANDARDIZED TEST PRACTICE

25. The diameter of a half dollar is $30\frac{3}{5}$ mm, and a dime is $17\frac{9}{10}$ mm in diameter. What is the difference between the two diameters?

   A $6\frac{2}{5}$ mm   **B** $6\frac{3}{10}$ mm   **C** $11\frac{6}{10}$ mm   **D** $12\frac{7}{10}$ mm

EXPLORATION AND EXTENSION

PORTFOLIO

BUILDING YOUR PROJECT The table shows the hours you spent as a volunteer at the library.

Week	1	2	3	4
Hours	$1\frac{2}{3}$	$1\frac{1}{3}$	$1\frac{1}{6}$	$2\frac{1}{6}$

26. How much longer did you spend at the library during Week 4 than Week 2?

27. How many hours did you work over the four weeks?

1. **CARS** A survey asked a group of car buyers to name their favorite car color. The results are shown at the right. Write the portion of car buyers who chose each color as a decimal, fraction, and percent. **(3.8)**

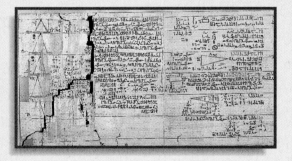

2. **FISHING** You buy a fishing pole for $115. You must pay a sales tax of 6%. What is the total cost of the fishing pole? **(4.8)**

In Exercises 3 and 4, use Guess, Check, and Revise to find ? . (5.3)

3. $\dfrac{13 + 10 + \boxed{?}}{3} = 9$

4. $\dfrac{8 + 11 + \boxed{?} + 24}{3} = 15$

ALGEBRA In Exercises 5–7, solve the proportion. (6.4)

5. $\dfrac{2}{3} = \dfrac{12}{x}$

6. $\dfrac{28}{36} = \dfrac{n}{9}$

7. $\dfrac{8}{m} = \dfrac{40}{75}$

In Exercises 8–10, divide. Then write the quotient in two ways. (2.4)

8. $82 \div 6$

9. $30 \div 7$

10. $126 \div 5$

HISTORY Connection

BROKEN NUMBERS

The word "fraction" comes from the Latin verb *frangere,* "to break," since they were considered broken numbers. Early Egyptian writings had symbols for only *unit fractions,* that is, fractions with numerators of 1. So, they would write $\dfrac{3}{4}$ as $\dfrac{1}{2} + \dfrac{1}{4}$.

Early *nonunit fractions* were written with the denominator over the numerator. The Hindu mathematician Brahmagupta (about 628 A.D.) argued that the numerator should be over the denominator.

1. Simplify the unit fractions.

   a. $\dfrac{1}{9} + \dfrac{1}{9}$

   b. $\dfrac{1}{14} + \dfrac{1}{14} + \dfrac{1}{7}$

   c. $\dfrac{1}{6} + \dfrac{1}{12} + \dfrac{1}{3}$

2. Find combinations of unit fractions for $\dfrac{3}{8}, \dfrac{2}{5},$ and $\dfrac{2}{7}$.

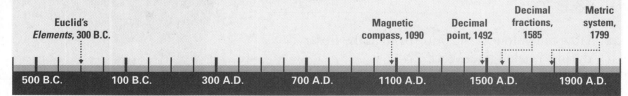

| | Euclid's Elements, 300 B.C. | | | | | Magnetic compass, 1090 | Decimal point, 1492 | Decimal fractions, 1585 | Metric system, 1799 |

| 500 B.C. | 100 B.C. | 300 A.D. | 700 A.D. | 1100 A.D. | 1500 A.D. | 1900 A.D. |

Ribbit!
Ribbit!

READ About It

Tree frogs protect themselves in many ways. For example, both the poison dart and the strawberry poison frogs protect themselves from predators by having poison in their skin. Other frogs, like the Taipei tree frog, protect themselves by changing color to match their surroundings.

Tree frogs can be identified by the sounds they make. The $1\frac{1}{2}$ in. stripeless tree frog makes a sound like a duck quacking. The $2\frac{7}{10}$ in. red-banded rubber tree frog calls with a trilling noise, and the $1\frac{4}{5}$ in. ornate tree frog's sound is almost like a cat's meow. The glade tree frog cries with a scream and a series of clacks, while the $2\frac{7}{20}$ in. foam-nest tree frog has a quiet chirp.

strawberry poison frog

WRITE About It

1. Write a sentence that orders the stripeless tree frog, red-banded rubber tree frog, ornate tree frog, and foam-nest tree frog from longest to shortest.

2. Measure the diameter of a nickel. Is the stripeless tree frog longer or shorter than a nickel? Explain.

3. How much longer is the red-banded rubber tree frog than the stripeless tree frog? Write your answer as a sentence.

4. The largest frog in the world is the Goliath frog. It is $11\frac{4}{5}$ in. long. Suppose that all of the frogs in Exercise 1 sat end to end in a line. Would the line be as long as a Goliath frog? Explain.

5. The Taipei tree frog is $\frac{3}{10}$ in. longer than the stripeless tree frog. How long is the Taipei tree frog? Explain.

poison dart frog

gaudy tree frog

Problem Solving with Fractions and Decimals

What you should learn:

Goal 1 How to use addition and subtraction of fractions to solve problems

Goal 2 How to use addition and subtraction of decimals to solve problems

Why you should learn it:

Knowing how to add and subtract fractions and decimals can help you find a distance you have traveled.

Goal 1 USING FRACTIONS TO SOLVE PROBLEMS

Example 1 Traveling on the Ocean

The map below shows the route traveled by a research ship gathering samples from the ocean floor.

Pacific

Ocean

Indonesia

Papua New Guinea

$319\frac{8}{9}$ mi

$193\frac{1}{3}$ mi

420 mi

N W E S

a. Find the total distance traveled by the ship.

b. How much farther north is the ship from where it began?

Solution

a. To find the total distance, add the three fractions.

$$193\frac{1}{3} + 420 + 319\frac{8}{9} = 193\frac{3}{9} + 420 + 319\frac{8}{9}$$

$$= 932\frac{11}{9}$$

$$= 933\frac{2}{9}$$

The total distance is $933\frac{2}{9}$ mi.

b. To find how much farther north the ship is, subtract the distance traveled south from the distance traveled north.

$$319\frac{8}{9} - 193\frac{1}{3} = 319\frac{8}{9} - 193\frac{3}{9}$$

$$= 126\frac{5}{9}$$

The ship is $126\frac{5}{9}$ mi farther north than when it began.

Example 2 Conducting Ocean Research

The underwater research vessel ALVIN will be diving 4000 m below sea level to conduct research. The trip cannot exceed 10 h. The time spent doing research depends on how long it takes to travel to and from 4000 m. As a general rule, subtract 1.25 h from the total dive time for each 1000 m of depth. How much time can ALVIN spend conducting research at 4000 m?

Solution

Understand the Problem
Use the rule given in the problem to figure out how much time ALVIN can spend at 4000 m.

Make a Plan
Find how many hours ALVIN will spend traveling to and from 4000 m. Then subtract the travel time from the total dive time.

Solve the Problem
Because 4000 m is 4×1000 m, find the total travel time by multiplying the time for 1000 m by 4.

$$\text{Travel time} = 4 \times 1.25$$
$$= 5 \text{ h}$$

ALVIN will spend 5 h in travel time.

Now subtract 5 h from the total dive time.

$$10 - 5 = 5 \text{ h}$$

Look Back
ALVIN will be able to spend 5 h at 4000 m.

Real Life...
Real Facts

Oceanography
The ocean covers more than 70% of the earth's surface.

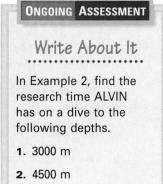

ONGOING ASSESSMENT

Write About It

In Example 2, find the research time ALVIN has on a dive to the following depths.

1. 3000 m

2. 4500 m

GUIDED PRACTICE

In Exercises 1–4, match the problem with its answer.

A. $1\frac{1}{2}$

B. $1\frac{3}{4}$

C. $6\frac{7}{8}$

D. $2\frac{7}{8}$

1. $2\frac{5}{8} + 4\frac{1}{4}$

2. $5 - 2\frac{1}{8}$

3. $1\frac{9}{10} - \frac{2}{5}$

4. $7\frac{1}{4} - 5\frac{2}{4}$

SUPER BOWL In Exercises 5–7, use the circle graph at the right. It shows how the tickets are divided up for the Super Bowl.

Super Bowl Tickets

NFC and AFC champions $\frac{14}{40}$

NFL office $\frac{1}{4}$

Divided among remaining teams $\frac{3}{10}$

Host city $\frac{1}{10}$

5. Which portion shows the largest number of tickets: the *NFL office* or the *remaining teams*? Use an area model to support your answer.

6. What is the difference of the tickets for the NFC and AFC champions and for the remaining teams? Explain.

7. What is the sum of all the fractions in the circle graph? Explain.

PRACTICE AND PROBLEM SOLVING

STOCK MARKET In Exercises 8 and 9, use the following information. On Tuesday, April 15, 1997, the price of stock for Nike Company was $56\frac{1}{2}$ dollars per share. On Wednesday, the stock rose $1\frac{7}{8}$ dollars per share, and on Thursday, it dropped $\frac{3}{8}$ dollar per share. On Friday, it dropped $3\frac{7}{8}$ dollars per share.

8. Find the stock's value on Wednesday.

9. Find the stock's value on Friday.

10. **ITALY** While you are writing a paper on Italy, you research the Leaning Tower of Pisa. You learn that the tower is leaning $14\frac{1}{2}$ ft and leans $\frac{1}{12}$ ft more every 20 years.

a. How much will the tower be leaning in 60 years?

b. How much will the tower be leaning in 100 years?

c. How many years ago was the tower leaning $14\frac{1}{3}$ ft?

HORSES The shoulder height of a horse is measured in hands. One hand equals 4 in. American quarter horses have an average shoulder height of 14.75 hands. Thoroughbreds have an average shoulder height of 16 hands.

Shoulder height

11. Write each average height in inches.

12. Write each average height in feet and inches.

13. Find the difference in the average heights.

14. An American quarter horse can run $\frac{1}{4}$ of a mile in $\frac{1}{3}$ of a minute. A thoroughbred can run 1 mile in $1\frac{1}{2}$ minutes. Which horse is faster? Explain.

STANDARDIZED TEST PRACTICE

15. Choose the best method to solve the problem. You have a board that is $10\frac{3}{4}$ ft long. You want to make a shelf that is $3\frac{3}{5}$ ft long and a shelf that is $2\frac{1}{2}$ ft long. How can you find how much of the board you will have left after making the two shelves?

    (A) Subtract $3\frac{3}{5}$ from $10\frac{3}{4}$, and then add the result to $2\frac{1}{2}$.

    (B) Add $3\frac{3}{5}$ and $2\frac{1}{2}$, and then subtract the result from $10\frac{3}{4}$.

    (C) Add $2\frac{1}{2}$ to $10\frac{3}{4}$, and then subtract $3\frac{3}{5}$ from the result.

    (D) Subtract $2\frac{1}{2}$ from $3\frac{3}{5}$, and then subtract the result from $10\frac{3}{4}$.

EXPLORATION AND EXTENSION

16. COMMUNICATING ABOUT MATHEMATICS (page 353) Despite their name, only 55 of the 135 known species of poison-dart frogs are known to be toxic. Native hunters only use three species to tip their darts. What fraction of the species are actually toxic? What fraction of the toxic frogs are used to get poison for darts?

WHAT *did you learn?*

WHY *did you learn it?*

Skills

7.1	Measure and rewrite lengths in the U.S. Customary system.	Compare measurements, such as the heights of people.
7.2	Find the least common denominator of two fractions.	Compare and order fractions.
7.3	Add and subtract fractions with different denominators.	Add measurements that have fractions.
7.4	Add and subtract mixed numbers.	Find dimensions to complete a project.
7.5	Use regrouping to subtract numbers with common denominators.	Find the difference in amounts of money.
7.6	Use regrouping to subtract numbers with different denominators.	Compare measurements, such as wrench sizes.
7.7	Use fractions and decimals to solve problems.	Find a distance traveled.

Strategies 7.1–7.7 Use problem solving strategies.   Solve real-life problems.

Using Data 7.1–7.7 Use tables and graphs.   Organize data and solve problems.

HOW *does it fit in the bigger picture of mathematics?*

In mathematics, it is important to notice that most difficult problems can be rewritten as a simpler problem.

Example Find $\frac{1}{2} + \frac{2}{5}$.

Solution

$$\frac{1}{2} + \frac{2}{5} = \frac{1 \cdot 5}{2 \cdot 5} + \frac{2 \cdot 2}{5 \cdot 2}$$ **Rewrite with common denominator.**

$$= \frac{5}{10} + \frac{4}{10}$$ **Multiply.**

$$= \frac{9}{10}$$ **Add.**

You learned how to add fractions with a common denominator. To add fractions with different denominators, you do not have to learn a new set of rules. Instead, you only have to learn how to rewrite the two fractions with a common denominator.

One of the most important strategies in math is to *rewrite a difficult problem as a simpler problem.*

VOCABULARY

- common denominator (p. 322)
- least common denominator (p. 323)
- least common multiple (p. 323)
- regrouping (p. 342)

7.1 THE U.S. CUSTOMARY SYSTEM

The U.S. Customary system is not a base-ten system. Multiply or divide to change units of measure.

Example 3 ft 6 in. = 36 in. + 6 in. = 42 in.   12 in. = 1 ft

1. Measure the length of the paper clip to the nearest $\frac{1}{8}$ in.

In Exercises 2–5, write the measurement in feet and inches.

2. 15 in.   **3.** 27 in.   **4.** 19 in.   **5.** 34 in.

7.2 LEAST COMMON DENOMINATORS

The least common denominator of two fractions is the least common multiple of their denominators.

Example Rewrite $\frac{3}{8}$ and $\frac{5}{6}$ with the least common denominator.

Solution $\frac{3}{8} = \frac{3 \cdot 3}{8 \cdot 3} = \frac{9}{24}$ $\frac{5}{6} = \frac{5 \cdot 4}{6 \cdot 4} = \frac{20}{24}$

In Exercises 6–9, rewrite the fractions with the least common denominator.

6. $\frac{2}{5}, \frac{1}{4}$ **7.** $\frac{5}{7}, \frac{3}{4}$ **8.** $\frac{1}{8}, \frac{3}{16}$ **9.** $\frac{11}{12}, \frac{1}{3}$

7.3 ADDING AND SUBTRACTING FRACTIONS

Examples **a.** $\frac{2}{9} + \frac{5}{9} = \frac{7}{9}$ Add numerators.

b. $\frac{3}{4} - \frac{1}{8} = \frac{6}{8} - \frac{1}{8}$ Rewrite with common denominator.

$= \frac{5}{8}$ Subtract.

10. You jog $\frac{7}{8}$ of a mile in the morning and $\frac{5}{8}$ of a mile at night. How many miles did you jog during the day?

7.4 ADDING AND SUBTRACTING MIXED NUMBERS

To add or subtract mixed numbers, first add or subtract the fractions, then add or subtract the whole numbers. If the fractions have different denominators, rename them with a common denominator.

Examples   **a.** $4\frac{1}{2} + 3\frac{1}{8} = 4\frac{4}{8} + 3\frac{1}{8}$ **Rewrite with common denominator.**

$$= 7\frac{5}{8}$$ **Add the fractions. Then add the whole numbers.**

b. $7\frac{5}{6} - 2\frac{2}{3} = 7\frac{5}{6} - 2\frac{4}{6}$ **Rewrite with common denominator.**

$$= 5\frac{1}{6}$$ **Subtract the fractions. Then subtract the whole numbers.**

In Exercises 11–13, add or subtract.

11. $1\frac{5}{7} + 5\frac{1}{7}$ **12.** $1\frac{3}{8} + 3\frac{1}{6}$ **13.** $4\frac{2}{3} - 1\frac{2}{9}$

7.5 COMMON DENOMINATORS

To subtract the fraction part of the mixed number, you may need to regroup the whole number.

Example $2\frac{1}{3} - \frac{2}{3} = 1\frac{4}{3} - \frac{2}{3} = 1\frac{2}{3}$

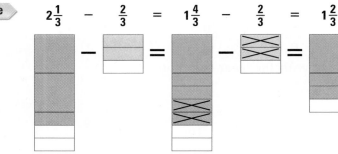

14. Subtract $2\frac{5}{6}$ from $7\frac{1}{6}$.   **15.** Find the difference of 12 and $3\frac{7}{9}$.

16. Your math book is $10\frac{1}{4}$ in. long, and your science book is $9\frac{3}{4}$ in. long. How much longer is your math book?

17. Last week, you baby-sat for $4\frac{1}{6}$ hours. This week, you spent $3\frac{5}{6}$ hours baby-sitting. How many more hours did you spend baby-sitting last week?

7.6 DIFFERENT DENOMINATORS

If the fraction parts of the mixed numbers have different denominators, you need to rename them using a common denominator. Then you can regroup them, if needed.

Example

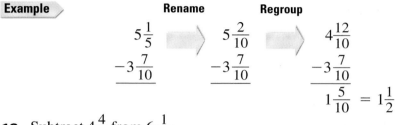

Rename	Regroup

$$5\frac{1}{5} \implies 5\frac{2}{10} \implies 4\frac{12}{10}$$

$$-3\frac{7}{10} \qquad -3\frac{7}{10} \qquad -3\frac{7}{10}$$

$$\overline{\qquad\qquad 1\frac{5}{10}} = 1\frac{1}{2}$$

18. Subtract $4\frac{4}{5}$ from $6\frac{1}{10}$.

19. You are tracking animals in the forest. The length of a woodchuck's track is $1\frac{1}{2}$ in. A raccoon's track is $4\frac{1}{4}$ in. long. How much longer is the raccoon's track?

7.7 PROBLEM SOLVING WITH FRACTIONS AND DECIMALS

Example As part of a science project, you estimate how your family uses water. The results are shown in the circle graph below. Find the sum of the fraction of water used by the dishwasher and faucets.

Solution Add $\frac{1}{40} + \frac{1}{10}$.

$$\frac{1}{40} + \frac{1}{10} = \frac{1}{40} + \frac{4}{40}$$

$$= \frac{5}{40}$$

$$= \frac{1}{8}$$

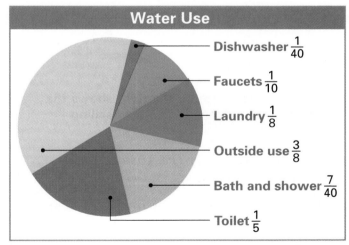

Water Use

Dishwasher $\frac{1}{40}$
Faucets $\frac{1}{10}$
Laundry $\frac{1}{8}$
Outside use $\frac{3}{8}$
Bath and shower $\frac{7}{40}$
Toilet $\frac{1}{5}$

In Exercises 20–22, use the circle graph at the right.

20. Which uses more water: toilet or bath and shower?

21. Add the fractions used by the dishwasher, faucets and laundry. How does this sum compare to the fraction used by the bath and shower?

22. Find the sum of all the fractions. What can you conclude?

In Exercises 1–3, complete the statement.

1. 48 in. = ? ft

2. ? in. = 4 yd

3. $1\frac{1}{2}$ ft = ? in.

In Exercises 4–6, find the least common denominator.

4. $\frac{1}{6}, \frac{2}{3}$

5. $\frac{3}{8}, \frac{5}{6}$

6. $\frac{3}{10}, \frac{3}{4}$

GEOMETRY **In Exercises 7–9, find the value of *x*.**

7. Perimeter = *x*

8. Perimeter = $10\frac{1}{8}$ m

9. Perimeter = *x*

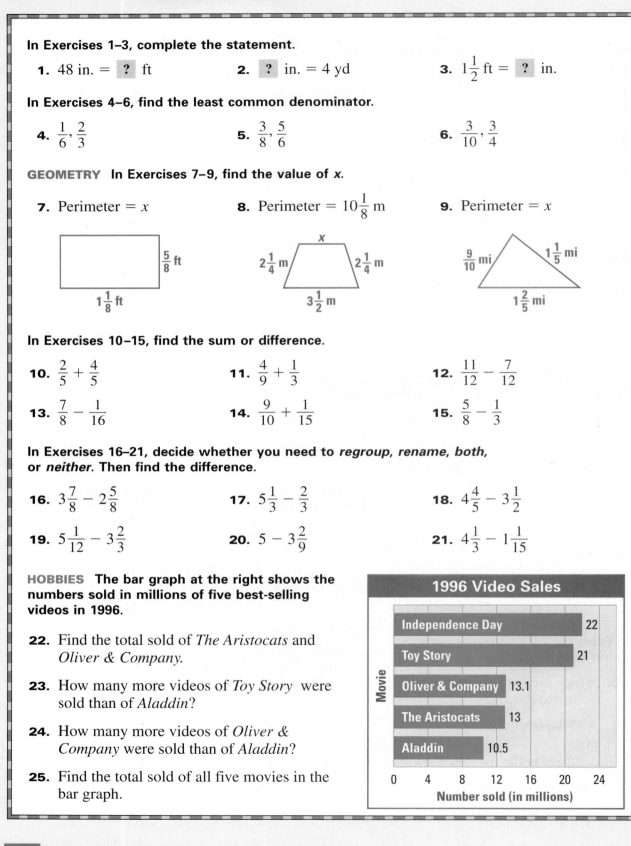

In Exercises 10–15, find the sum or difference.

10. $\frac{2}{5} + \frac{4}{5}$

11. $\frac{4}{9} + \frac{1}{3}$

12. $\frac{11}{12} - \frac{7}{12}$

13. $\frac{7}{8} - \frac{1}{16}$

14. $\frac{9}{10} + \frac{1}{15}$

15. $\frac{5}{8} - \frac{1}{3}$

In Exercises 16–21, decide whether you need to *regroup*, *rename*, *both*, or *neither*. Then find the difference.

16. $3\frac{7}{8} - 2\frac{5}{8}$

17. $5\frac{1}{3} - \frac{2}{3}$

18. $4\frac{4}{5} - 3\frac{1}{2}$

19. $5\frac{1}{12} - 3\frac{2}{3}$

20. $5 - 3\frac{2}{9}$

21. $4\frac{1}{3} - 1\frac{1}{15}$

HOBBIES **The bar graph at the right shows the numbers sold in millions of five best-selling videos in 1996.**

22. Find the total sold of *The Aristocats* and *Oliver & Company*.

23. How many more videos of *Toy Story* were sold than of *Aladdin*?

24. How many more videos of *Oliver & Company* were sold than of *Aladdin*?

25. Find the total sold of all five movies in the bar graph.

1996 Video Sales

Movie	Number sold (in millions)
Independence Day	22
Toy Story	21
Oliver & Company	13.1
The Aristocats	13
Aladdin	10.5

1. You measure 4 nails. The lengths of the nails are shown on the ruler. Which nail is $1\frac{7}{8}''$ long?

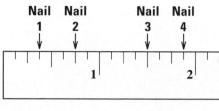

Nail 1   Nail 2   Nail 3   Nail 4

(A) Nail 1   (B) Nail 2
(C) Nail 3   (D) Nail 4

2. Four students live the following distances from school. Maria: $\frac{1}{2}$ mi, Jeremy: $\frac{3}{8}$ mi, Raoul: $\frac{4}{9}$ mi, and Charille: $\frac{5}{12}$ mi. Which of the following statements is *not* true?

(A) Maria lives the farthest from school.

(B) Charille lives farther from the school than Jeremy.

(C) Jeremy lives closer to the school than Raoul.

(D) Raoul lives closer to the school than Charille.

3. The sixth grade voted on their class trip. Out of the 60 students, 24 voted for an amusement park, 20 voted for a picnic, and 16 voted for a museum. What fraction voted for the amusement park?

(A) $\frac{1}{5}$ (B) $\frac{1}{4}$
(C) $\frac{1}{3}$ (D) $\frac{2}{5}$

4. Shannon practiced playing the piano for $\frac{3}{4}$ h on Monday and $\frac{5}{6}$ h on Wednesday. How many hours did she practice on the two days?

(A) $\frac{11}{12}$ h   (B) $1\frac{7}{13}$ h
(C) $1\frac{7}{12}$ h   (D) $2\frac{11}{12}$ h

5. Sean won the 400 m race at the swim meet with a time of $4\frac{3}{4}$ min. The second-place swimmer had a time of $4\frac{5}{6}$ min. How many minutes did Sean win by?

(A) $\frac{1}{2}$ min   (B) $\frac{1}{3}$ min
(C) $\frac{1}{6}$ min   (D) $\frac{1}{12}$ min

6. Lydia weighed $7\frac{2}{3}$ lb when she was born. When she was six months old, she weighed $18\frac{1}{2}$ lb. How much weight did she gain from birth to six months?

(A) $11\frac{1}{3}$ lb   (B) $11\frac{1}{6}$ lb
(C) $10\frac{5}{6}$ lb   (D) $10\frac{1}{6}$ lb

7. Which of the following does *not* equal $\frac{1}{4} + \frac{3}{8} + \frac{5}{6}$?

(A) $1\frac{8}{24}$ (B) $1\frac{11}{24}$
(C) $\frac{70}{48}$ (D) $\frac{35}{24}$

Multiplying and Dividing Fractions

MONUMENTS The Statue of Liberty, in New York, is one of many well-known American monuments. A monument is often built to help us remember some part of our history.

TECHNOLOGY

Technology resources accompanying this chapter:

- Interactive Real-Life Investigations
- Middle School Tutorial Software

CHAPTER THEME
Outdoor Recreation

ON THE WATER Lakes, ponds, and seashores are popular sites for outdoor activities such as swimming and boating.

HIKING is a healthy and enjoyable way to explore the outdoors.

Scenery and History

REAL LIFE
Recreation

The National Park Service manages recreational and scenic sites covering over 83,000,000 acres of land in the United States. (Source: U.S. Department of the Interior, National Park Service)

National Park Service Sites

Parks (national, historic, and military)	101
Historic sites and battlefields	89
Monuments and memorials	99
Preserves and reserves	18
Lake shores and seashores	14
Rivers	15
Other areas	38

Think and Discuss

1. How might you best display this data? Why?

2. Write two questions involving fractions about the data.

PORTFOLIO

CHAPTER PROJECT

Planning a Park Outing

PROJECT DESCRIPTION

Parks are places people go to enjoy their free time. Many public parks offer nature trails, swimming, picnic areas, and playground equipment. Plan a class trip to a park. Use the list of **TOPICS** on the next page to help you organize your plans.

GETTING STARTED

Talking It Over

- Discuss in your group what types of parks are in your area. What sorts of recreation do they offer? Is there an admission fee for the park? Is there a fee for any of the services or activities?

- Have you been to an outdoor park in your area? Who did you go with? What kinds of things did you do while you were there?

Planning Your Project

- **Materials Needed:** paper, pencils or pens

- Choose a park to visit. Make a booklet, and write your name and the park's name on the cover. Find out when the park is open, and what sorts of recreation it offers. Add pictures if you wish. As you complete the **BUILDING YOUR PROJECT** exercises, add the results to your booklet.

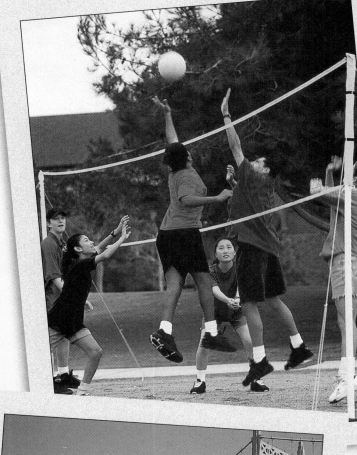

MAY

DAY	THURSDAY	FRIDAY	SATURDAY
	1	2	3
8		⑨ Class outing at Field Park	10
15		16	17
22		23	24
	30		31

BUILDING YOUR PROJECT

These are places throughout the chapter where you will work on your project.

TOPICS

8.1 Adjust the size of a recipe to feed a larger group. *p. 373*

8.2 Plan games for your outing. *p. 379*

8.3 Plan a sign for your outing. *p. 387*

8.4 Plan snacks for your outing. *p. 394*

8.5 Plan a sale to raise money for your outing. *p. 399*

8.6 Decide if you have time to walk the nature trail. *p. 404*

I N T E R N E T

To find out more about outdoor recreation, go to: **http://www.mlmath.com**

LAB 8.1

COOPERATIVE LEARNING

Investigating Fraction Multiplication

Materials Needed
- plain paper
- colored pencils or markers
- pencils or pens

The multiplication problem $3 \times \frac{1}{2}$ means the same as adding $\frac{1}{2}$ three times.

From the model, you can write the following.

$\frac{1}{2} + \frac{1}{2} + \frac{1}{2} = \frac{3}{2}$, or $1\frac{1}{2}$ **Repeated addition**

$3 \times \frac{1}{2} = \frac{3}{2}$, or $1\frac{1}{2}$ **Multiplication**

1. Use a repeated addition model to solve.

    a. $4 \times \frac{1}{3}$ **b.** $3 \times \frac{1}{4}$ **c.** $6 \times \frac{1}{3}$ **d.** $8 \times \frac{1}{2}$

Part B WRITING MULTIPLICATION PROBLEMS

2. Write the repeated addition problem shown by each model. Solve. Draw a sketch of the answer. Then rewrite each problem as a multiplication problem.

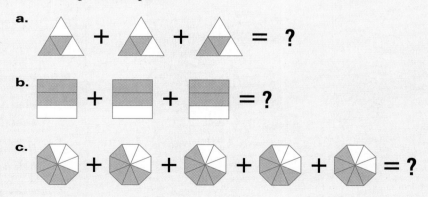

3. Discuss the results of Exercise 2 with others in your group. Did you write each answer as an improper fraction, as a whole number, or as a mixed number? Explain.

The area model below shows that $\frac{2}{5} \times 4 = \frac{8}{5}$, or $1\frac{3}{5}$.

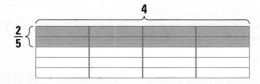

4. Draw an area model for each of the following. Copy and complete the table below. Discuss any patterns that you find.

   a. $\frac{2}{3} \times 2$ **b.** $\frac{3}{4} \times 2$ **c.** $\frac{5}{6} \times 3$

Problem	Width of Rectangle	Length of Rectangle	Area of Rectangle
Example	$\frac{2}{5}$	4	$\frac{8}{5} = 1\frac{3}{5}$
a.	?	?	?
b.	?	?	?
c.	?	?	?

NOW TRY THESE

In Exercises 5 and 6, use a repeated addition model to solve.

5. $4 \times \frac{2}{3}$ 6. $\frac{2}{5} \times 3$

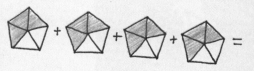

7. Write the repeated addition problem represented by each model shown at the right. Solve. How are the models alike? How are they different?

8. Sketch an area model for $\frac{3}{5} \times 4$. Label the dimensions. Find the area of the shaded rectangle. Is it easier to count the number of fifths in this model or in the model shown at the right? Explain.

9. Explain how to multiply $\frac{3}{7}$ by 4 without drawing a model.

Multiplying Fractions and Whole Numbers

What you should learn:

Goal 1 How to multiply fractions and whole numbers

Goal 2 How to use models for multiplication

Why you should learn it:

Knowing how to multiply a fraction and a whole number can help you work with data about your class. An example is finding the number of students who went to a water park.

TOOLBOX

Rewriting Improper Fractions as Mixed Numbers, page 645

Goal 1 MULTIPLYING FRACTIONS AND WHOLE NUMBERS

The process used to multiply fractions and whole numbers is different from the process used to multiply whole numbers.

MULTIPLYING FRACTIONS AND WHOLE NUMBERS

To find the product of a fraction and a whole number:

1. Multiply the numerator of the fraction by the whole number.
2. Write the result as a fraction with the original denominator.
3. Simplify, if possible.

Example 1 Multiplying with Fractions

Find each product. **a.** $\frac{2}{5} \times 3$ **b.** $2 \times \frac{1}{8}$

Solution

a. $\frac{2}{5} \times 3 = \frac{2 \times 3}{5}$ Multiply 2 times 3.

$= \frac{6}{5}$ Simplify numerator.

$= 1\frac{1}{5}$ Write as mixed number.

b. $2 \times \frac{1}{8} = \frac{2 \times 1}{8}$ Multiply 2 times 1.

$= \frac{2}{8}$ Simplify numerator.

$= \frac{1}{4}$ Simplify.

Example 2 Solving an Equation

Use mental math to solve for n in the problem $\frac{n}{6} \times 3 = \frac{15}{6}$.

Solution

You can solve this problem by asking the question:

   "What number can be multiplied by 3 to get 15?"

The answer is 5. So, the solution of the equation is $n = 5$.

Example 3 **Using a Set Model**

There are 24 students in your class. Two thirds of these went to a water park last summer. How many is that?

Solution

Method **1** Use a set model. Divide the model into thirds.

Since $\frac{1}{3}$ of 24 is 8, $\frac{2}{3}$ of 24 is 16. So, 16 students visited a water park.

Method **2** Use multiplication.

$$\frac{2}{3} \text{ of } 24 = \frac{2}{3} \times 24 \qquad \text{Translate "of" as "times."}$$

$$= \frac{2 \times 24}{3} \qquad \text{Multiply 2 times 24.}$$

$$= \frac{48}{3}, \text{ or } 16 \qquad \text{Simplify.}$$

So, 16 students went to a water park last summer.

Example 4 **Using an Area Model**

STRATEGY **DRAW A DIAGRAM** You can use an area model to find the product of a fraction and a whole number, like $3 \times \frac{2}{5}$.

Draw a model for **3**. Divide the model into **5** equal parts.

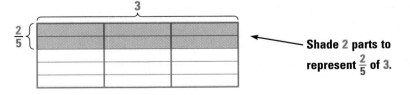

Shade **2** parts to represent $\frac{2}{5}$ of **3**.

Each small rectangle in the model represents $\frac{1}{5}$. There are 6 small shaded rectangles. So, the product is $\frac{6}{5}$, or $1\frac{1}{5}$.

Extra Practice, page 633

1. Write the multiplication problem shown by the model at the right. Then solve.

2. What is three eighths of ten?

3. Is $\frac{6}{7} \times 5 = 5 \times \frac{6}{7}$? Explain.

4. **ERROR ANALYSIS** Describe and correct the error shown at the right.

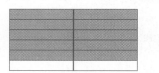

$$\frac{2}{3} \times 6 = \frac{12}{18} \quad \times$$

5. **MENTAL MATH** What whole number can be multiplied by $\frac{4}{5}$ to get $\frac{32}{5}$?

GEOMETRY In Exercises 6 and 7, solve the multiplication problem that is shown by the area model. Simplify, if possible.

6.

7.

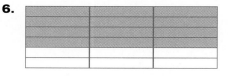

In Exercises 8–15, solve. Simplify, if possible.

8. $\frac{2}{7}$ of 3

9. $8 \times \frac{1}{12}$

10. $\frac{5}{8} \times 2$

11. $\frac{2}{9}$ of 6

12. $5 \times \frac{3}{4}$

13. $4 \times \frac{6}{11}$

14. $\frac{5}{10}$ of 10

15. $\frac{2}{3} \times 9$

ALGEBRA AND MENTAL MATH In Exercises 16–18, solve.

16. $\frac{m}{5} \times 2 = \frac{2}{5}$

17. $\frac{5}{9} \times n = \frac{20}{9}$

18. $5 \times \frac{7}{a} = \frac{35}{8}$

In Exercises 19–24, use the number line to complete the statement with the correct letter.

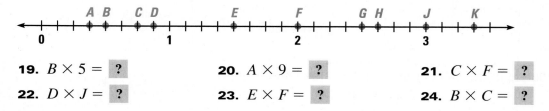

19. $B \times 5 =$?

20. $A \times 9 =$?

21. $C \times F =$?

22. $D \times J =$?

23. $E \times F =$?

24. $B \times C =$?

NUMBER SENSE In Exercises 25–27, write an example of a fraction times a whole number with an answer as described.

25. Greater than 1   **26.** Less than 1   **27.** Equal to 1

28. **NURSING** There are 50 nurses on the staff at a hospital. The staff is divided according to the shifts that the nurses work.

Investigation 8,
Interactive
Real-Life
Investigations

Day shift only: $\frac{8}{25}$ Evening shift only: $\frac{1}{5}$

Overnight shift only: $\frac{9}{50}$ Rotating shifts: $\frac{3}{10}$

Use a set model to find the number of nurses that work on each shift.

29. **SCIENCE** Use the information below to find the length of a rainbow trout and a coho salmon.

- *Channel catfish:* Length is 28 in.

- *Coho salmon:* Length is $\frac{6}{7}$ of a channel catfish.

- *Rainbow trout:* Length is $\frac{7}{12}$ of a coho salmon.

Real Life... **R**eal Facts

Catfish The channel catfish has tastebuds on its whiskers that help it to find food.

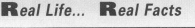

STANDARDIZED TEST PRACTICE

30. The total surface area of Earth is approximately 196,800,000 mi^2. Seven tenths of this is covered by water. How many square miles are covered by water?

(**A**) 14,000,000 mi^2 (**B**) 1,377,600 mi^2

(**C**) 13,776,000 mi^2 (**D**) 137,760,000 mi^2

EXPLORATION AND EXTENSION

PORTFOLIO

31. **BUILDING YOUR PROJECT** Find a recipe that includes fractional measurements and serves 6 or fewer people. Change it so it serves the number of students in your class. Record your results in your booklet.

Apple Crisp (serves 6)	
4 c. sliced apples	$\frac{1}{2}$ c. oats
$\frac{2}{3}$ c. packed brown sugar	$\frac{3}{4}$ t. cinnamon
$\frac{1}{2}$ c. flour	$\frac{3}{4}$ t. nutmeg
$\frac{1}{3}$ c. margarine or butter, softened	(directions on back)

Using Area Models for **Multiplication**

Materials Needed
- grid paper
- colored pencils or markers
- pencils or pens

Part A AREA MODELS WITH FRACTIONAL DIMENSIONS

Here are three possible area models for $\frac{4}{12}$.

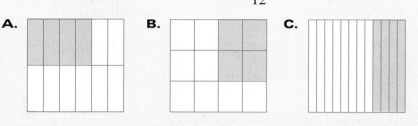

A.   B.   C.

To create each model, a square with an area of 1 square unit was divided into 12 equal parts. Then 4 of the parts were shaded to form a rectangle with an area of $\frac{4}{12}$.

Remember that a square with an area of 1 square unit must have 4 equal sides, each 1 unit long.

1. One way to construct model A is shown below. Work with a partner and follow these steps to draw model A on grid paper.

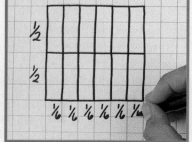

a. Draw a 6-by-6 square to represent 1 square unit. Why is a square of this size convenient?

b. Divide the square into 6 vertical parts and 2 horizontal parts. Label the distances.

c. Shade $\frac{4}{6}$ of the square. In a second color, shade $\frac{1}{2}$ of the square.

2. What is the length and width of the rectangle that is shaded in both colors? Label these dimensions.

3. Explain why the model shows that $\frac{1}{2} \times \frac{4}{6} = \frac{4}{12}$.

4. Repeat the process in Exercise 1 to form two-color rectangles for models B and C. Make your unit squares a convenient size. Find the length and width of each two-color rectangle. Label these dimensions.

5. Copy and complete the table at the right. Use the area models you have drawn. Do you see any patterns?

6. Find the length, width, and area of the two-color region. The area of the entire square is 1 square unit.

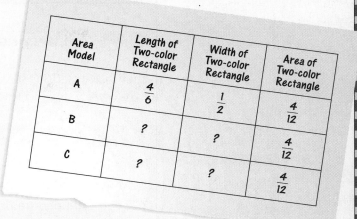

Area Model	Length of Two-color Rectangle	Width of Two-color Rectangle	Area of Two-color Rectangle
A	$\frac{4}{6}$	$\frac{1}{2}$	$\frac{4}{12}$
B	?	?	$\frac{4}{12}$
C	?	?	$\frac{4}{12}$

a. 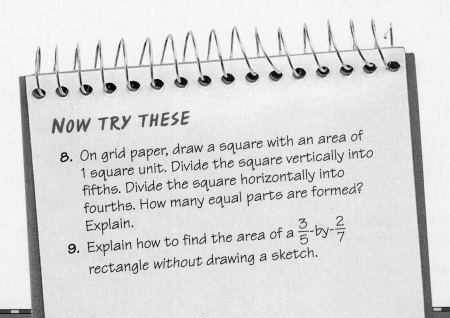 b. c.

7. **a.** Choose a pair of fractions not shown above. Use an area model of a unit square to draw a two-color rectangle with these dimensions. Label the dimensions and find the area.

 b. In a table similar to the one above, list the findings of your group and three other groups. What patterns do you see?

NOW TRY THESE

8. On grid paper, draw a square with an area of 1 square unit. Divide the square vertically into fifths. Divide the square horizontally into fourths. How many equal parts are formed? Explain.

9. Explain how to find the area of a $\frac{3}{5}$-by-$\frac{2}{7}$ rectangle without drawing a sketch.

8.2

Multiplying Fractions

What you should learn:

Goal 1 How to multiply fractions

Goal 2 How to use multiplication of fractions to solve real-life problems

Why you should learn it:

Knowing how to multiply fractions can help you make decisions about nutrition. An example is finding how much cheese is on two pieces of pizza.

TOOLBOX
Multiplying Fractions, page 647

Goal 1 MULTIPLYING FRACTIONS

Remember, fractions have numerators *and* denominators. You can use the following steps to find the product of two or more fractions.

FRACTION MULTIPLICATION

To multiply fractions:

1. Multiply the numerators.

2. Then multiply the denominators.

3. Simplify, if possible.

Example 1 Multiplying Fractions

a. $\dfrac{3}{4} \times \dfrac{3}{5} = \dfrac{3 \times 3}{4 \times 5}$ Multiply numerators and denominators.

$= \dfrac{9}{20}$ Simplify numerator and denominator.

The product of $\dfrac{3}{4}$ and $\dfrac{3}{5}$ is $\dfrac{9}{20}$.

b. $\dfrac{5}{8} \times \dfrac{2}{5} \times \dfrac{3}{2} = \dfrac{5 \times 2 \times 3}{8 \times 5 \times 2}$ Multiply numerators and denominators.

$= \dfrac{30}{80}$ Simplify numerator and denominator.

$= \dfrac{3}{8}$ Simplify.

The product of $\dfrac{5}{8}$, $\dfrac{2}{5}$, and $\dfrac{3}{2}$ is $\dfrac{3}{8}$.

Example 2 Solving an Equation

Use mental math to solve for n in the problem $\dfrac{3}{5} \times \dfrac{n}{8} = \dfrac{21}{40}$.

Solution

You need to find a number n such that $3 \times n = 21$. Using mental math, it follows that $n = 7$.

✔**Check:** $\dfrac{3}{5} \times \dfrac{7}{8} = \dfrac{21}{40}$

Goal 2 SOLVING REAL-LIFE PROBLEMS

You can use multiplication of fractions to solve real-life problems.

Question	Multiply fractions to solve.
What is $\frac{1}{2}$ of $\frac{3}{5}$ mile?	$\frac{1}{2} \times \frac{3}{5} = \frac{1 \times 3}{2 \times 5} = \frac{3}{10}$ mi
What is $\frac{2}{3}$ of $\frac{3}{4}$ cup?	$\frac{2}{3} \times \frac{3}{4} = \frac{2 \times 3}{3 \times 4} = \frac{6}{12} = \frac{1}{2}$ cup

Example 3 Finding a Serving Size

You make a small pizza that has $\frac{3}{4}$ cup of cheese on it. You cut the pizza into 6 pieces and eat 2 pieces. How much cheese did you eat?

REAL LIFE
Nutrition

Solution

You ate $\frac{2}{6}$ of $\frac{3}{4}$ cup of cheese.

$\frac{2}{6} \times \frac{3}{4} = \frac{2 \times 3}{6 \times 4}$ **Multiply numerators and denominators.**

$= \frac{6}{24}$ **Simplify numerator and denominator.**

$= \frac{1}{4}$ **Simplify.**

You ate $\frac{1}{4}$ cup of cheese.

✔**Check:** Use an Area Model

1. To show $\frac{3}{4}$, divide a square into 4 vertical parts and shade 3 parts.

2. To show $\frac{2}{6}$, divide the square into 6 horizontal parts. Using a different color, shade 2 parts.

3. In the completed model, 6 of the 24 parts are shaded with both colors. So, $\frac{2}{6} \times \frac{3}{4} = \frac{6}{24}$, or $\frac{1}{4}$. ✔

$\frac{3}{4}$

$\frac{2}{6}$

$\frac{3}{4}$

8.2 Exercises

Extra Practice, page 633

GUIDED PRACTICE

1. **PANCAKES** A pancake recipe calls for $\frac{3}{4}$ cup of milk. To make only half a recipe, how much milk should you use?

2. Multiply $\frac{2}{3}, \frac{1}{2},$ and $\frac{5}{7}$.

3. Find $\frac{3}{5}$ of $\frac{3}{4}$.

4. **ALGEBRA AND MENTAL MATH** Use mental math to solve for *n*.

   a. $\frac{5}{9} \times \frac{4}{n} = \frac{20}{63}$

   b. $\frac{9}{8} \times \frac{n}{4} = \frac{27}{32}$

5. **ERROR ANALYSIS** Describe and correct the error.

$$\frac{8}{9} \times \frac{2}{9} = \frac{16}{9} \ \times$$

PRACTICE AND PROBLEM SOLVING

GEOMETRY In Exercises 6–9, match the multiplication problem with the area model. Then find the product. Simplify, if possible.

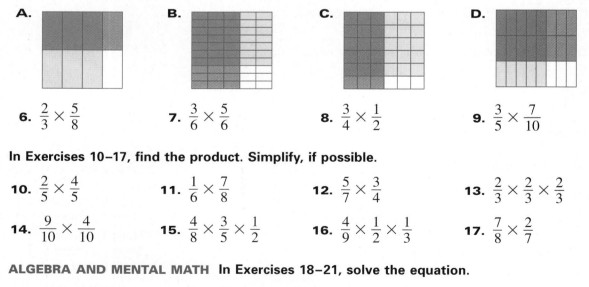

A.   **B.**   **C.**   **D.**

6. $\frac{2}{3} \times \frac{5}{8}$ 7. $\frac{3}{6} \times \frac{5}{6}$ 8. $\frac{3}{4} \times \frac{1}{2}$ 9. $\frac{3}{5} \times \frac{7}{10}$

In Exercises 10–17, find the product. Simplify, if possible.

10. $\frac{2}{5} \times \frac{4}{5}$ 11. $\frac{1}{6} \times \frac{7}{8}$ 12. $\frac{5}{7} \times \frac{3}{4}$ 13. $\frac{2}{3} \times \frac{2}{3} \times \frac{2}{3}$

14. $\frac{9}{10} \times \frac{4}{10}$ 15. $\frac{4}{8} \times \frac{3}{5} \times \frac{1}{2}$ 16. $\frac{4}{9} \times \frac{1}{2} \times \frac{1}{3}$ 17. $\frac{7}{8} \times \frac{2}{7}$

ALGEBRA AND MENTAL MATH In Exercises 18–21, solve the equation.

18. $\frac{4}{5} \times \frac{n}{5} = \frac{12}{25}$ 19. $\frac{2}{7} \times \frac{3}{x} = \frac{6}{28}$ 20. $\frac{3}{8} \times \frac{5}{y} = \frac{15}{56}$ 21. $\frac{1}{9} \times \frac{m}{10} = \frac{7}{90}$

In Exercises 22 and 23, use an area model to help you find the answer.

22. What is $\frac{2}{3}$ of $\frac{3}{4}$?

23. What is $\frac{4}{5}$ of $\frac{2}{3}$?

24. Is the following statement *true* or *false*? Explain.

$\frac{1}{3} + \frac{1}{3}$ is greater than $\frac{1}{3} \times \frac{1}{3}$.

25. REASONING Find four pairs of fractions whose products are $\frac{8}{45}$. Explain your process.

SCIENCE An ostrich egg is about $\frac{1}{2}$ ft long. Write the length of the indicated egg in feet.

26. A chickadee egg is about $\frac{1}{12}$ as long as an ostrich egg.

27. A blue jay egg is about $\frac{1}{6}$ as long as an ostrich egg.

28. A bald eagle egg is about $\frac{1}{2}$ as long as an ostrich egg.

29. MEASUREMENT Explain how to change a measurement from feet to inches. Compare each bird's egg length in feet to its length in inches. Use a table to organize your results.

Bald Eagles

The bald eagle, our national symbol, was declared an endangered species in 1967. Its comeback since that time has allowed it to be removed from the list of endangered species.

STANDARDIZED TEST PRACTICE

30. In Juneau, AK, $\frac{2}{3}$ of the 30 days in November are wet days. In June, there are $\frac{3}{4}$ as many wet days as in November. How many wet days are there in Juneau, AK in the month of June?

A 10 **B** 12 **C** 15 **D** 20

EXPLORATION AND EXTENSION

PORTFOLIO

31. MAKING CONNECTIONS Use fractions to find the area of the two-color region at the right. Then use decimals. Are your results the same? Explain.

32. BUILDING YOUR PROJECT Plan at least 3 games to be played at your park outing. Describe the dimensions of the playing fields. Include measurements that are fractions. Find the areas of the fields. Record your results in your booklet.

1. **ANIMAL SPEED** An owl flies 79 miles in 2 hours. What is the average speed of the owl? **(2.4)**

2. Write each measurement as a mixed number and as an improper fraction. **(6.6, 7.1)**

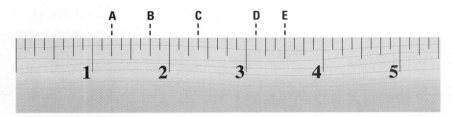

In Exercises 3–6, find the product. (4.4)

3. 9.25×1.8

4. 15.5×3.46

5. 75% of 80

6. 125% of 40

In Exercises 7–10, solve the proportion. (6.4)

7. $\dfrac{?}{6} = \dfrac{3}{18}$

8. $\dfrac{14}{35} = \dfrac{2}{?}$

9. $\dfrac{16}{?} = \dfrac{4}{7}$

10. $\dfrac{8}{9} = \dfrac{?}{54}$

In Exercises 11–14, simplify. (7.3)

11. $\dfrac{1}{3} + \dfrac{4}{3}$

12. $\dfrac{1}{2} + \dfrac{1}{3}$

13. $\dfrac{3}{8} - \dfrac{1}{8}$

14. $\dfrac{3}{8} - \dfrac{1}{4}$

CAREER Interview

SOUND ENGINEER

Rhea Vogel is the owner of Countdown Studios, a rehearsal and recording studio for musicians. In addition to handling administrative work, Rhea schedules the bands' rehearsals, operates the sound equipment, and employs engineers to do the recording.

Q **What led you to this career?**
As a singer, I wanted to understand the equipment used to amplify my voice so that I could control the sound.

Q **Does having a math background help you?**
Music is described by measures, beats per minute, time signatures, notes, and bars. To understand these terms, I must understand fractions and division and be able to compute quickly in my head.

Q **Has technology changed your job experience?**
Synthesizers and computers are used to write, perform, and record a lot of music today. Digital recording has greatly improved the quality of recorded sound.

Fraction Figures

Calculators treat fractions in many different ways. Some "fraction calculators" can display fractions, but most calculators display fractions as decimals. Some calculators have parentheses and some don't. If your calculator has parentheses, you can use it to multiply and divide fractions.

CALCULATOR TIP

Remember that a fraction can be interpreted as a division problem. For example, enter $\frac{3}{4}$ as

3 ÷ 4 = 0.75.

If your calculator is not a "fraction calculator," you can use the division key to enter a fraction.

Example ❶

Use a calculator to multiply $\frac{1}{3}$ by $\frac{3}{8}$.

Solution

Use the following keystrokes.

(1 ÷ 3) × (3 ÷ 8) =

The calculator will display 0.125. This is equal to $\frac{1}{8}$.

Example ❷

Use a calculator to multiply $1\frac{2}{3}$ by $\frac{3}{4}$.

Solution

Use the following keystrokes.

(1 + 2 ÷ 3) × (3 ÷ 4) =

The calculator will display 1.25. This is equal to $1\frac{1}{4}$.

Exercises

In Exercises 1–8, use a calculator with parentheses to find the products. If necessary, round your answers to thousandths.

1. $\frac{7}{8} \times \frac{2}{7}$ 2. $\frac{2}{5} \times \frac{1}{2}$ 3. $\frac{2}{3} \times \frac{6}{4}$ 4. $\frac{5}{4} \times \frac{3}{8}$

5. $1\frac{1}{2} \times \frac{3}{4}$ 6. $2\frac{1}{3} \times \frac{3}{8}$ 7. $1\frac{2}{3} \times \frac{3}{4}$ 8. $3\frac{3}{4} \times 5\frac{1}{2}$

9. **ERROR ANALYSIS** A friend used a calculator to multiply $1\frac{1}{2}$ by $\frac{1}{2}$.

   Your friend used the following keystrokes and got an answer of 1.25.

   1 + 1 ÷ 2 × 1 ÷ 2 =

   What did your friend do wrong? How could you fix it?

LAB 8.3

COOPERATIVE LEARNING

Investigating Mixed Number Multiplication

....

Materials Needed
- plain paper
- colored pencils or markers
- pencils or pens

Part A USING AREA MODELS TO MULTIPLY

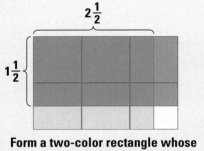
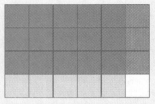

Form a two-color rectangle whose dimensions are $1\frac{1}{2}$ by $2\frac{1}{2}$.

Add grid lines. Then count the number of fourths in the two-color region.

1. Use the area models above to help you find the product of $1\frac{1}{2}$ and $2\frac{1}{2}$. Write a summary of your steps.

2. In Exercise 1, did you write the answer as a mixed number or as an improper fraction? Which form is easier for you to find with a model? Explain.

Part B DRAWING AREA MODELS

3. Copy the models shown below. Label the dimensions of the second model as improper fractions.

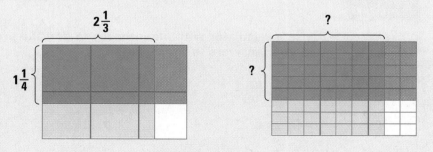

4. Write the multiplication problem that is shown by the models. Then use either model to help you find the product. Write a summary of your steps.

5. Draw an area model for each multiplication problem. Then find the product.

    a. $1\frac{2}{3} \times 2\frac{1}{2}$ **b.** $1\frac{2}{5} \times 1\frac{1}{2}$ **c.** $3\frac{3}{4} \times 2\frac{1}{3}$

6. Use the results of Exercise 5 to copy and complete the table below. Use improper fractions instead of mixed numbers for the length and the width.

Problem	Length of rectangle	Width of rectangle	Area of rectangle
$1\frac{1}{2} \times 2\frac{1}{2}$	$\frac{3}{2}$	$\frac{5}{2}$	$\frac{15}{4}$, or $3\frac{3}{4}$
$1\frac{2}{3} \times 2\frac{1}{2}$	?	?	?
$1\frac{2}{5} \times 1\frac{1}{2}$	?	?	?
$3\frac{3}{4} \times 2\frac{1}{3}$	?	?	?

7. With others in your group, discuss any patterns you see in the table. Record your observations.

NOW TRY THESE

8. Write the multiplication problem that is represented by the model below. Then find the product.

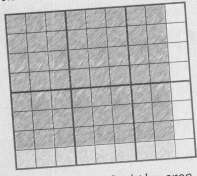

9. Explain how you could find the area of a $2\frac{3}{4}$-by-$1\frac{3}{5}$ rectangle without drawing a sketch.

8.3

Multiplying Mixed Numbers

What you should learn:

Goal 1 How to multiply mixed numbers

Goal 2 How to multiply mixed numbers to solve real-life problems

Why you should learn it:

Knowing how to multiply mixed numbers can help you keep records for your sports team. An example is comparing distances people run during track practice.

Goal 1 MULTIPLYING MIXED NUMBERS

You can use the following rule to multiply mixed numbers.

MULTIPLYING MIXED NUMBERS

To multiply mixed numbers:

1. Rewrite the mixed numbers as improper fractions.
2. Multiply the numerators and multiply the denominators.
3. Simplify, if possible.

Example 1 Multiplying Mixed Numbers

a. $1\frac{3}{4} \times 2\frac{1}{2} = \frac{7}{4} \times \frac{5}{2}$ Rewrite as improper fractions.

$= \frac{7 \times 5}{4 \times 2}$ Multiply.

$= \frac{35}{8}$ Simplify.

> **TOOLBOX**
>
> Rewriting Mixed Numbers as Improper Fractions, page 645

The product of $2\frac{1}{2}$ and $1\frac{3}{4}$ is $\frac{35}{8}$, or $4\frac{3}{8}$.

b. $3\frac{1}{2} \times \frac{2}{3} = \frac{7}{2} \times \frac{2}{3}$ Rewrite $3\frac{1}{2}$ as an improper fraction.

$= \frac{7 \times 2}{2 \times 3}$ Multiply.

$= \frac{14}{6}$ Simplify.

$= \frac{7}{3}$ Simplify fraction.

The product of $3\frac{1}{2}$ and $\frac{2}{3}$ is $\frac{7}{3}$, or $2\frac{1}{3}$.

c. $1\frac{5}{6} \times 3 = \frac{11}{6} \times 3$ Rewrite $1\frac{5}{6}$ as an improper fraction.

$= \frac{33}{6}$ Multiply.

$= \frac{11}{2}$ Simplify.

The product of $1\frac{5}{6}$ and 3 is $\frac{11}{2}$, or $5\frac{1}{2}$.

STUDY TIP

An area model can help you check your result. Here is an area model that shows the product in part (a) of Example 1.

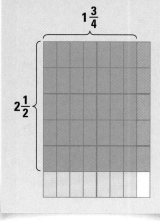

Goal 2 SOLVING REAL-LIFE PROBLEMS

Example 2 **Comparing Products**

Which person ran the farthest during track practice?

a. Pam ran $4\frac{1}{2}$ times around a $\frac{1}{2}$ mi track.

b. Josh ran 3 times around a $\frac{5}{6}$ mi track.

c. Dionne ran 2 times around a $1\frac{1}{4}$ mi track.

Solution

a. Find Pam's distance.

$$4\frac{1}{2} \times \frac{1}{2} = \frac{9}{2} \times \frac{1}{2} \qquad \text{Rewrite } 4\frac{1}{2} \text{ as an improper fraction.}$$

$$= \frac{9 \times 1}{2 \times 2} \qquad \text{Multiply.}$$

$$= \frac{9}{4} \qquad \text{Simplify.}$$

$$= 2\frac{1}{4} \text{ mi} \qquad \text{Pam's distance}$$

b. Find Josh's distance.

$$3 \times \frac{5}{6} = \frac{15}{6} \qquad \text{Multiply.}$$

$$= \frac{5}{2} \qquad \text{Simplify.}$$

$$= 2\frac{1}{2} \text{ mi} \qquad \text{Josh's distance}$$

c. Find Dionne's distance.

$$2 \times 1\frac{1}{4} = 2 \times \frac{5}{4} \qquad \text{Rewrite } 1\frac{1}{4} \text{ as an improper fraction.}$$

$$= \frac{10}{4} \qquad \text{Multiply.}$$

$$= \frac{5}{2} \qquad \text{Simplify.}$$

$$= 2\frac{1}{2} \text{ mi} \qquad \text{Dionne's distance}$$

Josh and Dionne tied for farthest distance.

ONGOING ASSESSMENT

Write About It
....

How do the following compare with Pam's, Josh's, and Dionne's distances in Example 2?

1. Chun ran $4\frac{1}{2}$ times around a $\frac{3}{4}$ mi track.

2. Charles ran $1\frac{1}{2}$ times around a $1\frac{2}{3}$ mi track.

GUIDED PRACTICE

1. Write the multiplication problem that is represented by the model at the right. Then find the product.

2. Multiply: $2\frac{1}{7} \times 2\frac{1}{3}$. Explain each step of your solution.

ERROR ANALYSIS In Exercises 3 and 4, describe and correct the error.

3.
$$2\frac{2}{3} \times 3\frac{4}{5} = 6\frac{8}{15} \quad \times$$

4.
$$4 \times 3\frac{3}{4} = 12\frac{3}{4} \quad \times$$

MEASUREMENT In Exercises 5 and 6, answer the question. Write the answer in hours. Then write the answer in hours and minutes.

5. What is $1\frac{1}{3}$ of 2 h?

6. What is $\frac{1}{2}$ of $3\frac{1}{2}$ h?

PRACTICE AND PROBLEM SOLVING

In Exercises 7 and 8, write the multiplication problem that is represented by the area model. Then find the product.

7.

8.

In Exercises 9–16, multiply. Simplify, if possible.

9. $1\frac{1}{2} \times 4\frac{1}{2}$

10. $2\frac{1}{6} \times 2$

11. $4\frac{2}{7} \times \frac{1}{5}$

12. $\frac{3}{4} \times 3\frac{3}{4}$

13. $9 \times 1\frac{7}{9}$

14. $2\frac{1}{3} \times 1\frac{2}{5}$

15. $1\frac{1}{8} \times 5\frac{1}{2} \times 1\frac{1}{3}$

16. $6\frac{2}{3} \times 2\frac{1}{2} \times \frac{4}{7}$

GEOMETRY In Exercises 17–19, find the area of the rectangle.

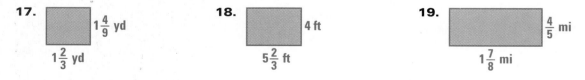

17. $1\frac{4}{9}$ yd, $1\frac{2}{3}$ yd

18. 4 ft, $5\frac{2}{3}$ ft

19. $\frac{4}{5}$ mi, $1\frac{7}{8}$ mi

20. **REASONING** Is $2\frac{1}{4} \times 3\frac{4}{5}$ greater than 8? Explain.

In Exercises 21–23, solve each problem. Then describe any patterns that you see. Write and solve the next two problems in the pattern.

21. $3\frac{1}{2} \times 3 = $? **22.** $1\frac{1}{7} \times \frac{1}{3} = $? **23.** $1\frac{1}{5} \times 1\frac{1}{4} = $?

$3\frac{1}{2} \times 4 = $? $1\frac{2}{7} \times \frac{1}{3} = $? $2\frac{1}{5} \times 1\frac{1}{4} = $?

$3\frac{1}{2} \times 5 = $? $1\frac{3}{7} \times \frac{1}{3} = $? $3\frac{1}{5} \times 1\frac{1}{4} = $?

SAILBOAT RACING In Exercises 24 and 25, use the following information. To practice for a sailing race, you sailed on five different courses. The length of each course and the number of times you sailed it are given in the table below.

Course	1	2	3	4	5
Length (miles)	$9\frac{1}{3}$	$7\frac{1}{2}$	$18\frac{1}{5}$	$5\frac{3}{4}$	$12\frac{3}{5}$
Number of Times Sailed	$2\frac{1}{2}$	$3\frac{1}{5}$	$\frac{6}{7}$	4	$2\frac{1}{7}$

24. On which course did you sail farthest?

25. How many *total* miles did you sail?

STANDARDIZED TEST PRACTICE

26. Which of the following improper fractions does *not* reduce to $3\frac{1}{6}$?

(A) $\frac{19}{6}$ **(B)** $\frac{38}{12}$ **(C)** $\frac{57}{18}$ **(D)** $\frac{76}{4}$

EXPLORATION AND EXTENSION

PORTFOLIO

27. a. BUILDING YOUR PROJECT A sign announcing the school play measures $9\frac{1}{4}$ in.-by-$7\frac{1}{2}$ in. Find the area of the sign.

b. Draw plans for a sign with fractional dimensions for your outing. Decide what the sign should say (for example, time and date, directions). Find the area of your sign.

Investigating Division of Fractions

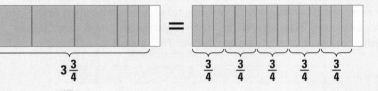

Part A USING MODELS FOR DIVISION

Materials Needed
- plain paper
- colored pencils or markers
- pencils or pens

You need to measure $3\frac{3}{4}$ cups of water. You have a container that holds $\frac{3}{4}$ cup. How many times do you need to fill the container? To find the answer, divide $3\frac{3}{4}$ by $\frac{3}{4}$, as shown in the following model.

1. Use the above model to help you rewrite the problem $3\frac{3}{4} \div \frac{3}{4}$ with no mixed numbers. Then solve.

2. The following model represents $2\frac{2}{5}$. Copy the model. Explain how you can use the model to rewrite the problem $2\frac{2}{5} \div \frac{4}{5}$ with no mixed numbers. Then solve.

3. Use a model to help you rewrite each division problem with no mixed numbers. Then solve.

   a. $2\frac{4}{7} \div \frac{3}{7}$ b. $2\frac{5}{8} \div \frac{3}{8}$ c. $4\frac{2}{3} \div \frac{2}{3}$

4. Describe any patterns you see in Exercises 1–3. With others in your group, discuss how you could solve these division problems without drawing a model.

5. Use the model below to help you solve the problem $1\frac{1}{2} \div \frac{3}{4}$.

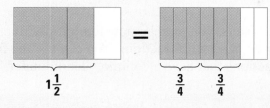

6. Copy and complete the table.

Mixed Numbers	Improper Fractions	Rewritten with Common Denominators	Solution
a. $2\frac{1}{2} \div \frac{5}{8}$	$? \div ?$	$? \div ?$	$?$
b. $3\frac{1}{2} \div 1\frac{1}{6}$	$? \div ?$	$? \div ?$	$?$

Part C PROBLEMS THAT DON'T DIVIDE EVENLY

7. Use the model below to help you solve the problem $2\frac{1}{2} \div \frac{3}{4}$.

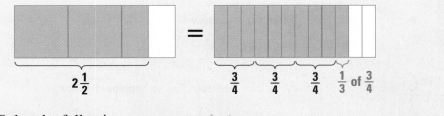

8. Solve the following problems.

a. $2\frac{1}{2} \div \frac{3}{8}$

b. $2\frac{1}{6} \div \frac{2}{3}$

c. $3\frac{1}{4} \div \frac{2}{3}$

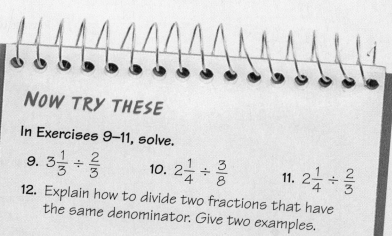

NOW TRY THESE

In Exercises 9–11, solve.

9. $3\frac{1}{3} \div \frac{2}{3}$ 10. $2\frac{1}{4} \div \frac{3}{8}$ 11. $2\frac{1}{4} \div \frac{2}{3}$

12. Explain how to divide two fractions that have the same denominator. Give two examples.

Dividing Fractions with Common Denominators

What you should learn:

Goal 1 How to divide fractions that have a common denominator

Goal 2 How to use division of fractions to solve real-life problems

Why you should learn it:

Knowing how to divide fractions can help you find measurements for a construction project. An example is cutting shelves.

Goal 1 DIVIDING FRACTIONS

In the last three lessons, you learned how to multiply fractions. Now you will explore division with fractions. You can use the following rule to divide fractions that have a common denominator.

DIVIDING WITH COMMON DENOMINATORS

To divide fractions that have a common denominator, divide the numerators.

Example: $\frac{15}{4} \div \frac{3}{4} = \frac{15}{3} = 5$

Sometimes you need to find the common denominator of the fractions before dividing.

Example 1 Dividing Fractions

Find the quotient.

a. $\frac{7}{3} \div \frac{1}{3}$ **b.** $4\frac{1}{2} \div \frac{3}{4}$ **c.** $2\frac{1}{3} \div \frac{1}{2}$

Solution

a. $\frac{7}{3} \div \frac{1}{3} = \frac{7}{1}$ Divide numerators.

$= 7$ Simplify.

b. $4\frac{1}{2} \div \frac{3}{4} = \frac{9}{2} \div \frac{3}{4}$ Rewrite $4\frac{1}{2}$ as an improper fraction.

$= \frac{18}{4} \div \frac{3}{4}$ Rewrite with common denominators.

$= \frac{18}{3}$ Divide numerators.

$= 6$ Simplify.

c. $2\frac{1}{3} \div \frac{1}{2} = \frac{7}{3} \div \frac{1}{2}$ Rewrite $2\frac{1}{3}$ as an improper fraction.

$= \frac{14}{6} \div \frac{3}{6}$ Rewrite with common denominators.

$= \frac{14}{3}$ Divide numerators.

$= 4\frac{2}{3}$ Simplify.

Example 2 **Real-Life Fractions**

You are cutting shelves from a $7\frac{1}{2}$ ft board. How many shelves can you cut of the given lengths?

a. Each shelf is $2\frac{1}{2}$ ft.   **b.** Each shelf is $1\frac{3}{4}$ ft.

Solution

a. Divide $7\frac{1}{2}$ by $2\frac{1}{2}$.

REAL LIFE
Woodworking

$$7\frac{1}{2} \div 2\frac{1}{2} = \frac{15}{2} \div \frac{5}{2}$$ Rewrite as improper fractions.

$$= \frac{15}{5}$$ Divide numerators.

$$= 3$$ Simplify.

You get 3 full shelves.

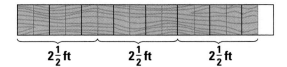

$2\frac{1}{2}$ ft $2\frac{1}{2}$ ft $2\frac{1}{2}$ ft

b. Divide $7\frac{1}{2}$ by $1\frac{3}{4}$.

$$7\frac{1}{2} \div 1\frac{3}{4} = \frac{15}{2} \div \frac{7}{4}$$ Rewrite as improper fractions.

$$= \frac{30}{4} \div \frac{7}{4}$$ Rewrite with common denominators.

$$= \frac{30}{7}$$ Divide numerators.

$$= 4\frac{2}{7}$$ Simplify.

You have enough wood to make 4 full shelves.

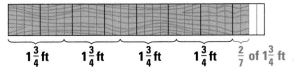

$1\frac{3}{4}$ ft $1\frac{3}{4}$ ft $1\frac{3}{4}$ ft $1\frac{3}{4}$ ft $\frac{2}{7}$ of $1\frac{3}{4}$ ft

Some wood is left over. The leftover wood is $\frac{2}{7}$ of the amount needed to make another $1\frac{3}{4}$ ft shelf.

ONGOING ASSESSMENT

Talk About It
....

1. Use division to find how many $\frac{3}{4}$ ft shelves you can make from a board $7\frac{1}{2}$ ft long.

2. Use an area model to find how many $1\frac{1}{4}$ ft shelves you can make from a board 8 ft long.

GUIDED PRACTICE

In Exercises 1 and 2, write the division problem that is shown by the model.

1.
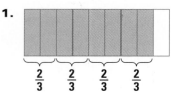

$\dfrac{2}{3}$ $\dfrac{2}{3}$ $\dfrac{2}{3}$ $\dfrac{2}{3}$

2.
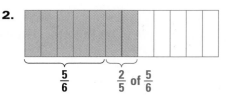

$\dfrac{5}{6}$ $\dfrac{2}{5}$ of $\dfrac{5}{6}$

In Exercises 3 and 4, complete the statement.

3. $\dfrac{18}{5} \div \boxed{?} = \dfrac{18}{3}$

4. $\boxed{?} \div \dfrac{4}{9} = \dfrac{15}{4}$

5. Write a real-life problem that can be solved using $\dfrac{5}{2} \div \dfrac{1}{2}$.

PRACTICE AND PROBLEM SOLVING

In Exercises 6 and 7, write the division problem that is shown by the model.

6.
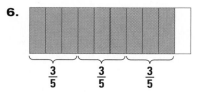

$\dfrac{3}{5}$ $\dfrac{3}{5}$ $\dfrac{3}{5}$

7.
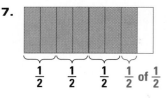

$\dfrac{1}{2}$ $\dfrac{1}{2}$ $\dfrac{1}{2}$ $\dfrac{1}{2}$ of $\dfrac{1}{2}$

In Exercises 8–15, find the quotient. Simplify, if possible.

8. $3\dfrac{1}{5} \div \dfrac{4}{5}$ **9.** $\dfrac{2}{3} \div 4\dfrac{2}{3}$ **10.** $\dfrac{17}{8} \div \dfrac{7}{8}$ **11.** $1\dfrac{9}{10} \div \dfrac{3}{10}$

12. $2\dfrac{7}{8} \div \dfrac{1}{2}$ **13.** $\dfrac{16}{3} \div \dfrac{1}{6}$ **14.** $4\dfrac{5}{6} \div \dfrac{1}{2}$ **15.** $\dfrac{13}{4} \div \dfrac{2}{3}$

COMMUNICATING In Exercises 16–21, use estimation to decide whether the quotient is *greater than 1* or *less than 1*. Explain your reasoning.

16. $\dfrac{4}{5} \div \dfrac{1}{5}$ **17.** $\dfrac{5}{4} \div 2$ **18.** $\dfrac{2}{3} \div \dfrac{1}{9}$

19. $\dfrac{3}{7} \div \dfrac{1}{14}$ **20.** $3\dfrac{2}{3} \div \dfrac{1}{6}$ **21.** $\dfrac{2}{9} \div 1\dfrac{1}{3}$

ALGEBRA AND MENTAL MATH In Exercises 22–24, solve.

22. $b \div \dfrac{1}{6} = 11$ **23.** $b \div \dfrac{1}{2} = \dfrac{13}{2}$ **24.** $1\dfrac{3}{4} \div b = \dfrac{7}{3}$

25. TRAVEL You are driving across South Dakota. You stop at the border and plan to stop every 100 mi. The distance across South Dakota on the map is $2\frac{13}{16}$ in. On the map, $\frac{3}{4}$ in. represents 100 mi. How many times will you stop *in* the state?

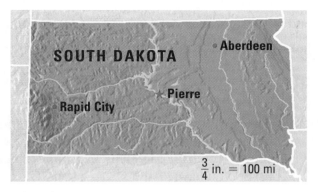

SOUTH DAKOTA Aberdeen
Pierre
Rapid City
$\frac{3}{4}$ in. = 100 mi

26. CD PLAYER After the batteries are charged, your portable CD player will run for $4\frac{1}{2}$ h. An average CD plays for $\frac{5}{6}$ h. How many CDs can you play before the batteries run down?

27. DIVISION PUZZLE Complete the puzzle below by finding the values of w, x, y, and z. Name the problem solving strategy or strategies you used.

$$w \times \frac{1}{2} = x, \quad x \times \frac{4}{5} = y, \quad y \times \frac{1}{3} = z, \quad z \times \frac{3}{4} = \frac{45}{4}$$

STANDARDIZED TEST PRACTICE

28. Solve for n in the problem $7\frac{1}{3} \div n = 66$.

   A $\frac{1}{9}$ **B** $\frac{1}{3}$ **C** $3\frac{1}{9}$ **D** 9

29. Which of the following statements is true?

   A $12 \div 2\frac{1}{2} > 5$ **B** $\frac{1}{8} \div \frac{1}{4} = \frac{1}{32}$

   C $\frac{2}{3} \div 6 < 1$ **D** $6\frac{3}{4} \div \frac{3}{4} = 6$

30. It takes you $1\frac{3}{4}$ h to type your final report for history class. The finished report is 14 pages long. Estimate the amount of time that you spent typing each page.

   A $\frac{1}{8}$ h   **B** $\frac{9}{64}$ h   **C** 8 h   **D** $24\frac{1}{2}$ h

EXPLORATION AND EXTENSION

BUILDING YOUR PROJECT You are making snacks for your outing. Each snack is a small bag that holds $\frac{2}{3}$ cup of fruit and nut mix. You are filling the bags from a container that holds $12\frac{5}{6}$ cups of the mix.

31. How many bags will you fill? Is this enough for each person in your class to get one?

32. If you won't have enough bags for your entire class, how many more cups of fruit and nut mix will you need? If you have too many bags, how much extra mix do you have?

33. Think of another snack you can make for your outing. Explain how to use division of fractions to make the snack.

34. **COMMUNICATING ABOUT MATHEMATICS (page 405)** A male bee hummingbird weighs $1\frac{3}{5}$ grams. A female bee hummingbird weighs $2\frac{3}{5}$ grams. How many times larger is the female than the male?

SPIRAL REVIEW

In Exercises 1–3, complete the statement using >, <, or =. (3.2)

1. 0.5 km ? 500 m

2. 1.2 cm ? 120 mm

3. 4.25 km ? 4250 cm

In Exercises 4 and 5, find the missing digits. (4.1, 4.2)

4.
$$\begin{array}{r} 63.\boxed{?} \\ +2\boxed{?}.4 \\ \hline \boxed{?}4.2 \end{array}$$

5.
$$\begin{array}{r} \boxed{?}5.29 \\ -\ 4.\boxed{?}\boxed{?} \\ \hline 1\boxed{?}.92 \end{array}$$

6. **SURVEYS** The table at the right shows the results of a survey that asked 40 people to name their favorite type of canned fruit. Draw an appropriate graph of the data. Explain why you chose the type of graph you did. (5.7)

Type of Canned Fruit	Number
Pineapple	20
Peaches	16
Pears	4

In Exercises 7–9, which fraction is *not* equivalent to any of the others? (6.3)

7. $\frac{3}{24}, \frac{1}{8}, \frac{9}{72}, \frac{8}{16}, \frac{6}{48}$

8. $\frac{18}{30}, \frac{6}{15}, \frac{27}{45}, \frac{3}{5}, \frac{21}{35}$

9. $\frac{12}{42}, \frac{6}{21}, \frac{10}{35}, \frac{4}{28}, \frac{2}{7}$

10. **GO CARTS** You and your friend are riding go carts. You travel $2\frac{1}{6}$ mi and your friend travels $1\frac{5}{6}$ mi. How much farther did you travel than your friend? (7.5)

Take this test as you would take a test in class. The answers to the exercises are given in the back of the book.

In Exercises 1–8, find the product or quotient. Simplify, if possible. (8.1–8.4)

1. $\frac{3}{8} \times 2$

2. $5 \times \frac{4}{7}$

3. $\frac{5}{9}$ of $\frac{1}{2}$

4. $\frac{1}{6} \times \frac{3}{4}$

5. $1\frac{1}{7} \times 3\frac{2}{3}$

6. $\frac{3}{7}$ of $2\frac{4}{5}$

7. $7\frac{1}{5} \div \frac{2}{5}$

8. $6\frac{1}{2} \div \frac{3}{4}$

ALGEBRA AND MENTAL MATH **In Exercises 9–14, solve.** (8.1, 8.2, 8.4)

9. $\frac{x}{4} \times 3 = \frac{9}{4}$

10. $y \times \frac{5}{6} = 10$

11. $\frac{1}{5} \times \frac{m}{3} = \frac{2}{15}$

12. $\frac{7}{n} \times \frac{4}{5} = \frac{28}{45}$

13. $a \div \frac{1}{7} = 6$

14. $2\frac{3}{8} \div b = \frac{19}{8}$

GEOMETRY **In Exercises 15–17, find the area.** (8.1–8.3)

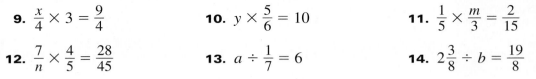

15. $\frac{9}{10}$ yd, 2 yd

16. $\frac{2}{5}$ mi, $\frac{7}{8}$ mi

17. $4\frac{1}{2}$ ft, $6\frac{2}{3}$ ft

In Exercises 18–25, find the product or quotient of the numbers shown on the number line. (8.1–8.4)

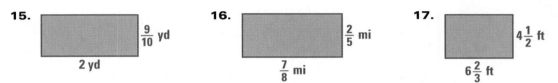

18. $K \times D$

19. $C \times B$

20. $J \times C$

21. $H \div E$

22. $K \div B$

23. $F \div C$

24. $G \times A$

25. $H \times J$

26. **STATISTICS** In a survey, 48 students were asked to name their favorite pudding flavor. One sixth of the students chose banana, three eighths chose chocolate, one third chose vanilla, and one eighth chose butterscotch. How many students chose each flavor? (8.1)

27. **DESSERTS** You are making pudding and need $4\frac{1}{2}$ cups of milk. You use a $\frac{3}{4}$ cup measuring cup. How many times do you need to fill the measuring cup to get the milk you need? (8.4)

8.5

Using Reciprocals to Divide Fractions

What you should learn:

Goal 1 How to use reciprocals to divide fractions

Goal 2 How to use division of fractions to solve real-life problems

Why you should learn it:

Knowing how to divide fractions can help you make comparisons of sizes. An example is comparing the sizes of two projects you made in art class.

Goal 1 USING RECIPROCALS

In Lesson 8.4, you learned one way to divide fractions. In this lesson, you will learn another way to divide fractions. It is called *multiply by the reciprocal*.

Two fractions are **reciprocals** if their product is 1. For example, $\frac{2}{5}$ and $\frac{5}{2}$ are reciprocals because

$$\frac{2}{5} \times \frac{5}{2} = \frac{2 \times 5}{5 \times 2} = \frac{10}{10} = 1.$$

USING RECIPROCALS TO DIVIDE FRACTIONS

To divide one fraction by another fraction, multiply the first fraction by the reciprocal of the second fraction.

$$\textbf{Example: } \frac{8}{3} \div \frac{2}{5} = \frac{8}{3} \times \frac{5}{2}$$
$$= \frac{40}{6}$$
$$= \frac{20}{3}, \text{ or } 6\frac{2}{3}$$

Example 1 Dividing Fractions

a. $\frac{3}{4} \div \frac{3}{8} = \frac{3}{4} \times \frac{8}{3}$ **Multiply by reciprocal.**

$\qquad\qquad = \frac{24}{12}$ **Multiply.**

$\qquad\qquad = 2$ **Simplify.**

b. $\frac{5}{3} \div \frac{1}{2} = \frac{5}{3} \times \frac{2}{1}$ **Multiply by reciprocal.**

$\qquad\qquad = \frac{10}{3}$ **Multiply.**

$\qquad\qquad = 3\frac{1}{3}$ **Simplify.**

c. $\frac{2}{3} \div \frac{8}{9} = \frac{2}{3} \times \frac{9}{8}$ **Multiply by reciprocal.**

$\qquad\qquad = \frac{18}{24}$ **Multiply.**

$\qquad\qquad = \frac{3}{4}$ **Simplify.**

TOOLBOX

Multiplying Fractions, page 647

Example 2 > **Comparing Areas**

You have made two mosaics as shown at the right. In terms of area, how *much larger* is the blue mosaic than the gold one? How *many times larger* is the area of the blue mosaic than the area of the gold one?

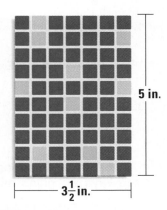

5 in.

$3\frac{1}{2}$ in.

Solution

Understand the Problem

Both questions ask you to compare area. So, you need to find the area of each mosaic.

Make a Plan

First, find the area of each mosaic. Then compare the areas to answer each question.

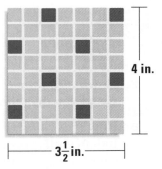

4 in.

$3\frac{1}{2}$ in.

Solve the Problem

$\text{Area} = 3\frac{1}{2} \times 4$ **Dimensions of gold mosaic**

$= 14 \text{ in.}^2$ **Area of gold mosaic**

$\text{Area} = 3\frac{1}{2} \times 5$ **Dimensions of blue mosaic**

$= \frac{35}{2}, \text{ or } 17\frac{1}{2} \text{ in.}^2$ **Area of blue mosaic**

Compare the areas. To find how *much larger* the blue mosaic is, subtract the area of the gold mosaic from the area of the blue one.

$$17\frac{1}{2} - 14 = 3\frac{1}{2}$$

The blue mosaic is $3\frac{1}{2}$ in.² larger.

To find how *many times larger* the blue mosaic is, divide its area by the area of the gold mosaic.

$$17\frac{1}{2} \div 14 = \frac{35}{2} \times \frac{1}{14}$$

$$= \frac{5}{4}, \text{ or } 1\frac{1}{4}$$

The blue mosaic is $1\frac{1}{4}$ times larger.

Look Back

✔**Check:** $14 + 3\frac{1}{2} = 17\frac{1}{2}$✔

$$14 \times \frac{5}{4} = 17\frac{1}{2}$✔$$

ONGOING ASSESSMENT

Talk About It
....

Suppose you made a red mosaic with dimensions of $3\frac{1}{2}$ in. by 10 in.

1. How *many times larger* is the red mosaic than the gold one?

2. How *many times larger* is the red mosaic than the blue one?

GUIDED PRACTICE

In Exercises 1 and 2, complete the statement.

1. The reciprocal of ? is $\frac{7}{5}$.

2. The reciprocal of $\frac{1}{9}$ is ? .

ERROR ANALYSIS In Exercises 3 and 4, describe and correct the error.

3. $\frac{7}{8} \div \frac{5}{6} = \frac{7}{8} \div \frac{6}{5}$ ✗

4. $\frac{5}{9} \div \frac{3}{5} = \frac{9}{5} \times \frac{3}{5}$ ✗

AUTO RACING The lengths of two motor speedways are given below.

Racetrack	Length
Indianapolis, Indiana	$\frac{5}{2}$ mi
Charlotte, North Carolina	$\frac{3}{2}$ mi

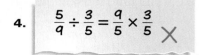

Real Life... **R**eal Facts

Indy 500 Every Memorial Day weekend, more than 250,000 spectators attend the Indianapolis 500 automobile race at the Indianapolis Motor Speedway.

5. How *much longer* is the Indianapolis speedway than the Charlotte speedway?

6. How *many times longer* is the Indianapolis speedway than the Charlotte speedway?

PRACTICE AND PROBLEM SOLVING

In Exercises 7–10, find the reciprocal of the number.

7. $\frac{4}{5}$

8. $\frac{7}{9}$

9. $\frac{11}{6}$

10. $\frac{1}{8}$

In Exercises 11–18, find the quotient. Simplify, if possible.

11. $\frac{5}{8} \div \frac{1}{6}$

12. $\frac{9}{10} \div \frac{2}{5}$

13. $\frac{7}{16} \div \frac{1}{4}$

14. $\frac{8}{9} \div \frac{2}{3}$

15. $\frac{14}{5} \div \frac{2}{3}$

16. $\frac{13}{10} \div \frac{3}{4}$

17. $\frac{22}{5} \div \frac{1}{3}$

18. $\frac{15}{4} \div \frac{5}{6}$

19. How many $\frac{1}{4}$ in. pieces of ribbon can you cut from $\frac{7}{8}$ yd of ribbon?

20. How many $\frac{2}{3}$ cup servings are in a $12\frac{1}{3}$ cup box of cereal?

FINDING A PATTERN **In Exercises 21–23, solve the equations. Then describe any patterns that you see.**

21. $\dfrac{7}{8} \div \dfrac{1}{2} = t$

$\dfrac{7}{8} \div \dfrac{1}{3} = t$

$\dfrac{7}{8} \div \dfrac{1}{4} = t$

22. $x \div \dfrac{1}{4} = \dfrac{36}{2}$

$x \div \dfrac{1}{5} = \dfrac{45}{2}$

$x \div \dfrac{1}{6} = \dfrac{54}{2}$

23. $\dfrac{7}{6} \div n = \dfrac{28}{6}$

$\dfrac{7}{6} \div n = \dfrac{21}{6}$

$\dfrac{7}{6} \div n = \dfrac{14}{6}$

24. **GARDENING** You are tying your tomato plants to stakes. You need $\dfrac{3}{4}$ ft of string for each plant. You have $8\dfrac{1}{4}$ ft of string. How many plants can you tie up?

25. The rectangle shown at the right has an area of $3\dfrac{3}{8}$ in.^{2}. Find the length of the rectangle.

$\dfrac{3}{4}$ in.

(A) 6 in. **(B)** $4\dfrac{1}{2}$ in. **(C)** $2\dfrac{5}{8}$ in. **(D)** $2\dfrac{17}{32}$ in.

26. Solve for x in the equation $\dfrac{3}{7} \div \dfrac{4}{5} = x$.

(A) $\dfrac{12}{35}$ **(B)** $\dfrac{15}{28}$ **(C)** $\dfrac{7}{12}$ **(D)** $\dfrac{15}{7}$

EXPLORATION AND EXTENSION

PORTFOLIO

27. **BUILDING YOUR PROJECT** To raise money for the outing, your class is selling bags of popcorn. Each bag takes $\dfrac{15}{4}$ min to pop.

a. How many bags can you pop in one hour?

b. Choose another item to sell. The time it takes to make each item should be a fraction. Find how many you can make in one hour.

8.6

Dividing with Mixed Numbers

What you should learn:

Goal 1 How to divide mixed numbers, fractions, and whole numbers

Goal 2 How to use division of mixed numbers to solve real-life problems

Why you should learn it:

Knowing how to divide mixed numbers can help you gather data for a science project. An example is finding the average height of a group of plants.

Goal 1 DIVIDING MIXED NUMBERS

To multiply mixed numbers, you first rewrite them as improper fractions. Use the same strategy to divide mixed numbers.

MIXED NUMBER DIVISION

To divide mixed numbers:

1. Rewrite the mixed numbers as improper fractions.
2. Multiply the first fraction by the reciprocal of the second.
3. Simplify, if possible.

Example 1 Dividing Mixed Numbers

a. $6\frac{1}{2} \div 2\frac{1}{2} = \frac{13}{2} \div \frac{5}{2}$ Rewrite as improper fractions.

$\phantom{6\frac{1}{2} \div 2\frac{1}{2}} = \frac{13}{2} \times \frac{2}{5}$ Multiply by reciprocal.

$\phantom{6\frac{1}{2} \div 2\frac{1}{2}} = \frac{26}{10}$ Multiply.

$\phantom{6\frac{1}{2} \div 2\frac{1}{2}} = \frac{13}{5}$, or $2\frac{3}{5}$ Simplify.

b. $3 \div 2\frac{1}{2} = 3 \div \frac{5}{2}$ Rewrite $2\frac{1}{2}$ as an improper fraction.

$\phantom{3 \div 2\frac{1}{2}} = 3 \times \frac{2}{5}$ Multiply by reciprocal.

$\phantom{3 \div 2\frac{1}{2}} = \frac{6}{5}$, or $1\frac{1}{5}$ Multiply.

c. $2\frac{1}{2} \div 3 = \frac{5}{2} \div \frac{3}{1}$ Rewrite as improper fractions.

$\phantom{2\frac{1}{2} \div 3} = \frac{5}{2} \times \frac{1}{3}$ Multiply by reciprocal.

$\phantom{2\frac{1}{2} \div 3} = \frac{5}{6}$ Multiply.

Notice that the reciprocal of a whole number is the fraction that has 1 as its numerator and the whole number as its denominator.

For example, the reciprocal of 3 is $\frac{1}{3}$.

Goal 2 **SOLVING REAL-LIFE PROBLEMS**

Example 2 **Finding an Average**

Your science class is conducting group experiments. Each group plants 5 corn seeds, using the same soil and the same amount of sunlight. But each group uses a different amount of water. After 2 weeks, the heights of the corn seedlings are measured and recorded. The heights for your group are shown at the right. What is the average height?

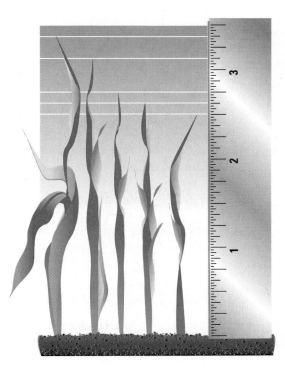

Solution

Begin by collecting the data. The heights are as follows:

$2\frac{1}{2}$ in.; $3\frac{1}{8}$ in.; $2\frac{3}{4}$ in.; $3\frac{3}{8}$ in.; $2\frac{5}{8}$ in.

Next, add the five heights.

$$\text{Total of heights} = 2\frac{1}{2} + 3\frac{1}{8} + 2\frac{3}{4} + 3\frac{3}{8} + 2\frac{5}{8}$$

$$= 2\frac{4}{8} + 3\frac{1}{8} + 2\frac{6}{8} + 3\frac{3}{8} + 2\frac{5}{8}$$

$$= 12\frac{19}{8}$$

$$= 12 + \frac{16}{8} + \frac{3}{8}$$

$$= 14\frac{3}{8} \text{ in.}$$

To find the average height, divide this total by 5.

$$\text{Average} = 14\frac{3}{8} \div 5 \qquad \text{Divide sum of heights by 5.}$$

$$= \frac{115}{8} \div 5 \qquad \text{Rewrite } 14\frac{3}{8} \text{ as an improper fraction.}$$

$$= \frac{115}{8} \times \frac{1}{5} \qquad \text{Multiply by reciprocal.}$$

$$= \frac{115}{40} \qquad \text{Multiply.}$$

$$= 2\frac{35}{40}, \text{ or } 2\frac{7}{8} \qquad \text{Simplify.}$$

The average height of the seedlings is $2\frac{7}{8}$ in.

ONGOING ASSESSMENT

Write About It

Divide. Show your work and describe each step.

1. $3\frac{3}{4} \div 5$

2. $6 \div 1\frac{1}{3}$

3. $3\frac{1}{2} \div 1\frac{1}{4}$

8.6 Exercises

Extra Practice, page 634

GUIDED PRACTICE

In Exercises 1 and 2, explain each step of the solution.

1. $2\frac{3}{5} \div 6 = \frac{13}{5} \div \frac{6}{1}$

$\qquad = \frac{13}{5} \times \frac{1}{6}$

$\qquad = \frac{13}{30}$

2. $4\frac{2}{3} \div 3\frac{1}{2} = \frac{14}{3} \div \frac{7}{2}$

$\qquad = \frac{14}{3} \times \frac{2}{7}$

$\qquad = \frac{28}{21}$

$\qquad = \frac{4}{3}$, or $1\frac{1}{3}$

3. Use two different methods to solve $5 \div 3\frac{3}{4}$. Which method do you prefer? Explain.

4. Divide $3\frac{1}{2}$ cakes among 28 students. Explain your method.

5. Does it matter which fraction you find the reciprocal of when dividing fractions? Give examples to support your answer.

PRACTICE AND PROBLEM SOLVING

CHILI COOK-OFF In Exercises 6–8, divide the chili evenly among the people.

6. Divide $24\frac{1}{2}$ oz among 5 people.

7. Divide $4\frac{1}{2}$ cups among 5 people.

8. Divide $5\frac{3}{4}$ cups among 6 people.

9. Copy the model. What mixed number does it represent? Divide the mixed number by 3 and show the results on your sketch.

In Exercises 10–13, match the problem with an equivalent problem.

A. $\frac{12}{5} \times \frac{3}{7}$ **B.** $\frac{18}{5} \times \frac{1}{3}$ **C.** $3 \div \frac{5}{3}$ **D.** $\frac{7}{3} \div \frac{12}{5}$

10. $3 \div 1\frac{2}{3}$ **11.** $2\frac{1}{3} \div 2\frac{2}{5}$ **12.** $2\frac{2}{5} \div 2\frac{1}{3}$ **13.** $3\frac{3}{5} \div 3$

In Exercises 14–22, find the quotient. Simplify, if possible.

14. $1\frac{2}{5} \div 1\frac{2}{3}$

15. $6\frac{2}{3} \div 1\frac{1}{4}$

16. $7 \div 8\frac{2}{5}$

17. $2 \div 2\frac{3}{8}$

18. $4\frac{1}{6} \div 5$

19. $3\frac{4}{5} \div 4$

20. $4\frac{1}{2} \div 2\frac{1}{3}$

21. $10 \div 5\frac{5}{7}$

22. $9\frac{1}{4} \div \frac{3}{8}$

NUMBER SENSE In Exercises 23–25, complete the statement with *sometimes*, *always*, or *never*.

23. The reciprocal of a fraction is _?_ less than the fraction itself.

24. A whole number divided by a mixed number is _?_ greater than 1.

25. A mixed number divided by a whole number is _?_ greater than 1.

FITNESS In Exercises 26–28, use the following information. You and three friends go to exercise at the gym. The table below shows the number of minutes each of you used a stairclimber and a stationary bicycle.

	Stair-climber	Stationary Bicycle
You	$10\frac{1}{5}$	$19\frac{1}{4}$
Felicia	$11\frac{7}{10}$	$22\frac{1}{6}$
Enrico	$9\frac{1}{2}$	$22\frac{5}{12}$
Kali	$10\frac{3}{5}$	$20\frac{1}{6}$

26. What is the average time for the stairclimber?

27. What is the average time for the stationary bicycle?

28. How many times more is the average time on the bicycle than the average time on the stairclimber?

BUTTERFLIES Use the table at the right showing the widths of three kinds of butterflies.

29. How many times wider is the monarch than the great purple hairstreak?

30. How many times wider is the tiger swallowtail than the great purple hairstreak?

31. Find the average width of the three types of butterflies.

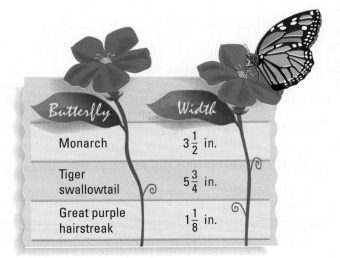

Butterfly	Width
Monarch	$3\frac{1}{2}$ in.
Tiger swallowtail	$5\frac{3}{4}$ in.
Great purple hairstreak	$1\frac{1}{8}$ in.

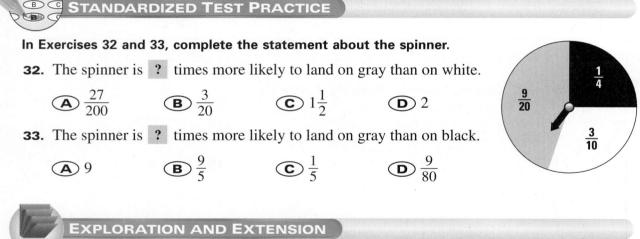
In Exercises 32 and 33, complete the statement about the spinner.

32. The spinner is ? times more likely to land on gray than on white.

(A) $\frac{27}{200}$ (B) $\frac{3}{20}$ (C) $1\frac{1}{2}$ (D) 2

33. The spinner is ? times more likely to land on gray than on black.

(A) 9   (B) $\frac{9}{5}$ (C) $\frac{1}{5}$ (D) $\frac{9}{80}$

EXPLORATION AND EXTENSION

PORTFOLIO

BUILDING YOUR PROJECT The park you visit has an $8\frac{1}{2}$ mi nature trail that starts and ends at the same place. You can walk $2\frac{1}{4}$ mi in an hour. You have $3\frac{1}{2}$ h until you have to start home.

34. Will you have enough time to walk the entire trail? Explain.

35. If you will not have enough time to walk the entire trail, at what mile marker should you turn around and start back? If you will have enough time, how much spare time will you have when you are done walking?

SPIRAL REVIEW

WORKING BACKWARD Copy and complete the diagram. (1.7)

1.
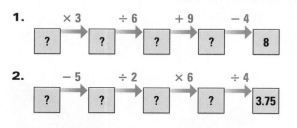

$\times 3 \qquad \div 6 \qquad + 9 \qquad - 4$

? → ? → ? → ? → 8

2.

$- 5 \qquad \div 2 \qquad \times 6 \qquad \div 4$

? → ? → ? → ? → 3.75

In Exercises 3–10, divide. (4.5–4.7, 8.4)

3. $45.9 \div 3$ **4.** $204.05 \div 11$ **5.** $50.32 \div 6.8$ **6.** $76.86 \div 4.5$

7. $680 \div 1000$ **8.** $7500 \div 100$ **9.** $\frac{9}{4} \div \frac{3}{4}$ **10.** $\frac{7}{2} \div \frac{5}{6}$

In Exercises 11–13, find the mean of the numbers. (5.3)

11. 28, 34, 55   **12.** 22, 19, 16, 27   **13.** 100, 46, 80, 81, 43

14. COOKING You want to double a spaghetti sauce recipe that uses $1\frac{7}{8}$ lb of tomatoes. How many pounds of tomatoes do you need? (7.4)

Hummingbirds: the Tiniest Birds

READ About It

With a length of only $2\frac{1}{4}$ inches, the bee hummingbird is the smallest type of bird in the world. It weighs only $1\frac{3}{5}$ grams.

While most types of hummingbirds are small, some are almost the size of a robin. For example, the giant hummingbird is $8\frac{1}{2}$ inches long and weighs 20 grams.

Hummingbirds are the only birds that can fly forward, backward, and upside down. While flying, their hearts beat 20 times per second. They take a breath every $\frac{1}{4}$ second.

Hummingbirds eat nectar and insects. In one day, they eat an amount equal to half their weight. Hummingbirds drink 8 times their weight in water each day.

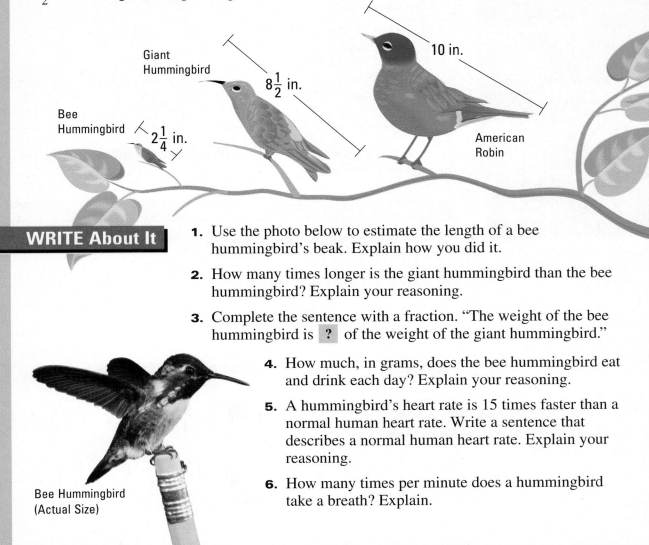

Giant Hummingbird

$8\frac{1}{2}$ in.

Bee Hummingbird

$2\frac{1}{4}$ in.

10 in.

American Robin

WRITE About It

1. Use the photo below to estimate the length of a bee hummingbird's beak. Explain how you did it.

2. How many times longer is the giant hummingbird than the bee hummingbird? Explain your reasoning.

3. Complete the sentence with a fraction. "The weight of the bee hummingbird is ? of the weight of the giant hummingbird."

4. How much, in grams, does the bee hummingbird eat and drink each day? Explain your reasoning.

5. A hummingbird's heart rate is 15 times faster than a normal human heart rate. Write a sentence that describes a normal human heart rate. Explain your reasoning.

6. How many times per minute does a hummingbird take a breath? Explain.

Bee Hummingbird (Actual Size)

Exploring the Area of a Right Triangle

What you should learn:

Goal 1 How to find the area of a right triangle

Goal 2 How to solve real-life area problems

Why you should learn it:

Knowing how to find the area of a right triangle can help you solve real-life problems.

In architecture, horizontal and vertical portions of structures meet at 90° angles.

Goal 1 FINDING THE AREA OF A RIGHT TRIANGLE

A 90° angle is a **right angle**. A triangle that has a right angle is a **right triangle**.

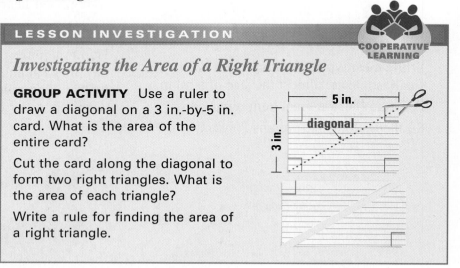

LESSON INVESTIGATION

Investigating the Area of a Right Triangle

GROUP ACTIVITY Use a ruler to draw a diagonal on a 3 in.-by-5 in. card. What is the area of the entire card?

Cut the card along the diagonal to form two right triangles. What is the area of each triangle?

Write a rule for finding the area of a right triangle.

In this investigation, you may have discovered the following rule for the area of a right triangle.

AREA OF A RIGHT TRIANGLE

The area of a right triangle is one half the product of its **base** and **height**.

$$\text{Area} = \frac{1}{2} \times \textbf{Base} \times \textbf{Height}$$

$$A = \frac{1}{2} \cdot b \cdot h$$

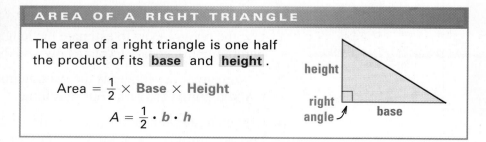

Example 1 Finding the Area of a Right Triangle

Find the area of the triangle at the right.

Solution

$$\text{Area} = \frac{1}{2} \times 4\frac{1}{2} \times 3\frac{1}{2}$$

$$= \frac{1}{2} \times \frac{9}{2} \times \frac{7}{2}$$

$$= \frac{63}{8}, \text{ or } 7\frac{7}{8} \text{ cm}^2$$

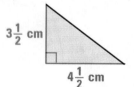

Example 2 Solving a Real-Life Problem

You want to plant grass in the region shown at the right. The seed package says that you can plant an area of 600 ft² for each pound of seed. How many pounds of grass seed do you need?

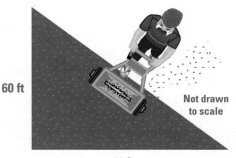

60 ft

Not drawn to scale

80 ft

Solution

First, find the area of the region to be planted.

Area $= \frac{1}{2} \cdot$ base $\cdot$ height

$\quad = \frac{1}{2} \cdot 80$ ft $\cdot 60$ ft

$\quad = 2400$ ft²

Then use a verbal model to write an equation that you can solve to find how many pounds of grass seed are needed for this area.

Verbal Model	$\dfrac{\textbf{Amount of}}{\textbf{seed needed}} = \dfrac{\textbf{Area to}}{\textbf{plant}} \div \dfrac{\textbf{Planting}}{\textbf{rate}}$	

Equation $\quad S = 2400 \text{ ft}^2 \div \dfrac{600 \text{ ft}^2}{1 \text{ lb}}$ Substitute.

$\qquad\qquad = 2400 \text{ ft}^2 \cdot \dfrac{1 \text{ lb}}{600 \text{ ft}^2}$ Multiply by reciprocal.

$\qquad\qquad = 4 \text{ lb}$ Simplify.

Example 3 Using Algebra and Mental Math

The triangle at the right has an area of 24 square units. Find the value of x.

6

x

Solution

Area $= \frac{1}{2} \cdot$ base $\cdot$ height

$24 = \frac{1}{2} \cdot 6 \cdot x$

$24 = 3 \cdot x$

Using mental math, the solution is $x = 8$.

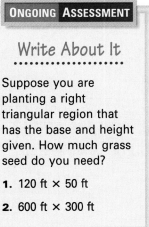

ONGOING ASSESSMENT

Write About It

Suppose you are planting a right triangular region that has the base and height given. How much grass seed do you need?

1. 120 ft × 50 ft

2. 600 ft × 300 ft

8.7 Exercises

Extra Practice, page 634

GUIDED PRACTICE

In Exercises 1–3, use the triangle at the right to match the measure with its description.

$2\frac{1}{4}$ in.
$3\frac{5}{6}$ in.

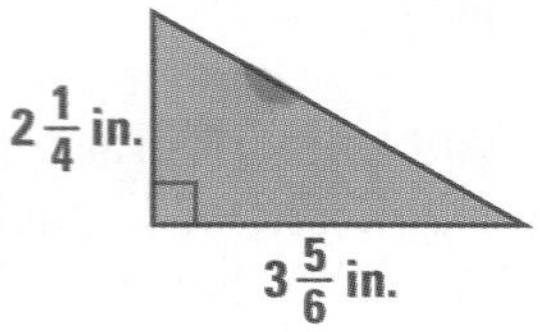

A. Base **B.** Height **C.** Area

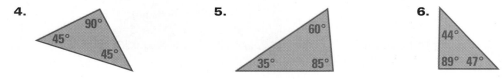

1. $4\frac{5}{16}$ in.^{2}

2. $3\frac{5}{6}$ in.

3. $2\frac{1}{4}$ in.

REASONING **In Exercises 4–6, decide whether the triangle is a right triangle. Explain.**

4.

90°
45°
45°

5.

60°
35°
85°

6.

44°
89°
47°

7. Give a real-life example of a right angle.

PRACTICE AND PROBLEM SOLVING

In Exercises 8–10, use a metric ruler to draw a right triangle that has the given base and height. Then find its area.

8. Base: $2\frac{1}{2}$ cm
Height: 3 cm

9. Base: 4 cm
Height: $3\frac{1}{2}$ cm

10. Base: $5\frac{1}{2}$ cm
Height: $2\frac{1}{2}$ cm

11. **FINDING A PATTERN** Find the areas for the triangles. Describe any patterns that you see. Draw the next two triangles that fit the pattern.

a.

0.5
0.5

b.

1.0
1.0

c.

1.5
1.5

d.

2.0
2.0

ALGEBRA AND MENTAL MATH **In Exercises 12–14, find the value of x.**

12. Area = 3 in.^{2}

x
$\frac{3}{4}$ in.

13. Area = 4.6 cm^2

2.3 cm
x

14. Area = 0.18 m^2

x
x

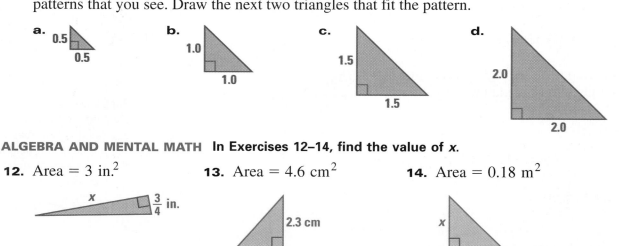

15. COMMUNITY SERVICE You are planting trees in a park shaped like the triangle shown at the right. Each tree needs $9\frac{1}{3}$ ft^2 of area to grow properly. How many trees can you plant?

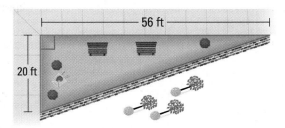

16. The base and height of the park are multiplied by 3. Which of the following is the number of trees you can plant? Explain.

A. 180   **B.** 270   **C.** 540

GEOMETRY In Exercises 17–19, the figure is made of right triangles. Find the area of the figure.

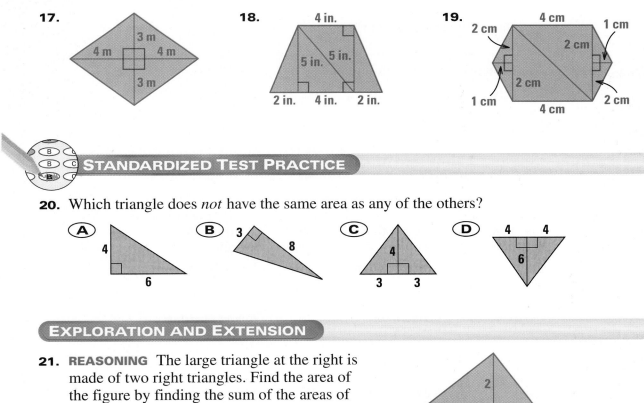

17.

18.

19.

STANDARDIZED TEST PRACTICE

20. Which triangle does *not* have the same area as any of the others?

EXPLORATION AND EXTENSION

21. REASONING The large triangle at the right is made of two right triangles. Find the area of the figure by finding the sum of the areas of the right triangles.

22. Draw another triangle that is not a right triangle. Then divide the triangle into two right triangles. Find the area of the larger triangle by the same method you used in Exercise 21.

WHAT did you learn?   ## WHY did you learn it?

		WHAT did you learn?	WHY did you learn it?
Skills	8.1	Multiply a fraction and a whole number.	Find a fractional amount of a group.
	8.2	Multiply fractions.	Find a fractional amount of a fraction.
	8.3	Multiply mixed numbers.	Compare performances.
	8.4	Divide fractions that have a common denominator.	Divide an amount into fractional portions.
	8.5	Use a reciprocal to divide fractions.	Compare areas.
	8.6	Divide mixed numbers.	Find averages of fractions.
	8.7	Find the area of a right triangle.	Find real-life areas.
Strategies	8.1–8.7	Use problem solving strategies.	Solve a wide variety of real-life problems.
Using Data	8.1–8.7	Use tables and graphs.	Organize data and solve problems.

HOW does it fit in the bigger picture of mathematics?

You have now studied operations with decimals *and* with fractions. Although the rules for adding, subtracting, multiplying, and dividing decimals and fractions have differences, they also have similarities. For example, think about how you would solve $1.3 + 2.4$ and $1\frac{3}{10} + 2\frac{4}{10}$. Do you see any similarities?

Decimals

$$\begin{array}{r} 1.3 \\ + 2.4 \\ \hline 3.7 \end{array}$$

Line up decimal places.
Add **tenths** and add **ones**.

Mixed Numbers

$$1\frac{3}{10} + 2\frac{4}{10} = 3\frac{7}{10}$$

Add **fractions**. Then add **whole numbers**.

Looking for similarities (or differences) in rules for operations with decimals and fractions helps you understand the rules. And understanding the rules helps you to be a better problem solver!

VOCABULARY

- **reciprocals** (p. 396)
- **right triangle** (p. 406)
- **height** (p. 406)
- **right angle** (p. 406)
- **base** (p. 406)

8.1 MULTIPLYING FRACTIONS AND WHOLE NUMBERS

Example

$$\frac{4}{5} \times 3 = \frac{4 \times 3}{5}$$ Multiply numerator by 3.

$$= \frac{12}{5}$$ Simplify the numerator.

$$= 2\frac{2}{5}$$ Rewrite as a mixed number.

1. A survey asked 32 students what they preferred to use for writing. Three fourths chose pencils, three sixteenths chose pens, and one sixteenth chose markers. How many students chose each?

2. Find $\frac{7}{8}$ of 3.

3. Find $\frac{3}{4}$ of 6.

4. Find $\frac{1}{9}$ of 3.

8.2 MULTIPLYING FRACTIONS

Example

$$\frac{2}{3} \times \frac{3}{5} = \frac{2 \times 3}{3 \times 5}$$ Multiply numerators and denominators.

$$= \frac{6}{15}$$ Simplify numerator and denominator.

$$= \frac{2}{5}$$ Simplify fraction.

5. Find $\frac{3}{4}$ of $\frac{1}{6}$.

6. Find $\frac{2}{3}$ of $\frac{4}{7}$.

7. Find $\frac{7}{8}$ of $\frac{1}{5}$.

8. In a survey of students in Grades 7–12, $\frac{19}{50}$ of the students said that they would choose a musician as a heroic figure. One half as many students said they would choose an actor as a heroic figure. What fraction of the students surveyed said they would choose an actor?

9. Sizes of eggs are defined by their weight per dozen. Large eggs weigh $\frac{4}{5}$ as much per dozen as jumbo eggs, and small eggs weigh $\frac{3}{4}$ as much per dozen as large eggs. Use this information to complete the statement.

Small eggs weigh ? *as much per dozen as jumbo eggs.*

8.3 MULTIPLYING MIXED NUMBERS

Example

$$1\frac{5}{6} \times 1\frac{1}{4} = \frac{11}{6} \times \frac{5}{4}$$ **Rewrite mixed numbers as improper fractions.**

$$= \frac{11 \times 5}{6 \times 4}$$ **Multiply numerators and denominators.**

$$= \frac{55}{24}$$ **Simplify numerator and denominator.**

$$= 2\frac{7}{24}$$ **Rewrite improper fraction as mixed number.**

10. An American elm is $28\frac{1}{8}$ m tall. Find the height of a red maple and a quaking aspen.

Red maple: Height is $\frac{4}{5}$ of an American elm.

Quaking aspen: Height is $\frac{5}{6}$ of a red maple.

8.4 DIVIDING FRACTIONS WITH COMMON DENOMINATORS

Example

$$\frac{6}{8} \div \frac{2}{8} = \frac{6}{2}$$ **Divide numerators.**

$$= 3$$ **Simplify.**

In Exercises 11–14, find the quotient. Simplify, if possible.

11. $4\frac{1}{5} \div \frac{3}{5}$ **12.** $\frac{8}{9} \div \frac{2}{3}$ **13.** $\frac{11}{15} \div \frac{6}{5}$ **14.** $7\frac{1}{8} \div \frac{3}{4}$

8.5 USING RECIPROCALS TO DIVIDE FRACTIONS

Two fractions are reciprocals if their product is 1.

Example $\frac{3}{7}$ and $\frac{7}{3}$ are reciprocals because $\frac{3}{7} \times \frac{7}{3} = \frac{21}{21} = 1$.

To divide one fraction by another fraction, multiply the first fraction by the reciprocal of the second fraction.

Example $\frac{3}{8} \div \frac{1}{6} = \frac{3}{8} \times \frac{6}{1} = \frac{18}{8} = \frac{9}{4}$, or $2\frac{1}{4}$

15. The reciprocal of $\frac{1}{12}$ is $\boxed{?}$.   **16.** Find $\frac{3}{8} \div \frac{2}{5}$.   **17.** Find $\frac{27}{2} \div \frac{5}{2}$.

8.6 DIVIDING WITH MIXED NUMBERS

To divide mixed numbers, first rewrite them as improper fractions. Then multiply the first fraction by the reciprocal of the second fraction. Simplify, if possible.

Example

$$3\frac{1}{3} \div 1\frac{5}{6} = \frac{10}{3} \div \frac{11}{6}$$ Rewrite mixed numbers as improper fractions.

$$= \frac{10}{3} \times \frac{6}{11}$$ Multiply by reciprocal.

$$= \frac{60}{33} = \frac{20}{11}, \text{ or } 1\frac{9}{11}$$ Simplify.

In Exercises 18–21, find the quotient. Simplify, if possible.

18. $4\frac{2}{5} \div 2\frac{3}{4}$ **19.** $3\frac{3}{7} \div \frac{9}{14}$ **20.** $8\frac{1}{3} \div 6$ **21.** $3\frac{1}{4} \div 1\frac{1}{2}$

22. A $12\frac{1}{2}$ cup box of cereal contains ? $\frac{3}{4}$ cup servings.

8.7 EXPLORING THE AREA OF A RIGHT TRIANGLE

The area of a right triangle is one half the product of its **base** and **height**.

Example

$$\text{Area} = \frac{1}{2} \times 3\frac{1}{8} \times 2\frac{2}{3}$$

$$= \frac{1}{2} \times \frac{25}{8} \times \frac{8}{3}$$

$$= \frac{200}{48} = \frac{25}{6}, \text{ or } 4\frac{1}{6} \text{ units}^2$$

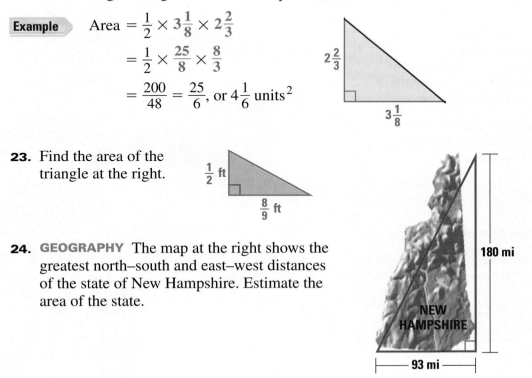

$2\frac{2}{3}$

$3\frac{1}{8}$

23. Find the area of the triangle at the right.

$\frac{1}{2}$ ft

$\frac{8}{9}$ ft

24. **GEOGRAPHY** The map at the right shows the greatest north–south and east–west distances of the state of New Hampshire. Estimate the area of the state.

180 mi

NEW HAMPSHIRE

93 mi

ALGEBRA In Exercises 1–3, evaluate the product when $n = 3$.

1. $\frac{5}{6}$ of n

2. $n \times 1\frac{9}{10}$

3. $16 \times \frac{n}{12}$

In Exercises 4 and 5, is the statement *true* or *false*? Explain.

4. The product of 3 and $\frac{1}{4}$ is $\frac{3}{12}$.

5. The reciprocal of $\frac{1}{7}$ is $\frac{7}{1}$.

In Exercises 6–9, find the product. Simplify, if possible.

6. $\frac{5}{8} \times \frac{1}{5}$

7. $4 \times \frac{3}{5}$

8. $3\frac{1}{6} \times \frac{2}{9}$

9. $2\frac{1}{3} \times 4\frac{3}{8}$

In Exercises 10–13, find the quotient. Simplify, if possible.

10. $\frac{11}{6} \div \frac{5}{6}$

11. $\frac{14}{5} \div \frac{3}{10}$

12. $2\frac{3}{4} \div \frac{3}{5}$

13. $5\frac{1}{2} \div 1\frac{5}{12}$

GEOMETRY In Exercises 14–16, find the area of the right triangle.

14.

15. $\frac{7}{8}$ cm $1\frac{1}{8}$ cm

16. $\frac{5}{6}$ mi $2\frac{3}{4}$ mi

$3\frac{1}{3}$ m

$5\frac{1}{6}$ m

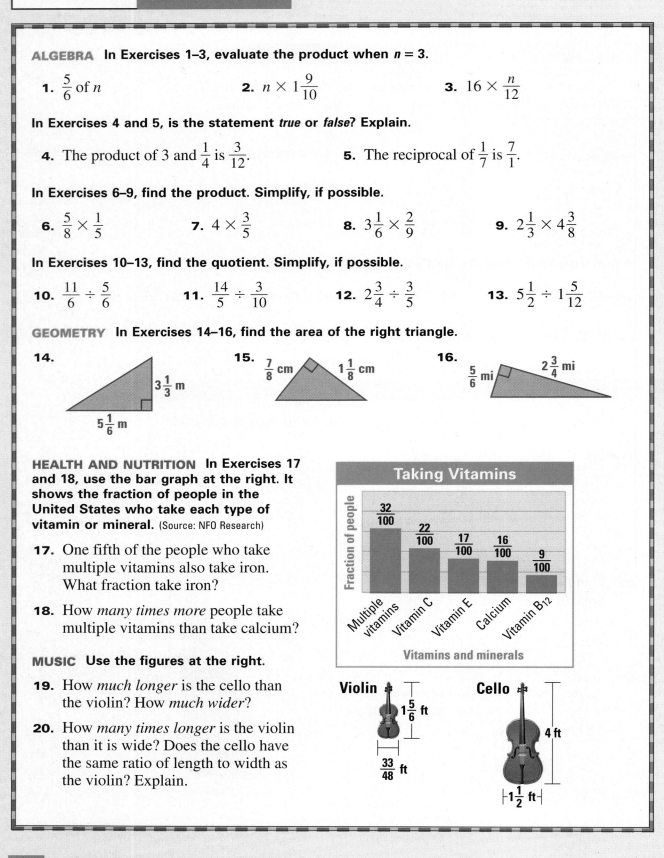

HEALTH AND NUTRITION In Exercises 17 and 18, use the bar graph at the right. It shows the fraction of people in the United States who take each type of vitamin or mineral. (Source: NFO Research)

17. One fifth of the people who take multiple vitamins also take iron. What fraction take iron?

18. How *many times more* people take multiple vitamins than take calcium?

MUSIC Use the figures at the right.

19. How *much longer* is the cello than the violin? How *much wider*?

20. How *many times longer* is the violin than it is wide? Does the cello have the same ratio of length to width as the violin? Explain.

Taking Vitamins

Fraction of people

$\frac{32}{100}$ $\frac{22}{100}$ $\frac{17}{100}$ $\frac{16}{100}$ $\frac{9}{100}$

Multiple vitamins / Vitamin C / Vitamin E / Calcium / Vitamin B₁₂

Vitamins and minerals

Violin $1\frac{5}{6}$ ft $\frac{33}{48}$ ft

Cello 4 ft $1\frac{1}{2}$ ft

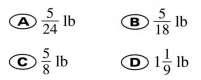

1. To make a wooden box, you buy a board that you can divide into four $6\frac{1}{3}$ in. pieces. How long is the board?

   A $1\frac{7}{12}$ in.   **B** 21 in.

   C $24\frac{1}{3}$ in.   **D** $25\frac{1}{3}$ in.

2. Jerome wants to divide $1\frac{3}{8}$ lb of peanuts evenly among himself and his two sisters. How many pounds of peanuts will each person receive?

   A $\frac{11}{24}$ lb   **B** $\frac{11}{16}$ lb

   C $2\frac{3}{4}$ lb   **D** $4\frac{1}{8}$ lb

3. A dressmaker has $\frac{2}{3}$ yd of ribbon to divide into 3 pieces of equal length. How long will each piece be?

   A 2 yd   **B** $\frac{2}{9}$ yd

   C $\frac{1}{6}$ yd   **D** $\frac{1}{9}$ yd

4. A bread recipe calls for 3 cups of flour. The only measuring cup you have holds $\frac{3}{4}$ cup. How many times do you have to fill it with flour to measure the correct amount?

   A 3 times   **B** 4 times
   C 6 times   **D** not possible

5. Solve for n: $\frac{7}{13} \times \frac{4}{n} = \frac{28}{39}$.

   A 1   **B** 3
   C 7   **D** 13

6. You and two friends are building a dog house and each has $\frac{5}{6}$ lb of nails. Your brother joins you, so you put your nails in a pile and divide them evenly among all four of you. How many nails does each receive?

   A $\frac{5}{24}$ lb   **B** $\frac{5}{18}$ lb

   C $\frac{5}{8}$ lb   **D** $1\frac{1}{9}$ lb

7. Elizabeth's remodeled room is $12\frac{1}{2}$ ft by $10\frac{2}{3}$ ft. How many square feet of carpet will she need in order to cover the floor?

   A $23\frac{1}{6}$ ft^2 **B** $120\frac{1}{3}$ ft^2

   C $121\frac{1}{6}$ ft^2 **D** $133\frac{1}{3}$ ft^2

8. You ride your bicycle $\frac{5}{8}$ mi in $\frac{1}{2}$ h. If you ride at the same pace for 3 h, how far will you travel?

   A $3\frac{3}{4}$ mi   **B** $1\frac{7}{8}$ mi

   C $\frac{15}{16}$ mi   **D** $\frac{5}{12}$ mi

9. A photograph is $5\frac{1}{2}$ in. by 7 in. If the photographer doubles both the length and the width, how many square inches will the area of the photograph be?

   A $70\frac{1}{2}$ in.^{2} **B** 77 in.^{2}

   C 140 in.^{2} **D** 154 in.^{2}

9

Geometry and Patterns

TECHNOLOGY

Technology resources accompanying this chapter:

- Interactive Real-Life Investigations
- Middle School Tutorial Software

LIFE SIZE ORIGAMI This origami model of a *Tyrannosaurus rex* skeleton was designed by Issei Yoshino. This life-size model was folded out of twenty-one 9 ft squares of paper.

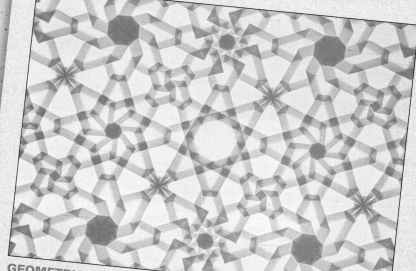

GEOMETRIC DESIGNS Models can represent real objects or geometric designs. This model by Chris Palmer recreates, in paper, a tiling pattern like the one on page 421.

CHAPTER THEME
Origami

PAPER FOLDING Origami is the Japanese art of folding paper. Many models are made from a single, square sheet of paper. Others may be made from paper that is not square or from more than one sheet of paper.

Origami

REAL LIFE
Art

Many origami models begin with the same series of folds, or *base*. The pattern of creases made when you fold two common bases are shown below.

Crane base

Frog base

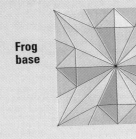

Think and Discuss

1. What are the different shapes that are formed by the creases in the diagrams?

2. In each diagram, which shapes are the same? Which are different?

3. How are the two patterns the same? How are they different?

Chapter Theme **417**

CHAPTER PROJECT

Folding Origami Shapes

PROJECT DESCRIPTION

Origami is the Japanese art of folding paper to form animals, flowers, and other figures without cutting the paper or adding anything to it. As the photos show, these figures can be simple or fantastically complex. You will make a collection of origami figures described in the **TOPICS** list.

GETTING STARTED

Talking It Over

- Have you ever folded paper to make a shape? Was it folded from a square piece of paper or some other shape?

- How can you make sharp, even folds?

- Most origami models are folded from square paper. How can you fold and cut a sheet of paper to make a square?

- Do you know anyone who does origami?

- What kinds of things are made of paper?

Planning Your Project

- **Materials Needed:** plain paper or origami paper, a large envelope or a shoebox

- Make at least five square pieces of paper and place them in a large envelope. You will use these to complete the **BUILDING YOUR PROJECT** exercises. You can use the envelope to store your completed figures.

- Decide with your teacher where the figures can be displayed when the project is complete. Plan how the display will be organized.

SAILBOAT

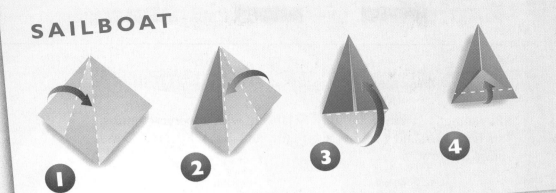

1   2   3   4   5

SWAN

1   2   3

4   5   6

INTERNET

To find out more about origami, go to:
http://www.mlmath.com

9.1 Exploring Geometric Figures

What you should learn:

Goal 1 How to describe geometric figures

Goal 2 How to identify geometric figures

Why you should learn it:

Knowing how to describe and identify geometric figures can help you describe pieces of art. An example is describing a Moorish tile pattern.

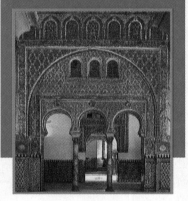

Goal 1 DESCRIBING GEOMETRIC FIGURES

In geometry, **points** are usually labeled with uppercase letters, such as A, B, and C. **Line segments** and **lines** are labeled as shown below.

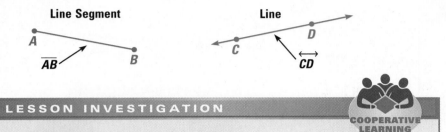

LESSON INVESTIGATION

COOPERATIVE LEARNING

Investigating Geometric Shapes

GROUP ACTIVITY Draw a figure on grid paper using line segments.

Describe the figure to a partner. (Do not show the figure to your partner.)

Your partner should use your description to draw the figure.

Compare your partner's drawing to your original figure.

You can name triangles and other shapes by naming the corners in the order they appear as you trace the outline of the shape.

Example 1 Estimating Lengths

For triangle RPQ below, describe how to move from point R to point P by staying on grid lines. Is $\overline{RP}$ longer than $\overline{RQ}$? Is $\overline{RP}$ longer than $\overline{RQ} + \overline{QP}$?

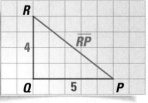

Solution

To move from point R to point P, move 4 units down and 5 units to the right.

By studying the diagram, you can see that $\overline{RP}$ is longer than $\overline{RQ}$ and $\overline{QP}$, but shorter than $\overline{RQ} + \overline{QP}$.

Goal 2 IDENTIFYING GEOMETRIC FIGURES

A **polygon** is a closed geometric figure that has straight sides. The name of a polygon tells you how many sides it has. For example, a triangle has 3 sides and a quadrilateral has 4 sides.

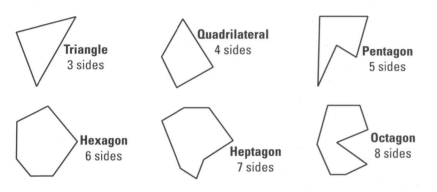

Triangle
3 sides

Quadrilateral
4 sides

Pentagon
5 sides

Hexagon
6 sides

Heptagon
7 sides

Octagon
8 sides

Some geometric figures are not polygons.

Figure is not closed.

One side is not straight.

Example 2 Identifying Polygons

The photo at the right shows part of a *mosaic* from Spain. How many different polygons can you find? Copy each different polygon. Name it and tell how many sides it has.

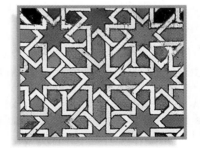

Solution

The mosaic has at least 6 different polygons.

hexagons
6 sides

octagons
8 sides

16-gon
16 sides

**Real Life...
Real People**

Chris Palmer is an artist and origami designer. He has developed a method to create geometric tilings by folding paper and fabric.

ONGOING ASSESSMENT

Talk About It

Find three examples of each polygon in your classroom.

1. Triangle

2. Pentagon

3. Heptagon

4. Is there a mosaic in your classroom?

9.1 *Exploring Geometric Figures*

 421

GUIDED PRACTICE

In Exercises 1–3, is the figure a polygon? If yes, name it. If not, explain why.

1. **2.** **3.**

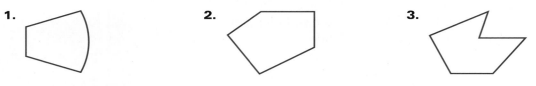

4. **COMMUNICATING** Write a description of how to move from the starting point, clockwise around the figure by staying on grid lines.

a. **b.**

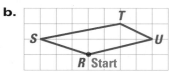

5. Estimate the perimeter of the shape in Exercise 13.

PRACTICE AND PROBLEM SOLVING

In Exercises 6–9, sketch two different polygons of the given shape.

6. Pentagon   **7.** Quadrilateral   **8.** Hexagon   **9.** Octagon

In Exercises 10 and 11, sketch the described figure on grid paper by connecting the points.

10. Start at *A*. Move left 3 and down 5 to *B*. Move right 5 and up 1 to *C*. Move up 4 and left 2 to *A*.

11. Start at *V*. Move right 1 to *W*. Move down 3 to *X*. Move left 1 to *Y*. Move left 1 and up 2 to *Z*. Move up 1 and right 1 to *V*.

Start at the point that is farthest to the left. Then, moving counterclockwise, describe how to move around the polygon.

12. **13.** **14.**

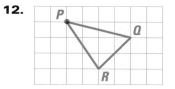 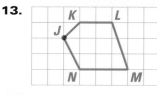 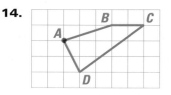

In Exercises 15 and 16, use the figure at the right.

15. Copy the figure and outline a pentagon, a hexagon, and two different sizes of quadrilaterals.

16. How many triangles can you find?

AREA In Exercises 17–19, each square in the grid represents 1 square unit. Find the area of the figure. (*Hint:* Count the squares.)

17. **18.** **19.**

STANDARDIZED TEST PRACTICE

20. Which figure is a polygon?

Ⓐ   Ⓑ   Ⓒ   Ⓓ

21. Which figure is a heptagon?

Ⓐ   Ⓑ   Ⓒ   Ⓓ

EXPLORATION AND EXTENSION

PORTFOLIO

22. BUILDING YOUR PROJECT Use the steps shown to make an origami cat. Draw its face. Name the different polygons you see on the front and back of the cat.

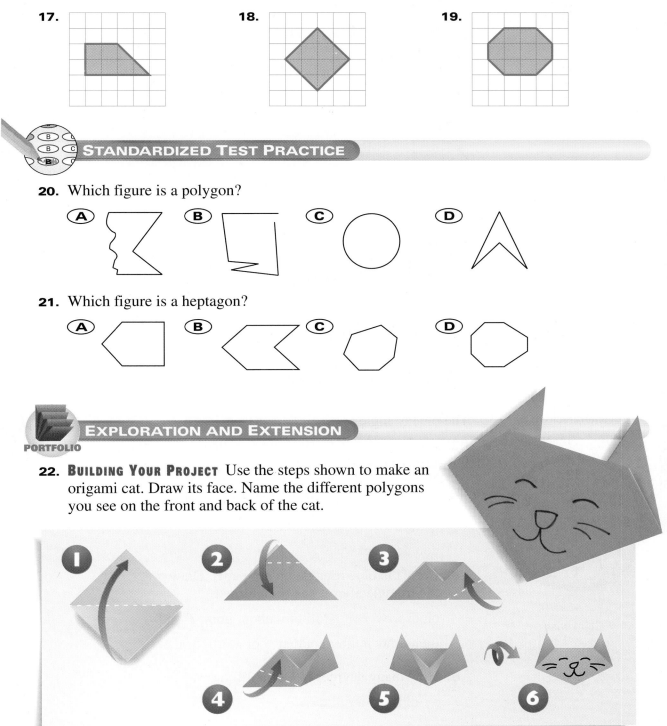

LAB 9.2

COOPERATIVE LEARNING

Investigating Turns and Angles

Materials Needed
- grid or dot paper
- pencils or pens
- scissors

Part A DESCRIBING TURNS

In the figures below, Felix turns about point *P*.

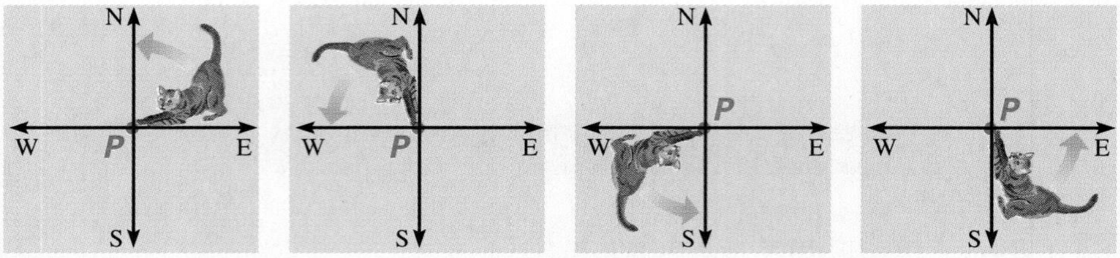

1. To start, which direction is Felix facing?

2. Which direction is Felix facing after making $\frac{1}{4}$ of a full turn? after making another $\frac{1}{4}$ of a full turn? after making another $\frac{1}{4}$ of a full turn?

3. If Felix made a full turn from his starting position, which direction would he be facing?

Part B TURNS AND ANGLES

Counterclockwise

Clockwise

The blue triangle at the right is turned $\frac{1}{4}$ of a full turn about point *P*. This turn is called a 90° turn. This is read as "a 90 degree turn."

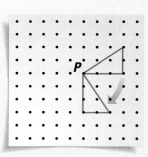

4. Compare the triangle's $\frac{1}{4}$ turn to Felix's $\frac{1}{4}$ turn. Which is clockwise? Which is counterclockwise?

5. Copy the blue triangle on dot paper. Draw the triangle after it has been turned clockwise $\frac{1}{2}$ of a full turn about point *P* and then draw it after another $\frac{3}{4}$ of a full turn.

6. How many degrees is $\frac{1}{2}$ of a full turn? $\frac{3}{4}$ of a full turn? a full turn?

7. In each drawing, the blue figure has been turned about point *P* to form the red figure. Use degrees to describe the turn. Was the figure turned clockwise or counterclockwise?

a.

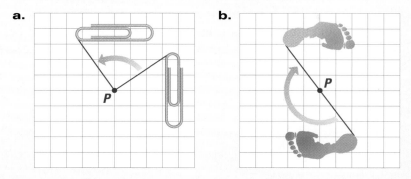

b.

8. Copy each figure on grid or dot paper. Trace and cut out the figure. Turn each figure about point *P* as indicated and trace each result.

a.

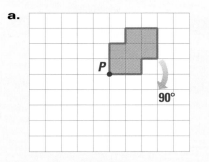

90°

b.

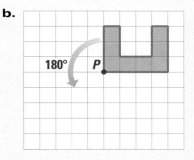

180° *P*

9. Draw a simple figure on grid or dot paper. Then draw the figure after it has been turned 90° clockwise. Draw the original figure after it has been turned 270° counterclockwise. What can you conclude?

NOW TRY THESE

In Exercises 10 and 11, draw a triangle on grid or dot paper. Label one of the corners of the triangle as point P. Trace the triangle and cut it out.

10. Turn the triangle 90° clockwise about point P. Then turn it another 180° clockwise. Trace the triangle's final position.

11. Turn the triangle 180° clockwise about point P. Then turn the triangle another 90° clockwise. Trace the final position of the triangle.

12. Compare the results of Exercises 10 and 11. Are they the same? What can you conclude?

9.2

Angles and **Their Measures**

What you should learn:

Goal 1 How to identify types of angles

Goal 2 How to use a protractor to measure angles

Why you should learn it:

Knowing how to measure angles can help you work with angles in real life.

Goal 1 TYPES OF ANGLES

A **ray** is part of a line. It begins at a point and extends in one direction without ending. An **angle** is formed by two rays that begin at the same point. This point is the **vertex** of the angle, and the rays are the **sides** of the angle.

The ray beginning at point A and passing through point B is written as $\overrightarrow{AB}$. The symbol "$\angle$" represents an angle. The angle at the right can be named as $\angle A$, $\angle BAC$, or $\angle CAB$.

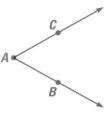

You can identify an angle as *acute, right,* or *obtuse* by its size. In the figure above $\angle A$ is acute because it is less than 90°.

TYPES OF ANGLES

Angles can be **acute**, **right**, or **obtuse**.

Acute angle	Right angle	Obtuse angle
Less than 90°	Exactly 90°	More than 90°

Example 1 Types of Angles

By observation, identify the types of the 4 angles in quadrilateral *DEFG*. Explain.

Solution

Angle	Type	Comment
$\angle D$, or $\angle EDG$	Right	Measure is 90°.
$\angle E$, or $\angle DEF$	Acute	Measure is less than 90°.
$\angle F$, or $\angle EFG$	Obtuse	Measure is greater than 90°.
$\angle G$, or $\angle FGD$	Acute	Measure is less than 90°.

Example 2 > Measuring an Angle

Use a protractor to measure the angle in the photo at the right.

Solution

Follow the steps that are outlined below. Notice that the angle does not have to have one side that is horizontal. Just turn the protractor until the 0° line is on one side of the angle.

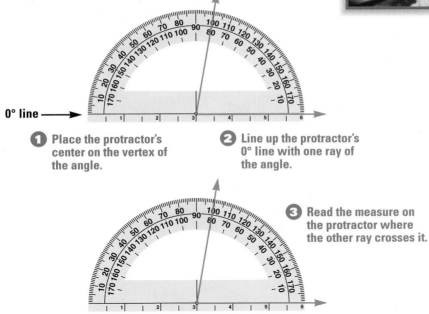

0° line ⟶

1 Place the protractor's center on the vertex of the angle.

2 Line up the protractor's 0° line with one ray of the angle.

3 Read the measure on the protractor where the other ray crosses it.

The measure of the angle is about 80°.

LESSON INVESTIGATION

COOPERATIVE LEARNING

Investigating Angle Measures

GROUP ACTIVITY Draw four angles on a sheet of paper. Label the angles as ∠A, ∠B, ∠C, and ∠D. Use a protractor to measure each angle. Write the results on another sheet of paper. Exchange angles with your partner and measure the angles your partner drew. Compare your results. Discuss any differences.

ONGOING ASSESSMENT

Write About It

1. Find an acute angle and an obtuse angle in this book or in your classroom. Use a protractor to measure them.

2. Find angles in your classroom. Without measuring, tell whether each angle appears to be acute, obtuse, or right.

In Exercises 1–3, use the blue angle at the right.
Write the given part of the angle.

1. The name of the angle

2. The two rays of the angle

3. The vertex of the angle

4. Give a real-life example of an acute angle.

5. Draw a triangle that has one obtuse angle.

6. In the drawing at the right, give the measure of the angle.

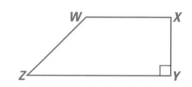

In Exercises 7–9, use the figure at the right to match the description of the angle with its name.

A. $\angle Y$ B. $\angle W$ C. $\angle Z$

7. Obtuse   8. Right   9. Acute

MEASUREMENT In Exercises 10–12, use a protractor to find the measure of $\angle JKL$.

10.

11.

12.

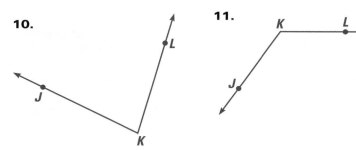
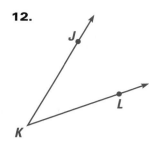

ESTIMATION In Exercises 13–19, use the figure at the right. Estimate the measure of the given angle. Choose from 15°, 45°, 60°, 90°, 95°, or 175°. Do not use a protractor.

13. $\angle DBF$ 14. $\angle CBF$ 15. $\angle ABF$

16. $\angle EBF$ 17. $\angle DBE$ 18. $\angle ABG$

19. Find the sum of the measures of angles $\angle FBG$, $\angle ABF$, and $\angle ABG$. What can you conclude?

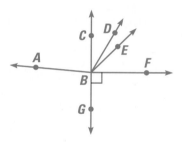

20. SCIENCE Use the photo at the right of a honeycomb from a beehive. Each cell of the honeycomb is in the shape of a hexagon. Are the angles of the hexagon *acute*, *right*, or *obtuse*?

For Exercises 21 and 22, imagine that you are in a place that has no right angles in it.

21. You have a scrap of paper with no right angles on it. Explain how you can fold your paper twice to create a right angle. Make a right angle.

22. Use the right angle you made in Exercise 21 to decide whether the given angle is *right*, *acute*, or *obtuse*.

a.   **b.**   **c.**

23. Use a protractor to find the measure of ∠ *LOM* and ∠ *MON*. What is the sum of the two measures?

24. REASONING Draw two angles side by side so the sum of their measures is 180°. (The diagram at the right is an example.)

  a. If one of the angles is acute, what must the other one be? Why?

  b. If one of the angles is right, what must the other one be? Why?

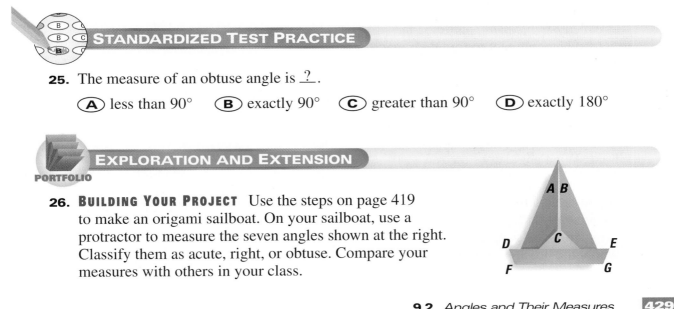

STANDARDIZED TEST PRACTICE

25. The measure of an obtuse angle is ___?___.

  A less than 90°   **B** exactly 90°   **C** greater than 90°   **D** exactly 180°

EXPLORATION AND EXTENSION

PORTFOLIO

26. BUILDING YOUR PROJECT Use the steps on page 419 to make an origami sailboat. On your sailboat, use a protractor to measure the seven angles shown at the right. Classify them as acute, right, or obtuse. Compare your measures with others in your class.

In Exercises 1–4, write the number as a fraction. (3.4)

1. 0.75　　　　　**2.** 0.2　　　　　**3.** 37%　　　　　**4.** 59%

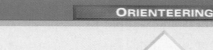 **ALGEBRA** **Use mental math to solve the equation. Then use a calculator to check your answer.** (4.6)

5. $p \times 100 = 5400$　　　**6.** $5900 \div m = 5.9$　　　**7.** $y \div 1000 = 0.3$

8. $0.75 \times n = 75$　　　**9.** $t \times 100 = 760{,}000$　　　**10.** $z \times 1000 = 57$

Find the mean and median of the data. (5.3, 5.4)

11. 25, 19, 33, 51　　　**12.** 69, 89, 31, 74, 82　　　**13.** 7, 10, 4

Decide whether the fractions are equivalent. (6.3)

14. $\dfrac{1}{3}, \dfrac{4}{12}$　　　　　**15.** $\dfrac{4}{5}, \dfrac{8}{15}$　　　　　**16.** $\dfrac{5}{10}, \dfrac{1}{2}$

17. **BIRDS** Use the following clues to find the size of each bird. (8.1)

- A blue jay is 30 cm.

- An American robin is $\dfrac{4}{5}$ of a blue jay.

- A northern cardinal is $\dfrac{5}{6}$ of an American robin.

- A house sparrow is $\dfrac{3}{4}$ of a northern cardinal.

Geography Connection

ORIENTEERING

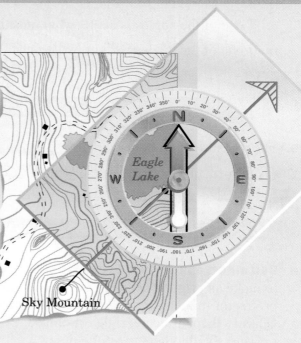

Using a compass helps people travel in the right direction and stay on course while hiking, biking, walking, or otherwise exploring the outdoors. In a sport called *orienteering*, participants use a map and compass to find their way through the woods on a set course, going from checkpoint to checkpoint to complete the course.

1. The compass is set on a straight course from Sky Mountain to Eagle Lake. What angle does the red *bearing line* show?

2. If you rotated the *bearing line* to set a course from Eagle Lake to Sky Mountain, what angle and direction would the bearing line show?

Great paper

AIRPLANES

READ About It

The National Air and Space Museum is in Washington, DC. In 1995, the museum had a Great Paper Airplane Contest. Each of the 75 contestants were given a kit to build a Whitewings Racer Sky Cub 95 glider. The gliders were made of balsa wood and paper and took about one half hour to assemble.

The classic paper airplane, whose pattern is shown below, does not take nearly as long to make. The folds on the pattern are numbered to show the folding order. The dashed lines are folded toward you so that the line ends up inside the fold. The dotted lines are folded away from you, so you can see the line after the paper is folded. After you make Fold #1, reopen the paper. The same line is Fold #4. Once the airplane is folded, you can make additional folds on the wings that help control the airplane's flight.

WRITE About It

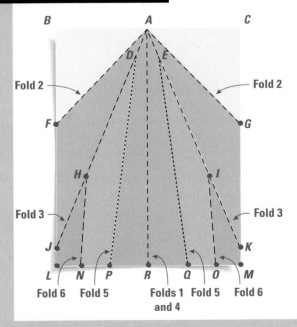

1. Copy the airplane pattern onto an $8\frac{1}{2}$ in.-by-11 in. sheet of paper. Are all of the measures of the angles in your copy the same as the ones in the book?

2. Describe the shape of the region.

   a. Purple region   **b.** Green region

   c. Blue region   **d.** Orange region

3. Write a sentence that describes two quadrilaterals of the same color that are exactly the same shape.

4. Name two triangles in the pattern that are exactly the same shape. Write a sentence that states whether the triangles are *obtuse*, *acute*, or *right*.

5. Use a protractor to measure ∠JAF and ∠AJF. Without measuring, state the measure of ∠AFJ. Explain your reasoning.

Exploring Congruent and Similar Figures

Congruent and similar shapes are often used in construction.

Goal ❶ CONGRUENT AND SIMILAR FIGURES

Two geometric figures are **congruent** if they have exactly the same shape and the same size. Two figures are **similar** if they have the same shape.

Similar, congruent	Similar, not congruent	Not similar, not congruent

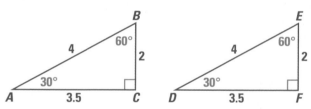

Same size and shape	Same shape but not same size	Not same size or shape

Two polygons are congruent if their angles *and* sides have the same measures. This means that if you place one figure on top of the other, they will match exactly. For example, triangle *ABC* is congruent to triangle *DEF*.

When you name congruent or similar figures, you should list corresponding points in the same order.

Example 1 Drawing Congruent Figures

Show how a square can be divided into 4 congruent parts.

Solution

STRATEGY **DRAW A DIAGRAM** There are many ways to solve this problem. Three are shown below.

Can you find other ways?

Example 2 **Comparing Quadrilaterals**

You work for a surveying company. You are asked to compare two plots of land shaped like the quadrilaterals below. You measure the sides and discover they have the same lengths. Are the quadrilaterals congruent? Are they similar?

REAL LIFE
Surveying

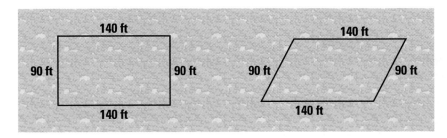

Solution

The quadrilaterals are *not* congruent or similar, because their angles do not have the same measure.

LESSON INVESTIGATION

Investigating Congruent Figures

COOPERATIVE LEARNING

GROUP ACTIVITY Many times in real life, you want to split something equally with another person. Can you find ways to divide each of the shapes into two congruent parts?

Trace and cut out each figure. If possible, draw lines that can be used to divide each figure into two congruent parts. Then cut along the lines and check to see whether the pieces in each pair are congruent.

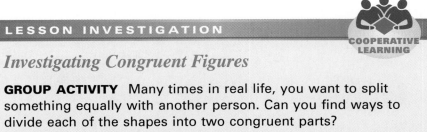

ONGOING ASSESSMENT

Talk About It
. . . .

1. Draw a triangle and measure its sides. How can you draw a triangle that is congruent to the one you drew?

2. Using only words, describe to a partner how to draw your triangle. Compare your triangle to your partner's drawing. Are they congruent? Switch roles and repeat the activity.

GUIDED PRACTICE

In Exercises 1–4, match the triangle with a similar triangle.

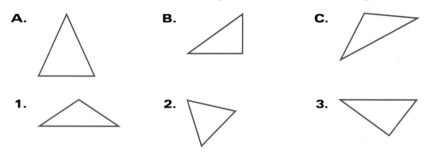

A.   **B.**   **C.**   **D.**

1.   **2.**   **3.**   **4.**

5. Show one way a rectangle can be divided into 2 congruent parts, into 3 congruent parts, and into 4 congruent parts.

6. **REASONING** Are the figures at the right congruent? similar? Why or why not?

7. **COMMUNICATING** Sketch two triangles that are congruent. Explain your method. Check your result by measuring the sides and angles of each triangle.

PRACTICE AND PROBLEM SOLVING

NATURE In Exercises 8 and 9, name the pair of figures that are similar.

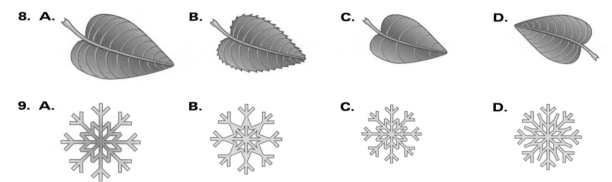

8. A.   **B.**   **C.**   **D.**

9. A.   **B.**   **C.**   **D.**

ALGEBRA AND MENTAL MATH In Exercises 10 and 11, the two figures are congruent. Find the missing lengths and angles.

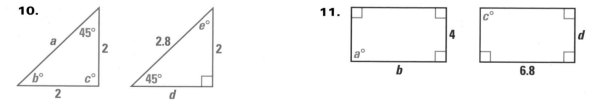

10.   **11.**

In Exercises 12–15, decide whether the figure can be divided into two congruent parts. Then decide whether the figure can be divided into three congruent parts. Sketch your results.

12. **13.** **14.** **15.**

16. REASONING Can two triangles be drawn with the same side lengths and different angle measures? Include sketches with your answer.

17. ART Identify any congruent polygons in the stained glass window shown at the right. Make a key that gives the name of each type of polygon.

18. Design your own stained glass window. Color any congruent polygons the same color.

STANDARDIZED TEST PRACTICE

19. The quadrilaterals shown at the right are congruent. Identify the longest line segment in quadrilateral *EFGH*.

    Ⓐ $\overline{EF}$ Ⓑ $\overline{FG}$

    Ⓒ $\overline{GH}$ Ⓓ $\overline{EH}$

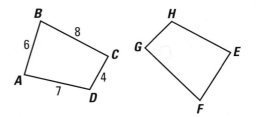

EXPLORATION AND EXTENSION

PORTFOLIO

20. BUILDING YOUR PROJECT Use the steps on page 419 to make an origami swan. The first two steps are shown below. Compare the swan to the sailboat you have made. During which steps are the swan and the sailboat congruent? Name the congruent triangles labeled in Step 2.

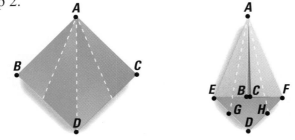

Materials Needed
- grid paper
- tracing paper
- colored pencils or markers
- straightedge
- protractor

Investigating Flips

Part **A** DESCRIBING AND DRAWING FLIPS

In Exercises 1 and 2, compare the two drawings of the cat. How are the drawings alike? different? Are they congruent?

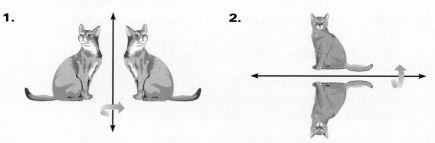

1.

2.

In Exercises 3–5, trace the partial figure. Then draw the other half of the figure by flipping the partial figure about the line.

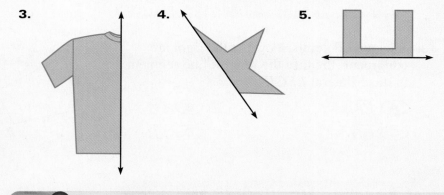

3.

4.

5.

Part **B** DRAWING A LINE

In Exercises 6 and 7, trace both figures. Then draw a line about which one figure could be flipped to produce the other figure. Explain how you can check your result by folding the paper.

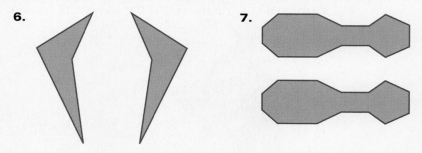

6.

7.

In Exercises 8 and 9, copy the figure on grid paper. Imagine what the figure would look like if it were flipped about the line. Draw the "flipped" figure. Use a ruler to measure the sides of both figures. Then use a protractor to measure the angles of both figures. How do the two figures compare?

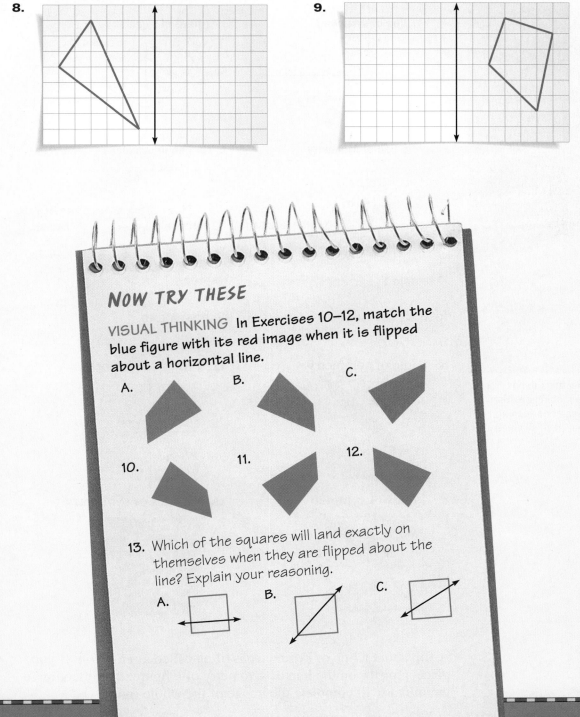

8.

9.

NOW TRY THESE

VISUAL THINKING In Exercises 10–12, match the blue figure with its red image when it is flipped about a horizontal line.

A.

B.

C.

10.

11.

12.

13. Which of the squares will land exactly on themselves when they are flipped about the line? Explain your reasoning.

A.

B.

C.

Line Symmetry

What you should learn:

Goal 1 How to identify line symmetry

Goal 2 How to use line symmetry to solve real-life problems

Why you should learn it:

Knowing how to identify line symmetry can help create designs, such as company logos or cheerleading formations.

People usually think things with symmetry look nice. Many sports, such as cheerleading, use poses that have symmetry.

Goal 1 IDENTIFYING LINE SYMMETRY

A figure has **line symmetry** if it can be flipped about a line and land exactly on itself. The line is called the **line of symmetry**.

1 line of symmetry

2 lines of symmetry

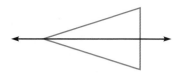

No line of symmetry

No line of symmetry

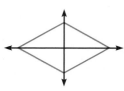

Example 1 Identifying Lines of Symmetry

Identify the lines of symmetry of the tile pattern.

Solution

a. 1 line of symmetry

b. 2 lines of symmetry

c. 4 lines of symmetry

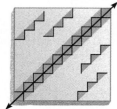

d. No lines of symmetry

A flip about a line of symmetry is often called a *reflection*. If you place a mirror on the line of symmetry of a figure, the reflection in the mirror will complete the image of the whole figure.

LESSON INVESTIGATION

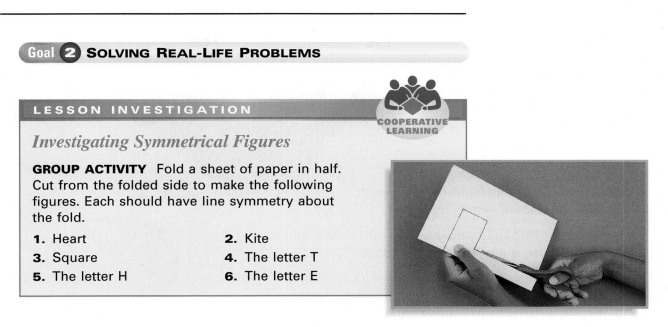

Investigating Symmetrical Figures

COOPERATIVE LEARNING

GROUP ACTIVITY Fold a sheet of paper in half. Cut from the folded side to make the following figures. Each should have line symmetry about the fold.

1. Heart
2. Kite
3. Square
4. The letter T
5. The letter H
6. The letter E

Example 2 Identifying Lines of Symmetry

REAL LIFE
Design

You are working with Alma and Joab to design a company logo. You begin by cutting figures out of folded paper as shown. How many lines of symmetry will each design have?

Yours

1 fold →

Alma's

2 folds

Joab's

3 folds

Solution

Your design will have one line of symmetry. Alma's will have two lines of symmetry. Joab's will have four lines of symmetry.

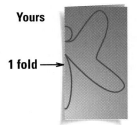
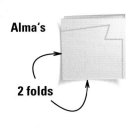
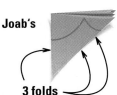

ONGOING ASSESSMENT

Talk About It

1. Find objects in your classroom that have line symmetry. Count the lines of symmetry in each.

2. Explain how you can trace a shape and fold the paper to find and check lines of symmetry.

GUIDED PRACTICE

In Exercises 1–3, draw a figure that has the given symmetry.

1. One line of symmetry

2. Two lines of symmetry

3. No line of symmetry

4. **SCIENCE** Trace the butterfly at the right. Draw any lines of symmetry.

5. Write your first and last names in capital block letters. Which letters, if any, have line symmetry?

6. A sheet of paper was folded in half twice and cut as shown. Draw what you think the paper will look like unfolded. Check your answer by folding and cutting a sheet of paper.

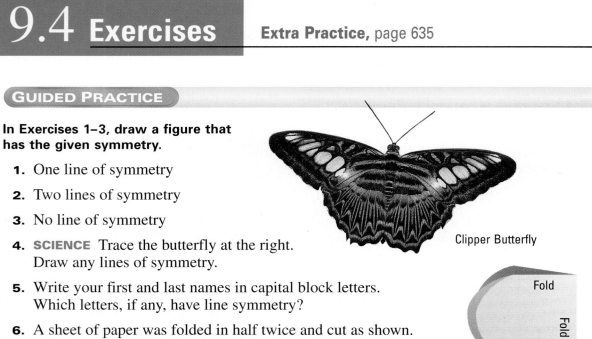

Clipper Butterfly

Fold

Fold

PRACTICE AND PROBLEM SOLVING

In Exercises 7–10, decide whether the quadrilateral has line symmetry. If it does, copy the figure and draw the line or lines of symmetry.

7.
8.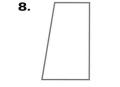
9.
10.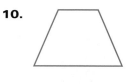

REASONING In Exercises 11–13, decide whether the red line is a line of symmetry for the figure. Explain.

11.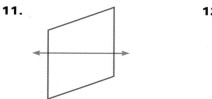
12.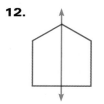
13.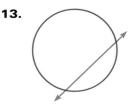

14. **ROAD SIGNS** Find three road signs (such as a stop sign) whose shapes have line symmetry. Draw the shapes of the signs. Draw any lines of symmetry.

WOODWORKING In Exercises 15–17, the designs are from woodworking projects such as cabinets and boxes. Decide whether the design has line symmetry. If it does, how many lines of symmetry does the design have?

15. 16. 17.

Tech Link

Investigation 9, Interactive Real-Life Investigations

In Exercises 18–20, complete the figure on a 5-by-5 grid of dot paper so that it has line symmetry. Sketch the line or lines of symmetry.

18. 19. 20.

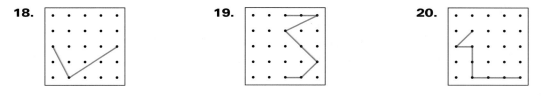

SCIENCE In Exercises 21–23, find the number of lines of symmetry in the flower.

21. 22. 23.

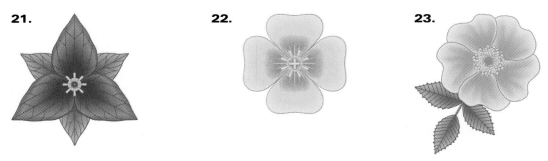

REASONING In Exercises 24–26, a sheet of paper was folded and cut as shown. Draw what you think the paper will look like unfolded. Check your answer by folding and cutting a sheet of paper.

24. 25. 26.

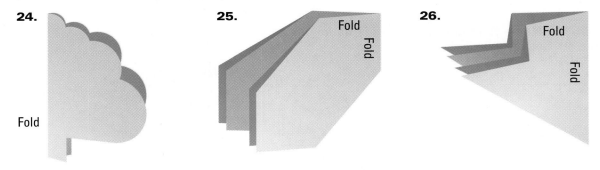

STANDARDIZED TEST PRACTICE

27. Which letter has a horizontal line of symmetry?

Ⓐ **A**   Ⓑ **C**   Ⓒ **Y**   Ⓓ **Z**

EXPLORATION AND EXTENSION

PORTFOLIO

28. BUILDING YOUR PROJECT Use the steps below to make an origami model of a dog. Does the polygon that makes the dog's face have line symmetry? Does the polygon that makes the dog's ear have line symmetry?

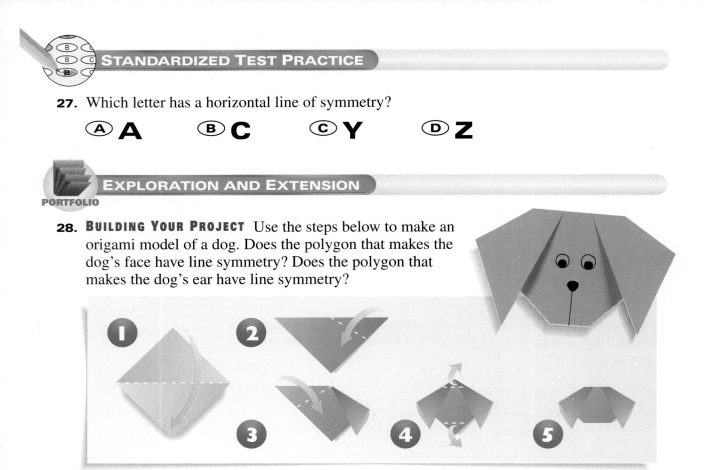

SPIRAL REVIEW

1. MAKING A LIST You are making a fruit salad with four different kinds of fruit. You can choose from grapes, pineapple, watermelon, cantaloupe, and strawberries. How many different kinds of fruit salad can you make? **(1.3)**

Order the numbers from least to greatest. (3.5, 6.5)

2. 6.15, 6.05, 6.051, 6.5, 6.01

3. $\frac{5}{7}, \frac{1}{2}, \frac{4}{7}, \frac{5}{6}$

Add, subtract, multiply, or divide. (7.4, 7.5, 8.3–8.5)

4. $4\frac{2}{5} + 3\frac{1}{2}$ **5.** $5 - 2\frac{3}{4}$ **6.** $1\frac{1}{6} \times \frac{4}{5}$ **7.** $\frac{2}{3} \div \frac{2}{9}$

GEOMETRY Name the figure and classify its angles as *acute*, *right*, or *obtuse*. (9.1, 9.2)

8. 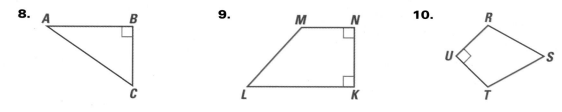   **9.**   **10.**

Take this test as you would take a test in class. The answers to the exercises are given in the back of the book.

In Exercises 1–3, describe how to move counterclockwise around the figure by staying on grid lines. Begin at *A*. (9.1)

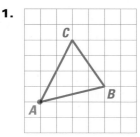
1.

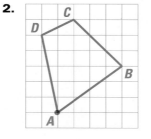
2.

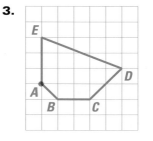
3.

4. Name each polygon. (9.1)

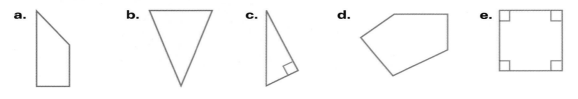

a.   b.   c.   d.   e.

Classify and measure the angle formed by the clock's hands. (9.2)

5.

6.

7.

Are the figures congruent? similar? Why or why not? (9.3)

8.   **9.**   **10.**

In Exercises 11–13, find the number of lines of symmetry. (9.4)

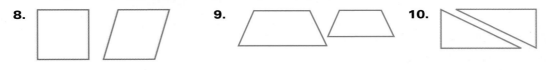

11.   **12.**   **13.**

14. ALPHABET Copy the letters that have line symmetry. Then draw the line or lines of symmetry. (9.4)

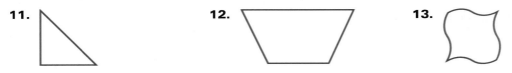

ABCDEFGHIJKLMNOPQRSTUVWXYZ

LAB 9.5

COOPERATIVE LEARNING

Materials Needed
- **paper**
- **cardboard**
- **pencils or pens**
- **ruler**
- **scissors**

Tilings in a Plane

A plane is a flat surface that extends in all directions without ending. A tiling, or tessellation, of a plane is a collection of tiles that fill the plane with no gaps or overlaps.

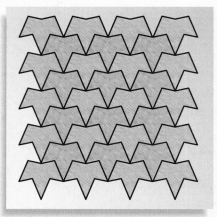

Part A MAKING TILINGS WITH TRIANGLES

1. The tiling shown below is made with congruent triangles.

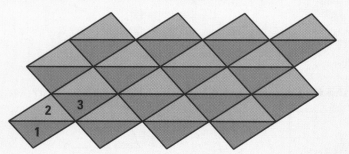

a. Explain how to move Triangle 1 so that it is exactly on top of Triangle 3. Do you have to turn or flip the triangle?

b. Explain how to move Triangle 1 so that it is exactly on top of Triangle 2. Do you have to turn or flip the triangle?

2. Have each person in your group draw a different triangle on cardboard to use as a pattern. Cut out your triangle. Use your triangular pattern to trace a tiling in the plane.

3. Could everyone create a tiling with their triangle? Discuss whether you think any triangle can be used to create a tiling.

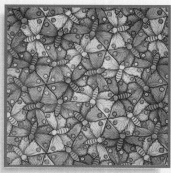

4. How can Quadrilateral 1 be moved so that it is exactly on top of Quadrilateral 2? exactly on top of Quadrilateral 3?

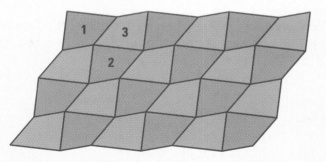

5. With others in your group, decide whether any quadrilateral can be used to tile a plane.

6. Decide whether any hexagon can be used to tile a plane. If not, find some hexagons that work and some that don't.

Part **C** MAKING TILINGS WITH ANIMAL SHAPES

7. Trace the shape at the right and cut it out. Use this shape to create a tiling. Explain your process. After you have made the tiling, draw features on the shapes so that each looks like an animal. Each tile must have the same features.

NOW TRY THESE

Copy each shape and make a pattern. Then decide whether the shape can be used to make a tiling. If it can, use the pattern to make a tiling.

8. 9. 10.

11. Make your own tiling. You can use a stencil, rubber stamps, or other shapes. Or you can make your own stencil from cardboard or heavy paper.

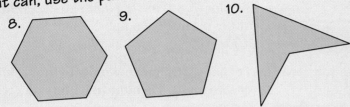

9.5

Slides in a Coordinate Plane

What you should learn:

Goal 1 How to plot points in a coordinate plane

Goal 2 How to identify slides in a coordinate plane

Why you should learn it:

Knowing how to use a coordinate plane can help you draw construction plans. An example is drawing plans for a building.

Engineers use coordinate planes to draw plans for buildings, automobiles, and machinery.

Goal 1 POINTS IN A COORDINATE PLANE

In a **coordinate plane**, you can use **ordered pairs** of numbers to name points. The numbers are the coordinates of the point. You can read "(x, y)" as "the ordered pair x, y."

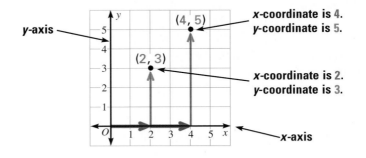

A coordinate plane has two axes, usually called the **x-axis** and the **y-axis**. When you name the coordinates of a point, always give the **x-coordinate** first and the **y-coordinate** second. The point where the axes meet is called the **origin**.

Example 1 Plotting Points

a. Plot the points represented by the ordered pairs (2, 4) and (5, 1).

b. Plot the points represented by the ordered pairs (4, 0) and (0, 3).

Solution

a.

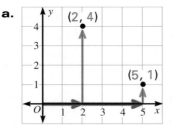

To plot (2, 4), move 2 units to the **right** of the origin. Then move 4 units **up**. Draw a dot to show the position of the point.

To plot (5, 1), move 5 units to the **right** of the origin. Then move 1 unit **up**.

b.

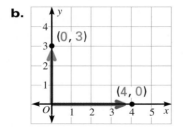

To plot (4, 0), move 4 units to the **right** of the origin. Then move 0 units **up**.

To plot (0, 3), move 0 units to the **right** of the origin. Then move 3 units **up**.

Example 2 Slides in a Coordinate Plane

Explain how you can **slide** triangle *ABC* to triangle *DEF*. What are the coordinates of each corner point or vertex of triangle *DEF*?

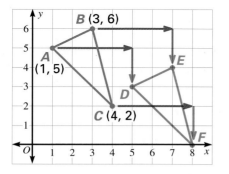

Solution

Slide triangle *ABC* 4 units to the right and 2 units down.

Point *A*: (1, 5)
Point *B*: (3, 6)
Point *C*: (4, 2)

Move 4 units right.
Move 2 units down.

Point *D*: (5, 3)
Point *E*: (7, 4)
Point *F*: (8, 0)

Example 3 Looking for a Pattern

a. In Example 2, you can find a pattern in the coordinates of triangle *ABC* and triangle *DEF*.

CONNECTION
Algebra

Geometry	Algebra
Move 4 units to the **right**.	Add 4 to the *x*-coordinate.
Move 2 units **down**.	Subtract 2 from the *y*-coordinate.

b. You can use a pattern to find the new coordinates of the point (2, 4) if you slide it 3 units to the right and 5 units up. To find the new coordinates, add 3 to the *x*-coordinate and add 5 to the *y*-coordinate.

New *x*-coordinate = 2 + 3   Move 3 units to the right.

New *y*-coordinate = 4 + 5   Move 5 units up.

The new point is (5, 9).

STUDY TIP

Use these guidelines to draw a coordinate plane.

1. Use grid paper.
2. Draw a horizontal line to be the x-axis. Label the line "x."
3. Draw a vertical line to be the y-axis. Label the line "y."
4. Label the grid lines on each axis with the numbers: 1, 2, 3, 4, . . .
5. Mark the origin.

ONGOING ASSESSMENT

Write About It
. . . .

Plot the points in the same coordinate plane. Connect the points to form a triangle.

1. *A*(1, 2), *B*(0, 5), *C*(1, 6)
2. *D*(8, 1), *E*(7, 4), *F*(9, 5)
3. *G*(5, 3), *H*(4, 6), *J*(5, 7)
4. Can you slide one of the triangles to form one of the other triangles? Explain.

9.5 Exercises

Extra Practice, page 636

GUIDED PRACTICE

In Exercises 1–4, use the grid at the right to complete the statement.

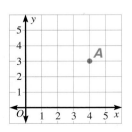

1. The grid is called a _?_.

2. The vertical line is called the _?_.

3. _?_ is the ordered pair of point *A*.

4. The first number of an ordered pair is called the _?_. Why?

5. **PARTNER ACTIVITY** You and a partner should each draw the same figure in a coordinate plane. Without your partner looking, sketch a slide of the figure. Label the coordinates of each vertex.

    Describe the slide to your partner. Your partner draws the new figure and names the coordinates of each vertex. Is your partner's slide correct? Repeat.

6. Plot the points *A*(2, 0), *B*(0, 2), *C*(3, 5), and *D*(5, 3) in a coordinate plane. Sketch the sides of figure *ABCD*. Name the figure.

PRACTICE AND PROBLEM SOLVING

In Exercises 7–10, match the ordered pair with its point.

7. (2, 2)   8. (3, 4)

9. $\left(4\frac{1}{2}, 0\right)$ 10. (0, 1)

In Exercises 11 and 12, plot each set of points in a coordinate plane. Connect the points to form polygons. Which polygons are slides of other polygons?

11. **a.** *H*(2, 6), *J*(1, 9), *K*(4, 7)

    b. *L*(1, 0), *M*(2, 3), *N*(4, 2)

    c. *P*(4, 5), *Q*(5, 8), *R*(7, 7)

    d. *S*(6, 1), *T*(5, 4), *U*(8, 2)

12. **a.** *H*(0, 0), *J*(0, 2), *K*(2, 3), *L*(2, 1)

    b. *M*(2, 4), *N*(4, 4), *P*(5, 2), *Q*(3, 2)

    c. *R*(5, 5.5), *S*(7, 6.5), *T*(7, 4.5), *U*(5, 3.5)

    d. *V*(6, 2), *W*(8, 3), *X*(8, 1), *Y*(6, 0)

13. **COMMUNICATING** Is a slide of a figure congruent to the original figure? Explain.

14. Draw a triangle in a coordinate plane. Label the coordinates of each vertex. Multiply the coordinates of each ordered pair by 2. Draw the triangle with the new ordered pairs. Is the new triangle a slide of the original? Explain.

COMMUNICATING **In Exercises 15–17, the blue figure slides to form the red figure. Describe the slide.**

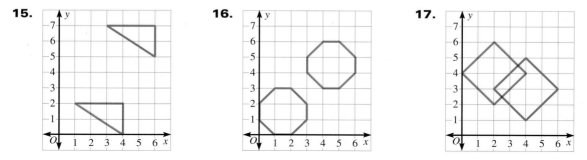

15.

16.

17.

18. A triangle has vertices (1, 4), (1, 2), and (3, 4). Slide the triangle 2 units right and 2 units down. Write the new coordinates of each vertex.

19. **MAKING A MAP** You leave home and ride your bike 3 blocks north and 2 blocks east to your friend's house. You both ride 3 blocks east and 5 blocks south to the movies, then 1 block south and 1 block west to the grocery store. Then you go home. Your house is located at (2, 5). Make a coordinate map showing the locations of the other places you stopped. On your map, 1 unit should equal 1 block.

STANDARDIZED TEST PRACTICE

20. Point A is slid 3 units left and 2 units down. What are the new coordinates of Point A?

    A (3, 2)　　**B** (4, 1)　　**C** (2, 3)　　**D** (1, 4)

EXPLORATION AND EXTENSION

TILES **In Exercises 21–24, do you need to slide, flip, or turn the first piece to match the second? Describe how to move the first shape so that it would be in the same place as the second shape.**

21. 1 and 2　　　　22. 1 and 3

23. 4 and 5　　　　24. 4 and 6

25. Trace or draw a pattern you have found. Identify shapes that are congruent. Do you need to slide, flip, or turn one to match the other?

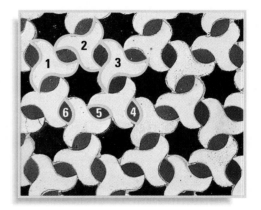

9.6

What you should learn:

Goal 1 How to identify triangles by their sides

Goal 2 How to identify triangles by their angles

Why you should learn it:

Knowing how to identify triangles can help you describe structures in real life.

In areas that get snow, houses often have steep roofs. The angle of the roofs keeps the snow from getting too deep.

Triangles

Goal 1 IDENTIFYING TRIANGLES BY THEIR SIDES

In this lesson, you will learn to classify triangles by their sides and by their angles.

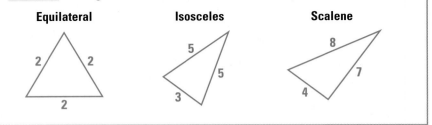

EQUILATERAL, ISOSCELES, AND SCALENE

An **equilateral** triangle has 3 sides of the same length.

An **isosceles** triangle has at least 2 sides of the same length.

A **scalene** triangle has 3 sides of different lengths.

The Venn diagram at the right shows how these three types of triangles are related. Notice that every equilateral triangle is also isosceles.

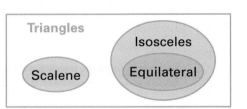

Example 1 Classifying Triangles

Classify the triangles in the diagram at the right as *equilateral, isosceles,* or *scalene.*

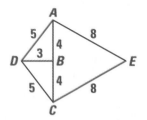

Solution

STRATEGY **MAKE A TABLE** You can use a table to organize the information about all four triangles in the figure.

Triangle	Side lengths	Type
ABD	3, 4, 5	Scalene
BCD	3, 4, 5	Scalene
ADC	5, 5, 8	Isosceles
ACE	8, 8, 8	Equilateral

Goal 2 IDENTIFYING TRIANGLES BY THEIR ANGLES

ACUTE, RIGHT, AND OBTUSE TRIANGLES

An **acute triangle** has 3 acute angles.

A right triangle has one right angle.

An **obtuse triangle** has one obtuse angle.

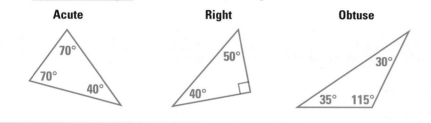

Acute   Right   Obtuse

Example 2 ▸ Identifying Triangles

In the diagram of the roof truss, identify an acute triangle, a right triangle, and an obtuse triangle.

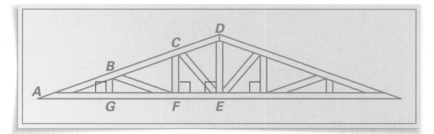

Solution

Triangle *ABG* is a right triangle. Triangle *ACE* is an obtuse triangle. Triangle *CDE* is an acute triangle.

LESSON INVESTIGATION

COOPERATIVE LEARNING

Investigating Types of Triangles

GROUP ACTIVITY Use pieces of straws cut to the following lengths: 1″, 2″, 2″, 3″, 3″, 3″, 4″, 4″, 5″.

Which lengths can be used to make a triangle? Record your results in a table. Classify each triangle as *equilateral*, *isosceles*, or *scalene*. Then classify each triangle as *acute*, *right*, or *obtuse*.

ONGOING ASSESSMENT

Write About It

1. Can a triangle have more than one right angle? more than one obtuse angle? Explain.

2. What can you conclude about the other two angles in a right or obtuse triangle?

9.6 Exercises

Extra Practice, page 636

GUIDED PRACTICE

In Exercises 1–3, use as many words as possible to describe the triangle: *equilateral, isosceles, scalene, obtuse, right,* or *acute*.

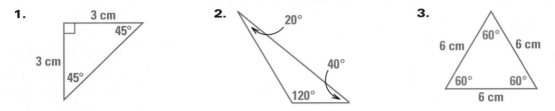

1.

3 cm
45°
3 cm
45°

2.

20°
40°
120°

3.

60°
6 cm
6 cm
60°
60°
6 cm

ACT IT OUT **In Exercises 4–6, use a 6 ft piece of string to make the indicated triangle. One person should stand at each vertex. Explain how you can determine the side lengths.**

4. Scalene

5. Equilateral

6. Isosceles

PRACTICE AND PROBLEM SOLVING

MEASUREMENT **In Exercises 7–9, use a centimeter ruler. Classify the triangle by the lengths of its sides.**

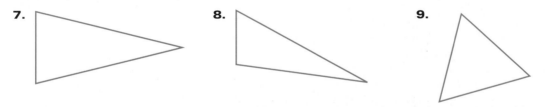

7.

8.

9.

In Exercises 10–13, sketch a triangle with the given description.

10. Acute and scalene

11. Acute and equilateral

12. Obtuse and isosceles

13. Right and scalene

ENGINEERING **Use the bridge support at the right. Use as many words as possible to describe each triangle: *equilateral, isosceles, scalene, obtuse, right,* or *acute.***

A
E
F
D
B
C

14. Triangle *BCF*

15. Triangle *ABC*

16. Triangle *CDF*

17. BUILDING BRIDGES Make your own design for a bridge support or find a picture of a bridge. Identify the triangles in your sketch or picture.

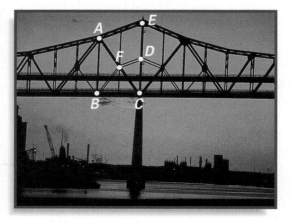

MEASUREMENT In Exercises 18–20, use a protractor to find the three angle measures. Then classify each triangle by the measures of its angles.

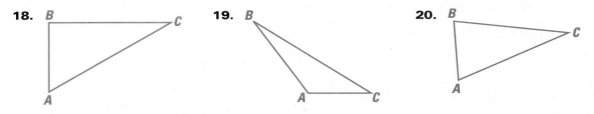

18.

19.

20.

SYMMETRY In Exercises 21–24, decide whether the triangle has line symmetry. If it does, copy the triangle and draw its line or lines of symmetry.

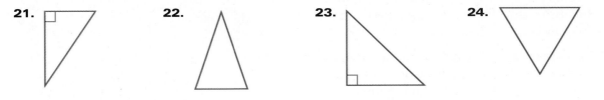

21.

22.

23.

24.

REASONING In Exercises 25 and 26, complete the statement using the words *sometimes*, *always*, or *never*.

25. A triangle can _?_ have 2 obtuse angles.

26. A right triangle _?_ has 2 acute angles.

27. **VISUAL THINKING** Draw an equilateral triangle. Label each vertex using *A*, *B*, and *C*. What are the different types of triangles that you can form by drawing a line from *A* to side $\overline{BC}$? Sketch your results.

28. **GEODESIC DOMES** A geodesic dome is a structure made using triangular braces. In the photo at the right, what type of triangles appear to be used in the structure of the roof?

Real Life... Real Facts

Geodesic Domes are made of triangular pieces. They require less material to build than traditional buildings of the same size.

29. Which triangle is isosceles and acute?

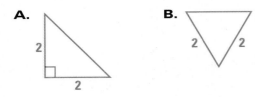

A.

B.

C.

D.

30. Which statement is *false*?

    (A) An isosceles triangle can never be a scalene triangle.

    (B) An acute triangle can also be a scalene triangle.

    (C) An obtuse triangle can also be an equilateral triangle.

    (D) A right triangle can also be an isosceles triangle.

EXPLORATION AND EXTENSION

PORTFOLIO

31. COMMUNICATING ABOUT MATHEMATICS (page 431) Fold an origami airplane. (There are many ways to do this.) Then, unfold the airplane. Use a ruler to trace the triangles. Identify them. Then write directions for folding your airplane.

32. BUILDING YOUR PROJECT Find directions for folding an origami model. You may be able to find a book about origami at the library or to find directions on the Internet. Follow the directions to fold the origami model.

SPIRAL REVIEW

In Exercises 1–3, complete the statement. Use +, −, ×, and ÷. (2.5)

1. 9 **?** 6 **?** 3 **?** 5 = 0   **2.** 7 **?** 8 **?** 4 **?** 2 = 7   **3.** 1 **?** 5 **?** 9 **?** 3 = 16

In Exercises 4–6, find the area of the figure. (4.4, 8.7)

4.

2.7 ft

2.7 ft

5.

4.15 in.

5.6 in.

6.

15.2 cm

11.4 cm

7. The data at the right shows the numbers of letters in the first names of the students in a classroom. Make a line plot of the data. (5.1)

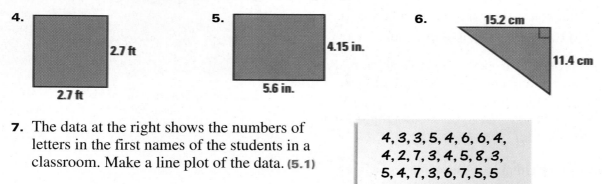

4, 3, 3, 5, 4, 6, 6, 4,
4, 2, 7, 3, 4, 5, 8, 3,
5, 4, 7, 3, 6, 7, 5, 5

8. You buy lunch meat to make subs for a class party. You order $2\frac{1}{4}$ lb of ham, $1\frac{1}{2}$ lb of turkey, and $\frac{3}{4}$ lb of salami. How many pounds of lunch meat did you buy? (7.4)

Red number cube shows 5.

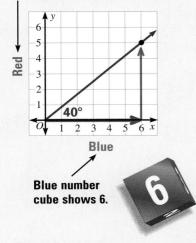

Blue

Blue number cube shows 6.

Red number cube shows 2.

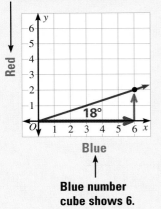

Blue

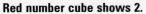

Blue number cube shows 6.

An Average Angle

Calculators can help you when you conduct experiments. For example, in the experiment below, you may want to use a calculator to find the mean, or average, of your results.

Example

Toss two number cubes (one blue and one red) 10 times. Record the results in a table. For each toss, plot a point on grid paper. Use the point to draw an angle, as shown below. Then use a protractor to measure the angle. Finally, find the average of the 10 angle measures.

Solution

The first toss of the number cubes is a blue 6 and a red 5. This angle is about 40°. The results of ten tosses are shown in the table below.

Toss	1	2	3	4	5	6	7	8	9	10
Blue	6	6	3	4	5	2	3	3	1	2
Red	5	2	3	5	1	6	5	1	1	1
Angle	40°	18°	45°	51°	11°	72°	59°	18°	45°	27°

You can use a calculator to find the mean of the angle measures. Begin by finding the sum of the measures.

40 ➕ 18 ➕ 45 ➕ 51 ➕ 11 ➕ 72 ➕ 59

➕ 18 ➕ 45 ➕ 27 ➕ (386.)

Then use mental math to divide by 10. The mean angle measure is 38.6°.

Exercises

1. Try the above experiment for yourself. What average angle measure do you get?

2. If the blue and red numbers are the same, what is the measure of the angle? Explain your reasoning.

3. If you tossed the number cubes 1000 times, what do you think the average angle measure would be? Explain.

LAB 9.7

COOPERATIVE LEARNING

Investigating Angles of a **Triangle**

Materials Needed
• ruler
• protractor
• pencils or pens
• paper

Part A MEASURING ANGLES OF RIGHT TRIANGLES

1. Use a ruler to draw two different right triangles on a sheet of paper. (Use the corners as the right angles.) Label the triangles as Right Triangle 1 and Right Triangle 2. Then label the angles of each triangle as ∠A, ∠B, and ∠C.

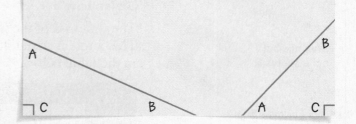

2. Copy the table below. Use a protractor to measure the angles. Complete the first two rows of the table.

Triangle	Measure of ∠A	Measure of ∠B	Measure of ∠C
Right Triangle 1	?	?	?
Right Triangle 2	?	?	?
Acute Triangle 1	?	?	?
Acute Triangle 2	?	?	?
Obtuse Triangle 1	?	?	?
Obtuse Triangle 2	?	?	?

3. What observations can you make about the angles in the triangles that are not right angles?

Part B ANGLES OF ACUTE AND OBTUSE TRIANGLES

4. Use your ruler to draw two different acute triangles and two different obtuse triangles. Label the angles of each triangle as ∠A, ∠B, and ∠C. Measure the angles of the four triangles. Complete your table from Exercise 2.

5. Look back at the data in your table. Add a fifth column to the table and label it *Sum of the Angles*. Add the measures of each triangle's angles and record the sum. Compare your group's results with other groups. What can you conclude?

6. Is it possible to draw a triangle that has a 10° angle and a 20° angle? If so, what would the measure of the third angle be?

7. Use a protractor to measure the angles of both triangles. What do you observe? Are the triangles congruent? similar? Explain.

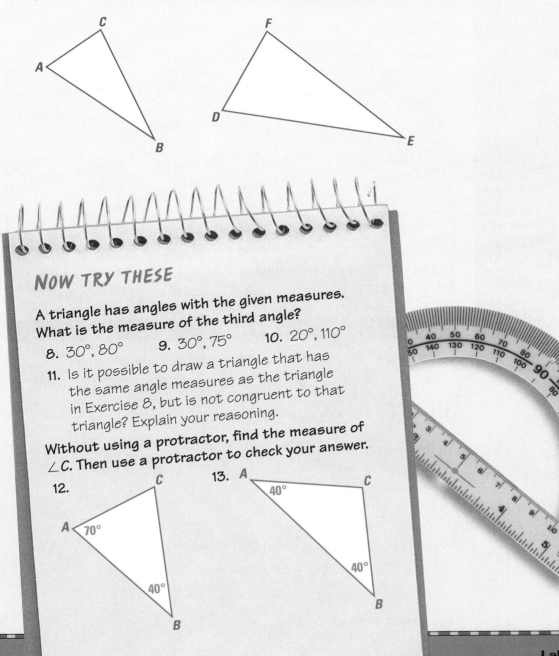

NOW TRY THESE

A triangle has angles with the given measures. What is the measure of the third angle?

8. 30°, 80°   9. 30°, 75°   10. 20°, 110°

11. Is it possible to draw a triangle that has the same angle measures as the triangle in Exercise 8, but is not congruent to that triangle? Explain your reasoning.

Without using a protractor, find the measure of ∠C. Then use a protractor to check your answer.

12.

13.

9.7

Exploring the Angles of a Triangle

What you should learn:

Goal ① How to measure the angles of a triangle

Goal ② How to use patterns to explore properties of the angles of a triangle

Why you should learn it:

Knowing how to measure the angles of a triangle can help you read maps.

Goal ① Measuring a Triangle's Angles

In this chapter you have learned about several different kinds of triangles. In this lesson, you will learn some things that are true of *every* triangle.

LESSON INVESTIGATION

Investigating the Angles of a Triangle

GROUP ACTIVITY Cut a triangle out of paper. Tear off the 3 corners and tape them next to each other as shown. What do you observe? Do you get the same result no matter what triangle you use?

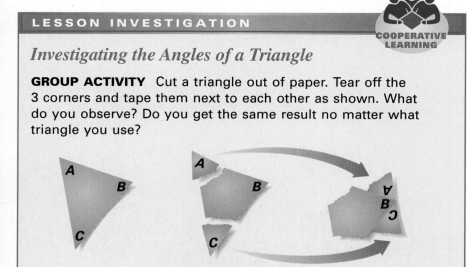

In Lab 9.7, or in this investigation, you may have discovered the following property.

ANGLES OF A TRIANGLE

The sum of the measures of the angles of a triangle is 180°.

Example 1 Finding the Measure of an Angle

To find the measure of ∠P, subtract the measures of ∠Q and ∠R from 180°.

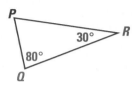

Measure of ∠P = 180° − Measure of ∠Q − Measure of ∠R

= 180 − 80 − 30

= 70

The measure of ∠P is 70°.

Example 2 Angles of a Right Triangle

Make a table showing the measures of the angles for the five right triangles below. Describe the pattern.

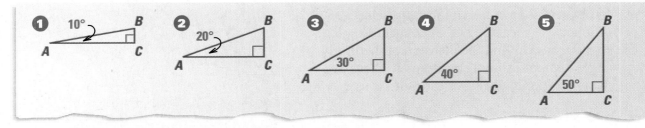

Solution

🔑 **STRATEGY** **MAKE A TABLE** For each triangle, find the measure of $\angle B$ by subtracting the measures of $\angle A$ and $\angle C$ from 180°.

Triangle	Measure $\angle A$	Measure $\angle C$	Measure $\angle B$
1	10°	90°	$180° - 10° - 90° = 80°$
2	20°	90°	$180° - 20° - 90° = 70°$
3	30°	90°	$180° - 30° - 90° = 60°$
4	40°	90°	$180° - 40° - 90° = 50°$
5	50°	90°	$180° - 50° - 90° = 40°$

🔑 **STRATEGY** **MAKE A GRAPH** One way to look for a pattern is to make a line graph of the measures of $\angle A$ and $\angle B$.

The points appear to be on a line. As the measure of $\angle A$ increases by 10°, the measure of $\angle B$ decreases by 10°. Also notice that the sum of the two measures is always 90°.

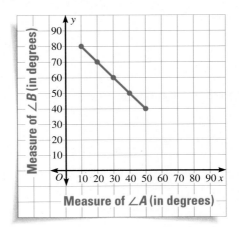

Measure of $\angle A$ (in degrees)

ONGOING ASSESSMENT

Write About It

In a right triangle, the sum of the acute angles is 90°.

1. Make a new table for the triangles in Example 2 using the fact above.

2. Do you get the same measures for $\angle B$ as in Example 2? Which method do you like better? Why?

In Exercises 1–4, use the figure at the right to match the angle with its measure. Explain your reasoning.

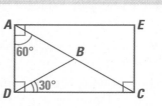

A. 120°   **B.** 60°   **C.** 30°   **D.** 90°

1. ∠ACD   **2.** ∠CBD   **3.** ∠ABD   **4.** ∠AEC

5. REASONING Draw a right triangle. Use a protractor to measure one of the acute angles. Explain how to find the measure of the third angle without using the protractor. Then use the protractor to check your result.

6. THE GREAT PYRAMID Each face of the Great Pyramid Khufu at Giza in Egypt has two 52° angles. What is the measure of the other angle?

The Pyramids of Giza in Egypt

COMMUNICATING In Exercises 7–9, decide whether a triangle could have the given angle measures. Explain your reasoning.

7. 115°, 35°, 30°   **8.** 55°, 90°, 45°   **9.** 61°, 55°, 64°

MEASUREMENT In Exercises 10–12, use a protractor to measure each angle of the triangle. Then find the sum of the measures.

10.   **11.**   **12.**

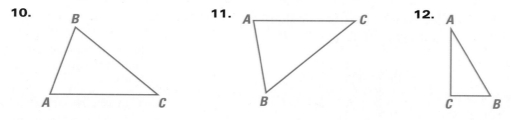

ALGEBRA AND MENTAL MATH In Exercises 13–15, use mental math to find the value of x.

13.   **14.**   **15.**

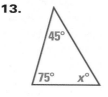

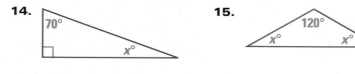

16. HIKING You are hiking on the trail in the diagram at the right. You begin at point *A* and hike southwest. When you get to point *B*, you turn to 135° and hike directly east.

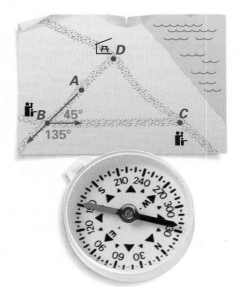

a. When you get to point *C*, you turn to face point *D*. How many degrees do you turn?

b. What is the measure of ∠*D*? How many degrees do you need to turn to get back to point *A*?

17. LOOKING FOR A PATTERN Copy and complete the table below for the measures of triangle *ABC*. Describe any patterns you see.

∠A	85°	80°	75°	70°	65°	60°
∠B	85°	80°	75°	70°	65°	60°
∠C	?	?	?	?	?	?

STANDARDIZED TEST PRACTICE

In Exercises 18 and 19, use the similar triangles below.

18. What is the measure of ∠*E*?

(A) 115°   **(B)** 80°

(C) 35°   **(D)** 30°

19. What is the measure of ∠*D*?

(A) 115°   **(B)** 80°

(C) 35°   **(D)** 30°

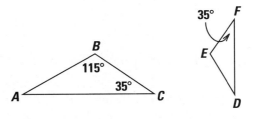

EXPLORATION AND EXTENSION

GEOMETRY The quadrilateral at the right has been divided into two triangles.

20. WRITING You know that the sum of the angles of each triangle is 180°. Explain how you can use this information to find the sum of the angles of the quadrilateral.

21. To check the result of Exercise 20, draw your own quadrilateral. Use a protractor to measure the angles. What is the sum?

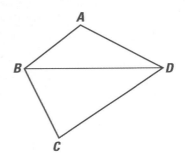

CHAPTER 9 Summary

WHAT did you learn?

Skills

9.1 Describe geometric figures and identify polygons.

9.2 Identify and measure acute, right, and obtuse angles.

9.3 Identify congruent and similar shapes and polygons.

9.4 Identify line symmetry in a figure.

9.5 Plot points and describe slides in a coordinate plane.

9.6 Identify triangles using sides and angles.

9.7 Find the sum of the measures of a triangle's angles.

Strategies **9.1–9.7** Use problem solving strategies.

Using Data **9.1–9.7** Use tables and graphs.

WHY did you learn it?

Describe a pattern, such as a mosaic tiling.

Measure angles used in real-life situations.

Compare the shapes of things, such as two plots of land.

Create symmetric designs.

Draw construction plans.

Describe triangles such as those used in the support for a roof.

Apply geometry in real-life situations.

Solve a wide variety of real-life problems.

Organize data and solve problems.

HOW does it fit in the bigger picture of mathematics?

In this chapter, you learned many new words, such as polygon, acute, obtuse, congruent, similar, coordinate, axis, isosceles, and scalene. These words form part of the *vocabulary* of *geometry*.

Every part of mathematics has its own vocabulary. For example, the vocabulary of fractions has words like numerator, equivalent, and denominator.

Learning vocabulary words is an important part of studying a new part of mathematics. You need to know vocabulary to be able to communicate with others—and communicating is much of what mathematics is about!

VOCABULARY

- point (p. 420)
- line segment (p. 420)
- line (p. 420)
- polygon (p. 421)
- ray (p. 426)
- angle (p. 426)
- vertex (p. 426)
- side (p. 426)
- acute angle (p. 426)

- obtuse angle (p. 426)
- congruent (p. 432)
- similar (p. 432)
- line symmetry (p. 438)
- line of symmetry (p. 438)
- coordinate plane (p. 446)
- ordered pair (p. 446)
- *x*-axis (p. 446)
- *y*-axis (p. 446)

- *x*-coordinate (p. 446)
- *y*-coordinate (p. 446)
- origin (p. 446)
- slide (p. 447)
- equilateral (p. 450)
- isosceles (p. 450)
- scalene (p. 450)
- acute triangle (p. 451)
- obtuse triangle (p. 451)

9.1 EXPLORING GEOMETRIC FIGURES

Example   A polygon is a closed geometric figure that has straight sides.

Triangle: 3 sides	Hexagon: 6 sides
Quadrilateral: 4 sides	Heptagon: 7 sides
Pentagon: 5 sides	Octagon: 8 sides

1. Sketch two different quadrilaterals.

In Exercises 2–5, state whether the shape is a polygon. If it is, name the polygon. If it is not, explain why not.

2.   **3.**   **4.**   **5.**

9.2 ANGLES AND THEIR MEASURES

Example   ∠*A*, ∠*B*, ∠*J*, and ∠*K* are acute.
∠*C* is right.
∠*L* is obtuse.

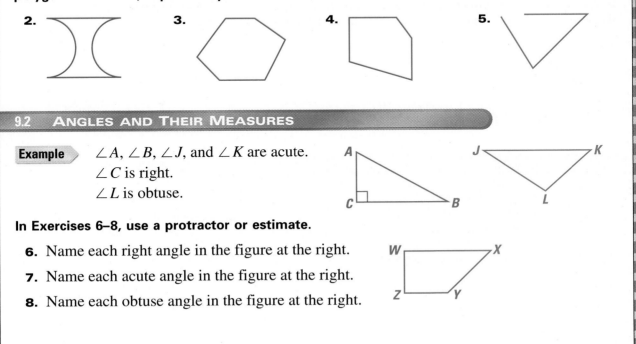

In Exercises 6–8, use a protractor or estimate.

6. Name each right angle in the figure at the right.

7. Name each acute angle in the figure at the right.

8. Name each obtuse angle in the figure at the right.

9.3 EXPLORING CONGRUENT AND SIMILAR FIGURES

Examples

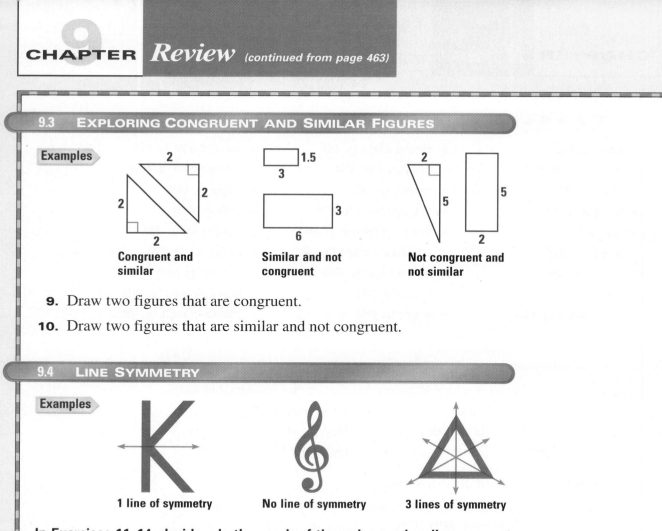

Congruent and similar

Similar and not congruent

Not congruent and not similar

9. Draw two figures that are congruent.

10. Draw two figures that are similar and not congruent.

9.4 LINE SYMMETRY

Examples

1 line of symmetry

No line of symmetry

3 lines of symmetry

In Exercises 11–14, decide whether each of the polygons has line symmetry. If it does, copy the figure and draw the line or lines of symmetry.

11. 12. 13. 14.

9.5 SLIDES IN A COORDINATE PLANE

Example To plot the ordered pair $(3, 2)$, move **3** units to the **right** of the origin and **2** units **up**.

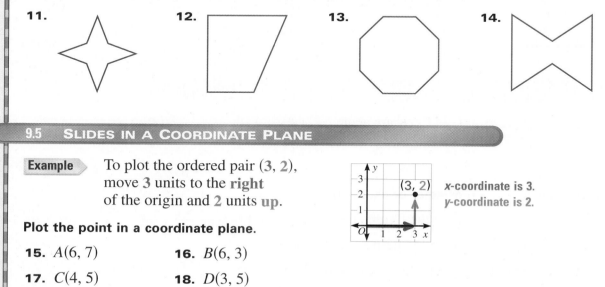

x-coordinate is 3.
y-coordinate is 2.

Plot the point in a coordinate plane.

15. $A(6, 7)$

16. $B(6, 3)$

17. $C(4, 5)$

18. $D(3, 5)$

Examples Triangle *ABC* is an obtuse, scalene triangle.

Triangle *JKL* is an acute, equilateral triangle.

Triangle *PQR* is a right, isosceles triangle.

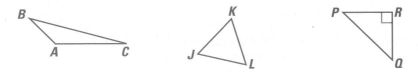

In Exercises 19–22, identify the triangle as *scalene*, *isosceles*, or *equilateral*.

19. **20.** **21.** **22.**

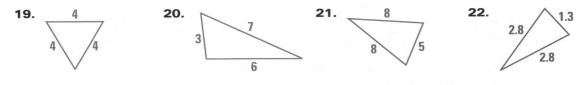

In Exercises 23–26, identify the triangle as *obtuse*, *right*, or *acute*.

23. **24.** **25.** **26.**

Example To find the measure of $\angle A$ use the fact that the sum of the measures of the angles of a triangle is 180°.

Measure of $\angle A = 180° - 35° - 55°$
$= 90°$

In Exercises 27–30, find the value of *x*.

27. **28.** **29.** **30.**

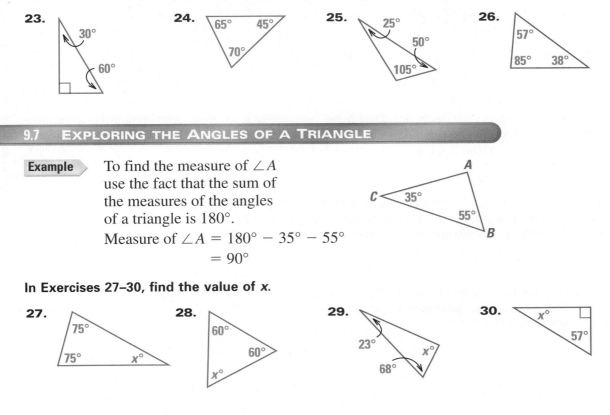

ALGEBRA In Exercises 1–4, match the polygon with its name.

A. Hexagon   **B.** Octagon   **C.** Quadrilateral   **D.** Pentagon

1.   **2.**   **3.**   **4.**

MEASUREMENT In Exercises 5–7, use a protractor to measure ∠*DEF*. What type of angle is it: *acute, right,* or *obtuse*?

5.   **6.**   **7.**

ALGEBRA In Exercises 8 and 9, the figures are congruent. Find the missing side and angle measures.

8.   **9.**

10. The digits from a calculator are shown at the right. Sketch the ones that have line symmetry. Then draw any lines of symmetry.

1234567890

In Exercises 11 and 12, plot the points in a coordinate plane. Connect the points to form a polygon. Then slide the polygon 3 units to the right and 4 units up. Write the coordinates of the new polygon.

11. $(0, 0), (4, 1), (3, 4)$ **12.** $(2, 1), (5, 1), (2, 4), (5, 6)$

KITES In Exercises 13 and 14, each kite is made from triangles. Classify the triangles as *scalene, isosceles,* or *equilateral.* Then find the measure of the angle marked *x*.

13.   **14.**

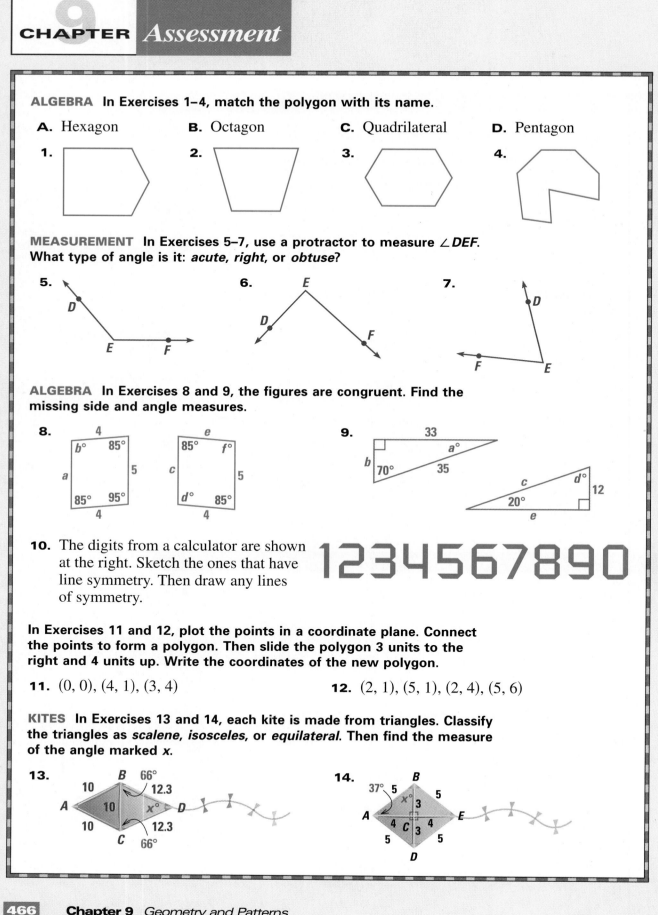

1. Which of the statements is always true about two similar polygons?

   A Their corresponding sides are the same length.

   B Their angles have the same measure.

   C They are the same size.

   D Their corresponding sides are different lengths.

2. If a figure has line symmetry, then ? .

   A it appears the same after it has been rotated 90° about the line of symmetry

   B it appears the same after it has been flipped over the line of symmetry

   C it appears the same after a slide across the line of symmetry

   D it is congruent to any other figure that has the same line of symmetry

3. If a triangle is isosceles, then ? .

   A one of its angles always measures 90°

   B all sides are different lengths

   C it always has three acute angles

   D two of its sides are the same length

4. All of the names apply to the figure except ? .

   A polygon

   B acute triangle

   C right triangle

   D isosceles triangle

5. Which of the following statements cannot be true of a triangle?

   A It is both acute and isosceles.

   B It is both obtuse and scalene.

   C It is both isosceles and equilateral.

   D It is both right and obtuse.

6. If one figure is a slide of another figure, which of the following statements is not true?

   A The figures are congruent to each other.

   B The figures are similar to each other.

   C The figures have the same coordinates.

   D The figures have the same number of lines of symmetry.

7. If you slide the point (3, 4) so that it lands on the point (1, 7), you would move it ? .

   A 2 units down and 3 units to the left

   B 2 units down and 3 units to the right

   C 3 units up and 2 units to the right

   D 3 units up and 2 units to the left

8. If two angles of a triangle measure 80° and 40°, which of the statements about the triangle cannot be true?

   A It is an obtuse triangle.

   B It has no lines of symmetry.

   C The third angle measures 60°.

   D It is an acute triangle.

1. Write the measure as a mixed number and as a fraction. (7.1)

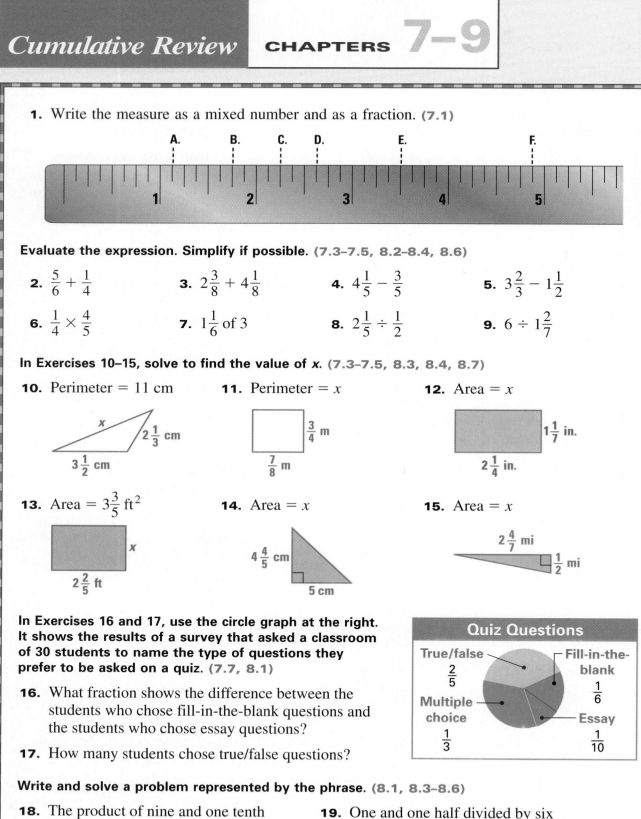

Evaluate the expression. Simplify if possible. (7.3–7.5, 8.2–8.4, 8.6)

2. $\dfrac{5}{6} + \dfrac{1}{4}$

3. $2\dfrac{3}{8} + 4\dfrac{1}{8}$

4. $4\dfrac{1}{5} - \dfrac{3}{5}$

5. $3\dfrac{2}{3} - 1\dfrac{1}{2}$

6. $\dfrac{1}{4} \times \dfrac{4}{5}$

7. $1\dfrac{1}{6}$ of 3

8. $2\dfrac{1}{5} \div \dfrac{1}{2}$

9. $6 \div 1\dfrac{2}{7}$

In Exercises 10–15, solve to find the value of x. (7.3–7.5, 8.3, 8.4, 8.7)

10. Perimeter = 11 cm

11. Perimeter = x

12. Area = x

13. Area = $3\dfrac{3}{5}$ ft^2

14. Area = x

15. Area = x

In Exercises 16 and 17, use the circle graph at the right. It shows the results of a survey that asked a classroom of 30 students to name the type of questions they prefer to be asked on a quiz. (7.7, 8.1)

Quiz Questions

True/false $\dfrac{2}{5}$ — Fill-in-the-blank $\dfrac{1}{6}$ — Multiple choice $\dfrac{1}{3}$ — Essay $\dfrac{1}{10}$

16. What fraction shows the difference between the students who chose fill-in-the-blank questions and the students who chose essay questions?

17. How many students chose true/false questions?

Write and solve a problem represented by the phrase. (8.1, 8.3–8.6)

18. The product of nine and one tenth

19. One and one half divided by six

20. Four fifths divided by three tenths

21. Two and one sixth multiplied by six sevenths

GEOMETRY In Exercises 22–24, name the polygon. Then classify and measure its angles. (9.1, 9.2)

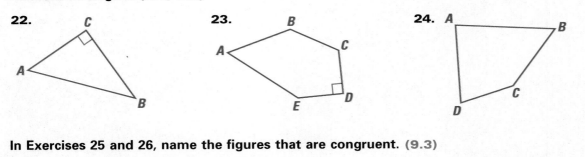

22.

23.

24.

In Exercises 25 and 26, name the figures that are congruent. (9.3)

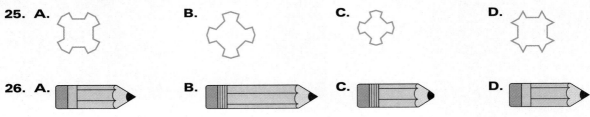

25. **A.** **B.** **C.** **D.**

26. **A.** **B.** **C.** **D.**

Complete the figure on a 5-by-5 grid of dot paper so that it has line symmetry. How many lines of symmetry does your figure have? (9.4)

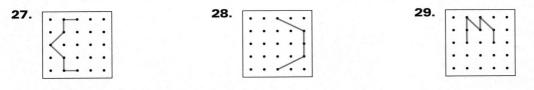

27.

28.

29.

Copy the figure onto grid paper. Use the description to slide it. (9.5)

30. Up 4 and right 3

31. Up 3 and left 4

32. Down 2 and left 1

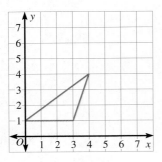

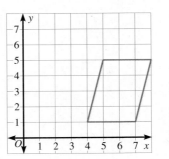

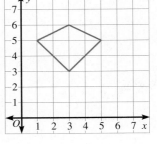

33. **UNICYCLING** Imagine that you are riding a unicycle on the path at the right. What type of angle is formed at your starting point? How far did you ride? (7.4, 9.2)

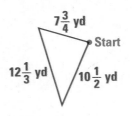

$7\frac{3}{4}$ yd

Start

$12\frac{1}{3}$ yd

$10\frac{1}{2}$ yd

Geometry and Measurement

TECHNOLOGY

Technology resources accompanying this chapter:

- Interactive Real-Life Investigations
- Middle School Tutorial Software

Mementos left by visitors to the **VIETNAM VETERANS MEMORIAL** are collected twice daily by park rangers. All items are saved and cataloged.

The United States **CAPITOL BUILDING** has 540 rooms.

CHAPTER THEME
Washington, DC

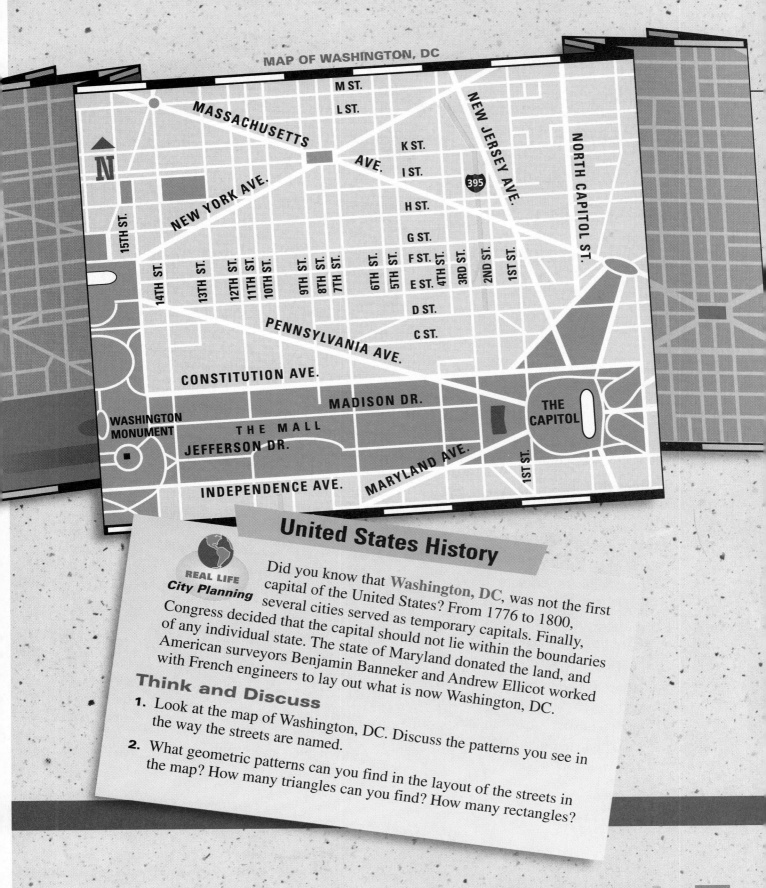

M ST.

L ST.

MASSACHUSETTS

NEW JERSEY AVE.

NORTH CAPITOL ST.

K ST.

AVE.

I ST.

395

NEW YORK AVE.

H ST.

G ST.

15TH ST.

14TH ST.
13TH ST.
12TH ST.
11TH ST.
10TH ST.
9TH ST.
8TH ST.
7TH ST.
6TH ST.
5TH ST.
F ST.
4TH ST.
E ST.
3RD ST.
2ND ST.
1ST ST.

D ST.

PENNSYLVANIA AVE.

C ST.

CONSTITUTION AVE.

MADISON DR.

THE CAPITOL

WASHINGTON MONUMENT

THE MALL

JEFFERSON DR.

1ST ST.

MARYLAND AVE.

INDEPENDENCE AVE.

United States History

REAL LIFE
City Planning

Did you know that Washington, DC, was not the first capital of the United States? From 1776 to 1800, several cities served as temporary capitals. Finally, Congress decided that the capital should not lie within the boundaries of any individual state. The state of Maryland donated the land, and American surveyors Benjamin Banneker and Andrew Ellicot worked with French engineers to lay out what is now Washington, DC.

Think and Discuss

1. Look at the map of Washington, DC. Discuss the patterns you see in the way the streets are named.

2. What geometric patterns can you find in the layout of the streets in the map? How many triangles can you find? How many rectangles?

PORTFOLIO

CHAPTER PROJECT

Planning a City

The ancient city of Titrus Hoyuk was built 4,500 years ago. It is one of the earliest known examples of city planning.

PROJECT DESCRIPTION

City planners work on the physical layout of cities and towns. Some cities, like Washington, DC, were carefully planned before they were built. Suppose you are given the chance to plan your own city. Many decisions need to be made about the city's layout. Making a map will help with these decisions. You will plan a city and make a map showing the information from the **TOPICS** listed on the next page.

GETTING STARTED

Talking It Over

- What features will your city have? Will there be parks? Will your city be large or small? Will there be a business district? a housing district?

- Where will your city be located? Where will the natural features, such as rivers and lakes, be found on your map? How much land will your city cover?

Planning Your Project

- **Materials Needed:** sheets of paper, colored pencils or markers.

- Think of a name for your city. Decide what scale your map will be and write it on the map. Draw in any geographic features that lie in the area. Use the five topics in the **BUILDING YOUR PROJECT** list on the next page to add more information to the map.

BUILDING YOUR PROJECT

These are places throughout the chapter where you will work on your project.

TOPICS

10.1 Lay out the major streets in your city. *p. 479*

10.2 Add special streets leading to landmarks. *p. 483*

10.3 Explore patterns in the city streets. *p. 489*

10.4 Find the area of the land enclosed by streets. *p. 496*

10.6 Include a park in your city plans. *p. 510*

I N T E R N E T

To find out more about city planning, go to:
http://www.mlmath.com

Investigating Lines

Materials Needed
- **dot paper**
- **colored pencils or markers**
- **ruler**

1. Use a ruler to copy the pattern of lines below onto dot paper. Lines that meet are *intersecting*. Lines that do not meet are *parallel*. Use the pattern of lines to name two parallel lines and two intersecting lines.

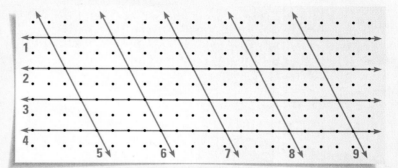

2. Color a small quadrilateral in your pattern of lines.

3. Use a second color to shade a larger quadrilateral.

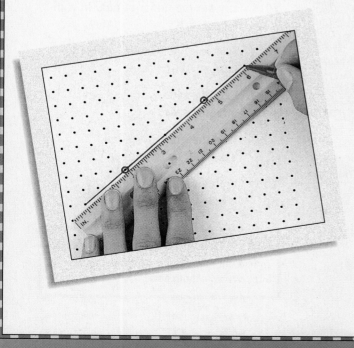

4. On dot paper, choose a dot and color it. Move 6 dots to the right and 4 dots up and color that dot. Draw a line through the colored dots, as shown at the left. Repeat the process twice, starting at dots that are not on the line you have drawn. What can you conclude about the three lines?

5. Repeat the process in Exercise 4, only begin by moving 8 dots to the left and 5 dots up. What can you conclude about these three lines?

6. With others in your group, create your own series of three lines, like those in Exercises 4 and 5. Explain your steps.

7. **a.** On dot paper, color a dot and label it *P*.

b. From point *P*, move right 6 dots and up 4 dots. Label the resulting point *Q*.

c. From point *P*, move right 4 dots and down 6 dots. Label the resulting point *R*.

d. Use a ruler to draw lines $\overleftrightarrow{PQ}$ and $\overleftrightarrow{PR}$.

e. Lines that form right angles are *perpendicular*. Tear off a corner of a piece of paper and use it to check that lines $\overleftrightarrow{PQ}$ and $\overleftrightarrow{PR}$ are perpendicular.

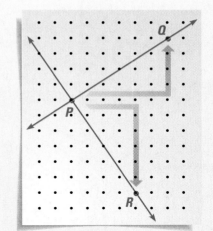

8. **a.** On dot paper, color a dot and label it *J*.

b. From point *J*, move right 8 dots and up 5 dots. Label the resulting point *K*.

c. From point *J*, move right 5 dots and down 8 dots. Label the resulting point *L*.

d. Use a ruler to draw lines $\overleftrightarrow{JK}$ and $\overleftrightarrow{JL}$.

What can you conclude about the two lines?

9. With others in your group, create your own pair of perpendicular lines, like those in Exercises 7 and 8. Explain your steps.

NOW TRY THESE

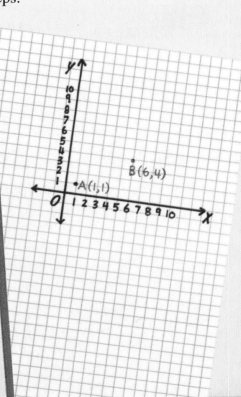

10. Copy the coordinate plane at the right.

a. Plot and label the following points.
A(1, 1), B(6, 4), C(2, 4), D(7, 7), E(3, 10), F(5, 1), G(2, 7)

b. Draw the following lines. Which pairs of lines are parallel? perpendicular? How can you tell?
$\overleftrightarrow{AB}$, $\overleftrightarrow{CD}$, $\overleftrightarrow{EB}$, $\overleftrightarrow{FG}$

c. Label points *P* and *Q* so that line $\overleftrightarrow{PQ}$ is parallel to $\overleftrightarrow{AB}$.

d. Label points *R* and *S* so that line $\overleftrightarrow{RS}$ is perpendicular to $\overleftrightarrow{AB}$.

Parallel, Intersecting, and Perpendicular Lines

What you should learn:

Goal 1 How to identify parallel and intersecting lines

Goal 2 How to identify perpendicular lines

Why you should learn it:

Knowing how to recognize parallel and perpendicular lines can help you make farming decisions. An example is measuring the distance between parallel crop rows.

Goal 1 PARALLEL AND INTERSECTING LINES

In a plane, two lines that never meet are **parallel** . Any two lines in a plane are either parallel or **intersecting** .

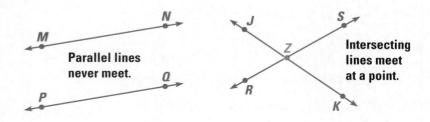

Parallel lines never meet.

Intersecting lines meet at a point.

In the above figures, lines $\overleftrightarrow{MN}$ and $\overleftrightarrow{PQ}$ are parallel, and lines $\overleftrightarrow{JK}$ and $\overleftrightarrow{RS}$ are intersecting.

Example 1 Parallel and Intersecting Lines

In the diagram below, which lines are intersecting? Which lines appear to be parallel?

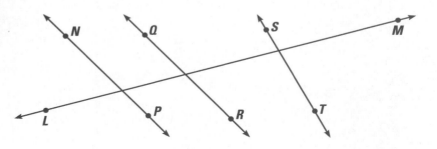

Solution

From the diagram, it is clear that line $\overleftrightarrow{LM}$ intersects the other three lines. To decide whether lines $\overleftrightarrow{NP}$, $\overleftrightarrow{QR}$, and $\overleftrightarrow{ST}$ are parallel or intersecting, you can use tracing paper and a ruler to trace the lines. If you trace the lines carefully and extend them far enough, you will find that line $\overleftrightarrow{ST}$ intersects lines $\overleftrightarrow{NP}$ and $\overleftrightarrow{QR}$. You will also find that lines $\overleftrightarrow{NP}$ and $\overleftrightarrow{QR}$ are parallel.

When lines intersect, they form angles. In Lesson 9.2 you learned how to measure angles with a protractor and classify them as acute, right, or obtuse.

Goal 2 PERPENDICULAR LINES

Two lines that meet at right angles
are **perpendicular** . There are many
examples of perpendicular lines in real
life. For example, the right side and the
top of this page are perpendicular. In
the figure to the right, lines $\overleftrightarrow{AB}$ and
$\overleftrightarrow{CD}$ are perpendicular to line $\overleftrightarrow{PQ}$.

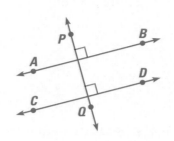

A right angle mark is used to show that
two lines are perpendicular. This is
shown in the diagram at the right.

Example 2 > **Parallel and Perpendicular Lines**

Fold a sheet of paper twice to produce two parallel lines, as shown
below at the left. Label these lines 1 and 2. Then fold the sheet of
paper twice the other way to produce another pair of parallel lines.
Label these lines 3 and 4. Which pairs of lines are perpendicular?

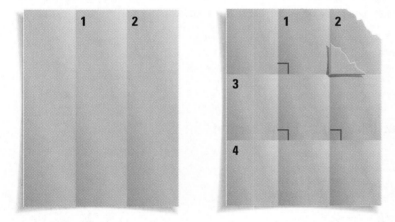

As shown above, the folds produce four pairs of perpendicular lines.

- Line 1 and line 3
- Line 1 and line 4
- Line 2 and line 3
- Line 2 and line 4

✔ **Check:** Tear off a corner of the paper and use it to check that the
lines meet at right angles.

ONGOING ASSESSMENT

Talk About It
....

1. In Example 2, name all
   the pairs of lines that
   appear parallel.

2. How can you tell if two
   lines are parallel?

10.1 Exercises

Extra Practice, page 636

GUIDED PRACTICE

In Exercises 1–3, match the lines with each correct description.

A. Perpendicular **B.** Intersecting **C.** Appear parallel

1.

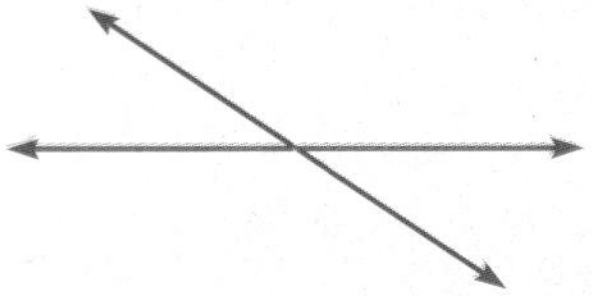

2.

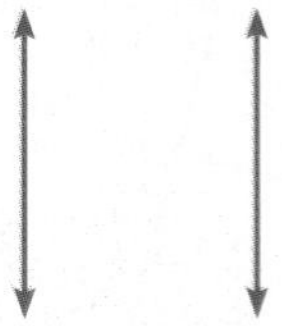

3.

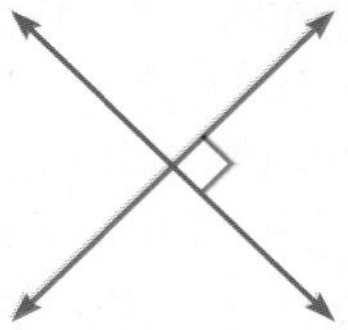

REASONING **In Exercises 4 and 5, decide whether the statement is *true* or *false.* Explain your reasoning.**

4. Perpendicular lines always intersect at right angles.

5. Intersecting lines always intersect at right angles.

6. Make a list of three pairs of parallel lines and three pairs of perpendicular lines that you can see in your classroom.

PRACTICE AND PROBLEM SOLVING

In Exercises 7–10, do the lines appear *parallel* or *intersecting*? Explain.

7.

8.

9.

10.

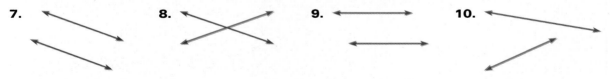

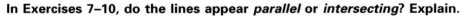

In Exercises 11–14, use the figure at the right to name each of the following.

11. Two lines that appear parallel

12. Two intersecting lines

13. A line that is perpendicular to two lines

14. A line that intersects three other lines

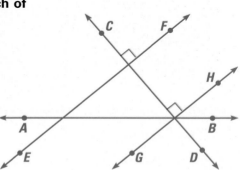

REASONING **In Exercises 15–17, complete the statement using *sometimes, always,* or *never.* Use a sketch to support your answer.**

15. Parallel lines _?_ meet.

16. Intersecting lines are _?_ perpendicular.

17. Perpendicular lines _?_ meet at right angles.

LETTER PUZZLE In Exercises 18–20, use the letter L at the right. When this letter is cut as shown, the pieces can be rearranged to form a square.

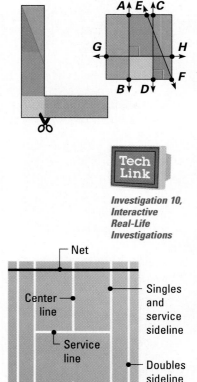

18. Which lines intersect $\overleftrightarrow{AB}$?

19. Which line appears parallel to $\overleftrightarrow{AB}$?

20. Which line is perpendicular to $\overleftrightarrow{AB}$?

21. NEWSPAPERS Your class is printing a newspaper. To make a layout sheet, start with an $8\frac{1}{2}$ in.-by-11 in. piece of paper. Draw a line parallel to the top edge of the paper that is $1\frac{1}{2}$ in. from the edge. Then draw lines parallel to the sides and bottom that are 1 in. from the edge. Explain the steps you used to draw the parallel lines.

Tech Link

Investigation 10, Interactive Real-Life Investigations

TENNIS In Exercises 22–24, use the diagram at the right. It shows the layout of a tennis court.

22. What lines on the tennis court are parallel to the net?

23. What lines on the tennis court are perpendicular to the net?

24. Explain how you know that the service line and the center line are perpendicular.

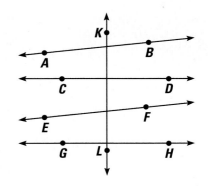

STANDARDIZED TEST PRACTICE

In Exercises 25 and 26, use the figure at the right.

25. How many lines appear parallel to line $\overleftrightarrow{AB}$?

    A 1   **B** 2

    C 3   **D** 4

26. Which lines appear perpendicular to line $\overleftrightarrow{KL}$?

    A $\overleftrightarrow{AB}$ and $\overleftrightarrow{GH}$ **B** $\overleftrightarrow{CD}$ and $\overleftrightarrow{EF}$

    C $\overleftrightarrow{EF}$ and $\overleftrightarrow{GH}$ **D** $\overleftrightarrow{CD}$ and $\overleftrightarrow{GH}$

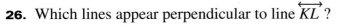

EXPLORATION AND EXTENSION

PORTFOLIO

27. BUILDING YOUR PROJECT Plan the basic layout of your city using parallel and perpendicular streets. Name the streets on your map. Is there a pattern to the way you named them? If so, describe it.

10.2

Angles

What you should learn:

Goal 1 How to identify supplementary and complementary angles

Goal 2 How to draw angles that have a given measure

Why you should learn it:

Knowing how to recognize supplementary and complementary angles can help you with design projects. An example is designing a stained-glass window.

Goal 1 SPECIAL ANGLES

In the figure at the right, the angle labeled 1 can be named $\angle 1$ or $\angle QPS$. Because $\angle 1$ and $\angle 2$ have the same vertex, it is better not to refer to either of the angles as $\angle P$.

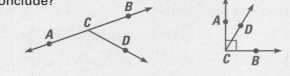

LESSON INVESTIGATION

Investigating Angles

GROUP ACTIVITY Copy the figures below. For each, use a protractor to measure $\angle BCD$ and $\angle ACD$. Repeat this process, redrawing each figure with *D* in a different location. What can you conclude?

In this investigation, you may have discovered that when two angles form a straight line, the sum of their measures is 180°. These angles are **supplementary** . When two angles form a right angle, the sum of their measures is 90°. These angles are **complementary** .

Example 1 Algebra Connection

Find the angle measure by solving for *x*.

a.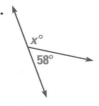

b.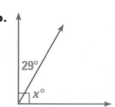

Solution

a. $x + 58 = 180$ **Supplementary angles**

        $x = 122$ **Mental math**

b. $x + 29 = 90$ **Complementary angles**

        $x = 61$ **Mental math**

In Lesson 9.2, you learned how to use a protractor to *measure* angles. You can also use a protractor to *draw* angles with a given measure.

Example 2 Using a Protractor

Draw an angle whose measure is 55°.

Solution

a. Begin by drawing a ray. Mark the end point of the ray. This is the vertex of the angle.

b. Line up the 0° line of the protractor with the ray. Place the protractor's center on the end point of the ray, or vertex.

c. Use the protractor and a pencil to mark a measure of 55°.

d. Use a ruler to draw the second ray of the angle.

If two angles have the same measure, then they are said to be **congruent** angles.

Example 3 Drawing Congruent Angles

Draw an angle that is congruent to the angle labeled $x°$ on the stained-glass pattern at the right.

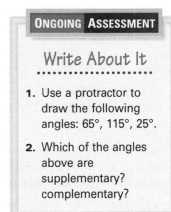

Solution

Using a protractor, you can find that the measure of x is 40°. To draw a congruent angle, use the steps in Example 2. The resulting angle will look like the figure at the right.

40°

Real Life... Real Facts

Stained Glass

Frank Lloyd Wright designed this stained-glass panel. It includes supplementary and complementary angles.

ONGOING ASSESSMENT

Write About It

1. Use a protractor to draw the following angles: 65°, 115°, 25°.

2. Which of the angles above are supplementary? complementary?

10.2 Exercises

Extra Practice, page 637

Guided Practice

In Exercises 1–5, use the figure at the right to complete the statements.

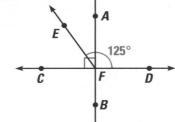

1. Lines $\overleftrightarrow{AB}$ and $\overleftrightarrow{CD}$ are _?_.
2. $\angle CFE$ and $\angle EFA$ are _?_ angles.
3. $\angle CFE$ has a measure of ? .
4. $\angle EFA$ has a measure of ? .
5. In the figure, name three pairs of supplementary angles.
6. Give a real-life example of two angles that are complementary and two angles that are supplementary.
7. **REASONING** Use the diagram at the right. The following steps give a logical argument that $\angle 1$ and $\angle 4$ are congruent. Discuss how you know each step is correct.
   a. The measure of $\angle 3$ is 55°.
   b. The measure of $\angle 4$ is 125°.
   c. $\angle 1$ and $\angle 4$ are congruent.

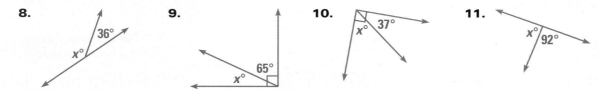

Given:
- $\angle 1$ and $\angle 3$ are supplementary.
- $\angle 3$ and $\angle 4$ are supplementary.
- The measure of $\angle 1$ is 125°.

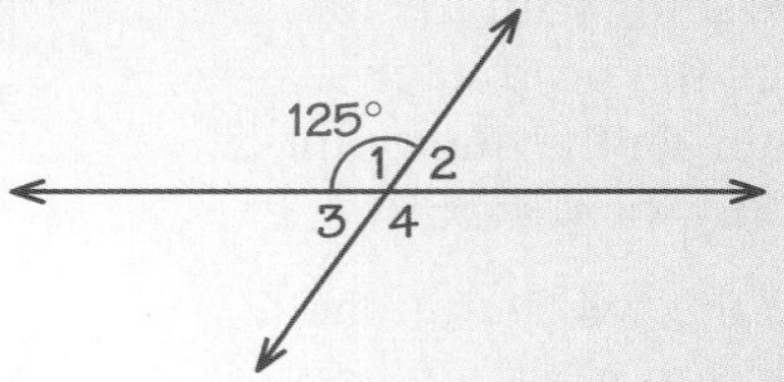

Practice and Problem Solving

ALGEBRA AND MENTAL MATH **In Exercises 8–11, find the angle measure by solving for *x*.**

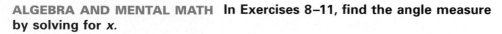

8.

9.

10.

11.

MEASUREMENT **In Exercises 12–15, find the measure of the angle that is complementary to the given angle. Use a protractor to draw both angles.**

12. 20°
13. 55°
14. 30°
15. 70°

MEASUREMENT **In Exercises 16–19, find the measure of the angle that is supplementary to the given angle. Use a protractor to draw both angles.**

16. 160°
17. 100°
18. 40°
19. 30°

In Exercises 20 and 21, decide whether the statement is *true* or *false*. Give examples to support your answer.

20. If two angles are complementary, then both must be acute.

21. If two angles are supplementary, then one must be acute and one must be obtuse.

LOGICAL REASONING In Exercises 22–25, use the diagram of an air hockey game shown at the right.

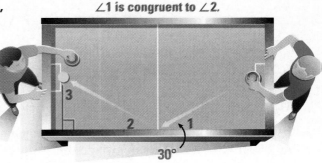

∠1 is congruent to ∠2.

22. Find the measure of ∠3. Explain your reasoning.

23. How are ∠1 and ∠2 related?

24. How are ∠2 and ∠3 related?

25. How are ∠1 and ∠3 related?

26. WASHINGTON, DC Look at the map of Washington, DC, on page 471. Notice how G Street, New Jersey Avenue, and 1st Street form a set of complementary angles. Find another set of complementary angles.

STANDARDIZED TEST PRACTICE

In Exercises 27 and 28, use the figure at the right.

27. Find the measure of the angle labeled $x°$.

Ⓐ 48°   Ⓑ 58°   Ⓒ 62°   Ⓓ 68°

28. Find the measure of the angle labeled $y°$.

Ⓐ 22°   Ⓑ 32°   Ⓒ 42°   Ⓓ 132°

EXPLORATION AND EXTENSION

PORTFOLIO

29. BUILDING YOUR PROJECT The map of Washington, DC, on p. 471, shows that Pennsylvania Avenue and New Jersey Avenue form spokes that lead to the Capitol Building. Think of a central point of interest for your city, and add a few streets leading directly to it. Do these streets form sets of complementary angles with any of the other streets?

In Exercises 1–3, write the fraction shown by the model. (6.1)

1. 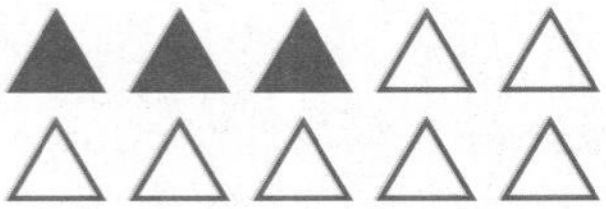 ▲ ▲ ▲ △ △
   △ △ △ △ △

2. 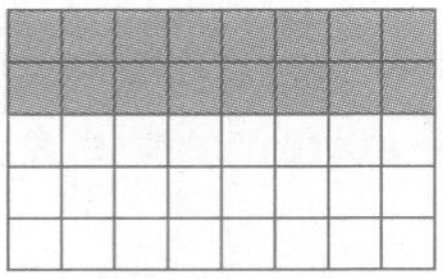 [grid model]

3. [rectangle model]

TECHNOLOGY In Exercises 4–8, use a calculator to help you rewrite the fraction as a decimal (round to nearest hundredth) and as a percent. (3.4, 3.6)

4. $\dfrac{4}{5}$ 5. $\dfrac{3}{8}$ 6. $\dfrac{2}{3}$ 7. $\dfrac{11}{20}$ 8. $\dfrac{15}{19}$

9. **WALKING** You are participating in a charity walk that is 15 mi long. It takes you $\dfrac{2}{5}$ h to walk 1 mi. (4.4, 8.1)

   a. How long will it take you to complete the charity walk?

   b. If you raise $4.75 for each mile that you walk, how much money will you raise after you complete the 15 mi?

HISTORY Connection

ALMANACS

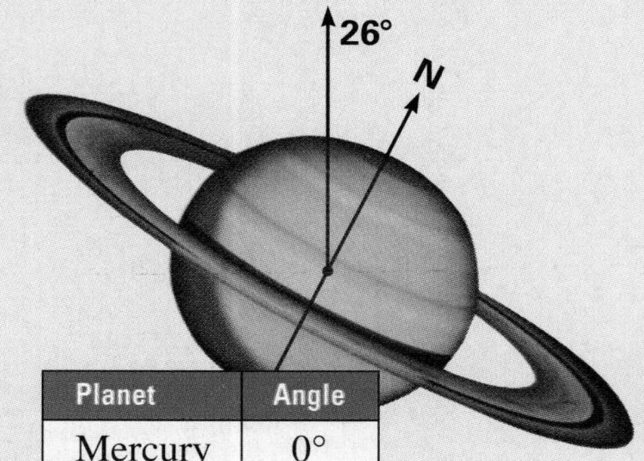

26°

N

Planet	Angle
Mercury	0°
Venus	3°
Earth	23°
Mars	25°
Jupiter	3°
Saturn	26°
Uranus	98°
Neptune	28°
Pluto	60°

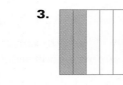

Benjamin Banneker, the son of a freed slave, was a writer, inventor, and mathematician. He taught himself the mathematics of star charts by reading borrowed textbooks. After being appointed to the surveying team that would plan the District of Columbia, Banneker was able to publish annual editions of almanacs from 1791 through 1802.

As each planet rotates around the sun, it is tilted at an angle. The picture shows that Saturn tilts at an angle of 26°.

1. Does Earth tilt more than Venus? Explain.

2. Using a protractor, draw a picture of what Earth looks like as it rotates around the sun.

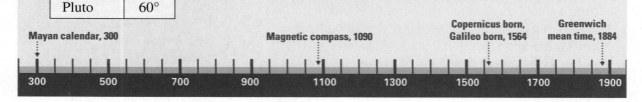

Mayan calendar, 300   Magnetic compass, 1090   Copernicus born, Galileo born, 1564   Greenwich mean time, 1884

300   500   700   900   1100   1300   1500   1700   1900

The Sum of the Angles

You know that the measures of the angles in a triangle add up to 180°. You will find that something similar happens with the angles of a quadrilateral.

Example

Draw three large quadrilaterals on a sheet of paper. Use a protractor to measure the angles of each quadrilateral. For each quadrilateral, find the sum of the angle measures.

Solution

Begin by drawing three quadrilaterals. Then measure the angles of each. An example is shown at the left. You can use a calculator to find the sum of the measures. Compare the sums.

Quadrilateral 1

95 [+] 80 [+] 55 [+] 130 [=]

Quadrilateral 2

60 [+] 120 [+] 60 [+] 120 [=]

Quadrilateral 3

90 [+] 90 [+] 90 [+] 90 [=]

Exercises

1. **PARTNER ACTIVITY** Try the above experiment with a partner. Make your quadrilaterals different from those above. Compare your totals with your partner's totals. Do you get the same results?

2. From the results of the example and Exercise 1, write a statement about the sum of the measures of the angles of a quadrilateral.

In Exercises 3–5, use a calculator to find the measure of the fourth angle. Then use a protractor to check your answer.

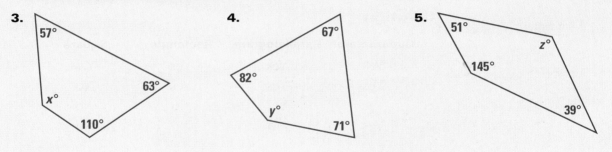

3.

57°
63°
$x°$
110°

4.

67°
82°
$y°$
71°

5.

51°
$z°$
145°
39°

10.3

Parallelograms

What you should learn:

Goal 1 How to identify parallelograms

Goal 2 How to use properties of parallelograms

Why you should learn it:

Knowing properties of parallelograms can help you find the sum of the angle measures of a parallelogram.

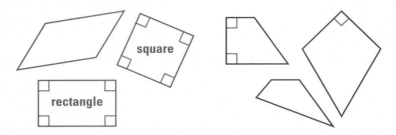

Goal 1 IDENTIFYING PARALLELOGRAMS

A **parallelogram** is a quadrilateral whose opposite sides are parallel. A **rectangle** is a special parallelogram that has four right angles. A **square** is a special rectangle that has four sides of the same length.

These are parallelograms.   **These are not parallelograms.**

square

rectangle

Example 1 Classifying Quadrilaterals

By inspection, decide whether each quadrilateral is a parallelogram, a rectangle, or a square.

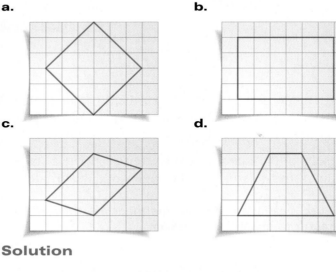

a.

b.

c.

d.

Solution

	Quadrilateral	Parallelogram	Rectangle	Square
a.	Yes	Yes	Yes	Yes
b.	Yes	Yes	Yes	No
c.	Yes	Yes	No	No
d.	Yes	No	No	No

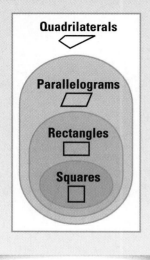

STUDY TIP

The Venn diagram below shows: all parallelograms are quadrilaterals; all rectangles are parallelograms; and all squares are rectangles.

Quadrilaterals

Parallelograms

Rectangles

Squares

Goal 2 **PROPERTIES OF PARALLELOGRAMS**

LESSON INVESTIGATION

Investigating Parallelograms

GROUP ACTIVITY Each person in your group should draw two parallelograms on grid paper. Use a ruler and a protractor to measure the sides and angles of your parallelograms. Discuss any patterns that you see.

COOPERATIVE LEARNING

Scissors Lift
Parallelograms are used when a part of a machine needs to stay level as it moves up and down. This scissors lift is an example.

In this investigation, you may have discovered the following properties of parallelograms.

PROPERTIES OF PARALLELOGRAMS

In a parallelogram,

1. opposite sides have the same length.
2. opposite angles have the same measure.

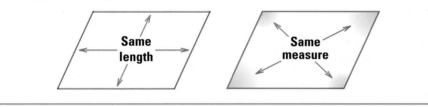

Same length

Same measure

Example 2 **Using Properties of Parallelograms**

In the parallelogram *ABCD*, you are given the measures of ∠*A* and ∠*B*.

a. Find the measures of ∠*C* and ∠*D*.

b. Find the sum of the measures of the four angles.

Solution

a. Because *ABCD* is a parallelogram, you know that opposite angles have the same measure.

Measure of ∠*C* = Measure of ∠*A* = 50°

Measure of ∠*D* = Measure of ∠*B* = 130°

b. The sum of the four angles is 50° + 130° + 50° + 130° = 360°.

ONGOING ASSESSMENT

Write About It
....

1. Draw a large parallelogram with a 60° angle.

2. Use a protractor to measure the other angles.

3. Explain how to find the measures *without* using a protractor.

In Exercises 1–4, match the polygon with the sentence or sentences that describe it. (You can use each sentence more than once.)

A. It has four right angles.

B. It has four sides of equal length.

C. It has four sides.

D. It has opposite sides that are parallel.

1. Square **2.** Quadrilateral **3.** Parallelogram **4.** Rectangle

5. **VISUAL THINKING** Use the figure at the right. Name one of each type of the polygons listed below.

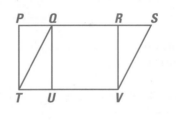

    a. Square   **b.** Parallelogram

    c. Rectangle   **d.** Quadrilateral

6. **ACT IT OUT** Thread four straws of equal length together with a string, as shown in the diagram at the right. Without bending the straws, can you arrange them to form a quadrilateral that is not a parallelogram? Can you form a rectangle that is not a square? Explain why or why not. (The straws must lie flat.)

In Exercises 7–10, describe the figure using one or more words from the following list: *square, rectangle, parallelogram, quadrilateral.*

7.    **8.** 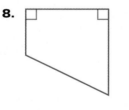   **9.** 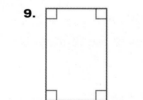   **10.**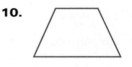

REASONING In Exercises 11–14, decide whether the statement is *true* or *false*. If false, support your answer with a drawing.

11. All rectangles are parallelograms.   **12.** All rectangles are squares.

13. All quadrilaterals are parallelograms.   **14.** All squares are parallelograms.

SYMMETRY Decide whether the quadrilateral has line symmetry. If so, copy it and draw the line or lines of symmetry.

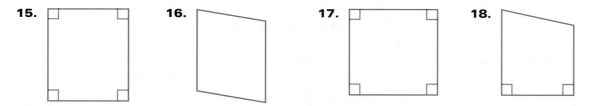

15.   16.   17.   18.

In Exercises 19–21, discuss whether the parallelogram is a *rectangle*, *square*, *both*, or *neither*. Then find the missing measures.

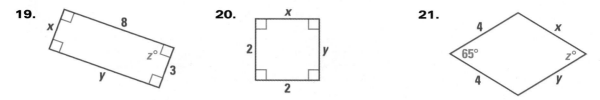

19.   20.   21.

22. **WASHINGTON, DC** Look at the map of Washington, DC, on page 471. Notice that Massachusetts and Pennsylvania Avenues seem to make a parallelogram with 3rd and 7th Streets. Measure the angles with a protractor to see if this is really a parallelogram.

STANDARDIZED TEST PRACTICE

23. One of the following statements is true. Which one?

    Ⓐ All quadrilaterals have four right angles.

    Ⓑ A parallelogram can have four right angles.

    Ⓒ A quadrilateral can have three obtuse angles.

    Ⓓ The sum of the angles of a parallelogram is 180°.

24. What is the sum of the angles of a quadrilateral?

    Ⓐ 90°   Ⓑ 180°   Ⓒ 360°   Ⓓ 720°

EXPLORATION AND EXTENSION

PORTFOLIO

25. **BUILDING YOUR PROJECT** Are there any streets that form nonrectangular parallelograms in your city? If not, add a street or two so that a nonrectangular parallelogram is formed. Measure the angles of the parallelogram.

LAB 10.4

Investigating the Area of a Triangle

Materials Needed
- grid paper
- colored pencils or markers
- ruler
- scissors

Part A CUTTING PARALLELOGRAMS INTO TRIANGLES

1. Draw a parallelogram on grid paper. (Each person in your group should try to draw a different one.) Cut it out. Draw a *diagonal* on the parallelogram. Cut along the diagonal to form two triangles. Compare the triangles. What can you conclude?

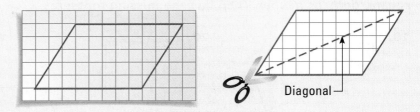

Diagonal

Part B FORMING RECTANGLES FROM TRIANGLES

2. Use the triangles you made in Exercise 1. Fold one of them to form a crease that is perpendicular to the longest side and goes through the opposite vertex. Cut along the crease. Rearrange the three pieces to form a rectangle.

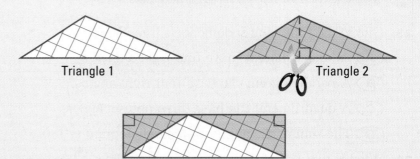

Triangle 1   Triangle 2

3. Measure the sides of your rectangle. What is its area?

4. How is the area of Triangle 1 related to the area of the rectangle? Use the area of the rectangle to find the area of Triangle 1.

5. Compare your results with the results of others in your group. What patterns do you observe?

6. a. Draw an acute triangle on grid paper. Draw one side on a grid line. Locate each vertex at a grid point. Then draw a rectangle that encloses the triangle. A sample is shown below.

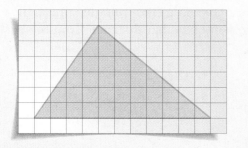 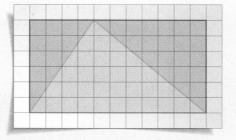

   b. Each small square on the grid is 1 unit by 1 unit. Find the area of your rectangle.

   c. Cut out your rectangle. Then cut the original triangle out of the rectangle. This should make three triangles: the original and two smaller triangles. Compare the original triangle to the two smaller triangles. What can you conclude? What is the area of the original triangle?

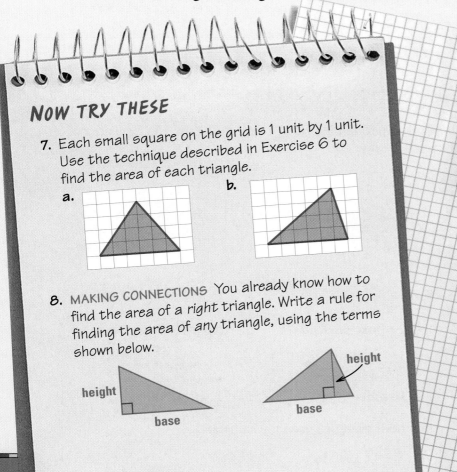

NOW TRY THESE

7. Each small square on the grid is 1 unit by 1 unit. Use the technique described in Exercise 6 to find the area of each triangle.

   a.   **b.**

8. MAKING CONNECTIONS You already know how to find the area of a right triangle. Write a rule for finding the area of any triangle, using the terms shown below.

height base

height base

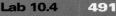

10.4 Area of a Triangle

What you should learn:

Goal 1 How to find the area of a triangle

Goal 2 How to use the area of a triangle to solve real-life problems

Why you should learn it:

Knowing how to find the area of a triangle can help you plan a project. An example is finding how much material you need to make a sail for a sailboat.

Goal 1 AREA OF A TRIANGLE

Any side of a triangle can be labeled as the triangle's **base**. The **height** of the triangle is the perpendicular distance from the base to the opposite vertex.

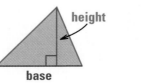 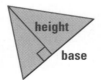

AREA OF A TRIANGLE

The **area** of a triangle is one half the product of the base and height of the triangle. An example is given.

$$\text{Area of Triangle} = \frac{1}{2} \times \textbf{base} \times \textbf{height}$$

$$= \frac{1}{2} \times 12 \times 7$$

$$= 42 \text{ units}^2$$

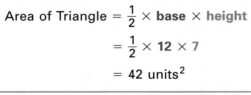

Example 1 Finding the Area of a Triangle

Each small square in the grid is 1 unit by 1 unit. Find the area of each triangle.

a. 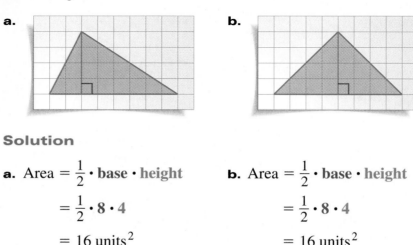 b.

Solution

a. Area $= \frac{1}{2} \cdot \textbf{base} \cdot \textbf{height}$

$= \frac{1}{2} \cdot 8 \cdot 4$

$= 16 \text{ units}^2$

b. Area $= \frac{1}{2} \cdot \textbf{base} \cdot \textbf{height}$

$= \frac{1}{2} \cdot 8 \cdot 4$

$= 16 \text{ units}^2$

Notice that both triangles have the same area.

STUDY TIP

Even though any side of a triangle can be labeled as its base, there is often one side that is the most convenient. For example, the side $\overline{AB}$ is most convenient in the triangle below.

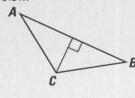

Example 2 Finding the Area of a Triangle

You are making sails for the sailboat shown below. How much material is in the two sails?

Solution

Each sail is a right triangle.

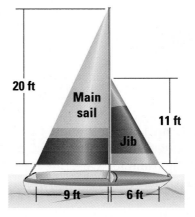

$$\text{Area of Jib} = \frac{1}{2} \cdot \text{base} \cdot \text{height}$$

$$= \frac{1}{2} \cdot 6 \cdot 11$$

$$= 33 \text{ ft}^2$$

$$\text{Area of Main Sail} = \frac{1}{2} \cdot \text{base} \cdot \text{height}$$

$$= \frac{1}{2} \cdot 9 \cdot 20$$

$$= 90 \text{ ft}^2$$

So, the total amount of material in the two sails is

$$33 + 90 = 123 \text{ ft}^2.$$

Example 3 Measuring a Triangle

You are using the piece of wood at the right for a project. Find its area.

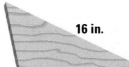
16 in.

Solution

Use a tool called a square to measure the height.

$$\text{Area} = \frac{1}{2} \cdot \text{base} \cdot \text{height}$$

$$= \frac{1}{2} \cdot 16 \cdot 5\frac{3}{4}$$

$$= \frac{1}{2} \cdot 16 \cdot \frac{23}{4}$$

$$= 46$$

The area is 46 in.^{2}

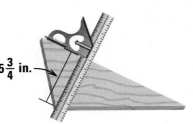
$5\frac{3}{4}$ in.

ONGOING ASSESSMENT

Talk About It
....

Draw a large obtuse triangle and have a partner draw a large acute triangle.

1. Use a ruler to find the area of your triangle.

2. Trade and find the area of your partner's triangle.

3. Compare your results.

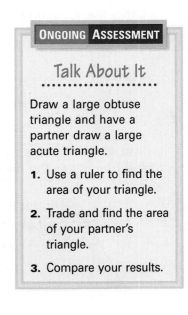

GUIDED PRACTICE

In Exercises 1–3, find the area of the triangle described.

1. base = 8, height = 6   **2.** base = 8, height = 3   **3.** base = 6, height = 3

4. ERROR ANALYSIS Your friend wants to find the area of the triangle below. Describe your friend's error.

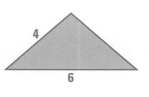

Area = $\frac{1}{2}$ × base × height

= $\frac{1}{2}$ × 6 × 4

= 12   ✗

5. COMMUNICATING Draw a triangle that has an area of 18 square units. What is the base and height of the triangle? Describe how you made the triangle.

6. COOKING The Greek dessert *baklava* is a pastry made with walnuts and honey that is sometimes cut into a triangle, as shown at the right. Find the area of the triangle.

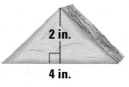

2 in.

4 in.

PRACTICE AND PROBLEM SOLVING

In Exercises 7–10, find the area of the triangle.

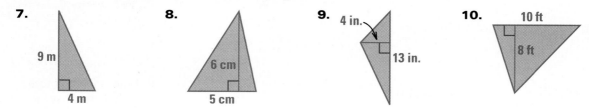

7. 9 m, 4 m

8. 6 cm, 5 cm

9. 4 in., 13 in.

10. 10 ft, 8 ft

MEASUREMENT Use a metric ruler to measure the base and the height of the triangle to the nearest centimeter. Find the area.

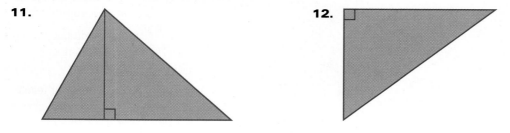

11.

12.

In Exercises 13–15, find the area of each polygon.

13.

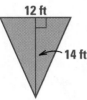

14.

15.

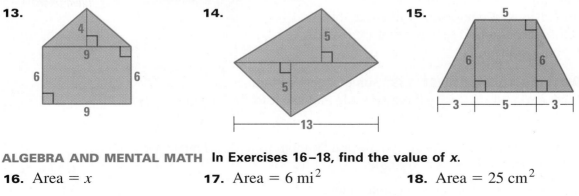

ALGEBRA AND MENTAL MATH **In Exercises 16–18, find the value of x.**

16. Area = x

17. Area = 6 mi^2

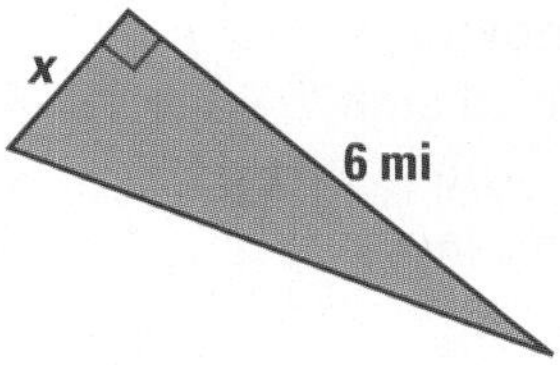

18. Area = 25 cm^2

12 ft

14 ft

x

6 mi

x

5 cm

19. **GREENHOUSE** You are helping build a greenhouse. The walls and the roof are made up of the two pieces shown below.

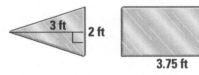

3 ft   **2 ft**   **2 ft**

3.75 ft

a. Find the area of each piece.

b. There are 27 triangular and 62 rectangular pieces that make up the walls and roof. Find the total area covered by the pieces of glass.

20. **GEOGRAPHY** The diagram shows the approximate dimensions of Nevada. Use a calculator to estimate the area of the state.

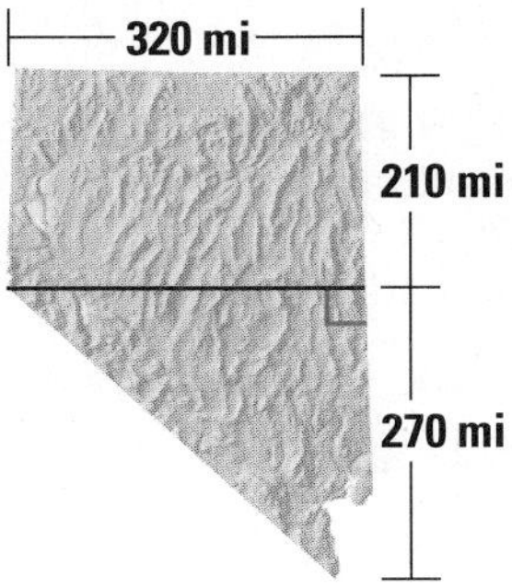

┣— **320 mi** —┫

210 mi

270 mi

STANDARDIZED TEST PRACTICE

21. The figure at the right is made up of a rectangle and congruent right triangles. Find its area.

6 mm

3 mm

9 mm

Ⓐ 54 mm^2 **Ⓑ** 81 mm^2

Ⓒ 98 mm^2 **Ⓓ** 108 mm^2

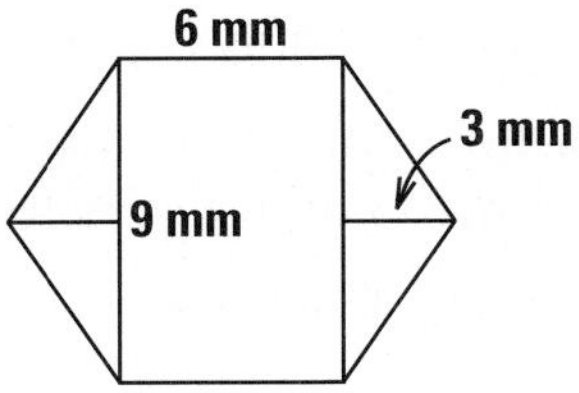

22. WASHINGTON, DC The Vietnam Veterans Memorial in Washington, DC, is formed by two granite walls that are equal in size. The diagram at the right shows the dimensions of one of the walls. Use this information to find the area that is covered by both walls.

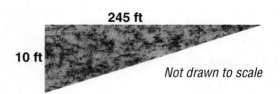

245 ft

10 ft

Not drawn to scale

23. BUILDING YOUR PROJECT Find some streets on your map that form a triangle. Identify the map scale and use it to find the area enclosed by the streets.

24. ACT IT OUT In your classroom, form a "human triangle." The triangle should be a right triangle.

  a. Have 3 people stand along one side of the triangle, 4 people along another side, and 5 people along the third side, as shown at the right. Outline your triangle using string or masking tape.

  b. What is the area of the triangle *in people*? This number of people should be able to comfortably stand inside the outline of the triangle.

  c. Find the area using the formula for the area of a triangle. How does this area compare to the area *in people*? Explain.

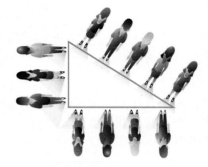

SPIRAL REVIEW

NUMBER THEORY In Exercises 1–3, find the least common multiple of the numbers. (7.2)

  1. 4, 7   **2.** 12, 15   **3.** 6, 8

ALGEBRA In Exercises 4–9, evaluate the expression. (2.5)

  4. $5 \times (4 + 3)$ **5.** $10 \times 5 - 2 \times 7$ **6.** $16 - 4 \div 2$

  7. $7 + 3 \times 5$ **8.** $10 \times 2 \times 3$ **9.** $(2 + 13) \div 5 + 1$

10. MAKING A MAP You leave home and ride your bike 3 blocks east and 4 blocks north to the post office. You then ride 2 blocks east and 1 block south to the grocery store. Finally, you ride 3 blocks west and 3 blocks south to your friend's house. (9.5)

  a. Make a coordinate map showing the locations of the places you stopped. Assume your house is located at the origin.

  b. How many blocks from you does your friend live?

Take this test as you would take a test in class. The answers to the exercises are given in the back of the book.

In Exercises 1–6, use the figure at the right to name a line or angle that fits the description. (10.1, 10.2)

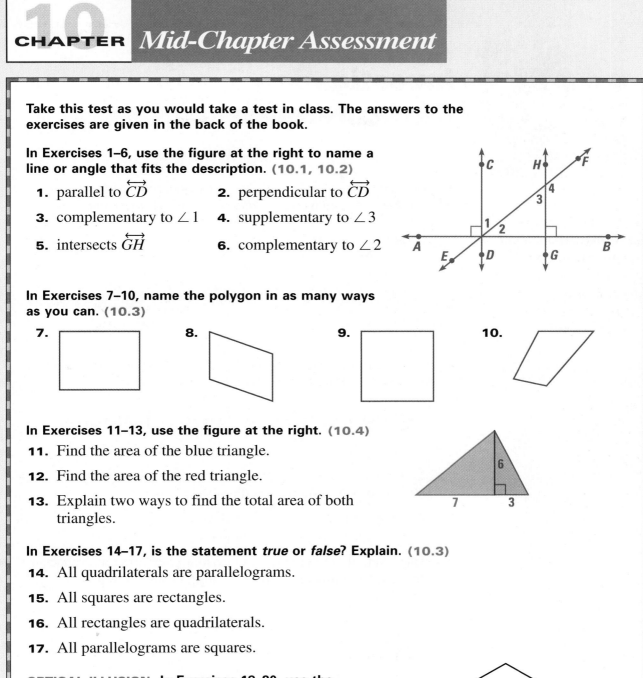

1. parallel to $\overleftrightarrow{CD}$

2. perpendicular to $\overleftrightarrow{CD}$

3. complementary to $\angle 1$

4. supplementary to $\angle 3$

5. intersects $\overleftrightarrow{GH}$

6. complementary to $\angle 2$

In Exercises 7–10, name the polygon in as many ways as you can. (10.3)

7.

8.

9.

10.

In Exercises 11–13, use the figure at the right. (10.4)

11. Find the area of the blue triangle.

12. Find the area of the red triangle.

13. Explain two ways to find the total area of both triangles.

In Exercises 14–17, is the statement *true* or *false*? Explain. (10.3)

14. All quadrilaterals are parallelograms.

15. All squares are rectangles.

16. All rectangles are quadrilaterals.

17. All parallelograms are squares.

OPTICAL ILLUSION In Exercises 18–20, use the optical illusion at the right. (10.3, 10.4)

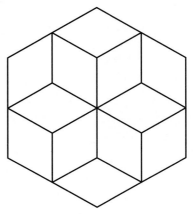

18. How many parallelograms are in the optical illusion?

19. Each parallelogram in the optical illusion can be divided into two acute triangles. If each triangle has a base of 10 units and a height of 8.7 units then find the area of each parallelogram.

20. Find the area of the optical illusion. (*Hint:* Use your answers from Exercises 18 and 19.)

LAB 10.5

Investigating Circumference

Materials Needed
• construction paper
• pencils or pens
• ruler
• scissors
• round can
• calculator

Throughout history, many people have wondered about the relationship between a circle's *diameter* and *circumference*.

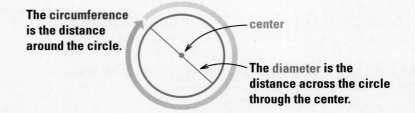

The circumference is the distance around the circle.

center

The diameter is the distance across the circle through the center.

In this lab, you can try experiments that were first tried thousands of years ago. See if you can discover the amazing result!

Part A CIRCUMFERENCE IN TERMS OF DIAMETER

1. Cut two 1 in. wide strips out of construction paper.

2. Use one of the strips to measure the diameter of the can. Cut this strip so it is exactly the length of the diameter.

3. Use the other strip to measure the circumference of the can. Cut this strip so that it wraps around the can exactly once.

4. Use your "diameter strip" to measure your "circumference strip." In terms of diameter strips, how long is the circumference strip?

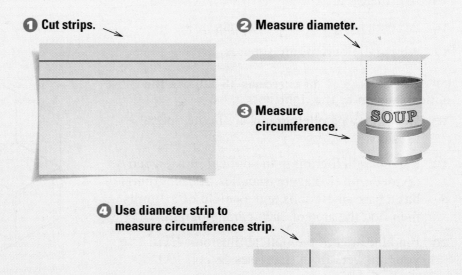

❶ Cut strips.

❷ Measure diameter.

❸ Measure circumference.

SOUP

❹ Use diameter strip to measure circumference strip.

5. a. Measure and cut a sheet of construction paper into eleven 1 in. strips. Mark and cut the strips as shown at the right.

b. One person should hold and tape each strip end to end so that it forms a circle. Another should use a ruler to measure the diameter of the circle to the nearest quarter inch.

c. A third person should record the results in a table. Do this for all eleven strips.

Circumference (in.)	3.5	4.0	4.5	5.0	5.5	6.0	6.5	7.0	7.5	8.0	8.5
Diameter (in.)	?	?	?	?	?	?	?	?	?	?	?
Circumference ÷ Diameter	?	?	?	?	?	?	?	?	?	?	?

6. **TECHNOLOGY** Complete the third row of your table. Round to the nearest tenth. With others in your group, discuss any patterns that you see. Can you see the amazing result that has fascinated people for thousands of years?

In Exercises 5 and 6, you may have discovered that the quotient of the circumference and the diameter is about 3 for *any* circle. The ancient Greeks called this quotient *pi*. It is written as π.

7. Use the results of your table to write a decimal approximation for π. To do this, use a calculator to find the average of the quotients in your table.

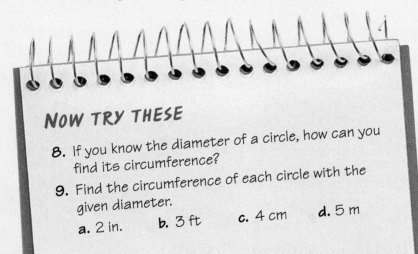

NOW TRY THESE

8. If you know the diameter of a circle, how can you find its circumference?

9. Find the circumference of each circle with the given diameter.

   a. 2 in.   **b.** 3 ft   **c.** 4 cm   **d.** 5 m

10.5

Circumference of a Circle

What you should learn:

Goal 1 How to find the circumference of a circle

Goal 2 How to use the circumference of a circle to solve real-life problems

Why you should learn it:

Knowing how to find the circumference of a circle can help you measure distances. An example is finding the distance around the Rotunda of the Capitol Building.

Goal 1 CIRCUMFERENCE OF A CIRCLE

Every point on a circle is the same distance from the center. The **diameter** of a circle is the distance across the circle through the center. The **circumference** is the distance around a circle.

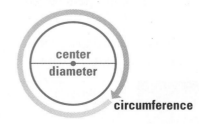

CIRCUMFERENCE OF A CIRCLE

To find the circumference of a circle, multiply the diameter by π. The symbol "π" is the Greek letter **pi**. A decimal approximation for π is 3.14.

$$\text{Circumference} = \pi \times \text{diameter} \qquad C = \pi \cdot d$$

Example 1 Finding Circumferences

Find the circumference of each circle.

a.

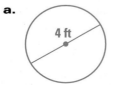

b.

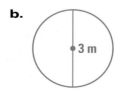

TOOLBOX

Multiplying with a Decimal, page 643

NEED TO KNOW

The reason the number *pi* is shown by the special symbol π is because its decimal representation has an unending number of digits that have no pattern. Here are some of the digits.

$\pi = 3.141592653589\ldots$

Solution

a. Circumference $= \pi \times$ **diameter**

$\approx 3.14 \times 4$ Diameter is 4 ft.

≈ 12.56 ft   Multiply.

The circumference is about 12.56 ft.

b. Circumference $= \pi \times$ **diameter**

$\approx 3.14 \times 3$ Diameter is 3 m.

≈ 9.42 m   Multiply.

The circumference is about 9.42 m.

Goal 2 SOLVING REAL-LIFE PROBLEMS

Example 2 **Estimating a Distance**

The diagram below shows the Rotunda of the Capitol Building. Around the edge of the Rotunda are 12 statues. About how far apart are the statues?

Solution

Circumference = $\pi \times$ diameter

$$\approx 3.14 \times 96$$

$$\approx 301.44 \text{ ft}$$

Divide 301.44 by 12 to find the distance between the statues.

$$\frac{301.44}{12} = 25.12 \text{ ft}$$

96 ft

The distance between the statues will be a small amount less than 25.12 ft. This is because the diameter of the circle formed by the statues is smaller than the diameter of the Rotunda.

**Real Life...
Real Facts**

Capitol Building
The painting at the top of the dome in the Rotunda was done by the Italian painter Constantino Brumidi. It is called *The Apotheosis of George Washington*.

Example 3 **Estimating an Age**

STRATEGY **WORK BACKWARD** A hemlock tree adds about $\frac{1}{4}$ in. to its diameter, d, each year. You find the circumference, C, of a tree to be 60 in. To estimate the age of the tree, find its diameter.

$$C = \pi \cdot d$$ Formula for circumference.

$$60 \approx 3.14 \cdot d$$ Substitute 60 for C and 3.14 for π.

$$\frac{60}{3.14} \approx d$$ Divide to undo multiplication.

$$19 \text{ in.} \approx d$$ Use a calculator. Round to the nearest inch.

Knowing the diameter, you can find the age of the tree.

$$d = \frac{1}{4} \text{ in.} \times (\text{age of tree})$$ Formula for age of a tree.

$$19 \approx \frac{1}{4} \text{ in.} \times (\text{age of tree})$$ Substitute 19 for d.

$$76 \approx \text{age of tree}$$ Divide to undo multiplication.

The tree is about 76 years old.

ONGOING ASSESSMENT

Write About It

Find the diameter of the circle, given the circumference. Show your work and explain your steps.

1. $C = 14$ ft

2. $C = 9$ m

10.5 *Circumference of a Circle* **501**

GUIDED PRACTICE

In Exercises 1–3, use the diagram at the right to match the name with the part of the circle. Then give a definition for the part.

A. *P*   **B.** *Q*   **C.** *R*

1. Diameter   **2.** Center   **3.** Circumference

4. Find the circumference of a circle with a diameter of 4.5 ft.

5. Find the diameter of the circle.

$C = 22$

PRACTICE AND PROBLEM SOLVING

MEASUREMENT In Exercises 6–9, find the circumference of the circle. Each square on the grid is 1 unit by 1 unit.

6.   **7.**   **8.**   **9.**

 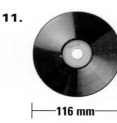 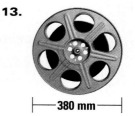 

TECHNOLOGY In Exercises 10–13, use a calculator to find the circumference.

10.   **11.**   **12.**   **13.**

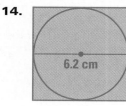 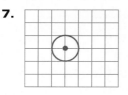 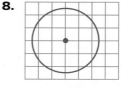 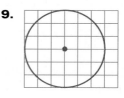

⊢— 1.5 ft —⊣   ⊢—116 mm—⊣   ⊢— 10.5 in. —⊣   ⊢—380 mm—⊣

REASONING In Exercises 14 and 15, use a calculator to find the perimeter and area of the quadrilateral.

14.   **15.**

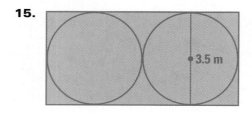

6.2 cm   3.5 m

In Exercises 16–19, find the circumference of a circle with the given diameter.

16. 10 in.   **17.** 20 in.   **18.** 8 ft   **19.** 16 ft

20. REASONING What happens to the circumference of a circle if you double its diameter? Use the results of Exercises 16–19 to support your answer.

21. SOAP BOX DERBY You are racing in the Soap Box Derby in a car with wheels that are 20 inches in diameter. Use a calculator to find about how many times your wheels will rotate in complete circles if the race is 1,000 ft. (*Hint:* Start by finding the circumference of the wheels, in feet.)

Real Life... **R**eal People

Danielle Del Farraro, 14, of Ohio, is the 1st two-time winner of the Soap Box Derby.

22. AMUSEMENT PARK You are spending the day at an amusement park. You ride a Ferris wheel that has a circumference of 785 ft. Find the diameter of the Ferris wheel.

STANDARDIZED TEST PRACTICE

23. A carousel has an outside diameter of 35 ft and an inside diameter of 20 ft. Which expression can you use to determine how far you will travel if you ride on the outer edge of the carousel?

- **(A)** 20π
- **(B)** 35π
- **(C)** $20^2\pi$
- **(D)** $35^2\pi$

EXPLORATION AND EXTENSION

24. EXPLORING CIRCLES The figure shows a 12 sided polygon inside a circle.

a. Use a calculator to find the perimeter of the polygon and the circumference of the circle. Compare the two numbers. What can you conclude?

b. Find the perimeter of a 16 sided polygon with each side measuring 0.78 in. surrounded by the same circle.

c. Is the perimeter of the 16 sided polygon closer to the circumference of the circle than the perimeter of the 12 sided polygon? Explain your reasoning.

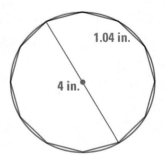

1.04 in.

4 in.

LAB 10.6

COOPERATIVE LEARNING

Investigating the Area of a Circle

Materials Needed
• paper
• pencils or pens
• scissors
• tape
• calculator

In Lesson 10.5, you learned that the diameter is the distance across the circle through the center. The distance from the center of the circle to a point on the circle is called the *radius* of the circle.

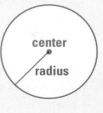

center
radius

The diameter of a circle is twice its radius.

Diameter = 2 × radius

1. Begin with a circle whose circumference is shaded. Follow the steps below. When you are done, you will have cut a circle into wedges and rearranged the wedges to form a figure that is almost rectangular.

1 Fold the circle in half, four times.

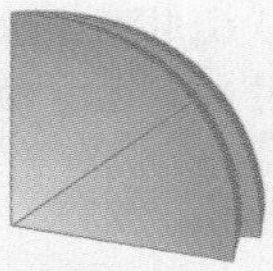

2 Cut the circle into 16 wedges.

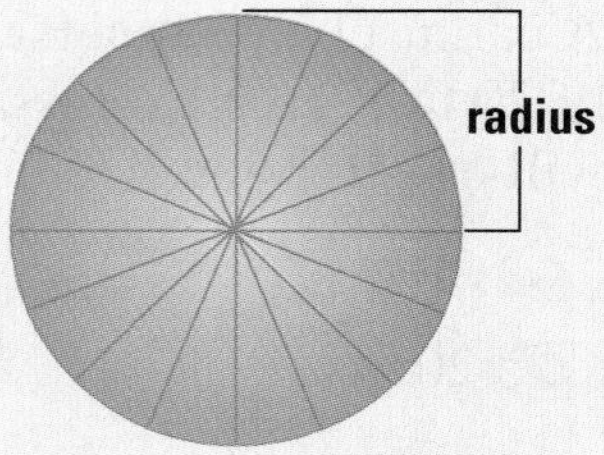

radius

3 Cut one wedge in half.

4 Rearrange the wedges as shown.

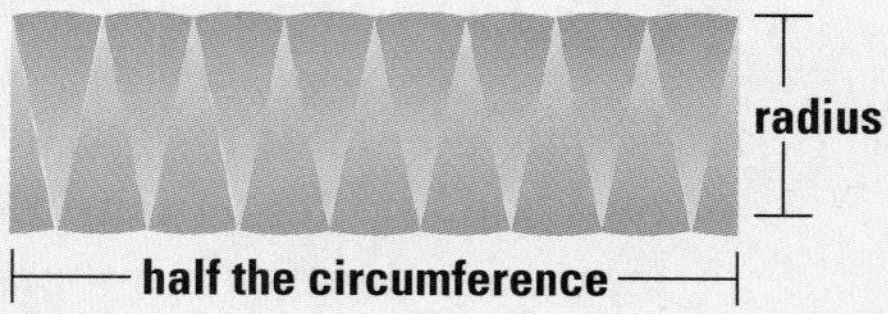

radius

half the circumference

2. With others in your group, discuss how to estimate the area of the rearranged wedges. What can you say about the area of a circle?

In Part A, you may have discovered that you can find the area of a circle by multiplying its radius by half the circle's circumference. Half the circumference is equal to multiplying half the diameter or the radius by π.

Area = radius $\times$ half the circumference

= radius $\times$ ($\pi \times$ radius)

= $\pi \times$ radius^2

This is read as "area equals pi times radius squared."

3. Use the formula to find the area of a circle with a radius of 4.

4. The circle below has a radius of 4. Follow the illustration to find how many 4-by-4 squares fit in the circle. How does this relate to your answer from Exercise 3?

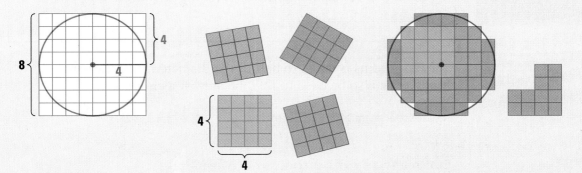

5. You want to draw a circle whose area is about 12 in.^{2} Estimate the radius of the circle you should draw. Explain your reasoning.

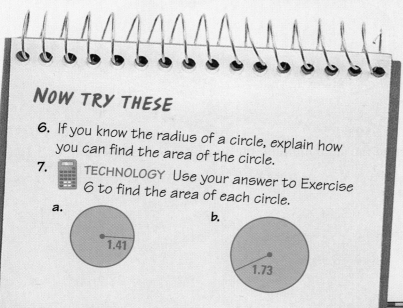

NOW TRY THESE

6. If you know the radius of a circle, explain how you can find the area of the circle.

7. TECHNOLOGY Use your answer to Exercise 6 to find the area of each circle.

a.

1.41

b.

1.73

10.6
Area of a **Circle**

What you should learn:

Goal 1 How to find the area of a circle

Goal 2 How to use the area of a circle to solve real-life problems

Why you should learn it:

Knowing how to find the area of a circle can help you compare the sizes of circular objects. An example is comparing the sizes of camera lenses.

Goal 1 AREA OF A CIRCLE

The **radius** of a circle is the distance between the center of the circle and a point on the circle. The radius of a circle is half its diameter.

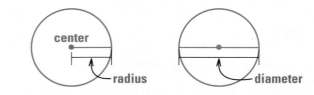

AREA OF A CIRCLE

To find the area of a circle, multiply the square of the radius by π. A decimal approximation for π is 3.14.

$$\text{Area} = \pi \times \text{radius}^2 \qquad A = \pi \cdot r^2$$

Since the radius is equal to half of the diameter, the following formula can also be used to find the area of a circle.

$$\text{Area} = \pi \times \left(\frac{1}{2} \times \text{diameter}\right)^2 \qquad A = \pi\left(\frac{1}{2} \cdot d\right)^2$$

Example 1 Finding the Area of a Circle

Find the area of each circle.

a.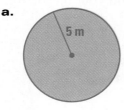
5 m

b.
6 ft

STUDY TIP

When you are finding the area of a circle, it helps to use a calculator. To find the area of the circle in part (a) of Example 1, you could use the following keystrokes.

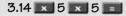

Solution

To find the area, multiply the square of the radius by π, or 3.14.

a. $\text{Area} = \pi \times \text{radius}^2$

$\approx 3.14 \times 5^2$

$\approx 3.14 \times 25$

$\approx 78.50 \text{ m}^2$

b. $\text{Area} = \pi \times \left(\frac{1}{2} \times \text{diameter}\right)^2$

$= \pi \times \left(\frac{1}{2} \times 6\right)^2$

$\approx 3.14 \times 3^2$

$\approx 3.14 \times 9$

$\approx 28.26 \text{ ft}^2$

Goal 2 SOLVING REAL-LIFE PROBLEMS

Example 2 Using the Area of a Circle

STRATEGY **DRAW A DIAGRAM** You just bought a poster of a circular piece of art. You are going to frame it using a mat so that only the circular piece of art shows. The mat is 30 in. long and 24 in. wide. The cut out circle has a diameter of 22 in. What is the area of the circular piece of art? What is the area of the mat?

Solution

Draw a diagram that shows the facts from the problem.

22 in. 24 in.

30 in. **Mat**

Use the diagram to visualize the problem.

From the diagram, you can see that the radius of the circle is half the diameter, or 11 in. To find the area of the circle, multiply the square of the radius by π.

Use arithmetic to find a solution.

$$\text{Area} = \pi \times \text{radius}^2 \qquad \text{Formula for area.}$$
$$\approx 3.14 \times 11^2 \qquad \text{Substitute 11 for radius and 3.14 for } \pi.$$
$$= 3.14 \times 121 \qquad \text{Square 11.}$$
$$= 379.94 \text{ in.}^2 \qquad \text{Use a calculator.}$$

The circular piece of art has an area of about 380 in.^{2}

To find the area of the mat, first find the area of the rectangle, as if there were no circle cut out.

$$\text{Area of rectangle} = \text{length} \times \text{width} \qquad \text{Formula for area.}$$
$$= 30 \times 24 \qquad \text{Substitute.}$$
$$= 720 \text{ in.}^2 \qquad \text{Multiply.}$$

Now subtract the area of the circle.

$$720 - 379.94 = 340.06 \text{ in.}^2$$

The area of the mat is about 340 in.^{2}

Real Life...
Real Facts

Circular Paintings
Frank Stella's *Sinjerli II* is an example of a circular painting. Most of his paintings include geometric figures.

ONGOING ASSESSMENT

Talk About It
· · · · · · · · · · · · · · · · · · · ·

Find the area of the circle described. Compare your answers with a partner.

1. Radius = 8 yd

2. Radius = 12 m

3. Diameter = 5 in.

GUIDED PRACTICE

In Exercises 1–4, match the name with the labeled part of the circle.

1. Diameter

2. Radius

3. Center

4. Area

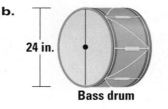

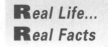

5. **DRUMS** A snare drum and a bass drum are shown below. The surface that is hit is called the drumhead. Find the area of each drumhead.

a.

7 in.

Snare drum

b.

24 in.

Bass drum

PRACTICE AND PROBLEM SOLVING

MEASUREMENT In Exercises 6–8, use a calculator to find the area of each object.

6.
7.5 in.

7.
1.75 ft

8.
10.6 mm

TECHNOLOGY In Exercises 9–11, find the area of the shaded region in each figure.

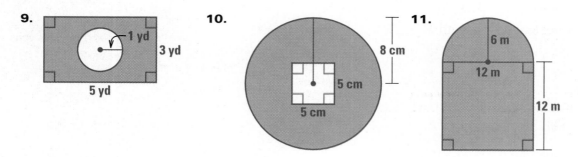

9.
1 yd
3 yd
5 yd

10.
8 cm
5 cm
5 cm

11.
6 m
12 m
12 m

REASONING In Exercises 12–14, complete the statement using *less than, greater than,* or *equal to.*

12. A circle with a radius of 3 m has an area _?_ 27 m².

13. A circle with a diameter of 10 in. has an area _?_ 100 in.²

14. A circle with a radius of 7 ft has an area _?_ a circle with a diameter of 13 ft.

GEOGRAPHY In Exercises 15 and 16, use a calculator and the map of the Arctic Circle.

15. What is the approximate area of the circle formed by the Arctic Circle?

16. What is the circumference of the Arctic Circle?

17. PHOTOGRAPHY The *diaphragm,* a circular opening behind the lens, operates with a camera's shutter to admit light into the camera. Will more light enter the camera if the diaphragm is set at a diameter of $\frac{1}{2}$ in. or if it is set at a radius of $\frac{3}{16}$ in.? Explain.

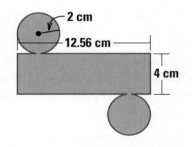

18. **SURFACE AREA** Calculate the area of the figure, using a calculator. Copy the figure, cut it out, and tape it together to form a three-dimensional figure. Can you name the figure? The area you calculated is the *surface area* of the three-dimensional figure.

STANDARDIZED TEST PRACTICE

19. A circular swimming pool has an area of 380 ft². What is the diameter of the pool?

(A) $5\frac{1}{2}$ ft   (B) 11 ft   (C) 22 ft   (D) 121 ft

20. Find the area of the shaded region.

(A) 5π cm²

(B) 75 cm²

(C) 75π cm²

(D) 100π cm²

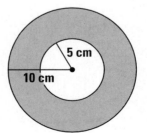

EXPLORATION AND EXTENSION

PORTFOLIO

21. The formula for the area of a circle is $\pi\left(\dfrac{1}{2} \cdot d\right)^2$, or $\pi \cdot r^2$. One formula uses the diameter and the other uses the radius. The formula for the circumference of a circle is $\pi \cdot d$. Rewrite this formula using the radius.

22. **WASHINGTON, DC** Both the Lincoln and Jefferson Memorials in Washington, DC, are enclosed by circular paths. The path around the Lincoln Memorial is about 317 ft in diameter. The path around the Jefferson Memorial is about 634 ft in diameter. Find the area enclosed by each path.

Jefferson Memorial

23. **BUILDING YOUR PROJECT** Suppose you want your city to have a circular park with a total area of about 500,000 ft². Estimate the diameter of your park. Add such a park to your map.

SPIRAL REVIEW

1. Find the mean, median, mode, and range of the data. **(5.1, 5.3, 5.4)**

    25, 35, 65, 55, 22, 50, 26, 50, 36, 35, 60, 48,
    55, 55, 45, 60, 48, 55, 45, 35, 52, 60, 40, 50

2. **INTERPRETING A GRAPH** A survey asked a group of students to name how they travel to school. The results are shown below. Estimate the portions shown in the graph. List your answers in decimals. **(3.3)**

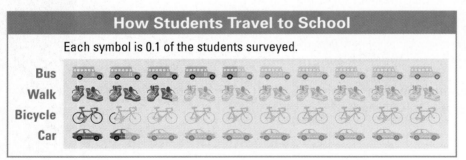

How Students Travel to School

Each symbol is 0.1 of the students surveyed.

Bus
Walk
Bicycle
Car

In Exercises 3 and 4, solve for x. (10.2)

3.

$x°$
$42°$

4.

$58°$ $x°$

Bicycles Built for View

READ About It

The amazing tricycle shown below was built by Arthur Dillon. Arthur and his son, Christopher, are shown riding the tricycle near their home in southern California. The tricycle is 22 ft long and 11 ft high.

Another one of Arthur Dillon's creations is shown below. Each of the two wheels on this bicycle has a diameter of 15 in. The bicycle rolls around the inside of a circular frame. The inside diameter of the frame is about $5\frac{1}{2}$ ft. Arthur can reach a speed of about 25 mi/h on this bicycle. Just don't get in his way. Brakes make the bike flip over, so Arthur left them off.

WRITE About It

1. The yellow frame on the *circular bicycle* is about 6 in. wide. What is the circumference of the outside of the frame?

2. Estimate the length of the spokes in the front and the rear wheels of the giant tricycle. Explain.

3. Write a sentence that compares the circumference of the front wheel to the circumference of each back wheel of the giant tricycle.

4. If you were buying strips of rubber to put around the outside of all three wheels of the giant tricycle, how many yards of rubber strips would you need? Explain.

Statistics and Circle Graphs

What you should learn:

Goal 1 How to make a circle graph

Goal 2 How to use a circle graph to organize real-life data

Why you should learn it:

Knowing how to make a circle graph can help you organize data. An example is organizing the results of a poll about ice skating.

Goal 1 MAKING A CIRCLE GRAPH

A **circle graph** shows data as parts of a circle. The parts are labeled as fractions, decimals, or percents. Because the entire circle graph represents one unit, the sum of all the parts must be 1 (or 100%).

To make a circle graph, you need to find the angle measure of each part. The sum of the angle measures of all the parts is 360°. So, to find $\frac{1}{4}$ of the circle, find $\frac{1}{4}$ of 360°.

$$\frac{1}{4} \text{ of } 360° = \frac{1}{4} \times 360° = 90°$$

Example 1 Making a Circle Graph

The 30 students on a school bus are asked which grade they are in. The results below can be organized with a circle graph.

Fifth Grade: 10 students   **Sixth Grade:** 10 students

Seventh Grade: 5 students   **Eighth Grade:** 5 students

To find the angle measure for the part that shows the fifth graders, multiply the fraction of fifth grade students by 360°.

$$\frac{10}{30} \times 360° = \frac{1}{3} \times 360°$$

$$= \frac{360°}{3}$$

$$= 120°$$

The angle measure for the part that shows the sixth graders will be the same since there are also 10 students from the sixth grade.

The other two grades have 5 students each.

$$\frac{5}{30} \times 360° = \frac{1}{6} \times 360°$$

$$= \frac{360°}{6}$$

$$= 60°$$

To make the circle graph, mark two 120° angles and two 60° angles. Label and shade each part. Finally, add a title to your graph.

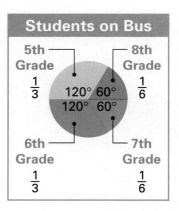

Students on Bus

5th Grade $\frac{1}{3}$ 8th Grade $\frac{1}{6}$

120° 60°
120° 60°

6th Grade $\frac{1}{3}$ 7th Grade $\frac{1}{6}$

TOOLBOX

Reading a Circle Graph, page 660

Goal 2 SOLVING REAL-LIFE PROBLEMS

To make a circle graph, you can use a protractor to draw and measure each part or you can use *circle graph paper*, shown at the right. On circle graph paper, the circle is divided into 72 parts. The angle measure of each part is

$$\frac{360°}{72} = 5°.$$

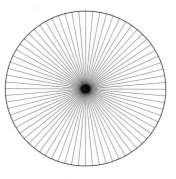

Example 2 — Making a Circle Graph

A survey asked 36 people who made New Year's resolutions to name the month in which they broke their resolution. Make a circle graph of the results.

Jan	Feb	Mar	Apr–Jun	Jul–Sep	Oct–Dec	Didn't break
9	6	6	3	3	3	6

Solution

January was the answer given by 9 people.

$$\frac{9}{36} \times 360° = \frac{1}{4} \times 360°$$
$$= \frac{360°}{4}$$
$$= 90°$$

February, March, and Didn't break were answers given by 6 people.

$$\frac{6}{36} \times 360° = \frac{1}{6} \times 360°$$
$$= \frac{360°}{6}$$
$$= 60°$$

Each of the other categories was answered by 3 people.

$$\frac{3}{36} \times 360° = \frac{1}{12} \times 360°$$
$$= \frac{360°}{12}$$
$$= 30°$$

The circle graph is at the right.

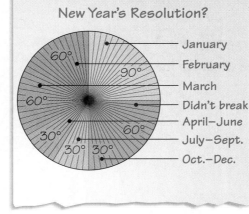

When Did You Break Your New Year's Resolution?

January
February
March
Didn't break
April–June
July–Sept.
Oct.–Dec.

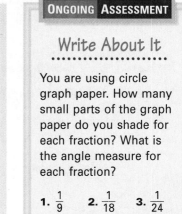

ONGOING ASSESSMENT

Write About It

You are using circle graph paper. How many small parts of the graph paper do you shade for each fraction? What is the angle measure for each fraction?

1. $\frac{1}{9}$ **2.** $\frac{1}{18}$ **3.** $\frac{1}{24}$

Extra Practice, page 638

GUIDED PRACTICE

ERROR ANALYSIS In Exercises 1 and 2, describe and correct the error.

1.

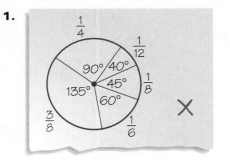

2.

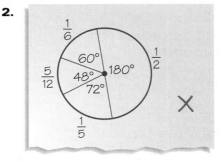

3. The list below shows the unordered steps to make a circle graph.
   Write the steps in order.

   A. Use circle graph paper to draw each part.   **B.** Find the degree of each part.

   C. Add up the fractions and angle measures.   **D.** Find the fraction for each part.

ENERGY SOURCES In Exercises 4–6, use the
circle graph at the right. The graph shows
how electricity is generated in the United
States. (Source: U.S. Dept. of Energy, *Annual Energy Review*, 1996)

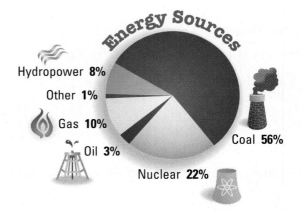

4. Show that the sum of the parts equals
   100%. Change the percents to fractions.
   Show that the sum of the parts equals 1.

5. Which sources combine to equal 35%?
   Show why.

6. Is the amount of electricity generated by
   coal greater than all the other sources
   combined? Explain.

PRACTICE AND PROBLEM SOLVING

Name the fraction or degree measure for each unknown part.

7.

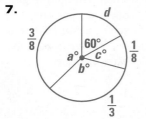

8.

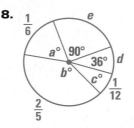

9. Students in three classes were asked to name their favorite fruit juice. The results were: orange, 24; grape, 18; apple, 12; cranberry, 12; and other, 6. Organize the data with a circle graph.

10. BOOKS A survey asked 48 students what type of book they like to read most. The results were: mystery, 18; autobiography, 16; science fiction, 8; and humor, 6. Organize the data with a circle graph.

11. ICE SKATING Students at an ice rink were asked what grade they are in. Organize the data at the right with a circle graph and a bar graph. Which two grades make up half the students at the rink? What graph did you use to answer the question?

Grade	4	5	6	7	8
Number of Students	15	40	30	20	15

12. AT THE BEACH A survey asked 20 people to name what they like to do most at the beach. Organize the following results with a circle graph.

Activity	Percent
Get a tan	25%
Swim	40%
Play volleyball	20%
Build a sand castle	5%
Other	10%

STANDARDIZED TEST PRACTICE

13. Write $\frac{2}{10}$ as a percent.

   A 20%   **B** 5%   **C** 2%   **D** $\frac{1}{5}$%

14. What fraction of a circle does 240° show?

   A $\frac{1}{3}$ **B** $\frac{2}{3}$ **C** $\frac{3}{2}$ **D** $\frac{12}{5}$

EXPLORATION AND EXTENSION

15. COMMUNICATING ABOUT MATHEMATICS Look at the picture of the tricycle on page 511. On the back wheel, 20 spokes meet in a circle around the rear axle. How many degrees does one section of the wheel show? How many degrees are in one section of a normal bicycle wheel with 20 spokes?

Solids, Surface Area, and **Volume**

Goal 1 FINDING SURFACE AREA

You might call the solid at the right a box. In geometry, it is called a **rectangular prism**. Each of the six *faces*, or sides, is a rectangle. The length, width, and height of the prism is labeled. If each face is a square, then the prism is called a **cube**.

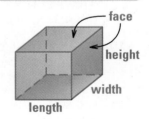

LESSON INVESTIGATION

Investigating Surface Area

GROUP ACTIVITY Use cubes to make the prisms shown below. For each prism, add the areas of the six faces. Record your results in a table. Describe the patterns you see.

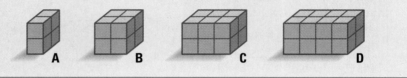

The **surface area** of a prism is found by adding the areas of the six faces of the prism.

Example 1 Finding the Surface Area of a Prism

Find the surface area of the rectangular prism.

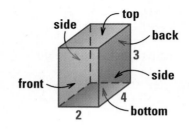

Solution

The front and back each have an area of 6 units^2. The top and bottom each have an area of 8 units^2. The two sides each have an area of 12 units^2.

$$\text{Surface Area} = 6 + 6 + 8 + 8 + 12 + 12$$
$$= 52 \text{ units}^2$$

The **volume** of a prism is a measure of how much space it occupies. Volume is measured in *cubic units,* or units^3.

Example 2 Exploring Volume

STRATEGY **LOOK FOR A PATTERN** Each small cube has a volume of 1 cubic unit. To find any patterns, the length, width, height, and volume of each prism can be organized in a table.

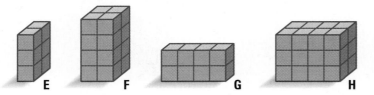

Prism	Length (units)	Width (units)	Height (units)	Volume (units^3)
E	1	2	3	6
F	2	2	4	16
G	4	1	2	8
H	4	2	3	24

In each case, you can get the volume by multiplying the length, width, and height.

VOLUME OF A PRISM

The volume of a rectangular prism is the product of its length, width, and height.

Volume = length × width × height   V = l · w · h

Example 3 Finding Volume

To find the volume of the prism at the right, use the formula given above.

Volume = length × width × height
      = 24 × 12 × 18
      = 5184 in.^{3}

18 in.
12 in.
24 in.

ONGOING ASSESSMENT

Write About It

1. Find the volume of the prisms *A*, *B*, *C*, and *D* on page 516.

2. Prism *D* is twice as big as prism *B*. Explain what "twice as big" means.

10.8 Exercises Extra Practice, page 638

GUIDED PRACTICE

In Exercises 1–4, use the rectangular prism at the right.

1. Identify the length, width, and height.

2. Is the prism also a cube? Explain.

3. Find the surface area of the prism.

4. Find the volume of the prism.

In Exercises 5–7, find the surface area and the volume of the prism.

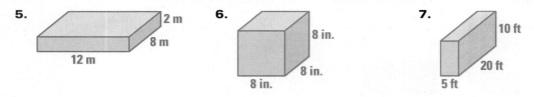

5. 2 m, 8 m, 12 m

6. 8 in., 8 in., 8 in.

7. 10 ft, 20 ft, 5 ft

8. **DRAWING A DIAGRAM** Draw a rectangular prism that has a length of 3 in., a width of 1 in., and a height of 2 in. Then find the surface area and the volume of the prism.

PRACTICE AND PROBLEM SOLVING

TECHNOLOGY In Exercises 9–16, find the surface area and volume of the rectangular prism.

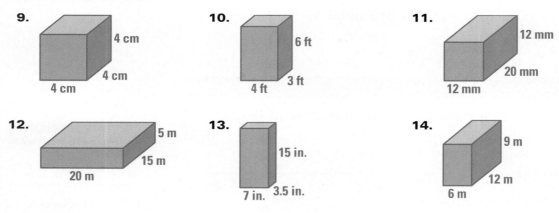

9. 4 cm, 4 cm, 4 cm

10. 6 ft, 4 ft, 3 ft

11. 12 mm, 20 mm, 12 mm

12. 5 m, 15 m, 20 m

13. 15 in., 7 in., 3.5 in.

14. 9 m, 6 m, 12 m

15. length = 16 in., width = 18 in., height = 18 in.

16. length = 2.4 cm, width = 3.9 cm, height = 1.1 cm

17. **REASONING** The volume of a rectangular prism is 1800 mm^3. It has a length of 10 mm and a width of 15 mm. Find the height of the rectangular prism.

PAINTING **In Exercises 18–20, use the following information.**

You are painting a room that is 17 ft long, 12 ft wide, and 8 ft high. The room has two windows and two doors. Both windows are 3 ft wide and 4 ft high. The doors are $3\frac{1}{2}$ ft wide and 7 ft high.

18. Find the total surface area of the room.

19. Find the area of the wall space in the room.

20. Find the volume of the room.

21. CONSTRUCTION A cube of bricks has a volume of 33,750 in.³ A single brick measures 8 in. long, $3\frac{3}{4}$ in. wide, and $2\frac{1}{4}$ in. high. How many bricks are in a cube of bricks?

22. **PETS** You have an aquarium that is 24 in. long, 12 in. wide, and 18 in. high.

   a. Find the volume of your aquarium.

   b. Two angelfish require an aquarium that can hold at least 25 gallons of water. If 1 gallon is equal to 231 in.³, then use a calculator to see if your aquarium will be suitable for two angelfish.

STANDARDIZED TEST PRACTICE

23. Which rectangular prism has the greatest volume?

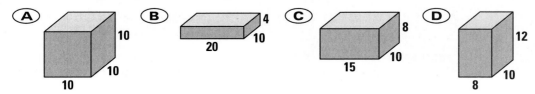

EXPLORATION AND EXTENSION

24. SURFACE AREA Use the prism at the right.

   a. Find the perimeter and area of the top face of the prism.

   b. Multiply the perimeter of the top face by the height of the prism. Then, add twice the area of the top face to the result.

   c. Find the surface area of the prism.

   d. What can you conclude? Does your conclusion hold for other rectangular prisms?

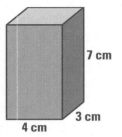

WHAT did you learn?

WHY did you learn it?

		WHAT did you learn?	WHY did you learn it?
Skills	10.1	Identify parallel, intersecting, and perpendicular lines.	Make decisions using properties of lines.
	10.2	Identify and draw angles.	Help you with design projects, such as stained-glass windows.
	10.3	Identify and use properties of parallelograms.	Find the sum of the angles of a parallelogram.
	10.4	Find the area of a triangle.	Calculate the amount of material needed for a project.
	10.5	Find the circumference of a circle.	Find the distance around a circular object.
	10.6	Find the area of a circle.	Compare the sizes of circular objects.
	10.7	Make a circle graph.	Organize the results of a survey.
	10.8	Find the surface area and volume of a rectangular prism.	Calculate volume of real-life objects, such as an aquarium.
Strategies	10.1–8	Use problem solving strategies.	Solve a wide variety of real-world problems.
Using Data	10.1–8	Use tables, graphs, and time lines.	Organize data and solve problems.

HOW does it fit in the bigger picture of mathematics?

To be successful in mathematics, you will need to remember what you studied. An example is remembering how to find the area of a triangle.

Method **1**   From memory, the formula for the area of a triangle is "one-half of the base times the height."

$$\text{Area} = \frac{1}{2} \cdot b \cdot h$$

Method **2**   In this chapter, you found that the area of a triangle is half the area of a rectangle.

$$\text{Area} = \frac{1}{2} \, (\text{area of a rectangle})$$
$$= \frac{1}{2} \, (b \cdot h)$$

Instead of memorizing, try to understand *why* properties are true.

V O C A B U L A R Y

- parallel (p. 476)
- intersecting (p. 476)
- perpendicular (p. 477)
- supplementary (p. 480)
- complementary (p. 480)
- congruent (p. 481)

- parallelogram (p. 486)
- rectangle (p. 486)
- square (p. 486)
- diameter (p. 500)
- circumference (p. 500)
- pi, π (p. 500)

- radius (p. 506)
- circle graph (p. 512)
- rectangular prism (p. 516)
- cube (p. 516)
- surface area (p. 516)
- volume (p. 517)

10.1   INVESTIGATING LINES

Parallel lines never meet. Intersecting lines meet at a point.
Perpendicular lines meet at right angles.

Examples

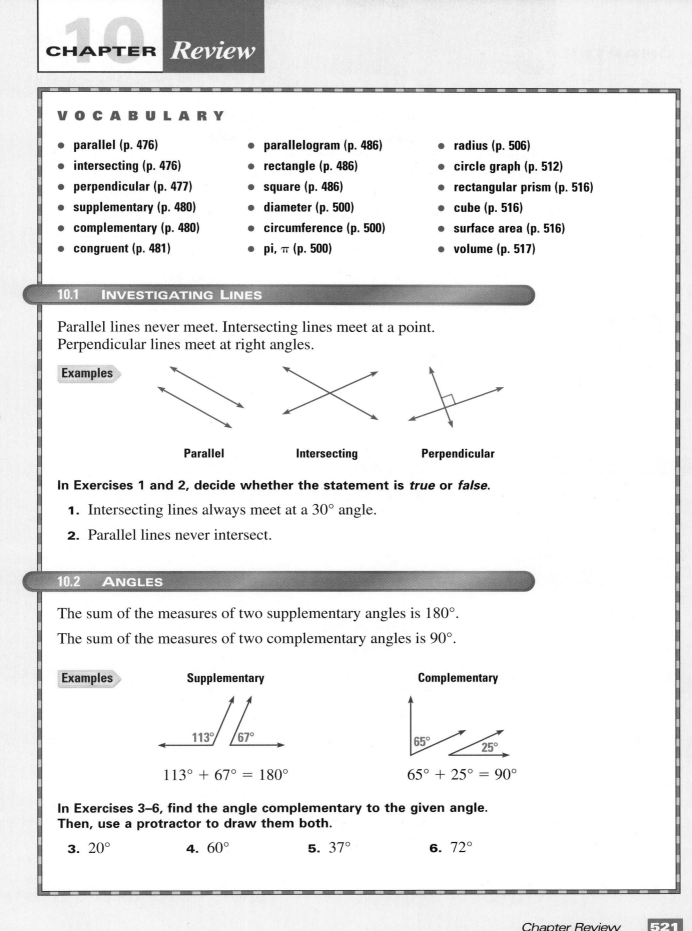

Parallel   Intersecting   Perpendicular

In Exercises 1 and 2, decide whether the statement is *true* or *false*.

1. Intersecting lines always meet at a 30° angle.

2. Parallel lines never intersect.

10.2   ANGLES

The sum of the measures of two supplementary angles is 180°.

The sum of the measures of two complementary angles is 90°.

Examples   Supplementary   Complementary

113° 67°   65°   25°

$113° + 67° = 180°$ $65° + 25° = 90°$

In Exercises 3–6, find the angle complementary to the given angle. Then, use a protractor to draw them both.

3. 20°   **4.** 60°   **5.** 37°   **6.** 72°

10.3 PARALLELOGRAMS

A parallelogram is a quadrilateral whose opposite sides are parallel. A rectangle is a special parallelogram that has 4 right angles. A square is a special rectangle that has 4 sides of equal length.

Examples

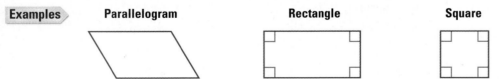

Parallelogram   Rectangle   Square

In Exercises 7–10, use the figure shown. Name one of each polygon described.

7. Square

8. Parallelogram

9. Rectangle

10. Quadrilateral

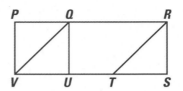

10.4 AREA OF A TRIANGLE

The area of a triangle is one half the product of its base and height.

Example

$$\text{Area} = \frac{1}{2} \times \textbf{base} \times \textbf{height}$$

$$= \frac{1}{2} \times 6 \times 3$$

$$= 9 \text{ m}^2$$

11. Find the area of the triangle.

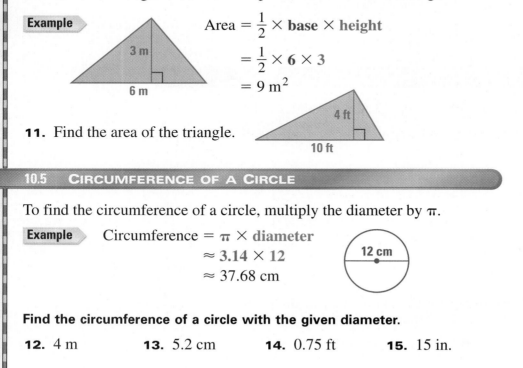

10.5 CIRCUMFERENCE OF A CIRCLE

To find the circumference of a circle, multiply the diameter by π.

Example   Circumference $= \pi \times \textbf{diameter}$

$$\approx 3.14 \times 12$$

$$\approx 37.68 \text{ cm}$$

Find the circumference of a circle with the given diameter.

12. 4 m   **13.** 5.2 cm   **14.** 0.75 ft   **15.** 15 in.

10.6 AREA OF A CIRCLE

Example Area $= \pi \times \text{radius}^2$
$\approx 3.14 \times 5^2$
$\approx 78.5 \text{ ft}^2$

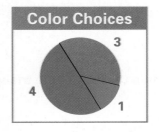

In Exercises 16–19, find the area of a circle with the given radius.

16. 10 cm   **17.** 15 ft   **18.** 2.6 m   **19.** 4 in.

10.7 STATISTICS AND CIRCLE GRAPHS

To make a circle graph, find the measure of each part's angle by multiplying 360° by the fraction of the total data for each part.

Example Out of 8 students, 4 like blue, 3 like red, and 1 likes green.

Blue $= \dfrac{4}{8}$ $\qquad \dfrac{4}{8} \times 360° = 180°$

Red $= \dfrac{3}{8}$ $\qquad \dfrac{3}{8} \times 360° = 135°$

Green $= \dfrac{1}{8}$ $\qquad \dfrac{1}{8} \times 360° = 45°$

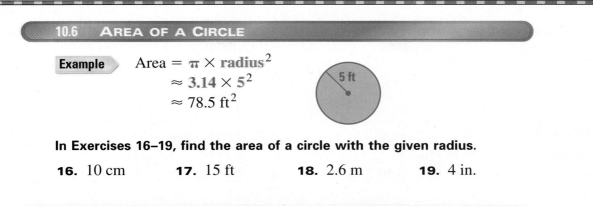

Color Choices

20. A survey asked people to name their favorite meal of the day. Out of the 45 people surveyed, 15 chose breakfast, 12 chose lunch, and 18 chose dinner. Organize the results in a circle graph.

10.8 SOLIDS, SURFACE AREA, AND VOLUME

Example Surface area $= 24 + 24 + 32 + 32 + 48 + 48$
$= 208 \text{ cm}^2$
Volume $=$ length $\times$ width $\times$ height
$= 6 \times 4 \times 8$
$= 192 \text{ cm}^3$

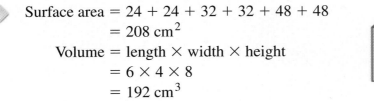

8 cm
4 cm
6 cm

In Exercises 21–23, find the surface area and volume of the given prism.

21. **22.** **23.**

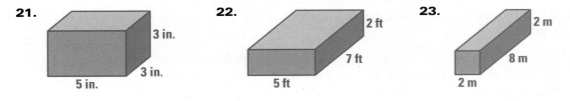

3 in.
3 in.
5 in.

2 ft
7 ft
5 ft

2 m
8 m
2 m

In Exercises 1–5, use the figure at the right.

1. Lines $\overleftrightarrow{ST}$ and $\overleftrightarrow{WX}$ are ___?___ lines.

2. Name two pairs of perpendicular lines.

3. $\angle 1$ and $\angle 2$ are ___?___ angles.

4. $\angle 5$ and $\angle 6$ are ___?___ angles.

5. Write an explanation of how you can determine that the measure of $\angle 4$ is 98°.

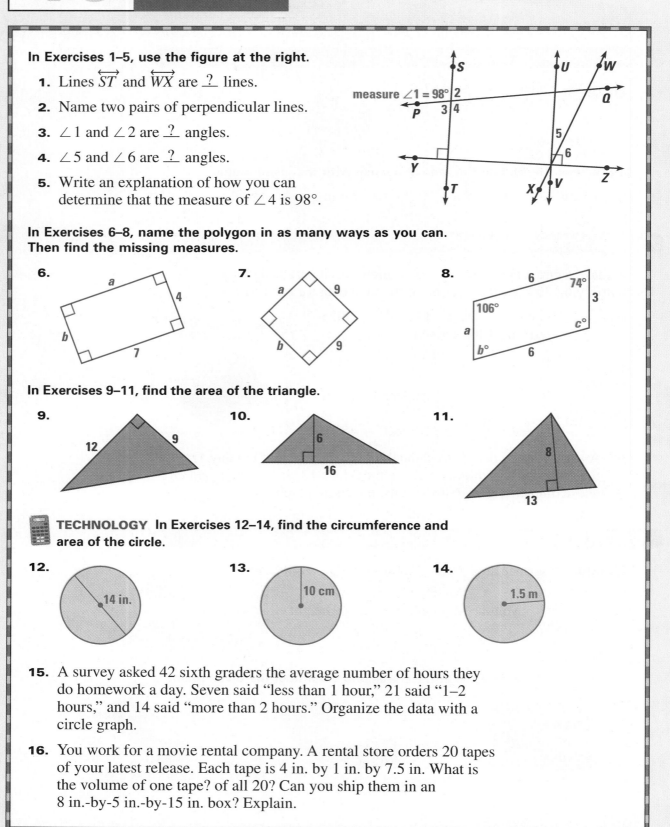

In Exercises 6–8, name the polygon in as many ways as you can. Then find the missing measures.

6.

7.

8.

In Exercises 9–11, find the area of the triangle.

9.

10.

11.

TECHNOLOGY **In Exercises 12–14, find the circumference and area of the circle.**

12.

13.

14.

15. A survey asked 42 sixth graders the average number of hours they do homework a day. Seven said "less than 1 hour," 21 said "1–2 hours," and 14 said "more than 2 hours." Organize the data with a circle graph.

16. You work for a movie rental company. A rental store orders 20 tapes of your latest release. Each tape is 4 in. by 1 in. by 7.5 in. What is the volume of one tape? of all 20? Can you ship them in an 8 in.-by-5 in.-by-15 in. box? Explain.

1. Nathan walks west up Franklin Street and turns north onto Penn Street to go to his friend's house. Which of the following do you know is true about Franklin and Penn Streets?

   (A) They are parallel.

   (B) They are one-way streets.

   (C) They have sidewalks.

   (D) They are perpendicular.

2. If two lines are perpendicular, which of the following statements is *not* true of the lines?

   (A) They intersect.

   (B) They form a right angle.

   (C) They form a square corner.

   (D) They form a 60° angle.

3. What is the perimeter of the square?

   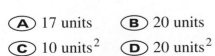

   (A) 17 units   (B) 20 units

   (C) 10 units^2 (D) 20 units^2

4. What is the next shape in the pattern?

   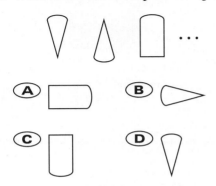

5. Mary wants to plant flowers around the outside of a circular garden that has a diameter of 4 ft. If the flowers have to be planted 6 in. from each other, about how many flowers should she buy?

   (A) 50   (B) 26

   (C) 25   (D) 12

6. An automobile tire is 25 in. when measured directly across the center. The radius of the tire is ? .

   (A) $12\frac{1}{2}$ in.   (B) $39\frac{1}{4}$ in.

   (C) 25 in.   (D) 78.5 in.

In Questions 7 and 8, use the circle graph below. It shows the results of a survey that asked what invention people thought was most important.

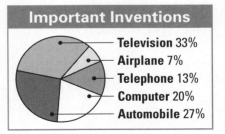

Important Inventions

- Television 33%
- Airplane 7%
- Telephone 13%
- Computer 20%
- Automobile 27%

7. What percent of the people surveyed said a computer was most important?

   (A) 80%   (B) 27%

   (C) 20%   (D) 10%

8. If there were 200 people surveyed, how many people said the television was most important?

   (A) 20   (B) 33

   (C) 59   (D) 66

CHAPTER
11

Integers and the Coordinate Plane

PENGUINS have short feathers but cannot fly. Several kinds of penguins live in Antarctica, where temperatures range from 0°F to −94°F.

TECHNOLOGY

Technology resources accompanying this chapter:
- Interactive Real-Life Investigations
- Middle School Tutorial Software

CHAPTER THEME
Antarctica

Life in Antarctica

REAL LIFE
Geography

A treaty signed in 1959 reserves Antarctica for scientific use. Several countries claim parts of Antarctica, and scientists from around the world operate research stations there. The fragile and unspoiled environment allows them to investigate topics ranging from the ozone layer to the origin of the universe.

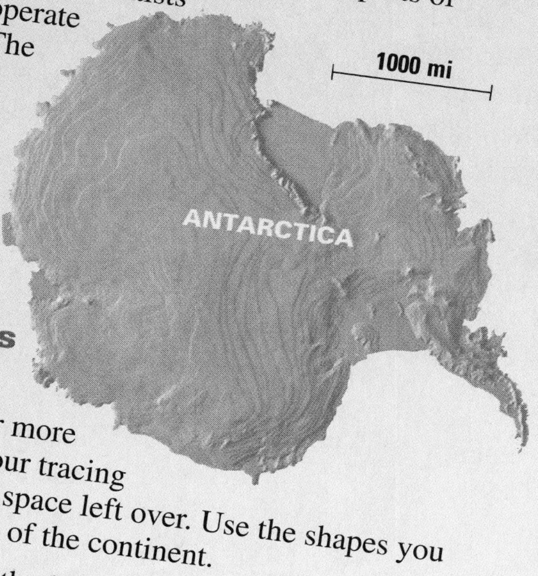

1000 mi

ANTARCTICA

Think and Discuss

1. Trace the continent of Antarctica. Draw one or more shapes that fit around your tracing with the least amount of space left over. Use the shapes you drew to estimate the area of the continent.

2. Do you think that this method will work for finding any area? Explain.

CHAPTER 11

PORTFOLIO

CHAPTER PROJECT

Research on Antarctica

PROJECT DESCRIPTION

Your school newspaper is starting a monthly science feature. You are going to write the first installment, and the topic that you are assigned is *Science in Antarctica*.

GETTING STARTED

Talking It Over

- In your group, talk about how you might find interesting facts about research in Antarctica. Do you have Internet access that you will be able to use? Will you use magazines or newspapers? books?

- Discuss which aspects of Science in Antarctica you want to pursue: climate, geology, and so on.

Planning Your Project

- **Materials Needed:** paper, pencils or pens, word processor (optional)

- Think of a name for your feature. Go to your library and look for interesting facts about Antarctica that you can include in your article. Think about how the facts you find will fit with the **TOPICS** listed on the next page. Make an outline for your article. After completing the **BUILDING YOUR PROJECT** exercises, use this outline to write your article.

BUILDING YOUR PROJECT

These are places throughout the chapter where you will work on your project.

TOPICS

11.1 Change temperatures in degrees Celsius to degrees Fahrenheit. *p. 535*

11.2 Find the average temperature for a week. *p. 541*

11.3 Find the height of an iceberg. *p. 550*

11.4 Locate the United States stations in Antarctica in a coordinate plane. *p. 557*

11.5 Estimate the distance traveled by the first explorers to reach the South Pole. *p. 562*

INTERNET

To find out more about Antarctica, go to:
http://www.mlmath.com

Investigating Integers

Part A ADDITION AND THE NUMBER LINE

Materials Needed
- calculator
- pencils and pens
- paper

1. Enter 6 on a calculator. Then repeatedly add 4 and write the numbers the calculator displays. Describe the pattern.

6 [+] 4 [=] (10.) [+] 4 [=] (14.) [+] 4 [=]
(18.) [+] 4 [=] (22.)

2. The number line below shows some answers from Exercise 1. Describe the number line pattern. Is the pattern moving to the right or to the left?

```
0  1  2  3  4  5  6  7  8  9  10 11 12 13 14 15 16 17 18 19
```

3. The pattern in Exercise 2 starts with 6, 10, 14, 18. Give the next three numbers in the pattern.

4. Did you use a calculator, a number line, or mental math to answer Exercise 3? Which method do you prefer? Explain.

5. Copy and complete the table. Describe any patterns that you find in the "First 8 answers" column.

Starting number	Repeated operation	Example	First 8 answers
3	Add 2.	3 [+] 2 [=]	5, 7, 9, 11, 13, 15, 17, 19
0	Add 5.	0 [+] 5 [=]	?
9	Add 3.	9 [+] 3 [=]	?

6. Plot the answers in the last column of each row of the table on a number line. Draw arrows to indicate the progression of the numbers. Do the arrows point left or right?

7. Complete the statement:
If you add 3 to a number, the result will lie __?__ units to the __?__ of the number on the number line.

8. Enter 17 on a calculator. Repeatedly subtract 2 and write the numbers the calculator displays. Describe the pattern.

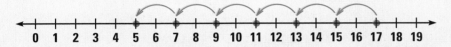

9. The number line below shows some of the answers from Exercise 8. Describe the number line pattern.

10. Copy and complete the table. Plot the answer in each row of the table on a number line. Describe each pattern.

Starting number	Repeated operation	Example	First 8 answers
27	Subtract 3.	27 ▬ 3 ▬	24, 21, 18, 15, 12, 9, 6, 3
45	Subtract 5.	45 ▬ 5 ▬	?
36	Subtract 4.	36 ▬ 4 ▬	?

11. Complete the statement:
If you subtract 3 from a number, the result will lie __?__ units to the __?__ of the number on the number line.

12. **TEMPERATURES** On a winter day, the temperature is falling 4 degrees each hour. The temperature at 3 P.M. is 8°F. Estimate the temperature at 6 P.M. and at 7 P.M.

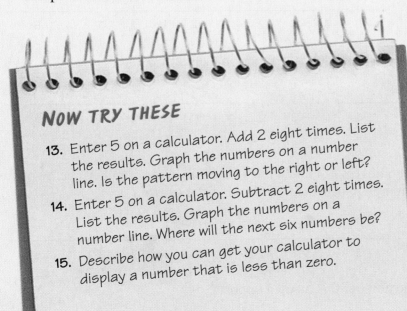

NOW TRY THESE

13. Enter 5 on a calculator. Add 2 eight times. List the results. Graph the numbers on a number line. Is the pattern moving to the right or left?

14. Enter 5 on a calculator. Subtract 2 eight times. List the results. Graph the numbers on a number line. Where will the next six numbers be?

15. Describe how you can get your calculator to display a number that is less than zero.

11.1

Graphing Integers on a **Number Line**

What you should learn:

Goal ① How to graph integers on a number line

Goal ② How to use integers to solve real-life problems

Why you should learn it:

Knowing how to use negative integers can help you understand a scientific report, such as one about temperatures in Antarctica.

Goal ① GRAPHING INTEGERS

The following numbers are **integers**.

  . . . , −4, −3, −2, −1, 0, 1, 2, 3, . . .

Integers are divided into three categories: **negative integers**, zero, and **positive integers**.

The symbol "−" used to represent negative numbers is a *negative sign.* You read "−4" as "negative four."

Example 1 Graphing on a Number Line

Graph −4, −1, 0, 2, and 4 on a number line.

Solution

Step ① Use a ruler to draw a straight line.

Step ② Mark several evenly spaced tick marks on the line and label them. Draw arrowheads on the ends of the line.

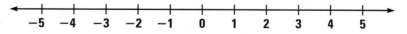

Step ③ Graph each number on the number line.

The integers −4 and 4 are **opposites**. On a number line, two integers that are opposites are the same distance from 0.

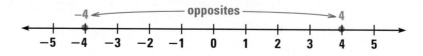

The number 0 is its own opposite.

Goal 2 ORDERING INTEGERS

It is helpful to know how to put integers in order from least to greatest. Often scientific data involve negative integers, and putting them in order can help you understand the data.

Example 2 Comparing and Ordering Integers

a. Name the integers between -7 and -3.
b. Order -1, -2, 4, -5, and 0 from least to greatest.

Solution

a. The integers between -7 and -3 are -6, -5, and -4.

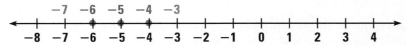

b. To order -1, -2, 4, -5, and 0 from least to greatest, begin by graphing the numbers on a number line.

To order the integers from least to greatest, read from left to right. The order is -5, -2, -1, 0, 4.

Example 3 Measuring Temperatures

You saw a television program called *Live from Antarctica*. A scientist on the program said that the temperature on the Celsius scale changed from $-15°$ to $-20°$. Did it get warmer or colder?

Solution

To compare $-15°C$ and $-20°C$, think of the thermometer as a number line.

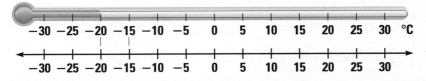

Because $-20°C$ is to the left of $-15°C$, $-20 < -15$. It got colder.

Scientists in Antarctica study climate, marine life, geology, and water currents. Here, Kristin Larson checks ice samples at McMurdo Station.

ONGOING ASSESSMENT

Talk About It
. . . .

Use a number line to order the numbers from least to greatest. Describe a real-life situation in which these numbers could occur.

1. -6, 2, 3, -3, -5

2. 0, -2, 2, -5, 5

GUIDED PRACTICE

1. List the integers in order from −4 to 4.

In Exercises 2–6, match the number with its location on the number line.

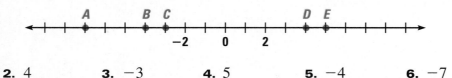

2. 4   **3.** −3   **4.** 5   **5.** −4   **6.** −7

7. NUMBER SENSE Tell which integer is the opposite of 10. Tell which integer is the opposite of −8.

PRACTICE AND PROBLEM SOLVING

LOOKING FOR A PATTERN In Exercises 8–10, graph the integers on a number line. Describe the pattern. Then list the next two integers in the pattern.

8. −6, −4, −2, 0, 2, ? , ?   **9.** −5, −3, −1, 1, 3, ? , ?   **10.** 2, −1, −4, −7, ? , ?

NUMBER SENSE In Exercises 11–18, use a number line to help you complete the statement using > or <.

11. 4 ? 0   **12.** 0 ? −1   **13.** −8 ? −6   **14.** −2 ? 2

15. 7 ? −1   **16.** 3 ? −3   **17.** −2 ? −1   **18.** −14 ? −4

NUMBER SENSE In Exercises 19–21, use a number line to help you order the integers from least to greatest.

19. 6, 1, −3, 3, −4   **20.** −2, 4, −9, −7, 0   **21.** −1, −6, −3, 0, −5

VISUAL THINKING In Exercises 22–25, match the number line with its description.

22.
```
←+—●—+—+—+—+—+—●—+→
  −3 −2 −1  0  1  2  3
```

A. Three integers that are 1 unit apart

23.
```
←+—●—+—+—+—+—●—+→
−10 −9 −8 −7 −6 −5 −4
```

B. Two integers that are 5 units apart

24.
```
←+—●—+—●—+—●—+→
 −8 −7 −6 −5 −4 −3 −2
```

C. Two integers that are opposites

25.
```
←+—●—●—●—+—+—+→
 −5 −4 −3 −2 −1  0  1
```

D. Three integers that are 2 units apart

In Exercises 26–33, write the described integer.

26. 3 more than −3

27. between −6 and −4

28. opposite of 6

29. opposite of −9

30. smallest positive integer

31. largest negative integer

32. 2 less than −7

33. 4 less than 10

34. Graph each integer in Exercises 26–33 on the same number line.

35. **SCIENCE** The lowest temperature recorded in Alaska was −80°F, in Prospect Creek Camp. The lowest temperature recorded in Montana was −70°F, in Rogers Pass. Which temperature is lower?

36. **COMMUNICATING** Beginning at 0 on a number line, graph the integer that is represented by the expression "one step forward and two steps back." If you repeat the instructions four more times, what integer will you end on?

Rogers Pass, Montana

37. Which group of numbers is plotted on the number line?

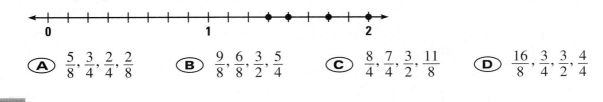

(A) $\frac{5}{8}, \frac{3}{4}, \frac{2}{4}, \frac{2}{8}$

(B) $\frac{9}{8}, \frac{6}{8}, \frac{3}{2}, \frac{5}{4}$

(C) $\frac{8}{4}, \frac{7}{4}, \frac{3}{2}, \frac{11}{8}$

(D) $\frac{16}{8}, \frac{3}{4}, \frac{3}{2}, \frac{4}{4}$

EXPLORATION AND EXTENSION

PORTFOLIO

38. **BUILDING YOUR PROJECT** You are online chatting with a scientist about Antarctica. The scientist says that the temperature is −8°C. Use the thermometers at the right to estimate this temperature on the Fahrenheit scale.

Include these temperatures in your article about Antarctica.

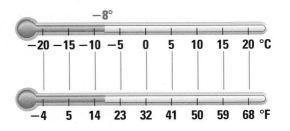

Investigating Integer Addition

Materials Needed
- **number counters**
- **pencils**
- **paper**

Part A ADDING TWO INTEGERS

You can use number counters to model addition. Tan counters represent positive integers and red counters represent negative integers.

You can use counters to find the sum $5 + 3$.

1

+5 ⊕ ⊕ ⊕ ⊕ ⊕

+3 ⊕ ⊕ ⊕

2 Count the total.

3 Write the result as an equation.

$5 + 3 = 8$

You can use counters to find the sum $(-5) + (-3)$.

1

−5 ⊖ ⊖ ⊖ ⊖ ⊖

−3 ⊖ ⊖ ⊖

2 Count the total.

3 Write the result as an equation.

$-5 + (-3) = -8$

1. Use counters to find the sum.

    a. $4 + 5$ **b.** $7 + 2$ **c.** $-3 + (-6)$ **d.** $-5 + (-5)$

Part B USING ZERO PAIRS

When you pair one tan counter and one red counter, the result is zero. This pair of counters is called a *zero pair*.

You can use counters to find the sum $3 + (-3)$.

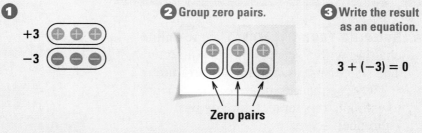

1

+3 ⊕ ⊕ ⊕

−3 ⊖ ⊖ ⊖

2 Group zero pairs.

3 Write the result as an equation.

$3 + (-3) = 0$

Zero pairs

2. Use counters to find the sum.

    a. $-2 + 2$ **b.** $4 + (-4)$ **c.** $6 + (-6)$ **d.** $1 + (-1)$

When you use number counters to add a positive integer and a negative integer, remember to remove all the zero pairs.

You can use counters to find the sum $-5 + 3$.

①

② Count remaining counters.

③ Write the result as an equation.

-5 ⊖⊖⊖⊖⊖

$+3$ ⊕⊕⊕

Remove zero pairs.

$-5 + 3 = -2$

3. Use counters to find the sum.

a. $-4 + 5$ **b.** $7 + (-2)$ **c.** $5 + (-8)$ **d.** $-7 + 2$

4. **NUMBER SENSE** With others in your group, discuss what you noticed about the sum of a positive integer and a negative integer.

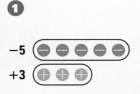

NOW TRY THESE

In Exercises 5–8, use counters to find the sum. Then write the result as an equation.

5. $-5 + (-2)$

6. $-3 + (-9)$

7. $-4 + 3$

8. $5 + (-5)$

In Exercises 9–11, match the addition problem with the description of its sum. Then use number counters to check your result.

9. $-4 + 5$

10. $3 + (-4)$

11. $-4 + 4$

A. A negative integer

B. Zero

C. A positive integer

Complete the statement using *sometimes, always,* or *never.* Give examples to support your answer.

12. The sum of two positive integers is ___?___ negative.

13. The sum of two negative integers is ___?___ negative.

14. The sum of a positive integer and a negative integer is ___?___ negative.

11.2

Adding Integers

What you should learn:

Goal 1 How to use a number line to add integers

Goal 2 How to use integer addition to solve real-life problems

Why you should learn it:

Knowing how to add integers can help you find averages, such as finding whether your average golf score is above or below par.

Miniature golf is one sport in which you try to get the lowest score.

Goal 1 ADDING INTEGERS

You can use a number line to add integers.

- When you add a *positive* number, move to the right.
- When you add a *negative* number, move to the left.

Example 1 Adding Two Integers

Use a number line to solve the addition problem.

a. $3 + 5$ **b.** $-4 + (-2)$ **c.** $-5 + 2$ **d.** $1 + (-6)$

Solution

a. Begin at 3.
Then move 5 units to the right.

The final position is 8. So, $3 + 5 = 8$.

b. Begin at -4.
Then move 2 units to the left.

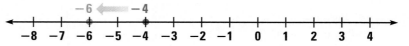

The final position is -6. So, $-4 + (-2) = -6$.

c. Begin at -5.
Then move 2 units to the right.

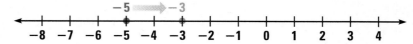

The final position is -3. So, $-5 + 2 = -3$.

d. Begin at 1.
Then move 6 units to the left.

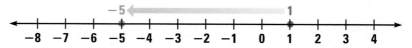

The final position is -5. So, $1 + (-6) = -5$.

There are many applications of negative integers.

Real-Life Situation	Number Model
A loss of ten dollars	−$10
Five feet below sea level	−5 ft
In football, a loss of six yards	−6 yd
A loss of 5 points	−5

Example 2 **Adding Integers**

REAL LIFE
Sports

In the game of miniature golf, your score for each hole is the number of strokes you take above or below par. (*Par* is the number of times you should hit the ball for each hole.)

Use the scorecard at the right that shows the number of strokes above or below par in the "Score" column.

a. Find your total score above or below par.

b. Find your average score above or below par per hole.

Hole	Par	Score
1	3	3
2	2	−1
3	4	4
4	3	3
5	3	−1
6	4	0
7	2	3
8	3	−2
9	3	0

Solution

a. Use a calculator to find the total.

Keystrokes   **Display**

So, your total score is 9. This means that you have taken 9 strokes above par for the game.

b. To find the average score above or below par, divide the total by the number of holes.

$$\text{Average} = \frac{\text{Total score}}{\text{Number of holes}}$$

$$= \frac{9}{9}$$

$$= 1$$

So, your average score per hole is 1 above par.

CALCULATOR TIP

To enter a negative number on a calculator, use the change-sign key: [+/−] .

ONGOING ASSESSMENT

Talk About It

1. Use a number line to find each sum. Do you get the same results as in Example 1?

   a. 5 + 3

   b. −2 + (−4)

   c. 2 + (−5)

   d. −6 + 1

2. What can you conclude?

GUIDED PRACTICE

ERROR ANALYSIS Describe and correct the error. Write the correct sum.

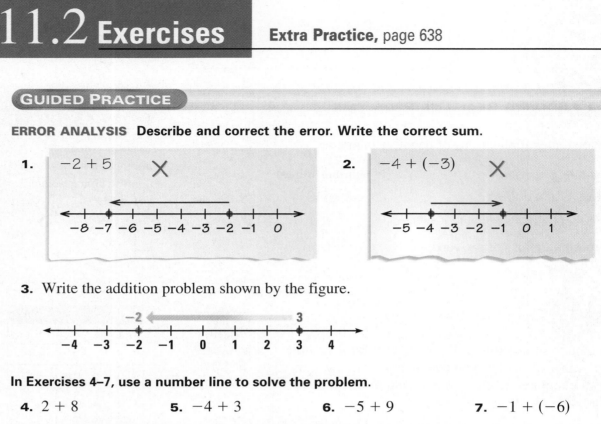

1. $-2 + 5$

2. $-4 + (-3)$

3. Write the addition problem shown by the figure.

In Exercises 4–7, use a number line to solve the problem.

4. $2 + 8$ **5.** $-4 + 3$ **6.** $-5 + 9$ **7.** $-1 + (-6)$

8. **NUMBER SENSE** How can the sum of a positive integer and a negative integer be positive? negative? zero? Give examples to support your answers.

PRACTICE AND PROBLEM SOLVING

Write the addition problem shown by the figure. Then solve.

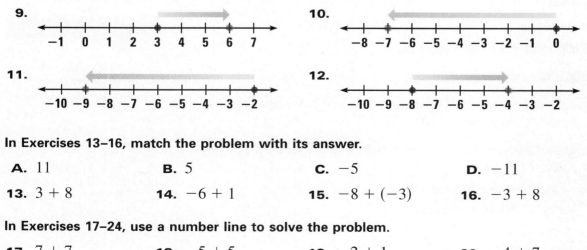

9.

10.

11.

12.

In Exercises 13–16, match the problem with its answer.

A. 11 **B.** 5 **C.** -5 **D.** -11

13. $3 + 8$ **14.** $-6 + 1$ **15.** $-8 + (-3)$ **16.** $-3 + 8$

In Exercises 17–24, use a number line to solve the problem.

17. $7 + 7$ **18.** $-5 + 5$ **19.** $-2 + 1$ **20.** $-4 + 7$

21. $-9 + (-5)$ **22.** $-4 + (-11)$ **23.** $-6 + 13$ **24.** $-15 + 8$

VISUAL THINKING Use a number line. Write the addition problem described. Then solve.

25. Start at 4. Move 5 units left, then 2 units right.

26. Start at −3. Move 1 unit left, then 5 units right. Move 1 unit left.

27. SAVINGS ACCOUNT In your savings account book, you record a deposit as a positive integer and a withdrawal as a negative integer. You then add to get a new balance.

Suppose you begin with $15 in your account. What will the new balance be after you do the following?

a. Deposit $7.　　　**b.** Then withdraw $11.

In Exercises 28 and 29, use a number line to determine how many total yards the tag football team gained or lost.

28. The team gains 6 yd, then gains 9 yd.

29. The team gains 8 yd, then loses 4 yd.

STANDARDIZED TEST PRACTICE

30. Which of the expressions is not equal to any of the others?

(A) −3 + 4 + (−1)　　　**(B)** 3 + (−4) + 1

(C) 5 + 2 + (−7)　　　**(D)** −5 + 7 + 2

EXPLORATION AND EXTENSION

PORTFOLIO

31. BUILDING YOUR PROJECT You are exploring data about temperatures in Antarctica. You find the morning temperatures for a week. They are shown at the right. What is the average morning temperature for the week? Explain. Include this fact in your article.

32. REASONING Write three different addition problems whose sums are −12.

Temperatures			
Sunday	−4°C	Thursday	6°C
Monday	−5°C	Friday	7°C
Tuesday	−1°C	Saturday	9°C
Wednesday	2°C		

MEASUREMENT Use a fraction to complete the statement. **(6.1)**

1. Sixteen minutes is ? of an hour.

2. Six inches is ? of a foot.

3. Three pints is ? of a gallon.

4. Four ounces is ? of a pound.

Is the proportion *true* or *false*? Explain your reasoning. **(6.4)**

5. $\dfrac{5}{6} = \dfrac{15}{18}$

6. $\dfrac{2}{9} = \dfrac{5}{27}$

7. $\dfrac{15}{45} = \dfrac{1}{3}$

8. $\dfrac{3}{4} = \dfrac{16}{20}$

Find the reciprocal of the number. **(8.5)**

9. $\dfrac{8}{9}$

10. $\dfrac{1}{6}$

11. $\dfrac{7}{12}$

12. $\dfrac{13}{16}$

13. **PREFERENCES** A survey asked a group of people to name the type of milk they drink. The results were: skim, 20; 1 percent, 35; 2 percent, 25; and whole, 20. Display the data with a circle graph. **(10.7)**

Use a number line to complete the statement using > or <. **(11.1)**

14. -10 ? 0

15. -3 ? -9

16. 6 ? -6

17. -5 ? 2

CAREER Interview

MARTIAL ARTIST

Kenn Perry is a martial artist with a green belt in American Kenpo. Perry not only studies karate, he trains others with disabilities. He is also involved with the Disability Awareness Project aimed at improving students' sensitivity toward people with disabilities.

Q How did you become interested in karate?
I always wanted to do karate but never thought that I could. Then I saw a flier in a rehabilitation hospital offering a class for people with disabilities. After taking that class, I continued training in a regular class.

Q What math skills do you apply in karate?
I always use logic. My math teacher told me that math is a perfectly logical science. She was right. I use logic to take apart the moves that an able-bodied person does and rebuild them for a person using a wheelchair.

Q Do you use any other math concepts in karate?
Yes, I was taught that there are 18 ways to attack. They can be described using a coordinate plane on which you are the origin and different lines through the origin represent different angles of attack. Geometry is a useful tool when describing motion.

Integer Addition

Most calculators have a special key for negative numbers. This key comes in two versions: a *change-sign key* or a *negative key*.

Change-sign key	+/–	Enter number first, then press this key.
Negative key	(-)	Press this key first, then enter number.

CALCULATOR TIP

On most calculators, the subtraction key ▬ cannot be used as a negative key. Typically you use the change-sign key +/– .

Example

Use a calculator to find the sum.

a. $-3 + 4$　**b.** $5 + (-2)$　**c.** $3 + (-6)$　**d.** $-2 + (-4)$

Solution

Keystrokes	Display	Type of Key
a. 3 +/– + 4 =	1.	Change-sign key
(-) 3 + 4 =	1.	Negative key
b. 5 + 2 +/– =	3.	Change-sign key
5 + (-) 2 =	3.	Negative key
c. 3 + 6 +/– =	−3.	Change-sign key
3 + (-) 6 =	−3.	Negative key
d. 2 +/– + 4 +/– =	−6.	Change-sign key
(-) 2 + (-) 4 =	−6.	Negative key

Exercises

In Exercises 1–16, use a calculator to find the sum. Then use a number line to check your result.

1. $5 + (-3)$　　**2.** $4 + (-7)$　　**3.** $-2 + 4$　　**4.** $-9 + 6$

5. $-2 + (-3)$　　**6.** $-7 + (-1)$　　**7.** $-9 + 7$　　**8.** $-5 + 8$

9. $2 + (-4)$　　**10.** $-4 + 1$　　**11.** $-3 + 9$　　**12.** $8 + (-3)$

13. $-5 + 7$　　**14.** $8 + (-6)$　　**15.** $6 + (-1)$　　**16.** $-8 + 5$

17. NUMBER SENSE Suppose you have a calculator that does not have a negative key. Using only ➕ , ➖ , ═ , and the number keys, show how you can get the calculator to display -5.

LAB 11.3

COOPERATIVE LEARNING

Materials Needed
- **number counters**
- **pencils**
- **paper**

Investigating Integer Subtraction

You can use number counters to subtract integers.

① Use counters to model the first number.

② If there are not enough counters to do the subtraction, add zero pairs so that you can do the subtraction.

③ Use the second number to decide how many counters to subtract.

④ Count the remaining counters. Write the result as an equation.

Part Ⓐ SUBTRACTING POSITIVE INTEGERS

You can use counters to find the difference $5 - 8$.

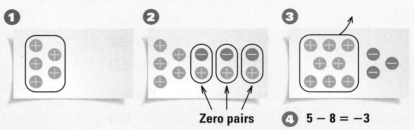

①   **②** Zero pairs   **③**   **④** $5 - 8 = -3$

1. Use counters to find the difference.

     a. $5 - 7$ **b.** $3 - 6$ **c.** $2 - 9$ **d.** $8 - 9$

Part Ⓑ SUBTRACTING NEGATIVE INTEGERS

You can use counters to find the difference $-2 - (-4)$.

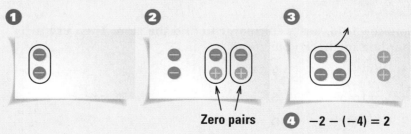

①   **②** Zero pairs   **③**   **④** $-2 - (-4) = 2$

2. Use counters to find the difference.

     a. $-3 - (-4)$ **b.** $-4 - (-6)$ **c.** $-5 - (-1)$ **d.** $-9 - (-5)$

3. In which parts of Exercise 2 did you add zero pairs to the model? Explain how to tell when you need to add zero pairs.

You can use counters to find the difference $5 - (-3)$.

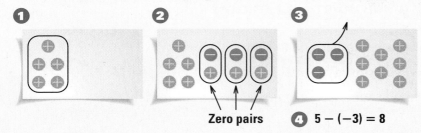

Zero pairs   ④ $5 - (-3) = 8$

4. Use number counters to find the difference.

    a. $6 - (-3)$ **b.** $4 - (-5)$ **c.** $2 - (-2)$ **d.** $1 - (-7)$

You can use counters to find the difference $-4 - 2$.

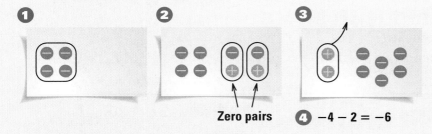

Zero pairs   ④ $-4 - 2 = -6$

5. Use number counters to find the difference.

    a. $-3 - 5$ **b.** $-2 - 6$ **c.** $-1 - 3$ **d.** $-8 - 1$

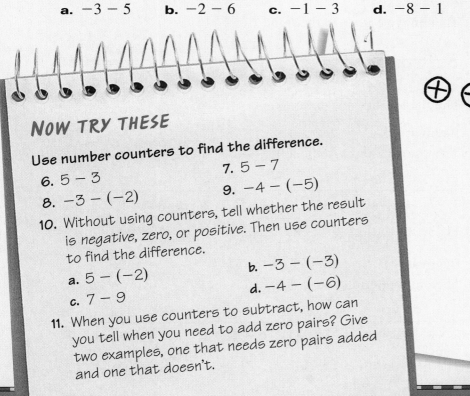

NOW TRY THESE

Use number counters to find the difference.

6. $5 - 3$

7. $5 - 7$

8. $-3 - (-2)$

9. $-4 - (-5)$

10. Without using counters, tell whether the result is negative, zero, or positive. Then use counters to find the difference.

    a. $5 - (-2)$ **b.** $-3 - (-3)$

    c. $7 - 9$ **d.** $-4 - (-6)$

11. When you use counters to subtract, how can you tell when you need to add zero pairs? Give two examples, one that needs zero pairs added and one that doesn't.

11.3

Subtracting Integers

What you should learn:

Goal 1 How to use a number line to subtract integers

Goal 2 How to use integer subtraction to solve real-life problems

Why you should learn it:

Knowing how to subtract integers can help you find distances. Another example is finding a change in temperature.

Goal 1 SUBTRACTING INTEGERS

You can use a number line to subtract integers.

- When you subtract a *positive* number, move left.
- When you subtract a *negative* number, move right.

Example 1 Subtracting Integers

Use a number line to find the difference.
a. $7 - 3$ **b.** $2 - (-4)$ **c.** $-3 - 2$ **d.** $-1 - (-5)$

Solution

a. Begin at 7.
Then move 3 units to the left.

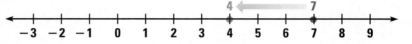

The final position is 4. So, $7 - 3 = 4$.

b. Begin at 2.
Then move 4 units to the right.

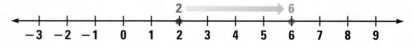

The final position is 6. So, $2 - (-4) = 6$.

c. Begin at -3.
Then move 2 units to the left.

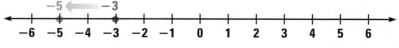

The final position is -5. So, $-3 - 2 = -5$.

d. Begin at -1.
Then move 5 units to the right.

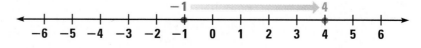

The final position is 4. So, $-1 - (-5) = 4$.

STUDY TIP

Compare the rules for subtracting on a number line with the rules for adding on a number line on page 538. Notice that with subtraction, you move the opposite direction that you move with addition.

In many real-life problems, smaller integers are subtracted from larger integers. When you subtract a smaller integer from a larger integer, the result represents the distance between the two numbers.

Example 2 **Subtracting Integers**

REAL LIFE
Temperature

At 1 P.M. the temperature was 5°C. By 5 P.M. it was −7°C. How many degrees did the temperature drop? Check your answer.

Solution

The number of degrees the temperature dropped is the difference between 5 and −7.

Begin at **5**. Then move **7** units to the right.

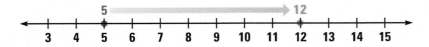

The final position is **12**, so $5 - (-7) = 12$.
The temperature dropped 12°.

✔**Check:** You can check this result by counting the number of degrees between 5 and −7 on the thermometers below. The number of degrees between 5 and −7 is 12. This is the same as the distance between 5 and −7 on a number line.

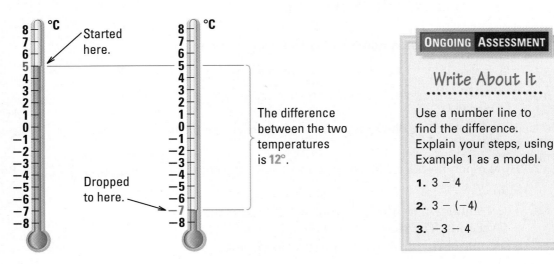

Started here.

Dropped to here.

The difference between the two temperatures is **12**°.

Real Life...
Real Facts

Ice Fishing

In a lake that is frozen, the best fishing is found near the bottom of the lake, not at the surface. Water near the bottom of the lake can be as warm as 39°F, so more fish swim there.

ONGOING ASSESSMENT

Write About It
....

Use a number line to find the difference. Explain your steps, using Example 1 as a model.

1. $3 - 4$

2. $3 - (-4)$

3. $-3 - 4$

GUIDED PRACTICE

In Exercises 1–4, use a number line. Start at 3. Write whether you should move *left* or *right* on the number line to solve.

```
←——+——+——+——+——+——+——+——+——+——+——+——+——+——→
   -6  -5  -4  -3  -2  -1   0   1   2   3   4   5   6
```

1. Subtract 2.   **2.** Add −2.   **3.** Add 2.   **4.** Subtract −2.

5. Repeat Exercises 1–4, starting at −3. How do your answers change?

6. **WRITING** Write a real-life problem that can be modeled by −10 − 25. Then solve the problem.

PRACTICE AND PROBLEM SOLVING

In Exercises 7–10, match the number line model with the subtraction problem that it represents.

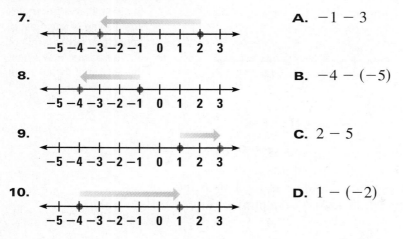

7.

A. −1 − 3

8.

B. −4 − (−5)

9.

C. 2 − 5

10.

D. 1 − (−2)

In Exercises 11–16, use a number line to find the difference.

11. −8 − 2   **12.** −2 − 5   **13.** 6 − (−5)

14. 2 − (−6)   **15.** −4 − (−9)   **16.** −7 − (−5)

MODEL ROCKET The diagram at the right shows the path of a model rocket.

17. How much higher is the rocket at its highest point than at ground level?

18. The countdown to liftoff of your model rocket starts at −5 seconds. The rocket reaches its highest point at 3 seconds after liftoff. How many seconds later is this?

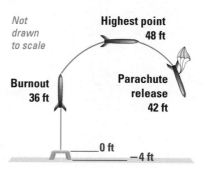

ALGEBRA In Exercises 19–21, evaluate the expression when $a = -5$.

19. $a - 5$ **20.** $6 - a$ **21.** $-3 - a$

Solve each subtraction problem. Describe any patterns you see.

22. $3 - 2 = \boxed{?}$

$3 - 1 = \boxed{?}$

$3 - 0 = \boxed{?}$

$3 - (-1) = \boxed{?}$

23. $3 - (-2) = \boxed{?}$

$2 - (-2) = \boxed{?}$

$1 - (-2) = \boxed{?}$

$0 - (-2) = \boxed{?}$

24. $-6 - 2 = \boxed{?}$

$-6 - 1 = \boxed{?}$

$-6 - 0 = \boxed{?}$

$-6 - (-1) = \boxed{?}$

25. INTEGER GAME Describe a strategy you could use to win this game.

Players take turns joining any two dots next to each other. Diagonals are not allowed. When a player makes a square, the player's initials go in the box. When all the squares are completed, find the scores by subtracting the numbers in each player's boxes from 25. The player with the highest score wins.

```
-3   2   4  -6  -2
 1   7  -4   3  -1
 5   3   6   2  -5
 3  -4   1   4  -3
 6  -1   2   5  -4
```

26. VOLCANOES Mauna Loa in Hawaii is one of the world's largest volcanoes. Its height above the surface of the ocean is about 4200 ft. The bottom of the volcano is on the ocean floor, about 25,800 ft below the surface of the ocean. Which estimate better describes the difference between the top and the bottom of the volcano? Explain.

A. 30,000 ft   **B.** 21,600 ft

Tech Link

Investigation 11, Interactive Real-Life Investigations

STANDARDIZED TEST PRACTICE

27. On a two-part test, Maria earned 35 points and 45 points but lost 2 points for forgetting to put her name on her paper. What was her total score?

Ⓐ 85   Ⓑ 82   Ⓒ 80   Ⓓ 78

28. In a football game, Joe gained 10 yd on one play, then lost 3 yd, and gained 5 yd. Find the total number of yards gained or lost.

Ⓐ 18   Ⓑ 15   Ⓒ 12   Ⓓ 10

29. When $x = -6$, $2 - x = \boxed{?}$.

Ⓐ -8 Ⓑ -4 Ⓒ 4   Ⓓ 8

EXPLORATION AND EXTENSION

30. BUILDING YOUR PROJECT You are on the Internet exploring data about icebergs. You discover the tip of an iceberg is 100 ft above sea level and the bottom of the iceberg is 500 ft below sea level.

a. Draw a vertical number line to represent these measures.

b. How could you use subtraction to find the total height of the iceberg? Include these facts in your article. Also include a sketch of an iceberg.

31. COMMUNICATING ABOUT MATHEMATICS The Maltese people took control of their own government in 1964. Use the number line on page 563 to find how many years this was after the first residents lived in Malta.

SPIRAL REVIEW

In Exercises 1–8, find the value of the exponent or the base. (3.7)

1. $49 = \boxed{?}^2$ **2.** $64 = 2^{\boxed{?}}$ **3.** $81 = \boxed{?}^4$ **4.** $125 = 5^{\boxed{?}}$

5. $16 = \boxed{?}^2$ **6.** $10{,}000 = 100^{\boxed{?}}$ **7.** $27 = \boxed{?}^3$ **8.** $100 = 10^{\boxed{?}}$

9. MOVIES A survey asked a group of 200 students to name their favorite type of movie. The favorite types were: comedy, 58%; suspense, 20%; drama, 15%; and westerns, 7%. How many students chose each type of movie? **(4.8)**

In Exercises 10–15, complete the statement using >, <, or =. (6.3, 6.5)

10. $\frac{6}{8}\ \boxed{?}\ \frac{3}{4}$ **11.** $\frac{3}{5}\ \boxed{?}\ \frac{2}{3}$ **12.** $\frac{5}{9}\ \boxed{?}\ \frac{1}{2}$

13. $\frac{3}{4}\ \boxed{?}\ \frac{3}{5}$ **14.** $\frac{4}{5}\ \boxed{?}\ \frac{20}{25}$ **15.** $\frac{7}{10}\ \boxed{?}\ \frac{7}{11}$

In Exercises 16–18, find the value of x. (9.7)

16. 75°, 70°, $x°$ **17.** 40°, $x°$ **18.** 25°, $x°$, 30°

In Exercises 19 and 20, find the circumference and the area of a circle with the given measure. (10.5, 10.6)

19. Diameter = 16 m **20.** Radius = 5 in.

Take this test as you would take a test in class. The answers to the exercises are given in the back of the book.

In Exercises 1–4, match the integer with the phrase that describes it. (11.1)

A. Opposite of -6

B. 1 less than -7

C. 1 more than -1

D. Between -7 and -5

1. -8 **2.** -6 **3.** 0 **4.** 6

NUMBER SENSE In Exercises 5–12, use a number line to complete the statement using > or <. (11.1)

5. -9 ? -5 **6.** -2 ? -3 **7.** -4 ? 0 **8.** 1 ? -1

9. 6 ? -6 **10.** -10 ? -3 **11.** -8 ? 2 **12.** -1 ? -7

In Exercises 13–20, use a number line to solve the problem. (11.2, 11.3)

13. $-3 + 5$ **14.** $-6 + 2$ **15.** $-1 + (-9)$ **16.** $-8 - (-2)$

17. $7 - 12$ **18.** $-5 - 6$ **19.** $4 - (-7)$ **20.** $9 - (-3)$

In Exercises 21 and 22, use a number line. Write the addition or subtraction problem described. Then solve. (11.2, 11.3)

21. Start at -7. Move 4 units right, then 2 units left.

22. Start at -3. Move 5 units left, then 1 unit right.

23. TEMPERATURE On a cold winter morning, you keep a record of the temperature at every hour. At 7:00 A.M., you record a temperature of $-12°$F. At 8:00 A.M., you record a temperature of $-8°$F. You forget to record the temperatures at 9:00 A.M. and 10:00 A.M. However, you do record the temperature for 11:00 A.M. to be 4°F. Use a number line to estimate the temperatures at 9:00 A.M. and 10:00 A.M. **(11.1)**

24. READING A BAR GRAPH You have a job walking dogs for your neighbors. The bar graph at the right shows how much money you earned and spent in five days. Find how much money you have at the end of the five days. **(11.2, 11.3)**

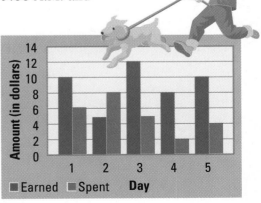

■ Earned ■ Spent   **Day**

25. WRITING Write a summary of what you have learned about integers. **(11.1–11.3)**

LAB 11.4

COOPERATIVE LEARNING

Investigating the Coordinate Plane

In Lesson 9.5, you plotted ordered pairs in a coordinate plane. Now that you have studied integers, you can enlarge the coordinate plane to include points that have negative coordinates.

Materials Needed
- graph paper
- pencils or pens
- ruler

Part Ⓐ **INTEGERS AND THE COORDINATE PLANE**

The coordinate plane below has coordinates that are positive, zero, and negative. The ordered pair (0, 0) is the origin.

To graph the point $B(-4, 2)$, start at the origin. Then, move 4 units to the left and 2 units up. The ordered pairs $A(3, 4)$, $C(-5, -4)$, $D(4, -5)$ can be graphed in a similar way.

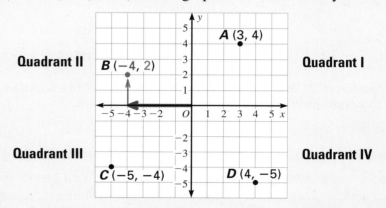

1. **a.** Copy the coordinate plane and the four points. Then plot the following six points.

   $M(-4, 3), N(4, 3), P(4, -3), Q\left(\frac{3}{2}, -3\right), R(-4, 0), S(-3, -4)$

   b. Name all of the points on the same vertical line.

   c. Name all of the points on the same horizontal line.

   d. Do the points $M, N, P,$ and S form the vertices of a rectangle? Explain.

2. Are the points $(1, -4)$ and $(-1, 4)$ the same point? Explain.

3. **a.** In which quadrant(s) can you graph a point in which the coordinates are equal?

   b. In which quadrant(s) can you graph a point in which the coordinates are opposites?

4. a. Draw a coordinate plane, as shown at the right. Then plot the figure. Write the coordinates of the labeled points.

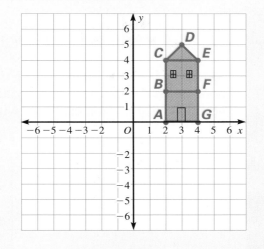

b. Slide the figure 6 units to the left and 2 units down. What are the new coordinates for points *A, B, C, D, E, F,* and *G*?

c. What patterns do you see in the *x*-coordinates? in the *y*-coordinates?

5. Now slide the new figure 2 units to the right and 4 units down. Then describe the slide you would need to move the figure back to its original position.

NOW TRY THESE

6. Copy the coordinate grid at the right on graph paper. Include the labels of the points. Write the coordinates of each of the 15 points. For example, point A has coordinates (6, 0).

7. Add these labeled points to your graph.
G(1, −3), H(1, −2), J(−6, −2), K(−7, −1), N(−3, 3), S(3, 3), V(4, 3), W(5, 2)

8. Connect the points in alphabetical order. Then connect W to A. What animal is formed?

9. Describe the slide that would move the tip of the animal's tail to the origin.

10. Describe a slide that would make all of the animal's x-coordinates and y-coordinates negative.

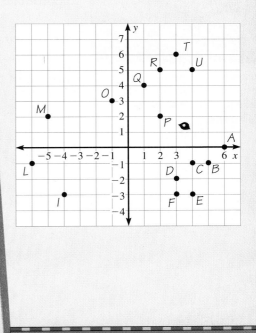

11.4

The Coordinate Plane

What you should learn:

Goal 1 How to plot points in a coordinate plane

Goal 2 How to use a coordinate plane to describe figures that have been slid or flipped

Why you should learn it:

Knowing how to plot points in a coordinate plane can help you understand how a computer works.

Computers are used by car designers and architects, to make it easier to visualize their plans.

Goal 1 USING A COORDINATE PLANE

In Lesson 9.5, you studied the coordinate plane. But in that lesson, none of the coordinates were negative. Now that you have studied negative integers, you can work with an expanded coordinate plane.

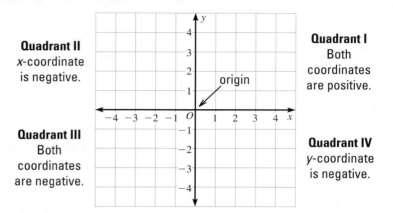

Quadrant II
x-coordinate is negative.

Quadrant I
Both coordinates are positive.

origin

Quadrant III
Both coordinates are negative.

Quadrant IV
y-coordinate is negative.

The x-axis and y-axis divide the plane into four regions called **quadrants** .

Example 1 Plotting Points

Plot points $A(-2, 3)$, $B(-4, 0)$, $C(-2, -4)$, and $D(1, -3)$ in a coordinate plane.

Solution

Begin by plotting point A. The x-coordinate is -2, so move 2 units to the left of the origin. The y-coordinate is 3, so move 3 units up.

To slide a figure on a coordinate plane, you move each point the same number of units in the same direction.

Example 2 **Moving Points on a Coordinate Plane**

You are using a computer drawing program. The coordinates of the figure on your screen are $A(-1, 3)$, $B(-3, 1)$, $C(-1, -2)$, and $D(-2, 1)$.

REAL LIFE
Computers

a. What are the new coordinates of the figure if you slide it 3 units to the right and 1 unit down?

b. What are the new coordinates of the figure if you flip it over the y-axis?

Solution

a. First, draw the figure. Slide it 3 units to the right and 1 unit down.

The coordinates of the new figure are $(2, 2)$, $(0, 0)$, $(2, -3)$, and $(1, 0)$.

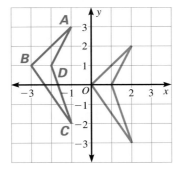

b. First, draw the figure. Then flip it over the y-axis.

The coordinates of the new figure are $(1, 3)$, $(3, 1)$, $(1, -2)$, and $(2, 1)$.

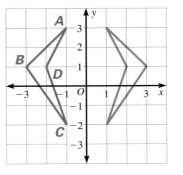

Real Life...
Real Facts

Galileo was the first spacecraft to orbit Jupiter. Winds greater than 400 mi/h have been detected there, as well as a new radiation belt about 31,000 mi above Jupiter.

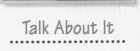
ONGOING ASSESSMENT

Talk About It
••••••••••••••••••••

Use the figure *ABCD* in Example 2. What are the new coordinates after you move the figure?

1. Slide left 3 units and up 4 units.

2. Slide right 4 units and down 2 units.

1. Write the ordered pairs for the points shown on the coordinate plane. Which of these points has a special name? What is that name?

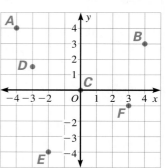

In Exercises 2–4, describe in words how to plot the point in a coordinate plane.

2. $(-3, 4)$ 3. $(2, 7)$ 4. $(-4, -6)$

5. Plot the points represented by the ordered pairs $A(-2, 2)$, $B(1, 2)$, $C(2, -2)$, and $D(-1, -2)$. Connect the sides of polygon $ABCD$. Then name the type of polygon.

PRACTICE AND PROBLEM SOLVING

In Exercises 6–9, name the quadrant that contains the point.

6. $(-9, 5)$ 7. $(1, 3)$ 8. $(-7.6, -3)$ 9. $(2, -2)$

In Exercises 10–12, plot the points represented by the ordered pairs. Connect the sides of the polygon. Then name the type of polygon.

10. $A(2, 1)$, $B\left(-2, -2\frac{3}{4}\right)$, $C(4, -2)$

11. $H(-5, -4)$, $I(-5, -2)$, $J(-1, 0)$, $K(-1, -6)$

12. $D(1, 0)$, $E(3, -2)$, $F(3, -5)$, $G(0, -5)$, $H(-2, -3)$

13. Name the coordinates of each vertex. Slide the figure 1 unit right and 2 units up. What are the new coordinates of each vertex?

14. Name the coordinates of each vertex. Flip the figure over the x-axis. What are the new coordinates of each vertex?

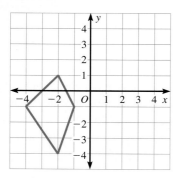

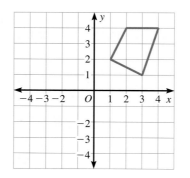

15. **VISUAL THINKING** Draw a triangle in the first quadrant. Flip the triangle over the y-axis. Compare the coordinates of the vertices of the two triangles.

In Exercises 16 and 17, plot the points represented by the ordered pairs. Connect the sides of the polygons. Describe the slide or flip.

16. Figure: $H(3, -1)$, $I(6, -1)$, $J(4, -3)$, $K(1, -3)$
Slide: $L(-4, 1)$, $M(-1, 1)$, $N(-3, -1)$, $O(-6, -1)$

17. Figure: $A(-5, 3)$, $B(-2, -1)$, $C(-7, -1)$
Flip: $D(5, 3)$, $E(2, -1)$, $F(7, -1)$

USING A MAP **A company has six stores in a city, as shown in the coordinate plane at the right. Each unit represents 5 mi.**

18. Where is the Headquarters located?

19. Which store is closest to the headquarters? Estimate its distance.

20. Which two stores are the same distance from the headquarters? Explain.

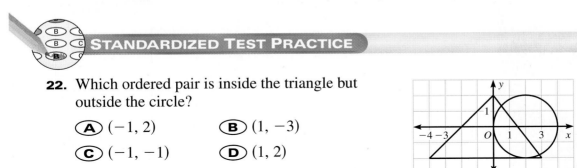

21. Store 1 decides to move its location to $(-7, -1)$. Describe the slide.

STANDARDIZED TEST PRACTICE

22. Which ordered pair is inside the triangle but outside the circle?

Ⓐ $(-1, 2)$ **Ⓑ** $(1, -3)$

Ⓒ $(-1, -1)$ **Ⓓ** $(1, 2)$

EXPLORATION AND EXTENSION

PORTFOLIO

23. a. BUILDING YOUR PROJECT To estimate the locations of the United States stations in Antarctica, draw a coordinate plane and label the axes from -16 to 16. Let the origin represent the South Pole. Each unit represents 100 mi.

b. Locate and label these stations: Amundsen-Scott Station (at South Pole), Palmer Station (1300 mi left and 700 mi up from origin), McMurdo Station (200 mi right and 800 mi down from origin). Include a map of these stations in your article.

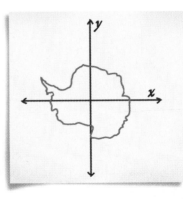

What you should learn:

Goal 1 How to create and describe patterns by evaluating expressions

Goal 2 How to use a coordinate plane to represent data

Why you should learn it:

Representing data in a coordinate plane can help you find patterns. An example is finding how many inches a corn plant grows each day.

In 1996, the United States produced about four times as much corn as wheat.

Patterns in the Coordinate Plane

Goal 1 EVALUATING INTEGER EXPRESSIONS

One of the important uses of algebra is to use expressions to represent patterns. To recognize the pattern, it helps to make a table.

Example 1 Evaluating Expressions

a. Evaluate $x - 2$ for the integers -3 through 3. Make a table.

b. Describe any patterns that you see.

x	-3	-2	-1	0	1	2	3
$x - 2$	?	?	?	?	?	?	?

Solution

a. Evaluate the expression $x - 2$ for the given values of x.

Value of x	Substitute	Simplify
-3	$-3 - 2$	$-3 - 2 = -5$
-2	$-2 - 2$	$-2 - 2 = -4$
-1	$-1 - 2$	$-1 - 2 = -3$
0	$0 - 2$	$0 - 2 = -2$
1	$1 - 2$	$1 - 2 = -1$
2	$2 - 2$	$2 - 2 = 0$
3	$3 - 2$	$3 - 2 = 1$

x	$x - 2$
-3	-5
-2	-4
-1	-3
0	-2
1	-1
2	0
3	1

b. **STRATEGY** **LOOK FOR A PATTERN** As the numbers in the first column increase by 1, the numbers in the second column also increase by 1.

Another pattern is that each number in the second column is 2 less than its matching number in the first column.

··

You can use mental math to find a value for y, given a value for x. To solve the equation $y = 3 - x$ when $x = 2$, substitute 2 for x:

$$y = 3 - x$$
$$= 3 - 2 = 1$$

So, when $x = 2$, $y = 1$ is a solution. This can be written as the ordered pair (2, 1). Notice that the solution has two values.

Sometimes graphing data, such as ordered pairs, can help you to see a pattern in the data.

Example 2 Graphing Solutions

Make a table of the solutions of the equation $y = 3 - x$. Use x-values for the integers -1 through 4. Write the solutions of the equation as ordered pairs. Graph the ordered pairs and describe the pattern.

Solution

Substitute each x-value into the equation to find the corresponding y-value. For example, when $x = -1$, $y = 4$. Make a table of the x-values and y-values.

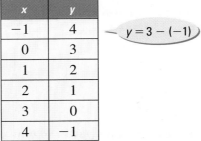

x	y
−1	4
0	3
1	2
2	1
3	0
4	−1

$y = 3 - (-1)$

Write each pair of x-values and y-values as an ordered pair.

$(-1, 4), (0, 3), (1, 2), (2, 1), (3, 0), (4, -1)$

Plot the ordered pairs on a coordinate plane.

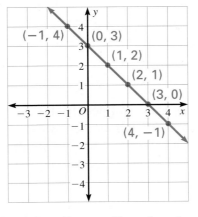

One pattern is that the points lie on a line. Another pattern is that each time x increases by 1, y decreases by 1.

ONGOING ASSESSMENT

Write About It
• • • • • • • • • • • • • • • • • • •

1. Rewrite the data in Example 1 as ordered pairs.

2. Plot the ordered pairs.

3. Describe the pattern.

GUIDED PRACTICE

1. Order the steps necessary to graph the solutions of an equation in the coordinate plane.

    A. Graph the ordered pairs.   **B.** Write as ordered pairs.

    C. Make a table of the data.   **D.** Evaluate the expression.

2. Copy and complete the table. Then write the data in the table as ordered pairs.

x	-2	-1	0	1	2
$x + 3$	?	?	?	?	?

In Exercises 3 and 4, use the coordinate plane at the right.

3. Describe the pattern of the points.

4. If the pattern continued, which of the following would be on the graph? Explain.

    A. $(-15, -15)$ **B.** $(15, -15)$

    C. $(-15, 15)$ **D.** $(15, 15)$

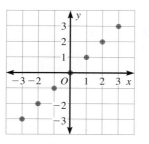

PRACTICE AND PROBLEM SOLVING

In Exercises 5 and 6, complete the table. Describe any patterns you see.

5.

x	$x + 4$
-3	?
-2	?
-1	?
0	?
1	?
2	?
3	?

6.

x	$4 - x$
-3	?
-2	?
-1	?
0	?
1	?
2	?
3	?

7. GRADES You are a teacher and decide to give a 2-point penalty for each day that homework is late. Complete the table below that shows the number of points a student will receive for a 10-point homework paper. Then plot the ordered pairs on a coordinate plane. Describe the pattern.

x	Days Late	0	1	2	3	4	5
y	Score	10	?	?	?	?	?

Evaluate the given expression for the integers −3 through 3. Record your results in a table. Graph the ordered pairs. Describe any patterns.

8. $x - 3$

9. $-5 + x$

10. $x - (-4)$

11. $x + (-2)$

In Exercises 12–14, match the equation to the pattern on the coordinate plane.

A.   **B.**   **C.**
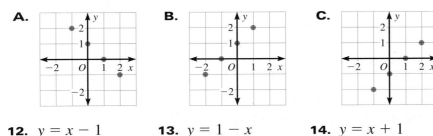

12. $y = x - 1$ **13.** $y = 1 - x$ **14.** $y = x + 1$

15. Write five ordered pairs that you think lie on a vertical line. Check your work by plotting the points. How can you tell whether two points lie on a vertical line?

16. **SCIENCE** The table shows the height (in inches) of a corn kernel after it is planted.

x	Day	1	2	3	4	5
y	Height	−3	−1.5	0	1.5	3

a. Write the data as ordered pairs.

b. Graph the ordered pairs. Use the graph to complete the statement: *A corn plant grows* ? *inches each day.*

c. How do you interpret a height of −3 in.?

Real Life...
Real Facts

Corn

In 1996, the state of Iowa produced about 1.6 billion bushels of corn.

STANDARDIZED TEST PRACTICE

Use the coordinate plane at the right.

17. Which equation matches the pattern of points on the line?

A $y = x - 2$ **B** $y = 2 - x$

C $y = x + 2$ **D** $y = -2 + x$

18. Which ordered pair is on the line?

A $(-1, 2)$ **B** $(2, 1)$

C $(3, 1)$ **D** $(3, -1)$

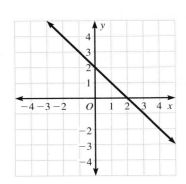

EXPLORATION AND EXTENSION

BUILDING YOUR PROJECT While researching the history of Antarctica, you discover that the first person to reach the South Pole was a Norwegian explorer named Roald Amundsen. Amundsen and British explorer Robert Scott raced to be the first to reach the South Pole. America's Amundsen-Scott research station, which is located just a few hundred yards from the South Pole, is named for these two men.

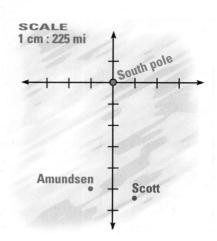

SCALE
1 cm : 225 mi

19. Amundsen set off from a location on the Ross Ice Shelf. He reached the South Pole on December 14, 1911. What ordered pair represents the approximate spot where Amundsen began his expedition?

20. Scott began his expedition on Ross Island, where McMurdy station is now located. He arrived at the South Pole 35 days after Amundsen. What ordered pair represents the approximate spot where Scott began his expedition?

21. Use a ruler and the scale to estimate the length of each expedition. Which expedition appears to be shorter? How much shorter?

SPIRAL REVIEW

In Exercises 1–8, add or subtract. (7.5)

1. $6\frac{2}{5} - 2\frac{4}{5}$

2. $10\frac{5}{8} + 4\frac{1}{4}$

3. $2\frac{7}{8} - 1\frac{1}{3}$

4. $3\frac{3}{4} + 5\frac{1}{6}$

5. $7\frac{2}{3} + 7\frac{1}{4}$

6. $1\frac{5}{6} + 10\frac{1}{8}$

7. $8\frac{1}{6} - 1\frac{5}{6}$

8. $5\frac{9}{10} - 3\frac{1}{2}$

PROBABILITY A square is evenly divided into 9 small squares. Three of the small squares are red, 2 are blue, and 4 are yellow. If a coin is tossed onto the square, what is the probability it will land on the given color? (The coin is retossed if it lands on a line.) (6.7)

9. Red

10. Yellow

11. Blue or red

ALGEBRA In Exercises 12–15, solve. (8.4, 8.5)

12. $t \div \frac{2}{5} = \frac{5}{2}$

13. $\frac{3}{4} \div n = \frac{9}{4}$

14. $\frac{4}{5} \div m = \frac{4}{15}$

15. $p \div \frac{1}{4} = \frac{4}{15}$

16. **WORKING BACKWARD** You take some money with you to the movies. You spend $\frac{2}{5}$ of the money on admission. You then spend $\frac{2}{3}$ of the money you have left on a snack and a beverage. You leave the movies with $3. How much money did you originally take to the movies? (1.7)

It's About
TIME

READ About It

The oldest pyramids in Egypt were built in about 2650 B.C. People used to think that these were the oldest large stone monuments in the world. But in 1972, the archeologist Colin Renfrew was able to show that some giant buildings on the island of Malta were about 1350 years older than the pyramids. These huge structures were built by Malta's first residents, who probably arrived in Malta about 5200 B.C. and disappeared in 2500 B.C.

After they disappeared, the island changed hands many times. Phoenicians colonized Malta in about 1000 B.C. Then, about 2090 years later, the island came under the control of Sicily. In 1530, Sicily gave the island to the Knights of Malta. They held the island for 268 years until Napoleon Bonaparte took over. Later, Malta became a colony of Great Britain. Finally, in 1964, the people of Malta took control of their own government and have held it ever since.

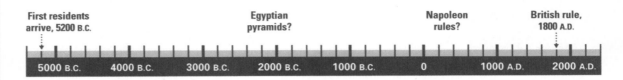

First residents arrive, 5200 B.C.		Egyptian pyramids?		Napoleon rules?	British rule, 1800 A.D.

5000 B.C.   4000 B.C.   3000 B.C.   2000 B.C.   1000 B.C.   0   1000 A.D.   2000 A.D.

Time Line of Events on Malta

WRITE About It

1. The time line shows two important events in Malta. Copy the time line and add six more events that are important in Malta's history. Label the dates to the left of 0 as negative numbers.

2. Stonehenge in England was built around 1800 B.C. Add Stonehenge and the first Egyptian pyramids to your time line. How many years older than each of these monuments are the ruins on Malta? Explain your reasoning.

3. How many years after the first residents arrived on Malta did they start building monuments? Write your answer as a sentence.

4. In what year did Sicily start to rule Malta? In what year did Napoleon Bonaparte invade Malta? Explain.

5. When the people of Malta regained control of their own island, how many years had it been since the original residents had been there? Explain.

11.6 Coordinate Geometry

What you should learn:

Goal 1 How to find areas of figures in a coordinate plane

Goal 2 How to find the midpoint of a line segment

Why you should learn it:

Understanding coordinate geometry can help you when studying maps. An example is finding the area of a piece of land.

Goal 1 AREAS IN THE COORDINATE PLANE

Coordinate geometry is the study of geometric figures in a coordinate plane. The coordinates of the points on the plane can be used to find lengths, perimeters, and areas.

To measure lengths, use the units given on the axes.

Example 1 Finding Areas

Find the area of each figure.

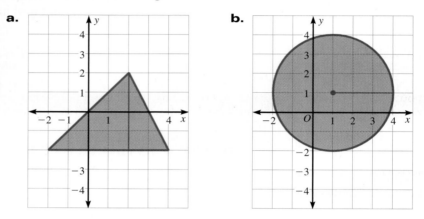

a. b.

Solution

a. This figure is a triangle. The base of the triangle is 6 units long, and the height is 4 units. Notice that area is always positive. Use the formula for the area of a triangle.

$$\text{Area} = \frac{1}{2} \cdot \text{base} \cdot \text{height} \qquad \text{Area of triangle}$$

$$= \frac{1}{2} \cdot 6 \cdot 4 \qquad \text{Substitute.}$$

$$= 12 \text{ units}^2 \qquad \text{Simplify.}$$

The area is 12 units^2.

b. This figure is a circle. The radius is 3 units long. Use the formula for the area of a circle.

$$\text{Area} = \pi \cdot (\text{radius})^2 \qquad \text{Area of circle}$$

$$\approx 3.14 \cdot 3^2 \qquad \text{Substitute.}$$

$$\approx 28.26 \text{ units}^2 \qquad \text{Simplify.}$$

The area is about 28.26 units^2.

STUDY TIP

There are two ways to find the length of the base of the triangle in part (a) of Example 1. You could count the squares that lie along the base, or you could use subtraction. On the x-axis, the distance from $x = 4$ to $x = -2$ is $4 - (-2)$, or 6.

The **midpoint** of a line segment is the point on the line segment that is halfway between the two endpoints.

Sometimes you can use inspection to find a midpoint of a line segment. At the right, the point $M(0, -1)$ is the midpoint of the line segment joining $P(-3, 0)$ and $Q(3, -2)$. It is easy to see that 0 is the x-coordinate because it is halfway between -3 and 3.

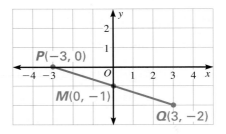

Example 2 **Finding Midpoints**

By inspection, find the midpoints of the sides of quadrilateral *EFGH*. The coordinates are $E(2, 3)$, $F(4, 1)$, $G(0, -3)$, and $H(-4, 1)$. Then connect the midpoints. What type of figure do you get?

Solution

Begin by plotting the four points in a coordinate plane. Connect the points to form quadrilateral *EFGH*. Use inspection to estimate where the midpoint of each side is.

The midpoint of $\overline{EF}$ appears to be the point $(3, 2)$.

The midpoint of $\overline{FG}$ appears to be the point $(2, -1)$.

The midpoint of $\overline{GH}$ appears to be the point $(-2, -1)$.

The midpoint of $\overline{HE}$ appears to be the point $(-1, 2)$.

When you connect the midpoints, you get a parallelogram.

ONGOING ASSESSMENT

Talk About It
••••••••••••••••••••

1. Use a ruler to draw several quadrilaterals on grid paper.

2. Find and connect the midpoints of the sides.

3. Do you always get a parallelogram?

11.6 Exercises

GUIDED PRACTICE

Use the figure at the right. Match the point or measurement with its description.

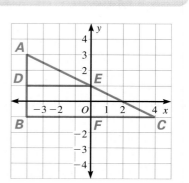

1. 12 units^2 **A.** Length of $\overline{AB}$

2. 4 units^2 **B.** Midpoint of $\overline{AB}$

3. 4 units   **C.** Midpoint of $\overline{BC}$

4. $(-4, 1)$ **D.** Perimeter of rectangle $BDEF$

5. 12 units   **E.** Area of triangle DEA

6. $(0, -1)$ **F.** Area of quadrilateral $AEFB$

PRACTICE AND PROBLEM SOLVING

AREA In Exercises 7–9, find the area of the figure.

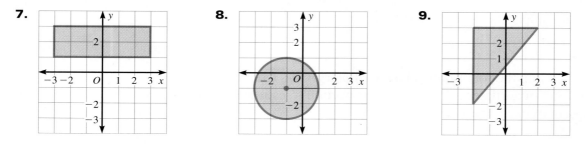

7.

8.

9.

GEOMETRY In Exercises 10–13, plot the ordered pairs and connect them to form a polygon. Find the area.

10. $(2, 5), (-3, 5), (-3, -2), (2, -2)$ 11. $(2, 0), (-1, 3), (-1, -5)$

12. $(2, 3), (4, -1), (-2, -1)$ 13. $(4, 1), (4, -2), (-3, -2), (-3, 1)$

Which is the best estimate of the figure's area? Explain.

14. **A.** 4 units^2 15. **A.** 12 units^2 16. **A.** 10 units^2

    B. 6 units^2 **B.** 14 units^2 **B.** 12 units^2

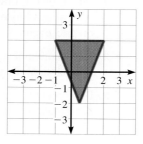
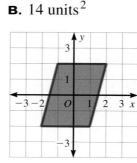
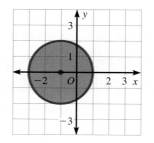

REASONING Find the coordinates of the midpoints of $\overline{PR}$ and $\overline{QS}$. Are the midpoints the same point? Explain.

17.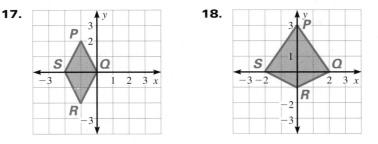

18.

19.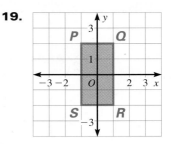

20. **LOOKING FOR A PATTERN** In the figure at the right, each smaller triangle is formed by connecting the midpoints of the sides of the next larger triangle. Find the area of each of the four triangles. Describe any patterns that you see. What would be the area of the next smaller triangle?

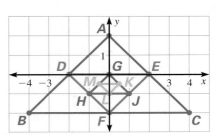

21. **LAND AREA** On a grid, each square unit is 2 mi by 2 mi. The coordinates of a piece of land are $(-3, 3)$, $(1, 3)$, and $(1, -3)$. What is the area in square units? in square miles?

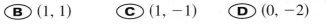

STANDARDIZED TEST PRACTICE

In Exercises 22 and 23, use the figure at the right.

22. Find the midpoint of the base of the triangle.

　Ⓐ $(0, 1)$　　Ⓑ $(1, 1)$　　Ⓒ $(1, -1)$　　Ⓓ $(0, -2)$

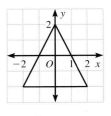

23. Find the area of the triangle.

　Ⓐ 8 units^2　　Ⓑ 16 units^2　　Ⓒ 20 units^2　　Ⓓ 32 units^2

EXPLORATION AND EXTENSION

24. **GROUP ACTIVITY** Draw a large triangle on cardboard. Find the midpoint of one side of the triangle. Draw a line from the midpoint to the opposite vertex. Repeat this for each of the other sides. The point where the three lines meet is the balance point of the triangle. Check it by carefully cutting out the triangle and balancing it on a pencil point.

Balance point

WHAT *did you learn?*

WHY *did you learn it?*

		WHAT did you learn?	WHY did you learn it?
Skills	11.1	Graph integers on a number line.	Understand a scientific report, such as a report about temperatures.
	11.2	Add integers.	Find averages, such as average above or below par in golf.
	11.3	Subtract Integers.	Help find changes in temperatures and in distances.
	11.4	Plot points on a coordinate plane. Slide and flip geometric figures on a coordinate plane.	Understand better how a computer works.
	11.5	Use a graph on the coordinate plane to represent data.	Find patterns in real life, such as the growth of a plant.
	11.6	Find the area of a figure on a coordinate plane. Find the midpoint of a line segment on a coordinate plane.	Study maps, and find the area of a piece of land.
Strategies	11.1–6	Use problem solving strategies.	Solve a wide variety of real-life problems.
Using Data	11.1–6	Use tables and graphs.	Organize data and solve problems.

HOW *does it fit in the bigger picture of mathematics?*

Throughout history, the number system we use has become more and more complicated. In this book, you have studied many types of numbers.

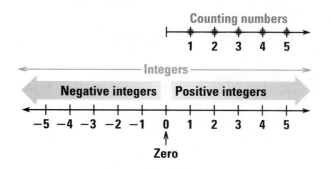

You can choose the form of a number that helps you solve a problem the easiest way.

VOCABULARY

- **integers (p. 532)**
- **negative integers (p. 532)**
- **positive integers (p. 532)**
- **opposites (p. 532)**
- **quadrants (p. 554)**
- **coordinate geometry (p. 564)**
- **midpoint (p. 565)**

11.1 GRAPHING INTEGERS ON A NUMBER LINE

Example

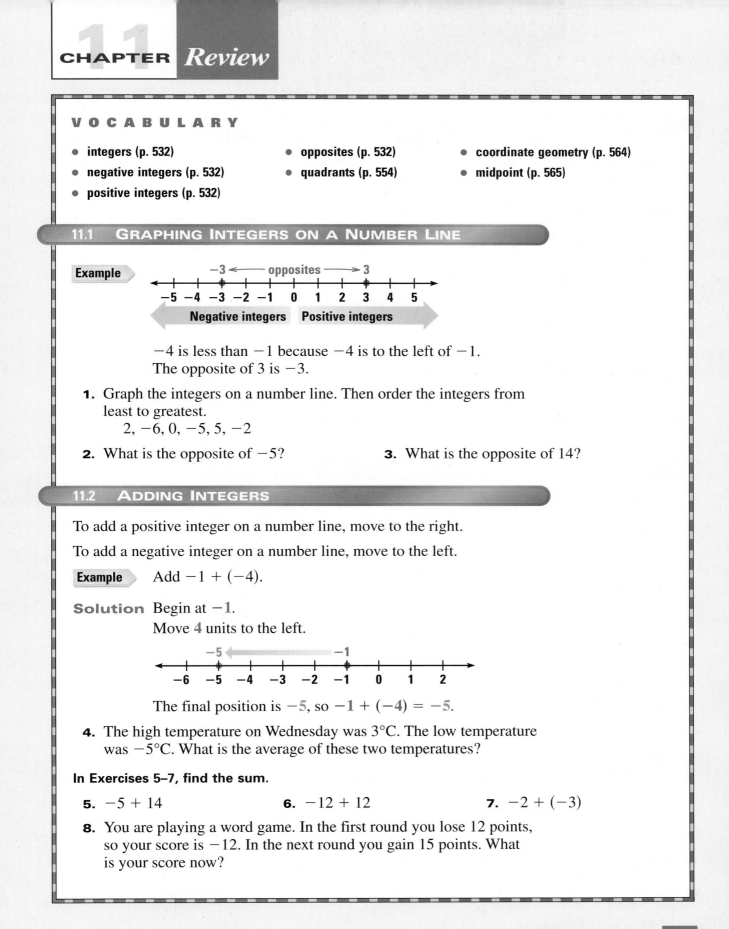

-4 is less than -1 because -4 is to the left of -1.
The opposite of 3 is -3.

1. Graph the integers on a number line. Then order the integers from least to greatest.
$2, -6, 0, -5, 5, -2$

2. What is the opposite of -5?

3. What is the opposite of 14?

11.2 ADDING INTEGERS

To add a positive integer on a number line, move to the right.

To add a negative integer on a number line, move to the left.

Example Add $-1 + (-4)$.

Solution Begin at -1.
Move 4 units to the left.

The final position is -5, so $-1 + (-4) = -5$.

4. The high temperature on Wednesday was 3°C. The low temperature was -5°C. What is the average of these two temperatures?

In Exercises 5–7, find the sum.

5. $-5 + 14$

6. $-12 + 12$

7. $-2 + (-3)$

8. You are playing a word game. In the first round you lose 12 points, so your score is -12. In the next round you gain 15 points. What is your score now?

11.3 SUBTRACTING INTEGERS

To subtract a positive integer on a number line, move to the left.

To subtract a negative integer on a number line, move to the right.

Example Subtract -2 from -3.

Solution Begin at -3.

Move 2 units to the right.

The final position is -1, so $-3 - (-2) = -1$.

Evaluate each expression when $t = -3$.

9. $t - (-7)$ **10.** $3 - t$ **11.** $-5 - t$ **12.** $t - 8$

13. $t - (-3)$ **14.** $0 - t$ **15.** $14 - t$ **16.** $-6 - t$

11.4 THE COORDINATE PLANE

Example To plot the point $(2, -1)$, move 2 units to the right of the origin along the x-axis and 1 unit below the origin along the y-axis.

In Exercises 17–20, write the ordered pair for the point.

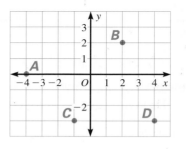

17. Point A **18.** Point B

19. Point C **20.** Point D

21. Name the quadrant that contains point C.

In Exercises 22–29, plot the point in a coordinate plane.

22. $(6, 1)$ **23.** $(-3, -3)$ **24.** $(0, 4)$ **25.** $(2, 0)$

26. $(-3, 0)$ **27.** $(-2, 3)$ **28.** $(4, -5)$ **29.** $(0, -1)$

11.5 PATTERNS IN THE COORDINATE PLANE

Plotting data in a coordinate plane can help you see patterns in the data.

Example

x	−3	−2	−1	0	1	2	3
x + 1	−2	−1	0	1	2	3	4

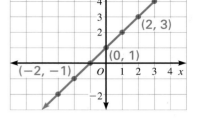

As the numbers in the first row increase by 1, the numbers in the second row increase by 1.

30. Complete the table, then graph the data in a coordinate plane. Describe any patterns.

x	−2	−1	0	1	2
4 − x	?	?	?	?	?

11.6 COORDINATE GEOMETRY

The midpoint of a line segment is the point on the line segment that is halfway between the two endpoints. You can use the coordinates of points in a plane to find perimeters and areas.

Example

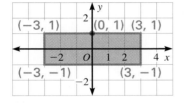

The midpoint of the segment between (−3, 1) and (3, 1) is (0, 1).

Area = base × height
= 6 × 2
= 12 units²

31. Find the midpoint of each side of the triangle at the right.

32. Find the area of the triangle at the right.

33. Write the coordinates of Sioux City and Waterloo. Then estimate the distance (in miles) in between the two cities.

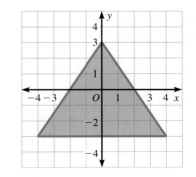

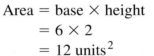

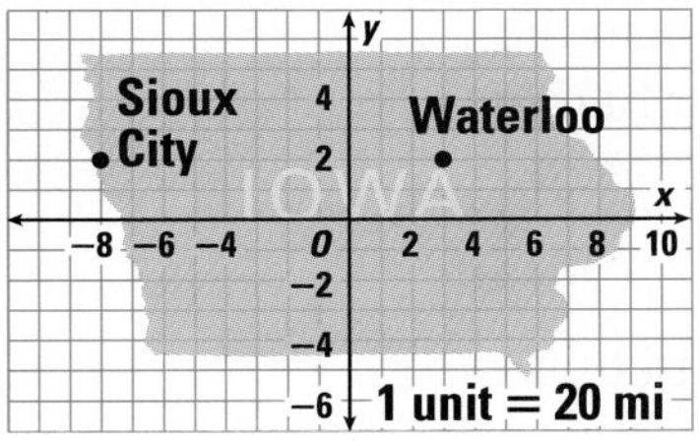

In Exercises 1–3, write the integer described by the phrase.

1. 2 more than -10 **2.** 4 less than 1 **3.** Opposite of 7

In Exercises 4–11, solve the problem.

4. $-5 + 11$ **5.** $-8 + 8$ **6.** $-6 + 22$ **7.** $-4 - (-9)$

8. $-7 - (23)$ **9.** $-4 - 4$ **10.** $5 - 10$ **11.** $3 - (-1)$

GEOMETRY **In Exercises 12 and 13, plot the points and connect them to form a polygon. Then name the type of polygon.**

12. $A(-1, 3), B(2, 0), C(-1, -1), D(-4, 2)$

13. $M(-7, -1), N(-3, 3), P(1, -1), Q(-3, -5)$

In Exercises 14 and 15, copy and complete the table. Then copy the graph at the right and use the data in the table to plot the ordered pairs. What do you notice?

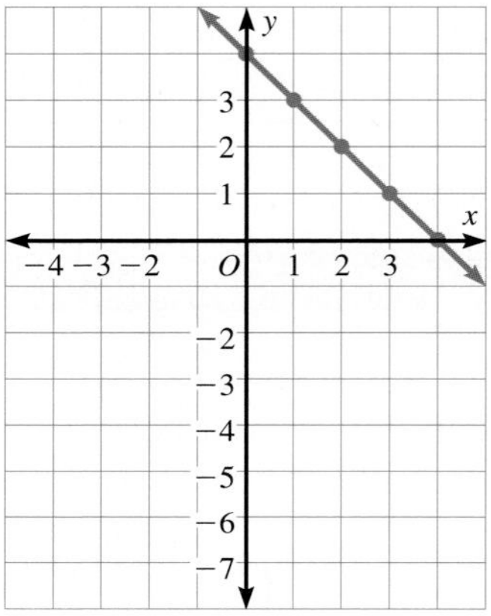

14.

x	−3	−2	−1	0	1	2	3
1 − x	?	?	?	?	?	?	?

15.

x	−3	−2	−1	0	1	2	3
x − 4	?	?	?	?	?	?	?

In Exercises 16–18, find the area of the figure.

16.

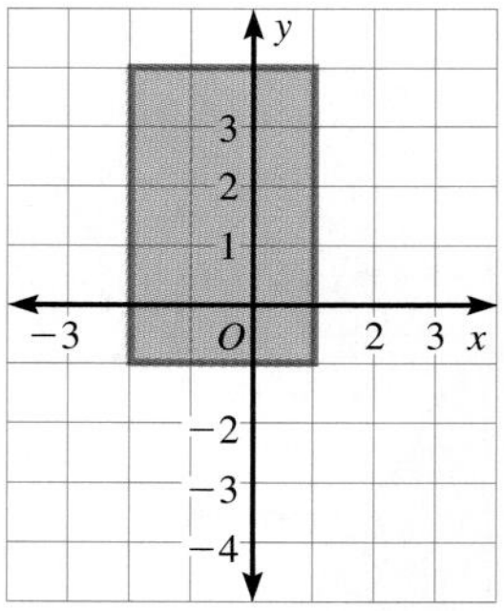

17.

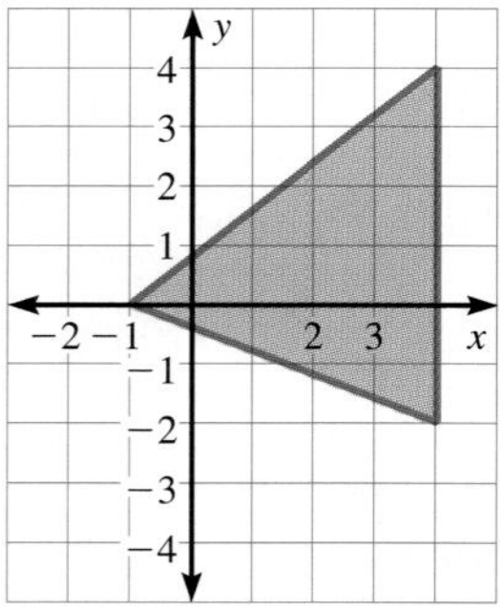

18.

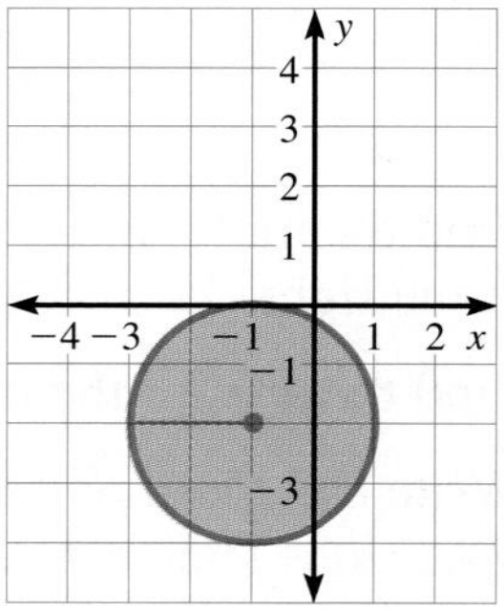

19. **SCIENCE** The temperature of dry ice is about 141°F less than the temperature of normal ice, which is 32°F. How would you find the temperature of dry ice? Explain your reasoning.

A. $141 - 32$ **B.** $32 - 141$

20. **WRITING** Write a summary about what you have learned in this chapter about the coordinate plane.

1. What is the next number in the following pattern?

   3, −2, −7, . . .

   A −6   **B** −8

   C −11   **D** −12

2. Which set of integers is ordered from least to greatest?

   A 1, −4, 5, −7, −9

   B −4, −7, −9, 5, 1

   C −9, −7, −4, 1, 5

   D −9, −7, 5, −4, 1

3. Juan borrowed $27 from Alyssa and returned $19. Which statement is true?

   A Alyssa owes Juan $8.

   B Juan owes Alyssa $6.

   C Juan owes Alyssa $8.

   D Juan owes Alyssa $46.

4. At 5 P.M. the temperature was −4°. At 10 P.M. the temperature was −21°F. How many degrees did the temperature drop?

   A 15°   **B** 17°

   C 23°   **D** 25°

5. What is the area of the triangle?

   A 7.5 units^2 **B** 22.5 units^2

   C 45 units^2 **D** 67.5 units^2

   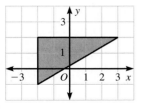

6. −9 + 5 + (−2) + 6 = ?

   A 0   **B** 4

   C 8   **D** 10

7. According to legend, Rome was founded in 753 B.C. The empire ended in 476 A.D. Estimate how many years Rome was an empire.

   A 1229 years   **B** 277 years

   C −277 years   **D** −1229 years

8. Which point has the coordinates (4, −2)?

   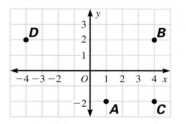

   A Point A   **B** Point B

   C Point C   **D** Point D

9. For which point is $x \le -1$ and $y \ge 2$?

   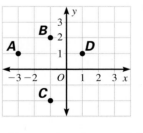

   A Point A   **B** Point B

   C Point C   **D** Point D

10. In which quadrant is the point (−5, 6)?

    A Quadrant I   **B** Quadrant II

    C Quadrant III   **D** Quadrant IV

Algebra: Equations
and Probability

LUCK AND STRATEGY both play a role in the outcome of many games. For example, in this computer solitaire game, you may start the game with a lucky board when the pieces are placed randomly. But you need to use your skill at analyzing the positions of the pieces in order to win.

CHAPTER THEME
Games

TECHNOLOGY

Technology resources accompanying this chapter:

• Interactive Real-Life Investigations

• Middle School Tutorial Software

STRATEGY *Go* is a game of strategy, like Chess and Checkers. You need to use strategy to outwit your opponent.

LUCK The outcome of some games is due to luck. There's no skill involved in guessing whether a tossed coin will land "heads" or "tails."

Heads or Tails

REAL LIFE
Games

One way to model "win-lose" games is to use coin tossing. A tree diagram for the 8 possible outcomes of tossing 3 coins is shown.

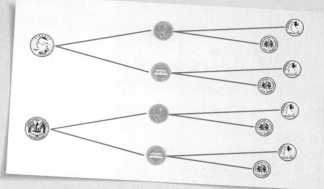

Think and Discuss

1. How many outcomes show *exactly* 2 heads? *at least* 2 heads?

2. Extend the tree pattern to show the possible outcomes for tossing 4 coins. How many outcomes are there?

PORTFOLIO

CHAPTER **PROJECT**

Games Around the World

PROJECT DESCRIPTION

Children of every nation play games. Some games involve luck and others require strategy. Mathematicians study games to explore strategy and probability and relate them to real-life situations. In your project, you will create a booklet about some games played around the world, using the list of **TOPICS** on the next page.

GETTING STARTED

Talking It Over

- In your group, talk about some of the different types of games that you like to play. Do any of them involve math? In what ways?

- Identify some games that everyone in your group knows how to play. Are there any special strategies you can use to increase your chances of winning? Explain. What are some examples of games that you need to be lucky to win?

Planning Your Project

- **Materials Needed:** paper, pencils or pens, colored pencils or pens

- Make a booklet from several pieces of paper. Think of a title and write it on the cover, along with your name. Add pictures if you wish. As you complete the **BUILDING YOUR PROJECT** exercises, add the results to a new page of your booklet. Use the library, Internet, or other resource to find more information on the games. Find some other games from around the world to include in your booklet.

BUILDING YOUR PROJECT

These are places throughout the chapter where you will work on your project.

TOPICS

I N T E R N E T

To find out more about games, go to:
http://www.mlmath.com

ALGEBRA CONNECTION

Investigating Equations

You can use algebra tiles to model expressions and to solve equations.

1
1

The smaller tile is a 1-by-1 square whose area is 1 square unit. It represents the number 1.

x
1

The larger tile is a 1-by-*x* rectangle whose area is *x* square units. It represents the variable *x*.

Part **A** MODELING EXPRESSIONS

Here are three expressions modeled with algebra tiles.

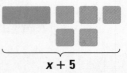

2*x* + 1   **2*x* + 4**   ***x* + 5**

1. Write the expression that is modeled by the tiles.

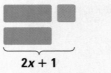

a.   **b.**   **c.**

2. Use algebra tiles to model each expression. Sketch each model.

    a. $3x + 4$ **b.** $4x + 5$ **c.** $x + 2$

Part **B** SOLVING EQUATIONS

Algebra tiles can also be used to solve equations. The example below shows how to solve the equation $x + 3 = 8$.

Model the equation with algebra tiles.

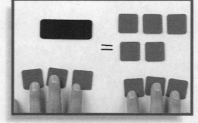

To get the *x*-tile by itself on one side of the equation, remove three 1-tiles from each side.

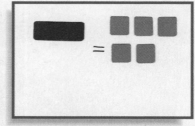

The solution is $x = 5$.

3. Write the equation that is being modeled. Then remove enough tiles from each side of the equation so that the *x*-tile is by itself on one side. What is the solution?

   a.   b.

   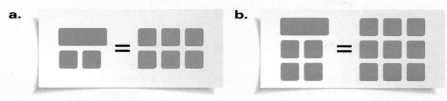

4. Use algebra tiles to solve each equation. Sketch the tiles that you used.

   a. $x + 5 = 12$ b. $x + 8 = 14$ c. $x + 2 = 17$

5. With others in your group, discuss how you knew the number of tiles to remove from each side in Exercise 4.

6. In the following model, two tiles are removed from each side of the equation. What operation does this represent? Explain your reasoning.

NOW TRY THESE

In Exercises 7–10, use algebra tiles to solve the equation. Sketch the tiles that you used.

  7. $x + 4 = 8$ 8. $x + 5 = 15$

  9. $x + 1 = 12$ 10. $x + 3 = 10$

11. REASONING Which of the following do you think is correct? Explain your reasoning.

    A. To solve $x + 3 = 7$, subtract 3 from the left side of the equation.

    B. To solve $x + 3 = 7$, subtract 3 from each side of the equation.

    C. To solve $x + 3 = 7$, subtract 3 from the right side of the equation.

$3x + 6$

12.1

Addition Equations

What you should learn:

Goal ① How to solve addition equations

Goal ② How to use addition equations to solve real-life problems

Why you should learn it:

Knowing how to solve addition equations can help you find temperature increases. An example is finding the increase in temperature from 12°C to 38°C.

Goal ① **SOLVING ADDITION EQUATIONS**

You can use the following rule to solve addition equations.

SOLVING AN ADDITION EQUATION

To solve an addition equation, subtract the same number from each side of the equation so that the variable will be by itself on one side of the equation.

Check your answer by substituting it for the variable in the original equation. Simplify both sides of the equation.

- If both sides of the equation are the same, then your answer is a correct solution.

- If both sides of the equation are not the same, then your answer is not a correct solution.

Example 1 **Solving Addition Equations**

Solve the equation.

a. $m + 4 = -8$ **b.** $3 = n + 5$

Solution

a.
$$
\begin{array}{ll}
m + 4 = -8 & \text{Write original equation.} \\
\underline{-4 \quad -4} & \text{Subtract 4 from each side.} \\
m = -12 & \text{Solution: } m \text{ is by itself.}
\end{array}
$$

✔**Check:** Substitute for the variable in the original equation.

$$
\begin{array}{ll}
m + 4 = -8 & \text{Write original equation.} \\
-12 + 4 \stackrel{?}{=} -8 & \text{Substitute } -12 \text{ for } m. \\
-8 = -8 & \text{Both sides are the same. ✔}
\end{array}
$$

b.
$$
\begin{array}{ll}
3 = n + 5 & \text{Write original equation.} \\
\underline{-5 \quad\quad -5} & \text{Subtract 5 from each side.} \\
-2 = n & \text{Solution: } n \text{ is by itself.}
\end{array}
$$

✔**Check:** Substitute for the variable in the original equation.

$$
\begin{array}{ll}
3 = n + 5 & \text{Write original equation.} \\
3 \stackrel{?}{=} -2 + 5 & \text{Substitute } -2 \text{ for } n. \\
3 = 3 & \text{Both sides are the same. ✔}
\end{array}
$$

When you use algebra to solve a real-life problem, you can use a verbal model. A **verbal model** uses words to represent a problem.

USING VERBAL MODELS

1. Write a verbal model for the problem.
2. Assign values to each label in the model. If you know the value, use a number. If you don't know the value, use a variable, like x.
3. Rewrite the verbal model as an equation, and then solve. Check your solution.

Example 2 Using a Verbal Model

The temperature is 12°C. How many degrees must the temperature increase to reach 38°C?

REAL LIFE
Temperature

Solution

Use a verbal model to represent the problem. Assign values to each label. Let x represent the unknown amount.

Verbal Model   Original temperature $+$ Increase $=$ New temperature

Labels   Original temperature (°C) $= 12$
Increase (°C) $= x$
New temperature (°C) $= 38$

Equation $12 + x = 38$

To solve this equation, subtract 12 from both sides of the equation.

$$
\begin{array}{rl}
12 + x = 38 & \text{Write original equation.} \\
\underline{-\,12 \qquad -\,12} & \text{Subtract 12 from both sides.} \\
x = 26 & \text{Solution: } x \text{ is by itself.}
\end{array}
$$

✔**Check:** The solution is 26, so the increase is 26°C. You can check $12 + 26 = 38$ by using a number line.

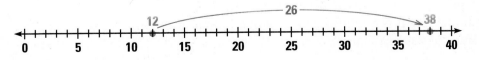

In Exercises 1–3, describe the steps used to solve the equation.

$$\begin{array}{ccc} \textbf{1. } x + 2 = & 9 \\ \underline{-2} & \underline{-2} \\ x & = & 7 \end{array}$$

$$\begin{array}{cc} \textbf{2. } -1 = m + 1 \\ \underline{-1} & \underline{-1} \\ -2 = m \end{array}$$

$$\begin{array}{ccc} \textbf{3. } t + 3 = & 0 \\ \underline{-3} & \underline{-3} \\ t & = & -3 \end{array}$$

4. Explain the basic strategy for solving an addition equation.

In Exercises 5–7, solve the equation. Then check your solution.

5. $5 + y = 4$

6. $3 + n = 6$

7. $a + 1 = -7$

8. Write the equation represented by the following sentence. *The sum of a number and 5 is −10*. Then solve the equation.

In Exercises 9–12, decide whether the given number is a solution to the equation. If not, give the correct solution.

9. $z + 2 = -7$

$z = -9$

10. $p + 6 = -1$

$p = -7$

11. $n + 5 = -3$

$n = -8$

12. $5 = m + 11$

$m = 6$

In Exercises 13–24, solve the equation. Then check your solution.

13. $x + 8 = 3$

14. $10 + a = 2$

15. $6 + y = 14$

16. $15 = t + 11$

17. $5 = 5 + m$

18. $9 + p = 0$

19. $n + 7 = 27$

20. $13 + b = 26$

21. $-2 + c = 8$

22. $p + 8 = 211$

23. $4 + q = 220$

24. $15 = 14 + z$

WRITING AN EQUATION In Exercises 25–29, write the equation represented by the sentence. Then solve the equation.

25. The sum of a number and 2 is 210.

26. The sum of a number and 16 is 1.

27. The sum of 5 and a number is 18.

28. The sum of 13 and a number is 0.

29. The sum of 9 and a number is −5.

30. GUESS, CHECK, AND REVISE I am a number between −5 and 5. When I am added to 8, the result is a multiple of 2. When I am added to 14, the result is a multiple of 5. What number am I?

GUESS, CHECK AND REVISE In Exercises 31 and 32, use the given numbers to make the equation true. Use each number only once.

31. ? + ? = ?

    −1, 2, −3

32. ? = ? + ?

    3, −2, 1

33. **BOWLING** You are saving money to buy a bowling ball that costs $64. You have saved $38. How much more money do you need to save? Use the verbal model to assign labels and write an equation to represent the problem. Then solve.

| Verbal Model | Amount saved | + | Amount left to save | = | Cost |

34. The bowling ball in Exercise 33 is on sale for $48. Which of the addition equations below represents the amount the bowling ball is discounted from the regular price? Explain your reasoning.

    A. $x + 48 = 64$ **B.** $x + 64 = -48$

Real Life... Real People

Bowling
Jeanne Maiden, of Tacoma, WA, set the Women's International Bowling Congress record of 20 perfect games and a record of 40 consecutive strikes.

STANDARDIZED TEST PRACTICE

35. Which equation does *not* have $x = -2$ as a solution?

    A $x + 5 = 3$ **B** $x + (-2) = -4$ **C** $x + 5 = 7$ **D** $x + (-1) = -3$

EXPLORATION AND EXTENSION

PORTFOLIO

36. **BUILDING YOUR PROJECT** Early settlers of Hawaii played the game of Lu-lu using playing pieces made from volcanic stone, marked on one side as shown at the right. You take a turn by tossing the pieces. If all 4 pieces land dot-side up, score 10 points and take another turn.

If all 4 pieces do not land dot-side up, toss the pieces that are dot-side down again. Add the number of dots showing on all 4 pieces to your score, and pass the pieces to the next player. The first player to reach exactly 100 wins. If your score is 79, can you win on your next turn? Explain, using an addition equation.

12.2

Subtraction Equations

What you should learn:

Goal 1 How to solve subtraction equations

Goal 2 How to solve real-life problems using subtraction equations

Why you should learn it:

Knowing how to solve subtraction equations can help you solve real-life problems, like finding an elevation.

Much of Amsterdam is below sea level. In areas like this, dikes are built to protect the land from being flooded with sea water.

Goal 1 SOLVING SUBTRACTION EQUATIONS

In Lesson 12.1, you learned how to write out steps to help solve addition equations. The process used to solve subtraction equations is similar.

> **SOLVING A SUBTRACTION EQUATION**
>
> To solve a subtraction equation, you add the same number to both sides of the equation so that the variable will be by itself on one side of the equation.

Remember to check your answer. Substitute it for the variable in the original equation. If both sides of the equation are the same after substituting, then your solution is correct.

Example 1 Solving a Subtraction Equation

Solve the equation.

a. $x - 5 = -6$ **b.** $-2 = m - 7$

Solution

a.
$$\begin{array}{ll} x - 5 = -6 & \text{Write original equation.} \\ \underline{+5 \quad +5} & \text{Add 5 to both sides.} \\ x \quad\;\; = -1 & \text{Solution: } x \text{ is by itself.} \end{array}$$

The solution is $x = -1$.

✔**Check:** Substitute for the variable in the original equation.

$$\begin{array}{ll} x - 5 = -6 & \text{Write original equation.} \\ -1 - 5 \overset{?}{=} -6 & \text{Substitute } -1 \text{ for } x. \\ -6 = -6 & \text{Both sides are the same. } ✔ \end{array}$$

b.
$$\begin{array}{ll} -2 = m - 7 & \text{Write original equation.} \\ \underline{+7 \quad\;\; +7} & \text{Add 7 to both sides.} \\ 5 = m & \text{Solution: } m \text{ is by itself.} \end{array}$$

The solution is $m = 5$.

✔**Check:** Substitute for the variable in the original equation.

$$\begin{array}{ll} -2 = m - 7 & \text{Write original equation.} \\ -2 \overset{?}{=} 5 - 7 & \text{Substitute 5 for } m. \\ -2 = -2 & \text{Both sides are the same. } ✔ \end{array}$$

Goal 2 SOLVING REAL-LIFE PROBLEMS

Example 2 Writing a Subtraction Equation

REAL LIFE
Elevation

You are visiting New Orleans. At the base of a building a sign says that the *elevation* is −5 ft. Elevation is the distance above or below sea level. The building is 22 ft tall. What is the elevation on the roof of the building?

Solution

One way to answer the question is to use a verbal model.

Verbal Model	$\dfrac{\text{Elevation}}{\text{on roof}} - \dfrac{\text{Height of}}{\text{building}} = \dfrac{\text{Elevation}}{\text{at base}}$

Labels
Elevation on roof (ft) $= x$
Height of building (ft) $= 22$
Elevation at base (ft) $= -5$

Equation $\quad x - 22 = -5$

To solve this equation, add 22 to each side.

$$
\begin{array}{ll}
x - 22 = -5 & \text{Write equation.} \\
\underline{\;+\,22 \quad +\,22\;} & \text{Add 22 to each side.} \\
x \qquad = 17 & \text{Solution: } x \text{ is by itself.}
\end{array}
$$

The elevation on the roof is 17 ft (above sea level).

✔**Check:** DRAW A DIAGRAM

1. Draw a building and label the base as −5.

2. Mark **22** units to the top of the building. Label the units as shown.

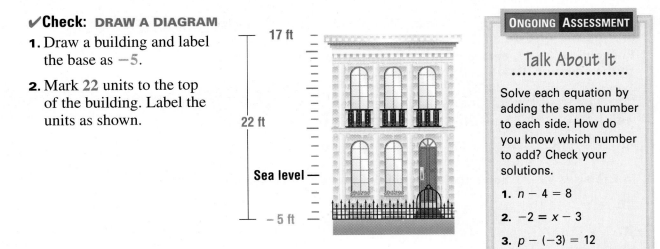

17 ft

22 ft

Sea level —

− 5 ft

ONGOING ASSESSMENT

Talk About It

Solve each equation by adding the same number to each side. How do you know which number to add? Check your solutions.

1. $n - 4 = 8$

2. $-2 = x - 3$

3. $p - (-3) = 12$

The drawing shows that the roof is **17 ft** above sea level.

GUIDED PRACTICE

In Exercises 1–3, decide whether you should add or subtract to solve the equation. Explain your reasoning. Then solve and check.

1. $t - 3 = 14$

2. $u + 5 = -33$

3. $-14 = s - 12$

In Exercises 4–6, use the following information. The temperature at 8 P.M. was 28°F. The temperature had fallen 5° from 5 P.M. What was the temperature at 5 P.M.?

4. Write a verbal model to represent the problem.

5. Let x represent the 5 P.M. temperature. Assign values. Then write the verbal model as an equation.

6. Solve the equation and answer the question.

ERROR ANALYSIS **In Exercises 7 and 8, describe and correct the error.**

7.
$$x - 8 = 7$$
$$x - 8 + (-8) = 7 + (-8)$$
$$x = -1 \quad \times$$

8.
$$x - (-6) = -5$$
$$x - (-6) - (-6) = -5 - (-6)$$
$$x = 1 \quad \times$$

PRACTICE AND PROBLEM SOLVING

WRITING **In Exercises 9–11, write a real-life problem that could be solved using the given equation.**

9. $n - 14 = 0$

10. $35 = t - 25$

11. $x - 6 = -12$

In Exercises 12–17, decide whether the given solution is a correct solution to the equation. If not, find the solution.

12. $x - 12 = 13$; $x = 25$

13. $x - 25 = -1$; $x = 24$

14. $-9 = x - 17$; $x = 26$

15. $-2 = x - 4$; $x = -2$

16. $x - 11 = -18$; $x = 27$

17. $14 = x - 7$; $x = 21$

In Exercises 18–26, solve the equation. Then check your solution.

18. $n - 5 = 16$

19. $t - 7 = 19$

20. $27 = p - 13$

21. $50 = x - 15$

22. $b - 14 = -2$

23. $s - 16 = -12$

24. $-3 = z - 18$

25. $-16 = y - 13$

26. $c - 6 = -20$

27. SCIENCE Earth is farthest from the sun in July. In January, when Earth comes nearest to the sun, it is about 3 million miles closer, at a distance of about 91 million miles. Use the verbal model to assign values to the labels. Write an equation that can be used to find Earth's distance from the sun in July. Then solve.

| Verbal Model | Distance in July | − | 3 million miles | = | Distance in January |

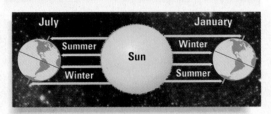

Real Life... Real Facts

July | January
Summer | Winter
Sun
Winter | Summer

Seasons
Changes in season are due to the tilt of Earth's axis, not its distance from the sun.

28. ART Your class is taking a field trip to an art museum. After driving 35 mi, you see a sign that says the museum is 15 mi away. Write a verbal model using subtraction to find the total distance to the museum. Assign labels. Then write the verbal model as an equation and solve.

STANDARDIZED TEST PRACTICE

29. Solve for *n* in the equation $n - 13 = -7$.

   (A) -20 **(B)** -6 **(C)** 6 **(D)** 20

30. Solve for *x* in the equation $x - 9 = -4$.

   (A) -13 **(B)** -5 **(C)** 5 **(D)** 13

EXPLORATION AND EXTENSION

PORTFOLIO

31. BUILDING YOUR PROJECT The Korean game of Ko-no is for 2 players. In one version, the first player has 2 black playing pieces and the other has 2 white pieces, as shown. To play the game, take turns moving a playing piece along a line segment to an open space. The game is over when a player is blocked and cannot move.

In another version, after you cover spaces with 14 playing pieces you have 11 open spaces. How many total spaces did you start with in this version? Explain, using a subtraction equation.

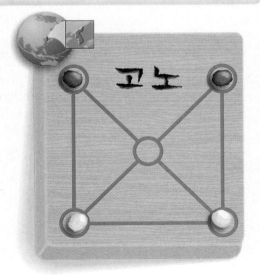

고노

ALGEBRA In Exercises 1–6, solve the equation using mental math. (2.2, 4.1, 4.2, 7.3)

1. $9 + x = 12$

2. $25 - y = 5$

3. $1.3 + m = 4.6$

4. $n - 0.8 = 1$

5. $a + \dfrac{1}{4} = 1$

6. $b - \dfrac{2}{7} = \dfrac{3}{7}$

WORKING BACKWARD In Exercises 7 and 8, copy and complete the model. (1.7, 11.2, 11.3)

7.

8.

WRITING In Exercises 9–11, tell whether there is a *rate* or a *ratio*. Then describe a real-life situation that it could represent. (6.2, 6.3)

9. $\dfrac{5 \text{ hours}}{8 \text{ hours}}$

10. $\dfrac{9 \text{ apples}}{14 \text{ students}}$

11. $\dfrac{3 \text{ yards}}{10 \text{ yards}}$

Science Connection

BAROMETERS

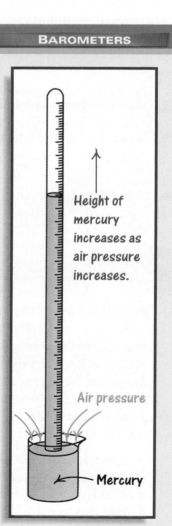

Barometers are used to measure the pressure of the atmosphere. Meteorologists often use them to help forecast the weather. Changes in air pressure indicate weather changes. When the air pressure rises, expect good weather. When it falls, bad weather is on the way.

The first barometer was made in 1643, using liquid mercury. Air presses on an open container of mercury, causing it to rise in a glass tube. As air pressure increases, the mercury rises. In an experiment in 1647, a mercury barometer was carried up a mountain in France. The height of the mercury column fell as the altitude rose, because air is thinner at higher altitudes. After this, people started to use barometers to estimate altitude as well as to measure atmospheric conditions.

Height of mercury increases as air pressure increases.

Air pressure

Mercury

Write an equation to represent the problem. Then solve it.

1. In the experiment described above, the height of the mercury at the top of the mountain was 26.3 in., which was 3.3 in. less than at the base of the mountain. How high was the mercury at the base of the mountain?

2. A weather forecaster notes that from morning to afternoon, the barometer falls by 0.8 in. to a reading of 30.1 in. What was the reading of the barometer in the morning?

Rolling Probabilities

Much of what is known about probability has been learned from doing experiments. Try the following experiment, which uses number cubes.

Example

Toss 1 blue and 1 red number cube and write the results as

$$x + (\textbf{Blue number}) = (\textbf{Red number}).$$

Solve the equation and write the results in a table. Repeat the experiment 20 times.

Solution

When we performed this experiment, our first toss was a blue 6 and a red 1, as shown at the left. The equation is $x + 6 = 1$ and the solution is $x = -5$. Check this with a calculator.

Keystrokes	Display	Type of Negative Key
5 **+/−** **+** 6 **=**	1.	Change-sign key
(−) 5 **+** 6 **=**	1.	Negative key

The tables summarize all 20 tosses.

Blue	6	4	1	3	5	2	1	4	4	4
Red	1	4	4	5	3	5	1	1	4	1

Blue	3	3	3	2	2	3	5	1	3	1
Red	5	3	1	4	2	6	6	3	4	5

Exercises

1. Find x for each result shown above. Use a calculator to check your answers.

2. **LINE PLOTS** Now do the experiment yourself. Use a line plot to organize your results.

3. Copy and complete the table at the right. In each square, write the solution.

    a. What are the possible solutions?

    b. Which solution is most likely? Explain.

	1	**2**	**3**	**4**	**5**	**6**
1	?	?	?	?	?	?
2	?	?	?	?	?	?
3	?	?	?	?	?	?
4	?	?	?	?	?	?
5	?	?	?	?	?	?
6	?	?	?	?	?	?

Why you should learn it:

Knowing how to solve equations can help you make a savings plan to buy an item you really want. An example is finding how much more money you need to save to buy a skateboard.

TOOLBOX

Adding and Subtracting Fractions, page 646

Equations with Fractions and Decimals

Goal 1 SOLVING EQUATIONS

To solve equations that include fractions or decimals, add or subtract so that the variable is by itself on one side of the equation.

Example 1 Solving Equations with Fractions

Solve for x in the equation $x + \dfrac{1}{5} = \dfrac{3}{5}$.

Solution

Subtract $\dfrac{1}{5}$ from both sides of the equation.

$$
\begin{array}{ll}
x + \dfrac{1}{5} = \dfrac{3}{5} & \text{Write original equation.} \\[2mm]
\underline{-\dfrac{1}{5} \quad -\dfrac{1}{5}} & \text{Subtract } \dfrac{1}{5} \text{ from both sides.} \\[2mm]
x \quad\;\; = \dfrac{2}{5} & \text{Solution: } x \text{ is by itself.}
\end{array}
$$

✔**Check:** $\dfrac{2}{5} + \dfrac{1}{5} = \dfrac{3}{5}$

Example 2 Solving Equations with Decimals

Solve the equation.

a. $n + 11.4 = 23.1$ **b.** $p - 7.8 = 12.5$

Solution

a. Subtract 11.4 from both sides of the equation.

$$
\begin{array}{ll}
n + 11.4 = \;\;\; 23.1 & \text{Write original equation.} \\
\underline{- 11.4 \quad - 11.4} & \text{Subtract 11.4 from both sides.} \\
n \quad\;\;\; = \;\;\; 11.7 & \text{Solution: } n \text{ is by itself.}
\end{array}
$$

✔**Check:** $11.7 + 11.4 = 23.1$

b. Add 7.8 to both sides of the equation.

$$
\begin{array}{ll}
p - 7.8 = \;\;\; 12.5 & \text{Write original equation.} \\
\underline{+ 7.8 \quad + 7.8} & \text{Add 7.8 to both sides.} \\
p \quad\;\;\; = \;\;\; 20.3 & \text{Solution: } p \text{ is by itself.}
\end{array}
$$

✔**Check:** $20.3 - 7.8 = 12.5$

Example 3 Real-Life Problems with Decimals

You have saved $52.35 for a skateboard that costs $84.75, including tax. How much more do you need to save?

Solution

One way to answer this question is to use a verbal model. Let x represent the unknown amount.

Verbal Model	Amount saved	+	Amount more to save	=	Total cost

Labels Amount saved (dollars) = **52.35**

Amount more to save (dollars) = x

Total cost (dollars) = **84.75**

Equation

$$52.35 + x = 84.75$$ Write equation.
$$-\,52.35 \qquad\quad -\,52.35$$ Subtract 52.35 from each side.
$$x = 32.40$$ Solution: x is by itself.

You need to save $32.40 more.

Example 4 Real-Life Problems with Fractions

For a woodworking project, you need a board that is $18\frac{3}{8}$ in. long. You find one that is $18\frac{3}{4}$ in. long. How much do you need to cut off?

Solution

Subtract the **length needed** from the **original length** to find the **amount to cut off**.

$$x = 18\frac{3}{4} - 18\frac{3}{8}$$ Write equation.

$$= 18\frac{6}{8} - 18\frac{3}{8}$$ Find common denominators and subtract.

$$= \frac{3}{8}$$ Solution: x is by itself.

You need to cut $\frac{3}{8}$ in. off the original board.

ONGOING ASSESSMENT

Write About It
....

Solve each equation. Show your work and explain each step.

1. $m + 4.3 = 3.7$

2. $y - 3\frac{1}{2} = 2\frac{1}{4}$

3. $5.1 + x = 2.5$

12.3 Exercises

Extra Practice, page 640

GUIDED PRACTICE

COMMUNICATING In Exercises 1–3, explain how to solve the equation.

1. $\frac{1}{6} + m = \frac{5}{6}$ **2.** $12.5 = z + 7.6$ **3.** $t - 9.4 = 3.8$

4. Write the equation represented by the following statement. *When you subtract one half from this number, you get two thirds.*

In Exercises 5–7, solve the equation. Then check the solution.

5. $n - \frac{3}{8} = 1$ **6.** $\frac{1}{2} + b = \frac{3}{5}$ **7.** $18 = x + 2.3$

8. FISHING You buy a fishing rod for $23.50. The total cost including sales tax is $24.91. Use the verbal model to find the amount you paid in sales tax.

Verbal Model $\dfrac{\text{Total}}{\text{cost}} = \text{Price} + \dfrac{\text{Sales}}{\text{tax}}$

PRACTICE AND PROBLEM SOLVING

In Exercises 9–12, match the equation with its solution.

A. $\frac{3}{5}$, or 0.6   **B.** $\frac{14}{5}$, or 2.8   **C.** $\frac{4}{5}$, or 0.8   **D.** $\frac{1}{2}$, or 0.5

9. $x - \frac{1}{5} = \frac{3}{10}$ **10.** $x + \frac{1}{5} = 1$ **11.** $13.5 + x = 14.1$ **12.** $1.6 = x - 1.2$

ERROR ANALYSIS In Exercises 13 and 14, describe the error. Then correct the error and solve the original equation.

13.
```
x + 4.6 =    7.8
  - 4.6    - 7.8
  x      =   0   ✗
```

14.
```
n - 5.6 =    8.8
  - 5.6    - 5.6
  n      =   3.2  ✗
```

In Exercises 15–26, solve the equation. Then check the solution.

15. $\frac{2}{7} + y = \frac{6}{7}$ **16.** $a - \frac{5}{8} = \frac{1}{8}$ **17.** $9.1 = 3.05 + p$

18. $m - \frac{2}{3} = \frac{3}{4}$ **19.** $s - 15.2 = 16.19$ **20.** $b - 32.96 = 7.04$

21. $q - \frac{4}{7} = \frac{2}{7}$ **22.** $\frac{4}{9} + b = \frac{8}{9}$ **23.** $h + 11.7 = 3.1$

24. $c + \frac{5}{12} = \frac{11}{12}$ **25.** $4.41 = w - 3.37$ **26.** $11.7 + k = 21.8$

2

FINDING A PATTERN In Exercises 27–29, solve each equation and describe the pattern for *t*. Then write the next two values of *t*.

27. $\frac{2}{7} = t + \frac{1}{7}$

$\frac{3}{7} = t + \frac{1}{7}$

$\frac{4}{7} = t + \frac{1}{7}$

28. $10.25 + t = 20.5$

$10.25 + t = 25.5$

$10.25 + t = 30.5$

29. $t - 1.8 = 35.1$

$t - 1.7 = 35.1$

$t - 1.6 = 35.1$

30. **MISSOURI** The rural portion of Missouri's population is represented by the fraction $\frac{8}{25}$. Tell whether each equation can be used to find the portion that is *not* rural. Explain.

a. $\frac{8}{25} + u = 1$

b. $100 = 0.32 + u$

c. $u + \frac{8}{25} = 100$

d. $0.32 + u = 1$

31. **IOWA** The portion of Iowa's population that is rural is represented by the decimal 0.4. Write an equation that can be used to find the portion that is not rural. Write the equation in decimal form and in fraction form. Then solve.

32. **WALK-A-THON** Your community is having a volunteer walk-a-thon of 4.25 mi. From 8:30 A.M. to 10:00 A.M. you walk 2.4 mi. How much farther will you walk? Write a verbal model, labels, and an equation to represent the problem.

STANDARDIZED TEST PRACTICE

33. Solve for *x* in the equation $x - \frac{3}{4} = \frac{1}{2}$.

A $\frac{1}{4}$　　**B** 1　　**C** $1\frac{1}{4}$　　**D** $1\frac{1}{2}$

34. Solve for *z* in the equation $z - 3.9 = 4.6$.

A -0.7　　**B** 0.7　　**C** 4.25　　**D** 8.5

35. You work as a quality control inspector. For a certain product, the minimum weight is 32.5 ounces. You weigh this product, and find that its weight is only 31.75 ounces. Which equation can be used to find how much more the product should weigh?

A $x + 32.5 = 31.75$　　**B** $x + 31.75 = 32.5$

C $31.75 + 32.5 = x$　　**D** $x - 32.5 = 31.75$

36. BUILDING YOUR PROJECT Magic Squares is a one-person game that is played on a square grid. Its origins trace back to many areas, including China, India, Egypt, and western Europe.

To play, complete the square. The sums of the 3 numbers in each horizontal, vertical, and diagonal row must be equal. Copy and complete the magic squares shown at the right.

37. COMMUNICATING ABOUT MATHEMATICS Use the information on page 607 to write an equation that you can solve to find out about what fraction of families do *not* own a video game system. Then solve the equation.

SPIRAL REVIEW

In Exercises 1 and 2, which number is not equivalent to any of the others? (3.4, 6.3, 6.4)

1. $\frac{12}{20}$, 6%, $\frac{6}{10}$, 0.6

2. 5.2, $\frac{13}{25}$, 52%, $\frac{52}{100}$

READING A TABLE In Exercises 3–6, use the table below. It shows the amount of money spent annually per person on home videos from 1992 through 1994 in the United States. (4.2, 4.5, 5.5)

3. Make a bar graph of the data.

4. Find the amount spent *per month* in 1992.

5. Find the amount spent *per week* in 1994. (Use 52 weeks in a year.)

6. How much more money per person was spent annually in 1994 than was spent in 1992?

Home Videos	
Year	Amount Spent
1992	$63.23
1993	$68.42
1994	$72.97

ALGEBRA AND MENTAL MATH In Exercises 7–10, complete the equation. (7.3, 8.1, 8.4)

7. $\frac{?}{8} + \frac{1}{8} = \frac{3}{4}$

8. $\frac{9}{10} - \frac{?}{10} = \frac{1}{5}$

9. $\frac{2}{3} \div \frac{1}{?} = 2$

10. $\frac{2}{5} \times \boxed{?} = \frac{4}{5}$

11. Plot the ordered pairs $A(-2, 4)$, $B(2, 0)$, $C(0, -2)$, and $D(-4, 2)$ in a coordinate plane. Connect the sides to make a polygon. Then name the polygon in as many ways as you can. (10.3, 11.4)

Take this test as you would a test in class. The answers to the exercises are given in the back of the book.

In Exercises 1–4, write whether you would add or subtract to solve the equation. Then solve and check. **(12.1, 12.2)**

1. $c + 5 = 11$ **2.** $p - 12 = 17$ **3.** $14 + m = -5$ **4.** $z - 7 = -2$

ERROR ANALYSIS In Exercises 5–7, describe and correct the error. **(12.1, 12.2)**

5.
$$
\begin{aligned}
-12 + x &= 21 \\
-12 \qquad &- 12 \\
\hline
x &= 9 \quad \times
\end{aligned}
$$

6.
$$
\begin{aligned}
x - 17 &= 16 \\
+ 17 \quad &+ 16 \\
\hline
x &= 0 \quad \times
\end{aligned}
$$

7.
$$
\begin{aligned}
-2 &= x + 5 \\
+ 2 \quad &+ 2 \\
\hline
x &= 7 \quad \times
\end{aligned}
$$

In Exercises 8–15, solve the equation. Check your solution. **(12.1–12.3)**

8. $x + 14 = -3$ **9.** $x - 16 = 25$ **10.** $x - 33 = -12$ **11.** $12 + x = -4$

12. $\dfrac{5}{9} + x = \dfrac{17}{3}$ **13.** $x + 5.67 = 9.11$ **14.** $x - \dfrac{1}{3} = \dfrac{5}{8}$ **15.** $x - 12.33 = 19.02$

In Exercises 16 and 17, choose the equation that you would use to answer the question. Then solve the equation and answer the question. **(12.3)**

16. **SPENDING** You and three friends are buying a chemistry set that costs $39.95. You pay for the set and receive $15.30 in change. How much money did you start with?

    A. $x - 39.95 = 15.30$ **B.** $x + 15.30 = 39.95$

17. **TENNIS** An official tennis ball must have a diameter that is at least $\dfrac{5}{2}$ in. The difference between the largest and smallest allowable diameters that it can have is $\dfrac{1}{8}$ in. How big can the diameter of an official tennis ball be?

    A. $x - \dfrac{5}{2} = \dfrac{1}{8}$ **B.** $x + \dfrac{1}{8} = \dfrac{5}{2}$

18. **FUNDRAISING** Your class is raising money by selling sandwiches. You have raised $284. The amount left to raise is $416.

Verbal Model	Total needed	−	Amount raised	=	Amount left to raise

Assign values to each label and write an equation. Then solve the equation to find the total amount your class needs to raise. **(12.2)**

12.4

What you should learn:

Goal 1 How to evaluate a function

Goal 2 How to write a rule for a function

Why you should learn it:

Knowing how to evaluate functions can help you find patterns in real life. An example is recognizing the pattern for the total cost of sending overnight mail.

Exploring Functions

Goal 1 EVALUATING FUNCTIONS

In mathematics a **function** is a rule that tells you how to perform one or more operations on a number, called the **input**, to produce a result called the **output**.

Input
x = 1

Function
y = x + 2

Output
y = 3

To find the output (*y*-value) for a given input (*x*-value), substitute the *x*-value into the function.

Example 1 Evaluating a Function

Find the output values of the function $y = x + 2$ for the input values of $x = -2, -1, 0\ 1$, and 2. Use a table to organize your results. Graph the results in a coordinate plane.

Solution

Input the x-value.	Substitute x-value in function.	Compute y-value as output.
$x = -2$	$y = -2 + 2$	$y = 0$
$x = -1$	$y = -1 + 2$	$y = 1$
$x = 0$	$y = 0 + 2$	$y = 2$
$x = 1$	$y = 1 + 2$	$y = 3$
$x = 2$	$y = 2 + 2$	$y = 4$

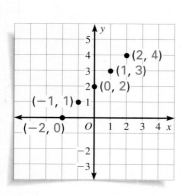

Write the data as ordered pairs. Use the input, or *x*-value, as the first number, and the output, or *y*-value, as the second number.

$$(-2, 0), (-1, 1), (0, 2), (1, 3), (2, 4)$$

Then graph each point, as shown at the left. Notice that all five points lie on a line.

Goal 2 WRITING A FUNCTION RULE

Example 2 Writing a Function Rule

Find the perimeter of each rectangle. Organize the results in a table, and describe the pattern. Using the length *L* as the input and the perimeter *P* as the output, write a rule for the function. Graph your results.

CONNECTION
Geometry

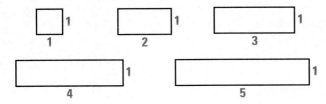

Solution

Length (input)	Height	Perimeter (output)
$L = 1$	1	$P = 1 + 1 + 1 + 1 = 4$
$L = 2$	1	$P = 2 + 1 + 2 + 1 = 6$
$L = 3$	1	$P = 3 + 1 + 3 + 1 = 8$
$L = 4$	1	$P = 4 + 1 + 4 + 1 = 10$
$L = 5$	1	$P = 5 + 1 + 5 + 1 = 12$

When the length is 1, the perimeter is 4. Each time the length increases by 1, the perimeter increases by 2. A rule that gives the perimeter is $P = 2 + 2 \cdot L$.

To graph the data in a coordinate plane, first write the **input** and **output** as ordered pairs.

$(1, 4), (2, 6), (3, 8),$

$(4, 10), (5, 12)$

In the graph you can see the same pattern that is described above. Each time *L* increases by 1, *P* increases by 2.

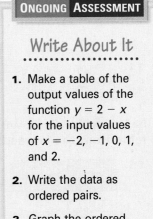

ONGOING ASSESSMENT

Write About It

1. Make a table of the output values of the function $y = 2 - x$ for the input values of $x = -2, -1, 0, 1,$ and 2.

2. Write the data as ordered pairs.

3. Graph the ordered pairs and describe the pattern.

GUIDED PRACTICE

1. Copy and complete the table at the right for $y = x - 8$.

Input x	Output y
9	?
8	?
7	?
6	?
5	?

In Exercises 2–4, use the following information.

You measured the daily temperatures (°C) for Oklahoma City from January through June. You find that the average temperature for each month can be modeled using the function $T = 4 \times m$. The variable m is the number of the month. That is, January = 1, February = 2, and so on.

2. Make a table that shows the temperatures from January through June.

3. Graph the data.

4. Do you think the same function could be a rule for the temperatures from July through December? Explain.

5. Write a function for the rule *For every carton of eggs you buy, you get 12 eggs.*

6. Use the graph at the right. Make a table of the inputs and outputs. Then write a function to represent the data.

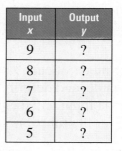

PRACTICE AND PROBLEM SOLVING

In Exercises 7–14, find the output values of the function for values of $m = 0, 1, 2,$ and 3. Use an input-output table to organize your results.

7. $y = 5 \times m$

8. $y = m + 10$

9. $y = m - 4$

10. $y = m - 1$

11. $y = m \cdot 3$

12. $y = 8 - m$

13. $y = 7 + m$

14. $y = (3 \times m) - 2$

In Exercises 15–17, write a function that will give the output y in the table from the corresponding input x. Then graph the data.

15.

Input x	Output y
0	0
1	3
2	6
3	9
4	12

16.

Input x	Output y
0	−6
1	−5
2	−4
3	−3
4	−2

17.

Input x	Output y
0	5
1	6
2	7
3	8
4	9

18. BUSINESS A company wants to send letters overnight using an express mail service. The cost per letter is $10.75. Make a table that shows the cost of sending 2, 4, 6, and 8 letters. Then write a function that you can use to find the cost of sending x letters.

Tech Link

Investigation 12, Interactive Real-Life Investigations

In Exercises 19–21, use the graph to make an input-output table. Then match the graph with the function that represents the data.

A. $y = x$ **B.** $y = x - 2$ **C.** $y = x + 2$

19.

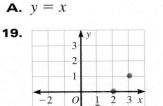

20.

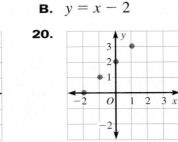

21.

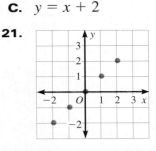

WRITING FUNCTIONS In Exercises 22–24, copy and complete the table. Describe the pattern. Write a rule for the function.

22. You are finding the area, y, of a triangle that has a height of x units and a base of 10 units.

23. Find the grade, y, of a quiz that has x questions answered correctly. Each correct answer gets a score of 3 points.

24. You have two cats. Ping is x years old. Pong is 2 years older. Find Pong's age, y.

Input x	Output y
1	?
2	?
3	?
4	?
5	?
6	?

STANDARDIZED TEST PRACTICE

25. Which function includes the ordered pairs (0, 0), (1, 5), (2, 10), (3, 15), (4, 20), and (5, 25) in its graph?

A $y = 5x$ **B** $y = x + 5$ **C** $y = 25 - x$ **D** $y = x \div 5$

EXPLORATION AND EXTENSION

26. GROUP ACTIVITY Use a watch with a second hand to find the number of times you can write your first name in 10 seconds, in 20 seconds, and in 30 seconds. Make an input-output table. Graph the data. Find a function to represent the number of times you can write your name in 1 second. Compare your function with others in your group.

Investigating Counting Techniques

Materials Needed
• pencils or pens
• paper

Part A USING A TABLE

1. You work at a restaurant that serves three types of tacos (bean, beef, and chicken). Each can be ordered with a hard shell or a soft shell. The number of different types of tacos a customer can order is shown in the table.

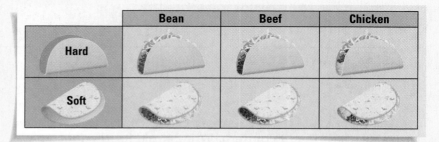

	Bean	Beef	Chicken
Hard			
Soft			

Explain how to use the table to count the number of different types of tacos that can be ordered.

2. Suppose you decide to add nacho shells as a third option. Draw a table that can be used to find the number of different types of tacos that are possible now.

Part B USING A TABLE

3. You are choosing uniforms for your new soccer team. You have five color choices for shorts and four color choices for shirts. The number of different color combinations is shown in the table. How many combinations are there?

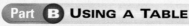

Shirts	Shorts				
	White	Blue	Yellow	Green	Black
Red					
White					
Blue					
Orange					

4. How many different color combinations are possible? Explain.

   a. Shorts: 6 color choices
      Shirts: 5 color choices

   b. Shorts: 7 color choices
      Shirts: 4 color choices

   c. Shorts: 5 color choices
      Shirts: 7 color choices

5. Your six-member band (keyboard, guitar, bass, drums, trumpet, saxophone) is playing at a show where you'll be joined by a four-member band (banjo, harmonica, fiddle, bongos) for one song. One person from each band will be chosen to play a solo. Use the table below to find the number of different solo combinations that are possible.

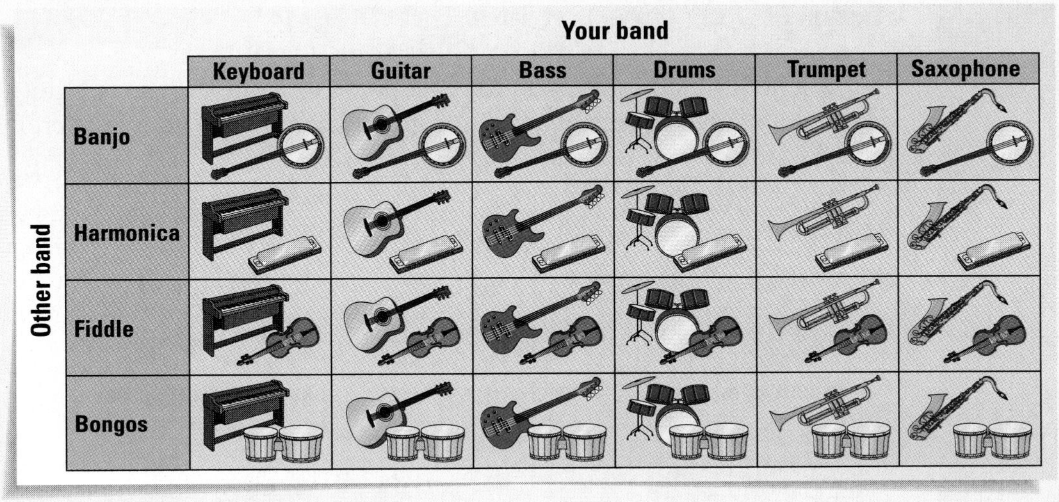

Your band

	Keyboard	Guitar	Bass	Drums	Trumpet	Saxophone
Banjo						
Harmonica						
Fiddle						
Bongos						

Other band (left side label)

6. How are the numbers of rows and columns in the table related to the number of possible combinations?

7. How many different instrument combinations are possible? Explain your reasoning.

    a. Your band:
        5 instruments
    Other band:
        4 instruments

    b. Your band:
        8 instruments
    Other band:
        3 instruments

NOW TRY THESE

8. You are voting for a committee to represent the sixth and seventh grades. For sixth grade, you can choose Luis, Ralph, Sue, or Alma. For seventh grade, you can choose Larry, Orlando, Carmen, or Flo. Use a table to show how many different committees you can choose.

9. GEOMETRY A rectangle has a width of n units and a length of m units. How many square units are in the rectangle? How does this question relate to the problems in this Lab?

10. You are choosing uniforms for the soccer team. You have n choices for shorts and m choices for shirts. How many different combinations are possible? Explain.

What you should learn:

 Goal 1 How to use a tree diagram

Goal 2 How to use the counting principle

Why you should learn it:

Knowing how to count the number of ways something can happen can help you figure out your options. An example is figuring out the different sets of fish you can choose.

Counting Techniques

Goal 1 USING TREE DIAGRAMS

There are several ways to count the number of possible combinations. One way is to make a list. Another way is to use a *tree diagram*.

Example 1 Using a List or a Tree Diagram

In the school lunch room, you have a choice of a hamburger or a hot dog and a choice of peas, carrots, or green beans. How many different lunches are possible?

Solution

Method 1 Make a list.

hamburger, peas   hamburger, carrots   hamburger, green beans

hot dog, peas   hot dog, carrots   hot dog, green beans

There are 6 different lunches possible.

Method 2 Use a **tree diagram**.

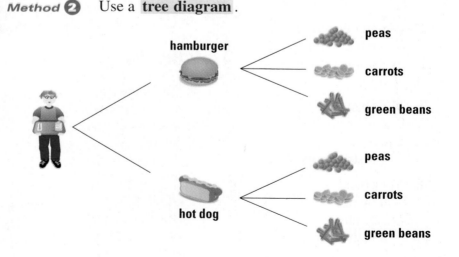

After drawing the tree diagram, you can count the number of different lunches by counting the number of *branches*. For example, the branch "hamburger and peas" represents one of the lunches. The diagram shows that six different lunches are possible.

Goal 2 THE COUNTING PRINCIPLE

Sometimes it is easy to use a list or a tree diagram to count the possibilities. In other cases, the **counting principle** can be helpful.

> **COUNTING PRINCIPLE**
>
> One item is to be selected from each of two or more sets. The total number of possible combinations is the product of the number of items in each set.

Example 2 Using the Counting Principle

A friend is giving you some fish from her aquarium so that she'll have room for new ones. Her tank has **2 guppies**, **3 swordtails**, and **5 tetras**. How many different sets of fish can you choose?

REAL LIFE
Fish

a. You want 1 guppy and 1 swordtail.

b. You want 1 guppy, 1 swordtail, and 1 tetra.

Solution

a. *Method* **1** Use the counting principle.

$$\underset{\text{guppies}}{\text{2 choices for}} \times \underset{\text{swordtails}}{\text{3 choices for}} = \underset{\text{sets of fish}}{\text{6 possible}}$$

Method **2** Use a tree diagram to show the 6 possible sets.

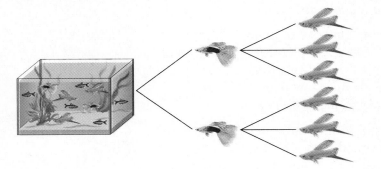

b. There are so many possible sets that making a tree diagram takes a long time. The counting principle is easier.

$$\underset{\text{guppies}}{\text{2 choices for}} \times \underset{\text{swordtails}}{\text{3 choices for}} \times \underset{\text{tetras}}{\text{5 choices for}} = \underset{\text{sets of fish}}{\text{30 possible}}$$

ONGOING ASSESSMENT

Write About It

1. In part (b) of Example 2, make a list of the 30 possible sets of fish. Use the following symbols.

   Guppies: G1, G2

   Swordtails: S1, S2, S3

   Tetras: T1, T2, T3, T4, T5

2. Which method do you prefer: the counting principle or making a list? Why?

---

1. You are buying a new bicycle. You have a choice of a touring bike, a mountain bike, or a racing bike. Each style comes in green or black. Complete the tree diagram at the right to find how many different bicycles you could choose.

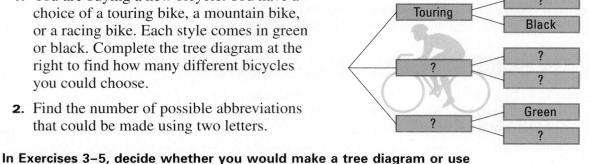

2. Find the number of possible abbreviations that could be made using two letters.

In Exercises 3–5, decide whether you would make a tree diagram or use the counting principle to find the number. Explain your choice. Then find the number.

3. The number of possible five-digit alarm codes

4. The number of possible combinations of heads and tails when tossing three pennies

5. The number of possible two-digit numbers on a baseball jersey

6. **THINKING SKILLS** Make up a problem that can be solved using the tree diagram at the right.

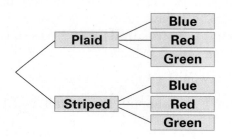

7. **REASONING** You are redecorating your room. You can choose from sky blue, pale green, or lemon yellow paint for the walls, and dark blue, forest green, or light brown carpeting. How many different ways can you redecorate?

8. **HISTORY** The first question on a history exam asks you to write about the Inca, Aztec, or Maya civilizations. The second question asks you to write about one of two Spanish explorers, Hernán Cortés or Francisco Pizarro. How many different combinations of two topics can you choose?

9. **COMMUNITY SERVICE** You are selling raffle tickets for a fund-raiser. The tickets are printed with all possible three-digit numbers using only the numbers 1 through 4. What is the probability that a ticket chosen at random is number 134?

10. **ENGLISH** How many possible words can you make using the prefixes *bi-* and *tri-* and the endings *cycle, annual, color, focal,* and *angular*?

11. **BAKING** You are baking a birthday cake for your friend. The choices for the cake are vanilla, chocolate, or marble. The choices for the filling are cherry or lemon. The frosting can be pink, white, or green. Use a tree diagram to find the probability that you make a chocolate cake with cherry filling and pink frosting, if you choose the cake, filling, and frosting at random.

In Exercises 12–15, use the counting principle to solve.

12. **MAPS** On a map, the numbers 1 through 12 appear across the top and the letters A through J appear down the side. You can locate a city using a number and a letter. How many different location labels are possible?

13. At summer camp, you have a choice of four morning activities, five afternoon activities, and three evening activities. If you are at camp for 60 days, will you ever have to spend two days doing the same three activities? Explain.

14. **VIDEO GAMES** You are playing a video car racing game. You can choose from 4 cars to drive, and from 12 courses to drive on. You can also choose 3 different viewpoints to display the race on the screen. How many different ways can you play the game?

15. Your brother offers to take you and a friend to the zoo, aquarium, or science museum as a birthday present. He can take you on Tuesday, Wednesday, or Saturday. You want to go with Terry, Dennis, Janelle, Rita, or Satchel.

a. How many ways can you take your birthday trip?

b. What is the probability that you go to the zoo with Rita, if you choose a friend and destination at random?

STANDARDIZED TEST PRACTICE

16. If a digit can appear more than once, how many four-digit numbers can be formed from the digits 6, 7, 8, and 9?

(A) 24 (B) 64 (C) 128 (D) 256

17. An apartment security system has a three-digit security code. You remember that the first digit is a 2 but forget the last two digits. At most, how many different codes must you enter before you find the correct one?

(A) 20 (B) 50 (C) 100 (D) 1000

PORTFOLIO

18. BUILDING YOUR PROJECT In one version of the Native American (Hopi) game Totolospi, 3 "cane dice" are used. A cane die is flat on one side and round on the other. Two players start at the circles at opposite ends of the board. They take turns tossing the 3 dice.

If 3 round sides land up, the player moves two lines. If 3 flat sides land up, the player moves one line. If a combination of round and flat sides is thrown, the player loses a turn. The player reaching the opposite circle first wins. How many different ways are there for the cane dice to land? Write an answer that uses a tree diagram.

19. TALENT SHOW Your school is having a talent show. To determine the order in which the five performers will appear, each person's name is chosen at random from a hat containing a card with each person's name.

    a. In how many different orders can the five performers appear?

    b. Does the counting principle work for this problem? Explain.

    c. Describe another situation where the counting principle cannot be used to find the correct number of combinations.

SPIRAL REVIEW

In Exercises 1–4, write the decimal as a fraction. (3.4)

1. 0.5 **2.** 0.9 **3.** 0.41 **4.** 0.75

GEOMETRY **In Exercises 5–7, solve for x. (9.7, 10.2)**

5. $32°$ $x°$ $28°$

6. $39°$ $x°$

7. $133°$ $x°$

FINDING A PATTERN **In Exercises 8 and 9, describe the pattern. Then write the next 3 numbers. (6.4, 7.3, 11.1)**

8. $\dfrac{1}{8}, \dfrac{1}{4}, \dfrac{3}{8}, \dfrac{1}{2},$? , ? , ?

9. $5, 2, -1, -4,$? , ? , ?

10. PROBABILITY A bag contains 5 blue marbles, 8 red marbles, 3 green marbles, and 2 yellow marbles. For each color, find the probability of choosing a marble of that color. (6.7)

Screen Play

READ About It

In 1995, Americans spent about $5 billion on 130 million video or computer games. At least one third of American families own a video game system, and others play games on home computers.

Video games often use equations, functions, and probability. Computer programmers make games by writing *computer code*. The code often includes equations that control things like the movement and speed of objects on the screen, and the scoring of the game.

Games are often designed to make random moves based on probability, to make playing the game more interesting. For example, many games have different levels of difficulty. A programmer making a game can control the difficulty by changing the probability that an event in the game occurs.

WRITE About It

1. Think about some of the video games you play. Describe some of the events in the game where things seem to happen randomly. Then describe some ways that the game acts like a function machine, where you supply the input.

2. You are a computer programmer designing a new game. Players score 10 points for hitting a circle, and lose 2 points for hitting a square.

   a. Suppose a player has x points. Write an equation to find P, the number of points a player has after hitting a circle.

   b. Suppose a player has z points. Write an equation to find S, the number of points a player has after hitting a square.

3. Explain how the equations you wrote in Exercise 2 represent functions.

4. How would you conduct a survey to find the experimental probability that a class member has a video game system at home? How many class members would you expect to have a game system at home?

12.6

Additional Probability Concepts

What you should learn:

Goal 1 How to find the probability of two independent events

Goal 2 How to solve real-life problems using probability

Why you should learn it:

Knowing how to find probabilities can help you play games. An example is finding the probability of winning a game.

Goal 1 FINDING PROBABILITIES

Mathematicians often explore probability by doing experiments. Here's one that you can try.

LESSON INVESTIGATION

Investigating Independent Events

GROUP ACTIVITY Put 3 blue marbles and 2 red marbles in a cup. Then put 1 blue marble and 1 red marble in another cup. Without looking, choose a marble from each cup. Record the colors in a table. Replace the marbles. Repeat the experiment 20 times. From your results, estimate the probability that both marbles will be red.

In this investigation, the two events (choosing a marble from each of the two cups) are **independent** because the occurrence of one event doesn't affect the occurrence of the other. An example of two real-life independent events is "Today is Thursday" and "It is raining."

PROBABILITY OF INDEPENDENT EVENTS

The probability that two independent events will occur is the product of their probabilities.

Example 1 Finding Probabilities

In the investigation above, what is the theoretical probability that both marbles will be red?

Solution

The probability of choosing a red marble from the first cup is $\frac{2}{5}$.

The probability of choosing a red marble from the second cup is $\frac{1}{2}$.

Because the events are independent, you can find the probability of choosing two red marbles by multiplying.

$$\frac{2}{5} \cdot \frac{1}{2} = \frac{2 \cdot 1}{5 \cdot 2} = \frac{2}{10}, \text{ or } \frac{1}{5}$$

The theoretical probability of choosing a red marble from both cups is $\frac{1}{5}$.

NEED TO KNOW

Events that are not independent are dependent. For example, the events "study for the test" and "get a good grade on the test" are dependent.

Example 2 Finding Probabilities

You are playing a game with a number cube and a spinner. What is the theoretical probability that you will get a 5 on the number cube *and* a blue region on the spinner?

NEED TO KNOW

Mathematicians refer to all of the different possible outcomes in a probability experiment as the "sample space."

Solution

Method **1** Multiply probabilities. The probability of getting a 5 on the number cube is $\frac{1}{6}$. The probability of getting a blue region on the spinner is $\frac{2}{5}$. Because the events are independent, the theoretical probability of getting a 5 *and* a blue region is

$$\frac{1}{6} \cdot \frac{2}{5} = \frac{1 \cdot 2}{6 \cdot 5} = \frac{2}{30}, \text{ or } \frac{1}{15}.$$

This means that you should get a 5 and a blue region about 1 out of every 15 times you toss the number cube and spin the spinner.

Method **2** STRATEGY **DRAW A DIAGRAM** Another way to find the theoretical probability is to draw a diagram showing all the possible outcomes.

You can see from the diagram that **2** of the 30 outcomes show a **5** and a **blue region**.

ONGOING ASSESSMENT

Talk About It

1. In Example 2, what is the theoretical probability of tossing an even number *and* landing on white? Solve the problem using a tree diagram.

2. Check your answer to Exercise 1 by using one of the methods in Example 2.

3. Which method do you prefer? Why?

GUIDED PRACTICE

1. What does it mean for events to be independent? Name two ways to find their probability.

In Exercises 2 and 3, are the events independent? Explain.

2. You like to play video games. You like to swim.

3. It is raining outside. You are holding an umbrella.

4. Find the theoretical probability of landing on green on both spinners shown at the right. Show how you can solve the problem by making a list.

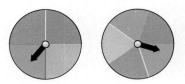

5. **GROUP ACTIVITY: THE GUESSING GAME**

   a. Choose a letter from A to C and a number from 1 to 15. Write your choices on a piece of paper. Ask others in your group to guess your combination (for example, "A3" or "C4") and write it down. After all guesses have been made, record each guess. Count the number of times the correct combination has been guessed.

   b. Repeat the experiment several times. Record your results in a table. From your results, estimate the probability of guessing the correct combination.

   c. Find the theoretical probability that the correct combination is chosen.

PRACTICE AND PROBLEM SOLVING

In Exercises 6–8, are the events independent? Explain your reasoning.

6. You studied 3 nights for your test. You do well on your test.

7. You own a dog. You like to roller skate.

8. You will play baseball this year. You buy a new pair of baseball shoes.

9. **BASKETBALL** You and a friend are shooting baskets. Your friend makes an average of 3 out of 5 and you make an average of 2 out of 3. What is the probability that both of you make your next basket?

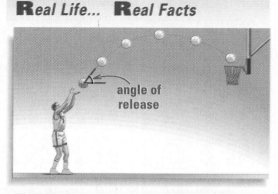

Real Life... **R**eal Facts

angle of release

Basketball Studies have indicated that the best angle of release for shooting a basketball is between 52° and 55°.

10. You are a contestant on a game show. You can win a trip to Mississippi or Tennessee. The letters of each state are placed in two separate bags. You choose one letter from each bag. To win, you must choose an "s" from each bag. What is the probability that you will win the trip?

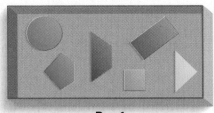

Box 1

GEOMETRY In Exercises 11 and 12, imagine that geometric figures are in two boxes as shown at the right. One figure is randomly selected from each box.

11. What is the probability that both selected figures are polygons?

12. What is the probability that both selected figures are parallelograms?

Box 2

STANDARDIZED TEST PRACTICE

13. A jar contains 6 red marbles, 5 blue marbles, 4 yellow marbles, 3 green marbles, 2 orange marbles, and 1 purple marble. If a marble is chosen without looking, what is the probability that it will be red?

     A $\frac{1}{2}$ **B** $\frac{2}{7}$ **C** $\frac{6}{23}$ **D** $\frac{1}{21}$

EXPLORATION AND EXTENSION

PORTFOLIO

14. BUILDING YOUR PROJECT The Nigerian game of Igba-Ita is played by 2 persons, each with 12 shells. Players put 2 shells into a circle on the ground, called a pot, to begin play (and each time the pot is won). The first player tosses 4 shells.

If 0, 2, or 4 shells land face up, the tosser wins the pot, and keeps tossing. If 1 or 3 shells land face up, the tosser adds 4 shells to the pot, and the other player becomes the tosser. The game is over when one player wins all the shells.

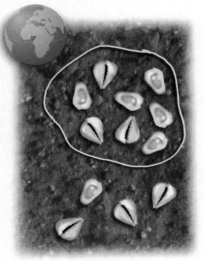

a. If the probability that a shell will land up is $\frac{11}{20}$, what is the probability of all four shells landing up?

b. What is the probability of all four shells landing down? Explain.

WHAT *did you learn?*   **WHY** *did you learn it?*

Skills	12.1	Solve addition equations.	Use a verbal model to find temperature increases.
	12.2	Solve subtraction equations.	Find the elevation of a building's roof.
	12.3	Solve equations with fractions or decimals.	Find how much money you need to save.
	12.4	Evaluate a function.	Find patterns in data, such as the perimeters of different rectangles.
	12.5	Solve counting problems.	Find the number of possible ways you can make a choice.
	12.6	Find the probability that two independent events will occur.	Understand the probability of an event such as winning a trip.
Strategies	12.1–6	Use problem solving strategies.	Solve a wide variety of real-life problems.
Using Data	12.1–6	Use tables and graphs.	Organize data and solve problems.

HOW *does it fit in the bigger picture of mathematics?*

One of the things you learned this year is that mathematics has many different parts. We hope this book has given you a passport to see several of these parts: number operations, algebra, geometry, statistics, and probability.

We also hope you have learned that there are many connections among the different parts of mathematics. New topics build on the skills that you have learned in the past. In this chapter you learned that you need to understand operations to do algebra, and that algebra helps you with probability.

In your future studies, we suggest that you continue to look for the many connections among the different parts of mathematics. Finding the connections helps you see more and more of the bigger picture of mathematics.

VOCABULARY

- verbal model (p. 581)
- function (p. 596)
- input (p. 596)
- output (p. 596)
- tree diagram (p. 602)
- counting principle (p. 603)
- independent events (p. 608)
- dependent events (p. 608)

12.1 SOLVING ADDITION EQUATIONS

Example

$$x + 6 = -3$$ Write original equation.
$$\underline{\quad -6 \qquad -6}$$ Subtract 6 from each side.
$$x \qquad = -9$$ Solution: *x* is by itself.

In Exercises 1–8, solve the equation. Then check your solution.

1. $n + 9 = -6$ **2.** $x + 4 = 2$ **3.** $z + 8 = 6$ **4.** $w + 6 = 9$

5. $x + 5 = 3$ **6.** $p + 7 = -3$ **7.** $f + 12 = -8$ **8.** $y + 10 = 3$

12.2 SOLVING SUBTRACTION EQUATIONS

Example

$$n - 4 = -7$$ Write original equation.
$$\underline{\quad +4 \qquad +4}$$ Add 4 to each side.
$$n \qquad = -3$$ Solution: *n* is by itself.

In Exercises 9–16, solve the equation. Then check your solution.

9. $y - 3 = -8$ **10.** $m - 5 = -2$ **11.** $d - 4 = -5$ **12.** $t - 8 = -12$

13. $y - 11 = 9$ **14.** $t - 7 = 7$ **15.** $d - 11 = 5$ **16.** $k - 4 = -5$

12.3 EQUATIONS WITH FRACTIONS AND DECIMALS

Examples

$$b + 12.7 = 16.3$$
$$\underline{\quad -12.7 \qquad -12.7}$$
$$b \qquad = 3.6$$

$$x - \frac{3}{5} = \frac{1}{5}$$
$$\underline{\quad +\frac{3}{5} \qquad +\frac{3}{5}}$$
$$x \qquad = \frac{4}{5}$$

17. You hike $3\frac{1}{2}$ mi of a trail and then rest. You will rest again at the 8-mile mark. Write and solve an equation that you can use to find the number of miles you must walk before resting.

18. During a field trip, you spend $12.25 for a shirt and have $3.50 left. Write an equation that you can use to find how much money you took on the trip. Then solve the equation.

12.4 EXPLORING FUNCTIONS

Example The table at the right shows the output values of the function $y = x - 6$ for $x = 0, 1, 2, 3, 4$.

Input: x	0	1	2	3	4
Output: y	-6	-5	-4	-3	-2

In Exercises 19–22, find the output values of the function for the input values of $x = -1, 0, 1, 2,$ and 3. Organize your results in a table.

19. $y = x - 3$ **20.** $y = x + 5$ **21.** $y = x + 3$ **22.** $y = x - 6$

12.5 COUNTING TECHNIQUES

Example How many different lunches are possible? Choose a **turkey** or **ham** sandwich, with **soup**, **chips**, or **salad**.

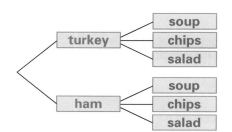

Counting Principle:

$$\begin{array}{c} 2 \text{ choices} \\ \text{of sandwich} \end{array} \times \begin{array}{c} 3 \text{ choices} \\ \text{of side order} \end{array} = \begin{array}{c} 6 \text{ different} \\ \text{lunches} \end{array}$$

23. A clothing store window displays figures wearing all possible combinations of 3 colors of T-shirts (red, yellow, blue) and 3 colors of shorts (blue, black, tan). How many figures are in the window?

12.6 ADDITIONAL PROBABILITY CONCEPTS

Examples 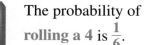 The probability of rolling a 4 is $\frac{1}{6}$.   The probability of spinning blue is $\frac{1}{4}$

The probability of **rolling a 4** *and* **spinning blue** is $\frac{1}{6} \cdot \frac{1}{4} = \frac{1}{24}$.

24. Using the spinner in the example above, what is the theoretical probability of getting red on one spin and purple on the next?

25. Are the events independent?

   a. You practice tennis every day. You are chosen for the tennis team.

   b. You have a quiz in math class. The sun is shining.

In Exercises 1–9, solve the equation. Then check the solution.

1. $p + 9 = 2$

2. $25 + s = 0$

3. $\dfrac{10}{11} = m + \dfrac{2}{11}$

4. $x + 20.8 = 30.03$

5. $32 + b = -8$

6. $n - \dfrac{2}{3} = \dfrac{4}{5}$

7. $y - 16.35 = 1.68$

8. $-19 = t - 18$

9. $-24 = z - 42$

In Exercises 10–12, use the graph to make a table of inputs and outputs. Then write a function to represent the data.

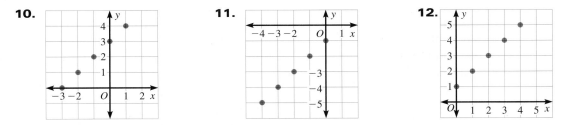

10.

11.

12.

13. WRITING AN EQUATION You lose 55 points in Round 2 of a card game. Your score is now -15 points. What was your score before Round 2? Write a verbal model using subtraction to represent the problem. Assign labels. Then write an equation and solve.

14. GARDENING You are planting flowers along a stone wall. After planting 11 flowers, you have 13 left. With how many plants did you start? Use a verbal model to represent the problem, and then solve.

15. BIRDS At the pet store, you want to buy 1 parakeet and 1 finch from cages that contain 16 parakeets and 12 finches. How many different pairs of birds can you select?

CHESS In Exercises 16–18, use the following information. In the game of chess, each player has 16 playing pieces in a box: 1 king, 1 queen, 2 rooks, 2 bishops, 2 knights, and 8 pawns. You and a friend decide to play. You each choose a piece from your box at random.

16. What is the theoretical probability that you both choose rooks?

17. What is the theoretical probability that you both choose pawns?

18. What is the theoretical probability that you choose a queen and your friend chooses a knight?

1. You and a friend are playing a board game. If you roll a 4 or a 1 on the number cube, you can send your friend back to start. What is the probability that you roll a 4?

   (A) $\frac{1}{6}$ **(B)** $\frac{1}{4}$

   (C) $\frac{1}{3}$ **(D)** $\frac{1}{2}$

2. Your club sold a total of $214.50 worth of candy to raise money. After paying for the candy, the club had $171.60 left. Which equation can you use to find how much the club paid for the candy?

   (A) $214.50 - x = 171.60$

   (B) $171.60 - x = 214.70$

   (C) $x - 171.60 = 214.50$

   (D) $214.50 + 171.60 = x$

3. You own 27 cassette tapes. You have 10 in your room, 5 in your school locker, and you loan the others to a friend. Which equation could you solve to find the number of cassette tapes your friend borrowed?

   (A) $x + 10 + 5 = 27$

   (B) $10 - x = 5$

   (C) $27 - 10 + x = 5$

   (D) $5 + x - 27 = 10$

4. Which of the following should you do to solve the equation $x - 22 = 43$?

   (A) Add 22 to each side.

   (B) Add 43 to each side.

   (C) Subtract 22 from each side.

   (D) Subtract 43 from each side.

5. At a cookout, you can put your hamburger in a white bun, a whole-grain bun, or pita bread. You can top it with either American, provolone, Swiss, or cheddar cheese. How many different cheeseburger-bread combinations can you make?

   (A) 3   **(B)** 4

   (C) 7   **(D)** 12

6. For her bedroom, Margie has a choice of a white, blue, or lavender rug, a pink or white bedspread, and white or lavender curtains. If she chooses colors at random, what is the probability that the rug, curtains, and bedspread will all be white?

   (A) 12   **(B)** 6

   (C) $\frac{1}{6}$ **(D)** $\frac{1}{12}$

7. Latisha earns money by baby-sitting and delivering newspapers. Last week she earned a total of $115.37. She earned $24.50 of the total by baby-sitting. Solve the equation $24.50 + x = 115.37$ to find how much she earned delivering newspapers.

   (A) $139.87   **(B)** $90.87

   (C) $4.71   **(D)** $-$90.87

8. You want to buy a CD player that costs $146. You have already saved $74. Which equation could you use to find the amount that you still need?

   (A) $x + 146 = 74$

   (B) $146 + 74 = x$

   (C) $74 + x = 146$

   (D) $x - 146 = 74$

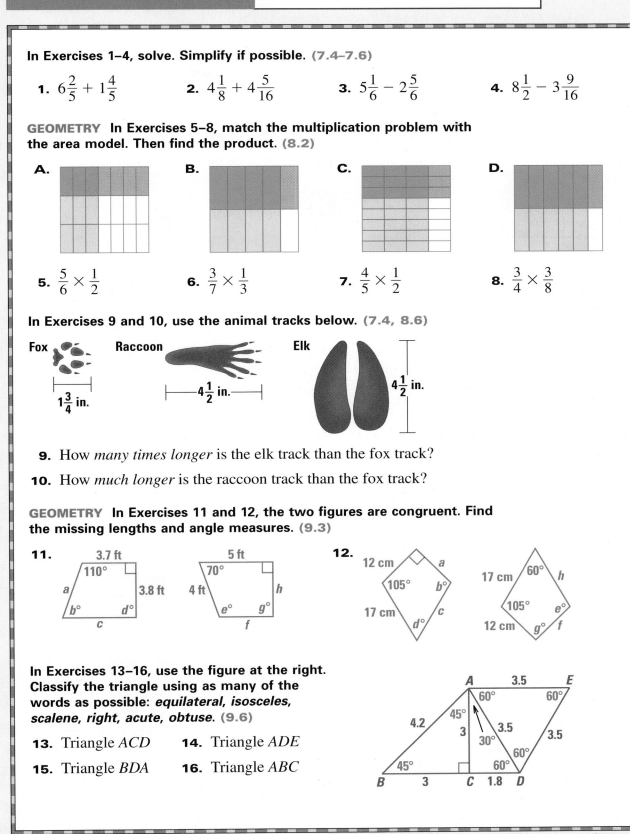

In Exercises 1–4, solve. Simplify if possible. (7.4–7.6)

1. $6\frac{2}{5} + 1\frac{4}{5}$

2. $4\frac{1}{8} + 4\frac{5}{16}$

3. $5\frac{1}{6} - 2\frac{5}{6}$

4. $8\frac{1}{2} - 3\frac{9}{16}$

GEOMETRY **In Exercises 5–8, match the multiplication problem with the area model. Then find the product. (8.2)**

A. **B.** **C.** **D.**

5. $\frac{5}{6} \times \frac{1}{2}$

6. $\frac{3}{7} \times \frac{1}{3}$

7. $\frac{4}{5} \times \frac{1}{2}$

8. $\frac{3}{4} \times \frac{3}{8}$

In Exercises 9 and 10, use the animal tracks below. (7.4, 8.6)

Fox $1\frac{3}{4}$ in.

Raccoon $4\frac{1}{2}$ in.

Elk $4\frac{1}{2}$ in.

9. How *many times longer* is the elk track than the fox track?

10. How *much longer* is the raccoon track than the fox track?

GEOMETRY **In Exercises 11 and 12, the two figures are congruent. Find the missing lengths and angle measures. (9.3)**

11. 3.7 ft, 110°, 3.8 ft, a, $b°$, $d°$, c; 5 ft, 70°, 4 ft, h, $e°$, $g°$, f

12. 12 cm, a, 105°, $b°$, 17 cm, c, $d°$; 17 cm, 60°, h, 105°, $e°$, 12 cm, $g°$, f

In Exercises 13–16, use the figure at the right. Classify the triangle using as many of the words as possible: *equilateral, isosceles, scalene, right, acute, obtuse*. (9.6)

13. Triangle *ACD*

14. Triangle *ADE*

15. Triangle *BDA*

16. Triangle *ABC*

In Exercises 17–22, use a number line to solve. (11.2, 11.3)

17. $-6 + 13$

18. $-4 + (-9)$

19. $-11 + 11$

20. $-8 - 7$

21. $4 - (-3)$

22. $-10 - (-3)$

In Exercise 23–25, find the area of the figure. (10.4, 10.6, 11.6)

23.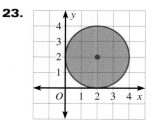

24.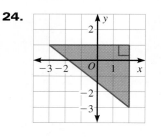

25.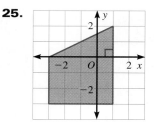

26. You threw a penny into a wishing well. The penny started 3 ft above the ground and landed 8 ft below ground. How many feet did the penny fall? Explain your steps. (11.3)

27. The top of a cash register receipt is torn off. The sales tax and the total are still showing. The sales tax is $3.36 and the total is $59.36. Write an equation that you can use to find the amount before tax. Then solve the equation. (12.1)

ALGEBRA In Exercises 28–33, solve the equation. Then check your solution. (12.1, 12.2, 12.3)

28. $5 + x = 31$

29. $12 = m - 3$

30. $z - 17 = -1$

31. $p - \dfrac{3}{8} = \dfrac{1}{2}$

32. $24.52 = t + 9.8$

33. $k - 6.67 = 34.05$

In Exercises 34 and 35, use a tree diagram to solve the problem. (12.5)

34. **PETS** You are buying a Labrador retriever puppy. You can choose a male or a female. You can also choose the color from yellow, chocolate, or black. What is the least number of Labrador retriever puppies that must be available for you to have all these choices?

35. **LUNCH** You are making a sandwich. You can choose from turkey, roast beef, or ham for the meat. You can also choose from white bread, rye bread, or sourdough bread. How many different sandwich combinations are there?

36. You and your friend each flip a coin. What is the probability that both coins will land heads up? (12.6)

37. **WRITING** Write a quiz about the top ten most important ideas you learned in math this year.

Student Resources

Table of Contents

x^2

%

$\dfrac{a}{b}$

6   10   8

EXTRA PRACTICE

Use after Lesson 1.1, page 4

Describe the pattern. Then write the next three numbers.

1. 100, 98, 96, 94,…

2. 1, 4, 7, 10,…

3. 1, 2, 4, 8,…

4. 1, 2, 4, 5,…

5. 0, 100, 5, 95,…

6. 3, 7, 11, 15,…

7. $\frac{1}{2}, \frac{2}{3}, \frac{3}{4}, \frac{4}{5}, \ldots$

8. $\frac{1}{3}, \frac{2}{5}, \frac{3}{7}, \frac{4}{9}, \ldots$

9. $\frac{1}{10}, \frac{1}{100}, \frac{1}{1,000}, \frac{1}{10,000}, \ldots$

Describe the pattern. Then write the next three letters.

10. A, C, E, G,…

11. A, Y, C, W,…

12. M, L, N, K,…

13. Z, V, R, N,…

14. Z, A, Y, B,…

15. B, D, F, H,…

Describe the pattern. Then sketch the next three figures.

16.   …   **17.**   …

Use after Lesson 1.2, page 8

The information below gives prices of apples at three different stores.

- Grocery Mart sells gala apples for $1.29/lb, red delicious apples for $.99/lb, and granny smith apples for $1.09/lb.

- Food Basket sells gala apples for $1.19/lb, red delicious apples for $.89/lb, and granny smith apples for $.99/lb.

- Fruit Farm sells all types of apples, including gala, red delicious, and granny smith, for $.99/lb.

1. Make a table for this data.

2. Compare the prices of apples at the three different stores.

3. Compare the prices of the three different types of apples.

Use after Lesson 1.3, page 12

In Exercises 1–4, make a list.

1. Make a list of the whole numbers from 1 through 60. Circle the multiples of 3. Color the multiples of 4. List the numbers that are both circled and colored. Describe the numbers in your list.

2. At a frozen yogurt stand you can order a small, medium, or large cup or cone of vanilla, raspberry, or swirl yogurt. List all the possible orders.

3. How many different ways can you make $.35 in change using quarters, dimes, and nickels? List all the possible ways.

4. Find a three-letter word that forms another word when the three letters are rearranged.

Use after Lesson 1.4, page 16

The graph at the right gives the fat content in 1 cup of milk for four types of milk.

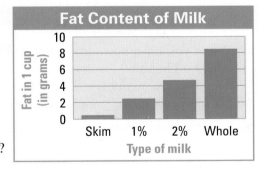

Fat Content of Milk

1. Which type of milk has about half as much fat as 2% milk?

2. Which type of milk has about 10 times more fat than skim milk?

3. About how many cups of skim milk can you drink for the same amount of fat as in 1 cup of whole milk?

Use after Lesson 1.5, page 22

1. How many different sizes of squares can be drawn in a 6-by-6 grid of dot paper?

2. Your bathroom floor measures 32 in. by 72 in. How many 8 in.-by-8 in. tiles are needed to cover the floor? Draw a diagram to show your solution.

3. Starting from home, you walk 6 blocks east, 3 blocks north, 2 blocks west, 4 blocks south, and you arrive at the mall. What is the shortest distance home if you walk north and west? Give two different routes.

Use after Lesson 1.6, page 28

Use mental math to solve.

1. $m + 11 = 54$ 2. $21 - p = 12$ 3. $k \cdot 4 = 28$ 4. $56 \div r = 8$

5. $n \div 6 = 9$ 6. $s \times s = 81$ 7. $13 \cdot 3 = a$ 8. $60 \div b = 5$

9. $43 - y = 23$ 10. $v + 12 = 62$ 11. $n = 27 - 10$ 12. $g \div 2 = 45$

Write an equation for the problem. Then solve.

13. You baby-sat 4 hours and earned $15. How much did you earn per hour?

14. After 5 friends left your party together, you counted 13 friends at the party. Before they left, how many friends were at the party?

Use after Lesson 1.7, page 34

Rewrite the equation as a question. Then solve the equation and check your answer.

1. $m \cdot 5 = 30$ 2. $18 - y = 10$ 3. $z + 7 = 13$ 4. $48 \div p = 12$

5. $11 + k = 28$ 6. $9 \times a = 63$ 7. $c - 4 = 8$ 8. $65 - w = 5$

Write an equation that represents the question. Then solve the equation and check your answer.

9. What number can be subtracted from 100 to get 43?

10. What number can be multiplied by 6 to get 66?

11. What number can be divided by 3 to get 15?

Use after Lesson 1.8, page 38

1. Every person in a club exchanges a dozen cookies with each member. If the club has eight members, how many cookies change hands?

2. When you have news to share, you call 2 friends. They call 2 other friends. Then they each call 2 other friends, and they each call 2 other friends. How many friends get the news? How many friends would get the news if everyone called 3 friends instead of 2?

3. Find the number of minutes in one year.

Use after Lesson 1.9, page 44

1. The circle graph at the right shows voter support for two candidates running for election. It is estimated that at least $\frac{3}{4}$ of the undecided voters will support Nilsen. Will this be enough for Nilsen to win the election? Explain.

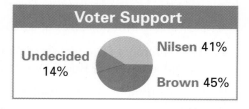

2. Find two consecutive numbers with a product of 1056.

3. Find two consecutive numbers with a sum of 253.

4. The number of ants in your ant farm doubles every 10 days. On the 61st day there are 640 ants in the farm. How many ants did you start with? How many will you have on day 81?

Use after Lesson 2.1, page 60

Write the number in words and in expanded notation.

1. 3095   2. 40,108   3. 4,004,400   4. 18,080,635

Write the number given by the expanded notation.

5. $5 \times 10{,}000 + 4 \times 100 + 6 \times 1$ 6. $6 \times 1000 + 2 \times 100 + 5 \times 10$

Write the number described by the words.

7. six hundred twenty-five thousand   8. eighty-seven million

9. nine thousand, two hundred three   10. forty thousand, sixty-one

Use after Lesson 2.2, page 66

Solve each problem without using a calculator. Show your work.

1. $325 + 387$ 2. $512 + 78$ 3. $432 + 987$ 4. $9235 + 6546$

5. $862 - 465$ 6. $526 - 379$ 7. $103 - 68$ 8. $6439 - 4985$

Find the perimeter of the figure.

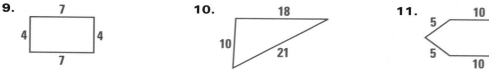

Use after Lesson 2.3, page 72

Write the multiplication problem that is shown by the area model.

1. Area is 32 square units.   **2.** Area is 20 square units.   **3.** Area is 27 square units.

Use mental math to solve.

4. $7 \cdot n = 56$ **5.** $a \cdot 4 = 48$ **6.** $6 \cdot w = 60$ **7.** $j \cdot 9 = 81$

8. Draw two different rectangles with an area of 30 cm^2.

9. Find the area of a rectangular room that measures 9 ft by 13 ft.

10. How many 2 ft-by-2 ft tiles will cover a floor with an area of 96 ft^2?

Use after Lesson 2.4, page 78

Write the division problem that is shown by the area model. Then write the quotient in two ways.

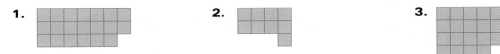

Divide. Then write the quotient in two ways.

4. $98 \div 9$ **5.** $46 \div 5$ **6.** $77 \div 8$ **7.** $64 \div 7$

8. $143 \div 6$ **9.** $398 \div 7$ **10.** $523 \div 5$ **11.** $452 \div 9$

12. Three sisters bought a gift for their parents for $57. If they divide the cost evenly, how much will each sister pay?

13. Peter drove 159 miles in about 3 hours. What was his average speed in miles per hour?

Use after Lesson 2.5, page 84

Evaluate each expression.

1. $4 \times 3 + 7$ **2.** $15 - 2 \times 3$ **3.** $6 \times (7 - 5)$ **4.** $48 \div 2 \div 6$

5. $9 + 3 \times 4 - 2$ **6.** $30 \div 3 + 12 \times 2$ **7.** $(52 + 8) \div 6 + 4$ **8.** $(4 + 8 \times 2) \div 4$

Write the expression that is described. Use parentheses if necessary. Then evaluate.

9. Add 10 to 6, then multiply the sum by 3.

10. Add 19 to the difference of 28 and 8.

11. Admission to a zoo costs $8 for adults and $5 for children. Write a numerical expression to show the admission cost for a family of 2 adults and 4 children. Then evaluate the expression.

Use after Lesson 2.6, page 88

Evaluate the expression in two ways.

1. $3(1 + 4)$ **2.** $5(4 + 2)$ **3.** $9(7 + 4)$ **4.** $8(7 + 12)$

5. $12(4 + 10)$ **6.** $6(11 + 6)$ **7.** $7(8 + 10)$ **8.** $14(2 + 3)$

Evaluate each expression when $n = 4$.

9. $8 \times n$ **10.** $n + 13$ **11.** $2 \times n + 5$ **12.** $3(n - 1)$

13. $10 \cdot n - 3$ **14.** $(6 + 5)n$ **15.** $6 \cdot n \div 2$ **16.** $100 - 9 \cdot n$

Use after Lesson 2.7, page 96

Write the number in the given base.

1. 42_5, base 10 **2.** 321_5, base 10 **3.** 11000_2, base 10 **4.** 10110_2, base 10

5. 73_{10}, base 5 **6.** 27_{10}, base 2 **7.** 46_{10}, base 2 **8.** 254_{10}, base 5

Use after Lesson 3.1, page 112

Write the number in expanded notation.

1. 27.8 **2.** 5.09 **3.** 0.75 **4.** 3.14

5. 9.067 **6.** 0.395 **7.** 298.1 **8.** 14.322

Write each cents amount as dollars.

9. 99¢ **10.** 300¢ **11.** 125¢ **12.** 4¢

Use after Lesson 3.2, page 116

Match the object with its measure.

A. 2 m **B.** 8 cm **C.** 17 mm **D.** 6.2 km

1. Width of a calculator **2.** Diameter of a dime

3. Height of Mt. McKinley **4.** Length of a sofa

Rewrite the measure in the given metric unit.

5. 5 cm (mm) **6.** 88 cm (m) **7.** 95,000 m (km) **8.** 74 mm (cm)

9. 0.7 km (m) **10.** 19 cm (mm) **11.** 9200 mm (m) **12.** 8.4 cm (mm)

Use after Lesson 3.3, page 124

Sketch a number-line model and a set model to show each number.

1. 0.3 **2.** 0.5 **3.** 1.4 **4.** 0.15

5. Club members set a goal to raise $1000. The diagram at the right shows the amount raised so far. How much money has been raised so far? How many dollar signs will there be when the goal is met?

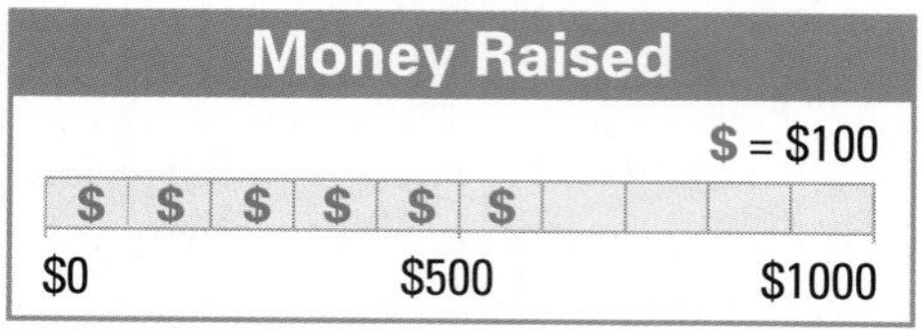

Money Raised

$	$	$	$	$	$				

$ = $100

$0 $500 $1000

Use after Lesson 3.4, page 128

Rewrite the number as a fraction, a decimal, and a percent.

1. 0.23

2. 19%

3. 88%

4. 0.4

5. 7%

6. 0.03

7. 1%

8. 0.317

9. $\dfrac{17}{100}$

10. $\dfrac{2}{10}$

11. 94%

12. 5%

Use after Lesson 3.5, page 134

Order the numbers from least to greatest.

1. 1.24, 1.04, 1.2, 1.4, 1.52

2. 0.23, 0.209, 0.229, 0.21, 0.22

3. 2.32, 3.01, 2.15, 2.99, 2.89

4. 4.1, 4.01, 4.8, 4.25, 4.81

5. Name the numbers represented by letters on the number line.

Use after Lesson 3.6, page 138

Round each number to the given place value.

1. 74 (tens)

2. 2195 (thousands)

3. 15,797 (hundreds)

4. 10,481 (thousands)

5. 7.081 (tenths)

6. 0.7235 (hundredths)

Round to the nearest dollar.

7. $24.95

8. $16.50

9. $2.25

10. $90.49

Use after Lesson 3.7, page 144

Find the missing value.

1. $3^? = 9$

2. $?^3 = 64$

3. $2^? = 16$

4. $10^? = 1000$

5. $?^3 = 125$

6. $3^? = 81$

7. $?^2 = 25$

8. $?^2 = 36$

Evaluate the expression.

9. $5 + 3^2$

10. $4 + 2 \times 5^2$

11. $(12 + 4) \div 4^2$

12. $9^2 \div 6$

Use after Lesson 3.8, page 148

Use a model to find the value.

1. 30% of 10 people at a party

2. 0.15 of 100 miles traveled

3. 0.2 of 40 pounds of potatoes

4. 25% of 60 dollars discounted

5. $\dfrac{3}{10}$ of 150 employees at a meeting

6. $\dfrac{22}{100}$ of 200 voters surveyed

7. Two hundred students were asked to name their favorite type of burrito. Half named bean, 30% named chicken, and the rest named beef. How many students named each type as their favorite?

Use after Lesson 4.1, page 166

Use vertical form to add.

1. $3.21 + 5.24$ **2.** $21.93 + 6.47$ **3.** $11.54 + 10.09$ **4.** $15.85 + 7$

5. $32.58 + 1.9$ **6.** $3.9071 + 28.26$ **7.** $0.0008 + 78.4$ **8.** $19.9 + 0.01$

Use the menu at the right.

9. You order a bagel with cream cheese and a small lemonade for lunch. How much does your lunch cost?

10. How much do 10 plain bagels cost? How many "free" bagels do you get when you order a dozen? Explain.

· · · · · · · · Bagels · · · · · · · ·		
Plain	with cream cheese	Dozen
$.65	$1.45	$6.50
· · · · · · · Lemonade · · · · · · ·		
Small	Medium	Large
$.75	$1.00	$1.25

Use after Lesson 4.2, page 170

Use vertical form to subtract.

1. $7.54 - 2.31$ **2.** $9.68 - 7.46$ **3.** $32.124 - 2.735$ **4.** $49.5 - 27.23$

5. $29.22 - 9.99$ **6.** $7 - 5.32$ **7.** $10 - 4.3$ **8.** $3.701 - 2.003$

Use the menu above.

9. How much does the cream cheese on a bagel cost?

10. You use a $10 bill to pay for a dozen bagels and a large lemonade. How much change should you receive?

Use after Lesson 4.3, page 176

Round the values to the nearest dollar and estimate the answer. Then estimate again by rounding to the nearest half dollar.

1. $7.23 + $2.65 **2.** $4.76 + $9.41 **3.** $12.40 - $9.80

4. $8.73 + $5.21 **5.** $19.32 - $7.86 **6.** $12.90 - $11.60

Estimate the answer by using front-end estimation. Then make your estimate better by using the "front" and "next" digits.

7. $1234 + 3342$ **8.** $4.32 + 5.51$ **9.** $5793 - 3112$

Use after Lesson 4.4, page 182

Find the product.

1. 1.3×4 **2.** 9.74×0.6 **3.** 6.44×3.9 **4.** 0.07×0.04

5. 32.1×0.23 **6.** 5.32×1.2 **7.** 0.8×0.4 **8.** 0.3×0.12

Write a multiplication problem that you could use to answer the question. Then answer the question.

9. What is 70% of 452? **10.** What is $\frac{9}{10}$ of 84? **11.** What is $\frac{32}{100}$ of 56?

12. What is 14% of 90? **13.** What is 0.5 of 65? **14.** What is 0.35 of 180?

Use after Lesson 4.5, page 188

Use long division to solve.

1. $3.87 \div 3$ **2.** $19.26 \div 6$ **3.** $10.7 \div 5$ **4.** $174.3 \div 3$

5. $170.1 \div 7$ **6.** $3.2 \div 50$ **7.** $18.8 \div 8$ **8.** $60.9 \div 3$

9. The length of a rectangle with area 220.98 cm^2 is 17.4 cm. Find the width of the rectangle.

Use after Lesson 4.6, page 192

Write the number as a power of 10.

1. 1000   **2.** 100,000   **3.** 10,000,000,000   **4.** 1,000,000,000,000

Solve the problem.

5. $932 \div 10$ **6.** 450×1000 **7.** $60,000 \div 10^3$ **8.** 43.32×10^4

Use mental math to solve. Then use a calculator to check.

9. $3.727 \times t = 3727$ **10.** $m \times 1000 = 660,000$ **11.** $k \div 100 = 0.739$

Use after Lesson 4.7, page 200

Divide. Check your answer by multiplying.

1. $8 \div 0.4$ **2.** $12.6 \div 0.3$ **3.** $0.9 \div 0.3$ **4.** $28 \div 2.8$

5. $0.6 \div 0.02$ **6.** $16.8 \div 2.1$ **7.** $7 \div 0.04$ **8.** $119.4 \div 0.3$

9. The area of a rectangle is 31 cm^2. The width is 6.5 cm. Find the length.

Use after Lesson 4.8, page 204

1. A jacket priced at $60 is on sale for 30% off the regular price. What is the discount? What is the sale price?

2. Ken earns $7 per hour and will get a 5% raise next month. What will his new hourly wage be?

3. Barbara has 15% of her earnings withheld from her paycheck for taxes. If her earnings are $875, how much will her paycheck be?

Use after Lesson 5.1, page 220

Make a line plot of the data. Find the most common number and the range of the data.

1. Scores on a 10 point quiz:

9, 8, 9, 5, 10, 6, 7, 8, 10, 7, 4, 9, 5, 10, 7, 8, 9, 8, 8, 10

2. Numbers of siblings of students in a sixth-grade class:

3, 1, 0, 1, 2, 1, 2, 0, 0, 2, 1, 1, 3, 1, 4, 1, 2, 1, 1, 0, 2, 0, 3, 1, 2

3. Average monthly wind speeds (mph) in Key West, Florida:

12, 12, 13, 13, 11, 10, 10, 9, 10, 11, 12, 12

Use after Lesson 5.2, page 224

Draw an ordered stem-and-leaf plot for the set of data.

1. Ages that teachers in a certain school retired:

   65, 61, 53, 47, 52, 54, 52, 56, 57, 48, 61, 64, 55, 59, 58, 62

2. Test scores of a sixth-grade class:

   72, 92, 93, 87, 80, 69, 79, 85, 76, 88, 97, 95, 68, 70, 91, 89, 94, 84, 98

3. Distances (in miles) of bike routes described in a book:

   20, 19, 16, 26, 23, 19, 10, 27, 18, 15, 21, 20, 22, 26, 24, 12, 29, 18

Use after Lesson 5.3, page 232

Find the mean of the numbers. Then check whether your answer is reasonable.

1. 24, 23, 28
2. 10, 11, 30
3. 21, 25, 23, 19
4. 26, 32, 33, 19
5. 11, 20, 17, 18
6. 7, 2, 7, 32, 7
7. 26, 31, 33, 28, 28
8. 19, 12, 16, 14, 18

9. Your test scores are 88, 85, 95, and 92. The highest possible score is 100. With the next test, can you raise your mean score to 94? Explain.

Use after Lesson 5.4, page 236

Find the median and mode of the data.

1. Numbers of club members who attend monthly meetings:

   25, 21, 30, 27, 22, 28, 33, 28, 20, 27, 29, 31

2. Lengths of phone calls listed on a phone bill (in minutes):

   4, 1, 1, 64, 1, 1, 23, 3, 10, 8, 12, 30, 1, 68, 4, 39, 3, 84, 1, 13, 1, 9, 14

3. Numbers of pages of best-selling paperback books:

   332, 503, 387, 309, 566, 524, 520, 914, 676, 287, 527, 447, 435

Use after Lesson 5.5, page 242

Draw a bar graph of the data. Choose an appropriate scale.

1. Annual rainfall (in inches) of cities in 6 different climates

Climate	in.
Polar	4
Cold temperate	15
Cool temperate	23
Warm temperate	16
Tropical (desert)	1
Tropical (monsoon)	103

2. Food wasted (in billions of pounds) in the U.S. in a year

Food	billion lb
Fats/oils	6.8
Meat, poultry, fish	8.2
Processed fruits/vegetables	8.3
Fresh fruits/vegetables	18.9
Fluid milk	17.4
Grain products	14.6

Use after Lesson 5.6, page 246

The chart below gives the population density in the U.S. from 1910 to 1990. Population density is the number of people per square mile of land.
(Source: U.S. Bureau of the Census)

Year	1910	1920	1930	1940	1950	1960	1970	1980	1990
Population Density	26.0	29.9	34.7	37.2	42.6	50.6	57.5	64.0	70.3

1. Draw a line graph for the data. Use the graph for Exercises 2–5.

2. In which decade did the population density increase the most?

3. In which decade did the population density increase the least?

4. Predict the population density in the U.S. in the year 2000.

5. About how many years did it take for the population density to double from the year 1910? When might it double again?

Use after Lesson 5.7, page 252

Draw a pictograph of the data.

1. Twenty people were asked to name their favorite season. The results were: spring, 3; summer, 8; fall, 4; winter, 5.

2. Fifty employees were asked how they travel to work. The results were: car, 25; bus, 15; walk, 10.

3. Ninety people were asked to name their favorite flower. The results were: tulip, 30; petunia, 20; rose, 35; lily, 5.

Match each data set described with each appropriate type of graph to represent the data. Explain your choice(s).

4. Hair colors of the students in your math class

5. Ages of the students in your math class

6. Heights of the students in your math class

7. Number of boys and girls in your math class

8. Number of students in your math class each year of school

A. Line plot

B. Stem-and-leaf plot

C. Bar graph

D. Line graph

E. Pictograph

Use after Lesson 6.1, page 268

What fraction of the model is shaded?

1. **2.** **3.** **4.**

Draw a diagram to represent the fraction of people in the U.S. with the given hair color.

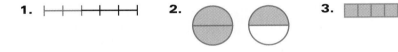

5. brown, $\frac{7}{10}$ **6.** blonde, $\frac{1}{7}$ **7.** black, $\frac{1}{10}$ **8.** red, $\frac{1}{16}$

Use after Lesson 6.2, page 274

Draw a diagram to help you divide. Write your answer as a fraction or mixed number.

1. Divide 4 cans of juice into 5 equal parts. **2.** Divide 5 pears into 7 equal parts.

3. Divide 6 sandwiches into 8 equal parts. **4.** Divide 7 bananas into 2 equal parts.

5. Divide 12 oranges into 8 equal parts. **6.** Divide 10 crackers into 4 equal parts.

Use the pattern of shapes at the right. Write each ratio.

7. squares to triangles **8.** triangles to circles

9. circles to squares **10.** triangles to all shapes

▲■●●■▲■▲●▲●
●▲■▲■●■▲●▲

Use after Lesson 6.3, page 278

Write two equivalent fractions represented by each diagram.

1. **2.** **3.** **4.**

Decide whether the ratios are equivalent.

5. $\dfrac{3}{4}, \dfrac{8}{12}$ **6.** $\dfrac{1}{3}, \dfrac{3}{10}$ **7.** $\dfrac{3}{8}, \dfrac{6}{16}$ **8.** $\dfrac{4}{5}, \dfrac{8}{10}$

Use after Lesson 6.4, page 282

Simplify the fraction.

1. $\dfrac{10}{15}$ **2.** $\dfrac{24}{42}$ **3.** $\dfrac{64}{72}$ **4.** $\dfrac{26}{54}$

5. $\dfrac{32}{64}$ **6.** $\dfrac{30}{75}$ **7.** $\dfrac{18}{12}$ **8.** $\dfrac{36}{18}$

Solve the proportion.

9. $\dfrac{1}{3} = \dfrac{x}{15}$ **10.** $\dfrac{3}{4} = \dfrac{6}{n}$ **11.** $\dfrac{a}{2} = \dfrac{17}{34}$ **12.** $\dfrac{5}{z} = \dfrac{10}{12}$

Use after Lesson 6.5, page 290

Complete the statement using > or <.

1. $\dfrac{4}{7} \; ? \; \dfrac{4}{9}$ **2.** $\dfrac{5}{11} \; ? \; \dfrac{6}{11}$ **3.** $\dfrac{17}{3} \; ? \; \dfrac{14}{3}$ **4.** $\dfrac{2}{5} \; ? \; \dfrac{2}{3}$

5. $\dfrac{3}{8} \; ? \; \dfrac{1}{3}$ **6.** $\dfrac{1}{4} \; ? \; \dfrac{4}{15}$ **7.** $\dfrac{8}{15} \; ? \; \dfrac{5}{9}$ **8.** $\dfrac{10}{6} \; ? \; \dfrac{12}{7}$

9. Draw a ruler from 0 to 1 in. Label these lengths on your ruler: 0, 1, $\dfrac{1}{2}, \dfrac{1}{4}, \dfrac{3}{4}, \dfrac{1}{8}, \dfrac{3}{8}, \dfrac{5}{8}, \dfrac{7}{8}$ in. Then write the lengths in order from least to greatest.

Use after Lesson 6.6, page 296

Draw a model to represent each number. Then rewrite the number.

1. $\dfrac{12}{5}$ **2.** $\dfrac{10}{3}$ **3.** $1\dfrac{7}{8}$ **4.** $2\dfrac{1}{4}$

Rewrite the improper fraction as a mixed number.

5. $\dfrac{21}{10}$ **6.** $\dfrac{35}{8}$ **7.** $\dfrac{16}{9}$ **8.** $\dfrac{27}{7}$

Rewrite the mixed number as an improper fraction.

9. $1\dfrac{2}{7}$ **10.** $2\dfrac{9}{20}$ **11.** $3\dfrac{1}{8}$ **12.** $2\dfrac{9}{10}$

Use after Lesson 6.7, page 302

Use the spinner below. Find the probability that the arrow will land in the region described.

1. yellow   **2.** blue   **3.** not red   **4.** red or yellow

Use the spinner at the right. Name an event that has the probability described.

5. likely to occur   **6.** not likely to occur

7. cannot occur   **8.** must occur

Use after Lesson 7.1, page 318

Complete the statement.

1. 2 ft = ? in.   **2.** 1 yd = ? in.   **3.** 9 ft = ? yd   **4.** 12 in. = ? yd

5. 4 yd = ? ft   **6.** 30 in. = ? ft   **7.** 2 yd = ? in.   **8.** $3\dfrac{1}{2}$ ft = ? in.

Write each height in inches.

9. 3'9"   **10.** 4'9"   **11.** 5'6"   **12.** 6'2"

Write each height in feet and inches.

13. 46"   **14.** 54"   **15.** 61"   **16.** 77"

Use after Lesson 7.2, page 322

Find the least common multiple of the two numbers.

1. 2, 5   **2.** 3, 8   **3.** 4, 6   **4.** 12, 9

Find the least common denominator. Then use the least common denominator to rewrite the fractions.

5. $\dfrac{1}{2}, \dfrac{2}{3}$ **6.** $\dfrac{1}{5}, \dfrac{1}{8}$ **7.** $\dfrac{1}{12}, \dfrac{1}{8}$ **8.** $\dfrac{1}{9}, \dfrac{1}{6}$

9. $\dfrac{5}{12}, \dfrac{1}{4}$ **10.** $\dfrac{9}{11}, \dfrac{1}{2}$ **11.** $\dfrac{5}{7}, \dfrac{1}{5}$ **12.** $\dfrac{4}{15}, \dfrac{2}{5}$

Use after Lesson 7.3, page 330

Add or subtract.

1. $\frac{5}{8} + \frac{1}{8}$ 2. $\frac{1}{5} + \frac{3}{5}$ 3. $\frac{5}{6} + \frac{5}{12}$ 4. $\frac{3}{8} + \frac{1}{4}$

5. $\frac{2}{3} + \frac{13}{18}$ 6. $\frac{2}{5} + \frac{3}{4} + \frac{1}{2}$ 7. $\frac{1}{7} + \frac{5}{7} + \frac{6}{7}$ 8. $\frac{3}{8} + \frac{1}{12} + \frac{1}{4}$

9. $\frac{5}{7} - \frac{2}{7}$ 10. $\frac{5}{9} - \frac{1}{9}$ 11. $\frac{1}{3} - \frac{2}{9}$ 12. $\frac{17}{20} - \frac{3}{10}$

13. $\frac{7}{8} - \frac{2}{3}$ 14. $\frac{9}{10} - \frac{4}{15}$ 15. $\frac{1}{2} - \frac{4}{9}$ 16. $\frac{7}{2} - \frac{7}{10}$

Use after Lesson 7.4, page 336

Add or subtract.

1. $2\frac{2}{9} + 5\frac{5}{9}$ 2. $7\frac{3}{11} + 4\frac{6}{11}$ 3. $3\frac{4}{7} + 1\frac{6}{7}$ 4. $6\frac{7}{12} + 5\frac{5}{12}$

5. $10\frac{3}{5} - 4\frac{1}{10}$ 6. $1\frac{18}{27} + 7\frac{7}{9}$ 7. $5\frac{17}{26} - 2\frac{7}{13}$ 8. $9\frac{1}{32} + 3\frac{3}{4}$

9. $4\frac{9}{17} - 1\frac{5}{17}$ 10. $8\frac{9}{10} - 3\frac{3}{10}$ 11. $2\frac{7}{11} - 1\frac{4}{11}$ 12. $6\frac{5}{7} - 4\frac{3}{7}$

13. From a board that is $20\frac{1}{2}$ in. long, Sam needs to cut two $4\frac{1}{8}$ in. long pieces. He needs at least 12 in. left. Is the board long enough?

Use after Lesson 7.5, page 342

Subtract. Then simplify, if possible.

1. $15 - 3\frac{1}{5}$ 2. $4 - \frac{7}{9}$ 3. $8 - 7\frac{3}{4}$ 4. $5\frac{2}{7} - 1\frac{4}{7}$

5. $11\frac{7}{12} - 10\frac{11}{12}$ 6. $21\frac{1}{6} - 15\frac{5}{6}$ 7. $12\frac{4}{21} - 9\frac{8}{21}$ 8. $30 - 6\frac{2}{15}$

9. A 10 cup canister is filled with sugar. If you use $3\frac{1}{4}$ cups of sugar to make a cake, how much will be left in the canister?

Use after Lesson 7.6, page 348

1. Put the steps for solving $4\frac{1}{8} - 1\frac{3}{4}$ in order.

   A. $3\frac{9}{8} - 1\frac{6}{8}$ **B.** $2\frac{3}{8}$ **C.** $4\frac{1}{8} - 1\frac{3}{4}$ **D.** $4\frac{1}{8} - 1\frac{6}{8}$

Subtract. Then simplify, if possible.

2. $4\frac{4}{9} - 1\frac{1}{18}$ 3. $13\frac{4}{11} - 5\frac{6}{11}$ 4. $8\frac{3}{14} - 2\frac{1}{7}$ 5. $9\frac{1}{4} - 3\frac{1}{3}$

6. $11\frac{3}{5} - \frac{5}{12}$ 7. $7\frac{1}{8} - 4\frac{3}{8}$ 8. $3\frac{2}{3} - \frac{4}{9}$ 9. $19\frac{7}{16} - 5\frac{1}{4}$

10. A recipe requires $4\frac{1}{2}$ cups of dry rice. You have only $2\frac{3}{4}$ cups. How much more dry rice do you need for the recipe?

Use after Lesson 7.7, page 354

In Exercises 1–6, use the table at the right.

Month	Rainfall (in inches)
January	$\frac{3}{4}$
February	$1\frac{3}{4}$
March	2
April	$2\frac{1}{8}$
May	$4\frac{1}{2}$
June	$3\frac{7}{8}$

1. How much more rain fell in the month with the most rainfall than in the month with the least rainfall?

2. What was the total rainfall in the six month period?

3. How much more rain fell in February than in January?

4. How much more rain fell in March than in February?

5. How much more rain fell in April than in March?

6. How much more rain fell in May than in April?

Use after Lesson 8.1, page 370

Use a model to help you find the answer.

1. What is $\frac{2}{3}$ of 12?   2. What is $\frac{2}{5}$ of 20?   3. What is $\frac{7}{8}$ of 10?

Find the product. Simplify, if possible.

4. $9 \times \frac{2}{3}$ 5. $\frac{3}{5} \times 35$ 6. $4 \times \frac{1}{8}$ 7. $\frac{4}{9} \times 12$

8. $15 \times \frac{2}{7}$ 9. $\frac{5}{11} \times 6$ 10. $5 \times \frac{7}{15}$ 11. $\frac{11}{12} \times 8$

Use after Lesson 8.2, page 376

Find the product. Simplify, if possible.

1. $\frac{1}{2} \times \frac{3}{8}$ 2. $\frac{5}{6} \times \frac{3}{4}$ 3. $\frac{1}{5} \times \frac{1}{3}$ 4. $\frac{4}{9} \times \frac{1}{6}$

5. $\frac{9}{10} \times \frac{3}{10}$ 6. $\frac{2}{7} \times \frac{1}{2} \times \frac{3}{4}$ 7. $\frac{10}{11} \times \frac{17}{100}$ 8. $\frac{3}{7} \times \frac{1}{2} \times \frac{2}{3}$

9. You have a piece of fabric that is $\frac{3}{4}$ yd long. If you cut it in half, how long will each piece be?

Use after Lesson 8.3, page 384

Write the answer in hours. Then write the answer in hours and minutes.

1. What is $1\frac{1}{2}$ of 5 hours?   2. What is $3\frac{1}{3}$ of 6 hours?   3. What is $\frac{2}{3}$ of $8\frac{1}{2}$ hours?

Multiply. Simplify, if possible.

4. $\frac{1}{2} \times 2\frac{3}{5}$ 5. $1\frac{2}{9} \times 4\frac{1}{2}$ 6. $4 \times 7\frac{1}{2}$ 7. $2\frac{1}{8} \times 1\frac{4}{9}$

8. $6\frac{2}{3} \times 2\frac{1}{4}$ 9. $3\frac{1}{4} \times \frac{3}{10}$ 10. $8\frac{1}{5} \times 10$ 11. $9\frac{1}{2} \times \frac{1}{3}$

Find the area of a rectangle with the given dimensions.

12. 6 in. by $2\frac{1}{8}$ in.   13. $4\frac{1}{2}$ ft by $1\frac{1}{6}$ ft   14. $2\frac{1}{2}$ yd by $3\frac{1}{4}$ yd   15. $1\frac{3}{4}$ mi by $\frac{3}{10}$ mi

Use after Lesson 8.4, page 390

Complete the statement.

1. $\dfrac{16}{5} \div \boxed{?} = \dfrac{16}{2}$

2. $\dfrac{4}{5} \div \dfrac{2}{5} = \boxed{?}$

3. $\boxed{?} \div \dfrac{12}{8} = \dfrac{21}{12}$

4. $\boxed{?} \div \dfrac{7}{10} = \dfrac{18}{7}$

5. $1\dfrac{2}{3} \div \dfrac{2}{3} = \boxed{?}$

6. $\dfrac{6}{8} \div \dfrac{1}{8} = \boxed{?}$

7. $\dfrac{4}{5} \div 1\dfrac{1}{5} = \boxed{?}$

8. $6\dfrac{2}{7} \div \dfrac{5}{7} = \boxed{?}$

9. How many $2\dfrac{1}{2}$ ft shelves can you cut from a $10\dfrac{1}{2}$ ft board?

Use after Lesson 8.5, page 396

Find the reciprocal of the number.

1. $\dfrac{3}{7}$

2. $\dfrac{11}{12}$

3. 4

4. $\dfrac{1}{6}$

Find the quotient. Simplify, if possible.

5. $\dfrac{1}{8} \div \dfrac{1}{4}$

6. $\dfrac{3}{5} \div \dfrac{2}{7}$

7. $\dfrac{8}{9} \div 2$

8. $\dfrac{3}{8} \div 4$

9. $\dfrac{2}{5} \div \dfrac{1}{5}$

10. $\dfrac{3}{4} \div \dfrac{5}{8}$

11. $9 \div \dfrac{1}{3}$

12. $\dfrac{1}{5} \div \dfrac{1}{15}$

13. How many $\dfrac{2}{3}$ cup servings are there in an 8 cup pitcher of juice?

Use after Lesson 8.6, page 400

Find the quotient. Simplify, if possible.

1. $1\dfrac{4}{7} \div 2\dfrac{2}{3}$

2. $3\dfrac{1}{2} \div 5\dfrac{4}{5}$

3. $2\dfrac{2}{3} \div 4$

4. $5\dfrac{1}{2} \div 2\dfrac{1}{3}$

5. $1\dfrac{2}{5} \div \dfrac{3}{4}$

6. $2\dfrac{6}{7} \div \dfrac{1}{7}$

7. $9 \div 4\dfrac{1}{4}$

8. $2\dfrac{5}{9} \div 2$

9. You are making tablecloths for picnic tables by cutting a 32 ft strip of cloth into $6\dfrac{1}{4}$ ft pieces. How many tables can you cover completely?

Use after Lesson 8.7, page 406

Find the area of a right triangle with the given dimensions.

1. Base: 4 in.; height: $2\dfrac{1}{8}$ in.

2. Base: $3\dfrac{1}{6}$ cm; height: 2 cm

3.

4.

5.

The figure is made of right triangles. Find the area of the figure.

6.

7.

8.

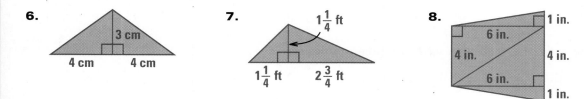

Use after Lesson 9.1, page 420

State whether the shape is a polygon. If it is, name the polygon. If it is not, explain why.

1. **2.** **3.**

4. Draw two different hexagons. Estimate which perimeter is greater.

Sketch the described figure on grid paper by connecting the points. Name the figure.

5. Start at *P*. Move right 2 and down 4 to *Q*. Move right 4 to *R*. Move right 2 and up 4 to *S*. Move left 2 and up 4 to *T*. Move left 4 to *V*. Move left 2 and down 4 to *P*.

6. Start at *L*. Move right 3 to *M*. Move up 4 to *N*. Move left 3 and down 4 to *L*.

Use after Lesson 9.2, page 426

Write the name of the angle. State whether it is acute, right, or obtuse. Then use a protractor to measure the angle.

1. **2.** **3.**

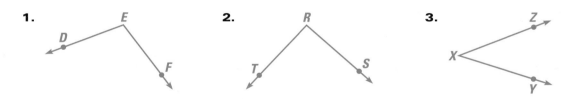

Use after Lesson 9.3, page 432

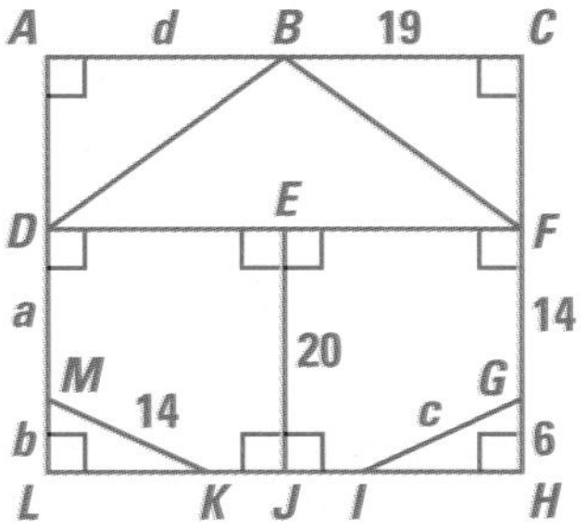

Use the figure at the right. All right triangles in the figure have angles of 30° and 60°.

1. Find the missing lengths *a*, *b*, *c*, and *d*.

2. Name a polygon congruent to polygon *EFGIJ*.

3. Name two congruent quadrilaterals.

4. Name two pairs of congruent triangles.

5. Name two similar, but not congruent, polygons.

Use after Lesson 9.4, page 438

Decide whether the figure has line symmetry. If it does, copy the figure and draw the line or lines of symmetry.

1. **2.** **3.** **4.**

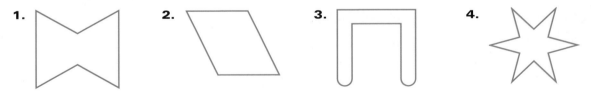

Use after Lesson 9.5, page 446

Plot the given points in a coordinate plane. Connect the points to form a polygon. Then slide the polygon 3 units right and 2 units up. Write the coordinates of the new polygon.

1. (0, 0), (1, 4), (6, 3), (2, 0)   **2.** (0, 1), (0, 4), (2, 6), (4, 4), (4, 1)

3. (1, 5), (3, 6), (3, 2), (1, 1)   **4.** (2, 1), (5, 0), (8, 1), (6, 5), (4, 5)

Plot both sets of points in a coordinate plane. Connect the points to form triangles. Then describe the slide from Triangle 1 to Triangle 2.

5. Triangle 1: (1, 4), (3, 8), (5, 4)   **6.** Triangle 1: (5, 3), (5, 6), (10, 6)
    Triangle 2: (7, 2), (11, 2), (9, 6)   Triangle 2: (0, 0), (0, 3), (5, 3)

7. Triangle 1: (2, 3), (3, 6), (6, 3)   **8.** Triangle 1: (6, 1), (5, 3), (7, 4)
    Triangle 2: (0, 3), (1, 6), (4, 3)   Triangle 2: (3, 6), (2, 3), (1, 5)

Use after Lesson 9.6, page 450

Use as many words as possible to describe the triangle: *equilateral, isosceles, scalene, obtuse, right,* or *acute*.

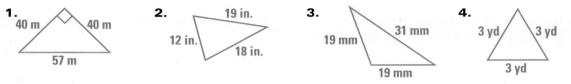

1. 40 m, 40 m, 57 m   **2.** 19 in., 12 in., 18 in.   **3.** 31 mm, 19 mm, 19 mm   **4.** 3 yd, 3 yd, 3 yd

Use after Lesson 9.7, page 458

Decide whether a triangle could have the given angle measures.

1. 45°, 66°, 69°   **2.** 52°, 43°, 87°   **3.** 37°, 15°, 128°

4. 108°, 10°, 12°   **5.** 112°, 57°, 10°   **6.** 8°, 168°, 4°

Find the value of x.

7.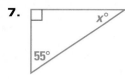

8.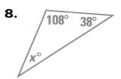

9.

Use after Lesson 10.1, page 476

Use the figure at the right. Do the lines appear *parallel* or *intersecting*? Are the lines perpendicular?

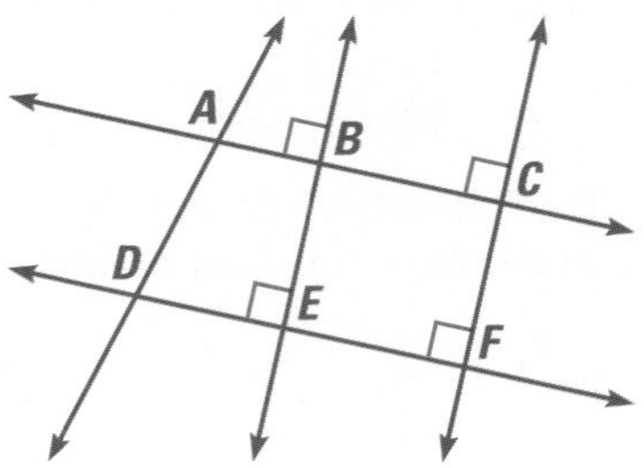

1. $\overleftrightarrow{AB}$ and $\overleftrightarrow{BE}$ **2.** $\overleftrightarrow{CF}$ and $\overleftrightarrow{DE}$

3. $\overleftrightarrow{AD}$ and $\overleftrightarrow{BC}$ **4.** $\overleftrightarrow{AB}$ and $\overleftrightarrow{CF}$

5. $\overleftrightarrow{CF}$ and $\overleftrightarrow{AD}$ **6.** $\overleftrightarrow{AC}$ and $\overleftrightarrow{DF}$

7. $\overleftrightarrow{BE}$ and $\overleftrightarrow{AD}$ **8.** $\overleftrightarrow{EF}$ and $\overleftrightarrow{AD}$

Use after Lesson 10.2, page 480

Find the measure of the angle that is supplementary to the given angle. Then use a protractor to draw both angles.

1. 75°   **2.** 160°   **3.** 135°   **4.** 90°

Use the diagram at the right. Use as many words as possible to describe the pair of angles: *congruent, complementary, supplementary.*

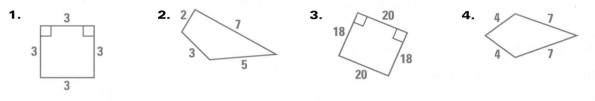

5. $\angle CFD$ and $\angle DFE$ **6.** $\angle CBF$ and $\angle FBE$

7. $\angle ABC$ and $\angle ABG$ **8.** $\angle BFE$ and $\angle CFD$

Use after Lesson 10.3, page 486

Name the figure in as many ways as you can using the words *polygon, quadrilateral, parallelogram, rectangle,* **and** *square.*

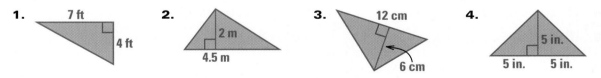

1. 3, 3, 3, 3   **2.** 2, 7, 3, 5   **3.** 20, 18, 18, 20   **4.** 4, 7, 4, 7

Use after Lesson 10.4, page 492

Find the area of the triangle.

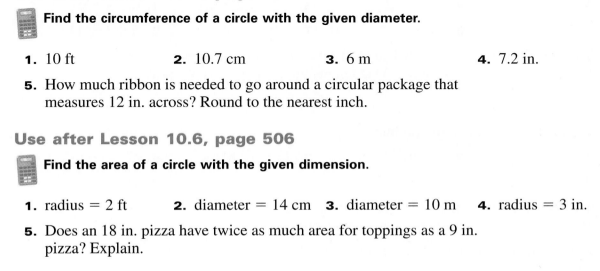

1. 7 ft, 4 ft   **2.** 2 m, 4.5 m   **3.** 12 cm, 6 cm   **4.** 5 in., 5 in., 5 in.

Use after Lesson 10.5, page 500

Find the circumference of a circle with the given diameter.

1. 10 ft   **2.** 10.7 cm   **3.** 6 m   **4.** 7.2 in.

5. How much ribbon is needed to go around a circular package that measures 12 in. across? Round to the nearest inch.

Use after Lesson 10.6, page 506

Find the area of a circle with the given dimension.

1. radius = 2 ft   **2.** diameter = 14 cm   **3.** diameter = 10 m   **4.** radius = 3 in.

5. Does an 18 in. pizza have twice as much area for toppings as a 9 in. pizza? Explain.

Use after Lesson 10.7, page 512

1. The composition of Earth is given in the table at the right. Organize the data with a circle graph.

2. At a birthday party, 50 guests were asked if they wanted cake, ice cream, both, or neither. The results were: cake, 12; ice cream, 5; both, 30; neither, 3. Organize the data with a circle graph. Label each part with a percent.

Composition of Earth	
Oxygen	46.6%
Silicon	27.7%
Aluminum	8.1%
Iron	5.0%
Calcium	3.6%
Other	9.0%

Use after Lesson 10.8, page 516

Find the surface area and volume of the rectangular prism.

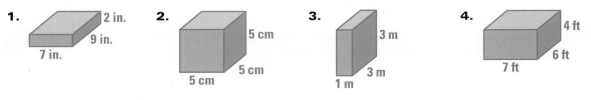

1. 2 in. 9 in. 7 in.

2. 5 cm 5 cm 5 cm

3. 3 m 3 m 1 m

4. 4 ft 6 ft 7 ft

Use after Lesson 11.1, page 532

Complete the statement with > or < .

1. $6 \, ? \, -4$ 2. $-12 \, ? \, 5$ 3. $0 \, ? \, -9$ 4. $-8 \, ? \, -2$ 5. $-7 \, ? \, -11$

Graph the integers on a number line. Describe the pattern. Then list the next two integers in the pattern.

6. $15, 10, 5, 0, -5, \, ? \, , \, ? \, , \ldots$

7. $-2, 2, 6, 10, 14, \, ? \, , \, ? \, , \ldots$

8. $10, 7, 4, 1, -2, \, ? \, , \, ? \, , \ldots$

9. $-8, -6, -4, -2, 0, \, ? \, , \, ? \, , \ldots$

Use after Lesson 11.2, page 538

Use a number line to solve the problem.

1. $4 + (-9)$ 2. $-5 + 12$ 3. $-11 + (-3)$ 4. $0 + (-5)$

5. $-2 + 2$ 6. $17 + (-2)$ 7. $-9 + (-8)$ 8. $5 + (-11)$

9. The thermometer showed $-8°F$ at 8:00 A.M. The temperature is expected to rise 15°F by noon. What temperature is expected at noon?

Use after Lesson 11.3, page 546

Use a number line to solve the problem.

1. $3 - 7$ 2. $5 - 12$ 3. $13 - (-8)$ 4. $-7 - (-14)$

5. $0 - 10$ 6. $-7 - (-5)$ 7. $-9 - 9$ 8. $16 - 22$

9. The temperature at 5:00 P.M. was 6°F. It is expected to drop 20°F overnight. What is the expected low temperature overnight?

10. During the day, the temperature rose from $-2°F$ to 7°F. How much did it rise?

Use after Lesson 11.4, page 554

1. Plot the following points in a coordinate plane:
$A(-3, 4)$, $B(2, 6)$, $C(0, -5)$, $D(-5, -2)$, $E(3, -1)$, $F(6, 0)$, $G(-2, 2)$

Plot both sets of points in a coordinate plane. Connect the points to form triangles. Then describe the slide or the flip from Triangle 1 to Triangle 2.

2. Triangle 1: $(-6, -1)$, $(-6, -4)$, $(-1, -4)$
Triangle 2: $(0, 1)$, $(0, -2)$, $(5, -2)$

3. Triangle 1: $(1, 1)$, $(3, 2)$, $(4, -3)$
Triangle 2: $(-1, 1)$, $(-3, 2)$, $(-4, -3)$

Use after Lesson 11.5, page 558

Evaluate the given expression for the integers -3 through 3. Record your results in a table. Graph the ordered pairs. Describe any patterns you see.

1. $y = x + 5$ **2.** $y = 4 - x$ **3.** $y = 0 - x$ **4.** $y = 3 + x$

5. $y = x - 2$ **6.** $y = x - 1$ **7.** $y = 6 + x$ **8.** $y = x - 4$

Use after Lesson 11.6, page 564

Plot the ordered pairs and connect them. Name the polygon. Find the area.

1. $(5, 7)$, $(6, 3)$, $(2, 3)$ **2.** $(-5, -3)$, $(-2, -3)$, $(-2, -7)$, $(-5, -7)$

Find the area of the figure.

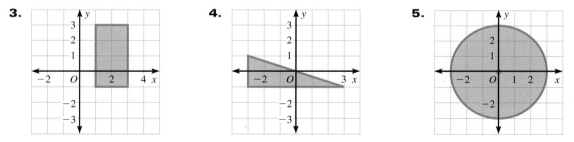

3.   **4.**   **5.**

6. Find the midpoint of each side of the rectangle in Exercise 3 above.

Use after Lesson 12.1, page 580

Solve the equation. Then check your solution.

1. $3 = 7 + n$ **2.** $y + 4 = -9$ **3.** $-4 = x + 3$ **4.** $-12 + p = 5$

Write the equation represented by the sentence. Then solve the equation.

5. The sum of a number and 7 is 5.   **6.** The sum of a number and 1 is -10.

Use after Lesson 12.2, page 584

Solve the equation. Then check your solution.

1. $z - 13 = -19$ **2.** $10 = c - 4$ **3.** $d - 9 = 11$ **4.** $p - 1 = -5$

5. $t - 7 = -12$ **6.** $-8 = b - 17$ **7.** $16 = n - 5$ **8.** $z - 4 = -9$

Use with Lesson 12.3, page 590

Solve the equation. Then check your solution.

1. $\frac{3}{10} + n = \frac{7}{10}$ **2.** $s + 0.92 = 2.48$ **3.** $a + \frac{1}{4} = \frac{7}{8}$ **4.** $y - 1.22 = 8.17$

5. $\frac{5}{6} + w = 2\frac{1}{3}$ **6.** $5.67 + v = 7.74$ **7.** $x - 4.85 = 6.25$ **8.** $d - \frac{5}{12} = \frac{11}{12}$

9. After depositing your paycheck of $157.50, you have $303.13 in your account. How much was in the account before the deposit?

Use with Lesson 12.4, page 596

Find the output values of the function for values $x = 0, 1, 2,$ and 3. Use a table to organize your results.

1. $y = x - 1$ **2.** $y = x + 7$ **3.** $y = 4 - x$ **4.** $y = 14 + x$

5. $y = x + 33$ **6.** $y = x - 3$ **7.** $y = x - 1$ **8.** $y = -5$

Use the graph to make a table of inputs and outputs. Then write a function to represent the data.

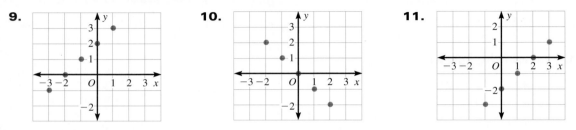

9.   **10.**   **11.**

Use with Lesson 12.5, page 602

Make a tree diagram or use the counting principle to solve.

1. When buying sneakers, you can choose low-tops or high-tops, black or white, with black, white, red or blue laces. How many different sneakers can you buy?

2. Your school is selling shirts with your school name on the front. You can choose a T-shirt or a sweatshirt, blue or gold, size small, medium, or large. How many different types of shirts are there?

3. For an English literature class you need to read one book from each of 3 lists. The lists include 10 classics, 8 adventures, and 6 poetry collections. In how many ways can you complete your assignment?

Use with Lesson 12.6, page 608

In Exercises 1 and 2, are the events independent? Explain your reasoning

1. You like cake.
You have green socks.

2. You ran 10 miles.
You are out of breath.

3. You roll two number cubes. What is the probability that both number cubes show an even number?

TOOLBOX

Adding and Subtracting Whole Numbers and Decimals

When you add or subtract whole numbers or decimals, remember to line up the decimal places.

Example 1   **Add 0.59 and 0.3.**

Solution   Rewrite 0.3 as 0.30, and line up the decimal places.

$$
\begin{array}{r}
0.59 \\
+\ 0.30 \\
\hline
0.89
\end{array}
$$
   The sum is 0.89.

Example 2   **Subtract 8 from 47.**

Solution   Line up the digits in the **ones** place. Then think:
$47 = 40 + 7 = 30 + 17$.

$$
\begin{array}{r}
{}^{3}\cancel{4}{}^{1}7 \\
-\ \ 8 \\
\hline
39
\end{array}
$$
   $17 - 8 = 9$

The difference is 39.

PRACTICE AND PROBLEM SOLVING

Find each sum or difference.

1. $\begin{array}{r} 23 \\ +\ 59 \\ \hline \end{array}$ 2. $\begin{array}{r} 2.3 \\ +\ 5.7 \\ \hline \end{array}$ 3. $\begin{array}{r} 0.66 \\ -\ 0.37 \\ \hline \end{array}$

4. $\begin{array}{r} 81 \\ -\ 43 \\ \hline \end{array}$ 5. $\begin{array}{r} 0.04 \\ +\ 0.88 \\ \hline \end{array}$ 6. $\begin{array}{r} 34 \\ -\ 17 \\ \hline \end{array}$

7. $0.55 + 0.36$ 8. $4.9 + 2.6$ 9. $5.0 - 1.3$

10. $4.2 - 0.8$ 11. $27 + 9$ 12. $0.31 - 0.06$

13. A button with a diameter of 0.79 cm fits into a buttonhole with a length of 0.9 cm. How much longer is the buttonhole than the diameter of the button?

14. Two of the buttons in Exercise 13 are next to each other. What is the total distance across the two buttons?

15. Anna had $10.00 and spent $3.25 on a magazine. How much money did she have left?

Multiplying and Dividing with Whole Numbers

When you multiply or divide, remember to focus on one digit at a time.

Example 1 Find 57 × 64.

Solution

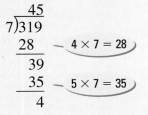

$$\begin{array}{r} 57 \\ \times\ 64 \\ \hline 228 \\ 342 \\ \hline 3648 \end{array}$$

$4 \times 5 + 2 = 22$ — 228 — $4 \times 7 = 28$

$6 \times 5 + 4 = 34$ — $6 \times 7 = 42$

The product is 3648.

Example 2 Find 319 ÷ 7.

Solution

$$\begin{array}{r} 45 \\ 7\overline{)319} \\ 28 \\ \hline 39 \\ 35 \\ \hline 4 \end{array}$$

$4 \times 7 = 28$

$5 \times 7 = 35$

The quotient is 45 R4.

PRACTICE AND PROBLEM SOLVING

In Exercises 1–16, find the product or quotient.

1. $\begin{array}{r} 42 \\ \times\ 17 \end{array}$

2. $\begin{array}{r} 557 \\ \times\ 16 \end{array}$

3. $\begin{array}{r} 39 \\ \times\ 51 \end{array}$

4. 823 ÷ 8

5. $4\overline{)205}$

6. 32 × 85

7. $7\overline{)139}$

8. $7\overline{)140}$

9. $6\overline{)515}$

10. 40 × 90

11. $3\overline{)975}$

12. 56 × 44

13. the product of thirty-five and twenty-seven

14. three hundred seventy-five divided by eight

15. the product of fifty-two and itself

16. three divided into two hundred seventy-one

17. A block of cheese is 235 mm long. How many complete 17 mm slices can you serve? As a remainder, do you have more or less than half a slice?

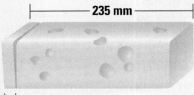

235 mm

17 mm

Multiplying and Dividing with Decimals

When you multiply or divide with decimals, it is important to place the decimal point in the correct place. You can use the numbers in the problem to find out where to place the decimal point.

Example 1   **Find the product 25.1 × 0.13.**

Solution   Perform the multiplication. Then count the number of decimal places in each factor.

$$
\begin{array}{r}
25.1 \\
\times\ 0.13 \\
\hline
753 \\
2\,51\ \ \\
\hline
3.263
\end{array}
$$

     1 decimal place
     2 decimal places
     3 decimal places

The sum of the number of decimal places is 3, so the product is 3.263.

Example 2   **Find the quotient 33.6 ÷ 7.**

Solution   You are dividing by a whole number, so the decimal point in the quotient is directly above the decimal point in the dividend.

$$7\overline{)33.6}$$

Divide as for whole numbers.

$$
\begin{array}{r}
4.8 \\
7\overline{)33.6} \\
\underline{28\ \ }\ \\
56 \\
\underline{56} \\
0
\end{array}
$$

PRACTICE AND PROBLEM SOLVING

Find each product or quotient.

1. $\begin{array}{r} 23.2 \\ \times\ 2.8 \\ \hline \end{array}$

2. 1.57×3.1

3. $\begin{array}{r} 14.4 \\ \times\ 57 \\ \hline \end{array}$

4. $3\overline{)68.1}$

5. $8\overline{)10.8}$

6. $172.8 \div 6$

7. $3\overline{)0.0153}$

8. $36.18 \div 9$

9. 2.002×3.5

10. 5.83×0.6

11. $2\overline{)32.64}$

12. $3\overline{)2.196}$

13. The length of a rectangle is 3.6 cm and its width is 2.4 cm. Area = length × width, so what is the area of the rectangle?

2.4 cm

3.6 cm

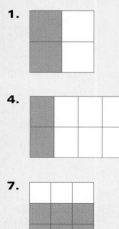

Equivalent Fractions

Equivalent fractions are different fractions that stand for the same number.

Example 1   Show that $\frac{2}{3}$ and $\frac{8}{12}$ are equivalent fractions.

Solution   Start with a sheet of paper. Fold the width into thirds. Then shade two of the parts to represent $\frac{2}{3}$.

Next, fold the length into fourths. The paper is folded into twelfths, so the shaded part represents $\frac{8}{12}$.

Since the same amount is shaded, the fractions $\frac{2}{3}$ and $\frac{8}{12}$ are equivalent.

PRACTICE AND PROBLEM SOLVING

Write two equivalent fractions to represent each diagram.

1.   **2.**   **3.**

4.   **5.**   **6.**

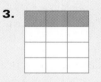
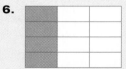

7.   **8.**   **9.**

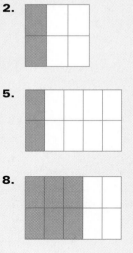
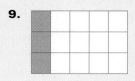

In Exercises 10–21, find the missing number.

10. $\dfrac{?}{10} = \dfrac{1}{2}$ **11.** $\dfrac{6}{?} = \dfrac{1}{2}$ **12.** $\dfrac{10}{?} = \dfrac{1}{2}$

13. $\dfrac{1}{3} = \dfrac{?}{9}$ **14.** $\dfrac{?}{30} = \dfrac{1}{3}$ **15.** $\dfrac{1}{3} = \dfrac{5}{?}$

16. $\dfrac{1}{5} = \dfrac{?}{10}$ **17.** $\dfrac{?}{25} = \dfrac{1}{5}$ **18.** $\dfrac{1}{5} = \dfrac{4}{?}$

19. $\dfrac{6}{?} = \dfrac{1}{6}$ **20.** $\dfrac{1}{6} = \dfrac{?}{24}$ **21.** $\dfrac{1}{6} = \dfrac{5}{?}$

Rewriting Fractions Greater than One

A number such as $3\frac{5}{6}$ that can be written as the sum of a whole number and a fraction is a *mixed number*. A fraction such as $\frac{23}{6}$ that is greater than or equal to one is an *improper fraction*.

Example 1 Write $\frac{23}{6}$ as a mixed number.

Solution $\frac{23}{6}$ means divide 23 by 6.

$$6\overline{)23} \quad \frac{3}{} \quad \frac{18}{5}$$

$$\frac{23}{6} = 3 \text{ R5, or } 3\frac{5}{6}$$

Example 2 Write $3\frac{5}{6}$ as a improper fraction.

Solution *Method* **1** $3 = \frac{3 \times 6}{1 \times 6} = \frac{18}{6}$

So, $3\frac{5}{6} = \frac{18}{6} + \frac{5}{6} = \frac{18 + 5}{6} = \frac{23}{6}$.

Method **2** $3\frac{5}{6} = \frac{(3 \times 6) + 5}{6} = \frac{23}{6}$

PRACTICE AND PROBLEM SOLVING

Write each fraction as a mixed number. Simplify if possible.

1. $\frac{10}{3}$ **2.** $\frac{11}{7}$ **3.** $\frac{15}{2}$ **4.** $\frac{29}{5}$

5. $\frac{110}{100}$ **6.** $\frac{12}{8}$ **7.** $\frac{29}{4}$ **8.** $\frac{21}{9}$

9. $\frac{35}{20}$ **10.** $\frac{64}{24}$ **11.** $\frac{14}{6}$ **12.** $\frac{58}{15}$

Write each mixed number as an improper fraction.

13. $7\frac{1}{2}$ **14.** $4\frac{7}{8}$ **15.** $1\frac{7}{50}$ **16.** $10\frac{2}{7}$

17. $8\frac{3}{10}$ **18.** $5\frac{18}{25}$ **19.** $15\frac{1}{3}$ **20.** $17\frac{5}{6}$

21. You have $3\frac{3}{4}$ bags of pretzels and want to give $\frac{1}{4}$ bag to each of 20 people on a field trip. Do you have enough pretzels? Explain.

22. A company uses $\frac{1}{4}$ yd of cloth to make a bean bag. How many bean bags can be made from a bolt of cloth that is $12\frac{3}{4}$ yd long?

Adding and Subtracting Fractions

When you add or subtract fractions that have a common denominator, you use that denominator and add or subtract the numerators.

When you add or subtract fractions with different denominators, first, rewrite the problem using equivalent fractions that have the same denominator.

Example 1 Find $\frac{1}{5} + \frac{3}{5}$.

Solution The fractions have a common denominator. You can add the numerators.

$$\frac{1}{5} + \frac{3}{5} = \frac{1+3}{5} = \frac{4}{5}$$

Example 2 Find $\frac{5}{8} - \frac{1}{4}$.

Solution The least common denominator for $\frac{5}{8}$ and $\frac{1}{4}$ is 8. First, find an equivalent fraction for $\frac{1}{4}$.

$$\frac{1}{4} = \frac{1 \times 2}{4 \times 2} = \frac{2}{8}$$

Then substitute and subtract.

$$\frac{5}{8} - \frac{1}{4} = \frac{5}{8} - \frac{2}{8} \qquad \text{Substitute } \tfrac{2}{8} \text{ for } \tfrac{1}{4}.$$

$$= \frac{5-2}{8} \qquad \text{Subtract numerators.}$$

$$= \frac{3}{8} \qquad \text{Simplify.}$$

PRACTICE AND PROBLEM SOLVING

Find each sum or difference. Write each answer in simplest form.

1. $\frac{1}{6} + \frac{3}{6}$ 2. $\frac{5}{8} - \frac{1}{8}$ 3. $\frac{2}{7} + \frac{4}{7}$

4. $\frac{7}{10} - \frac{2}{5}$ 5. $\frac{4}{9} - \frac{1}{3}$ 6. $\frac{1}{2} + \frac{1}{6}$

7. $\frac{3}{4} - \frac{5}{16}$ 8. $\frac{15}{16} - \frac{3}{8}$ 9. $\frac{1}{4} + \frac{3}{8}$

10. What is the width of a metal washer if the radius of the hole is $\frac{2}{5}$ cm and the radius from the center to the outside edge of the washer is $\frac{9}{10}$ cm?

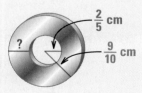

11. On the first day of a car trip, a family drove $\frac{1}{5}$ of the way. On the next day they drove $\frac{4}{15}$ of the way. How much of the way have they gone? How much of the way is left?

Multiplying and Dividing Fractions

To multiply two fractions, you multiply the numerators and multiply the denominators. To divide by a fraction, you can multiply by the reciprocal of the divisor.

Example 1 Find $\frac{3}{5} \times \frac{7}{12}$.

Solution Multiply the numerators and multiply the denominators. Simplify the product if possible.

$$\frac{3}{5} \times \frac{7}{12} = \frac{3 \times 7}{5 \times 12}$$

$$= \frac{21}{60}, \text{ or } \frac{7}{20}$$

Example 2 Find $6 \div \frac{2}{3}$.

Solution Multiply by the reciprocal. The reciprocal of $\frac{2}{3}$ is $\frac{3}{2}$.

$$6 \div \frac{2}{3} = 6 \times \frac{3}{2} \qquad \text{Multiply by the reciprocal.}$$

$$= \frac{6}{1} \times \frac{3}{2} \qquad \text{Write 6 as } \frac{6}{1}.$$

$$= \frac{18}{2}, \text{ or } 9 \qquad \text{Simplify.}$$

PRACTICE AND PROBLEM SOLVING

Find each product or quotient. Simplify the result if possible.

1. $\frac{2}{7} \times \frac{4}{9}$ 2. $3 \div \frac{1}{6}$ 3. $7 \div \frac{1}{3}$

4. $11 \div \frac{1}{5}$ 5. $\frac{1}{3} \times \frac{5}{8}$ 6. $\frac{6}{7} \times \frac{1}{3}$

7. $2 \div \frac{2}{5}$ 8. $\frac{3}{10} \times \frac{5}{6}$ 9. $1 \div \frac{1}{2}$

10. The width of a rectangle is $\frac{2}{3}$ ft and the length is $\frac{3}{4}$ ft. What is the area in square feet?

Area = length × width

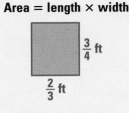

$\frac{3}{4}$ ft

$\frac{2}{3}$ ft

11. The area of a rectangle is 4 cm^2 and the width is $\frac{4}{5}$ cm. Divide 4 by $\frac{4}{5}$ to find the length of the rectangle.

Area ÷ length = width

$\frac{4}{5}$ cm

?

12. What is the product of the fraction $\frac{3}{7}$ and its reciprocal?

Estimating and Addition

You can get an estimate for a sum by looking at the numbers from left to right.

Example 1   **Estimate the sum: 675 + 310 + 477.**

Solution   Round each number to the
hundreds' place, and add.

$$\begin{array}{r} 700 \\ 300 \\ + 500 \\ \hline 1500 \end{array}$$

The sum of 675 + 310 + 477 is *about* 1500.

Example 2   **Find a closer estimate of the sum in Example 1.**

Solution   Add the digits in the **greatest** place. Then round the **remaining parts** of the numbers and add their sum to your first result.

$$\begin{array}{r} 675 \\ 310 \\ + 477 \\ \hline 1300 \end{array} \qquad \begin{array}{r} 80 \\ 10 \\ + 80 \\ \hline 170 \end{array}$$

A closer estimate is **1300 + 170** = 1470. So the sum of 675 + 310 + 477 is *about* 1470.

PRACTICE AND PROBLEM SOLVING

1. What is the difference between the estimate in Example 1 and the exact sum?

2. What is the difference between the estimate in Example 2 and the exact sum?

In Exercises 3–5, estimate each sum using only the digits in the greatest place.

3. $\begin{array}{r} 5733 \\ 2726 \\ + 4102 \end{array}$
   4. $\begin{array}{r} 348 \\ 477 \\ + 312 \end{array}$
   5. $\begin{array}{r} 2995 \\ 6161 \\ + 5510 \end{array}$

In Exercises 6–12, estimate the sum using the method shown in Example 2.

6. $\begin{array}{r} 4889 \\ 9005 \\ + 2127 \end{array}$
   7. $\begin{array}{r} 539 \\ 226 \\ + 912 \end{array}$
   8. $\begin{array}{r} 2004 \\ 8990 \\ + 7413 \end{array}$

9. 517 + 741 + 382 + 190

10. 43,507 + 65,880 + 34,231

11. 4456 + 7201 + 2102 + 3781

12. 976 + 463 + 187

Estimating and Subtraction

You can get an estimate of a difference by looking at the digits in the problem from left to right.

Example 1   **Estimate the difference.**

$$
\begin{array}{r}
37{,}143 \\
-\ 12{,}657 \\
\end{array}
$$

Solution   Subtract the digits in the **greatest** place:

$$
\begin{array}{r}
37{,}143 \\
-\ 12{,}657 \\
\hline
20{,}000 \\
\end{array}
$$

Then round the **remaining parts** of the numbers and subtract.

$$
\begin{array}{r}
7000 \\
-\ 3000 \\
\hline
4000 \\
\end{array}
$$

Add this difference to your first result.
The estimate is **20,000 + 4000** = 24,000.
So, 37,143 − 12,657 is *about* 24,000.

PRACTICE AND PROBLEM SOLVING

1. What is the actual difference in the Example, and how close is the estimate?

Estimate each difference using the method shown in Example 1.

2. $\begin{array}{r} 8521 \\ -\ 2375 \end{array}$ 3. $\begin{array}{r} 57{,}852 \\ -\ 26{,}749 \end{array}$ 4. $\begin{array}{r} 992 \\ -\ 452 \end{array}$

5. $\begin{array}{r} 77{,}806 \\ -\ 22{,}051 \end{array}$ 6. $\begin{array}{r} 651{,}308 \\ -\ 270{,}509 \end{array}$ 7. $\begin{array}{r} 8701 \\ -\ 4695 \end{array}$

8. $\begin{array}{r} 2723 \\ -\ 2485 \end{array}$ 9. $\begin{array}{r} 76{,}832 \\ -\ 39{,}595 \end{array}$ 10. $\begin{array}{r} 43{,}027 \\ -\ 17{,}985 \end{array}$

11. $\begin{array}{r} 4766 \\ -\ 2581 \end{array}$ 12. $\begin{array}{r} 9234 \\ -\ 4087 \end{array}$ 13. $\begin{array}{r} 57{,}276 \\ -\ 13{,}904 \end{array}$

14. A few years ago, when a family purchased a used car, the reading on the odometer was 55,707 miles. Now the odometer reading is 88,851. Use the method shown in Example 1 to estimate the number of miles the family has driven the car.

Estimating and Multiplication

You can estimate a product by finding a *low estimate* and a *high estimate*.

Example 1   **Find a low and high estimate for the product.**

$$7 \times \$12.37$$

Solution   For the low estimate, round the dollar amount *down*.

$$7 \times \$12.00 = \$84.00$$

For the high estimate, round the dollar amount *up*.

$$7 \times \$13.00 = \$91.00$$

The product of 7 and $12.37 is between $84 and $91.

Example 2   **Find a low and high estimate for the product.**

$$27 \times 44$$

Solution   For the low estimate, round both factors *down*.

$$20 \times 40 = 800$$

For the high estimate, round both factors *up*.

$$30 \times 50 = 1500$$

The product of 27 and 44 is between 800 and 1500.

PRACTICE AND PROBLEM SOLVING

Find a low and high estimate for each product.

1.   39
   $\times\ 21$

2.   82
   $\times\ 45$

3.   12
   $\times\ 79$

4. 563
   $\times\ 7$

5.   807
   $\times\ 15$

6.   395
   $\times\ 48$

7. $23.47
   $\times\ \ \ 6$

8. $785.23
   $\times\ \ \ \ \ 6$

9. $279
   $\times\ \ 6$

10. $230.48
   $\times\ \ \ \ \ 9$

11. $32.82
   $\times\ \ \ \ 18$

12. $117.50
   $\times\ \ \ \ \ 49$

13. The dimensions of a rectangle are 58 in. by 31 in. Find a low estimate and a high estimate for the area of the rectangle.

Area = length × width

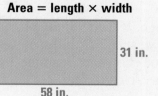

31 in.

58 in.

Estimating and Division

To find high and low estimates for division problems you can use numbers that divide with no remainder.

Example 1 | **Find low and high estimates for 2350 ÷ 7.**

Solution | Replace 2350 with numbers that are divisible by 7.

For the low estimate:

$$\frac{300}{7)2100}$$

For the high estimate:

$$\frac{400}{7)2800}$$

The quotient is between 300 and 400.

Example 2 | **Find low and high estimates for $3.75 ÷ 8.**

Solution | Replace $3.75 with numbers that are divisible by 8.

For the low estimate:

$$\frac{0.40}{8)3.20}$$

For the high estimate:

$$\frac{0.50}{8)4.00}$$

The quotient is between $.40 and $.50.

PRACTICE AND PROBLEM SOLVING

Find a low and a high estimate for each division.

1. $4)\overline{180}$

2. $6)\overline{537}$

3. $3)\overline{235}$

4. $5.95 ÷ 6

5. $8.15 ÷ 8

6. $12.35 ÷ 7

7. 2795 ÷ 5

8. $4.05 ÷ 9

9. 3512 ÷ 4

10. 4817 ÷ 7

11. $23.97 ÷ 6

12. 8739 ÷ 9

13. The area of a rectangle is 435 cm^2 and the width is 8 cm. Find a low and a high estimate for the length of the rectangle.

Area ÷ length = width

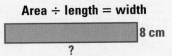

? | 8 cm

14. **RESTAURANTS** You go to a restaurant with seven friends. The bill for the meal comes to $51.50. Find a low and high estimate for each person's share of the bill.

TOOLBOX

Perimeter

The distance around a figure is called its *perimeter*.

Example 1

Find the perimeter.

a.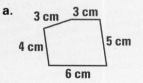

b.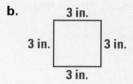

Solution

a. $6 + 4 + 3 + 3 + 5 = 21$

The perimeter is 21 cm.

b. There are 4 sides.
$4 \times 3 = 12$
The perimeter is 12 in.

PRACTICE AND PROBLEM SOLVING

Find the perimeter of each figure.

5. a square with sides that are 5 cm

6. a rectangle with two sides that are 5 in. and two sides that are 4 in.

7. a hexagon with all 6 sides of 2.0 cm

8. an octagon with all 8 sides of $\frac{1}{2}$ ft

9. a figure whose sides are 2 m, 3 m, 6 m, 4 m, and 3 m long

10. Which rectangle has the greater perimeter? Explain.

TOOLBOX

Area

The *area* of a figure is the number of square units needed to cover it. Area is measured in square units such as in.^{2}, yd^2, cm^2, and m^2.

Example 1   **Find the area of the rectangle at the right.**

Solution   One way to find the area is to cover the rectangle with 1 cm-by-1 cm square tiles. You would need 18 tiles, so the area is 18 cm^2. Another way is to use the formula for the area of a rectangle.

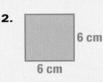

Area of a rectangle = length × width

             = 6 cm × 3 cm

             = 18 cm^2

PRACTICE AND PROBLEM SOLVING

In Exercises 1–8, find the area of each rectangle.

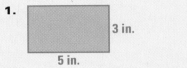
1. 3 in. 5 in.

2. 6 cm 6 cm

3. 2 ft $2\frac{1}{2}$ ft

4. a rectangle with length = 65 cm and width = 3 cm

5. a rectangle with length = 0.8 m and width = 0.2 m

6. a square with side = 12 ft

7. a rectangle with length = 14 in. and width = half of length

8. Find the area of the figure at the right.

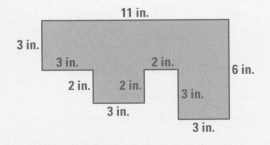

11 in.

3 in.

3 in.   2 in.

2 in.   2 in.   6 in.

3 in.

3 in.

3 in.

In Exercises 9–11, find the area of the rectangle. Then find the area of each triangle. (*Hint:* All of the triangles in each rectangle have the same area.)

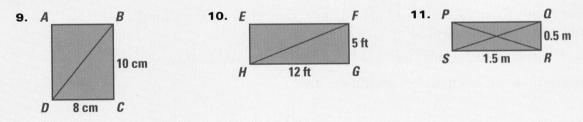

9.   A   B   10 cm   D   8 cm   C

10.   E   F   5 ft   H   12 ft   G

11.   P   Q   0.5 m   S   1.5 m   R

Equivalent Measures

When you measure an object, you can use many different units. Here are some equivalent expressions for length, weight, and capacity.

Length	Weight	Capacity
1 ft = 12 in.	1 lb = 16 oz	1 qt = 4 c
1 yd = 3 ft	1 T = 2000 lb	1 gal = 4 qt
1 yd = 36 in.		

Example 1 Use the chart above to find each missing number.

a. 10 ft = $\underline{?}$ in.   **b.** 2 T = $\underline{?}$ lb   **c.** 5 gal = $\underline{?}$ qt

Solution

a. 1 ft = 12 in., so 10 × (1 ft) = 10 × (12 in.).

$$10 \text{ ft} = 120 \text{ in.}$$

b. 1 T = 2000 lb, so 2 × (1 T) = 2 × (2000 lb).

$$2 \text{ T} = 4000 \text{ lb}$$

c. 1 gal = 4 qt, so 5 × (1 gal) = 5 × (4 qt).

$$5 \text{ gal} = 20 \text{ qt}$$

PRACTICE AND PROBLEM SOLVING

Find each missing number.

1. 5 yd = $\underline{?}$ ft
2. 5 yd = $\underline{?}$ in.
3. 12 lb = $\underline{?}$ oz

4. 16 T = $\underline{?}$ lb
5. 7 qt = $\underline{?}$ c
6. 17 gal = $\underline{?}$ qt

7. $3\frac{1}{2}$ ft = $\underline{?}$ in.
8. $7\frac{2}{3}$ yd = $\underline{?}$ ft
9. 12.5 T = $\underline{?}$ lb

10. $15\frac{3}{4}$ lb = $\underline{?}$ oz
11. $9\frac{1}{4}$ qt = $\underline{?}$ c
12. 2.75 gal = $\underline{?}$ qt

13. How many inches are there in 3 feet and 7 inches?

14. How many feet are there in 2 yards and 2 feet?

15. How many ounces are there in 6 pounds and 12 ounces?

16. How many quarts are there in 5 gallons and 2 quarts?

17. Jesse is 5 ft 4 in. tall. Maria is 66 in. tall. Who is taller? How many inches taller?

18. For a party, Andrew needed 12 qt of orange juice. How many gallons of orange juice did he need?

19. Suzanne has a recipe that call for $3\frac{1}{2}$ lb of canned tomatoes. How many 28 oz cans of tomatoes should she use?

TOOLBOX

Estimating Lengths

A useful skill in estimating lengths is to figure out how many times a shorter object will fit across a longer object.

Example 1 In this diagram, about how many helmets will fit across the bench?

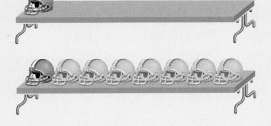

Solution If you make or imagine several copies of the helmet, you can see that about 8 helmets will fit across the bench.

PRACTICE AND PROBLEM SOLVING

Using this paper clip as one unit, estimate the length of each object.

1.

2.

3.

4. the length of your thumb

5. the length of your shoe

6. the height of this page

7. the wire that made the paper clip, after straightening it

Choose whether you would use *inches*, *feet*, or *miles* to estimate each length.

8. the distance to your State Capital Building

9. the length of a computer keyboard

10. the length of a surfboard

11. the length of a pencil

12. the height of a flagpole

13. the distance an athlete can run in 15 minutes

14. the length of your little finger

15. the length of a school bus

TOOLBOX

Ratio

A ratio is a comparison of two quantities that have the same unit of measure. As an example, the ratio of 8 cm to 5 cm can be written as 8 to 5, 8:5, or $\frac{8}{5}$.

Example 1   Find the missing number in $\frac{8}{5} = \frac{?}{55}$.

Solution   Use equivalent fractions.

Looking at the denominators, $5 \times 11 = 55$.

$$\frac{8}{5} = \frac{8 \times 11}{5 \times 11} = \frac{88}{55}$$

The missing number is 88.

Example 2   Find the missing number in $\frac{60}{30} = \frac{4}{?}$.

Solution   Use equivalent fractions.

Looking at the numerators, $60 \div 15 = 4$.

$$\frac{60}{30} = \frac{60 \div 15}{30 \div 15} = \frac{4}{2}$$

The missing number is 2.

PRACTICE AND PROBLEM SOLVING

For each ratio, write two equal ratios.

1. $\frac{2}{3}$

2. $\frac{8}{6}$

3. $4:1$

4. $12:22$

5. 4 to 2

6. 2 to 4

7. $5:5$

8. $\frac{18}{10}$

9. 1 to 3

Write the missing number for each pair of equal ratios.

10. $\frac{18}{3} = \frac{6}{?}$

11. $\frac{330}{?} = \frac{110}{10}$

12. $\frac{15}{?} = \frac{300}{1000}$

13. $\frac{3}{5} = \frac{?}{20}$

14. $\frac{9}{7} = \frac{?}{21}$

15. $\frac{18}{3} = \frac{12}{?}$

16. $\frac{?}{6} = \frac{20}{24}$

17. $\frac{5}{12} = \frac{?}{72}$

18. $\frac{?}{17} = \frac{9}{51}$

In Exercises 19–24, list the two ratios that are equal.

19. $\frac{2}{5}, \frac{6}{11}, \frac{4}{10}$

20. $\frac{9}{6}, \frac{3}{2}, \frac{12}{10}$

21. $\frac{5}{20}, \frac{1}{3}, \frac{4}{12}$

22. $\frac{6}{12}, \frac{12}{24}, \frac{3}{4}$

23. $\frac{10}{12}, \frac{12}{15}, \frac{4}{5}$

24. $\frac{14}{7}, \frac{10}{2}, \frac{16}{8}$

Percent

Percent means "per hundred." It is a ratio that compares a number to 100.

Example 1 **Write 75% as a fraction and as a decimal.**

Solution Start by writing 75% as $\frac{75}{100}$.

The fraction can be simplified.

$$\frac{75}{100} = \frac{75 \div 25}{100 \div 25}$$

$$= \frac{3}{4}$$

Also, $\frac{75}{100}$ is "seventy-five hundredths" and can be written as 0.75.

Example 2 **Find 50% of 60.**

Solution 50% is $\frac{50}{100}$ which is equal to $\frac{1}{2}$.

$\frac{1}{2} \times 60 = 30$ **Multiply to find a percent or fraction of a number.**

PRACTICE AND PROBLEM SOLVING

In Exercises 1–4, draw a ten-by-ten square on grid paper. Color the given percent of the square.

1. 15%   **2.** 6%   **3.** 74%   **4.** 33%

Write each percent as a fraction in simplest terms and as a decimal.

5. 25%   **6.** 80%   **7.** 5%

8. 84%   **9.** 2%   **10.** 35%

Find each percent.

11. 25% of 200   **12.** 50% of 50   **13.** 50% of 100

14. 75% of 20   **15.** 100% of 12   **16.** 0% of 7

17. 1% of 100   **18.** 100% of 30   **19.** 40% of 40

20. 15% of 60   **21.** 80% of 40   **22.** 40% of 80

Write each number as a percent.

23. $\frac{3}{5}$ **24.** 0.45   **25.** $\frac{1}{10}$

26. 0.79   **27.** $\frac{1}{20}$ **28.** 0.09

Average and Range

Example 1   **The table at the right gives prices of 7 pairs of shoes and 6 coats.**

a. Which has the smaller range, the shoes or the coats?

b. Which has the larger average?

Price of Shoes	Price of Coats
38	35
38	42
38	42
41	44
43	46
51	55
59	

Solution   **a.** The range is the difference between the largest and smallest numbers.

Range for shoes = \$59 − \$38 = \$21.

Range for coats = \$55 − \$35 = \$20.

The coat prices have a smaller range.

b. To find the average, find the sum of the prices and divide by the number of prices.

$$\text{Average shoe price} = \frac{38 + 38 + 38 + 41 + 43 + 51 + 59}{7}$$

$$= \frac{308}{7} = \$44$$

$$\text{Average coat price} = \frac{35 + 42 + 42 + 44 + 46 + 55}{6}$$

$$= \frac{264}{6} = \$44$$

The averages are the same.

PRACTICE AND PROBLEM SOLVING

Combine all 13 prices from the data for shoes and coats above.

1. What is the range?

2. To the nearest dollar, what is the average?

Give the range and average of each set of data.

3. 19, 23, 17, 13

4. 52, 21, 135, 76

5. 43, 64, 58, 93, 72

6. 3, 6, 1, 8, 2, 4, 3, 0, 9

7. 178, 234, 209, 167

8. 1025, 1431, 1378

The table gives the lengths in minutes of 14 movies.

Comedies	95	107	92	115	110	95	100
Adventures	93	95	100	125	90	98	127

9. What is the range for the comedies?

10. What is the range for the adventures?

11. What is the average length for the comedies?

12. What is the average length for all 14 movies?

Reading Bar Graphs and Pictographs

Some of the ways to display data are *bar graphs*, *double bar graphs*, and *pictographs*.

Example 1 A school collected data on the numbers of students who have dogs or cats as pets. Do more students in the sixth grade or in the fifth grade have cats?

Dogs and Cats

Solution The bar for the fifth graders is longer than the bar for the sixth graders, so more fifth graders have cats.

PRACTICE AND PROBLEM SOLVING

In Exercises 1–8, use the bar graph in the Example.

1. Which bar for cats is the shortest?

2. Which grade has the smallest number of students with cats?

3. How are Questions 1 and 2 related?

4. Which bar for dogs is the tallest?

5. Which grade has the largest number of students with dogs?

6. How are Questions 4 and 5 related?

7. Which grade has the smallest difference between their two bars?

8. Which grade has the largest difference between their two bars?

A sixth grade class counted the number of students who were wearing blue. They collected the data in the pictograph. Use the pictograph in Exercises 9–11.

Blue Clothing

9. Were more students wearing blue jeans or blue shirts?

10. What piece of clothing was least likely to be blue?

11. There were 21 students wearing blue. How do you know that some students were wearing more than one piece of blue clothing?

Reading Circle and Line Graphs

A line graph helps you see trends over time. A *circle graph* helps you compare parts to the whole.

Example 1 A class of students collected data on all the web sites they visited. Which day had the greatest increase from the previous day? Which category represented the most sites?

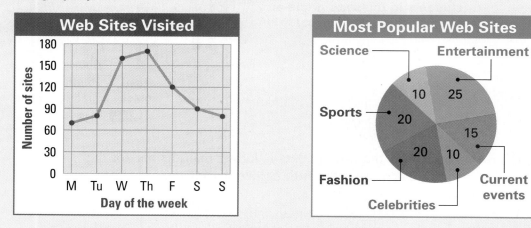

Solution The steepest line in the line graph is from Tuesday to Wednesday. The students recorded 80 sites on Tuesday and 160 sites on Wednesday, for a difference of 80 sites. In the circle graph, the largest category is Entertainment, with 25 of the 100 sites.

PRACTICE AND PROBLEM SOLVING

In Exercises 1–4, use the line graph above.

1. How many sites were visited on Friday?

2. From Thursday to Friday, did the number of sites increase or decrease?

3. For which two days did students visit the same number of sites?

4. From Monday to Tuesday the number of sites increased by 10. What other two consecutive days had the same increase?

In Exercises 5–8, use the circle graph above.

5. The Science sites make up what fraction of the total number of sites visited by the students?

6. The Fashion sites make up what fraction of the total number of sites visited by the students?

7. Which categories can represent $\frac{1}{5}$ of all the sites?

8. List a combination of sites that can represent $\frac{1}{2}$ of all the sites.

U.S. CUSTOMARY MEASURES

■ LENGTH

12 inches (in.) = 1 foot (ft)

3 feet = 1 yard (yd)

36 inches = 1 yard

5280 feet = 1 mile (mi)

1760 yards = 1 mile

■ CAPACITY

1 cup (c) = 8 fluid ounces (fl oz)

2 cups = 1 pint (pt)

2 pints = 1 quart (qt)

2 quarts = 1 half-gallon

4 quarts = 1 gallon (gal)

■ WEIGHT

16 ounces (oz) = 1 pound (lb)

2000 pounds = 1 ton

■ AREA

144 square inches (in.^2) = 1 square foot (ft^2)

9 ft^2 = 1 square yard (yd^2)

640 acres = 1 mi^2

■ VOLUME

1728 cubic inches (in.^3) = 1 cubic foot (ft^3)

27 ft^3 = 1 cubic yard (yd^3)

■ TIME

60 seconds (s) = 1 minute (min)

3600 seconds = 1 hour (h)

60 minutes = 1 hour

24 hours = 1 day

7 days = 1 week

360 days = 1 business year

365 days = 1 year

366 days = 1 leap year

10 years = 1 decade

10 decades = 1 century = 100 years

■ CONVERTING MEASUREMENT WITHIN THE U.S. CUSTOMARY SYSTEM

When you rewrite a measurement in another unit, you can use the relationships between the units.

STUDY TIP

To change $\frac{7}{10}$ of a mile to feet:

$\frac{7}{10}$ of a mile = 0.7 of a mile

= 0.7 × 1 mi

= 0.7 × 5280 ft

= 3696 ft

STUDY TIP

To change $\frac{1}{2}$ of a gallon to quarts:

$\frac{1}{2}$ of a gallon = 0.5 of a gallon

= 0.5 × 1 gal

= 0.5 × 4 qt

= 2 qt

METRIC MEASURES

In the metric system, the units are related by powers of 10.

Table of Units				
PREFIX	**POWER of 10**	**LENGTH**	**CAPACITY**	**MASS**
kilo (k)	1000 units	kilometer	kiloliter*	kilogram
hecto (h)	100 units	hectometer*	hectoliter*	hectogram*
deka (da)	10 units	dekameter*	dekaliter*	dekagram*
	1 unit	meter	liter	gram
deci (d)	0.1 unit	decimeter*	deciliter*	decigram*
centi (c)	0.01 unit	centimeter	centiliter*	centigram*
milli (m)	0.001 unit	millimeter	milliliter	milligram
*These units are seldom used.				

■ LENGTH

10 millimeters (mm) = 1 centimeter (cm)

10 cm = 1 decimeter (dm)

100 cm = 1 meter (m)

1000 m = 1 kilometer (km)

100,000 cm = 1 km

■ AREA

100 square millimeters (mm^2) =
  1 square centimeter (cm^2)

10,000 cm^2 = 1 square meter (m^2)

1,000,000 m^2 = 1 square kilometers (km^2)

■ CAPACITY

1000 milliliter (mL) = 1 liter (L)

10 deciliter (dL) = 1 L

■ MASS

1000 milligrams (mg) = 1 gram (g)

1000 g = 1 kilogram (kg)

■ VOLUME

1,000,000 cubic centimeters (cm^3) =
  1 cubic meter (cm^3)

1 cm^3 = 1 mL

1000 cm^3 = 1 L

■ CONVERTING MEASURES WITHIN THE METRIC SYSTEM

Use the relationships between units, which are shown in the table at the top of this page, to convert measures within the Metric System.

STUDY TIP

When you rewrite a measurement using a smaller unit, you multiply.

0.24 m = ? cm

In the Table of Units, there are 2 steps from meters to centimeters, so multiply by 10^2, or 100.

0.24 m × 100 = 24 cm

STUDY TIP

When you rewrite a measurement using a larger unit, you divide.

3500 mg = ? kg

In the Table of Units, there are 6 steps from milligrams to kilograms, so divide by 10^6, or 1,000,000.

3500 mg ÷ 1,000,000 = 0.0035 kg

SYMBOLS

■ ARITHMETIC AND ALGEBRA

$=$	Is equal to
$\neq$	Is not equal to
$>$	Is greater than
$<$	Is less than
$\approx$	Is approximately equal to

$$\left.\begin{array}{l} a \times b \\ a \cdot b \\ a(b) \\ ab \end{array}\right\} \quad a \text{ times } b$$

a^n	A number a raised to the nth power
( )	Grouping symbols
5, or $+5$	Positive 5
-5	Negative 5
$\sqrt{a}$	Square root of a number a
$\dfrac{a}{b}$	Ratio of a to b or a $\div$ b
$3.\overline{7}$	The repeating decimal 3.777...

■ GEOMETRY

(a, b)	Ordered Pair a, b
$\sim$	Is similar to
$\cong$	Is congruent to
$\overleftrightarrow{AB}$	Line AB
$\overrightarrow{AB}$	Ray AB
$\overline{AB}$	Segment AB
$\angle A$	Angle A
π	Pi (≈ 3.14)
	Perpendicular lines
	Right angle

FORMULAS AND NUMBER PROPERTIES

Formulas

Perimeter and Circumference

$P = 4 \cdot s$	Square (*p. 67*)
$P = 2 \cdot \ell + 2 \cdot w$	Rectangle (*p. 67*)
$C = \pi \cdot d$	Circle (*p. 500*)
$C = \pi \cdot 2 \cdot r$	Circle (*p. 500*)

Area

$A = s^2$	Square (*p. 73*)
$A = \ell \cdot w$	Rectangle (*p. 73*)
$A = \frac{1}{2} \cdot b \cdot h$	Triangle (*p. 492*)
$A = \pi \cdot r^2$	Circle (*p. 506*)
$A = \pi \cdot \left(\frac{1}{2} \cdot d \right)^2$	Circle (*p. 506*)

Surface area

Surface area of a prism = Sum of the areas of the faces (*p. 516*)

Volume

$V = s^3$	Cube (*p. 517*)
$V = \ell \cdot w \cdot h$	Rectangular prism (*p. 517*)

Miscellaneous

Amount of tax = Tax rate × Cost $\qquad$ Amount of tax (*p. 183*)

$$\text{Number of possible combinations} = \text{Number of items in one set} \times \text{Number of items in another set}$$ Counting Principle (*p. 603*)

Number properties

Let a, b, and c, represent any numbers.

$a \cdot (b + c) = a \cdot b + a \cdot c$	Distributive Property (*p. 88*)
$a + b = b + a$	Commutative Property of Addition (*p. 92*)
$a \cdot b = b \cdot a$	Commutative Property of Multiplication (*p. 92*)
$a + (b + c) = (a + b) + c$	Associative Property of Addition (*p. 92*)
$a \cdot (b \cdot c) = (a \cdot b) \cdot c$	Associative Property of Multiplication (*p. 92*)

GLOSSARY

acute angle (p. 426) An angle whose measure is between 0° and 90°.

acute triangle (p. 451) A triangle with three acute angles.

algebra (p. 28) A branch of mathematics in which letters or variables are used to represent some numbers.

angle (p. 426) A figure formed by two rays that begin at the same point. The rays are the *sides* of the angle, and the point is the *vertex* of the angle.

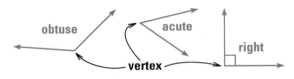

area (p. 73) A measure of how much surface is covered by a figure. Area is measured in *square* units.

area model (p. 72, p. 382) A model used to display the product or quotient of two numbers.

$$3 \times 4 = 12$$

area model (p. 122, p. 374) A model used to show fractional parts of a whole. A unit square represents the number one.

$$\frac{5}{8}$$

Associative Property of Addition (p. 92) If a, b, and c are any numbers, then $(a + b) + c = a + (b + c)$.

Associative Property of Mutiplication (p. 92) If a, b, and c are any numbers, then $(a \times b) \times c = a \times (b \times c)$.

average (p. 232) The sum of a set of numbers divided by how many numbers are in the set. It is also called the *mean*.

bar graph (p. 16) A graph that organizes a collection of data by using bars. The lengths of the bars show how quantities compare.

base of a power (p. 144) A number that is used as the factor in repeated multiplication. For example, in the expression 2^3, 2 is the base.

base of a triangle (p. 406) Any side of a triangle. *See* **triangle**.

base-ten pieces (p. 64) Counting pieces used to represent place values of base-ten numbers.

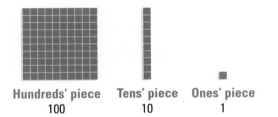

| Hundreds' piece | Tens' piece | Ones' piece |
| 100 | 10 | 1 |

base-ten system (p. 60) A number system in which each place value is 10 times larger than the place value to its right.

center of a circle (p. 500) The point inside a circle that is the same distance from all points on the circle.

centimeter (p. 116) A metric system unit of length equal to 0.01 meter.

circle (p. 500) A closed curve in a plane for which every point is the same distance from a given point called the *center*.

circle graph (p. 512) A graph that displays fractional parts of a data collection as parts of a circle. The whole circle represents the entire collection.

circumference (p. 500) The distance around a circle.

common denominator (p. 322) The same denominator used in two or more fractions. For example, $\frac{1}{4}$ and $\frac{3}{4}$ have a common denominator of 4.

common multiple (p. 323) A number that is a multiple of two or more numbers. For example, 24 is a common multiple of 3 and 4 because it is a multiple of 3 and a multiple of 4.

Commutative Property of Addition (p. 92) If a and b are any numbers, then changing the order in which they are added will not change the sum; that is $a + b = b + a$. For example, $3 + 4 = 4 + 3$.

Commutative Property of Multiplication (p. 92) If a and b are any numbers, then changing the order in which they are multiplied will not change the product; that is $a \times b = b \times a$. For example, $5 \times 6 = 6 \times 5$.

comparing fractions (p. 290) Deciding whether one fraction is greater or lesser than another.

complement of a probability (p. 303) The probability that an event will not happen is the complement of the probability that it will happen.

complementary angles (p. 480) Two angles whose measures have a sum of 90°.

congruent angles (p. 481) Angles that have exactly the same measure.

congruent figures (p. 432) Figures that have exactly the same size and shape.

coordinate geometry (p. 564) The study of geometric figures in a coordinate plane.

coordinate plane (p. 446, p. 554) A plane formed by a horizontal number line called the *x*-axis, and a vertical number line called the *y*-axis.

coordinates (p. 446) The two numbers of an ordered pair that locate a point in a coordinate plane.

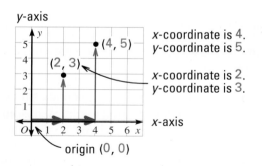

Counting Principle (p. 603) When one item is selected from each of two or more sets, the total number of combinations is the product of the number of items in each set.

cube (p. 516) A rectangular prism whose six faces are congruent squares.

data (p. 5) A collection of numbers or facts.

decimal point (p. 166) A symbol that establishes place value.

denominator (p. 268) The number below the line in a fraction. It tells into how many pieces the whole has been divided. For example, the denominator of $\frac{2}{3}$ is 3.

dependent events (p. 608) Events for which the occurrence of one event will change the probability of the occurrence of another event.

diagonal (p. 490) A segment that connects two vertices of a polygon and is not a side.

diameter (p. 500) The distance across a circle through its center.

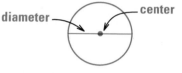

discount (p. 204) The amount by which a regular price is reduced.

Distributive Property (p. 88) If a, b, and c are any numbers, then $a \times (b + c) = a \times b + a \times c$. For example, $3 \times (4 + 5) = 3 \times 4 + 3 \times 5$.

divide (p. 78) To find a quotient of two numbers.

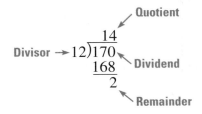

dividend (p. 78) *See* **divide.**

divides evenly (p. 78) Division with a whole-number quotient, or zero remainder.

divisor (p. 78) *See* **divide.**

equation (p. 28) A mathematical sentence with an equal sign "=" in it.

equilateral triangle (p. 450) A triangle that has 3 sides of the same length.

equivalent fractions (p. 278) Fractions that represent the same number. For example, $\frac{1}{2} = \frac{25}{50}$.

evaluate (p. 84) To find the value of an expression.

expanded notation (p. 60) A number written as the sum of each digit times a power of 10. For example, $374 = (3 \times 100) + (7 \times 10) + (4 \times 1)$.

experimental probability (p. 302) A probability based on the frequency of outcomes that have occurred after performing an experiment many times.

exponent (p. 144) The number of times a base is used as a factor. For example, in the expression 2^3, 3 is the exponent.

expression (p. 84) A collection of numbers or variables that can be linked by addition, subtraction, multiplication, and division symbols.

factor (p. 144) A number that divides another number evenly. For example, 1, 2, 3, 4, 6, and 12 are all factors of 12.

flip (p. 436) An operation that moves a figure about a line so that its new position is its mirror image on the opposite side of the line.

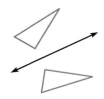

front-end estimation (p. 177) An estimating strategy that uses the front digits of given numbers.

front digits (p. 177) The leading digits of a number. For example, in 16,248 the front digits are 16.

function (p. 596) A rule that tells how to perform one or more operations on a number called the *input* to produce a result called the *output*.

grouping symbols (p. 84) Parentheses or brackets that group parts of an expression.

height of triangle (p. 406) *See* **triangle**.

heptagon (p. 421) A 7-sided polygon.

hexagon (p. 421) A 6-sided polygon.

horizontal bar graph (p. 243) A bar graph that uses horizontal bars.

improper fraction (p. 296) A fraction that is greater than or equal to 1. For example, $\frac{4}{3}$ and $\frac{8}{8}$ are improper fractions.

independent events (p. 608) Events for which the occurrence of one event will not affect the occurence of the other event.

input (p. 596) A number on which a function operates.

integers (p. 532) The set of whole numbers and their opposites.

intersecting lines (p. 476) Lines that meet at a point.

isosceles triangle (p. 450) A triangle that has at least 2 sides of the same length.

key (p. 224) An explanation of the symbols used in a graph or stem-and-leaf plot.

kilometer (p. 116) A metric system unit of length equal to 1000 meters.

least common denominator (p. 323) The least common multiple of the denominators of two or more fractions. For example, the least common denominator of $\frac{1}{2}$ and $\frac{2}{3}$ is 6.

least common multiple (p. 323) The smallest common multiple of two or more numbers. For example, 6 is the least common multiple of 2 and 3.

line (p. 420) A straight path extending without end in two directions.

line graph (p. 246) A graph that uses line segments to connect data points. It can show how data changes over time.

line of symmetry (p. 438) A line that divides a figure into two parts, each of which is the mirror image of the other.

line plot (p. 220) A diagram that uses a number line to show frequency of data.

line segment (p. 420) A part of a line consisting of two endpoints and all the points between them.

line symmetry (p. 438) The property of a figure that indicates it can be flipped about a line and land exactly on itself.

mean (p. 232) The sum of a set of numbers divided by how many numbers are in the set. It is also called the *average*.

median (p. 236) The middle number (or the average of the two middle numbers) of a set of numbers that have been written in numerical order.

meter (p. 116) The basic unit of length in the metric system.

metric system (p. 116) An international base-ten measuring system.

midpoint (p. 565) The point on a line segment that is halfway between the two endpoints.

millimeter (p. 116) A metric system unit of length equal to 0.001 meter.

mixed number (p. 268) The sum of a whole number and a fraction. For example, $6\frac{3}{5}$ is a mixed number.

mode (p. 237) The number (or numbers) that appears most often in a set of data.

multiple of a number (p. 13) The product of the number and any whole number greater than zero. For example, 3, 6, 9, and 12 are multiples of 3.

negative integer (p. 532) An integer less than 0.

negative sign (p. 532) The symbol "–" used to represent negative numbers.

number-line model (p. 124) A model used to show fractional parts of a whole.

numerator (p. 268) The number above the line in a fraction. It represents the number of equal portions out of the whole.

numerical expression (p. 84) A collection of numbers linked by mathematical operations.

obtuse angle (p. 426) An angle whose measure is greater than 90° and less than 180°.

obtuse triangle (p. 451) A triangle that has one obtuse angle.

octagon (p. 421) An 8-sided polygon.

opposites (p. 532) Two numbers that are the same distance from 0 on a number line. For example, 4 and −4 are opposites.

order of operations (p. 85) A procedure for evaluating expressions that have more than one operation.

ordered pair (p. 446) A pair of numbers that locates a point in a coordinate plane. *See* **coordinates**.

ordering (p. 134) Arranging numbers from least to greatest or greatest to least.

origin (p. 446) The point (0, 0) on the coordinate plane. It is the intersection of the *x*-axis and the *y*-axis. *See* **coordinates**.

output (p. 596) The number produced by evaluating a function using a specific input.

parallel lines (p. 476) Lines in the same plane that never meet.

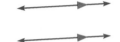

parallelogram (p. 22, p. 486) A quadrilateral whose opposite sides are parallel.

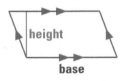

Pascal's Triangle (p. 6) A number arrangement.

```
                    1
Row 1 ─────────▶  1   1
Row 2 ────────▶ 1   2   1
Row 3 ───────▶ 1   3   3   1
Row 4 ─────▶ 1   4   6   4   1
           1   5   10   10   5   1
         1   6   15   20   15   6   1
       1   7   21   35   35   21   7   1
```

pentagon (p. 421) A 5-sided polygon.

percent (p. 129) The value of a ratio that compares a number to 100. *Percent* means "per hundred."

perimeter (p. 67) The distance around a figure. Perimeter is measured in units.

perpendicular lines (p. 477) Two lines that meet at a 90°, or right, angle.

pi (π) (p. 500) The number that represents the ratio of the circumference of a circle to its diameter, approximately 3.14.

pictograph (p. 252) A graph that uses pictures or symbols to represent data.

place-value system (p. 60) A number system in which the value of a digit is determined by its place in a number. For example, the 5 in 156 shows 5 tens, or fifty.

plane (p. 444) A flat surface that extends in all directions without ending.

point (p. 420) A position in space represented by a dot.

polygon (p. 421) A closed geometric figure that has straight sides.

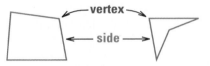

positive integer (p. 532) An integer greater than 0.

power (p. 144) An expression such as 4^2 that has a base (4) and an exponent (2).

powers of 10 (p. 144) The numbers 10^1, 10^2, 10^3, 10^4, ... They can also be written as 10, 100, 1000, 10,000, ...

prism (p. 516) A solid figure with two congruent and parallel faces and whose sides are polygons.

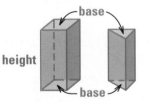

probability of an event (p. 302, p. 309) A ratio of the number of favorable outcomes to the number of possible outcomes. Probabilities are between 0 and 1.

product (p. 72) The result obtained by multiplying two or more numbers.

proportion (p. 283) An equation stating that two ratios are equivalent.

protractor (p. 427) A device used to measure angles.

quadrant (p. 554) One of the four regions in a coordinate plane formed by the coordinate axes.

quadrilateral (p. 22) A 4-sided polygon.

quotient (p. 78) *See* **divide.**

radius (p. 506) The distance between the center of a circle and a point on the circle.

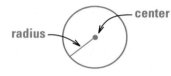

range (p. 221) The difference between the greatest number and the least number in a set of data.

ratio (p. 275) A comparison of two numbers by division.

ray (p. 426) Part of a line that begins at a point and extends in one direction without ending.

reciprocals (p. 396) Two numbers whose product is one. For example, $\frac{4}{3}$ is the reciprocal of $\frac{3}{4}$.

rectangle (p. 486) A parallelogram that has four right angles.

rectangular prism (p. 516) A prism with 6 faces, each a rectangle.

regroup (p. 66, p. 342) To rewrite a form of a number as an equivalent form. For example, $3\frac{2}{3}$ can be rewritten as $2\frac{5}{3}$.

remainder (p. 78) *See* **divide.**

rename (p. 348) To rewrite numbers in another form. For example, $3\frac{1}{3}$ can be renamed as $3\frac{2}{6}$.

right angle (p. 406, p. 426) An angle that measures 90°.

right triangle (p. 406, p. 451) A triangle that has a right angle.

rounding a number (p. 176) Replacing a number with another one of approximately the same value that is easier to use. For example, 387 rounded to the nearest ten is 390; 387 rounded to the nearest hundred is 400.

scale (p. 243) The numbers on the axes of a graph.

scale drawing (p. 246) A drawing whose measurements are proportional to the actual dimensions.

scalene triangle (p. 121) A triangle that has three sides of different lengths.

set model (p. 124) A model used to show fractional parts of a whole.

side of an angle (p. 426) *See* **angle.**

similar figures (p. 432) Figures that have the same shape, but not necessarily the same size.

simplest form of a fraction (p. 282) A fraction is in simplest form if the only common factor of the numerator and denominator is 1.

simplify a fraction (p. 282) To rewrite a fraction so that it is in simplest form.

slide (p. 447) To move a figure without turning or flipping.

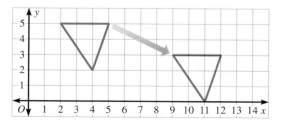

solution of an equation (p. 28) The value of the variable that makes the equation true.

solve a proportion (p. 283) To find the value of the variable in a proportion. For example, if $\frac{2}{3} = \frac{x}{9}$, then the solution is $x = 6$.

spreadsheet (p. 229) A software program used for organizing and analyzing data.

square (p. 486) A rectangle with four sides of the same length.

stem-and-leaf plot (p. 224) A method of organizing data in increasing or decreasing order.

supplementary angles (p. 480) Two angles whose measures have a sum of 180°.

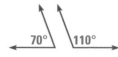

surface area (p. 516) The sum of the areas of all the faces of a three-dimensional figure.

tally sheet (p. 218) A table used to list the numbers of times different outcomes occur.

tessellation (p. 444) Repeating congruent figures that cover a surface without overlapping or leaving holes.

theoretical probability (p. 302) A probability that is found by counting and classifying all possible outcomes.

tiling (p. 444) A tessellation.

tree diagram (p. 602) A diagram that shows total possible outcomes. Outcomes are listed along the "branches" of the diagram.

triangle (p. 421) A 3-sided polygon.

turn (p. 424) An operation that turns a figure a given angle (clockwise or counter-clockwise) about a point (a rotation).

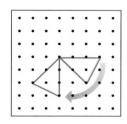

unit (p.67) A standard of measurement.

variable (p. 89) A letter that can be replaced by any number.

variable expression (p. 89) An expression that has at least one variable.

Venn Diagram (p. 450, p. 486) A diagram that uses shapes to show relationships among sets of objects or numbers.

verbal model (p. 581) A model that uses words to represents a problem.

vertex of an angle (p. 426) *See* **angle**.

vertical bar graph (p. 243) A bar graph that uses vertical bars.

vertical form (p. 166, p. 170) A form for adding, subtracting, multiplying, or dividing numbers in which place values are aligned vertically.

volume (p. 517) A measure of how much space is occupied by a solid figure. Volume is measured in cubic units.

x-axis (p. 446) The horizontal axis in a coordinate plane.

x-coordinate (p. 446) The first number of an ordered pair.

y-axis (p. 446) The vertical axis in a coordinate plane.

y-coordinate (p. 426) The second number of an ordered pair.

zero pair (p. 536) Two counters that result in zero when paired.

acute angle/ángulo agudo (p. 426) Angulo que mide entre 0° y 90°.

acute triangle/triángulo agudo (p. 451) Triángulo con tres ángulos agudos.

algebra/álgebra (p. 28) Rama de las matemáticas en la que se usan letras o variables para representar a algunos números.

angle/ángulo (p. 426) Figura formada por dos rayos que comienzan en el mismo punto. Los rayos son los *lados* del ángulo y el punto es el *vértice* del ángulo.

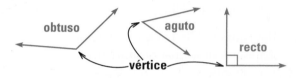

area/área (p. 73) Medida de la superficie cubierta por una figura. El área se mide en unidades *cuadradas*.

area model/modelo de área (p. 72, p. 382) Modelo usado para exhibir el producto o cociente de dos números.

$$3 \times 4 = 12$$

area model/modelo de área (p. 122, p. 374) Modelo usado para mostrar las partes fraccionarias de un entero. Un cuadrado unitario representa al número uno.

$$\frac{5}{8}$$

Associative Property of Addition/propiedad asociativa de la adición (p. 92) Para cualesquier números a, b, y c $(a + b) + c = a + (b + c)$.

Associative Property of Mutiplication/ propiedad asociativa de la multiplicación (p. 92) Para cualesquier números a, b, y c $(a \times b) \times c = a \times (b \times c)$.

average/promedio (p. 232) Suma de los números de un conjunto dividida entre la cantidad de números del conjunto. También se le llama *media*.

bar graph/gráfico de barras (p. 16) Gráfico que organiza un conjunto de datos usando barras, en el cual la longitud de las barras muestra una comparación entre cantidades.

base of a power/base de una potencia (p. 144) Número que se usa como factor en una multiplicación repetida. Por ejemplo, en la expresión 2^3, 2 es la base.

base of a triangle/base de un triángulo (p. 406) Cualquier lado de un triángulo. *Ver* **triangle/triángulo**.

base-ten pieces/elementos en base diez (p. 64) Elementos de conteo usados para representar valores de lugares de números en base diez.

Cuadrado Grande Centenas	Tira Decenas	Cuadra Pequén Unidad
100	10	1

base-ten system/sistema en base diez (p. 60) Sistema numérico donde cada valor de lugar en la cantidad es 10 veces mayor que el valor de lugar que se encuentra a su derecha.

center of a circle/centro de un círculo (p. 500) Punto interior a un círculo que está a la misma distancia de todos los puntos del círculo.

centimeter/centímetro (p. 116) Unidad del sistema métrico con una longitud igual a la centésima parte de un metro.

circle/círculo (p. 500) Curva cerrada en un plano cuyos puntos están todos a la misma distancia de un punto dado llamado *centro*.

circle graph/gráfica circular (p. 512) Gráfico que muestra las partes fraccionarias de un conjunto de datos como partes de un círculo. La totalidad del círculo representa la totalidad del conjunto de datos.

circumference/circunferencia (p. 500) Distancia alrededor de un círculo.

common denominator/común denominador (p. 322) Igual denominador usado en dos o más fracciones. Por ejemplo, $\frac{1}{4}$ y $\frac{3}{4}$ tienen un común denominador que es 4.

common multiple/común múltiplo (p. 323) Número que es múltiplo de dos o más números. Por ejemplo, 24 es común múltiplo de 3 y de 4 porque es múltiplo de 3 y múltiplo de 4.

Commutative Property of Addition/propiedad conmutativa de la adición (p. 92) Para dos números cualesquiera a y b, cambiar el orden en que se los suma no cambiará la suma; esto es, $a + b = b + a$. Por ejemplo, $3 + 4 = 4 + 3$.

Commutative Property of Multiplication/ propiedad conmutativa de la multiplicación (p. 92) Para dos números cualesquiera a y b, cambiar el orden en que se los multiplica no cambiará el producto; esto es, $a \times b = b \times a$. Por ejemplo, $5 \times 6 = 6 \times 5$.

comparing fractions/comparar fracciones (p. 290) Decidir si una fracción es mayor o menor que otra.

complement of a probability/complemento de una probabilidad (p. 303) La probabilidad de que un acontecimiento no ocurra es el complemento de la probabilidad de que el acontecimiento sí ocurra.

complementary angles/ángulos complementarios (p. 480) Dos ángulos cuyas medidas suman 90°.

congruent angles/ángulos congruentes (p. 481) Angulos que tienen exactamente la misma medida.

congruent figures/figuras congruentes (p. 432) Figuras que tienen exactamente el mismo tamaño y la misma forma.

coordinate geometry/geometría de coordenadas (p. 564) Estudio de las figuras geométricas en un plano de coordenadas.

coordinate plane/plano de coordenadas (pp. 446, 554) Plano formado por una línea numérica horizontal llamada eje de las x y una línea numérica vertical llamada eje de las y.

coordinates/coordenadas (p. 446) Dos números de un par ordenado que ubican un punto en un plano de coordenadas.

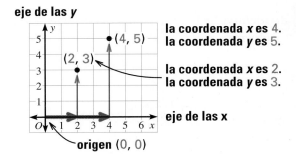

Counting Principle/principio de conteo (p. 603) Cuando se selecciona un elemento de cada uno de dos o más conjuntos, el número total de combinaciones posibles es el producto del número de elementos de cada conjunto.

cube/cubo (p. 516) Prisma rectangular cuyas seis caras son cuadrados congruentes.

data/datos (p. 5) Conjunto de números o hechos.

decimal point/punto o coma decimal (p. 166) Símbolo que establece un valor de lugar.

denominator/denominador (p. 268) Número situado debajo de la línea de una fracción y que indica en cuántas piezas se ha dividido el entero. Por ejemplo, el denominador de $\frac{2}{3}$ es 3.

dependent events/sucesos dependientes (p. 608) Sucesos tales que la ocurrencia de uno de ellos afecta la probabilidad de la ocurrencia del otro.

diagonal/diagonal (p. 490) Segmento que conecta dos vértices de un polígono pero no es uno de sus lados.

diameter/diámetro (p. 500) Distancia a través de un círculo que pasa por su centro.

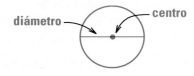

discount/descuento (p. 204) Importe en el que se reduce un precio habitual.

Distributive Property/propiedad distributiva (p. 88) Para números cualesquiera *a, b* y *c,* $a \times (b + c) = a \times b + a \times c$. Por ejemplo, $3 \times (4 + 5) = 3 \times 4 + 3 \times 5$.

divide/dividir (p. 78) Hallar el cociente de dos números.

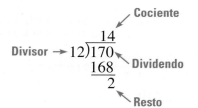

dividend/dividendo (p. 78) *Ver* **divide/dividir.**

divides evenly/división exacta (p. 78) División cuyo cociente es un número entero y cuyo resto o residuo es cero.

divisor/divisor (p. 78) *Ver* **divide/dividir.**

equation/ecuación (p. 28) Expresión matemática que incluye un signo de igual "=".

equilateral triangle/triángulo equilátero (p. 450) Triángulo que tiene tres lados de la misma longitud.

equivalent fractions/fracciones equivalentes (p. 278) Fracciones que representan el mismo número. Por ejemplo, $\frac{1}{2} = \frac{25}{50}$.

evaluate/evaluar (p. 84) Hallar el valor de una expresión.

expanded notation/notación expandida (p. 60) Número escrito como la suma de cada dígito multiplicado por una potencia de 10. Por ejemplo, $374 = (3 \times 100) + (7 \times 10) + (4 \times 1)$.

experimental probability/probabilidad experimental (p. 302) Probabilidad basada en la frecuencia de los resultados que han ocurrido después de realizar un experimento muchas veces.

exponent/exponente (p. 144) Número de veces que una base se usa como factor. Por ejemplo, en la expresión 2^3, 3 es el exponente.

expression/expresión (p. 84) Conjunto de números o variables que pueden relacionarse mediante signos de adición, sustracción, multiplicación y división.

factor/factor (p. 144) Número que divide a otro en forma exacta. Por ejemplo, 1, 2, 3, 4, 6 y 12 son factores de 12.

flip/voltear (p. 436) Operación que mueve una figura en relación con una línea de forma tal que la nueva posición es su imagen especular al otro lado de la línea.

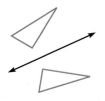

front-end estimation/valoración frontal (p. 177) Estrategia de valoración que usa los dígitos frontales de ciertos números.

front digits/dígitos frontales (p. 177) Dígitos principales de un número. Por ejemplo, en 16.248 los dígitos frontales son 16.

function/función (p. 596) Regla que indica cómo realizar una o más operaciones en un número llamado *entrada* para lograr un *resultado*.

grouping symbols/símbolos de agrupamiento (p. 84) Paréntesis curvos o rectos que agrupan partes de una expresión.

height of triangle/altura de un triángulo (p. 406) *Ver* **triangle/triángulo.**

heptagon/heptágono (p. 421) Polígono de siete lados.

hexagon/hexágono (p. 421) Polígono de seis lados.

horizontal bar graph/gráfico de barras horizontal (p. 243) Gráfico de barras que usa barras horizontales.

improper fraction/fracción impropia (p. 296) Fracción que es mayor o igual que 1. Por ejemplo, $\frac{4}{3}$ y $\frac{8}{8}$ son fracciones impropias.

independent events/sucesos independientes (p. 608) Sucesos tales que la ocurrencia de uno de ellos no afecta la ocurrencia del otro.

input/entrada (p. 596) Número sobre el cual opera una función.

integers/enteros (p. 532) Conjunto de números no fraccionarios y sus opuestos.

intersecting lines/líneas intersectadas (p. 476) Líneas que se cruzan en un punto.

isosceles triangle/triángulo isósceles (p. 450) Triángulo que tiene al menos 2 lados de la misma longitud.

key/clave (p. 224) Explicación de los símbolos usados en una gráfica o en un gráfico de hojas y nervaduras.

kilometer/kilómetro (p. 116) Unidad del sistema métrico con una longitud igual a 1.000 metros.

least common denominator/mínimo común denominador (p. 323) Mínimo común múltiplo de los denominadores de dos o más fracciones. Por ejemplo, el mínimo común denominador de $\frac{1}{2}$ y $\frac{2}{3}$ es 6.

least common multiple/mínimo común múltiplo (p. 323) Mínimo común múltiplo de dos o más números. Por ejemplo, el mínimo común múltiplo de 2 y 3 es 6.

line/línea (p. 420) Camino recto que se extiende sin fin en dos direcciones.

line graph/gráfica de líneas (p. 246) Gráfica que usa segmentos de línea para conectar puntos de datos. Puede mostrar cómo cambian los datos con el tiempo.

line of symmetry/línea de simetría (p. 438) Línea que divide una figura en dos partes, cada una de las cuales es la imagen especular de la otra.

line plot/gráfico de líneas (p. 220) Diagrama que usa una línea de números para mostrar la frecuencia de datos.

line segment/segmento de línea (p. 420) Parte de una línea que consta de dos puntos finales y todos los puntos entre éstos.

line symmetry/simetría lineal (p. 438) Propiedad de una figura que indica que puede ser girada en torno a una línea y volver exactamente a su posición inicial.

mean/media (p. 232) Suma de un conjunto de números dividida entre la cantidad de números que hay en el conjunto. También se le llama *promedio*.

median/mediana (p. 236) Número medio (o promedio de los dos números medios) de un conjunto de números que han sido escritos en orden numérico.

meter/metro (p. 116) Unidad básica de longitud del sistema métrico.

metric system/sistema métrico (p. 116) Sistema internacional de medición de base 10.

midpoint/punto medio (p. 565) Punto de un segmento de línea que está a mitad de camino entre los dos puntos extremos.

millimeter/milímetro (p. 116) Unidad del sistema métrico con una longitud igual a una milésima parte de un metro.

mixed number/número mixto (p. 268) Suma de un número entero y una fracción. Por ejemplo, $6\frac{3}{5}$ es un número mixto.

mode/modo (p. 237) Número(s) de un conjunto de datos que aparece(n) con mayor frecuencia en un conjunto de datos.

multiple of a number/múltiplo de un número (p. 13) Producto de dicho número y cualquier número entero mayor que cero. Por ejemplo, 3, 6, 9 y 12 son múltiplos de 3.

negative integer/entero negativo (p. 532) Cualquier entero inferior o igual a 0.

negative sign/signo negativo (p. 532) Símbolo "–" usado para representar números negativos.

number-line model/modelo de números y líneas (p. 124) Modelo usado para mostrar partes fraccionarias de un entero.

numerator/numerador (p. 268) En una fracción, el número situado encima de la línea que representa el número de partes iguales del entero.

numerical expression/expresión numérica (p. 84) Conjunto de números vinculados por operaciones matemáticas.

obtuse angle/ángulo obtuso (p. 426) Angulo que mide más de 90° y menos de 180°.

obtuse triangle/triángulo obtuso (p. 451) Triángulo que tiene un ángulo obtuso.

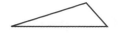

octagon/octágono (p. 421) Polígono de ocho lados.

opposites/opuestos (p. 532) Dos números situados a la misma distancia del 0 en una línea numérica. Por ejemplo, 4 y −4 son opuestos.

order of operations/orden de las operaciones (p. 85) Procedimiento para evaluar las expresiones que tienen más de una operación.

ordered pair/par ordenado (p. 446) Par de números que ubica a un punto en un plano de coordenadas. *Ver* **coordinates/coordenadas.**

ordering/ordenar (p. 134) Disponer números de menor a mayor o de mayor a menor.

origin/origen (p. 446) En un plano de coordenadas, el punto (0,0). Es la intersección entre el eje de las *x* y el eje de las *y. Ver* **coordinates/coordenadas**.

output/salida (p. 596) Número obtenido al evaluar una función usando una entrada específica.

parallel lines/líneas paralelas (p. 476) Líneas en un mismo plano que nunca se encuentran.

parallelogram/paralelogramo (p. 22, p. 486) Cuadrilátero cuyos lados opuestos son paralelos.

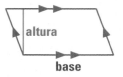

Pascal's Triangle/Triángulo de Pascal (p. 6) Disposición de números.

```
                    1
Línea 1 ────►    1    1
Línea 2 ────►  1    2    1
Línea 3 ──►  1    3    3    1
Línea 4 ─►  1    4    6    4    1
          1    5    10    10    5    1
        1    6    15    20    15    6    1
      1    7    21    35    35    21    7    1
```

pentagon/pentágono (p. 421) Polígono de cinco lados.

percent/porcentaje (p. 129) Valor de una razón aritmética que compara un número con 100. *Porcentaje* significa "por cada cien".

perimeter/perímetro (p. 67) Distancia en torno a una figura. El perímetro se mide en unidades de longitud.

perpendicular lines/líneas perpendiculares (p. 477) Dos líneas que se cruzan en ángulo de 90° o ángulo recto.

pi/pi (π) (p. 500) Número aproximadamente igual a 3,14 que representa la relación entre la circunferencia de un círculo y su diámetro.

pictograph/pictografía (p. 252) Gráfica que usa imágenes o símbolos para representar datos.

place-value system/sistema de valores de lugares (p. 60) Sistema numérico en el cual el valor de un dígito se determina por su lugar en un número. Por ejemplo, el 5 de 156 indica 5 decenas o cincuenta en tanto que el 5 de 35 indica 5 unidades.

plane/plano (p. 444) Superficie plana que se extiende en todas direcciones de manera sin fin.

point/punto (p. 420) Símbolo que representa una posición en el espacio.

polygon/polígono (p. 421) Figura geométrica cerrada que tiene lados rectos.

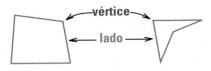

positive integer/entero positivo (p. 532) Todo entero mayor que cero.

power/potencia (p. 144) Expresión tal como 4^2, que tiene una base (4) y un exponente (2).

powers of 10/potencias de 10 (p. 144) Los números 10^1, 10^2, 10^3, 10^4, ... que también pueden escribirse como 10, 100, 1000, 10.000.

prism/prisma (p. 516) Figura sólida con dos caras congruentes y paralelas y cuyos lados son polígonos.

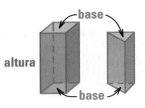

probability of an event/probabilidad de un suceso (p. 302, p. 309) Relación entre el número de resultados favorables y el número de posibles resultados. Las probabilidades varían entre 0 y 1.

product/producto (p. 72) Resultado obtenido al multiplicar dos o más números.

proportion/proporción (p. 283) Ecuación que indica que dos relaciones son equivalentes.

protractor/transportador (p. 427) Instrumento usado para medir ángulos.

quadrant/cuadrante (p. 554) Cada una de las cuatro regiones de un plano de coordenadas formadas por los ejes de coordenadas.

quadrilateral/cuadrilátero (p. 22) Polígono de cuatro lados.

quotient/cociente (p. 78) *Ver* **divide/dividir.**

radius/radio (p. 506) Distancia entre el centro de un círculo y cualquier punto sobre la circunferencia.

range/rango (p. 221) Diferencia entre los valores máximo y mínimo de un conjunto de datos numéricos.

ratio/razón (p. 275) Comparación entre dos números por medio de una división.

ray/rayo (p. 426) Parte de una línea que comienza en un punto y continúa de manera sin fin en una dirección.

reciprocals/números recíprocos (p. 396) Dos números cuyo producto es 1. Por ejemplo, $\frac{4}{3}$ es el número recíproco de $\frac{3}{4}$.

rectangle/rectángulo (p. 486) Paralelogramo que tiene cuatro ángulos rectos.

rectangular prism/prisma rectangular (p. 516) Prisma con seis caras, cada una de las cuales es un rectángulo.

regroup/reagrupar (p. 66, p. 342) Reescribir el formato de un número en un formato equivalente. Por ejemplo, $3\frac{2}{3}$ puede reescribirse como $2\frac{5}{3}$.

remainder/resto (p. 78) *Ver* **divide/dividir.**

rename/renombrar (p. 348) Reescribir números en otro formato. Por ejemplo, $3\frac{1}{3}$ puede renombrarse como $3\frac{2}{6}$.

right angle/ángulo recto (p. 406, p. 426) Angulo que mide 90°.

right triangle/triángulo recto (p. 406, p. 451) Triángulo con un ángulo recto.

rounding a number/redondear un número (p. 176) Sustituir un número por otro de aproximadamente el mismo valor y que sea más fácil de usar. Por ejemplo, 387 redondeado a la decena más próxima es 390; 387 redondeado a la centena más próxima es 400.

scale/escala (p. 243) Números que figuran en los ejes de una gráfica.

scale drawing/dibujo a escala (p. 246) Dibujo cuyas medidas son proporcionales a las dimensiones reales.

scalene triangle/triángulo escaleno (p. 121) Triángulo que tiene sus lados de diferentes longitudes.

set model/modelo de conjunto (p. 124) Modelo utilizado para mostrar las partes fraccionarias de un todo.

side of an angle/lado de un ángulo (p. 426) *Ver* **angle/ángulo.**

similar figures/figuras semejantes (p. 432) Figuras que tienen la misma forma pero no necesariamente el mismo tamaño.

simplest form of a fraction/forma más simple de una fracción (p. 282) Una fracción está en su forma más simple si el único factor común del numerador y el denominador es 1.

simplify a fraction/simplificar una fracción (p. 282) Reescribir una fracción en su forma más simple.

slide/deslizar (p. 447) Mover una figura sin girarla ni voltearla.

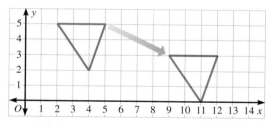

solution of an equation/solución de una ecuación (p. 28) Valor de la variable que hace que se cumpla la ecuación.

solve a proportion/resolver una proporción (p. 283) Hallar el valor de la variable de una proporción. Por ejemplo, si $\frac{2}{3} = \frac{x}{9}$, la solución es $x = 6$.

spreadsheet/hoja electrónica de cálculo (p. 229) Programa de computación usado para organizar y analizar datos.

square/cuadrado (p. 486) Rectángulo con cuatro lados de la misma longitud.

stem-and-leaf plot/gráfico de hojas y nervaduras (p. 224) Método de organizar datos en forma creciente o decreciente.

supplementary angles/ángulos suplementarios
(p. 480) Dos ángulos cuyas medidas suman
180°.

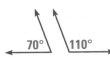

surface area/área de la superficie (p. 516)
Suma de las áreas de todas las caras de una
figura tridimensional.

tally sheet/planilla de recuento (p. 218) Tabla
usada para listar la cantidad de veces que
ocurren diferentes resultados.

tessellation/mosaico (p. 444) Figuras congruentes repetidas que cubren una superficie sin
traslaparse ni dejar vacíos.

theoretical probability/probabilidad teórica
(p. 302) Probabilidad que se determina
contando y clasificando todos los resultados
posibles.

tiling/embaldosado (p. 444) Mosaico.

tree diagram/diagrama de árbol (p. 602)
Diagrama que muestra el total de resultados
posibles y en el que los resultados se enumeran
a lo largo de las "ramas" del diagrama.

triangle/triángulo (p. 421)
Polígono de tres lados.

turn/giro (p. 424) Operación que gira una figura
en un ángulo dado (hacia la derecha o hacia la
izquierda) en relación con un punto (rotación).

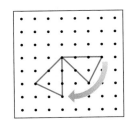

unit/unidad (p. 67) Patrón de medición

variable/variable (p. 89) Letra que puede ser
sustituida por cualquier número.

variable expression/expresión variable (p. 89)
Expresión que tiene por lo menos una variable.

Venn Diagram/Diagrama de Venn
(p. 450, p. 486) Diagrama que usa formas para
mostrar relaciones entre conjuntos de objetos o
números.

verbal model/modelo verbal (p. 581) Modelo
que usa palabras para representar un problema.

vertex of an angle/vértice de un ángulo (p. 426)
Ver angle/ángulo.

vertical bar graph/gráfico de barras vertical
(p. 243) Gráfico de barras que usa barras
verticales.

vertical form/formato vertical (p. 166, p. 170)
Forma de sumar, restar, multiplicar o dividir
números en la que los valores de lugar están
alineados verticalmente.

volume/volumen (p. 517) Medida del espacio
ocupado por una figura sólida. El volumen se
mide en unidades *cúbicas*.

x-axis/eje de las x (p. 446) Eje horizontal de un
plano de coordenadas.

x-coordinate/coordenada x (p. 446) Primer
número de un par ordenado.

y-axis/eje de las y (p. 446) Eje vertical de un
plano de coordenadas.

y-coordinate/coordenada y (p. 426) Segundo
número de un par ordenado.

zero pair/par cero (p. 536) Dos contadores que
al formar un par resultan en cero.

ENGLISH-TO-SPANISH GLOSSARY

PRIME FACTORIZATION

A **prime number** is a whole number greater than one with exactly two factors, 1 and the number itself. For example, 2, 3, 5, 7, 11, 13, and 17 are prime numbers.

The **prime factorization** of a whole number expresses that number as a product of prime numbers. You can use a *tree diagram* to write the prime factorization of a whole number.

The prime factorization of 6 is 2×3, because 2 and 3 are prime numbers. The prime factorization of 45 is $3 \times 3 \times 5$, or $3^2 \times 5$, because 3 and 5 are prime numbers.

Example 1 > Finding a Prime Factorization

Write the prime factorization of 315.

Solution

Use a tree diagram. Test prime numbers to see if they are divisors, and then write the number as a product. Continue factoring until only prime numbers remain in product.

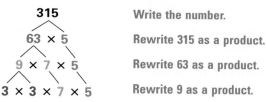

315	Write the number.
63 × 5	Rewrite 315 as a product.
9 × 7 × 5	Rewrite 63 as a product.
3 × 3 × 7 × 5	Rewrite 9 as a product.

The prime factorization of 315 is $3 \times 3 \times 7 \times 5$, or $3^2 \times 7 \times 5$, because 3, 7, and 5 are all prime numbers.

Example 2 > Writing a Prime Factorization

Write the prime factorization of 75.

Solution

$$75 = 15 \times 5 \qquad\qquad 75 = 3 \times 25$$
$$ = 5 \times 3 \times 5 \qquad\qquad = 3 \times 5 \times 5$$
$$ = 5^2 \times 3 \qquad\qquad\quad = 3 \times 5^2$$

Both factorizations give the same prime factors.

GCF and LCM

The **greatest common factor** (**GCF**) of two whole numbers is the greatest whole number that is a factor of each number. The GCF is equal to the product of all common prime factors of the numbers.

Example 3 Finding the GCF of Two Whole Numbers

Find the greatest common factor of 36 and 84.

Solution

Method **1**   Make a list of each number's factors.
36: **1, 2, 3, 4, 6,** 9, **12,** 18, 36
84: **1, 2, 3, 4, 6,** 7, **12,** 14, 21, 28, 42, 84

The **common** factors are 1, 2, 3, 4, 6, and 12. The *greatest* common factor of 36 and 84 is 12.

Method **2**   Find the product of all **common** prime factors.
$36 = 2 \times 2 \times 3 \times 3$ prime factorization of 36
$84 = 2 \times 2 \times 3 \times 7$ prime factorization of 84

The common prime factors of 36 and 84 are 2, 2, and 3. So, the GCF of 36 and 84 is $2 \times 2 \times 3$, or 12.

As you learned in Lesson 7.2, the **least common multiple** (**LCM**) of two whole numbers is the smallest whole number (not including zero) that is a multiple of each number. Use the method shown in Example 4 to find the LCM, or the method shown on page 323.

Example 4 Finding the LCM of Two Whole Numbers

Find the least common multiple of 42 and 60.

Solution

First, find the prime factorization of each number.

$42 = 2 \times 3 \times 7$ prime factorization of 42
$60 = 2 \times 2 \times 3 \times 5$ prime factorization of 60

To find the least common multiple, find the product of all the prime factors that are needed to write each factorization. Use the highest power of each prime number that appears in either factorization.

2, 3, 7   prime factors of 42
2, 2, 3, 5   prime factors of 60

The LCM of 42 and 60 is $2^2 \times 3 \times 7 \times 5$, or 420.

All the prime factors of 42 and 60 are in the factorization of the LCM.

In Exercises 1–4, tell whether the number is prime. If it is not a prime number, write it as a product of two prime numbers.

1. 23   **2.** 51   **3.** 39   **4.** 29

ERROR ANALYSIS In Exercises 5 and 6, identify the error. Then draw a new tree diagram to find the correct prime factorization.

5.   **6.**

In Exercises 7–10, copy and complete the tree diagam. Then write the prime factorization represented by the diagram.

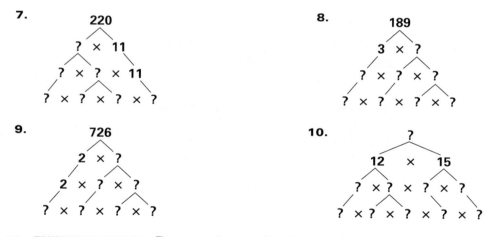

11. THINKING SKILLS Because the number 2 can only be written as a product of itself and 1, it is a prime number. Can any other even numbers be prime numbers? Explain.

In Exercises 12–17, use a tree diagram to find the prime factorization of the number. If the number is prime, write *prime*.

12. 24   **13.** 96   **14.** 105

15. 31   **16.** 64   **17.** 91

In Exercises 18–23, find the number with the given prime factorization.

18. $2 \times 3 \times 5$ **19.** $2^2 \times 5^2$ **20.** $2 \times 5 \times 13$

21. $2^4 \times 11$ **22.** $2 \times 3 \times 7^2$ **23.** $2 \times 3^2 \times 5$

In Exercises 24–29, find all of the factors of each number. Then identify the greatest common factor of the numbers.

24. 56, 70

25. 27, 45

26. 44, 65

27. 176, 550

28. 162, 243

29. 104, 455

In Exercises 30–35, identify the greatest common factor of the two numbers by finding the product of their common prime factors.

30. 57, 78

31. 80, 99

32. 375, 735

33. 200, 950

34. 189, 441

35. 644, 805

36. Andrew has 98 trading cards. Jeffrey has 21 trading cards. Each package that they bought had the same number of cards. What is the largest possible number of cards that could come in each package?

37. Ed Greene is assigning group reports to his two history classes. Each group must have the same number of students. His morning class has 18 students, and his afternoon class has 24 students. What is the largest possible number of students per group?

In Exercises 38–40, tell whether the statement is *true* or *false*. If the statement is false, change it to make it true.

38. The least common multiple of 6 and 10 is 60.

39. The least common multiple of 10 and 20 is 20.

40. The least common multiple of 39 and 52 is 13.

In Exercises 41–46, list the first 10 multiples of each number. Then find the least common multiple.

41. 4, 6

42. 12, 15

43. 8, 9

44. 18, 90

45. 25, 30

46. 28, 24

In Exercises 47–52, find the least common multiple of the numbers.

47. 21, 49

48. 32, 160

49. 36, 125

50. 81, 87

51. 135, 225

52. 168, 539

53. FILTERS An air purifier needs to have its secondary filter changed every 4 months. Its primary filter must be changed every 18 months. After how many months will both filters need to be changed at the same time?

54. GARDENING You plant 18 seedlings per row of one type of flower and 24 seedlings per row of another type. You want to plant an equal number of each type of flower. What is the least number of each type of flower that you can plant?

INDEX

INDEX

INDEX

INDEX

Credits

Cover Image

Photography by Ralph Mercer

Stock Photography

vi Mark Harwood/Tony Stone Images (t); Frank Siteman/Stock Boston (b); **vii** Ken Musgrave (t); Alan Levenson/Tony Stone Images (b); **viii** Gabe Palmer/The Stock Market (t); John Eastcott/Yva Momatiuk/The Image Works (b); **ix** Susan Lapides (t); Don Smetzer/ Tony Stone Images (b); **x** David Young-Wolff/PhotoEdit (t); David Young-Wolff/PhotoEdit (b); **xi** C.J. Allen/ Stock Boston (t); Patti McConville/The Image Bank (b); **xii** Kagan/Monkmeyer Press Photo (t); Bob Daemmrich/ The Image Works (b); **xiii** Dean Abramson/Stock Boston (t); David Young-Wolff/PhotoEdit (b); courtesy Chris Palmer (b); **xv** Ping Amranand/Uniphoto (t); Llewelyn/ Uniphoto (b); **xvi** Franz Lazi (t); Galen Rowell (b); **xvii** Phyllis Picardi/The Picture Cube (t); Paul Griffin/Stock Boston (b); **xix** Dan McCoy/Rainbow (t); Michael Mancuso/ Omni-Photo Communications (tl); Marian Beacon/ Animals, Animals (tr); Doris De Witt/Tony Stone Images (bl); Telegraph Colour Library/FPG International (bc); NASA (br); **xx** Zigy Kaluzny/Tony Stone Images (t); Rob Crandall/Rainbow (c); Susan Lapides (bl); Bohdan Hrynewych/Stock Boston (bc); Collection of the Carole and Barry Kaye Museum of Minatures (br); **xxi** David Young-Wolff/PhotoEdit (t); **xxii** Lawrence Migdale/Stock Boston (t); Mike Clemmer (c); David Young-Wolff/PhotoEdit (b); **xxvi** Francois Gohier/Photo Researchers, Inc. (t); Dana White/PhotoEdit (c); David Young-Wolff/PhotoEdit (b); **xxvii** David Young-Wolff/ PhotoEdit (b); **xxviii** David Wells/The Image Works; **1** Mark E. Gibson (tl); Dwight Cendrowski (tr); **2** Frank Siteman/Stock Boston (t); **3** School Division, Houghton Mifflin Company (b, tr); Dana White/PhotoEdit (bm); **4** Tom Pantages; **7** Ron Vesely; **8** Bob Daemmrich/Stock Boston; **12** Grantpix/Monkmeyer Press Photo; **14** Mark Harwood/Tony Stone Images; **15** Elena Rooraid/ PhotoEdit; **16** Bob Daemmrich/The Image Works; **22** Lawrence Migdale/Stock Boston; **24** William Blizzard/Uniphoto ;
29 E.R. Degginger/Earth Scenes; **30** Tommy Dodson/Unicorn Stock Photo; **31** Mark Gamba/The Stock Market; **33** Mark Sherman/Photo Network; **34** Jeff Greenberg/The Picture Cube; **37** Bob Daemmrich/The Image Works; **38** Jose Carrillo/ PhotoEdit;
43 Collection of the Carole and Barry Kaye Museum of Miniatures (t); courtesy Central Point Photography/Hall of Flame; **54** Jonathan Nourok/Tony Stone Images (t); Alfred Pasieka/Science Photo Library/Photo Researchers, Inc. (b); **55** Ken Musgrave; **56** Alan Levenson/Tony Stone Images; **57** Zigy Kaluzny/Tony Stone Images (tl); Richard Pasley/Stock Boston (tr); School Division, Houghton Mifflin Company (b); **59** Tom Benton/Impact Visuals (t); School Division, Houghton Mifflin Company (br);
61 F. Rossotto/The Stock Market; **66** Amanda Merullo/ Stock Boston; **69** David Young-Wolff/Tony Stone Images; **70** Stock Montage, Inc.; **71** Damian Strohmeyer/ Allsport USA; **72** Michael Rosenfeld/Tony Stone Images; **75** Geoff Tompkinson/Photo Researchers, Inc.; **78** John Coletti/The Picture Cube; **81** Lori Adamski Peek/Tony Stone Images; **84** George Chan/Tony Stone Images; **87** Doris DeWitt/Tony Stone Images (t); Tony Freeman/PhotoEdit (b); **88** Paula Lerner/Woodfin Camp & Associates; **89** Preuss/ The Image Works; **91** L. Kolvoord/The Image Works; **93** Sally Cassidy/The Picture Cube (t); University of Istanbul Library (b); **96** Robert Daemmrich/Tony Stone Images; **97** Michael Holford; **99** Doug Menuez; **106** Gabe Palmer/The Stock Market (inset); **106-107** David Frazier Photography (background); **107** David R. Frazier Photography (tr);

SELECTED ANSWERS

Chapter 1

1.1 Exercises, pp. 6–7

1. Each number is eight more than the previous one. **3.** No; yes; 104 is divisible by eight so it would be on the list. **5.** Each number is two more that the previous one; 9, 11, 13. **7.** Each number is the previous one times 3; 405, 1215, 3645. **9.** The denominator of each fraction is two times the previous one; $\frac{1}{32}, \frac{1}{64}, \frac{1}{128}$.
11. Each letter is the third letter in the alphabet after the previous letter; M, P, S. **13.** Working from the end of the alphabet, each letter is the second letter after the previous letter in the list; R, P, N.

15.

17. 8, 16, 32, 64, 128; the sum is the power of 2 whose exponent is the row number. **19.** If *n* is the number of digits, the product contains the digits from 1 to *n*, then back to 1. **21.** C

1.2 Exercises, pp. 10–11

1.

	Parker	Whittier	Madison
Bicycle	$89.00	$99.00	$84.00
Movie ticket	$5.50	$7.00	$4.75
Rollerblades	$48.50	$54.00	$47.25

5. a. limes and oranges **b.** 1995
7. elementary school

1.3 Exercises, pp. 14–15

1.
1 **2** 3 **4** (5) **6** 7 **8** 9 (10)
11 **12** 13 **14** (15) **16** 17 **18** 19 (20)
21 **22** 23 **24** (25) **26** 27 **28** 29 (30)
31 **32** 33 **34** (35) **36** 37 **38** 39 (40)
41 **42** 43 **44** (45) **46** 47 **48** 49 (50)

They are all multiples of 10.
3. shorts and blue T-shirt, shorts and white T-shirt, shorts and knit shirt, jeans and blue T-shirt, jeans and white T-shirt, jeans and knit shirt, sweat pants and blue T-shirt, sweat pants and white T-shirt, sweat pants and knit shirt

5. even **7.** odd **9.** 30 and 60; yes; no; yes
11. 6, 7, 8, 9, 10, 11, 12 **13.** 684
15. 24 numbers **17.** C

1.4 Exercises, pp. 18–20

1. *Sample answer:* annual U.S. consumption of gasoline from 1990 to 1995 **3.** 44 people
5. a. hiking **b.** camping, hiking, skiing, sailing
7. a. Never; it is the largest part of the circle.
b. Yes, these two parts of the circle are about the same size. **9.** *Sample answer:* 75, 190, 240, 420, 520; the graph may show the projected number of households, out of 1000, that are connected to the Internet. **11.** less; graph **13.** D

Spiral Review, p. 20

1. 9×7 **3.** 4×9 **5.** 8×7 **7.** 5×15
9. yes **11.** yes **13.** no **15.** yes **17.** $108

Mid-Chapter Assessment, p. 21

1. B **2.** A **3.** C **4.** 6 weeks **5.** bread, eggs, oranges **6.** bread, eggs, and oranges in 1995; chicken in 1993 **7.** 32 ways **8.** tell problems
9. *Sample answer:* Men and women rated *share common interests* and *spend time* similarly. Women rated *talk frequently*, *listen to problems*, and *tell problems* somewhat higher than men.
10. 32

1.5 Exercises, pp. 24–25

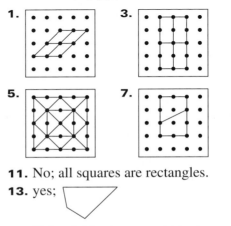

11. No; all squares are rectangles.
13. yes;

15. Yoko; 3 blocks **17.** 4 blocks west **19.** D

1.6 Exercises, pp. 30–31

1. equation   **3.** *Sample answer:* I chose *n* for the *number* of cans.   **5.** $t = 3\frac{1}{2} \cdot 336$; 1176 hours
7. 7   **9.** 7   **11.** 23   **13.** 6   **15.** 3   **17.** 32
19. $17 - x = 5$; 12   **21.** $x \div 2 = 18$; 36
23. 15, 20, 25, 30; *d* increases by 5.   **25.** 14, 16, 18, 20; *d* increases by 2.   **27.** $s = 350 - 134$; 216   **29.** $14 + p = 21$; 7 points
31. $180 \div p = 6$; 30 min   **33.** B

Spiral Review, p. 32

1. 53.8   **3.** 13.8   **5.** 54.73   **7.** 16.67
9. *Sample answer:* 11 in.   **11.** *Sample answer:* 7 in.   **13.** 0.5   **15.** 1.75

Using a Calculator, p. 33

1–9. *Sample answers are given.*   **1.** 2.7; 2.704
3. 2; 1.901   **5.** 3.75; 3.936   **7.** 4.1; 4.16
9. about $18; $17.985; yes

1.7 Exercises, pp. 36–37

1. 20, 12, 20   **3.** What number can you subtract from 54 to get 48? 6   **5.** What number can you divide 42 by to get 6? 7   **7.** 32, 4, 0, 0   **9.** 27, 35, 7, 21   **11.** 19   **13.** 83   **15.** 11   **17.** 6
19. 112   **21.** 3   **23.** $n + 18 = 27$; 9
25. $7 \cdot y = 105$; 15   **27.** $m \cdot 12 = 60$; 5
29. 42 m   **31.** C

1.8 Exercises, pp. 40–41

1. solve a simpler problem   **3.** make a list
5. First, find how many rings would be exchanged in a club with two members.   **7. a.** 25 squares
b. 16 squares   **c.** 3×3, 4×4, 5×5; nine 3×3 squares, four 4×4 squares, one 5×5 square   **d.** 55 squares
9.

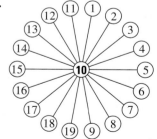

11. A

Spiral Review, p. 42

1. 4584   **3.** 1222   **5.** 13,484   **7.** go on vacation   **9.** 14 tokens

1.9 Exercises, pp. 46–47

1. *Sample answer:* Drawing a Diagram or Using a Graph; both methods would help one visualize the problem.   **3.** *Sample answer:* Find two consecutive numbers whose sum is 243.
5. a. 146 and 147   **b.** 26 and 27   **c.** 12, 13, and 14   **7.** *Sample answer:* 7 minutes; I used Drawing a Diagram. This helped me realize I needed 7 lines.   **9.** 1990: $4\frac{1}{2}$; 1991: 5; 1992: $4\frac{1}{2}$; 1993: $5\frac{1}{2}$; 1994: $4\frac{1}{2}$
11. 16 pieces;

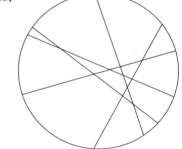

Chapter 1 Review, pp. 49–51

1. The numbers increase by the consecutive integers 5, 6, 7, … ; 61, 70, 80.
3.

2000	999	651

5. 1990
7. 18 cards;

9. 54   **11.** $9 + s = 25$; $16   **13.** What number can you divide by 3 to get 21? 63   **15.** First, find the number of seconds in a day and then multiply this number by 365.   **17.** 2160 mm, or 2.16 m

Chapter 2

2.1 Exercises, pp. 62–63

1. no **3.** CCCLXII **5.** False; each place gets larger to the left. **7.** 640 **9.** 44,040 **11.** five; two **13.** three; twenty-five **15.** D **17.** C **19.** 865 **21.** 386

23.

Province	Place value position of 5
Nova Scotia	ones
New Brunswick	tens
Manitoba	ten thousands
Saskatchewan	ten thousands
British Columbia	tens
Quebec	hundred thousands

25. 10,759 **27.** B

2.2 Exercises, pp. 68–69

1. *Sample answer:* without regrouping: $33 + 12 = 45$; with regrouping: $47 + 15 = 62$ **3.** 22 **5.** 32 **7.** 264 **9.** 38 **11.** 1161 **13.** 2334 **15.**

$$\begin{array}{r} 570 \\ -\,246 \\ \hline 324 \end{array}$$

17.

$$\begin{array}{r} 5268 \\ -\,681 \\ \hline 4587 \end{array}$$

19. 51 **21.** 175 **23.** 5000 **25.** 0.4 m **27.** $49 + 35$ **29.** $25 - 16$ **31.** false **33.** B **35.** B

Spiral Review, p. 70

1. 4200 **3.** 500 **5.** 66 **7.** 8 **9.** 4, 8, 12, 16, 20, 24, 28, 32, 36, 40, 44, 48 **11.** 10, 20, 30, 40, 50 **13.** pounds **15.** pounds or tons **17.** ounces

Using a Calculator, p. 71

1. 308 **3.** 316 **5.** 1280 **7.** Each list has either all even numbers or an even number of odd numbers. **9.** 282

2.3 Exercises, pp. 74–75

1. $7 \cdot 9 = 63$ **3.** 96,250 mi^2 **5.** $2 \cdot 2 = 4$ **7.** $6 \cdot 8 = 48$

9. ; 48 square units

11. ; 52 square units

13. Bathroom, 27 tiles; Laundry, 14 tiles; Hallway, 18 tiles **15.** 5 **17.** even **19.** odd

21. $n = 2, 4, 8$; as the product doubles, n doubles. **23.** system B **25.** B

2.4 Exercises, pp. 80–81

1. dividend, 27; divisor, 4 **3.** $6\frac{3}{4} = 6$ R3 **5.** A; 2 R1, $2\frac{1}{6}$ **7.** $52 \div 4 = 13$ **9.** 9 R3, $9\frac{3}{4}$ **11.** 14 R1, $14\frac{1}{3}$ **13.** 23 R4, $23\frac{4}{5}$ **15.** 61 R1, $61\frac{1}{4}$ **17.** $50 \div 3$ **19.** 2 R4 or $2\frac{4}{5}$ **21.** 3 R6 or $3\frac{3}{4}$ **23.** $7\frac{1}{4}$ ft **25.** He divided $45 \div 720$; the display should read 16. **27.** $2\frac{1}{2}$; a fraction, because you are referring to a fraction of a mile **29.** C

Spiral Review, p. 82

1. $p = 34$ in.; $A = 66$ in.^{2} **3.** $p = 28$ ft; $A = 49$ ft^2 **5.** 110 **7.** 70 **9.** 25 **11.** 50 **13.** 70 **15.** 1110 **17.** 2000 **19.** 27, 35, 43 **21.** $n = 80 \div 15$; $n = 5$ R5; a remainder, showing that you have 5¢ left over

Mid-Chapter Assessment, p. 83

1. 41,035 **2.** 6209 **3.** 590 **4.** four thousand, fifty-four **5.** thirty thousand, eight hundred seventy **6.** six hundred fifty-two thousand, one **7.** 20 **8.** 16

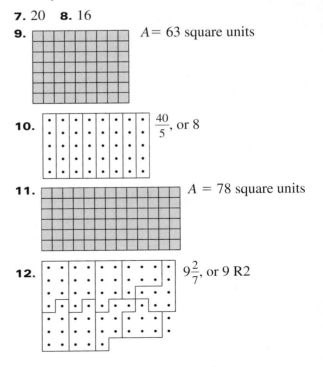

9. $A = 63$ square units

10. $\frac{40}{5}$, or 8

11. $A = 78$ square units

12. $9\frac{2}{7}$, or 9 R2

13. 20 **14.** 36 **15.** 85 **16.** 7 **17.** 4
18. 50 **19.** about 250 to 300
20. contemporary, about 500 fewer
21. contemporary, about 800 more

2.5 Exercises, pp. 86–87

1. B **3.** A **5.** $5 \times (9 - 3) + 12 \div 6 = 32$
7. 2 **9.** 56 **11.** 3 **13.** 18 **15.** 50 **17.** 3
19. 15 **21.** $5 \cdot (17 - 8) = 45$
23. $25 - 4 \cdot 5 = 5$ **25.** $7 + 2 \cdot 9 = 25$
27. $9 + 4 \div 2 = 11$ **29.** $+, \times, -$
31. $\times, +, \div$ **33.** $4 \cdot 43 + 30 \cdot 4 \cdot 2 = \$412$
35. $20 \cdot 18 + 5 = 365$ days; this is the same
number as in our year (except leap years).

2.6 Exercises, pp. 90–91

3. $70 + 56 = 126$ or $7 \cdot 18 = 126$; *sample
answer:* I prefer the first way because mental
math is easier for me.
5. $3(4 + 7) = 3 \times 11 = 33$ or $3 \times 4 + 3 \times 7 = 12 + 21 = 33$ **7.** $6(8 + 1) = 6 \times 9 = 54$ or
$6 \times 8 + 6 \times 1 = 48 + 6 = 54$ **9.** $4(25 + 5) = 4 \times 30 = 120$ or $4 \times 25 + 4 \times 5 = 100 + 20 = 120$ **11.** $2(15 + 50) = 2 \times 65 = 130$ or
$2 \times 15 + 2 \times 50 = 30 + 100 = 130$ **13.** C, 36;
answers are the same. **15.** D, 56; answers are
the same. **17.** $5 \cdot 5 = 5 \cdot 4 + 5 \cdot 1; 25 = 20 + 5$
19. 144 **21.** 371 **23.** 4 **25.** 4
27. $60(70 + 2) = 4320$ ft^2 **29. a.** $410
b. $240 **31.** D **33.** C

Spiral Review, p. 92

1. No; *sample answer:* 5 ft east, 2 ft north,
2 ft west, 7 ft south, 4 ft west, 1 ft south, 8 ft east,
1 ft south **3.** 15 **5.** 40 **7.** three hundred
twenty-seven **9.** fifty-six thousand, four
hundred

2.7 Exercises, pp. 98–99

1. A **3.** 123_5 **5.** 0, 1, 2, 3, 4, 5 **7.** The digit 6
is not possible in base five. **9.** 78 **11.** 232
13. 624 **15.** 300_5 **17.** 1034_5 **19.** 2220_5
21. 9 **23.** 15 **25.** 17 **27.** 1011_2 **29.** 11111_2
31. 27 **33.** 62 **35.** C

Chapter 2 Review, pp. 101–103

1. six hundred eighty thousand, two hundred one
3. 5003 **5.** 246 **7.** 21 ft **9.** $5 \times 2 = 10$

11. 16 R2, $16\frac{1}{3}$ **13.** 9 R1, $9\frac{1}{3}$ **15.** 5 **17.** 1
19. $5(7) + 4$, \$39 **21.** 56 **23.** 4 **25.** 30
27. 111100_2; 220_5 **29.** 1011_2; 21_5

Chapter 3

3.1 Exercises, pp. 114–115

1. C **3.** A **5.** 678¢ **7.** 112 hundredths,
11.2 tenths, 1.12 ones **9.** 121 hundredths,
12.1 tenths, 1.21 ones **11.** *Sample answer:*
5.8 tenths; 58 hundredths **13.** ones **15.** tenths
17. 12.52 **19.** 500.03 **21.** 0.005
23. $(2 \times 10) + (3 \times 1) + (9 \times 0.1) + (3 \times 0.01) + (6 \times 0.001)$ **25.** true **27.** true
29. \$.57, 57¢ **31.** \$121.00, 12,100¢
33. 5000¢; 5000¢ is equal to \$50. **35.** A

3.2 Exercises, pp. 118–119

1. No; for example, there are 12 rather than
10 in. in a foot. **3.** mm **5.** m **7.** 10 **9.** B
11. D **13.** 1000 **15.** 0.25 **17.** mm
19. 40 mm by 20 mm; 120 mm
21. *Sample answer:* 10.5 dm **23.** *Sample
answer:* 6.5 m; a sewing pattern to make drapes
requires 6.5 m of fabric per pair of drapes.
25. *Sample answer:* 3.6 km; the average school
bus commute for students is 3.6 km. **27.** *Sample
answer:* 10 m; the high diving board at the pool is
10 m. **29.** = **31.** > **33.** > **35.** *Allosaurus*
is 5 times as long as *Orintholestes*.

Spiral Review, p. 120

1. one thousand, four hundred thirty-two **3.** nine
and fifty-five hundredths
5. $(2 \times 1000) + (1 \times 100) + (6 \times 10) + (7 \times 1)$
7. $(2 \times 10,000) + (4 \times 100) + (5 \times 10)$
9. $(3 \times 100,000) + (6 \times 1000) + (5 \times 100) + (2 \times 10)$ **11.** 14 **13.** 3 **15.** 10
17. 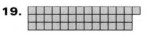 **19.**

21. $25 + 12 \cdot 45$; \$565

Using a Calculator, p. 121

1. 73.1 mm, 0.0731 m **3.** 9241 mm, 9.241 m
5. 45 in., 3.75 ft **7.** 86.4 in., 7.2 ft **9.** Metric;
you can convert by moving the decimal point.

3.3 Exercises, pp. 126–127

1. 27 hundredths **3.** 6 tenths

5.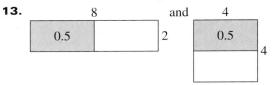

7. ○ ○ ○ ○ ○ **9.** a grid with 100 small squares
○ ○ ○ ○ ○

11. a number line with 10 parts

13.

8 and 4

| 0.5 | | 2 |

| 0.5 | | 4 |

15. $0.3 + 0.5 = 0.8$ **17.** Great Britain, 0.35; Italy, 0.25; Japan, 0.25; Australia, 0.1 **19.** C

3.4 Exercises, pp. 130–131

1. 0.56 **3.** 56% **5.** fifteen hundredths **7.** 0.5, 50%, $\frac{5}{10}$ **9.** 0.65, $\frac{65}{100}$, 65% **11.** $\frac{55}{100}$ **13.** $\frac{43}{100}$
15. $\frac{401}{1000}$ **17.** $\frac{49}{10,000}$ **19.** $\frac{39}{100}$ **21.** true
23. true **25.** false; $0.01 = 1\%$ **27.** true
29. 24% **31.** 85% **33.** 7% **35.** 60%
37. $\frac{35}{100}$, 35% **39.** $\frac{82}{100}$, 82% **41.** 20%
43. 70% **45.** D

Spiral Review, p. 132

1. 10 sandwiches **3.**

$$268 \atop \underline{-107} \atop 161$$

5. $4(7) = 28$ or $4(5) + 4(2) = 28$ **7.** $8(20) = 160$ or $8(9) + 8(11) = 160$ **9.** $7(11) = 77$ or $7(9) + 7(2) = 77$ **11.** cm **13.** 0.5

Mid-Chapter Assessment, p. 133

1.

2.

3.

4. 205 **5.** 0.30 **6.** 5.15 **7.** 560 **8.** m
9. 0.0123

10.

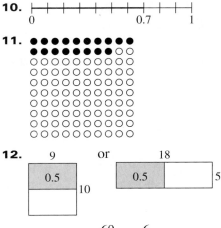

11.

12.

9 or 18

| 0.5 | | 10 |

| 0.5 | | 5 |

13. 0.6 or 0.60, $\frac{60}{100}$ or $\frac{6}{10}$, 60%

14. 0.29, $\frac{29}{100}$, 29% **15.** 0.74, $\frac{74}{100}$, 74%

16.

Event	Men's	Women's
High jump	2.45 m	2.09 m
Long jump	8.95 m	7.52 m
Discus	74.10 m	76.80 m

17. Discus **18.** VCR, 80%; Cellular phone, 50%; E-mail, 30%

3.5 Exercises, pp. 136–137

1. *A*, 1.6; *B*, 2.1; *C*, 1.1; *D*, 0.2; *E*, 0.8
3. *Sample answer:* 6.51, 6.56, 6.59 **5.** 0.02, 0.2, 0.25, 0.5, 2.5 **7.** 6.08, 6.12, 6.18, 6.8, 6.82
9. 0.026, 0.06, 0.126, 0.2, 0.26 **11.** 1.107, 1.69, 1.709, 1.76, 1.9 **13.** $>$ **15.** $<$ **17.** $=$
19. $=$ **21.** C, A, B, E, D **23.** C **25.** B
27. 0.2 **29.** 0.2, 0.23, 0.3 **31.** 917.2, 917.203, 917.22, 917.26, 917.267

3.6 Exercises, pp. 140–142

1. *Sample answer:* when determining interest earned in a bank account; when deciding how to divide a lunch bill among friends **3.** 4.524
5. 4.5 **7.** *Sample answer:* No; they must begin with the digit immediately to the right of the place they wish to round to. Since the hundredths' digit is a 4, round down to 6.3.
9.

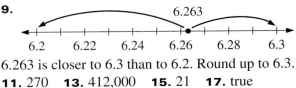

6.263 is closer to 6.3 than to 6.2. Round up to 6.3.
11. 270 **13.** 412,000 **15.** 21 **17.** true

19. false; 5.4 **21.** 22,000 **23.** 80 **25.** $25
27. $2 **29.** $95 **31.** $67 **33.** Penny, 0.7;
Nickel, 2.7; Dime, 1.6 **35.** 9; base **37.** 2; acid
39. 7; acid **41.** 14 **43.** 41 **45.** 7 **47.** 7
49. 6.4 **51.** 53.1° **53.** B

Spiral Review, p. 142

1. Lee, Chris, Pat; Lee, Pat, Chris; Chris, Pat,
Lee; Chris, Lee, Pat; Pat, Lee, Chris; Pat, Chris,
Lee **3.** 8 R1 or $8\frac{1}{4}$ **5.** 24 R4 or $24\frac{4}{9}$ **7.** 8
9. 12 **11.** 109 **13.** 27 **15.** 4.57 **17.** 10.050

3.7 Exercises, pp. 146–147

1. 22 **3.** 22^6 **5.** $(2 \times 10^3) + (9 \times 10^2) +$
$(9 \times 10) + (3 \times 1)$ **7.** 2 **9.** 3 **11.** 9 **13.** 2
15. 625 **17.** 729 **19.** 0.000001 or $\frac{1}{1,000,000}$
21. 12,167 **23.** 14,641 **25.** 43,046,721
27. 3,748,096 **29.** $(7 \times 10) + (5 \times 1)$
31. $(1 \times 10^3) + (3 \times 10)$ **33.** 49; 50
35. 2197; 2200 **37.** 8 cm **39.** 10 mm
41. 10^2 **43.** 27 **45.** 7 **47.** 84 people **49.** C

3.8 Exercises, pp. 150–151

1. 390 students **3.** 0.4, $\frac{4}{10}$, 40% **5.** 0.35, $\frac{35}{100}$, 35%
7. 0.6, $\frac{6}{10}$, 60% **9.** $9 **11.** 200 **13.** A: 20
students; B: 15 students; C: 10 students; D: 5
students **15.** Yes; 55% is greater than half, and
100 is half of 200. More than 100 people prefer
watching at home. **17.** A

Chapter 3 Review, pp. 153–155

1. fifteen and ninety-two hundredths
3. $(5 \times 10^2) + (4 \times 10) + (1 \times 1) + (9 \times 0.1) +$
(9×0.01) **5.** kilometers **7.** 5.2 **9.** 20 m,
2000 cm, 20,000 mm **11.** 0.8 **13.** $\frac{81}{100}$
15. 0.227 **17.** 10.54, 10.82, 10.94, 10.97, 11.06
19. 216 **21.** 79 **23.** 18 books

Chapters 1–3 Cumulative Review, pp. 158–159

1.

Figure	Perimeter	Area
1	4	1
2	6	2
3	8	3
4	10	4
5	12	5
6	14	6

The perimeters increase by 2 and the areas
increase by 1. **3.** No, all parallelograms have
4 sides. **5.** 26 **7.** 27 **9.** 6 **11.** 10, 70, 14, 8
13. 815 **15.** 57.5 **17.** small squares **19.** 25
21. $4(15) = 60$ or $4(9) + 4(6) = 60$
23. $7(20) = 140$ or $7(8) + 7(12) = 140$
25.

▲▲▲▲▲▲▲▲▲▲
▲▲▲▲▲▲▲▲▲▲
▲▲▲▲△△△△△△
△△△△△△△△△△
△△△△△△△△△△
△△△△△△△△△△
△△△△△△△△△△
△△△△△△△△△△
△△△△△△△△△△
△△△△△△△△△△

27. true **29.** false **31.** 6.9 **33.** 8000
35. Magic, 73%; Knicks, 57%; Heat, 51%;
Bullets, 48%; Celtics, 10% **37.** 0.1, 0.48, 0.51,
0.57, 0.73 **39.** 6 weeks

Chapter 4

4.1 Exercises, pp. 168–169

1.
$$\begin{array}{r} 2.45 \\ + 2.38 \\ \hline 4.83 \end{array}$$
3. *Sample answer:* $4.22 + 6.23 = 10.45$,
$5 + 5.45, 7.10 + 3.35$
5.
$$\begin{array}{r} 1.23 \\ + 0.36 \\ \hline 1.59 \end{array}$$
7. 9.36 **9.** 16.75
11.
$$\begin{array}{r} 6.07 \\ + 3.84 \\ \hline 9.91 \end{array}$$
13.
$$\begin{array}{r} 4.20 \\ + 2.1 \\ \hline 6.3 \end{array}$$
15. 31 **17.** 18.94 m
19. 122.312; 123.423; 124.534; the first number
increases by 1.111. The second number is always
94.3. The answer increases by 1.111. The next
two problems are $31.345 + 94.3 = 125.645$ and
$32.456 + 94.3 = 126.756$. **21.** 1st row: 22.18;
2nd row: 14.26, 7.92; 3rd row: 8.92, 5.34, 2.58;
4th row: 4.52, 4.4, 0.94, 1.64 **23.** 3.02

4.2 Exercises, pp. 172–173

1. $2.45 - 2.38 = 0.07$ **3.** correct; 0.15
5.
$$\begin{array}{r} 1.01 \\ - 0.34 \\ \hline 0.67 \end{array}$$
7. B; 1.19 **9.** 2.69% **11.** 4.45
13. 3.819 **15.** 2.11 **17.** 0.49 **19.** 3.302

21. 5.697 **23.** Pacific; East Central; 15.7 gallons per person **25.** *Sample answer:* People drink more water in the Southwest because the climate is sunnier and drier than in the Northeast. **27.** yes; $18.74 + \$.01 = \$18.75, \$18.75 + \$.25 = \$19.00, \$19.00 + \$1.00 = \$20.00$

Spiral Review, p. 174

1. $\frac{1}{12}, \frac{1}{15}, \frac{1}{18}$; the numerator is always 1. The denominator increases by 3.

3.
$$\begin{array}{r} 469 \\ + 135 \\ \hline 604 \end{array}$$
5.
$$\begin{array}{r} 89 \\ \times\ 2 \\ \hline 178 \end{array}$$

7. three thousand two hundred twelve
9. 170 **11.** 125 blocks; 5^3

Using a Calculator, p. 175

1. 2 milks @ \$0.89 each = \$1.78; 2 ice teas @ \$1.45 each = \$2.90; total bill = \$25.97

4.3 Exercises, pp. 178–179

1. rounding and front-end estimation; *sample answer:* rounding: to estimate the cost of buying several items at a store to make sure you have enough money; front-end estimation: if you make \$2.25 per hour gardening, you will make at least \$8 if you work for 4 hours. **3.** 13.02 **5.** 60 **7.** 700 **9.** 100 **11.** 9300 **13.** 2900 **15.** \$25.00; \$25.50 **17.** \$12.00; \$12.50 **19.** \$9.00; \$8.00 **21.** 300; 440 **23.** 0; 60 **25.** 1000; 1700 **27.** ≈9 units **29.** ≈5 units or 4.5 units **31.** 3 sets **33.** D

4.4 Exercises, pp. 184–185

1. 3 **3.** 6 **5.** 176 **7.** C; since $52 \times 2 = 104$, the product 122.2 (C) is closest. Also, the product should have 2 decimal places; however, the last place is a 0 ($2 \times 5 = 0$) and therefore does not appear. **9.** B; since $5 \times 0.2 = 1$, the product 1.222 is closest to the estimate. **11.** 10.25 **13.** 16.1001 **15.** 400; 1000; 1600; 1800; 1900; 1980; the product gets closer to 2000. **17.** 3 **19.** 3.77 mm^2 **21.** 0.80064 cm^2 **23.** 1.43787 **25.** 0.6176 **27.** 0.299268 **29.** 72.7824 **31.** 10.16 cm **33.** 1.016 cm **35.** 50.8 cm **37.** 30.48 cm **39.** $0.3 \times 6 = 1.8$ **41.** $0.48 \times 6.75 = 3.24$ **43.** $0.43 \times 9.5 = 4.085$ **45.** \$683.60 **47.** C **49.** B

Spiral Review, p. 186

1. 18 **3.** 10 **5.** $27 - (9 - 4) + 2 = 24$ **7.** $12 \div (6 + 6) \times 7 = 7$ **9.** 9.4, 9.45, 9.5, 9.54 **11.** 3 **13.** 5 **15.**   **17.** 57; 93

Mid-Chapter Assessment, p. 187

1. 9.23 **2.** \$4.43 **3.** 3.95 **4.** 9.18 **5.** 11.62 **6.** \$24.27 **7.** \$11; rounding **8.** 26,000; front-end or rounding **9.** \$29.00; rounding **10.** 3.5 **11.** 4.56 **12.** 35.90 **13.** 3.06 **14.** 0.54 **15.** 0.05 **16.** 12.57 **17.** 33.6 **18.** 36.48 **19.** $0.8 \times 75 = 60$ **20.** $0.5 \times 37 = 18.5$ **21.** $0.35 \times 46 = 16.10$ **22.** about \$7; ice cream **23.** lasagna, garden salad, soda and pie; Guess, check, and revise **24.** \$11.67

4.5 Exercises, pp. 190–191

1. $3.42 \div 3 = 1.14$ **3.** *Sample answer:* Line up the decimal places in the quotient with the decimal places in the dividend. Use the same steps you would use for long division with whole numbers. **5.** about 3; 3.25 **7.** about 1; 1.15 **9.** $3.9 \div 3 = 1.3$ **11.** 5.8 **13.** 4.78 **15.** 3 **17.** The quotient is halved. **19.** never; $0.9 \div 2 = 0.45$ **21.** \$1.45 per week **23.** books **25.** D

4.6 Exercises, pp. 194–195

1. Move the decimal point the same number of places as there are 0's. Move right when multiplying, move left when dividing. *Sample answer:* $4.3 \times 100 = 430$; move decimal point 2 places to the right. $39.6 \div 1000 = 0.0396$; move decimal point 3 places to the left. **3.** 4.2 **5.** 1.7 **7.** 9000 **9.** 230 **11.** 23.7 **13.** 1200 **15.** 110,000 **17.** 0.004 **19.** 79.9 **21.** 0.462 **23.** 0.52 **25.** 18,000 **27.** 250 **29.** 40 **31.** 10 **33.** 518 **35.** 1000 **37.** > **39.** < **41.** < **43.** 6.4 acres **45. a.** 50,000,000,000,000 **b.** 100,000,000,000; 0.2% **47.** C

Spiral Review, p. 196

1. 52 **3.** 6% **5.** − **7.** < **9.** 64 **11.** 216

4.7 Exercises, pp. 202–203

1. "Quotient" should read "divisor." **3.** 22
5. 220 **7.** 10 **9.** 100 **11.** 13 **13.** 15.7
15. 11.25 **17.** 1570 **19.** 2000 **21.** 219
23. 4.5 m **25.** carrot: 15.6 lb; cucumber:
20.2 lb; onion: 12.4 lb; radish: 38.2 lb; pumpkin:
997.8 lb; zucchini: 65.1 lb **27.** 20; 200
29. $5.38/m **31.** $8.07/m **33.** C

4.8 Exercises, pp. 206–207

1. B **3.** A **5.** 30 **7.** 24 **9.** 36 **11.** $15;
$22.50 **13.** $1; $5 **15.** 5,000,000
17. 500,000 **19.** 54 **21.** 33 **23.** 852,390
25. 768,180 **27.** A

Chapter 4 Review, pp. 209–211

1. $1.80 **3.** $.96 **5.** $38.50; $38.00 **7.** $12;
$11 **9.** $360.50; $360.00 **11.** yes **13.** 55.822
15. 78 **17.** pigeon: 1.61 km/min; butterfly:
0.54 km/min; honeybee: 0.27 km/min
19. 27,500 **21.** $3.17 **23.** 36.125 **25.** 42.6
27. 18.4 **29.** $6.60 **31.** set size 100: $11.50;
set size 500: $50.43; set size 1000: $91.25

Chapter 5

5.1 Exercises, pp. 222–223

1. A **3.** B
5.

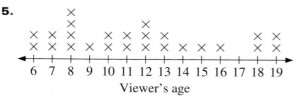

Viewer's age

7.

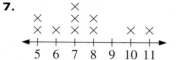

most common: 7; smallest: 5; largest: 11; range: 6

9.

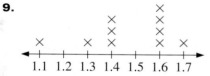

most common: 1.6; smallest: 1.1; largest: 1.7;
range: 0.6

11. *Sample answer:* Meat-eating mammals
probably have a tooth on the left for each one on
the right side of the mouth. **13.** 3, 4 **15.** 3
17. D

5.2 Exercises, pp. 226–227

1. The "stem" of a piece of data is the leftmost
digit. The "leaf" is any remaining digits to the
right of the stem. **3.** 7.1, 7.2, 7.7, 8.2, 8.5, 8.6,
8.8, 8.9, 9.0, 9.3, 9.4, 9.4, 9.8 **5.** B
7. 3, 4, and 5
9.

0	2 3 5 9
1	0 5 6 7
2	3 4
3	0 1 1 4 8 9
4	2
5	6 9 9

11. Record High December Temps (°F), by State

6	8 9
7	0 3 4 4 4 5 7
8	0 1 3 3 4 5 5
9	0 4

Key: 7 | 3 = 73
13. 74°F **15.** C

Spiral Review, p. 228

1. $5 + n = 27$; 22 **3.** $(3 \times 1000) + (2 \times 100) +$
(5×1) **5.** $(8 \times 1) + (2 \times 0.1) + (5 \times 0.01)$
7. 4.4 m **9.** 1.25 m **11.** $\frac{54}{100} = \frac{27}{50}$ **13.** $\frac{87}{100}$
15. $8.75; $26.24

5.3 Exercises, pp. 234–235

1. 7 **3.** 33 **5.** 6.2 **7.** 8 **9.** 6 **11.** 36
13. 54 **15.** 93 **17.** 190 **19.** 30 **21.** *Sample
answer:* 2, 5, 10, 15, 18; the five numbers must
have a sum of 50, because 50 divided by 5 yields
a mean of 10. **23.** 132 visitors; 153 visitors
25. B

5.4 Exercises, pp. 238–239

1. range: 142; median: 50; mode: 70; mean: 55.8
3. False; there is no mode. **5.** median: 46.5;
mode: 45 **7.** median: 12; modes: 11, 12 **9.** B
11. range: 251; median: 143; mode: 111
13. *Sample answer:* the median; because this is
the "middle" length **15.** 23, 25, 26, 28, 28

17. mean: 26; median: 23.5; modes: 20 and 40; *sample answer:* the mode is not the best measure because there are two modes that are far apart.
19. B

Spiral Review, p. 240

1. 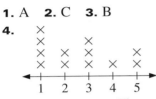 **3.**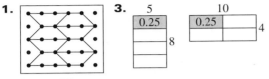

5. 2 **7.** 65

Mid-Chapter Assessment, p. 241

1. A **2.** C **3.** B

4.
```
  ×
  ×       ×
  ×  ×  ×       ×
  ×  ×  ×  ×  ×
  ┼──┼──┼──┼──┼─
  1  2  3  4  5
```

5. *Sample answer:* The most common number of wins is 1, and the range of the data is 4. **6.** 1; of teams that have won at least one Super Bowl, more have won only 1 than 2, 3, 4, or 5 games.

7. Margin of Victory in Super Bowl Games

```
0 | 1 3 4 4 4 5 7 9
1 | 0 0 0 2 3 4 6 7 7 7 7 8 9 9
2 | 1 2 3 5 9
3 | 2 5 6
4 | 5
Key: 4 | 5 = 45
```

1, 3, 4, 4, 4, 5, 7, 9, 10, 10, 10, 12, 13, 14, 16, 17, 17, 17, 17, 18, 19, 19, 21, 22, 23, 25, 29, 32, 35, 36, 45

8. 49ers **9.** Giants; they won by only one point.
10. 44 **11.** 28 **12.** 74 **13.** mean: 15.875, median: 12; mode: 10; *sample answer:* The median best describes the data because it is in the middle of the values.

5.5 Exercises, 244–245

1. *Sample answer:* 10's **3.** false **5.** The bars are different widths. **7.** A **9.** B

11. *Sample answer:*

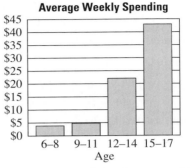

13. A bar graph is a better tool because a line plot would require over 3000 Xs, which would be difficult to draw and to read.

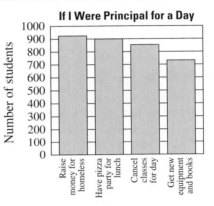

5.6 Exercises, pp. 248–249

1. The scale from one year to the next is not uniform. **3.** Yes; the line always slopes upward from left to right. **5.** *Sample answer:* 20

7.

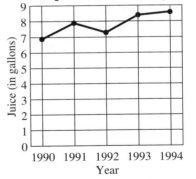

9. *Sample answers:* New car sales deceased from 1989 to 1991, then increased yearly until 1994, and dropped off in 1995. Used car sales were steady, around $30 million, from 1989–1991. From 1991–1995, sales steadily increased by $5 to $10 million per year.

11. *Sample answers:* possibly, because the sales of used cars are increasing while new car sales are decreasing; or, no, because more people will always prefer to buy new cars **13.** D

Spiral Review, p. 250

1. 12 **3.** 18 **5.** 34.5 **7.** 3.8 **9.** 2 **11.** 27
13. 14.32 **15.** 8.77 **17.** false; 0.048 **19.** true
21. Number of States Visited by 20 Students

```
0 | 1 2 3 5 6 6 8 9
1 | 1 3 4 4 5 8
2 | 0 2 7
3 | 1 8
4 | 0
```
Key: 3 | 1 = 31

1, 2, 3, 5, 6, 6, 8, 9, 11, 13, 14, 14, 15, 18, 20, 22, 27, 31, 38, 40

5.7 Exercises, pp. 254–255

1. misleading, symbols have different sizes
3. misleading, no key included **5.** line plot; *sample answer:* ages of the members of a youth basketball team **7.** D **9.** A **11.** C
13.

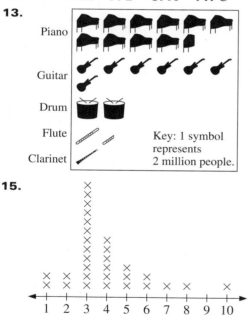

15.

A line plot will work. A stem-and-leaf plot will not work because nearly all the data are single digits.

17. Stem-and-leaf plot:
Average Daily High Temperature (°F)
for Baltimore, MD

```
4 | 0 4 5
5 | 4 6
6 | 4 7
7 | 4 9
8 | 3 5 7
```
Key: 8 | 3 = 83
Line graph:

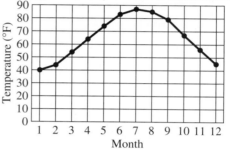

Average Daily Temperatures for Baltimore, MD

Chapter 5 Review, pp. 257–259

1.

3. 34 **5.** 35 **7.** 0.995
9.

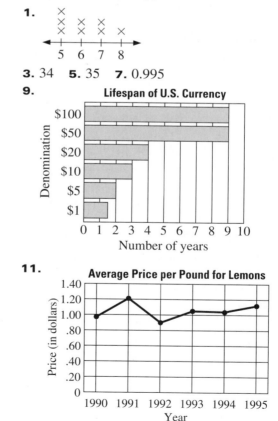

Lifespan of U.S. Currency

11.

Average Price per Pound for Lemons

1990–1991

Chapter 6

6.1 Exercises, pp. 270–271

1. No; the triangles are not all the same size.

3. mixed number   **5.** C   **7.** B   **9.** yes; $\frac{2}{3}$

11. yes; $\frac{4}{8}$ **13.** yes; $\frac{2}{10}$

15.
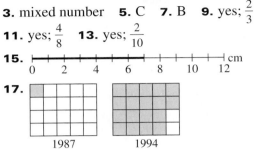

17.

1987   1994

19. the second litter   **21.** the second group

23. D

6.2 Exercises, pp. 276–277

1. Cut each sandwich into 5 pieces and divide the pieces equally among the 4 people; $\frac{4}{5}$.   **3.** $\frac{7}{4}$

5. 24 coins   **7.** $\frac{3}{5}$ **9.** $\frac{2}{4}$ dollar   **11.** $\frac{8}{6}$ pies

13. *Sample answer:* the ratio of the distance from your town to each of two nearby cities

15. *Sample answer:* the ratio of the width to the length of your house   **17.** $\frac{12}{25}$ **19.** $\frac{8}{12}$ **21.** $\frac{40}{41}$

6.3 Exercises, pp. 280–281

1. *Sample answer:* $\frac{3}{5}, \frac{12}{20}$

3.

5. yes, $\frac{1}{6} = \frac{1 \cdot 2}{6 \cdot 2} = \frac{2}{12}$ **7.** yes, $\frac{5}{8} = \frac{5 \cdot 3}{8 \cdot 3} = \frac{15}{24}$

9. $\frac{2}{3} = \frac{2 \cdot 2}{3 \cdot 2} = \frac{4}{6}$ or $\frac{2}{3} = \frac{2 \cdot 3}{3 \cdot 3} = \frac{6}{9}$ **11.** C; *sample answer:* $\frac{16}{28}$ **13.** A; *sample answer:* $\frac{6}{8}$ **15.** 1

17. 42   **19.** *Sample answer:* $\frac{8}{22}, \frac{12}{33}, \frac{16}{44}$

21. *Sample answer:* $\frac{1}{9}, \frac{8}{72}, \frac{12}{108}$ **23.** true

25. science, 6; English, 8; computer science, 4; math, 6   **27.** 4 students   **29.** Yes; Mark types $\frac{6 \text{ pages}}{36 \text{ min}} = \frac{1}{6}$ page per minute. Melissa types $\frac{5 \text{ pages}}{30 \text{ min}} = \frac{1}{6}$ page per minute.   **31.** C

6.4 Exercises, pp. 284–285

1. C   **3.** B   **5.** $\frac{3}{7}, \frac{9}{21}, \frac{6}{14}; \frac{3}{7}$ **7.** 12   **9.** $\frac{4}{16}; \frac{1}{4}$

11. $\frac{3}{8}; \frac{3}{8}$ **13.** not possible   **15.** 1   **17.** 7

19. $\frac{5}{8}$ **21.** not possible   **23.** not possible

25. False; these are not equivalent fractions.

27. 30   **29.** 8   **31.** 12   **33.** $\frac{28}{8} = \frac{7}{x}$; 2

35. No; $\frac{100}{5}$ and $\frac{150}{8}$ are not equivalent fractions.

37. D

Spiral Review, p. 286

1.

3. 20 tiles   **5.** 1.35   **7.** $\frac{8}{12}$ **9.** $\frac{2}{3}$ **11.** 0.49

13. 0.7

Mid-Chapter Assessment, p. 287

1. A   **2.** C   **3.** D   **4.** B   **5.** $\frac{2}{3}$ cake

6. $\frac{8}{5}$ pizzas   **7.** $\frac{6}{10}$ **8.** $\frac{3}{5}$ **9.** $\frac{9}{15}$ **10.** Yes; $\frac{6}{10}$, $\frac{3}{5}$, and $\frac{9}{15}$ are all equivalent fractions.   **11.** ratio; *sample answer:* the ratio of the width to the length of a patio   **12.** rate; *sample answer:* your driving speed on a local road   **13.** ratio; *sample answer:* the ratio of horses in stable A to horses in stable B   **14.** $\frac{5}{28}$ **15.** $\frac{5}{7}$ **16.** $\frac{2}{6}$ **17.** 8 ft

18. 1   **19.** 50   **20.** 45

6.5 Exercises, pp. 292–294

1. *Sample answer:* Use rectangular models, find equivalent fractions with the same denominator, or convert to a decimal. I like using the rectangular models. They help me visualize the solution.

3.

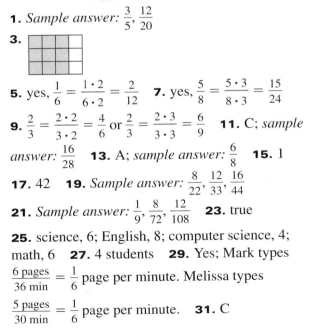

Model for $\frac{1}{5}$ Model for $\frac{1}{6}$

$\frac{1}{5}$ has six squares, so it is greater than $\frac{1}{6}$ with only 5 squares. Looking at the unshaded parts, you see that $\frac{4}{5}$ has 24 squares, which is less than the 25 squares of $\frac{5}{6}$. So, $\frac{5}{6} > \frac{4}{5}$.

5. $\frac{1}{3} < \frac{1}{2}, \frac{3}{4} > \frac{1}{2}; \frac{3}{4}$ **7.** $\frac{5}{6}, \frac{4}{5}; \frac{5}{6}$ **9.** $\frac{3}{4}$ **11.** $\frac{4}{6}$
13. $\frac{3}{10}, \frac{2}{5}, \frac{5}{10}, \frac{4}{5}$ **15.** $\frac{1}{10}, \frac{1}{2}, \frac{6}{10}, \frac{4}{5}$ **17.** $>$
19. $>$ **21.** *Sample answer:* $\frac{9}{10}$
23. *Sample answer:* $\frac{1}{2}$ **25.** *Sample answer:* $\frac{1}{3}$
27. *Sample answer:* $\frac{4}{10}$
29. $\frac{1}{7}$; fractions with the same numerator decrease as the denominators increase.   **31.** $\frac{3}{4}$
33. $\frac{7}{12}, \frac{4}{6}, \frac{3}{4}$ **35.** greater   **37.** A

Spiral Review, p. 294

1. 24 meals   **3.** 1   **5.** 121   **7.** 58.56   **9.** $\frac{6}{10}; \frac{3}{5}$
11. $\frac{150}{100}; \frac{3}{2}$ **13.** 8.3, 8.32, 8.35, 8.45, 8.53
15. 2.01, 2.015, 2.05, 2.105, 2.15

Using a Calculator, p. 295

1. $\frac{8}{11}$; thousandths   **3.** $\frac{3}{22}$; thousandths   **5.** $\frac{11}{19}$; thousandths   **7.** $\frac{9}{23}$; hundredths   **9.** yes, the decimal displays are the same. $0.\overline{7} = 0.\overline{7}$
11. Yes, the decimal displays are the same. $0.857 = 0.857$ **13.** Your friend's; using decimals to compare, $\frac{17}{31} > \frac{16}{37}$.

6.6 Exercises, pp. 298–299

1. *Sample answer:* It is greater than or equal to one.   **3.** $\frac{7}{2}$ **5.** $5\frac{2}{3}$ **7.** always   **9.** sometimes
11. $2\frac{4}{6}; \frac{16}{6}$ **13.** D   **15.** C   **17.** $1\frac{5}{9}$ **19.** $3\frac{1}{2}$
21. $1\frac{3}{8}$ **23.** $4\frac{5}{6}$ **25.** $\frac{7}{4}$ **27.** $\frac{11}{3}$ **29.** $\frac{13}{6}$
31. $\frac{23}{6}$ **33.** $3\frac{1}{3}$ h; mixed number, as it is easier to understand   **35.** B

Spiral Review, p. 300

1. $30   **3.** 1.4 in.   **5.** 7¢

6.7 Exercises, pp. 304–305

1. $\frac{3}{10}$ **3.** $\frac{1}{2}$ **5.** Yes; a number must be either odd or even. So, the probability of not odd is the same as that for even.   **7.** C   **11.** $\frac{1}{3}$ **13.** $\frac{3}{10}$
15. B   **17.** C   **19.** $\frac{1}{4}$; 0.25   **21.** $\frac{1}{2}$ **23.** C

Chapter 6 Review, pp. 307–309

1. $\frac{19}{8}; 2\frac{3}{8}$ **3.** $\frac{3}{7}$ **5.** $4   **7.** $\frac{5}{4}$, or $1\frac{1}{4}$ oranges
9. *Sample answer:* $\frac{12}{14}, \frac{18}{21}, \frac{24}{28}$ **11.** $\frac{1}{3}$ ft
13. $.36   **15.** $\frac{1}{2}, \frac{2}{3}, \frac{5}{6}$ **17.** ; $\frac{11}{6}$
19. $\frac{8}{16}$ or $\frac{1}{2}$ **21.** 1

Chapters 1–6 Cumulative Review, pp. 312–313

1. 12   **3.** 5   **5.** 3   **7.** 3   **9.** 16   **11.** 27
13. 1.39   **15.** $\frac{16}{24}$ **17.** 70   **19.** 48   **21.** 14
23. 0.01, 0.011, 0.02, 0.1, 0.11   **25.** $\frac{1}{2}, \frac{4}{7}, \frac{2}{3}, \frac{4}{5}$
27. 1600   **29.** 15   **31.** 7.85   **33.** 8.5
35. 6, 14, 14; 14
39. Average Maximum Weights (in pounds) of Breeds of Sporting Dogs

```
2 | 8
3 | 4
4 | 0 0 5 5 5
5 | 0 0 5
6 | 0 5 5
7 | 0 0 0 5 5 5 5
8 | 0 0 0 0 5
Key: 2 | 8 = 28
```

41. 28 lb   **43.** 27%   **45.** *Sample answer:* line graph; it should enable you to see the changes in the number of cellular phones over the years.
47. 12 calls

Chapter 7

7.1 Exercises, pp. 320–321

1. $\frac{3}{4}$ in.   **3.** $\frac{1}{8}, \frac{2}{8}, \frac{3}{8}, \frac{4}{8}, \frac{5}{8}, \frac{6}{8}, \frac{7}{8}, \frac{8}{8}$; each number increases by $\frac{1}{8}$.   **5.** 2   **7.** $2\frac{5}{8}$ in.; C   **9.** $4\frac{1}{2}$ in.; E
11. $1\frac{1}{8}$ in.; A   **13.** $\frac{7}{8}$ in.   **15.** *Sample answer:* a kitchen table   **17.** *Sample answer:* a desk
19. 6′3″   **21.** $4′5\frac{1}{2}″$ **23.** 3   **25.** 180   **27.** 18
29. 23 yd   **31.** $7\frac{3}{8}$ in.   **33.** D

7.2 Exercises, pp. 324–325

1. C; this model represents $\frac{1}{4}$.   **3.** False; 15 is also a common multiple and it is less than 30.

5. False; for example, 4 is the least common multiple of 2 and 4 not 8.

7. multiples of 5: 5, 10, 15, 20, 25, 30, 35, 40, 45, 50; multiples of 8: 8, 16, 24, 32, 40, 48, 56, 64, 72, 80; least common multiple: 40 **9.** multiples of 5: 5, 10, 15, 20, 25, 30, 35, 40, 45, 50; multiples of 6: 6, 12, 18, 24, 30, 36, 42, 48, 54, 60; least common multiple: 30

11. **13.**

15. $12; \frac{4}{12}, \frac{11}{12}$ **17.** $30; \frac{5}{30}, \frac{21}{30}$ **19.** $\frac{1}{12}\left(\frac{2}{24}\right)$, $\frac{1}{6}\left(\frac{4}{24}\right), \frac{3}{8}\left(\frac{9}{24}\right), \frac{5}{12}\left(\frac{10}{24}\right), \frac{2}{3}\left(\frac{16}{24}\right), \frac{5}{6}\left(\frac{20}{24}\right), \frac{7}{8}\left(\frac{21}{24}\right)$, $\frac{11}{12}\left(\frac{22}{24}\right)$; WELL DONE **21.** $\frac{4}{10}, \frac{3}{10}, \frac{3}{10}$

23. $\frac{3}{12}$, or $\frac{1}{4}$ **25.** B

Spiral Review, p. 326

1. a. $(3 \times 0.75) + (4 \times 0.25) + (2 \times 0.5)$
b. $4.25 **3.** = **5.** < **7.** 12.46 **9.** 1.68
11. 1000 **13.** 10,000 **15.** 12 black pens

Using a Calculator, p. 327

1. B **3.** A **5.** 7 **7.** 20 **9.** 6
11. 2213.4 tons, or 4,426,800 lb

7.3 Exercises, pp. 332–333

1. always; *sample answer:* $\frac{3}{7} - \frac{1}{7} = \frac{2}{7}$

3. sometimes; *sample answer:* The least common denominator of $\frac{1}{3}$ and $\frac{1}{5}$ is 15 and of $\frac{1}{4}$ and $\frac{1}{2}$ is 4.

5. a. Numerators were not multiplied by same factor as denominators; $\frac{1}{3} + \frac{3}{5} = \frac{1 \cdot 5}{3 \cdot 5} + \frac{3 \cdot 3}{5 \cdot 3} = \frac{5}{15} + \frac{9}{15} = \frac{14}{15}.$ **b.** Denominators were added; $\frac{2}{3} + \frac{1}{6} = \frac{4}{6} + \frac{1}{6} = \frac{5}{6}.$

7. ;

$\frac{2}{4} - \frac{2}{6} = \frac{1}{6}$ **9.** $\frac{2}{20}$, or $\frac{1}{10}$ **11.** $\frac{16}{10}$, or $1\frac{3}{5}$ **13.** $\frac{8}{21}$

15. *Sample answer:* $\frac{3}{10}$ **17.** *Sample answer:* $\frac{1}{8}$, $\frac{1}{8}$ **19.** *Sample answer:* $\frac{1}{6}$ **21.** $\frac{25}{12}$, or $2\frac{1}{12}$ yd

23. $\frac{3}{4}$; no **25.** 1; yes

7.4 Exercises, pp. 338–339

1. sum: $8\frac{7}{8}$ in.; difference: $2\frac{3}{8}$ in. **3.** Rewrite fractions with common denominator. Subtract fractions. Then subtract whole numbers. Simplify fraction. **5.** C **7.** A **9.** $6\frac{8}{9} - 2\frac{4}{9}; 4\frac{4}{9}$

11. $3\frac{6}{8} + 1\frac{1}{2}; 5\frac{1}{4}$ **13.** $3\frac{1}{2}$ **15.** $11\frac{1}{5}$ **17.** $4\frac{1}{15}$

19. $9\frac{19}{24}$ **21.** 6 **23.** $1\frac{2}{8}$, or $1\frac{1}{4}$ **25.** $\frac{1}{5}$ **27.** $1\frac{6}{8}$; $1\frac{5}{8}$; $1\frac{4}{8}$; as the number being subtracted increases by $\frac{1}{8}$, the difference decreases by $\frac{1}{8}$. **29.** $8\frac{1}{5}$; $8\frac{2}{5}$; $8\frac{3}{5}$; as the number being subtracted decreases by $\frac{1}{5}$, the difference increases by $\frac{1}{5}$. **31.** $3\frac{3}{5}$ and $2\frac{1}{5}$

33. C

Spiral Review, p. 340

1. 120 ways **3.** array of 100 triangles **5.** 106
7. 86 **9.** $\frac{1}{2}$ **11.** $\frac{1}{5}$ **13.** $\frac{37}{9}$ **15.** $\frac{67}{10}$

Mid-Chapter Assessment, p. 341

1. $1\frac{7}{8}$ in., $\frac{15}{8}$ in. **2.** $2\frac{1}{8}$ in.; $\frac{17}{8}$ in. **3.** 76 in.
4. no **5.** yes **6.** no **7.** yes **8.** E **9.** C
10. D **11.** A **12.** F **13.** B **14.** 1 **15.** $\frac{4}{15}$
16. $\frac{7}{18}$ **17.** $\frac{11}{12}$ **18.** 1 **19.** $\frac{3}{8}$ **20.** 6 **21.** $7\frac{1}{2}$
22. $4\frac{3}{5}$ **23.** She lost $\frac{1}{5} + \frac{1}{4} = \frac{9}{20}$, which is less than half of her baby teeth.

7.5 Exercises, pp. 344–345

1. B **3.** A **5.** $2\frac{3}{4}$ yd^2 **7.** 8 **9.** 5 **11.** =
13. < **15.** $14\frac{2}{3}$ yd **17.** $2\frac{5}{12}$ **19.** $1\frac{4}{5}$ **21.** $1\frac{8}{9}$
23. $2\frac{3}{5}$ **25.** $2\frac{1}{3}$ h **27.** $3\frac{1}{3}$ h **29.** A

7.6 Exercises, pp. 350–351

1. Rename; the denominators are different; $2\frac{5}{12}$.

3. Rename; the denominators are different; $1\frac{1}{4}$.

5. D, B, C, A **7.** C **9.** A **11.** $2\frac{19}{24}$ **13.** $2\frac{13}{24}$
15. $11\frac{7}{15}$ **17.** $4\frac{5}{6}$ **19.** $1\frac{87}{100}$ mi **21.** $\frac{18}{25}$ mi
23. $2\frac{1}{2}$ in. **25.** D

Spiral Review, p. 352

1. red: 0.6, $\frac{3}{5}$, 60%; green: 0.25, $\frac{1}{4}$, 25%; blue: 0.1, $\frac{1}{10}$, 10%; purple: 0.05, $\frac{1}{20}$, 5% **3.** 4
5. 18 **7.** 15 **9.** 4 R2 or $4\frac{2}{7}$

7.7 Exercises, pp. 356–357

1. C **3.** A **5.** remaining teams; $\frac{3}{10}=\frac{6}{20}$ $\frac{1}{4}=\frac{5}{20}$

7. 1; the circle represents a whole so its parts must have a sum of 1. **9.** $54\frac{1}{8}$ dollars per share
11. American quarter horses: 59 in.; thoroughbreds: 64 in. **13.** 5 in. **15.** B

Chapter 7 Review, pp. 359–361

1. $1\frac{1}{8}$ in. **3.** 2 ft 3 in. **5.** 2 ft 10 in. **7.** $\frac{20}{28}$, $\frac{21}{28}$
9. $\frac{11}{12}$, $\frac{4}{12}$ **11.** $6\frac{6}{7}$ **13.** $3\frac{4}{9}$ **15.** $8\frac{2}{9}$ **17.** $\frac{1}{3}$ h
19. $2\frac{3}{4}$ in. **21.** $\frac{1}{4}$; it is $\frac{3}{40}$ more.

Chapter 8

8.1 Exercises, pp. 372–373

1. $2 \times \frac{5}{6}$; $\frac{5}{3}$, or $1\frac{2}{3}$ **3.** Yes; *sample answer:* Both are equal to $\frac{30}{7}$. **5.** 8 **7.** $\frac{2}{3} \times 4 = \frac{8}{3}$, or $2\frac{2}{3}$
9. $\frac{2}{3}$ **11.** $\frac{4}{3}$, or $1\frac{1}{3}$ **13.** $\frac{24}{11}$, or $2\frac{2}{11}$ **15.** 6
17. 4 **19.** *G* **21.** *E* **23.** *J* **25.** *Sample answer:* $\frac{5}{6} \times 5$; $4\frac{1}{6}$ **27.** *Sample answer:* $\frac{1}{9} \times 9$
29. salmon: 24 in.; trout: 14 in.

8.2 Exercises, pp. 378–379

1. $\frac{3}{8}$ cup **3.** $\frac{9}{20}$ **5.** *Sample answer:* The denominator of the solution should be the product of the denominators of the two factors: $\frac{8}{9} \times \frac{2}{9} = \frac{16}{81}$.
7. C; $\frac{5}{12}$ **9.** B; $\frac{21}{50}$ **11.** $\frac{7}{48}$ **13.** $\frac{8}{27}$ **15.** $\frac{3}{20}$
17. $\frac{1}{4}$ **19.** 4 **21.** 7 **23.** $\frac{8}{15}$;

25. *Sample answer:* $\frac{1}{3}$ and $\frac{8}{15}$; $\frac{2}{3}$ and $\frac{4}{15}$; $\frac{4}{9}$ and $\frac{2}{5}$; $\frac{2}{9}$ and $\frac{4}{5}$; find two fractions so that the product of the numerators is 8 and the product of the denominators is 45. **27.** $\frac{1}{12}$ ft
29. Multiply the number of feet times 12.

Egg Type	ft	in.
ostrich	$\frac{1}{2}$	6
chickadee	$\frac{1}{24}$	$\frac{1}{2}$
blue jay	$\frac{1}{12}$	1
bald eagle	$\frac{1}{4}$	3

Spiral Review, p. 380

1. 39.5 mi/h **3.** 16.65 **5.** 60 **7.** 1 **9.** 28
11. $\frac{5}{3}$, or $1\frac{2}{3}$ **13.** $\frac{1}{4}$

Using a Calculator, p. 381

1. 0.25 **3.** 1 **5.** 1.125 **7.** 1.25 **9.** The friend left out the parentheses. The problem should be entered as $(1 + 1 \div 2) \times (1 \div 2) = 0.75$.

8.3 Exercises, pp. 386–387

1. $3\frac{1}{3} \times 2\frac{1}{2} = \frac{10}{3} \times \frac{5}{2} = \frac{50}{6} = \frac{25}{3}$, or $8\frac{1}{3}$
3. *Sample answer:* The mixed numbers need to be written as the improper fractions $\frac{8}{3}$ and $\frac{19}{5}$ before multiplying. This gives $\frac{152}{15}$, or $10\frac{2}{15}$. **5.** $2\frac{2}{3}$ h, or 2 h 40 min **7.** $2\frac{1}{2} \times 2\frac{1}{2} = \frac{25}{4}$, or $6\frac{1}{4}$ **9.** $\frac{27}{4}$, or $6\frac{3}{4}$ **11.** $\frac{6}{7}$ **13.** 16 **15.** $\frac{33}{4}$, or $8\frac{1}{4}$ **17.** $\frac{65}{27}$ yd², or $2\frac{11}{27}$ yd² **19.** $\frac{3}{2}$ mi², or $1\frac{1}{2}$ mi² **21.** $10\frac{1}{2}$, 14, $17\frac{1}{2}$; you add $3\frac{1}{2}$ to find the next answer. The next two problems are $3\frac{1}{2} \times 6 = 21$ and $3\frac{1}{2} \times 7 = 24\frac{1}{2}$.
23. $1\frac{1}{2}$, $2\frac{3}{4}$, 4; you add $1\frac{1}{4}$ to find the next answer. The next two problems are $4\frac{1}{5} \times 1\frac{1}{4} = 5\frac{1}{4}$ and $5\frac{1}{5} \times 1\frac{1}{4} = 6\frac{1}{2}$. **25.** $112\frac{14}{15}$ mi

8.4 Exercises, pp. 392–393

1. $2\frac{2}{3} \div \frac{2}{3} = 4$ **3.** $\frac{3}{5}$ **7.** $1\frac{3}{4} \div \frac{1}{2} = 3\frac{1}{2}$ **9.** $\frac{1}{7}$
11. $6\frac{1}{3}$ **13.** 32 **15.** $4\frac{7}{8}$ **17.** less than 1
19. greater than 1 **21.** less than 1 **23.** $\frac{13}{4}$
25. 3 **27.** $w = \frac{225}{2}$, $x = \frac{225}{4}$, $y = 45$, $z = 15$;

sample strategies: work backward; guess, check, and revise **29.** C

Spiral Review, p. 394

1. = **3.** > **5.** $\begin{array}{r} 15.29 \\ -\,4.37 \\ \hline 10.92 \end{array}$ **7.** $\frac{8}{16}$ **9.** $\frac{4}{28}$

Mid-Chapter Assessment, p. 395

1. $\frac{3}{4}$ **2.** $\frac{20}{7}$, or $2\frac{6}{7}$ **3.** $\frac{5}{18}$ **4.** $\frac{1}{8}$ **5.** $\frac{88}{21}$, or $4\frac{4}{21}$
6. $\frac{6}{5}$, or $1\frac{1}{5}$ **7.** 18 **8.** $\frac{26}{3}$, or $8\frac{2}{3}$ **9.** 3 **10.** 12
11. 2 **12.** 9 **13.** $\frac{6}{7}$ **14.** 1 **15.** $1\frac{4}{5}$ yd^2
16. $\frac{7}{20}$ mi^2 **17.** 30 ft^2 **18.** 2 **19.** $\frac{1}{6}$ **20.** $1\frac{1}{3}$
21. 3 **22.** 9 **23.** $2\frac{2}{3}$ **24.** $\frac{1}{3}$ **25.** $6\frac{2}{3}$
26. banana: 8; chocolate: 18; vanilla: 16; butterscotch: 6 **27.** 6

8.5 Exercises, pp. 398–399

1. $\frac{5}{7}$ **3.** It should be multiplication by the reciprocal instead of division by the reciprocal, $\frac{7}{8} \div \frac{5}{6} = \frac{7}{8} \times \frac{6}{5} = \frac{42}{40} = \frac{21}{20}$. **5.** 1 mi **7.** $\frac{5}{4}$
9. $\frac{6}{11}$ **11.** $\frac{15}{4}$, or $3\frac{3}{4}$ **13.** $\frac{7}{4}$, or $1\frac{3}{4}$ **15.** $\frac{21}{5}$, or $4\frac{1}{5}$ **17.** $\frac{66}{5}$, or $13\frac{1}{5}$ **19.** 126 **21.** $\frac{14}{8}$; $\frac{21}{8}$; $\frac{28}{8}$; *sample answer:* Numerators increase by 7.
23. $\frac{1}{4}$; $\frac{1}{3}$; $\frac{1}{2}$; *sample answer:* Denominators decrease by one. **25.** B

8.6 Exercises, pp. 402–404

1. Rewrite as improper fractions; Multiply by reciprocal; Multiply. **3.** $\frac{4}{3}$; *sample answer:*
$5 \div 3\frac{3}{4} = 5 \div \frac{15}{4} = \frac{20}{4} \div \frac{15}{4} = \frac{20}{15}$, or $1\frac{1}{3}$;
$5 \div 3\frac{3}{4} = 5 \div \frac{15}{4} = 5 \times \frac{4}{15} = \frac{20}{15}$, or $1\frac{1}{3}$ **5.** yes
7. $\frac{9}{10}$ cup per person

9. $2\frac{1}{4}$; $2\frac{1}{4} \div 3 = \frac{3}{4}$

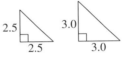

11. D **13.** B **15.** $\frac{16}{3}$, or $5\frac{1}{3}$ **17.** $\frac{16}{19}$ **19.** $\frac{19}{20}$
21. $\frac{7}{4}$, or $1\frac{3}{4}$ **23.** sometimes **25.** sometimes
27. 21 minutes **29.** $3\frac{1}{9}$ **31.** $3\frac{11}{24}$ in. **33.** B

Spiral Review, p. 404

1. 6, 18, 3, 12 **3.** 15.3 **5.** 7.4 **7.** 0.68 **9.** 3
11. 39 **13.** 70

8.7 Exercises, pp. 408–409

1. C **3.** B **5.** No; it does not contain a 90° angle. **9.** 7 cm^2 **11. a.** 0.125 units^2
b. 0.5 units^2 **c.** 1.125 units^2 **d.** 2.0 units^2
Sample answer: If you multiply the base and height of a right triangle by a given number, then you are multiplying its area by that number squared. For example, if you double the base and height, then you quadruple the area.

13. 4 cm **15.** 60 **17.** 24 m^2 **19.** 20 cm^2

Chapter 8 Review, pp. 411–413

1. pencils: 24; pens: 6; markers: 2 **3.** $\frac{9}{2}$, or $4\frac{1}{2}$
5. $\frac{1}{8}$ **7.** $\frac{7}{40}$ **9.** $\frac{3}{5}$ **11.** 7 **13.** $\frac{11}{18}$ **15.** 12
17. $\frac{27}{5}$, or $5\frac{2}{5}$ **19.** $\frac{16}{3}$, or $5\frac{1}{3}$ **21.** $\frac{13}{6}$, or $2\frac{1}{6}$
23. $\frac{2}{9}$ ft^2

Chapter 9

9.1 Exercises, pp. 422–423

1. No; it has a curved side. **3.** yes; hexagon
5. about 12 units **11.**

13. Start at J, move down 2 and right 1 to N, right 3 to M, left 1 and up 3 to L, left 2 to K, left 1 and down 1 to J. **17.** 6 units^2 **19.** 10 units^2
21. C

9.2 Exercises, pp. 428–429

1. *Sample answers:* $\angle P$, $\angle QPR$, or $\angle RPQ$ **3.** *P*
7. B **9.** C **11.** 125° **13.** 60° **15.** 175°
17. 15° **19.** 360°; the sum of the measures of all angles that surround a point is 360°.
21. Fold paper from top to bottom; fold again from left to right so the first fold lines match. The corner where the folds meet makes a right angle.
23. 135°, 45°; 180° **25.** C

Spiral Review, p. 430

1. $\frac{3}{4}$ **3.** $\frac{37}{100}$ **5.** 54 **7.** 300 **9.** 7600 **11.** 32, 29 **13.** 7, 7 **15.** no **17.** blue jay: 30 cm; American robin: 24 cm; northern cardinal: 20 cm; house sparrow: 15 cm

9.3 Exercises, pp. 434–435

1. C **3.** B
5. *Sample answer:*

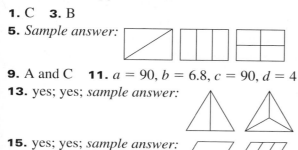

9. A and C **11.** $a = 90$, $b = 6.8$, $c = 90$, $d = 4$
13. yes; yes; *sample answer:*

15. yes; yes; *sample answer:*

17. a: triangle, b: triangle, c: right triangle

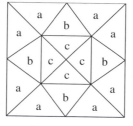

19. B

9.4 Exercises, pp. 440–442

7. no **9.** yes;

11. No, flipping about the line does not give an exact match. **13.** No, flipping about the line does not give an exact match.
15. yes; 2 **17.** no
19. *Sample answer:* **21.** 3

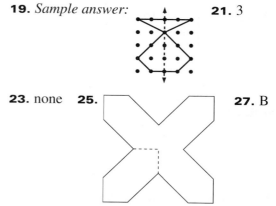

23. none **25.**

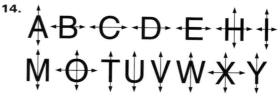

27. B

Spiral Review, p. 442

1. 5 **3.** $\frac{1}{2}, \frac{4}{7}, \frac{5}{7}, \frac{5}{6}$ **5.** $2\frac{1}{4}$ **7.** 3
9. Quadrilateral *KLMN*; $\angle N$ and $\angle K$ are right, $\angle M$ is obtuse, and $\angle L$ is acute.

Mid-Chapter Assessment, p. 443

1. Start at *A*, move right 4 up 1 to *B*, up 3 left 2 to *C*, left 2 down 4 to *A*. **2.** Start at *A*, move right 4 up 3 to *B*, up 3 left 3 to *C*, left 2 down 1 to *D*, down 5 right 1 to *A*. **3.** Start at *A*, move down 1 right 1 to *B*, right 2 to *C*, right 2 up 2 to *D*, up 2 left 5 to *E*, down 3 to *A*. **4. a.** quadrilateral
b. triangle **c.** right triangle **d.** pentagon
e. quadrilateral or rectangle **5.** right, 90°
6. acute, 60° **7.** obtuse, 120° **8.** neither; different size and shape **9.** similar; same shape, different size **10.** congruent and similar; same size and shape **11.** 1 **12.** 1 **13.** 2
14.

A B C D E H I
M O T U V W X Y

9.5 Exercises, pp. 448–449

1. coordinate plane **3.** (4, 3) **7.** *R* **9.** *S*

11.

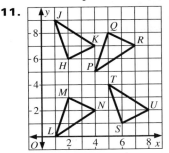

Triangle *HJK* is a slide of triangle *STU*, and triangle *LMN* is a slide of triangle *PQR*.
13. Yes; it has the same side lengths and angle measures. **15.** left 2 units, down 5 units
17. left 2 units, up 1 unit

19.

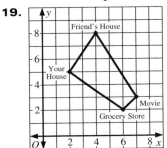

9.6 Exercises, pp. 452–454

1. right, isosceles **3.** acute, equilateral
7. isosceles **9.** equilateral
11.   **13.**   **15.** right, scalene

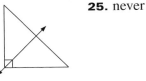

19. 124°, 32°, 24°; obtuse **21.** no
23. yes; **25.** never

27. 2 right triangles, or 1 acute and 1 obtuse;

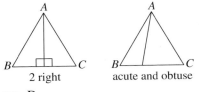

2 right   acute and obtuse

29. B

Spiral Review, p. 454

1. $9 + 6 - 3 \times 5 = 0$ **3.** $1 + 5 \times 9 \div 3 = 16$
5. 23.24 in.²

7.

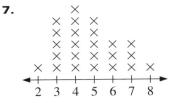

Using a Calculator, p. 455

3. *Sample answer:* about 45, because there are an equal number of rolls that will give an angle greater than 45° as there are rolls that will give an angle less than 45°

9.7 Exercises, pp. 460–461

1. C **3.** B **5.** Angle measures will vary; third angle measures 180° minus the sum of 90° and the other acute angle. **7.** Yes, sum is 180°.
9. Yes, sum is 180°. **11.** ∠*A* is 80°, ∠*B* is 60°, ∠*C* is 40°; 180° **13.** 60 **15.** 30 **17.** 10°, 20°, 30°, 40°, 50°, 60°; as the measures of ∠*A* and ∠*B* decrease by 5° each, the measure of ∠*C* increases by 10°. **19.** D

Chapter 9 Review, pp. 463–465

3. yes; hexagon **5.** No; figure is not closed.
7. ∠*X* **9.**

11. yes;   **13.** yes;

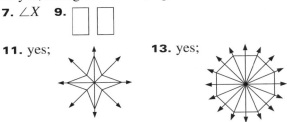

15, 17.

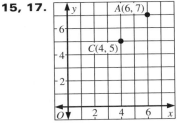

19. equilateral **21.** isosceles **23.** right
25. obtuse **27.** 30 **29.** 89

Chapters 7–9 Cumulative Review, pp. 468–469

1. A: $1\frac{1}{8}$ in., $\frac{9}{8}$ in.; B: $1\frac{3}{4}$ in., $\frac{7}{4}$ in.;
C: $2\frac{1}{4}$ in., $\frac{9}{4}$ in.; D: $2\frac{5}{8}$ in., $\frac{21}{8}$ in.; E: $3\frac{1}{2}$ in., $\frac{7}{2}$ in.;
F: $4\frac{7}{8}$ in., $\frac{39}{8}$ in. **3.** $6\frac{1}{2}$ **5.** $2\frac{1}{6}$ **7.** $3\frac{1}{2}$ **9.** $4\frac{2}{3}$

11. $3\frac{1}{4}$ m   **13.** $1\frac{1}{2}$ ft   **15.** $\frac{9}{14}$ mi^2
17. 12 students   **19.** $1\frac{1}{2} \div 6 = \frac{1}{4}$
21. $2\frac{1}{6} \times \frac{6}{7} = 1\frac{6}{7}$ **23.** pentagon; $\angle A$: acute, 55°;
$\angle B$: obtuse, 135°; $\angle C$: obtuse, 120°; $\angle D$: right,
90°; $\angle E$: obtuse, 140°;   **25.** A and B
27. 2;   **29.** 1;

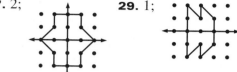

31.

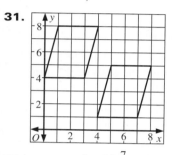

33. acute angle; $30\frac{7}{12}$ yd

Chapter 10

10.1 Exercises, pp. 478–479

1. B   **3.** A, B   **5.** False; intersecting lines can
intersect at any angle.   **7.** parallel; because they
never meet   **9.** parallel; because they never meet
11. $\overleftrightarrow{EF}$, $\overleftrightarrow{GH}$ **13.** $\overleftrightarrow{CD}$ **15.** never   **17.** always
19. $\overleftrightarrow{CD}$ or $\overleftrightarrow{FH}$ **21.** I measured $1\frac{1}{2}$ in. from the
top edge twice and drew a line connecting those
points. I repeated the process using the other
edges and 1 in.   **23.** center line, singles and
service sideline, doubles sideline   **25.** A

10.2 Exercises, pp. 482–483

1. perpendicular   **3.** 55°   **5.** *Sample answer:*
$\angle CFE$, $\angle EFD$; $\angle AFD$, $\angle DFB$; $\angle DFB$, $\angle BFC$
7. a. $\angle 1$ and $\angle 3$ are supplementary ($= 180°$),
therefore, $\angle 3 = 180° - 125° = 55°$.   **b.** $\angle 3$
and $\angle 4$ are supplementary ($= 180°$), therefore,
$\angle 4 = 180° - 55° = 125°$.   **c.** $\angle 1 = 125°$ and
$\angle 4 = 125°$, therefore, they are congruent.
9. 25°   **11.** 88°

13. 35°;   **15.** 20°;

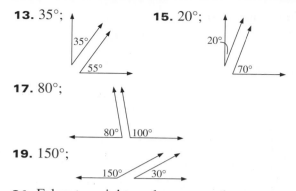

17. 80°;

19. 150°;

21. False; two right angles are supplementary.
23. $\angle 1$ and $\angle 2$ are congruent.   **25.** $\angle 1$ and $\angle 3$
are complementary angles.   **27.** D

Spiral Review, p. 484

1. $\frac{3}{10}$ **3.** $\frac{2}{5}$ **5.** 0.38, 38%   **7.** 0.55, 55%
9. a. 6 h   **b.** $71.25

Using a Calculator, p. 485

1. Answers should be close to 360°.   **3.** 130°
5. 125°

10.3 Exercises, pp. 488–489

1. A, B, C, D   **3.** C, D   **5.** *Sample answers are
given.* **a.** *QRVU* **b.** *QSVT* **c.** *PQUT* **d.** *PSVT*
7. parallelogram, quadrilateral   **9.** rectangle,
parallelogram, quadrilateral   **11.** true
13. false;   **15.** yes;

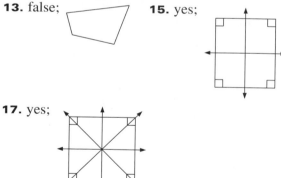

17. yes;

19. rectangle; $x = 3$, $y = 8$, $z° = 90°$
21. neither; $x = 4$, $y = 4$, $z° = 65°$ **23.** B

10.4 Exercises, pp. 494–495

1. 24 units^2 **3.** 9 units^2 **5.** *Sample answer:*
base, 4 units; height, 9 units   **7.** 18 m^2
9. 26 in.^{2} **11.** 7.5 cm^2 **13.** 72 units^2
15. 48 units^2 **17.** 2 mi   **19. a.** 3 ft^2, 7.5 ft^2
b. 546 ft^2 **21.** B

Spiral Review, p. 496

1. 28   **3.** 24   **5.** 36   **7.** 22   **9.** 4

Mid-Chapter Assessment, p. 497

1. $\overleftrightarrow{GH}$ **2.** $\overleftrightarrow{AB}$ **3.** $\angle 2$ **4.** $\angle 4$ **5.** $\overleftrightarrow{AB}$, $\overleftrightarrow{EF}$
6. $\angle 1$ **7.** quadrilateral, parallelogram, rectangle
8. quadrilateral, parallelogram   **9.** quadrilateral,
parallelogram, rectangle, square
10. quadrilateral   **11.** 9 units^2 **12.** 21 units^2
13. *Sample answer:* add each separate area
together, or add together each base then multiply,
$\left(\frac{1}{2}\right)(10)6$.   **14.** False; quadrilaterals have four
sides which are not necessarily parallel.
15. True; squares have four angles which
measure 90°.   **16.** True; all rectangles have four
sides.   **17.** False; not all parallelograms have
four sides of the same length or four angles which
measure 90°.   **18.** 12   **19.** 87 square units   **20.**
1044 square units

10.5 Exercises, pp. 502–503

1. *B*   **3.** *A*   **5.** 7 units   **7.** 6.28 units
9. 18.84 units   **11.** 364.24 mm
13. 1193.81 mm   **15.** $P = 21$ m, $A = 24.5$ m^2
17. 62.8 in.   **19.** 50.24 ft   **21.** about 191 times
23. B

10.6 Exercises, pp. 508–509

1. A   **3.** B   **5. a.** 153.86 in.^{2} **b.** 452.16 in.^{2}
7. 9.62 ft^2 **9.** 11.86 yd^2 **11.** 200.52 m^2
13. less than   **15.** about 8,346,897 mi^2
17. diameter of $\frac{1}{2}$ in.; $\frac{1}{2} = \frac{8}{16}$; radius $= \frac{1}{2} \cdot \frac{8}{16} =$
$\frac{4}{16}$; $\frac{4}{16} > \frac{3}{16}$ **19.** C

Spiral Review, p. 510

1. mean: 46.125, median: 49, mode: 55, range: 43
3. 48°

10.7 Exercises, pp. 514–515

1. $\frac{1}{12} \neq 40°$; it should be $\frac{1}{12} = 30°$.   **3.** D, B, C, A
5. nuclear, oil, and gas; $22 + 10 + 3 = 35$
7. $a° = 135°$, $b° = 120°$, $c° = 45°$, $d = \frac{1}{6}$

9.   Favorite Fruit Juice
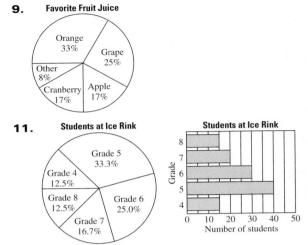

11.   Students at Ice Rink

grades 5 and 7; circle graph (33.3% + 16.7% =
50%)
13. A

10.8 Exercises, pp. 518–519

1. $l = 6$ cm, $w = 4$ cm, $h = 8$ cm   **3.** 208 cm^2
5. S.A. $= 272$ m^2, V $= 192$ m^3 **7.** S.A. $= 700$ ft^2,
V $= 1000$ ft^3 **9.** S.A. $= 96$ cm^2, V $= 64$ cm^3
11. S.A. $= 1248$ mm^2, V $= 2880$ mm^3
13. S.A. $= 364$ in.^{2}, V $= 367.5$ in.^{3}
15. S.A. $= 1800$ in.^{2}, V $= 5184$ in.^{3} **17.** 12 mm
19. 391 ft^2 **21.** 500   **23.** C

Chapter 10 Review, pp. 521–523

1. false
3. 70°;   **5.** 53°;

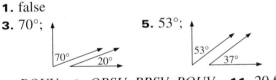

7. *PQUV*   **9.** *QRSU, PRSV, PQUV*   **11.** 20 ft^2
13. 16.33 cm   **15.** 47.10 in.   **17.** 706.50 ft^2
19. 50.24 in.^{2} **21.** S.A. $= 78$ in.^{2}, V $= 45$ in.^{3}
23. S.A. $= 72$ m^2, V $= 32$ m^3

Chapter 11

11.1 Exercises, pp. 534–535

1. $-4, -3, -2, -1, 0, 1, 2, 3, 4$ **3.** C   **5.** B
7. -10; 8
9.

increases by 2; 5, 7
11. $>$ **13.** $<$ **15.** $>$ **17.** $<$
19. $-4, -3, 1, 3, 6$ **21.** $-6, -5, -3, -1, 0$ **23.** B

25. A **27.** −5 **29.** 9 **31.** −1 **33.** 6
35. −80°F **37.** C

11.2 Exercises, pp. 540–541

1.

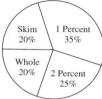

−4 −3 −2 −1 0 1 2 3 4

5 was subtracted instead of added; 3.
3. 3 + (−5) **5.** −1 **7.** −7 **9.** 3 + 3; 6
11. −2 + (−7); −9 **13.** A **15.** D **17.** 14
19. −1 **21.** −14 **23.** 7 **25.** 4 + (−5) + 2; 1
27. a. $22 **b.** $11 **29.** gained 4 yd

Spiral Review, p. 542

1. $\dfrac{4}{15}$ **3.** $\dfrac{3}{8}$ **5.** true; $\dfrac{15}{18} = \dfrac{5 \cdot 3}{6 \cdot 3}$

7. true; $\dfrac{15}{45} = \dfrac{1 \cdot 15}{3 \cdot 15}$ **9.** $\dfrac{9}{8}$ **11.** $\dfrac{12}{7}$

13.

Milk Preference

Skim 20%
1 Percent 35%
Whole 20%
2 Percent 25%

15. > **17.** <

Using a Calculator, p. 543

1. 2 **3.** 2 **5.** −5 **7.** −2 **9.** −2 **11.** 6 **13.** 2
15. 5 **17.** *Sample answer:* 0 − 5 = −5

11.3 Exercises, pp. 548–549

1. left **3.** right **5.** left, left, right, right;
answers remain the same. **7.** C **9.** D **11.** −10
13. 11 **15.** 5 **17.** 52 ft **19.** −10 **21.** 2
23. 5, 4, 3, 2; the number from which −2 is being
subtracted decreases by one and the difference
decreases by one. **25.** *Sample answer:* Try to
box negative numbers, since subtracting a negative
number results in addition. **27.** D **29.** D

Spiral Review, p. 550

1. 7 **3.** 3 **5.** 4 **7.** 3 **9.** 116, comedy;
40, suspense; 30, drama; 14, westerns **11.** <
13. > **15.** > **17.** 50 **19.** 50.24 m, 200.96 m²

Mid-Chapter Assessment, p. 551

1. B **2.** D **3.** C **4.** A **5.** < **6.** > **7.** <
8. > **9.** > **10.** < **11.** < **12.** > **13.** 2
14. −4 **15.** −10 **16.** −6 **17.** −5 **18.** −11

19. 11 **20.** 12 **21.** −7 + 4 − 2; −5
22. −3 − 5 + 1; −7 **23.** −4°F; 0°F **24.** $20

11.4 Exercises, pp. 556–557

1. $A(-4, 4)$, $B(4, 3)$, $C(0, 0)$, $D\left(-3, 1\dfrac{1}{2}\right)$,
$E(-2, -4)$, $F(3, -1)$; C; origin **3.** right 2 units,
up 7 units

5.

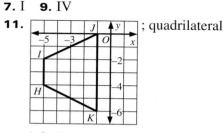

; parallelogram

7. I **9.** IV

11.

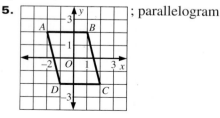

; quadrilateral

13. (−2, 1), (−1, −1), (−2, −4), (−4, −1); (−1, 3),
(0, 1), (−1, −2), (−3, 1) **15.** The *x*-coordinates
are opposites. The *y*-coordinates remain the same.
17. flip over the *y*-axis **19.** Store 4;
about 15 miles **21.** right 1 unit, down 5 units

11.5 Exercises, pp. 560–561

1. D, C, B, A **3.** *Sample answer:* For each
point, the *x*-coordinate and *y*-coordinate are the
same. **5.** 1, 2, 3, 4, 5, 6, 7; as the numbers in the
first column increase by 1, the numbers in the
second column increase by 1. **7.** 8, 6, 4, 2, 0; as
the numbers in the first column increase by 1, the
numbers in the second column decrease by 2.

9.

x	$-5 + x$
−3	−8
−2	−7
−1	−6
0	−5
1	−4
2	−3
3	−2

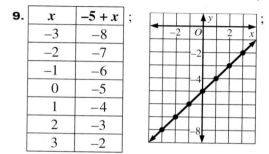

All points lie on a straight line. As the *x* values increase by 1, the −5 + *x* values also increase by 1.

11.

x	$x + (-2)$
-3	-5
-2	-4
-1	-3
0	-2
1	-1
2	0
3	1

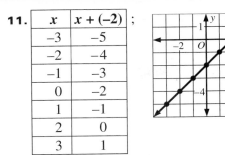

All points lie on a straight line. As the x values increase by 1, the $x + (-2)$ values also increase by 1.

13. A   **15.** *Sample answer:* (2, -3), (2, 0), (2, 1), (2, 2), (2, 4); *x*-coordinates must be the same for each point.   **17.** B

Spiral Review, p. 562

1. $3\frac{3}{5}$ **3.** $1\frac{13}{24}$ **5.** $14\frac{11}{12}$ **7.** $6\frac{1}{3}$ **9.** $\frac{1}{3}$ **11.** $\frac{5}{9}$
13. $\frac{1}{3}$ **15.** $\frac{1}{15}$

11.6 Exercises, pp. 566–567

1. F   **3.** A   **5.** D   **7.** 12 units^2 **9.** 10 units^2

11.

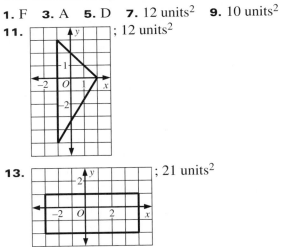

; 12 units^2

13. ; 21 units^2

15. A   **17.** (-1, 0), (-1, 0); same   **19.** (0, 0), (0, 0); same   **21.** 12 units^2; 48 mi^2 **23.** A

Chapter 11 Review, pp. 569–571

1.

;
-6, -5, -2, 0, 2, 5
3. -14   **5.** 9   **7.** -5   **9.** 4   **11.** -2   **13.** 0
15. 17   **17.** (-4, 0)   **19.** (-1, -3)   **21.** III

23, 25, 27, 29.

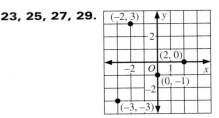

31. (0, -3), (2, 0), (-2, 0)   **33.** (-8, 2), (3, 2); about 220 mi

Chapter 12

12.1 Exercises, pp. 582–583

1. Write original equation. Subtract 2 from each side. Solution: x is by itself.   **3.** Write original equation. Subtract 3 from each side. Solution: t is by itself.   **5.** -1   **7.** -8   **9.** yes   **11.** yes
13. -5   **15.** 8   **17.** 0   **19.** 20   **21.** 10
23. 216   **25.** $x + 2 = 210$; 208
27. $5 + x = 18$; 13   **29.** $9 + x = -5$; -14
31. $-3 + 2 = -1$
33. Labels: Amount saved ($) = 38; Amount left to save ($) = x; Cost ($) = 64; Equation: $38 + x = 64$; $x = 26$, so you need to save $26.   **35.** C

12.2 Exercises, pp. 586–587

1. Add 3 so that t will be by itself on one side of the equation; $t = 17$.   **3.** Add 12 so that s will be by itself on one side of the equation; $s = -2$.
5. Temperature at 5 P.M. (°F) = x; Amount of temperature fall (°F) = 5; Temperature at 8 P.M. (°F) = 28; $x - 5 = 28$ **7.** 8 should be added to both sides instead of -8; $x = 15$.   **9.** *Sample answer:* After the hurricane passed, the water level dropped 14 feet to the average sea level. How high was the storm tide?   **11.** *Sample answer:* From midnight to 6 A.M., the temperature dropped 6°C to -12°C. What was the temperature at midnight?   **13.** yes   **15.** no; 2   **17.** yes
19. 26   **21.** 65   **23.** 4   **25.** -3
27. Labels: Distance in July (million mi) = x; Distance in January (million mi) = 91; Equation: $x - 3 = 91$; $x = 94$, so Earth is about 94 million mi from the sun in July.   **29.** C

Spiral Review, p. 588

1. 3 **3.** 3.3 **5.** $\frac{3}{4}$ **7.**

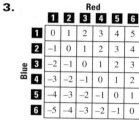

9. ratio; *sample answer:* It takes you 5 hours per week to clean the house and 3 hours to do the yard work. What is the ratio of the time spent cleaning to the total spent working inside and out?

11. ratio; *sample answer:* A deck has a width of 3 yards and a length of 10 yards. What is the ratio of the width to the length?

Using a Calculator, p. 589

1. x for top table: –5, 0, 3, 2, –2, 3, 0, –3, 0, –3; x for bottom table: 2, 0, –2, 2, 0, 3, 1, 2, 1, 4

3.

Blue \ Red	1	2	3	4	5	6
1	0	1	2	3	4	5
2	–1	0	1	2	3	4
3	–2	–1	0	1	2	3
4	–3	–2	–1	0	1	2
5	–4	–3	–2	–1	0	1
6	–5	–4	–3	–2	–1	0

a. –5, –4, –3, –2, –1, 0, 1, 2, 3, 4, 5

b. 0; of the 36 possible outcomes, 0 occurs 6 times, which is more than any other outcome.

12.3 Exercises. pp. 592–593

1. Subtract $\frac{1}{6}$ from each side to leave m by itself on one side of the equation. **3.** Add 9.4 to each side to leave t by itself on one side of the equation. **5.** $1\frac{3}{8}$ **7.** 15.7 **9.** D **11.** A

13. The same number, 4.6, should have been subtracted from both sides; $x = 3.2$. **15.** $\frac{4}{7}$

17. 6.05 **19.** 31.39 **21.** $\frac{6}{7}$ **23.** –8.6

25. 7.78 **27.** $\frac{1}{7}, \frac{2}{7}, \frac{3}{7}$; the sum and t both increase by $\frac{1}{7}$ each time; $\frac{4}{7}, \frac{5}{7}$. **29.** 36.9, 36.8, 36.7; the number subtracted from t and t both decrease by 0.1 each time; 36.6, 36.5.

31. Let $x =$ the portion that is not rural. Then $x + 0.4 = 1$, or $x + \frac{2}{5} = 1$, so $x = 0.6$, or $\frac{3}{5}$.

33. C **35.** B

Spiral Review, p. 594

1. 6%

3.

5. about $1.40 **7.** 5 **9.** 3 **11.** quadrilateral, rectangle, parallelogram

Mid-Chapter Assessment, p. 595

1. subtract; 6 **2.** add; 29 **3.** subtract; –19

4. add; 5 **5.** 12 should be added to both sides, not subtracted; $x = 33$. **6.** The same number, 17, should have been added to both sides; $x = 33$.

7. 5 should be subtracted from both sides instead of adding 2; $x = -7$. **8.** –17 **9.** 41 **10.** 21

11. –16 **12.** $\frac{46}{9}$ **13.** 3.44 **14.** $\frac{23}{24}$ **15.** 31.35

16. A; $x = 55.25$, so you started with $55.25.

17. A; $x = 2\frac{5}{8}$, so the maximum diameter is $2\frac{5}{8}$ in.

18. Labels: Total needed ($) = t; Amount raised ($) = 284; Amount left to raise ($) = 416; Equation: $t - 284 = 416$; the solution is $t = 700$, so the class needs to raise $700.

12.4 Exercises, pp. 598–599

1. 1, 0, –1, –2, –3

3.

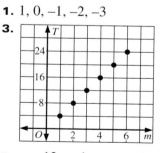

5. $y = 12x$, where $x =$ the number of cartons and $y =$ the number of eggs

SELECTED ANSWERS

7.

Input, m	Output, y
0	0
1	5
2	10
3	15

9.

Input, m	Output, y
0	−4
1	−3
2	−2
3	−1

11.

Input, m	Output, y
0	0
1	3
2	6
3	9

13.

Input, m	Output, y
0	7
1	8
2	9
3	10

15. $y = 3x$;

17. $y = x + 5$;

19.

Input, x	Output, y	; B
0	−2	
1	−1	
2	0	
3	1	

21.

Input, x	Output, y	; A
−2	−2	
−1	−1	
0	0	
1	1	
2	2	

23. y: 3, 6, 9, 12, 15, 18; each time x increases by 1, y increases by 3; $y = 3x$.   **25.** A

12.5 Exercises, pp. 604–605

1.

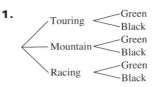

3. *Sample answer:* Use the counting principle, since there will obviously be many choices; 100,000.   **5.** *Sample answer:* Use the counting principle, since there will obviously be many choices; 90.   **7.** 9   **9.** $\frac{1}{64}$ **11.** $\frac{1}{18}$ **13.** No; there are 60 different combinations of activities, so you can have a different combination for each of the 60 days.   **15. a.** 45   **b.** $\frac{1}{15}$ **17.** C

Spiral Review, p. 606

1. $\frac{1}{2}$ **3.** $\frac{41}{100}$ **5.** 120   **7.** 47   **9.** Each number is 3 less than the preceding number; −7, −10, −13.

12.6 Exercises, pp. 610–611

1. Two events are independent when the outcome of one of them does not affect the outcome of the other. To find the probability of independent events, you can make a list or draw a diagram of all the possible outcomes, or you can multiply the probabilities of the events.   **3.** No; you generally will be holding an umbrella only if it is raining or you think that it might rain.   **5. b.** The probabilities should average about $\frac{1}{45}$.   **c.** $\frac{1}{45}$ **7.** Yes; whether you own a dog doesn't affect whether you like to roller skate, and vice versa.   **9.** $\frac{6}{15}$, or $\frac{2}{5}$ **11.** $\frac{5}{8}$ **13.** B

Chapter 12 Review, pp. 613–614

1. -15 **3.** -2 **5.** -2 **7.** -20 **9.** -5 **11.** -1

13. 20 **15.** 16 **17.** $3\frac{1}{2} + x = 8; 4\frac{1}{2}$, so you must walk $4\frac{1}{2}$ mi.

19.

Input, x	Output, y
-1	-4
0	-3
1	-2
2	-1
3	0

21.

Input, x	Output, y
-1	2
0	3
1	4
2	5
3	6

23. 9 **25. a.** no **b.** yes

Chapters 7–12 Cumulative Review, pp. 617–618

1. $8\frac{1}{5}$ **3.** $2\frac{1}{3}$ **5.** D; $\frac{5}{12}$ **7.** B; $\frac{4}{10}$, or $\frac{2}{5}$ **9.** $2\frac{4}{7}$

11. $a = 4$ ft, $b° = 70°$, $c = 5$ ft, $d° = 90°$, $e° = 110°$, $f = 3.7$ ft, $g° = 90°$, $h = 3.8$ ft

13. scalene, right **15.** scalene, acute

17. 7;

+ 13

-6 -4 -2 0 2 4 6 8

19. 0;

+ 11

-12 -10 -8 -6 -4 -2 0

21. 7;

$- (-3)$

0 2 4 6 8

23. 12.56 units^2 **25.** 16 units^2 **27.** $x + 3.36 = 59.36$; the solution is 56, so you spent $56 before tax. **29.** 15 **31.** $\frac{7}{8}$ **33.** 40.72

35. 9;

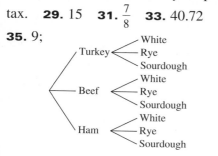